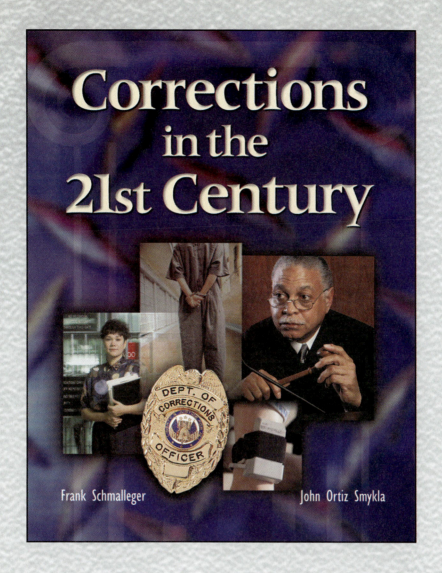

# Corrections
## in the
## 21st Century

Frank Schmalleger

John Ortiz Smykla

**Frank Schmalleger, Ph.D.**

Director
The Justice Research Association

**John Ortiz Smykla, Ph.D.**

Professor, Department of Criminal Justice
The University of Alabama

**Glencoe McGraw-Hill**

New York, New York    Columbus, Ohio    Woodland Hills, California    Peoria, Illinois

**Library of Congress Cataloging-in-Publication Data**

Schmalleger, Frank.
    Corrections in the 21st century / Frank Schmalleger, John Ortiz Smykla.
      p. cm.
    Includes bibliographical references and index.
    ISBN 0-02-802567-9
    1. Corrections--Vocational guidance--United States.  I. Smykla, John Ortiz. II. Title.

    HV9471 .S36 2000
    364.6'023'73--dc21

                                    99-054915

*Glencoe/McGraw-Hill*

A Division of The **McGraw-Hill** Companies

*Corrections in the 21st Century*
Student Text

Send all inquiries to:
Glencoe/McGraw-Hill
21600 Oxnard Street
Woodland Hills, CA 91367

ISBN 0-02-802567-9 (student text)
ISBN 0-02-802574-1 (student text with tutorial CD-ROM)

Printed in the United States of America.

2  3  4  5  6  7  8  9  10   027   07  06  05  04  03  02  01

# Brief Contents

# Expanded Contents

# 2 Sentencing: To Punish or To Reform? 32

**3**

# Punishments: A Brief History 62

# 4 Jails: Way Stations Along the Justice Highway 88

## 5 Diversion and Probation: Alternatives to Imprisonment    122

## 8   The Staff World: Managing the Prison Population   220

# 9 The Inmate World: Living Behind Bars 246

# 10 Legal Aspects: Prisons and the Courts 272

# 11 The Prison Environment: Issues and Concerns 308

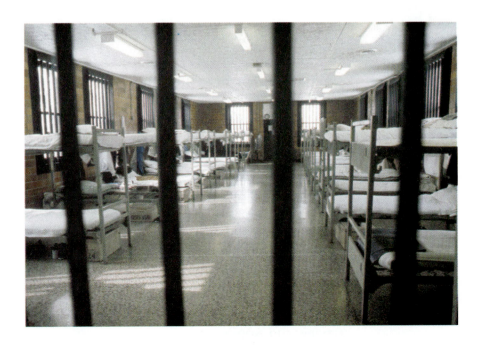

# 14 Juvenile Corrections: End of an Era? 400

FRANKLIN COUNTY JUVENILE DETENTION CENTER

Juvenile Release Only

# 15 The Victim: Role in the Correctional Process 426

## 16 Careers: Your Future in Corrections 452

# Inside Your Book

This book was designed for you to help you learn. It contains 16 chapters, divided into sections. This structure, together with numerous special features, helps you learn and apply the concepts that can help lead you to a career as a corrections professional.

## Previewing Chapter Concepts

The chapter opener introduces the key concepts to be learned.

The **opening photograph** sets the stage for the chapter content and provides a visual connection to the chapter.

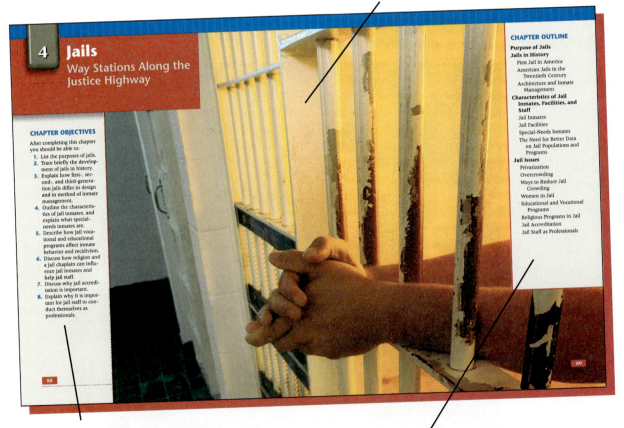

**Chapter objectives** alert you to the major concepts to learn. Turn the objectives into questions, and, as you read the chapter, look for the answers to the questions.

A **chapter outline** introduces the topics that will be discussed. Scan the outline to familiarize yourself with the subject matter.

# Developing Chapter Concepts

The chapter text explains correctional concepts in a structured, visual format and provides a comprehensive overview of correctional practices.

The **heading structure** shows the relationship among the topics in a section and breaks the material into easily digestible segments of information. Scan the headings to locate the information that will help you answer the questions you formed from the chapter objectives.

Concepts are depicted in **visual format** to make them easier to understand.

**Key terms** are also defined in the margin to make it easy for you to learn them.

**Key terms** are defined when introduced and are printed in boldface to make them easy to find.

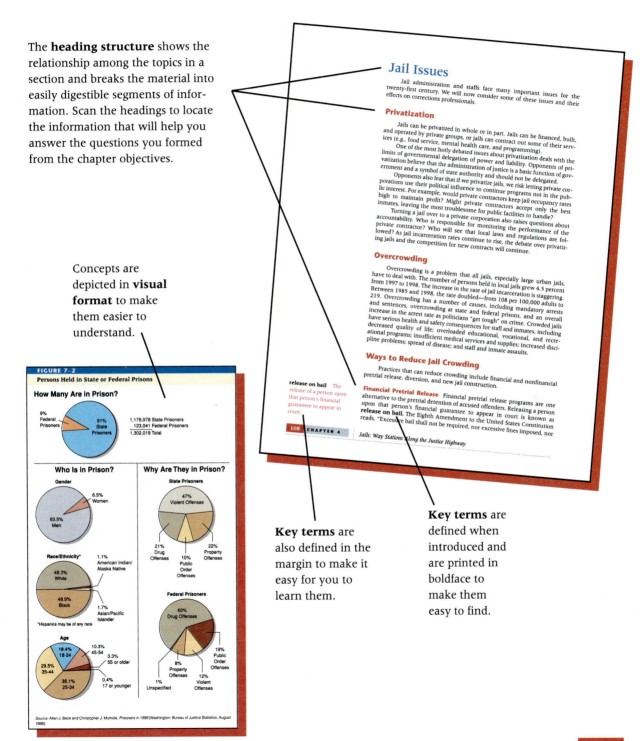

## Jail Issues

Jail administration and staffs face many important issues for the twenty-first century. We will now consider some of these issues and their effects on corrections professionals.

### Privatization

Jails can be privatized in whole or in part. Jails can be financed, built, and operated by private groups, or jails can contract out some of their services (e.g., food service, mental health care, and programming).

One of the most hotly debated issues about privatization deals with the limits of governmental delegation of power and liability. Opponents of privatization believe that the administration of justice is a basic function of government and a symbol of state authority and should not be delegated.

Opponents also fear that if we privatize jails, we risk letting private corporations use their political influence to continue programs not in the public interest. For example, would private contractors keep jail occupancy rates high to maintain profit? Might private contractors accept only the best inmates, leaving the most troublesome for public facilities to handle?

Turning a jail over to a private corporation also raises questions about accountability. Who is responsible for monitoring the performance of the private contractor? Who will see that local laws and regulations are followed? As jail incarceration rates continue to rise, the debate over privatizing jails and the competition for new contracts will continue.

### Overcrowding

Overcrowding is a problem that all jails, especially large urban jails, have to deal with. The number of persons held in local jails grew 4.5 percent from 1997 to 1998. The increase in the rate of jail incarceration is staggering. Between 1985 and 1998, the rate doubled—from 108 per 100,000 adults to 219. Overcrowding has a number of causes, including mandatory arrests and sentences, overcrowding at state and federal prisons, and an overall increase in the arrest rate as politicians "get tough" on crime. Crowded jails have serious health and safety consequences for staff and inmates, including decreased quality of life; overloaded educational, vocational, and recreational programs; insufficient medical services and supplies; increased discipline problems; spread of disease; and staff and inmate assaults.

### Ways to Reduce Jail Crowding

Practices that can reduce crowding include financial and nonfinancial pretrial release, diversion, and new jail construction.

**release on bail** The release of a person upon that person's financial guarantee to appear in court.

**Financial Pretrial Release** Financial pretrial release programs are one alternative to the pretrial detention of accused offenders. Releasing a person upon that person's financial guarantee to appear in court is known as **release on bail**. The Eighth Amendment to the United States Constitution reads, "Excessive bail shall not be required, nor excessive fines imposed, nor

108 CHAPTER 4     *Jails: Way Stations Along the Justice Highway*

FIGURE 7–2
Persons Held in State or Federal Prisons

**How Many Are in Prison?**

9% Federal Prisoners
91% State Prisoners

1,178,978 State Prisoners
123,041 Federal Prisoners
1,302,019 Total

**Who Is in Prison?**

Gender
6.5% Women
93.5% Men

Race/Ethnicity*
48.3% White
48.9% Black
1.1% American Indian/Alaska Native
1.7% Asian/Pacific Islander

*Hispanics may be of any race

Age
18.4% 18-24
29.5% 35-44
38.1% 25-34
10.3% 45-54
3.3% 55 or older
0.4% 17 or younger

**Why Are They in Prison?**

State Prisoners
47% Violent Offenses
21% Drug Offenses
10% Public Order Offenses
22% Property Offenses

Federal Prisoners
60% Drug Offenses
19% Public Order Offenses
12% Violent Offenses
8% Property Offenses
1% Unspecified

Source: Allen J. Beck and Christopher J. Mumola, *Prisoners in 1998* (Washington: Bureau of Justice Statistics, August 1999).

# Reinforcing Chapter Concepts

In-text examples, graphics, and special features enhance and strengthen your learning about major concepts and practices in corrections.

**Policy implications** alert you to the issues facing corrections professionals.

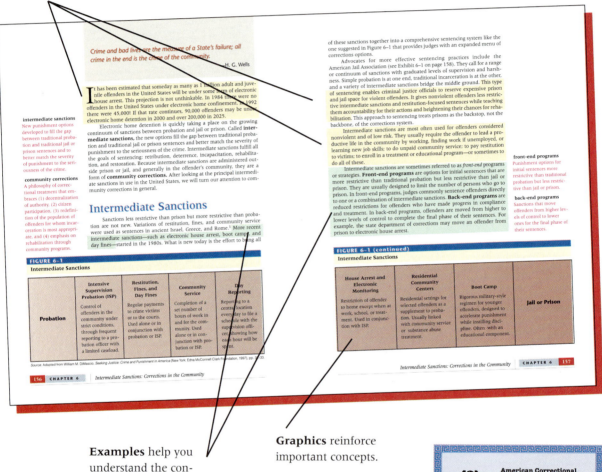

*Crime and bad lives are the measure of a State's failure; all crime in the end is the crime of the community.*

— H. G. Wells

It has been estimated that someday as many as 1 million adult and juvenile offenders in the United States will be under some form of electronic house arrest. This projection is not unthinkable. In 1984 there were no offenders in the United States under electronic home confinement. In 1992 there were 45,000! If that rate continues, 90,000 offenders may be under electronic home detention in 2000 and over 200,000 in 2025.

Electronic home detention is quickly taking a place on the growing continuum of sanctions between probation and jail or prison. Called **intermediate sanctions**, the new options fill the gap between traditional probation and traditional jail or prison sentences and better match the severity of punishment to the seriousness of the crime. Intermediate sanctions fulfill all the goals of sentencing: retribution, deterrence, incapacitation, rehabilitation, and restoration. Because intermediate sanctions are administered outside prison or jail, and generally in the offender's community, they are a form of **community corrections**. After looking at the principal intermediate sanctions in use in the United States, we will turn our attention to community corrections in general.

**intermediate sanctions**
New punishment options developed to fill the gap between traditional probation and traditional jail or prison sentences and to better match the severity of punishment to the seriousness of the crime.

**community corrections**
A philosophy of correctional treatment that embraces (1) decentralization of authority, (2) citizen participation, (3) redefinition of the population of offenders for whom incarceration is most appropriate, and (4) emphasis on rehabilitation through community programs.

## Intermediate Sanctions

Sanctions less restrictive than prison but more restrictive than probation are not new. Variations of restitution, fines, and community service were used as sentences in ancient Israel, Greece, and Rome.[1] More recent intermediate sanctions—such as electronic house arrest, boot camp, and day fines—started in the 1980s. What is new today is the effort to bring all of these sanctions together into a comprehensive sentencing system like the one suggested in Figure 6–1 that provides judges with an expanded menu of corrections options.

Advocates for more effective sentencing practices include the American Jail Association (see Exhibit 6–1 on page 158). They call for a range or continuum of sanctions with graduated levels of supervision and harshness. Simple probation is at one end, traditional incarceration is at the other, and a variety of intermediate sanctions bridge the middle ground. This type of sentencing enables criminal justice officials to reserve expensive prison and jail space for violent offenders. It gives nonviolent offenders less restrictive intermediate sanctions and restitution-focused sentences while teaching them accountability for their actions and heightening their chances for rehabilitation. This approach to sentencing treats prisons as the backstop, not the backbone, of the corrections system.

Intermediate sanctions are most often used for offenders considered nonviolent and of low risk. They usually require the offender to lead a productive life in the community by working, finding work if unemployed, or learning new job skills; to do unpaid community service; to pay restitution to victims; to enroll in a treatment or educational program—or sometimes to do all of these.

Intermediate sanctions are sometimes referred to as *front-end* programs or strategies. **Front-end programs** are options for initial sentences that are more restrictive than traditional probation but less restrictive than jail or prison. They are usually designed to limit the number of persons who go to prison. In front-end programs, judges commonly sentence offenders directly to one or a combination of intermediate sanctions. **Back-end programs** are reduced restrictions for offenders who have made progress in compliance and treatment. In back-end programs, offenders are moved from higher to lower levels of control to complete the final phase of their sentences. For example, the state department of corrections may move an offender from prison to electronic house arrest.

**front-end programs**
Punishment options for initial sentences more restrictive than traditional probation but less restrictive than jail or prison.

**back-end programs**
Sanctions that move offenders from higher levels of control to lower ones for the final phase of their sentences.

**FIGURE 6-1**
Intermediate Sanctions

| Probation | Intensive Supervision Probation (ISP) | Restitution, Fines, and Day Fines | Community Service | Day Reporting |
|---|---|---|---|---|
| | Control of offenders in the community under strict conditions, through frequent reporting to a probation officer with a limited caseload. | Regular payments to crime victims or to the courts. Used alone or in conjunction with probation or ISP. | Completion of a set number of hours of work in and for the community. Used alone or in conjunction with probation or ISP. | Reporting to a central location every day to file a schedule with the supervision officer, showing how each hour will be spent. |

Source: Adapted from William M. DiMascio, *Seeking Justice: Crime and Punishment in America* (New York: Edna McConnell Clark Foundation, 1997), pp. 19–30.

**FIGURE 6-1 (continued)**
Intermediate Sanctions

| House Arrest and Electronic Monitoring | Residential Community Centers | Boot Camp | Jail or Prison |
|---|---|---|---|
| Restriction of offender to home except when at work, school, or treatment. Used in conjunction with ISP. | Residential settings for selected offenders as a supplement to probation. Usually linked with community service or substance abuse treatment. | Rigorous military-style regimen for younger offenders, designed to accelerate punishment while instilling discipline. Often with an educational component. | |

156    CHAPTER 6    Intermediate Sanctions: Corrections in the Community

Intermediate Sanctions: Corrections in the Community    CHAPTER 6    157

**Examples** help you understand the concepts being presented.

**Graphics** reinforce important concepts.

Chapter content focuses on developing professionalism among corrections practitioners.

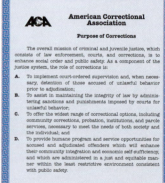

**American Correctional Association**

**Purpose of Corrections**

The overall mission of criminal and juvenile justice, which consists of law enforcement, courts, and corrections, is to enhance social order and public safety. As a component of the justice system, the role of corrections is:

A. To implement court-ordered supervision and, when necessary, detention of those accused of unlawful behavior prior to adjudication;

B. To assist in maintaining the integrity of law by administering sanctions and punishments imposed by courts for unlawful behavior;

C. To offer the widest range of correctional options, including community corrections, probation, institutions, and parole services, necessary to meet the needs of both society and the individual; and

D. To provide humane program and service opportunities for accused and adjudicated offenders which will enhance their community integration and economic self-sufficiency, and which are administered in a just and equitable manner within the least restrictive environment consistent with public safety.

Special features reinforce effective correctional practices and professional skills.

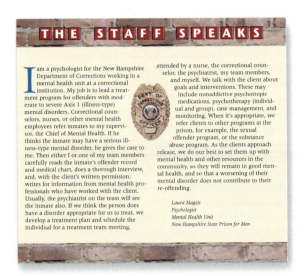

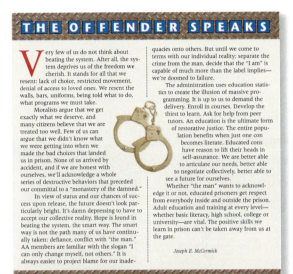

**The Staff Speaks** presents corrections professionals describing in their own words their work in the corrections profession.

**The Offender Speaks** presents offenders describing in their own words their experiences and reactions to the correctional system.

**Career Profile** highlights the training, educational background, and job responsibilities of current corrections professionals.

**Job Ads** focus on selected employment offerings from the wide range of opportunities in the field of corrections.

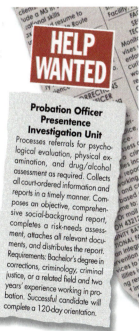

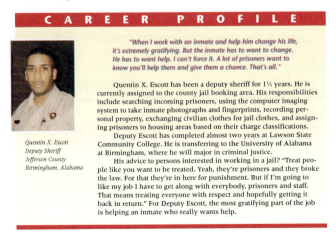

# Reviewing and Applying Chapter Concepts

End-of-chapter exercises and activities encourage you to apply what you have learned.

**Summary by Chapter Objectives** sums up the chapter's major themes. The summary is organized by chapter objectives and provides you with general answers to the questions you posed when you began the chapter.

**Questions for Review** reexamine key points presented in the chapter. These questions test your knowledge of the chapter concepts and can help you review for exams.

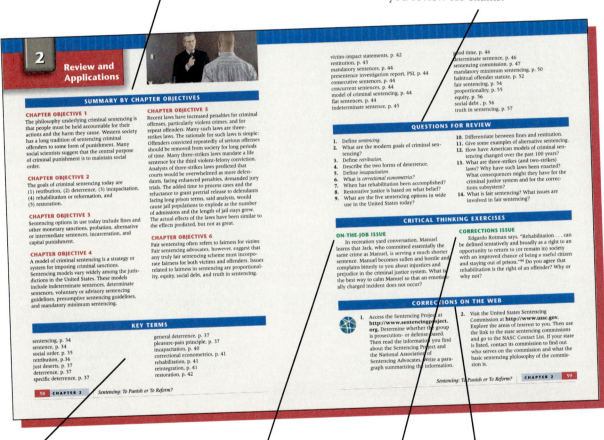

**Key Terms** listing consolidates the corrections vocabulary presented in the chapter. If you can't remember what a term means, the page reference alerts you to the location of its definition in the chapter.

**On-the-Job Issues** present workplace scenarios that encourage you to apply chapter concepts and develop decision-making skills.

**Corrections Issues** provide topics of concern in the corrections field that encourage you to develop critical thinking skills.

**Corrections on the Web** activities encourage you to learn from the vast array of information available on the Internet.

# Other Ways for You to Learn

To assist you in learning and applying corrections concepts, the *Corrections in the 21st Century* instructional program provides several study resources in addition to the textbook.

## Tutorial With Simulation Applications CD-ROM

A browser-based version of the textbook on CD-ROM includes key terms review, practice tests, and review games. Simulations present real-world situations for you to apply chapter concepts.

### Interactive Browser-Based Content
Chapter content is delivered in html format with topic search capabilities and links to other chapters.

### Application Simulations
Chapter concepts and issues are explored and applied through application simulations, which pose real-world situations to which you are asked to respond. You receive immediate feedback regarding the appropriateness of your choices.

### Chapter Review Game
A chapter review program in a game format helps you prepare for tests and quizzes.

### Glencoe Online
If you have Internet access, clicking on this button will start up a browser and connect to the Glencoe *Corrections in the 21st Century* Study Center Web Site.

## *Corrections in the 21st Century*
## Study Center Web Site

This unique study center site contains a wealth of current event material and multiple reinforcement and assessment tools. Visit it at: **http://www.corrections.glencoe.com**. Here is what you will find:

Chapter Resources
- Practice Tests
- Crossword Puzzles
- Concentration Games
- Interactive Exercises
- E-homework
- New Items
- Links to Corrections sites

Student Newsletter
Career Builder
Site Map

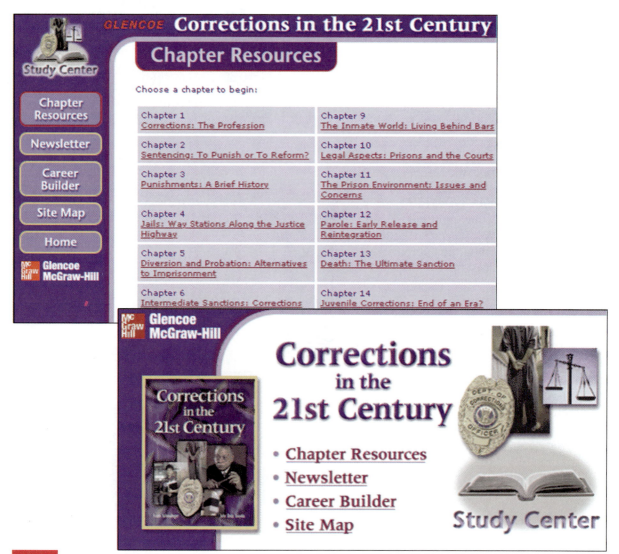

# How to Study Corrections

*Corrections in the 21st Century* is divided into 16 chapters and is organized to provide a logical approach to understanding how the corrections system operates in the United States. Chapter 1 contains important background information for topics presented elsewhere in the book. It presents a brief overview of the criminal justice system, with emphasis on the role of corrections in the system. Chapter 1 also introduces the theme of professionalism that is carried throughout the text.

Chapter 2 discusses the goals of sentencing and describes the types of punishments imposed on convicted offenders. Chapter 3 presents a brief history of punishments for crime and explains how incarceration came to be used as a criminal punishment. Chapters 4, 5, 6, and 7 focus on the institutional and non-institutional ways of punishing criminals. Chapters 8, 9, 10, and 11 describe the people and environments of living behind bars. Chapter 12 focuses on the concerns of early release and reintegration into society. Chapter 13 discusses the issues of the ultimate punishment, the death penalty. Chapter 14 focuses on juvenile corrections; Chapter 15 on victims; and Chapter 16 on careers in corrections.

Corrections, like any other course, builds in stages. Information presented in later chapters often assumes knowledge of information introduced in earlier chapters. You cannot afford to fall behind and then expect to catch up in one massive cramming session.

To get off to a good start, prepare yourself before the course begins by setting learning goals, organizing your time, studying your syllabus, and examining your own learning style.

## Set Learning Goals for Yourself

The purpose of setting goals is to understand exactly what you plan to accomplish. Ask yourself what you want out of this course. Is it a specific grade? Perhaps you need an A or a B to keep up your grade average. Perhaps you need a certain body of knowledge from this course to get into a higher level course. Perhaps you need a specific set of skills. You may be taking this course to meet a requirement for your job, to attain a personal career goal, or simply to satisfy your curiosity about the subject. Be forewarned, however: if you set your goals too low, you are likely to achieve only those low goals. For example, if you are not interested in the course but are taking it only because it is required of all majors, you should not be disappointed if you earn less than an A or a B.

## Organize Your Time

Now that you have set your goals, you need to organize your time to accomplish them. Time management allows you to meet your goals and still have time for activities. It helps you work smarter, not just harder. As a rule of thumb, for every class hour, allow two study hours. If an exam is coming up, allow more study time. Plan to study when you are most alert. You will retain information longer if you study on a regular basis, rather than during one or two cramming sessions. Either before or after a study session, have some fun! Timely breaks from studying enhance the learning process.

## Study Your Syllabus

Usually the course syllabus is available on the first day of class, but sometimes it is available sooner. If you can get a copy early, you will be that much ahead. The syllabus is your map for navigating the course. It should define the goals or objectives of the course, specify the textbook and supporting materials to be used, and explain course requirements, including the method or formula for determining final grades. The syllabus will also include a course schedule indicating when particular topics will be covered, what material needs to be read for each class, and when tests will be given. Other useful information on a course syllabus may include the instructor's name, office location, phone number, and office hours and, perhaps, the types of extra credit or special projects you may complete. Keep the syllabus in your notebook or organizer at all times. Review it at the beginning of each class and study session so you will know what course material will be covered and what you will be expected to know. Write down important due dates and test dates on your calendar.

# Eight-Step Study Plan to Maximize Your Learning

This plan is based on research that shows that people learn—and remember—best when they have repeated exposure to the same material. This technique not only helps you learn better but can also reduce anxiety by allowing you to become familiar with material step by step. You will go over material at least six times before you take an exam.

## Step 1: Use a Reading Strategy

In most cases, you will be asked to read material before each class. The SQ3R (Survey, Question, Read, Recite, and Review) method can help you get the most out of the material in every chapter of your book. Reading the material before class will acquaint you with the subject matter, arouse your interest in the subject, and help you know what questions to ask in class.

**Survey**   By surveying an assignment, you are preparing yourself for a more thorough reading of the material.

*Read the Chapter Title, the Chapter Objectives, and the Chapter Outline*   What topics does the chapter cover? What are the learning objectives? Do you already know something about the subject?

*Read the Summary by Chapter Objectives*   This will give you an overview of what is covered in the chapter.

*Look for Key Terms*   Key terms are the words associated with the important concepts covered in the chapter. Key terms are printed in boldface type in the text. Definitions of the key terms appear in the margins near the text in which they are introduced.

**Question**   Turn the chapter objectives into questions. For example, if the objective is, "Explain prisoner classification and its purposes." turn it into a question by asking yourself, "What is prisoner classification and what are its purposes?" Look for the answers to your questions as you read the chapter. By beginning the study of a chapter with questions, you will be more moti-

| | | **SQ3R Reading System** | |
|---|---|---|
| **Letter** | **Meaning** | **Reading Activity** |
| S | Survey | Survey the assigned reading material. Pay attention to the title, objectives, outline, key terms, and summary. |
| Q | Question | Find the major heads. Try to make questions out of these heads. |
| 3 R | (1) Read | Read the material, section by section. |
| | (2) Recite | After reading a section or part, try to briefly summarize aloud what you have read. Make sure your summary answers the question you formed for the section's head. |
| | (3) Review | After reading the entire assigned material, review your question heads. Make sure you can recall your original question and your answers. If you cannot, go back and reread that section. |

vated to read the chapter to find the answers. To make sure your answers are correct, consult the summary at the end of the chapter.

You can also write a question mark in pencil in the margin next to any material you don't understand as you read the chapter. Your goal is to answer all your questions and erase the question marks before you take an exam.

**Read**  Before you begin a thorough reading of the material, make sure that you are rested and alert and that your reading area is well-lighted and ventilated. This will not only make your reading time more efficient but help you understand what you read.

*Skim the Material*  Generally, you will need to read material more than once before you really understand it. Start by skimming, or reading straight through, the material. Do not expect to understand everything at once. You are getting the big picture and becoming familiar with the material.

*Read, Highlight, Outline*  The second time, read more slowly. Take time to study explanations and examples. Highlight key terms, important concepts, numbered lists, or other items that will help you understand the material. Most students use colored highlighting markers for this step. Put question marks in pencil in the margin beside any points or concepts you don't understand.

Outline the chapter in your notebook. By writing the concepts and definitions into your notebook, you are using your tactile sense to reinforce your learning and to remember better what you read. Be sure you state concepts and definitions accurately. You can use brief phrases or take more extensive notes for your outline, depending on the material.

*Apply What You Read*  In criminal justice, as in other courses, you must be able to apply what you read. The critical thinking exercises at the end of each chapter allow you to do this. Complete those exercises when you have finished studying the chapter.

**Recite**  In this step, you do a self-check of what you have learned in reading the chapter. Go back to the questions you formed from the chapter objectives and see if you can answer them. Also, see if you can answer the Questions for Review at the end of each chapter. Try explaining the material to a friend so that he or she understands it. These exercises will reveal your strengths and weaknesses.

**Review**  Now go back and review the entire chapter. Erase any question marks that you have answered. If you still don't understand something, put a Post-it by it or mark it in your text. These items are the questions you can ask in class.

## Step 2: Combine Learning Styles in Class

Think of the time you spend in class as your opportunity to learn by listening and participating. You are combining many learning styles in one experience. Knowing your preferred learning styles can increase your effectiveness in school or at work. Look at the chart on page xxvii to determine your preferred learning styles.

### Attendance: More Than Just Showing Up

Your attitude is a critical element. Attend class *ready to learn*. That means being prepared by having read and reread the assignment, having your questions ready, and having your note-taking materials organized.

Because corrections, like other courses, builds in stages, it is important for you to attend every class. You cannot ask questions if you are not there. And you may miss handouts, explanations, or key points that often are included on a test.

One final note. If you cannot attend a class, call the instructor or a classmate to find out what you have missed. You do not want to show up the next day and find out the instructor is giving a test!

### Attention: Active Listening and Learning

During most classes, you spend more time listening than you do reading, writing, or speaking. Learning by listening, however, calls for you to become an active listener and to participate in the class. Here are some active listening strategies for you to implement:

*Desire to Listen*  You must want to be a better listener and realize that listening is an active rather than a passive process.

| TYPE OF INTELLIGENCE | CHARACTERISTICS | LEARNER LIKES |
|---|---|---|
| **Verbal/Linguistic Learner** | Learns through words and language, written and spoken. Loves to read and write. Also tends to enjoy talking. | reading; answering questions; writing essays; discussion groups; playing word games |
| **Logical/Mathematical Learner** | Looks for patterns when solving problems. Creates a set of standards and follows them when researching in a sequential manner. | problem solving; experiments; working with numbers; asking questions; exploring patterns and relationships |
| **Visual/Spatial Learner** | Relies on sense of sight and being able to visualize an object, to create mental images. Learns through pictures, charts, graphs, diagrams, and art. | drawing, building, designing, creating things; jig saw puzzles; daydreaming; watching videos; looking at photos; drawing maps and charts |
| **Kinesthetic/Bodily Learner** | Learning is related to physical movement and the brain's motor cortex, which controls bodily motion. Eager to solve problems physically. | hands-on methods; demonstrating skill in crafts; tinkering; displaying physical endurance; performing; challenging self physically |
| **Interpersonal Learner** | Likes group work and working cooperatively to solve problems. Learns through person-to-person relationships and communication. | talking to people; joining groups; playing cooperative games; solving problems as part of a group; volunteering help when others need it. |
| **Intrapersonal Learner** | Enjoys opportunity to reflect and work independently. Often would rather work on his or her own than in a group. | working alone; pursuing own interests; daydreaming; keeping a journal or diary; independent assignments |
| **Naturalistic Learner** | Learns by observing, understanding, and organizing patterns in the natural environment. Has a strong connection to nature. | observing the world around them; spending time outdoors and working with plants, animals, and other parts of the natural environment |
| **Musical/Rhythmic Learner** | Recognizes tonal patterns, including various environmental sounds. Has a sensitivity to rhythm and beats. | Singing and humming; listening to music; playing an instrument; moving body when music is playing, making up songs |

*Be Open and Willing to Learn* Be open to different points of view, different styles of lecturing, and learning new ideas. Don't make up your mind that the instructor is wrong and that you are going to challenge what is said. It is easy to misinterpret the meaning of a message if you are defensive, bored, judgmental, or emotionally upset.

*Postpone Judgment* Don't judge your instructor or his or her message based on clothes, reputation, voice, or teaching style. Go to class with an open mind and focus on the message, the course content, and your performance.

*Be mindful* Being mentally and physically alert is vital for active listening. Focus your attention, concentrate on the subject, and keep your mind in the present.

*Use Empathy and Respect* Focus on understanding the message and viewpoint of the speaker. Look for common views and ways that you are alike rather than different.

*Observe* Observe your instructor and watch for obvious verbal and nonverbal clues about what information is important. Repetition, writing information on the board, and handouts give clues to important information. Watch for words that signal important information.

*Predict and Ask Questions* Keep yourself alert by predicting and asking yourself questions. What are the main points of the lecture? Do the examples clarify the concept? What test questions could be asked about this material?

*Look as If You Are Listening* Sit up, keep your spine straight, and uncross your legs. Maintain eye contact, and lean slightly forward. Don't lean back, cross your legs, or look bored. Respond with nods, smiles, and open facial expressions. Participate in discussions or when asked questions.

*Reduce Distractions* Don't sit next to friends or someone who likes to talk or is distracting. Sit near the front. Carry a bottle of water with you to sip if your energy starts to lag.

*Be Quiet* Be quiet while the instructor is speaking. Don't interrupt or talk to classmates. Really listen until the instructor is finished.

**Participation** In reading the material before class, you will have made a list of questions. If those questions are not answered in class, then ask your instructor to answer them. If the instruc-

tor makes a point you do not understand, jot it down and ask him or her to explain it as soon as you can.

**Note Taking** Why take notes? We forget nearly 60 percent of what we hear within one hour after we hear it. Memory is highly unreliable. This is why taking notes during class is so important.

Note taking involves both listening and writing at the same time. You must learn not to concentrate too much on one and forget the other. Follow these tips for taking good notes.

*Listen for and Record Main Ideas* You do not need to write down everything your instructor or other students say. By reading your assignment before class, you will know what the main topics are. Listen for those topics when your instructor goes over the material in class, then take notes on what he or she says about them. If the instructor emphasizes the importance of a topic for a test, be sure to make a note of this information as well (for example, "This section is really important for exam"). If you think you have missed a point, either ask your instructor to repeat or rephrase it right away, or mark the point with a question mark and ask your instructor about it later.

*Use Outline Style and Abbreviations* Set up your notes in outline style, and use phrases instead of complete sentences. Use abbreviations of symbols whenever possible (& for and, w for with, and so on). This technique will help you write faster to keep up with the instructor.

## Step 3: Review Class Notes

Listening and taking notes are critical steps in learning, but reviewing your notes is equally important. Remember: Repetition reinforces learning. The more times you go over material, the better you learn it.

**Fill in the Blanks** As soon as possible after a class, review your notes to fill in any missing information. Make sure you do it the same day. Sometimes you may be able to recall the missing information. If you can't, check your textbook or ask to see another student's notes to obtain what you need. Spell out important abbreviations that you may not recognize later.

**Highlight Important Information**  Marking different types of information helps organize your notes. You want to find what you need when you need it. Try these suggestions for highlighting your notes.

1. Use different colored highlighting pens to mark key terms, important Supreme Court decisions, and other kinds of information. Then, you will know that green, for example, always indicates key terms; blue indicates Supreme Court decisions; and so on. This method will help you find specific information quickly and easily.
2. Write a heading such as "Costs of Incarceration" at the beginning of each key topic. These headings can either correspond to those in the chapter, or you may make up your own headings to help you remember key information.

## Step 4: Reread the Text

After reviewing your notes, you are ready to reread the chapter to fix the concepts in your mind.

## Read for Details

- Go over the key points and main ideas carefully. Make sure you understand them thoroughly and can explain them to someone in your own words.
- Review the Chapter Objectives (that you have turned into questions) and the Questions for Review. Make sure you can answer all the questions and that you understand your answers.

## Mark Your Text

- Highlight any important terms or concepts you may have missed in your previous reading.
- Highlight any figures or tables you feel contain information that is important to remember.
- Erase any question marks in the margin that represent questions you have answered.
- Use Post-it notes to mark anything of which you are still unsure. Ask questions about those points in the next class, talk them over with other students, or make an appointment to meet with your instructor to discuss your questions.

## Step 5: Get Help if Necessary

What if you have read the material, taken notes, and asked questions, and you still do not understand the material? You can get further help. As soon as it becomes apparent that you need some help, ask for it. If you wait until the semester is nearly over, it may be too late. Here are several sources of help.

**Your Instructor**  Most instructors are willing to spend extra time with students who need help. Find out what your instructor's office hours are and schedule an appointment to go over the material in more detail. You may need several sessions. Remember to take notes during those sessions.

**Study Groups**  Join a study group in your class, or start your own. What one person does not learn, another does. Study groups take advantage of each member's expertise. You can often learn best by listening and talking to others in such groups. Chances are that, together, you will be able to master the material better than any one of you could alone. This is an example of power in numbers.

**Learning Labs**  Many schools have learning labs that offer individual instruction or tutoring for students who are having trouble with course material. Ask your instructor or classmates for information about the learning labs in your college or university.

**Private Tutors**  You might consider getting help from a private tutor if you can afford the fee. Although this route will cost you more, it may take only a few sessions to help you understand the material and keep up with the class. Check with your instructor about the availability of private tutors.

## Step 6: Study Creatively for Tests

If you have read your assignments, attended class, taken notes and reviewed them, answered the Questions for Review, and completed the Critical Thinking Exercises, then you have been studying for tests all along. This kind of preparation means less stress when test time comes around.

**Review: Bringing It All Together**  You should enter all exam dates on your calendar so that you know well in advance when to prepare for a test. If you plan extra time for study during the week, you will not have to cram the night before the test.

During that week, bring together all your textbook notes, all your handouts, and other study materials. Reread them, paying particular attention to anything you marked that the instructor emphasized or that you had trouble understanding.

In addition to studying the Summary by Chapter Objectives, Key Terms, and Questions for Review at the end of each chapter, it is a good idea to make a summary sheet of your own that lists all the major points and other information that will be covered on the test. If you have quizzes or tests you have already taken, review them as well. Focus on the material you either missed or did not do well on before.

Do not hesitate to ask the instructor for information about the test, in particular:

- The types of test items he or she will use (multiple-choice, true-false, matching, fill-in-the-blanks, short answer, essay)
- What material, if any, will be emphasized, and what material, if any, will not be included
- How much time you will have to take the test

## Step 7: Test-Taking Strategies

No matter how well you prepare for a test, you will feel some anxiety just before and even during the exam. This is natural—everybody feels this way. The guidelines in this section will help you manage your anxiety so that you can do your best.

**Before the Test: Get Ready**  Use this checklist to help you prepare the night before or a few hours before an exam.

- Gather supplies: unless instructed otherwise, at least 2 sharpened pencils with good erasers, a

watch for timing yourself, and other items if you need them (such as a blue book for essay exams).
- If the test is in your first class, get up at least an hour before the exam to make sure you will be fully awake.
- Eat well before the test, but avoid having a heavy meal, which can make you sleepy.
- Arrive early to review your notes and study materials. Remember: luck favors the prepared!

**During the Test: Go for It!**  Memorize these strategies to help you during the exam.

- Follow the directions. Listen carefully to the instructor's directions and read the printed directions carefully. Ask questions if the directions are unclear.
- Preview the test. Take a few minutes to look over the entire test. This will give you an idea of how much time to allot to each of the components.
- Do the easier sections first. If you get stumped on a question, skip it for now. You can come back to it later. Finish with the harder sections.
- Go back over the test. If you finish ahead of time, double-check your work and look for careless errors. Make sure your writing is legible if you are taking an essay exam or an exam that requires short answers. Make sure that your name and other information the instructor requires are on the test papers.

## Step 8: Reviewing Your Results

Never throw away any of your quizzes or tests. Tests give you direct feedback on your progress in the course. Whether the test is a weekly quiz or a mid-term, do not just look at the grade and put the paper in your file or notebook. Use the results of each quiz or test to help you achieve your goals.

**Learn From Your Successes**  First review the test for those questions you answered correctly. Ask yourself the following questions:

- What are my strongest areas? You will know which topics to spend less time studying for the next exam.

- What types of items did I find easiest to answer (multiple-choice, true-false, etc.)? You might want to start with these types of items on the next exam, giving you more time to work on the harder items.

**Learn From Your Mistakes**  Look over your errors, and ask yourself these questions:

- What types of items did I miss? Is there a pattern (for instance, true-false items, Supreme Court decisions)?
- Did I misunderstand any items? Was it clear to me what each item was asking for?
- Were my mistakes the result of carelessness? Did I read the items incorrectly or miss details? Did I lose track of time? Was I so engrossed in a test section that I forgot to allow myself enough time to get through the entire test at least once?

Look back through the textbook, your notes, class handouts, and other study materials to help you understand how and why you made the mistakes you did. Ask your instructor or classmates to go over your test with you until you know exactly why you missed the items. Evaluating your errors can show you where you need help and what to watch out for in the next test.

**Refine Your Action Plan: The Learning Spiral**  You can think of the eight-step action plan as an upward spiral. Each time you travel a full cycle of the plan, you accumulate more knowledge and experience. You go one turn higher on the spiral.

Use your test feedback and classroom work to help you refine your plan. Perhaps you need to spend more time reading the textbook or reviewing key terms. Perhaps you did not allow enough time for study during the week. Or you might need extra help from your instructor, your classmates, or tutors. Make adjustments in your plan as you tackle the next part of the course.

# Acknowledgments

Writing a textbook requires a great deal of help and support. We would like to acknowledge and thank the many individuals on whom we relied. Special thanks go to Dennis Stevens at the University of Massachusetts at Boston for his research on the special features and to Jody Klein-Saffran at the Federal Bureau of Prisons and Gary Bayens at Washburn University for their contributions to Chapters 12 (Parole) and Chapter 14 (Juvenile Corrections), respectively. We also gratefully acknowledge the contributions of the following individuals who helped in the development of textbook.

Tom Austin
Shippensburg University
Shippensburg, PA

Sharon Beck
University of Alabama at
   Birmingham
Birmingham, AL

Robert Bohm
University of Central Florida
Orlando, FL

Shelby Chandler
University of Alabama
Tuscaloosa, AL

Barbara Dahlbach
University of Alabama
Tuscaloosa, AL

E. Dorworth
Montgomery College
Rockville, MD

Lynn Fortney
EBSCO Subscription Services
Birmingham, AL

Donna Hale
Shippensburg University
Shippensburg, PA

Tavis Hardin
North Birmingham Elementary
   School
Birmingham, AL

Stephanie Holloway
University of Alabama
Tuscaloosa, AL

Julius Koefoed
Kirkwood Community College
Cedar Rapids, IA

Noelle Koval
Linda Nolen Learning Center
Alabaster, AL

Walter B. Lewis
St. Louis Community College at
   Meramec
Kirkwood, MO

Jess Maghan
University of Illinois at Chicago
Chicago, IL

Justine McNutt
University of Alabama
Tuscaloosa, AL

Alvin Mitchell
Delgado Community College
New Orleans, LA

Sarah Nordin
Solano Community College
Suisun City, CA

Michael F. Perna
Broome Community College
Binghamton, NY

Scott Plutchak
University of Alabama at
   Birmingham
Birmingham, AL

Sally Reeves
University of Alabama
Tuscaloosa, AL

William Selke
Indiana University
Bloomington, IN

John Sloan
University of Alabama at
   Birmingham
Birmingham, AL

Anthony C. Trevelino
Camden County College
Blackwood, NJ

Shela R. Van Ness
University of Tennessee at
   Chattanooga
Chattanooga, TN

Gennaro F. Vito
University of Louisville
Louisville, KY

Ed Whittle
Florida Metropolitan University
   at Tampa College
Tampa, FL

Robert R. Wiggins
Cedarville College
Cedarville, OH

Finally, we would like to express our appreciation to our publishing team at Glencoe/McGraw-Hill, whose vision, guidance, and support helped bring this project to fruition. Working with them has been an honor.

*Frank Schmalleger*
*John Ortiz Smykla*

# About the Authors

**Frank Schmalleger** is director of the Justice Research Association, a private consulting firm and think tank focusing on issues of crime and justice. The Justice Research Association is based in Hilton Head Island, South Carolina.

Dr. Schmalleger holds a bachelor's degree from the University of Notre Dame and both a master's and a doctorate in sociology from The Ohio State University with a special emphasis in criminology. From 1976 to 1994, he taught criminal justice courses at the University of North Carolina at Pembroke, serving for many years as a tenured full professor. For the last 16 of those years, he chaired the Department of Sociology, Social Work, and Criminal Justice. As an adjunct professor with Webster University in St. Louis, Missouri, Schmalleger helped develop a graduate program in security management and loss prevention. He taught courses in that curriculum for more than a decade, focusing primarily on computer and information security. Schmalleger has also taught in the New School for Social Research's on-line graduate program, helping to build the world's first electronic classrooms for criminal justice distance learning.

Frank Schmalleger is the author of numerous articles and many books, including *Criminal Justice Today* (Prentice Hall, 2001); *Criminal Law Today* (Prentice Hall, 1999); *Criminology Today* (Prentice Hall, 1999); *Crime and the Justice System in America: An Encyclopedia* (Greenwood, 1997); *Computers in Criminal Justice* (Wyndham Hall, 1991); *Criminal Justice Ethics* (Greenwood Press, 1991); *Finding Criminal Justice in the Library* (Wyndham Hall, 1991); and *Ethics in Criminal Justice* (Wyndham Hall, 1990). He is founding editor of the journal *The Justice Professional* and serves as imprint advisor for Greenwood Publishing Group's criminal justice reference series.

Schmalleger is also the creator of a number of award-winning Web sites. He is a member of the Advisory Board of APB Online, an innovative web-based criminal justice news service, where he also runs the CJ Professionalism Channel. He is founder and codirector of the Criminal Justice Distance Learning Consortium, a project of the Justice Research Association.

**John Ortiz Smykla** has been a professor of criminal justice at the University of Alabama since 1977, serving as chair of the department from 1986 to 1996. Using multimedia, he teaches undergraduate and graduate courses in research methods and corrections and has supervised more than 50 master's and doctoral students. He has taught two-way interactive corrections courses across several campuses of the University of Alabama system .

Smykla earned the interdisciplinary social science Ph.D. in criminal justice, sociology, and anthropology from Michigan State University. He holds bachelor's and master's degrees in sociology from California State University in Northridge. A former juvenile probation officer, Smykla conducted research with the Federal Bureau of Prisons in Pleasanton, California.

Dr. Smykla is the author of *Community-Based Corrections: Principles and Practices* (Macmillan, 1981) and *Probation and Parole: Crime Control in the Community* (Macmillan, 1984), co-author of *Executions in the United States, 1608–1995: The Espy File* (University of Michigan, 1995), co-editor of *Intermediate Sanctions: Sentencing in the 1990s* (Anderson, 1995), and editor of *Coed Prison* (Human Sciences Press, 1984). He serves on the editorial boards of a number of journals, including *Women & Criminal Justice*, *American Journal of Criminal Justice*, *Criminal Justice Review*, and *Journal of Crime and Justice*. He has published more than 40 research articles on jails, probation, parole, intermediate sanctions, same-sex and coed prisons, capital punishment, and juvenile corrections. He has delivered more than 50 conference papers in the United States and abroad.

Dr. Smykla is a member of the Academy of Criminal Justice Sciences and the Southern Criminal Justice Association. In 1996, the Southern Criminal Justice Association named him educator of the year. In 1997, he served as chair of the ACJS annual program committee. In 2000, he served as president of the Southern Criminal Justice Association. A supporter of community involvement, Smykla is a volunteer in the burn unit of Children's Hospital, Birmingham. In 1999, the nursing staff nominated him for volunteer of the year.

# Dedication

For Malia Hope
—Frank Schmalleger


A mi esposa, Evelyn, con amor siempre
—John Ortiz Smykla

# 1 Corrections
## The Profession

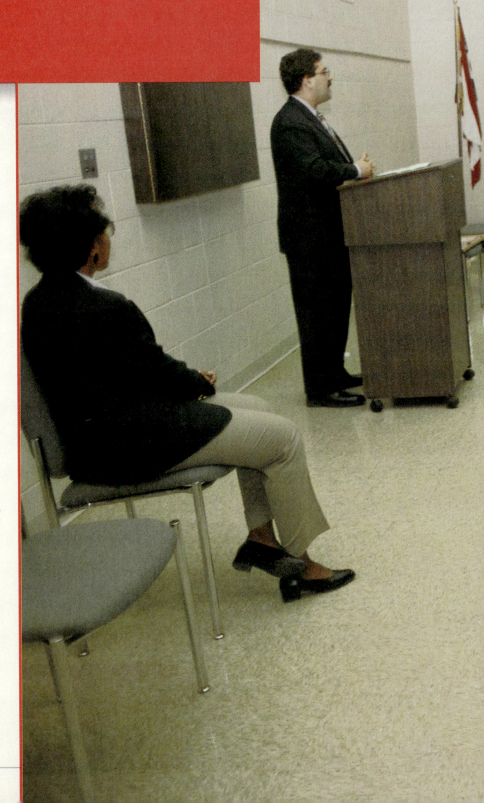

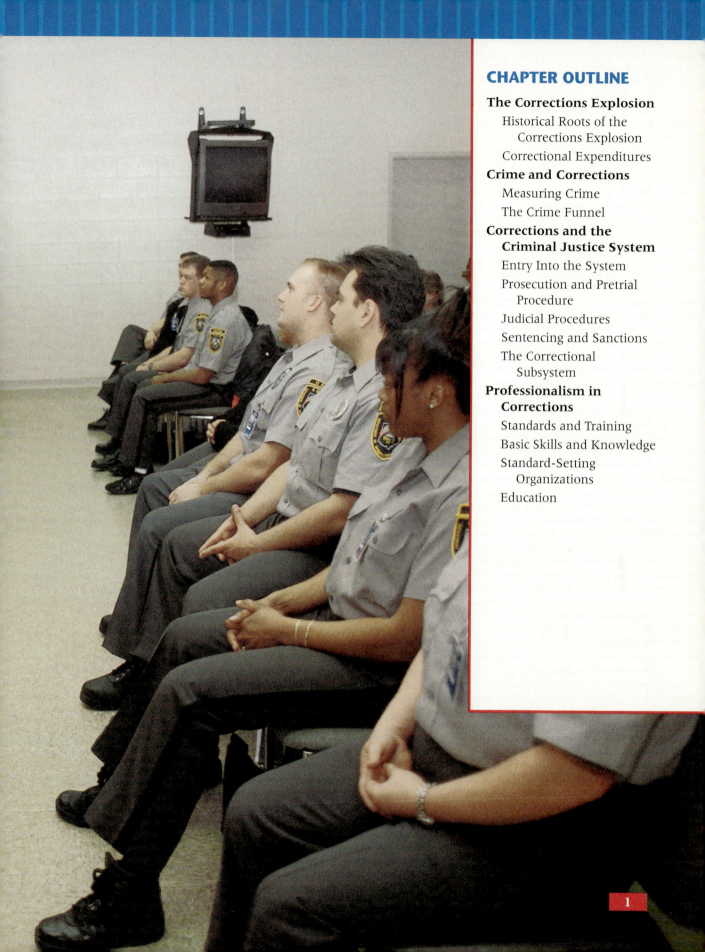

*Changes in the institutions and the correctional system as a whole require that correctional officers be capable of interacting with offenders and with colleagues in a manner which reflects attitudinal change and a knowledge base different from that generally accepted in the past.*

—P. H. Hahn

For decades, Father Patrick Moloney fought against drugs and was a prominent advocate for the homeless on New York City's Lower East Side.[1] These days, however, the Irish-born Catholic priest is known as federal prisoner 28251-0545. He spends his days behind bars and barbed wire at the Federal Correctional Institution at Loretto waiting for his 51-month sentence to expire.

Moloney was convicted of hiding $2 million, part of a $7.4 million Brink's armored car robbery in 1993. Prosecutors claim that the 64-year-old priest has ties to the Irish Republican Army—an allegation they have never been able to prove. Moloney now performs his priestly duties at a prison—one built, ironically, on the site of a former Franciscan seminary in Pennsylvania's Allegheny Mountains. "I spent my whole life fighting drugs—heroin, cocaine, crack, and marijuana," Father Moloney said in a recent interview. "Now I am in a cell with five other men, all of whom are convicted dealers." The priest has maintained his innocence, although all appeals of his conviction and sentence have been denied.

Because of prison regulations, Moloney cannot wear a clerical collar, is officially barred from conducting church services, and is not permitted to hear the confessions of other prisoners. On a typical day, he is assigned to cleaning toilets and shower stalls. Unofficially, however, Moloney conducts masses for some of the inmates at Loretto, leads a few men in group prayers, and counsels inmates in need of a receptive ear. Sometimes inmates ask the priest for special blessings. "When sending out their appeals they ask me to bless the document and pour holy water over it," said Moloney. "I tell them, 'I blessed mine and it didn't do anything for me.' "

**correctional clients**

Prison inmates, probationers, parolees, offenders assigned to alternative sentencing programs, and those held in jails.

Father Moloney's story illustrates the fact that **correctional clients,** as prison inmates, probationers, parolees, and those held in jails are called, are not all the same. Correctional clients are as diverse as the forms of criminal behavior that result in their encounters with the criminal justice system. The characteristics of the correctional population in the United States today are described generally in Figure 1–1.

# The Corrections Explosion

Not long ago, Fox Butterfield, a staff writer for the *New York Times*, wrote an editorial in which he noted: "It has become a comforting story: for five straight years, crime has been falling, led by a drop in murder. So why is the number of inmates in prisons and jails around the nation still going up? Last year [1996], it reached almost 1.7 million, up about seven percent a year since 1990."[2]

## FIGURE 1–1

### Characteristics of the Correctional Population

## Correctional Population

In the United States, almost 6 million adults (about 2.9% of the resident U.S. adult population) are under some form of correctional supervision

| | |
|---|---|
| 1,210,034 | in state and federal prisons |
| 664,847 | in local jails |
| 3,261,888 | on probation |
| 685,033 | on parole |

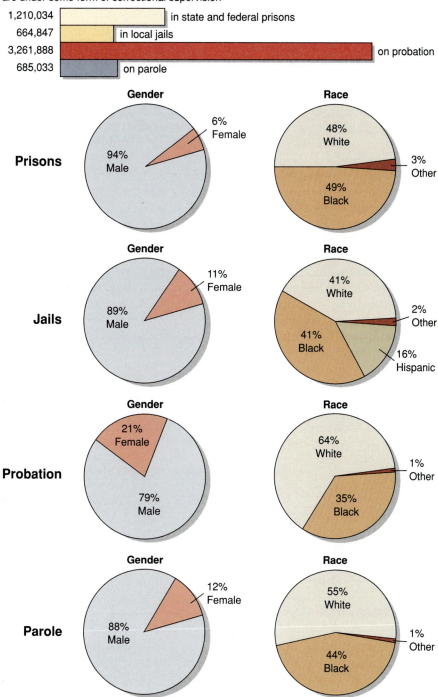

**Gender** (Prisons): 94% Male, 6% Female

**Race** (Prisons): 48% White, 49% Black, 3% Other

**Gender** (Jails): 89% Male, 11% Female

**Race** (Jails): 41% White, 41% Black, 16% Hispanic, 2% Other

**Gender** (Probation): 79% Male, 21% Female

**Race** (Probation): 64% White, 35% Black, 1% Other

**Gender** (Parole): 88% Male, 12% Female

**Race** (Parole): 55% White, 44% Black, 1% Other

*Sources:* Allen J. Beck and Christopher J. Mumola, *Prisoners in 1998* (Washington: Bureau of Justice Statistics, August 1999); Thomas P. Bonczar and Lauren E. Glaze, *Probation and Parole in the United States, 1998* (Washington: Bureau of Justice Statistics, August 1999, revised October 13, 1999); Darrell K. Gilliard and Allen J. Beck, *Prison and Jail Inmates at Midyear 1998,* Bureau of Justice Statistics Bulletin (Washington: Office of Justice Programs, March 1999).

As Butterfield observes, one amazing fact stands out from all the information about corrections. While serious crime in the United States has consistently declined throughout much of the 1990s, the number of people under correctional supervision in this country—not just the number of convicted offenders sent to prison—has continued to climb. Crime rates are approximately 15 percent lower today than they were in 1980. They are at their lowest level in 20 years. But the number of people on probation is up almost 300 percent since 1980, the nation's prison population has increased by more than 400 percent, and the number of persons on parole has increased by almost the same proportion. Figure 1–2 illustrates these trends.

The question is, why? Why the steady increase in correctional populations in the face of declining crime rates? The answer to this question, like the answers to most societal enigmas, is far from simple. Pursuit of the answer is important, however. As Franklin Zimring, director of the Earl Warren Legal Institute at the University of California at Berkeley, points out, "The change in the number of inmates tells us . . . about our feelings about crime and criminals."[3]

The answer has a number of dimensions. First, it is important to recognize that get-tough-on-crime laws, such as the three-strikes (and two-strikes) laws that were enacted in many states in the mid-1990s have fueled rapid increases in prison populations. The conservative attitudes that gave birth to those laws are still with us. Noted criminal justice scholar John P. Conrad summarizes today's mood this way: "There is an unprecedented consensus on the necessity for strengthening criminal justice. This consensus can be summed up in one sentence. Criminals must be locked up and kept off the streets."[4] Conrad goes on to explain: "The vast expansion of corrections today has not come about without good cause. For the citizen on the streets, there is only one reasonable response to the violence he or she fears. Lock them up, and hang the expense."[5]

Sources: FBI, *Crime in the United States, 1998* (Washington: U.S. Government Printing Office, 1999); Thomas P. Bonczar and Lauren E. Glaze, *Probation and Parole in the United States, 1998* (Washington: Bureau of Justice Statistics, 1999); Allen J. Beck and Christopher J. Mumola, *Prisoners in 1998* (Washington, Bureau of Justice Statistics, 1999).

## FIGURE 1–2

### Trends in Corrections Since 1980

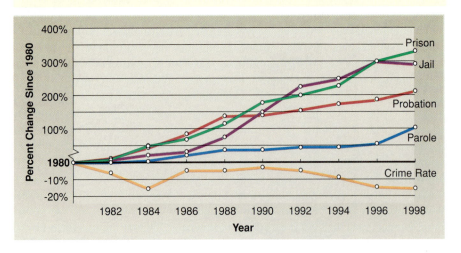

## TABLE 1-1

### Number of Prisoners by Offense

| Type of Offense | State | Federal |
|---|---|---|
| Violent Offenses | 494,349 | 13,021 |
| Property Offenses | 230,177 | 5,964 |
| Drug Offenses | 216,254 | 55,069 |
| Public-Order Offenses | 103,344 | 13,026 |
| | 1,044,124 | 87,080 |

*Source:* Adapted from Christopher J. Mumola, *Substance Abuse and Treatment, State and Federal Prisoners, 1997,* (Washington: BJS, January 1999).

A second reason correctional populations are rapidly increasing can be found in the nation's War on Drugs. The War on Drugs has led to the arrest and conviction of a large proportion of the country's populace, resulting in larger correctional populations in nearly every jurisdiction (especially within the federal correctional system). In Table 1–1, compare the total number of individuals incarcerated for drug offenses with, for example, the total incarcerated for property offenses. Drug arrests continue to increase. Although they account for a large proportion of the nation's correctional population, they do not figure into the FBI's calculations of the nation's rate of serious crimes. Hence, the War on Drugs goes a long way toward explaining the growth in correctional populations even while the rate of "serious crime" in the United States appears to be declining.

Third, parole authorities, fearing civil liability and public outcry, have become increasingly reluctant to release inmates, contributing to a further expansion of prison populations. Fourth, as some observers have noted, the corrections boom has created its own growth dynamic.[6] As ever greater numbers of people are placed on probation, the likelihood of probation violations increases. Prison sentences for more violators result in larger prison populations. When inmates are released from prison, they swell the numbers of those on parole, leading to a larger number of parole violations, which in turn fuels further prison growth. Statistics show that the number of criminals being sent to prison for at least the second time has increased steadily, rising to 35 percent of the total number of admissions in 1995, from 18 percent in 1980.[7]

## Historical Roots of the Corrections Explosion

Seen historically, the growth of correctional populations may be more the continuation of a long-term trend than the result of recent social conditions. A look at the data shows that correctional populations have continued to grow through widely divergent political eras and economic conditions. Census reports show an almost relentless increase in the rate of imprisonment over the past 150 years. In 1850, for example, only 29 people were imprisoned in this country for every 100,000 persons in the population.[8] By 1890 the rate had risen to 131 per 100,000. The rate grew slowly until 1980, when the rate of imprisonment in the United States stood at 153 per 100,000. At that point, a major shift in the use of imprisonment began. While crime rates rose sharply in the middle to late 1980s, the rate of imprisonment rose far more dramatically. Today the rate of imprisonment in this country is about 500 per 100,000 persons, and it shows no signs of declining.[9] Figure 1–3 illustrates changes in the rate of imprisonment over the past 150 years. Probation statistics—first available in 1935—show an even more amazing rate of growth. Although only 59,530 offenders were placed on probation throughout the United States in 1935, more than 3 million people are on probation today.[10]

FIGURE 1–3

## Rate of Imprisonment in the United States, 1850–2000

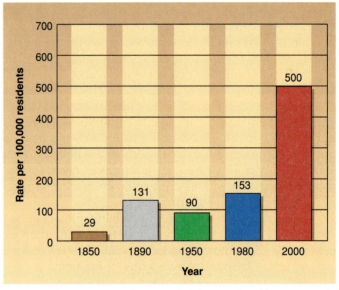

*Sources:* Margaret Werner Cahalan, *Historical Corrections Statistics in the United States, 1850–1984* (Washington: U.S. Department of Justice, 1986); Allen J. Beck and Christopher J. Mumola, *Prisoners in 1998* (Washington: BJS, 1999).

## Correctional Expenditures

Growing correctional populations also mean heightened costs. Budgetary allocations for corrections have grown in step with correctional populations. In 1965, the nation spent $1 billion on correctional services—including funding for juvenile institutions and programs. Thirty years later, in 1996, a staggering $22.8 billion was allocated to state and federal correctional budgets—with many additional dollars going to alternative programs for juveniles.[11] Most of the money spent on corrections today (about 75 percent) funds the day-to-day activities of correctional programs and institutions. Another 10 percent is allocated for the construction of new facilities—mostly prisons and jails.

As the trend continues toward ever greater use of correctional services, state and federal allocations are expected to continue to expand. The federal government alone spent $2.8 billion on correctional activities and services in 1996, $3.2 billion in 1997, and $3.3 billion in 1998. Federal expenditures on corrections are expected to exceed $3.8 billion by 2002,[12] and state correctional budgets are expected to rise proportionately.

The costs of running America's constantly expanding prison systems have begun to impose an enormous burden on government at all levels. Already, California and Florida spend more on incarceration than on higher education.[13]

On the flip side, growing correctional populations and increasing budgets have led to a dramatically expanding correctional workforce, and to enhanced employment opportunities within the field. According to historical reports, persons employed in the corrections field totaled approximately 27,000 in 1950.[14] By 1975 the number had risen to about 75,000. The most current statistics available show that the number of correctional officers alone has grown to more than 180,000.[15] When probation and parole officers, correctional administrators, and other corrections professionals are added, the total stands at nearly 340,000.[16] Figure 1–4 shows some of the employment possibilities in corrections.

New prisons mean jobs and can contribute greatly to the health of local economies. Some economically disadvantaged towns—from Tupper Lake, in the Adirondack Mountains of upstate New York, to Edgefield, South Carolina—are cashing in on the prison boom, having successfully competed to become sites for new prisons. The competition for new prison facilities is reminiscent of the efforts states made some years ago to attract new automobile factories and other industries.

## FIGURE 1–4

### Careers in Corrections

| Careers | Careers | Careers |
|---|---|---|
| academic teacher | field administrator | psychologist |
| activity therapy administrator | fugitive apprehension officer | recreation coordinator |
| business manager | human services counselor | social worker |
| case manager | job placement officer | statistician |
| chaplain | mental health clinician | substance abuse counselor |
| correctional officer | parole caseworker | unit leader |
| classification officer | parole officer | victim advocate |
| clinical social worker | presentence investigator | vocational instructor |
| children's services counselor | probation officer | warden/superintendent |
| chemical dependency manager | program officer | youth services coordinator |
| dietary officer | programmer/analyst | youth supervisor |
| drug court coordinator | program specialist | |

# Crime and Corrections

**felony**  A serious criminal offense; specifically, one punishable by death or by incarceration in a prison facility for more than a year.

The crimes that bring people into the American correctional system include felonies, misdemeanors, and minor law violations that are sometimes called *infractions.*

Felonies are serious crimes. Murder, rape, aggravated assault, robbery, burglary, and arson are felonies in all jurisdictions within the United States, although the names for these crimes may differ from state to state. A general way to think about felonies is to remember that a **felony** is a serious crime whose commission can result in confinement in a state or federal correctional institution for more than a year.

In some states a felony conviction can result in the loss of certain civil privileges. A few states make conviction of a felony and the resulting incarceration grounds for uncontested divorce. Others prohibit convicted felony offenders from running for public office or owning a firearm, and some exclude them from professions such as medicine, law, and police work.

**misdemeanor**  A relatively minor violation of the criminal law, such as petty theft or simple assault, punishable by confinement for one year or less.

Huge differences in the treatment of specific crimes exist between states. Some crimes classified as felonies in one part of the country may be misdemeanors in another. In still other states they may not even be crimes at all! Such is the case with some drug law violations, and with social order offenses such as homosexual acts, prostitution, and gambling.

**Misdemeanors,** which compose the second major crime category, are relatively minor violations of the criminal law. They include crimes such as petty theft (the theft of items of little worth), simple assault (in which the victim suffers no serious injury, and in which none was intended), breaking and entering, the possession of burglary tools, disorderly conduct, disturbing the peace, filing a false crime report, and writing bad checks (although the amount for which the check is written may determine the classification of this offense). In general, misdemeanors can be thought of as any crime punishable by a year or less in confinement.

Within felony and misdemeanor categories, most states distinguish between degrees, or levels of seriousness. Texas law, for example, establishes five felony classes and three classes of misdemeanor—intended to guide judges in assessing the seriousness of particular criminal acts. The Texas penal code then specifies categories into which given offenses fall.

**infraction**  A minor violation of state statute or local ordinance punishable by a fine or other penalty, but not by incarceration, or by a specified, usually very short term of incarceration.

A third category of crime is the **infraction.** The term, which is not used in all jurisdictions, refers to minor violations of the law that are less serious than misdemeanors. Infractions may include such violations of the law as jaywalking, spitting on the sidewalk, littering, and certain traffic violations, including the failure to wear a seat belt. People committing infractions are typically ticketed—that is, given citations—and released, usually upon a promise to appear later in court. Court appearances may be waived upon payment of a small fine, which is often mailed in.

## Measuring Crime

Two important sources of information on crime for correctional professionals are the FBI's Uniform Crime Reports (UCR) and the Bureau of Justice Statistics' National Crime Victimization Survey (NCVS). Corrections professionals closely analyze these data to forecast the numbers and types of correctional clients to expect in the future. The forecasts can be used to project the need for different types of detention and rehabilitation services and facilities.

**Uniform Crime Reports**   The FBI's Uniform Crime Reports (UCR) are published annually. Individual reports are often referred to by their official title, *Crime in the United States.* The UCR contains information on eight major crimes: murder, forcible rape, robbery, aggravated assault, burglary, larceny-theft, motor vehicle theft, and arson. These major crimes are divided into two subcategories: **violent crime** and **property crime.** Violent crime consists of murder, forcible rape, robbery, and aggravated assault. Burglary, larceny-theft, motor vehicle theft, and arson fall into the property crime category. Table 1–2 summarizes the crimes reported to police in the eight index crime categories.

The data, gathered from police agencies across the country, include only the crimes known to the police. Unreported or undiscovered crimes, which might outnumber those reported to the police, are not included in the UCR.

The sum total of all major crimes provides a national **crime index,** useful in comparing the occurrence of major crimes over time. The UCR also

**violent crime**
Interpersonal crime that involves the use of force by offenders or results in injury or death to victims. In the FBI's Uniform Crime Reports, violent crimes are murder, forcible rape, robbery, and aggravated assault.

**property crime**
Burglary, larceny, automobile theft, and arson as reported in the FBI's Uniform Crime Reports.

**crime index**   An annual statistical tally of major crimes known to law enforcement agencies in the United States.

## TABLE 1–2

### Major Crimes Known to the Police, 1998

| Offense | Number | Rate per 100,000 | Clearance Rate |
|---|---|---|---|
| **Violent Crimes** | | | |
| Murder | 16,914 | 6.3 | 69% |
| Forcible rape | 93,103 | 34.4 | 50% |
| Aggravated assault | 974,402 | 360.5 | 59% |
| Robbery | 446,625 | 165.2 | 28% |
| Total Personal Crimes | 1,531,044 | 566.4 | 49% |
| **Property Crimes** | | | |
| Burglary | 2,329,950 | 862.0 | 14% |
| Larceny-theft | 7,373,886 | 2,728.1 | 19% |
| Motor vehicle theft | 1,240,754 | 459.0 | 14% |
| Arson[1] | 78,094 | 39.0 | 16% |
| Total Property Crimes | 11,022,684 | 4,088.1 | 17% |
| U.S. Total | 12,553,728 | 4,654.5 | 21% |

1. Only fires determined through investigation to have been willfully or maliciously set are classified as arsons.

*Source:* Adapted from FBI, *Crime in the United States, 1998* (Washington: U.S. Government Printing Office, 1999).

**crime rate**  The number of index offenses reported for each unit of population.

reports a **crime rate** each year. The rate of crime is calculated by dividing the total number of major crimes by the population of the United States. The result is expressed as the number of crimes per 100,000 people. Crime rate comparisons provide a more realistic portrayal of changes in crime over time—and of the likelihood of victimization—than do simple comparisons of crime index totals.

The FBI reported that a total of 12.5 million major crimes occurred throughout the United States in 1998. The 1998 crime rate of 4,615.5 offenses per 100,000 United States inhabitants was the lowest since 1984. Regionally, the crime rate was 5,223 offenses per 100,000 inhabitants in the South; 4,879 in the West; 4,379 in the Midwest; and 3,474 in the Northeast. The violent crime rate in 1998 was 566 per 100,000, while the rate of property crimes was 4,049 offenses per 100,000.

If we look at Table 1–2, we see that 16,914 murders were recorded in 1998. The murder rate was 6.3 offenses per 100,000 inhabitants. According to supplemental data in the UCR, 76 percent of murder victims in 1998 were male and 88 percent were persons 18 years old or older. Of victims whose race was known, 50 percent were white and 48 percent were black. Eighty-nine percent of murderers were male, and 89 percent were 18 or older. Of murderers whose race was known, 49 percent were black, and 49 percent were white.

The UCR includes supplemental data for each index crime. Such data, along with the crime index totals, offers corrections personnel a glimpse of the background, makeup, and motivation of the offenders who may eventually become clients of the correctional system.

The UCR also includes data on the numbers of arrests in the United States for all types of crimes. Offenses not included in the crime index are called Part II offenses. Law enforcement agencies made an estimated 14.5 million arrests in 1998 for all offenses except traffic violations. The highest arrest count for a specific crime category was 1.6 million arrests for drug abuse violations. Larceny-theft and simple assaults each registered 1.3 million arrests. Arrests for driving under the influence numbered 1.4 million. In 1998 the nationwide rate of arrest was 5,534 per 100,000 people.

Most crimes reported to the police are not solved. Crimes that are solved are said to be *cleared.* For the UCR, a known offense is considered *cleared* or *solved* when a law enforcement agency has charged at least one person with the offense or when a suspect has been identified and located but circumstances have prevented charging the suspect.

The *clearance rate* is the number of offenses cleared, divided by the number of offenses known by police. Law enforcement agencies nationwide recorded a 21 percent crime index clearance rate in 1998. The clearance rate for violent crimes was 49 percent; for property crimes, 17 percent. Among crime index offenses, the clearance rate was highest for murder (69 percent), and lowest for burglary and motor vehicle theft (14 percent each). For many consensual crimes, such as prostitution, gambling, and drug abuse, rates of arrest are lower still. Table 1–2 shows the clearance rates for the index crimes reported in 1998. The clearance rates for individual index crimes help corrections professionals know the types and numbers of clients to expect in the correctional system.

**National Incident-Based Reporting System (NIBRS)** The FBI is implementing a new crime reporting program called the National Incident-Based Reporting System, or NIBRS. Under the new system, many details will be gathered about each criminal incident. Included among them will be information on place of occurrence, weapon used, type and value of property damaged or stolen, personal characteristics of the offender and the victim, the nature of any relationship between the two, disposition of the complaint, and so on. The new reporting system gathers data on 22 general offenses: arson, assault, bribery, burglary, counterfeiting, vandalism, narcotic offenses, embezzlement, extortion, fraud, gambling, homicide, kidnapping, larceny, motor vehicle theft, pornography, prostitution, robbery, forcible sex offenses, nonforcible sex offenses, receiving stolen property, and weapons violations. Data will also be gathered on bad checks, vagrancy, disorderly conduct, driving under the influence, drunkenness, nonviolent family offenses, liquor law violations, "peeping Tom" activity, runaway, trespass, and a general category of all other criminal law violations.

The FBI began accepting crime data in NIBRS format in January 1989. Although NIBRS was intended to replace the old system by 1999, delays have been frequent. It will be a few more years before all police departments report their crime data to the FBI in NIBRS format.

**National Crime Victimization Survey (NCVS)** The nation's second crime measuring tool is the National Crime Victimization Survey (NCVS).[17] The NCVS was begun by the Bureau of Justice Statistics (BJS) in 1973. It provides a detailed picture of crime incidents, victims, and trends. The survey collects detailed information on the frequency and nature of the crimes of rape, sexual assault, personal robbery, aggravated and simple assault, household burglary, theft, and motor vehicle theft. It does not measure homicide or commercial crimes (such as burglaries of stores).

*Racial minorities are overrepresented among all segments of the correctional population in comparison with the ethnic makeup of America. What is the cause of this lopsided ethnic representation?*

To gather data for the NCVS, U.S. Census Bureau personnel each year interview all household members at least 12 years old in a national representative sample of approximately 49,000 households. The total sample contains about 101,000 persons. The NCVS collects information on crimes suffered by individuals and households, whether or not those crimes were reported to law enforcement agencies. It estimates the proportion reported for each type of crime covered by the survey, and it summarizes the reasons that victims give for reporting or not reporting. For many types of offenses, the NCVS shows more crimes being committed than does the UCR. There are, however, some crimes—homicides and assaults—in which the police count more crimes than does the NCVS. Table 1–3 shows total victimizations reported by the NCVS for 1998. Compare the totals for similar categories in Table 1–3 and Table 1–2. This comparison will help you understand the importance of knowing the source and the manner of compilation of the data you use to make corrections decisions.

The NCVS provides information about victims (age, sex, race, ethnicity, marital status, income, and educational level), offenders (sex, race, approximate age, and victim-offender relationship), and crimes (time, place, weapons, injuries, and economic consequences). Questions also cover the

## TABLE 1–3

### Criminal Victimizations, 1998

| Type of Crime | Number of Victimizations |
| --- | --- |
| All Crimes | 31,307,000 |
| Personal crimes[1] | 8,412,000 |
| Crimes of violence | 8,116,000 |
| Completed violence | 2,564,000 |
| Attempted/threatened violence | 5,553,000 |
| Rape/sexual assault | 333,000 |
| Robbery | 886,000 |
| Completed/property taken | 610,000 |
| Attempted to take property | 277,000 |
| Assault | 6,897,000 |
| Personal theft[2] | 298,000 |
| Property crimes | 22,895,000 |
| Household burglary | 4,054,000 |
| Motor vehicle theft | 1,138,000 |
| Theft | 17,703,000 |

1. The NCVS is based on interviews with victims and therefore cannot measure murder.

2. Includes pocket picking, purse snatching, and attempted purse snatching not shown separately.

Source: Adapted from Callie M. Rennison, Criminal Victimization, 1998 (Washington: U.S. Department of Justice, July 1999).

experiences of victims with the criminal justice system, self-protective measures used by victims, and possible substance abuse by offenders. NCVS data are published annually under the title *Criminal Victimization in the United States.*

According to the most recent NCVS,[18] U.S. residents age 12 or older experienced approximately 31.3 million crimes in 1998. Seventy-three percent of those crimes, or 22.9 million, were property crimes; 26 percent (8.1 million) were crimes of violence; and 1 percent were crimes of personal theft. NCVS findings show that in 1998, Americans age 12 or older experienced fewer violent and property crimes than in any other year since 1973, when the NCVS began.

## The Crime Funnel

Not all crimes are reported, and not everyone who commits a reported crime is arrested, so relatively few offenders enter the criminal justice system. Of those who do, some are not prosecuted (perhaps because the evidence against them is insufficient), others plead guilty to lesser crimes, and others are found not guilty. Some who are convicted are diverted from further processing by the system or may be fined or ordered to counseling. Hence, the proportion of criminal offenders who eventually enter the correctional system is small, as Figure 1–5 shows.[19]

### FIGURE 1–5
### The Crime Funnel

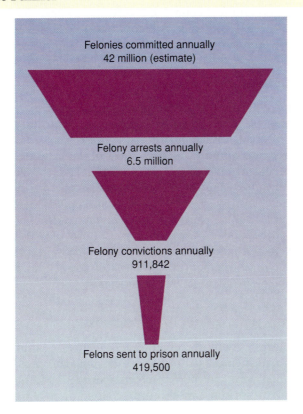

Felonies committed annually
42 million (estimate)

Felony arrests annually
6.5 million

Felony convictions annually
911,842

Felons sent to prison annually
419,500

*Sources:* Statistics compiled from Bureau of Justice Statistics data. Felonies include violent crimes, attempted personal victimizations, selected property crimes (such as burglary and motor vehicle theft), and various drug offenses. The estimated number of felonies committed annually is calculated from NCVS data, FBI data on drug and other felonies, and general knowledge about unreported crimes. Also see Bureau of Justice Statistics, *Felony Sentences in the United States, 1994* (Washington: BJS, 1997).

# Corrections and the Criminal Justice System

Corrections is generally considered the final stage in the criminal justice process. Some aspects of corrections, however, come into play early in the process. We have been talking about the criminal justice *process*. Keep in mind, however, that although the term **criminal justice** can be used to refer to the justice *process*, it can also be used to describe our *system* of justice. Criminal justice agencies, taken as a whole, are said to compose the **criminal justice system.** As you already probably know, the components of the criminal justice system are (1) police, (2) courts, and (3) corrections. Each component, because it contains a variety of organizations and agencies, can be termed a subsystem. The subsystem of corrections, for example, includes prisons, agencies of probation and parole, jails, and a variety of alternative programs. Since the activities of criminal justice agencies routinely involve other system components, the word *system* encompasses not only the agencies of justice, but also the interrelationships among those agencies.

The *process* of criminal justice involves the activities of the agencies that make up the criminal justice system. The process of criminal justice begins when a crime is discovered or reported.

Court decisions based on the due process guarantees of the U.S. Constitution require that specific steps be taken in the justice process. Although the exact nature of those steps varies among jurisdictions, the description that follows portrays the most common sequence of events in response to serious criminal behavior. Figure 1–6 on pages 16–17, a diagram of the American criminal justice system, indicates the relationship among the stages in the criminal justice process.

## Entry Into the System

The criminal justice system does not respond to most crime because, as previously discussed, much crime is not discovered or is not reported to the police.[20] Law enforcement agencies learn about crimes from the reports of citizens, through discovery by a police officer in the field, or through investigative and intelligence work. Once a law enforcement agency knows of a crime, the agency must identify and arrest a suspect before the case can proceed. Sometimes a suspect is found at the scene; sometimes, however, identifying a suspect requires an extensive investigation. Often no one is identified or apprehended—the crime goes unsolved. If an offender is arrested, booked, and jailed to await an initial appearance, the intake, custody, confinement, and supervision aspects of corrections first come into play at this stage of the criminal justice process.

## Prosecution and Pretrial Procedure

After an arrest, law enforcement agencies present information about the case and about the accused to the prosecutor, who decides whether to file formal charges with the court. If no charges are filed, the accused must be released. The prosecutor can also drop charges after filing them. Such a

**criminal justice** The process of achieving justice through the application of the criminal law and through the workings of the criminal justice system. Also, the study of the field of criminal justice.

**criminal justice system** The collection of all the agencies that perform criminal justice functions, whether operations or administration or technical support. The basic divisions of the criminal justice system are police, courts, and corrections.

Very few of us do not think about beating the system. After all, the system deprives us of the freedom we cherish. It stands for all that we resent: lack of choice, restricted movement, denial of access to loved ones. We resent the walls, bars, uniforms, being told what to do, what programs we must take.

Moralists argue that we get exactly what we deserve, and many citizens believe that we are treated too well. Few of us can argue that we didn't know what we were getting into when we made the bad choices that landed us in prison. None of us arrived by accident, and if we are honest with ourselves, we'll acknowledge a whole series of destructive behaviors that preceded our committal to a "monastery of the damned."

In view of status and our chances of success upon release, the future doesn't look particularly bright. It's damn depressing to have to accept our collective reality. Hope is found in beating the system, the smart way. The smart way is not the path many of us have continually taken: defiance, conflict with "the man." AA members are familiar with the slogan "I can only change myself, not others." It is always easier to project blame for our inadequacies onto others. But until we come to terms with our individual reality; separate the crime from the man, decide that the "I am" is capable of much more than the label implies—we're doomed to failure.

The administration uses education statistics to create the illusion of massive programming. It is up to us to demand the delivery. Enroll in courses. Develop the thirst to learn. Ask for help from peer tutors. An education is the ultimate form of restorative justice. The entire population benefits when just one con becomes literate. Educated cons have reason to lift their heads in self-assurance. We are better able to articulate our needs, better able to negotiate collectively, better able to see a future for ourselves.

Whether "the man" wants to acknowledge it or not, educated prisoners get respect from everybody inside and outside the prison. Adult education and training at every level—whether basic literacy, high school, college or university—are vital. The positive skills we learn in prison can't be taken away from us at the gate.

*Joseph E. McCormick*

choice is called *nolle prosequi,* and when it happens, a case is said to be "nolled" or "nollied."

A suspect charged with a crime must be taken before a judge or magistrate without unnecessary delay. At the initial appearance, the judge or magistrate informs the accused of the charges and decides whether there is probable cause to detain the accused. Often, defense counsel is also assigned then. If the offense charged is not very serious, the determination of guilt and the assessment of a penalty may also occur at this stage.

FIGURE 1–6

## The Criminal Justice System

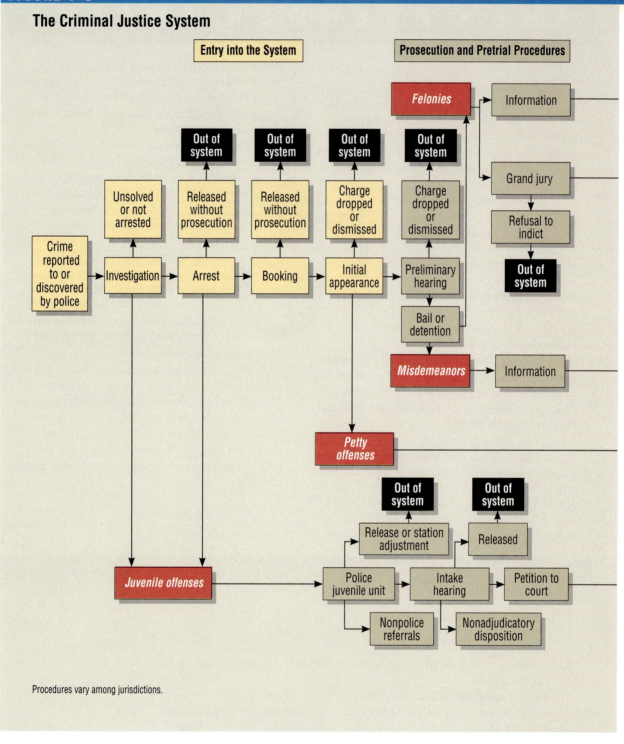

Entry into the System

Prosecution and Pretrial Procedures

Procedures vary among jurisdictions.

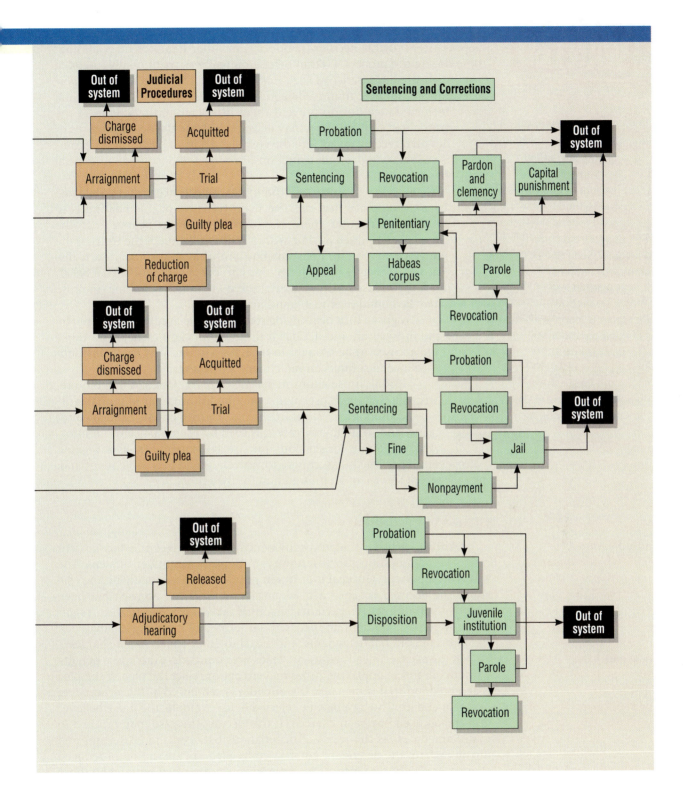

In some jurisdictions, a pretrial-release decision is made at the initial appearance, but this decision may occur at other hearings or at another time during the process. Pretrial release on bail was traditionally intended to ensure appearance at trial. However, many jurisdictions today permit pretrial detention of defendants accused of serious offenses and deemed dangerous, to prevent them from committing crimes in the pretrial period. The court may decide to release the accused on his or her own recognizance, into the custody of a third party, on the promise of satisfying certain conditions, or after the posting of a financial bond.

In many jurisdictions, the initial appearance may be followed by a preliminary hearing. The main function of this hearing is to determine whether there is probable cause to believe that the accused committed a crime within the jurisdiction of the court. If the judge or magistrate does not find probable cause, the case is dismissed. However, if the judge finds probable cause for such a belief, or if the accused waives the right to a preliminary hearing, the case may be bound over to a grand jury.

A grand jury hears evidence against the accused, presented by the prosecutor, and decides if there is sufficient evidence to cause the accused to be brought to trial. If the grand jury finds sufficient evidence, it submits an indictment to the court.

Not all jurisdictions make use of grand juries. Some require, instead, that the prosecutor submit an information (a formal written accusation) to the court. In most jurisdictions, misdemeanor cases and some felony cases proceed by the issuance of an information. Some jurisdictions require indictments in felony cases. However, the accused may choose to waive a grand jury indictment and, instead, accept service of an information for the crime.

## Judicial Procedures

**adjudication** The process by which a court arrives at a final decision in a case.

**Adjudication** is the process by which a court arrives at a decision in a case. The adjudication process, however, involves a number of steps. The first is arraignment. Once an indictment or information is filed with the trial court, the accused is scheduled for arraignment. If the accused has been detained without bail, corrections personnel take him or her to the arraignment. At the arraignment, the accused is informed of the charges, advised of the rights of criminal defendants, and asked to enter a plea to the charges.

**nolo contendere** A plea of "no contest." A no-contest plea may be used where a defendant does not wish to contest conviction. Because the plea does not admit guilt, however, it cannot provide the basis for later civil suits.

If the accused pleads guilty or pleads **nolo contendere** (accepts a penalty without admitting guilt), the judge may accept or reject the plea. If the plea is accepted, no trial is held and the offender is sentenced at this proceeding or at a later date. The plea may be rejected if, for example, the judge believes that the accused has been coerced. If this occurs, the case may proceed to trial. Sometimes, as the result of negotiations between the prosecutor and the defendant, the defendant enters a guilty plea in expectation of reduced charges or a light sentence. *Nolo contendere* pleas are often entered by those who fear a later civil action, and who therefore do not want to admit guilt.

If the accused pleads not guilty or not guilty by reason of insanity, a date is set for trial. A person accused of a serious crime is guaranteed a trial by jury. However, the accused may ask for a bench trial, in which the judge, rather than a jury, serves as the finder of fact. In both instances, the prosecution and defense present evidence by questioning witnesses, and the judge decides issues of law. The trial results in acquittal or conviction of the original charges or of lesser included offenses.

## Sentencing and Sanctions

After a guilty verdict or guilty plea, sentence is imposed. In most cases the judge decides on the sentence, but in some states, the sentence is decided by the jury, particularly for capital offenses, such as murder.

To arrive at an appropriate sentence, a court may hold a sentencing hearing to consider evidence of aggravating or mitigating circumstances. In assessing the circumstances surrounding a criminal act, courts often rely on presentence investigations by probation agencies or other designated authorities. Courts may also consider victim impact statements.

The sentencing choices available to judges and juries frequently include one or more of the following:

- The death penalty
- Incarceration in a prison, a jail, or another confinement facility
- Community service
- Probation—in which the convicted person is not confined but is subject to certain conditions and restrictions
- Fines—primarily as penalties for minor offenses
- Restitution—which requires the offender to provide financial compensation to the victim

In many states, laws mandate that persons convicted of certain types of offenses serve a prison term. Most states permit the judge to set the sentence length within certain limits, but some states have determinate sentencing laws (discussed in Chapter 2). Such laws specify the sentence that must be served, and these sentences cannot be altered by a parole board.

After the trial, a defendant may request appellate review of the conviction or the sentence. In many criminal cases, appeals of a conviction are a matter of right; all states with the death penalty provide for automatic appeal of cases involving a death sentence. However, under some circumstances in some jurisdictions, appeals are in the discretion of the appellate court, which may grant or deny a defendant's petition for a **writ of** *certiorari.* Prisoners may also appeal their sentences through civil rights petitions and writs of *habeas corpus,* in which they claim unlawful detention.

**writ of** *certiorari*   A writ issued by an appellate court to obtain from a lower court the record of its proceedings in a particular case.

## The Correctional Subsystem

After conviction and sentencing, most offenders enter the correctional subsystem. Before we proceed with our discussion, it is best to define the term *corrections.* As with most words, a variety of definitions can be found.

In 1967, for example, the President's Commission on Law Enforcement and Administration of Justice wrote that *corrections* means "America's prisons,

**institutional corrections**  That aspect of the correctional enterprise that "involves the incarceration and rehabilitation of adults and juveniles convicted of offenses against the law, and the confinement of persons suspected of a crime awaiting trial and adjudication."

**noninstitutional corrections** (also *community corrections*)  That aspect of the correctional enterprise that includes "pardon, probation, and parole activities, correctional administration not directly connectable to institutions, and miscellaneous [activities] not directly related to institutional care."

jails, juvenile training schools, and probation and parole machinery. . . . " It is "that part of the criminal justice system," said the Commission, "that the public sees least of and knows least about."[21]

A few years later, in 1975, the National Advisory Commission on Criminal Justice Standards and Goals said in its lengthy volume on corrections, "Corrections is defined here as the community's official reactions to the convicted offender, whether adult or juvenile."[22] The Commission noted that "this is a broad definition and it suffers . . . from several shortcomings."

We can distinguish between institutional corrections and noninstitutional corrections. A 1997 report by the Bureau of Justice Statistics (BJS) says that **institutional corrections** "involves the confinement and rehabilitation of adults and juveniles convicted of offenses against the law and the confinement of persons suspected of a crime awaiting trial and adjudication."[23] BJS goes on to say that "correctional institutions are prisons, reformatories, jails, houses of correction, penitentiaries, correctional farms, workhouses, reception centers, diagnostic centers, industrial schools, training schools, detention centers, and a variety of other types of institutions for the confinement and correction of convicted adults or juveniles who are adjudicated delinquent or in need of supervision. [The term] also includes facilities for the detention of adults and juveniles accused of a crime and awaiting trial or hearing." According to BJS, **noninstitutional corrections,** which is sometimes called *community corrections*, includes "pardon, probation, and parole activities, correctional administration not directly connectable to institutions, and miscellaneous [activities] not directly related to institutional care."

As all these definitions show, in its broadest sense, the term *corrections* encompasses each of the following components, as well as the process of interaction among them:

- The *purpose* and *goals* of the correctional enterprise
- Jails, prisons, correctional institutions, and other *facilities*
- Probation, parole, and alternative and diversionary *programs*
- Federal, state, local, and international correctional offices and *agencies*
- Counseling, educational, health care, nutrition, and many other *services*
- Correctional *clients*
- Corrections *volunteers*
- Corrections *professionals*
- Fiscal appropriations and *funding*
- Various aspects of criminal and civil *law*
- Formal and informal *procedures*
- Effective and responsible *management*
- Community *expectations* regarding correctional practices
- The machinery of *capital punishment*

**corrections**  All the various aspects of the pretrial and postconviction management of individuals accused or convicted of crimes.

When we use the word *corrections,* we include all of these elements. Fourteen elements, however, make for an unwieldy definition. Hence, for purposes of discussion, we will say that **corrections** refers to all the various aspects of the pretrial and postconviction management of individuals accused or convicted of crimes. Central to this perspective is the recognition

**EXHIBIT 1–1**

# American Correctional Association

## Purpose of Corrections

The overall mission of criminal and juvenile justice, which consists of law enforcement, courts, and corrections, is to enhance social order and public safety. As a component of the justice system, the role of corrections is:

**A.** To implement court-ordered supervision and, when necessary, detention of those accused of unlawful behavior prior to adjudication;

**B.** To assist in maintaining the integrity of law by administering sanctions and punishments imposed by courts for unlawful behavior;

**C.** To offer the widest range of correctional options, including community corrections, probation, institutions, and parole services, necessary to meet the needs of both society and the individual; and

**D.** To provide humane program and service opportunities for accused and adjudicated offenders which will enhance their community integration and economic self-sufficiency, and which are administered in a just and equitable manner within the least restrictive environment consistent with public safety.

that corrections—although it involves a variety of programs, services, facilities, and personnel—is essentially a management activity. Rather than stress the role of institutions or agencies, this definition emphasizes the human dimension of correctional activity—especially the efforts of the corrections professionals who undertake the day-to-day tasks. Like any other managed activity, corrections has goals and purposes. Exhibit 1–1 details the purpose of corrections as identified by the American Correctional Association (ACA).

**The Societal Goals of Corrections**   The ACA statement about the purpose of corrections is addressed primarily to corrections professionals. It recognizes, however, that *the* fundamental purpose of corrections "is to enhance social order and public safety." In any society, social order and public safety depend on effective social control. Some forms of social control take the form of customs, norms, and what sociologists refer to as *mores.*

*The percentage of women under correctional supervision, although still relatively small, has doubled over the past 10 years. How does this increase in female offenders affect institutional corrections?*

**mores**   Cultural restrictions on behavior that forbid serious violations of a group's values—such as murder, rape, and robbery.

**folkways**   Time-honored ways of doing things. Although they carry the force of tradition, their violation is unlikely to threaten the survival of the social group.

**criminal law** (also called *penal law*)   That portion of the law that defines crimes and specifies criminal punishments.

**Mores** are behavioral standards that embody a group's values and the violation of which is a serious wrong. They generally forbid such activities as murder, rape, and robbery. **Folkways,** in contrast, are time-honored ways of doing things. Although folkways carry the force of tradition, their violation is unlikely to threaten the survival of the group.

Societal expectations, whatever form they take, are sometimes enacted into law. The **criminal law,** also called **penal law,** is the body of rules and regulations that define public offenses, or wrongs committed against the state or society, and specify punishments for those offenses. Social control, social order, and public safety are the ultimate goals of criminal law.

The correctional subsystem is crucial in enforcing the dictates of the law because the rewards and punishments it carries out play a significant role in society's control of its members.

# Professionalism in Corrections

What is a professional? It isn't easy to say, but we seem to know when we encounter one. Professionals can exist in any field—even a field without clear-cut standards of professionalism, or one in which other professionals are rare. Professionalism and professional attitudes are important in just about any field because they win the respect and admiration of others, and because they make one a trusted participant in almost any endeavor. We need not limit this discussion to individuals, however. It is possible for a field of endeavor to be recognized as a profession. The legal profession, the medical profession, the nursing profession, and many other fields are now recognized as occupations in which people hold themselves to high standards. Not every participant in these fields is without faults, of course, but the public generally recognizes that, taken as a whole, those who call themselves doctors, for example, can be expected to act professionally and responsibly.

Only a few decades ago, some writers bemoaned the fact that the field of corrections had not achieved professional status. Luckily, much has changed over the past few decades. By 1987, Bob Barrington, who was then the executive director of the International Association of Correctional Officers, was able to proclaim, in a discussion about prisons, that "correctional facilities . . . run smoothly and efficiently for one basic reason: the professional and forward-thinking attitudes and actions of the correctional officers employed."[24]

Barrington noted the dawning of an age of professionalism in corrections. Professionalism, he noted, is rapidly becoming the foundation on which the practice of modern corrections rests. As Barrington wrote, today's correctional officers can say: "I am a corrections professional, and corrections is a profession in its own right."[25] Corrections professionals, added Barrington, ought to be proud to proclaim, "My profession is corrections!"

Some writers on American criminal justice have said that the hallmark of a true profession is "a shared set of principles and customs that transcend self-interest and speak to the essential nature of the particular calling or trade."[26] This definition recognizes the selfless nature of professional work. Hence, "professionals have a sense of commitment to their professions that is usually not present among those in occupational groups."[27] Work within a profession is viewed more as a 'calling' than as a mere way of earning a living. "Professionals have a love for their work that is above that of employment merely to receive a paycheck."[28]

Although it is important to keep formal definitions in mind, for our purposes we will define a **profession** as an occupational group granted high social status by virtue of the personal integrity of its members. We can summarize the *attitude* of a true professional by noting that it is characterized by:

- A spirit of public service and interest in the public good.
- The fair application of reason and the use of intellect to solve problems.
- Self-regulation through a set of internal guidelines by which professionals hold *themselves* accountable for their actions.
- Continual self-appraisal and self-examination.
- An inner sense of professionalism (i.e., honor, self-discipline, commitment, personal integrity, and self-direction).
- A commitment to lifelong learning and lifelong betterment within the profession.

Most professional occupations have developed practices that foster professionalism among their members.

**Programmer/Analyst**
Plans, develops, and implements computerized database systems, using own knowledge and guidelines established by department of corrections. Prepares system specifications to meet user requirements. Creates test data and programs, ensures uniformity of data definitions, and maintains standards for data dictionaries. Required qualifications include graduation from an accredited institution with a bachelor's or master's degree in civil engineering, computer operations, programming, computer science, business, business administration, engineering, mathematics, statistics, or statistical analysis.

**profession** An occupational group granted high social status by virtue of the personal integrity of its members.

## Standards and Training

Through training, new members of a profession learn the core values and ideals, the basic knowledge, and the accepted practices central to the profession. Setting training standards ensures that the education is uniform. Standards also mandate the teaching of specialized knowledge. Standards supplement training by:

- Setting minimum requirements for entry into the profession.
- Detailing expectations for those involved in the everyday life of correctional work.
- Establishing basic requirements for facilities, programs, and practices.

From the point of view of corrections professionals, training is a matter of personal responsibility. A lifelong commitment to a career ensures that those who think of themselves as professionals will seek the training needed to enhance their job performance.

Historically, professional corrections organizations and their leaders have recognized the importance of training. It was not until the late 1970s, however, that the American Correctional Association (ACA) Commission on Accreditation established the first training standards. The commission:

# THE STAFF SPEAKS

I had been a warden for several months when I discovered that it was extremely difficult to obtain basic training for in-service corrections officers. The problem essentially revolved around the cost associated with sending officers to the existing academy, some six hours away, and the overtime required to replace them for four weeks. Our solution was to develop a regional basic training academy at Mercyhurst College in Erie, Pennsylvania. Since the inception of this academy, we have made the training available to students who are not currently employed by any correctional agency. This collaborative effort between the county, the college, and our state oversight agency will produce officers who are not only well trained, but are also invested, both financially and mentally, in the corrections field. These individuals tend to see employment in a prison or jail as not just a job, but a career. I strongly encourage other correctional systems to develop a similar program or to make similar arrangements in order to enhance both custodial service and community involvement in their correctional enterprise. It's a win-win situation all the way around.

*Warden Art Amann*
*Director of Corrections*
*Erie, PA*

- Specified standards for given positions within corrections.
- Identified essential training topics.
- Set specific numbers of hours for preservice (120) and annual inservice training (40).
- Specified basic administrative policy support requirements for training programs.[29]

Following ACA's lead, virtually every state now requires at least 120 hours of preservice training for correctional officers working in institutional settings; many states require more. Probation and parole officers are required to undergo similar training in most jurisdictions, and correctional officers working in jails are similarly trained.

## Basic Skills and Knowledge

In 1990, the Professional Education Council of the American Correctional Association developed a model entry test for correctional officers. The test was intended to increase professionalism in the field and to provide a standard criminal justice curriculum.[30]

The council suggested that the test could act "as a quality control measure for such education, much as does the bar exam for attorneys." The standard entry test was designed to "reveal the applicant's understanding of the structure, purpose, and method of the police, prosecution, courts, institutions, probation, parole, community service, and extramural programs." It was also designed to "test for knowledge of various kinds of corrections programs, the role of punitive sanctions and incapacitation, and perspective on past experience and current trends."

More recently, in 1997, Mark S. Fleisher of Illinois State University identified four core traits essential to effective work in corrections.[31] The traits are:

- **Accountability** "Correctional work demands precision, timeliness, accountability and strong ethics." Students may drift into patterns of irresponsibility during their college years. Once they become correctional officers, however, they need to take their work seriously.
- **Strong Writing Skills** Because correctional officers must complete a huge amount of paperwork, they need to be able to write well. They should also be familiar with the "vocabulary of corrections."
- **Effective Presentational Skills** "A correctional career requires strong verbal skills, and an ability to organize presentations." Effective verbal skills help officers interact with their peers, inmates, and superiors.
- **A Logical Mind and the Ability to Solve Problems** Such skills are essential to success in corrections because problems arise daily. Being able to solve them is a sign of an effective officer.

In sum, we can say that a **corrections professional** is a dedicated person of high moral character and personal integrity, who is employed in the field of corrections, and takes professionalism to heart. He or she understands

**corrections professional**
A dedicated person of high moral character and personal integrity who is employed in the field of corrections and takes professionalism to heart.

*Melanie Estes*
*Day Youth Counselor*
*United Methodist Family*
*Services*
*Richmond, VA*

*"Working with troubled juveniles is challenging and rewarding, especially with abandoned and abused children. I'm not kidding anyone when I say that it is hard to maintain a healthy balance between friend and caretaker. But one of the greatest experiences I ever had is to help helpless children."*

Melanie Estes has been with the agency for one year and is currently one of two senior counselors. She completed a four-year degree in Criminal Justice in 1997 and is planning to attend graduate school in social work at Virginia Commonwealth University.

As a youth counselor, Melanie assists in developing, implementing, evaluating, and modifying individual and group treatment plans. She ensures that daily routine and expectations are followed in the residential home. It is also her responsibility to plan, oversee, and evaluate daily and weekly schedules of agency program activities. She is the liaison between the agency and the residents' social workers, probation officers, parents, and any others that may be involved in the youths' treatment. She keeps all parties informed of residents' progress.

As a staff member, Melanie's foremost duty is to act as a change agent for clients in the program. She believes that it is important that staffers learn that their interactions and interventions with one another are as crucial to the habilitative process as their interactions and interventions with youth. As a team member, she is asked to evaluate her coworkers' performance and to provide support, feedback, and training for other team members. Once a month, she is the chairperson and recorder for the weekly team meeting.

---

the importance of standards, training, and education, and the need to be proficient in the skills required for success in the correctional enterprise. The corrections professional recognizes that professionalism leads to the betterment of society, to enhanced social order, and to a higher quality of life for all.

## Standard-Setting Organizations

A number of standard-setting organizations and agencies in the field of corrections have developed models of professionalism. Among them are the American Correctional Association (ACA), the American Probation and Parole Association (APPA), the American Jail Association (AJA), and the federal Bureau of Prisons (BOP). Although the first three of these groups are **professional associations,** BOP is the agency that runs the federal prison system.

Standard-setting organizations like these offer detailed sets of written principles for correctional occupations and corrections administration. The ACA, the APPA, and the AJS, for example, all have developed standards to guide training and to clarify what is expected of those working in correc-

**professional associations** Organized groups of like-minded individuals who work to enhance the professional status of members of their occupational group.

**EXHIBIT 1-2**

# Federal Bureau of Prisons (BOP)

## Mission Statement

It is the mission of the Federal Bureau of Prisons to protect society by confining offenders in the controlled environments of prison and community-based facilities that are safe, humane, and appropriately secure, and that provide work and other self-improvement opportunities to assist offenders in becoming law-abiding citizens.

*Source:* Federal Bureau of Prisons, July 1998.

tions. Moreover, many professional associations have developed codes of ethics, outlining what is moral and proper conduct. Some of these codes will appear in later chapters.

Correctional associations also offer training, hold meetings and seminars, create and maintain job banks, and produce literature relevant to corrections. They sometimes lobby legislative bodies in an attempt to influence the development of new laws that affect corrections.

The BOP is especially significant as a standard-setting organization because its standards have wide influence. BOP standards govern the day-to-day activities of BOP personnel and institutions. They are also often studied closely by state departments of corrections, which frequently adapt the standards for their own use. Exhibit 1–2 is the Bureau's mission statement.

We will also present ACA policies in future chapters. The ACA policies, like BOP standards, are important because they guide the development of training and because they influence the work environment of many agencies and institutions.

## Education

Besides basic job skills and job-specific training, education is another component of true professionalism. Training, by itself, can never make one a true professional, because complex decision-making skills are essential for success in any occupation involving intense interpersonal interaction—and they can be acquired only through general education. Education builds critical-thinking skills, it allows the application of theory and ethical principles to a multitude of situations that are constantly in flux, and it provides insights into on-the-job difficulties.

Correctional education that goes beyond skills training is available primarily from two-year and four-year colleges that offer corrections curricula and programs of study. The day will come when at least a two-year degree will be required for entry into the corrections profession.

## SUMMARY BY CHAPTER OBJECTIVES

### CHAPTER OBJECTIVE 1

Although crime rates are at their lowest level in more than 20 years, correctional populations have been increasing because of get-tough-on-crime attitudes, the nation's War on Drugs, and the increasing reluctance of parole authorities, fearing civil liability and public outcry, to release inmates.

### CHAPTER OBJECTIVE 2

Growing correctional populations mean increasing costs. Budgetary allocations for corrections have grown in step with correctional populations. Growth in correctional populations and in spending has also led to a dramatically expanding correctional workforce, and to enhanced employment opportunities within the field.

### CHAPTER OBJECTIVE 3

The crimes that bring people into the American correctional system include felonies, which are relatively serious criminal offenses; misdemeanors, which are less serious crimes; and infractions, which are minor law violations.

### CHAPTER OBJECTIVE 4

Two important sources of crime statistics are the FBI's Uniform Crime Reports (UCR), published annually under the title *Crime in the United States,* and the National Crime Victimization Survey (NCVS), published by the Bureau of Justice Statistics under the title *Criminal Victimization in the United States.* The UCR reports information on eight major crimes: murder, forcible rape, robbery, aggravated assault, burglary, larceny, automobile theft, and arson. The NCVS provides a detailed picture of crime incidents, victims, and trends. While UCR data are based upon crime reports made to the police, NCVS data are derived from annual nationwide surveys of American households.

### CHAPTER OBJECTIVE 5

Criminal justice agencies are said to make up the criminal justice system. The main components of the criminal justice system are (1) police, (2) courts, and (3) corrections. Each can be considered a subsystem of the criminal justice system.

### CHAPTER OBJECTIVE 6

The major components of the corrections subsystem are jails, probation, parole, and prisons. Jails and prisons are examples of institutional corrections, while probation and parole are forms of non-institutional corrections.

### CHAPTER OBJECTIVE 7

The term *criminal justice* can be used to refer to our *system* of justice, or it can refer to the activities that take place during the justice *process.* Criminal justice agencies, taken together, make up the criminal justice system. Since the activities of criminal justice agencies routinely involve other agencies, the word *system* encompasses not only the agencies of justice, but also the relationships among those agencies. The justice process, on the other hand, refers to the events that unfold as a suspect is processed by the criminal justice system.

### CHAPTER OBJECTIVE 8

Corrections refers to all aspects of the pretrial and postconviction management of individuals accused or convicted of crimes.

### CHAPTER OBJECTIVE 9

Professionalism in corrections is important because it can win the respect and admiration of others outside of the field. Moreover, professionals are regarded as trusted participants in any field of endeavor.

correctional clients, p. 2
felony, p. 8
misdemeanor, p. 8
infraction, p. 8
violent crime, p. 9
property crime, p. 9
crime index, p. 9
crime rate, p. 10

criminal justice, p. 14
criminal justice system, p. 14
adjudication, p. 18
*nolo contendere*, p. 18
writ of *certiorari*, p. 19
institutional corrections, p. 20
noninstitutional corrections,
  p. 20

corrections, p. 20
mores, p. 22
folkways, p. 22
criminal law, p. 22
penal law, p. 22
profession, p. 23
corrections professional, p. 25
professional associations, p. 26

## QUESTIONS FOR REVIEW

1. Compare crime rates with correctional populations over time. What differences stand out? How might you explain them?

2. What three major categories of crime are discussed in this chapter? Explain the differences between them. Why is it important for corrections professionals to understand these differences?

3. Compare and contrast the Uniform Crime Reports and the National Crime Victimization Survey. What are the major differences? What are the similarities? What is the significance of these sources of information to the field of corrections?

4. What are the major components of the criminal justice system? Why did we say that the term *criminal justice* can be used to refer either to our system of justice or to the activities that take place during the justice *process?*

5. According to the ACA, what are the four fundamental purposes of corrections?

6. Explain how the UCR calculates its yearly crime rate.

7. According to the UCR, when is a crime considered *cleared* or *solved?*

8. What is the major difference between the original UCR system and the new system—NIBRS?

9. List four components of the corrections subsystem.

10. What is the function of a preliminary hearing?

11. Name and describe the first step in the adjudication process.

12. List at least five sentencing choices available to a judge or jury.

13. Based on the ACA statement defining corrections, what is the *fundamental* purpose of corrections?

14. Define criminal law.

15. List five characteristics of a true professional.

## CRITICAL THINKING EXERCISES

### ON-THE-JOB ISSUE

Today is the first day of your job as a correctional officer. A severe statewide shortage of officers required you to begin work immediately. You are scheduled to attend the training academy in three months. You are ushered into a meeting with the warden. He welcomes you to his facility and gives you a brief pep talk. He asks if you have any concerns. You tell him, "Well, I feel a little uneasy. I haven't gone through the academy yet." "Don't worry," he says, "all our new recruits get on-the-job experience before a slot in the acad-

emy opens up. You'll do fine!" He shakes your hand and leads you to the door.

After you leave the warden's office, you are given a set of keys and a can of mace. The shift supervisor, a sergeant, gives you a brief tour of the prison. Then he tells you that as you learn your job, you will spend most of your time with another officer; though pairing up will not always be possible.

The officer you are assigned to accompany is named Harold Gates. At first, you follow Officer Gates across the compound, getting more familiar with the layout of the facility. Then you spend an uneventful afternoon working with Officer Gates in the yard.

At 4:30, Officer Gates instructs you to make sure that all inmates have left the classroom building in preparation for a "count." As you enter the building, you encounter a group of six inmates heading toward the door. Before you can move to the side, one of the inmates walks to within an inch of you and stares at you. The others crowd in behind him. You can't move. You are pinned to the door by the men.

The man directly in front of you is huge—over six feet tall and about 280 pounds. His legs look like tree trunks, and his arms are held away from his body by their sheer bulk. You're staring at a chest that could easily pass as a brick wall. With a snarl he growls, "What do you want?"

1. How will you respond? Would you feel more confident responding to a situation like this if you had had some training?
2. If you tell the inmates that it's time for a count, and to move along, what will you do next? Will you ask anyone for guidance in similar future situations, or just chalk the encounter up as a learning experience? Who might you talk to about it?
3. Suppose you were a manager or supervisor at this facility. How would you handle the training of new recruits?

## CORRECTIONS ISSUES

1. Dianne Carter, President of the National Academy of Corrections, once said, "Too often in corrections, only worker skills are targeted for training, and the organization misses a significant opportunity to communicate its vision and mission."[32] Do you agree or disagree with this statement? Why?
2. Harold Williamson, a writer in the corrections field has noted, "Higher levels of professionalization require greater amounts of training and usually involve increased specialization when compared to lesser professionalized activity. Higher levels of professionalization also involve the learning of more abstract knowledge and information."[33] Do you agree? Why or why not?

## CORRECTIONS ON THE WEB

 Access the Web sites of the following professional corrections organizations. For each one, determine the organization's mission, membership, services offered, and benefits of membership. Then, using the information you have gathered, decide whether you, as a correctional professional, should be a member of the organization, and whether the agency with which you are associated should be a member. Explain the reasons for your answers.

**American Correctional Association**
http://www.corrections.com/aca

**American Jail Association**
http://www.corrections.com/aja

**American Probation and Parole Association**
http://www.csg.org/appa

**International Association of Correctional Officers**
http://www.acsp.uic.edu/iaco/about.htm

**National Sheriffs' Association (includes jailers)**
http://www.sheriffs.org

## ADDITIONAL READINGS

DiMascio, William M., *Seeking Justice: Crime and Punishment in America*. New York: The Edna McConnell Clark Foundation, 1997.

Gilbert, M. J., "Correctional Training Standards: A Basis for Improving Quality and Professionalism," in Ann Dargis (ed.), *State of Corrections: Proceedings of ACA Annual Conference, 1989*. Lanham, MD: ACA, 1990, pp. 44–58.

Haas, Kenneth C., and Geoffrey P. Alpert. *The Dilemmas of Corrections: Contemporary Readings*, 2d ed. Prospect Heights, IL: Waveland Press, 1991.

Josi, Don A. and Dale K. Sechrest, *The Changing Career of the Professional Officer: Policy Implications for the 21st Century*. Boston: Butterworth-Heineman, 1998.

# ENDNOTES

1. Details for this story come from Selwyn Raab, "A Shadow Priest Who Ministers to His Fellow Convicts," *New York Times* News Service, August 17, 1997.
2. Fox Butterfield, "Crime Keeps on Falling, but Prisons Keep on Filling," *New York Times* News Service, September 28, 1997.
3. Quoted ibid.
4. John P. Conrad, "The Pessimistic Reflections of a Chronic Optimist," *Federal Probation,* Vol. 55, No. 2, 1991, p. 4.
5. Ibid., p. 8.
6. See, for example, Jory Farr, "A Growth Enterprise." http://www.press-enterprise.com/focus/prison/html/a growth industry.html
7. Bureau of Justice Statistics, *Correctional Populations in the United States* (Washington: U.S. Department of Justice, May 1997).
8. Margaret Werner Cahalan, *Historical Corrections Statistics in the United States, 1850–1984* (Washington: U.S. Department of Justice, 1986).
9. Allen J. Beck and Christopher J. Mumola, *Prisoners in 1998* (Washington: BJS, 1999).
10. Thomas P. Bonczar and Lauren E. Glaze, *Probation and Parole in the United States, 1998* (Washington: BJS, 1999).
11. Kathleen Maguire and Ann L. Pastore (eds.), *Sourcebook of Criminal Justice Statistics.* Online, available: http://www.albany.edu/sourcebook, posted October 15, 1997.
12. Ibid., Table 1.11.
13. Butterfield.
14. Cahalan.
15. Greg Wees, "Fewer Correctional Officer Positions Created in 1996," *Corrections Compendium,* August 1996, pp. 12–14.
16. Statistics courtesy of David M. Wakefield at the American Correctional Association, fax transmission, June 12, 1998. Preliminary data for the table "Personnel in Adult and Juvenile Corrections" in ACA, *Vital Statistics in Corrections* (forthcoming).
17. Some of the material in this section is adapted from Bureau of Justice Statistics, *The Nation's Two Crime Measures* (Washington: U.S. Department of Justice, November 1995).
18. Callie Marie Rennison, "Criminal Victimization 1998: Changes 1997–98, With Trends 1973–98." (Washington: BJS, 1999).
19. The figure may be somewhat misleading, however, because an offender who commits a number of crimes may be prosecuted for only one.
20. Much of the following material is adapted from Bureau of Justice Statistics, *Report to the Nation on Crime and Justice,* 2d ed. (Washington: BJS, 1988), pp. 56–58.
21. President's Commission on Law Enforcement and Administration of Justice, *The Challenge of Crime in a Free Society* (Washington: U.S. Government Printing Office, 1967), p. 159.
22. National Advisory Commission on Criminal Justice Standards and Goals, *Corrections* (Washington: U.S. Government Printing Office, 1975), p. 2.
23. Bureau of Justice Statistics, *Correctional Populations in the United States, 1995* (Washington: U.S. Government Printing Office, 1997).
24. Bob Barrington, "Corrections: Defining the Profession and the Roles of Staff," *Corrections Today,* August 1987, pp. 116–120.
25. Ibid., paraphrased.
26. Arlin Adams, *The Legal Profession: A Critical Evaluation,* 93 DICK. L. REV. 643 (1989).
27. Harold E. Williamson, *The Corrections Profession* (Newbury Park, CA: Sage, 1990), p. 79.
28. Adams.
29. Ibid., p. 20.
30. P. P. Lejins, "ACA Education Council Proposes Correctional Officer Entry Tests," *Corrections Today,* Vol. 52, No. 1 (February 1990), pp. 56, 58, 60.
31. Mark S. Fleisher, "Teaching Correctional Management to Criminal Justice Majors," *Journal of Criminal Justice Education,* Vol. 8, No. 1, Spring 1997, pp. 59–73.
32. Dianne Carter, "The Status of Education and Training in Corrections," *Federal Probation,* Vol. 55, No. 2 (June 1991), pp. 17–23.
33. Williamson.

# 2 Sentencing
## To Punish or To Reform?

**CHAPTER OBJECTIVES**

After completing this chapter you should be able to:

1. Describe sentencing philosophy and identify the central purpose of criminal punishment.
2. Name the five goals of criminal sentencing.
3. List and explain the sentencing options in general use today.
4. Explain what a model of criminal sentencing is and identify models in use today.
5. Describe three-strikes laws and their impact on the correctional system.
6. Identify and explain some major issues related to fair sentencing.

STEPHEN J. SUNDVOLD

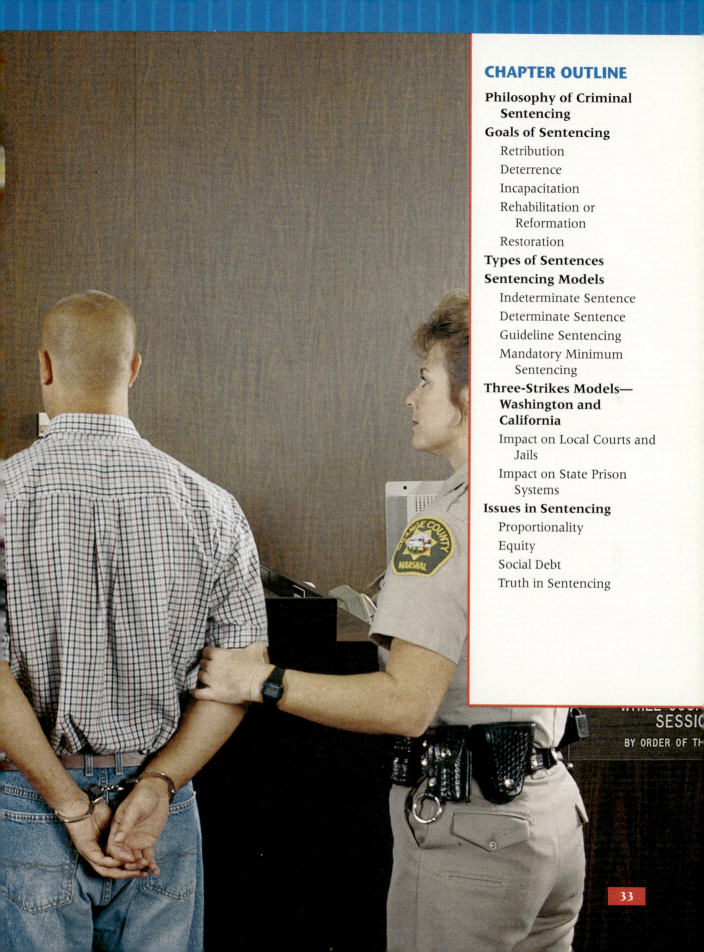

*We will not punish a man because he hath offended, but that he may offend no more; nor does punishment ever look to the past, but to the future; for it is not the result of passion, but that the same thing be guarded against in time to come.*

—Seneca (3 B.C.–A.D. 65)

On Halloween day 1997, 19-year-old British *au pair* Louise Woodward was sentenced to life in prison for second-degree murder.[1] One day earlier, a Massachusetts jury had found Woodward guilty of killing 8-month-old Matthew Eappen, a child in her care. Medical testimony at Woodward's trial convinced the jury that the boy died from injuries he had received while being severely shaken. According to medical experts, the boy's head had also been slammed against a wall. The child died five days later in a local hospital. Prosecutors argued that Woodward had fatally injured the boy during a fit of rage induced by his constant crying. Under Massachusetts law, Woodward, who denied hurting the boy, would have been eligible for parole in 15 years.

In an astonishing turnabout, Woodward was released a week later by state superior court judge Hiller B. Zobel, who overturned her murder conviction, reducing it to involuntary manslaughter. Woodward was sentenced to the time she had already served—279 days in jail. The judge ruled that Woodward's second-degree murder conviction had been a "miscarriage of justice," and concluded that "it is time to bring the judicial part of this extraordinary matter to a compassionate conclusion." The Woodward case, while relatively unusual, demonstrates judicial power in the determination of sentences.

Most criminal convictions, however, are not overturned. On the day before Woodward was convicted, the South Carolina Supreme Court upheld an 8-year prison sentence for Cornelia Whitner. Whitner had pleaded guilty in 1992 to child neglect after giving birth to a baby with measurable amounts of cocaine in its blood. Finding that a viable fetus is a "person" covered by the state's child-abuse laws, the state supreme court upheld the criminal prosecution of pregnant women who use drugs.[2] Ms. Whitner's attorneys planned to appeal the decision to the U.S. Supreme Court. "If women who use drugs during pregnancy can be prosecuted for child abuse," they asked, "what about women who drink or smoke while pregnant, or fail to get prenatal care?"

Although these cases are significantly different in many ways, both highlight the role of sentencing in the justice process. **Sentencing** is a court's imposition of a penalty on a convicted offender. A **sentence** is the penalty imposed.

This chapter concerns itself with the nature, history, purpose, and philosophy of criminal sentencing. One of the most crucial issues surrounding sentencing is whether to punish or to reform. The punish or reform debate has a long history and continues to concern many people today. We turn now to an examination of the history of sentencing philosophy.

**sentencing** The imposition of a criminal sanction by a sentencing authority, such as a judge.

**sentence** The penalty a court imposes on a person convicted of a crime.

# Philosophy of Criminal Sentencing

One of the most crucial issues in sentencing is whether to punish or to reform. The punish-or-reform debate has a long history and continues to concern many people today. Western society has a long tradition of punishing criminal offenders. Historically, offenders were banished, exiled, killed, or physically abused. Corporal, or physical, punishments became common during the Middle Ages, replacing executions as the preferred penalty. Physical punishments such as flogging and mutilation, though severe in themselves, prevented rampant use of the death penalty. Eventually, as we shall see in later chapters, imprisonment and a variety of other sentencing alternatives replaced corporal punishments as criminal sanctions.

Even so, the sentencing of offenders is still intimately associated with historical notions of punishment. Crimes are frequently seen as *deserving* of punishment. We often hear it said that the criminal must "pay his or her debt to society," or that "criminals deserve to be punished." John Conrad puts it another way: "The punishment of the criminal is the collective reaction of the community to the wrong that has been done."[3] Conrad goes on to say, "It is the offender's lot to be punished."

Philosophers have long debated *why* a wrongful act should be punished. Many social scientists suggest that criminal punishment maintains and defends the **social order.** By threatening potential law violators and by making the lives of violators uncomfortable, they say, punishments reduce the likelihood of future or continued criminal behavior.

Still, one might ask, instead of punishing offenders, why not offer them psychological treatment, or educate them so that they are less prone to future law violation? The answer to this question is far from clear. Although criminal sentencing today has a variety of goals, and educational and treatment programs are more common now in corrections, punishment still takes center stage in society's view. Some writers, like Conrad, have suggested that society will always *need* to punish criminals because punishment is a natural response to those who break social taboos.[4] Others disagree, arguing that an enlightened society will choose instead to reform law breakers through humanitarian means.

**social order** The smooth functioning of social institutions, the existence of positive and productive relations between individual members of society, and the orderly functioning of society as a whole.

# Goals of Sentencing

In late 1997, Chautauqua County, New York, District Attorney Jim Subjack announced that he would pursue charges of reckless endangerment against 20-year-old Nushawn Williams. Williams, a convicted drug dealer, was accused of infecting as many as 103 teenage girls and young women with the AIDS virus in a series of drugs-for-sex encounters.[5] Subjack said that Williams had sex with the women while knowing he was HIV positive, keeping a journal of his many "conquests." The prosecutor charged Williams with reckless endangerment for each sexual encounter, and with first-degree assault for each partner who subsequently became infected. He was also charged with statutory rape for allegedly having sex with a 13-year-old girl, who later tested positive for the virus. "It takes an individual with no regard for human life to do something like this," Subjack said.

The Williams case demonstrates a crucial component of contemporary sentencing philosophy: that people must be held accountable for their actions, and for the harm they cause. From this perspective, the purpose of the criminal justice system is to identify persons who have acted in intentionally harmful ways and (where a law is in place) to hold them accountable for their actions by imposing sanctions. Seen this way, our justice system is primarily an instrument of retribution.

Sentencing also has a variety of other purposes. As shown in Table 2–1, the modern goals of sentencing are: (1) retribution, (2) deterrence, (3) incapacitation, (4) rehabilitation or reformation, and (5) restoration.

## Retribution

**retribution** A sentencing goal that involves revenge against a criminal perpetrator.

One of the earliest goals of criminal sentencing was **retribution,** the payment of a debt to society and, thus, atonement for a person's offense.

### TABLE 2–1

#### Goals of Criminal Sentencing

| Goal | Rationale |
| --- | --- |
| Retribution | Punishment is appropriate for wrongdoing. <br> Punishment serves a purpose for both society and the wrongdoer. <br> Wrongdoers should be punished. |
| Deterrence | Punishment will prevent future wrongdoing by the offender and by others. <br> Punishment must outweigh the benefits gained by wrongdoing. |
| Incapacitation | Some wrongdoers cannot be changed and need to be segregated from society. <br> Society has the responsibility to protect law-abiding citizens from those whose behavior cannot be controlled. |
| Rehabilitation or Reformation | Society needs to help offenders learn how to behave appropriately. <br> Without learning acceptable behavior patterns, offenders will not be able to behave appropriately. |
| Restoration | Crime is primarily an offense against human relationships, and secondarily a violation of a law. <br> All those who suffered because of a crime should be restored to their previous sense of well-being. |

*Sentencing: To Punish or To Reform?*

Historically, retribution was couched in terms of "getting even," and it has sometimes been explained as "an eye for an eye, and a tooth for a tooth." *Retribution* literally means "paying back" the offender for what he or she has done. It is often equated with vengeance or revenge. Retribution, in a very fundamental way, expresses society's disapproval of criminal behavior and implies the payment of a debt to society.

Retribution remains one of the central goals of sentencing today—although it is now often expressed as **just deserts.** Just-deserts advocates claim that criminal acts are *deserving* of punishment and that justice is served by the imposition of appropriate punishments on criminal-law violators. As one contemporary author explains it, "Many of us have turned to retribution not only as the object of punishment, but as a basis for making sentences fair and equitable."[6] Even so, it is not always easy to determine just how much punishment is enough.

## Deterrence

A second goal of criminal sentencing is **deterrence.** Deterrence is the discouragement or prevention of crimes similar to the one for which an offender is being sentenced. Two forms of deterrence can be identified: specific and general.

**Specific deterrence** is the deterrence of the individual being punished from committing additional crimes. Long ago, specific deterrence was achieved through corporal punishments that maimed offenders in ways that precluded similar crimes in the future. Spies had their eyes gouged out and their tongues removed, rapists were castrated, thieves had their fingers or hands cut off, and so on. Even today, in some countries that follow a strict Islamic code, the hands of habitual thieves are cut off as a form of corporal punishment.

**General deterrence** occurs when the punishment of an individual serves as an example to others who might be thinking of committing a crime—thereby dissuading them from their planned course of action. The **pleasure-pain principle** is central to modern discussions of general deterrence. The pleasure-pain principle assumes that the threat of loss to anyone convicted of a crime should outweigh the potential pleasure to be gained by committing the crime.

For punishment to be effective as a deterrent, it must be relatively certain, swiftly applied, and sufficiently severe. *Certainty, swiftness,* and *severity* of punishment are not always easy to achieve. The crime funnel, described in Chapter 1, demonstrates that most offenses do not end in arrest and most arrests do not end in incarceration. Although it may not be easy for all offenders to get away with crime, the likelihood that any individual offender will be arrested, successfully prosecuted, and then punished is far smaller than deterrence advocates would like it to be. When an arrest does occur, an offender is typically released on bail, and because of an overcrowded court system, the trial, if any, may be a year or so later. Moreover, although the severity of punishments has increased in recent years, modern punishments are rarely as severe as those of earlier centuries. Arguments over just how much punishment is enough to deter further violations of the criminal law rarely lead to any clear conclusion.

**just deserts** The punishment deserved. A just-deserts perspective on criminal sentencing holds that criminal acts are *deserving* of punishment and that justice is best served by the imposition of appropriate punishments on criminal-law violators.

**deterrence** The discouragement or prevention of crimes similar to the one for which an offender is being sentenced; a goal of criminal sentencing.

**specific deterrence** The deterrence of the individual being punished from committing additional crimes.

**general deterrence** The use of the example of individual punishment to dissuade others from committing crimes.

**pleasure-pain principle** The idea that actions are motivated primarily by a person's desire to seek pleasure and avoid pain.

Well, here I am, about 2½ years into my life sentence in prison. The worst part so far for me has been the loneliness. It really gets to me sometimes. I'm close to 3000 miles away from my family, and I'm locked away from the people I hold dear and love. I really don't have anyone right now. I think my family is still digesting the fact that I'm in prison. I don't hear from them very often. They've never been ones to write, and I guess I really haven't, either.

I don't have a lot of human contact because I'm locked up in a single cell with a steel door. When the door shuts, I'm left to myself. I do get out about an hour a day, which includes 20 minutes for each meal. I also get out to exercise three times a week for 1½ hours. Other than that, it's cell time.

With all the time I have alone in my cell, my brain works overtime. I think about my life over and over again. I think about the good times and the bad times. It all comes out when you're left to yourself. Your mind goes in so many directions. I think about all the people I've hurt over the years, whether physically, emotionally, or financially. I'm just now feeling the pain that I caused so many years ago to so many people. My mind makes me remember the things that I don't want to remember. Then I have to deal with them internally.

I think about my crime every day of my life. I took a human life. What makes a man do that? I don't really know. All I can remember is the anger I felt and the hurt feelings. I can remember my heart hurting so bad that I couldn't function normally anymore. I cried all the time and I couldn't eat or sleep. At first it was all jealousy and then it was anger and pain. I guess it all came to a head that night. I had never felt that much rage before in my life. When it was over, I was holding a lifeless body in my arms. I couldn't speak or move. All I could feel was my soul leaving my body. It was an emptiness that I hope I never feel again. It was like I too had died that night.

So many what-ifs go through my mind these days. What if I wasn't an alcoholic? What if I hadn't lost my temper? What if I'd had the will to turn and walk away? So many what-ifs.

I often think about what effect all this has had on my friends and family. I remember the day I was sentenced like it was yesterday. It was one of the hardest times of my life. I knew ahead of time what I was getting, but it didn't make it any easier. The tears, the stares, the looks, and the glares were all directed in court from people who were once my friends. It was the final stop on the road of heartbreak and misery. I was sentenced to life so I couldn't hurt anyone else ever again (or at least I thought so). I called home that afternoon to let my family know that it was all over and that I was going down for life. My father told me that my Mom had tried to kill herself by putting a .38 in her mouth. By a miracle of God, my Dad had called home at that very moment and talked her out of it. He made it home in time to save her life. She was so depressed about me, plus she was addicted to painkillers because she had so many back operations. I wanted so much to comfort her, but I couldn't. I didn't know how. I didn't know how to get in touch with my feelings. I guess my pain and suffering tried to reach out for another victim, but luckily God intervened that time.

I think all the pain that I ever caused people comes back to me twofold. I experience all the pain that I caused and then some.

I remember the time I saw my father cry. It was a day I'll never forget. It was a day or two after I was arrested and a week before I was extradited to Arizona when he came to visit me in the county jail in Pennsylvania. I was so nervous knowing that he was coming that day. We hadn't talked in years. He didn't like me much at all because I had disappointed him so many times over the years. I couldn't blame him. I was a failure in his eyes as well as mine. I walked down the hallway to where my father was sitting. I sat down in a chair and looked at him through the glass that separated us. He looked so broken and so sad. We picked up the phones and started to talk. The tears just started to run down his face. I had a lump in my throat so that I couldn't swallow. My heart was bleeding inside and the pain was unbearable to see a rock of a man crumble before me because of what I had done. I wanted to end my life right there. My father didn't deserve what I was putting him through. He tried so hard to be a good father. He was strict but fair. I know it wasn't easy for him. I was his stepson. All through my childhood, he never treated me like less than his own son. We were just two very different people, and I rebelled against him every chance I could. As I looked into my father's eyes, I wished that he could hug me and I could cry too. I wanted to release all of this pain. We talked for a while and then he left. I knew I might never see him again.

I never wanted to cause my family pain again. I never want to cause a tear. I can't change what I've done with my life, but I sure can change myself. I can be a person that people can be proud to know. For the first time in my life, I'm drug- and alcohol-free. It's all new

to me, and it's a great feeling. I can't remember a time I wasn't high since I was 15 years old.

I guess I should thank God for letting me live for 31 years. I tried to destroy myself so many times with drugs, alcohol, and suicide attempts. I lived on the edge of life most of my life, and occasionally I fell off. In a way, prison has saved my life. I would have died at a young age from drugs or alcohol, or maybe the suicide attempts would have worked sooner or later. I guess in a sense I'm lucky. I know it's a strange way to look at things, but that's the way I see it. I'm just thankful I was able to overcome all the demons in my life. I'm a better person now. I'm responsible, caring, and able to be kind. I guess that's all part of growing up and that's what I've done the past few years. I still have a long way to go, but it's a start.

I guess my mind did work overtime on this story. It's sad, but a true part of my life. I tried to clear these things from my mind, but I couldn't. The mind never forgets. It's always there. Sometimes it just reminds you of an event or an experience, just to keep you humble, and when you sleep, it's there to haunt you through your dreams.

The mind is so awesome. I want to share my knowledge and all my thoughts and feelings with someone. It's time. I don't want to be lonely anymore. I'm going to place an ad in the newspaper for a pen pal. I need to get on with the rest of my life. I want to find the woman of my dreams, my best friend. I now know I'm a human being.

*George Killian, #82256*
*ASPC-Eyman Complex*
*Meadows Unit*
*Florence, Arizona*

## Incapacitation

**incapacitation** The use of imprisonment or other means to reduce an offender's capability to commit future offenses; a goal of criminal sentencing.

Many believe that the huge increase in the number of correctional clients has helped lower the crime rate by incapacitating more criminals. Many of these criminals are behind bars, and others are on supervised regimens of probation and parole. **Incapacitation** restrains offenders from committing additional crimes by isolating them from free society. A 1997 report by the National Center for Policy Analysis, for example, observed that a "major reason for [the] reduction in crime is that crime has become more costly to the perpetrators. The likelihood of going to prison for committing any type of major crime has increased substantially."[7] The center reported that over the previous four years:

- The murder rate dropped 23 percent as the probability of going to prison for murder rose 17 percent.
- Rape decreased 12 percent as the probability of imprisonment increased 9 percent.
- Robbery decreased 21 percent as the probability of imprisonment increased 14 percent.
- Aggravated assault decreased 11 percent as the probability of imprisonment increased 5 percent.
- Burglary decreased 15 percent as the probability of imprisonment increased 14 percent.

The report claims that "the best overall measure of the potential cost to a criminal of committing crimes is *expected punishment*." Expected punishment, said the report, "is the number of days in prison a criminal can expect to serve for committing a crime." The center calculated expected punishment by multiplying the median sentence imposed for each crime by the probabilities of being apprehended, prosecuted, convicted, and sentenced.

*As a goal of sentencing, incapacitation restrains offenders from committing more crimes by isolating them from society. Does this threat of isolation from society encourage law-abiding behavior?*

Crime rates are declining, said the report, because expected prison stays are significantly longer today than two decades ago for every category of serious crime.

According to the center, "between 1980 and 1995, expected punishment more than doubled for murder and nearly tripled for rape. It increased by about three-fourths for burglary and larceny/theft and increased 60 percent for motor vehicle theft."

A number of studies have claimed to show that incapacitating offenders through incarceration is cost-effective. Such studies conclude that imprisoning certain types of offenders (especially career or habitual offenders) results in savings by eliminating the social costs of the crimes offenders would be likely to commit if they were not imprisoned. Those social costs include monetary loss, medical costs of physical injury, and time lost from work.

One of the most frequently cited studies attempting to quantify the net costs of incarceration was done by Edwin W. Zedlewski.[8] Zedlewski used a Rand Corporation survey of inmates in three states (Michigan, Texas, and California) to estimate the number of crimes each inmate would commit if not imprisoned. In the survey, the average respondent reported committing anywhere from 187 to 287 crimes annually just before being incarcerated. To calculate the cost associated with each crime, Zedlewski divided the total criminal justice expenditures in the United States by the total number of crimes committed in the United States. From this he concluded that the average crime "cost" $2,300. Multiplying $2,300 by the 187 crimes estimated to be committed annually by a felon, Zedlewski calculated that society saves $430,100 per year for each felon who is incarcerated. Figuring that incarceration costs society about $25,000 per prisoner per year, he concluded that prisons produce a cost-benefit return to society of 17 to 1 ($17 saved for every $1 spent)—leading him to strongly support increased incarceration.

Three years after Zedlewski's work, well-known criminologist John DiIulio performed a cost-benefit analysis, using a survey of Wisconsin prisoners. The study, called "Crime and Punishment in Wisconsin," led to the conclusion that prisons saved taxpayers in Wisconsin approximately $2 for every dollar they cost.[9]

Studies such as those by Zedlewski and DiIulio are part of the growing field of correctional econometrics. **Correctional econometrics** is the study of the cost-effectiveness of various correctional programs and related reductions in the incidence of crime.[10]

# Rehabilitation or Reformation

The goal of **rehabilitation** or reformation is to change criminal lifestyles into law-abiding ones. Rehabilitation has been accomplished when an offender's criminal patterns of thought and behavior have been replaced by allegiance to society's values. Rehabilitation focuses on medical and psychological treatments and on social skills training, all designed to "correct" the problems that led the individual to crime.

A subgoal of rehabilitation is **reintegration** of the offender with the community. Reintegrating the offender with the community means making the offender a productive member of society—one who contributes to the

**correctional econometrics** The study of the cost-effectiveness of various correctional programs and related reductions in the incidence of crime.

**rehabilitation** The changing of criminal lifestyles into law-abiding ones by "correcting" the behavior of offenders through treatment, education, and training; a sentencing goal.

**reintegration** The process of making the offender a productive member of the community.

general well-being of the whole. *Social integration* might be another way to express this goal.

During the 1970s, rehabilitation came under harsh criticism, even though it had been the primary rationale for punishing offenders since the early 1900s. Some states abandoned rehabilitation altogether or de-emphasized it in favor of the goals of retribution and incapacitation. In other states, attempts at rehabilitation continued. Today some governments and private organizations are returning to a belief in rehabilitation, emphasizing treatment and education. According to Edgardo Rotman, "In order to neutralize the desocializing potential of prisons, a civilized society is forced into rehabilitative undertakings. These become an essential ingredient of its correctional system taken as a whole. A correctional system" with no "interest in treatment," says Rotman, "means . . . de-humanization and regression."[11]

## Restoration

In recent years, a new goal of criminal sentencing, known as **restoration,** has developed. Restorative justice is based on the belief that criminal sentencing should involve restoration and justice for all involved in or affected by crime. Hence, while advocates of restorative justice believe that the victim should be restored by the justice process, they also suggest that the offender and society should participate in the restoration process.

A restorative justice perspective allows judges and juries to consider **victim-impact statements** in their sentencing decisions. These are descriptions of the harm and suffering that a crime has caused victims and their survivors. Also among the programs being introduced on behalf of victims and their survivors are victim assistance and victim-compensation programs.

Other efforts at restoration place equal emphasis on victims' rights and needs and on the successful reintegration of offenders into the community. Restorative justice seeks to restore the health of the community, repair the harm done, meet victims' needs, and require the offender to contribute to those repairs. Thus, the criminal act is condemned, offenders are held accountable, offenders and victims are involved as participants, and repentant offenders are encouraged to earn their way back into the good graces of society.

**restoration** The process of returning to their previous condition all those involved in or affected by crime—including victims, offenders, and society; a recent goal of criminal sentencing.

**victim-impact statement** A description of the harm and suffering that a crime has caused victims and survivors.

# Types of Sentences

Legislatures establish the types of sentences that can be imposed. The U.S. Congress and the 50 state legislatures each decide what is against the law and define crimes and their punishments in the jurisdictions in which they have control. Sentencing options in wide use today include the following:

- fines and other monetary sanctions
- probation
- alternative or intermediate sanctions such as day fines, community service, electronic monitoring, and day reporting centers
- incarceration
- death penalty

As punishment for unlawful behavior, fines have a long history. By the fifth century B.C., Greece, for example, had developed an extensive system of fines for a wide variety of offenses.[12] Under our modern system of justice, fines are usually imposed as punishment for misdemeanors and infractions. When imposed on felony offenders, fines are frequently combined with another punishment, such as probation or incarceration.

Fines are only one type of monetary sanction in use today. Others include the court-ordered payment of the costs of trial, victim restitution, various fees, forfeitures, donations, and confiscations. **Restitution** consists of payments made by a criminal offender to his or her victim as compensation for the harm caused by the offense. While fines are usually paid to the government, restitution may be paid directly to the victim (or paid to the court and turned over to the victim). Some innovative courts have ordered offenders to donate specified amounts to specified charities in lieu of a fine.[13] Restitution is an example of a restorative-justice sentencing option.

With a sentence of probation, the convicted offender continues to live in the community, but must comply with court-imposed restrictions on his or her movements. Alternative or intermediate sentencing options usually combine probation with some other punishment, such as community service or house arrest with electronic monitoring. A sentence of incarceration, or total confinement away from the community, is used when the community needs to be protected from further criminal activity by an offender. The death penalty, or capital punishment, is the ultimate sentence. Figure 2–1 displays recent trends in three sentencing options compared with parole.

The sentence is generally imposed by the judge. Sentencing responsibility can also be exercised by the jury, or a group of judges, or it may be man-

**restitution** Payments made by a criminal offender to his or her victim (or to the court, which then turns them over to the victim) as compensation for the harm caused by the offense.

## FIGURE 2–1

### Adults on Probation, in Jail or in Prison, or on Parole

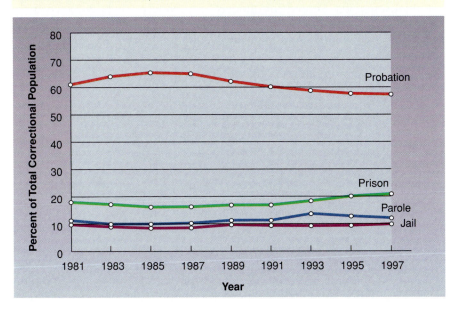

*Source:* Adapted from Kathleen Maguire and Ann L. Pastore (eds.), *Sourcebook of Criminal Justice Statistics 1997* (Washington: Bureau of Justice Statistics, October 1998), p. 464.

dated by statute. **Mandatory sentences** are those that are required by law under certain circumstances—such as conviction of a specified crime or of a series of offenses of a specified type. Mandatory sentences may add prison time to sentences for offenders who carried weapons during the commission of their crimes, who used or possessed illegal drugs, or who perpetrated crimes against elderly victims. Such sentences allow judges no leeway in sentencing.

Even when there is no mandatory sentence, judges cannot impose just any sentence. They are still limited by statutory provisions. They also are guided by prevailing sentencing goals. A judge usually considers a **presentence investigation report**, sometimes called a **PSI**. This report, prepared by the probation department attached to a court, is a social and personal history as well as an evaluation of the offender. Finally, judges' sentencing decisions are influenced by their own personal convictions and characteristics.

Once the sentence is chosen, the judge must decide how it will be served, especially if more than one sentence is being imposed. Sentences can be consecutive or concurrent. **Consecutive sentences** are served one after the other. When a person is convicted of multiple offenses, a judge might impose, for example, a sentence of 10 years for one offense and 20 years for another. If the sentences are to run consecutively, the offender will begin serving the second sentence only after the first one expires. **Concurrent sentences** are served together. If the sentences in the example are to run concurrently, the 10-year sentence will expire when the offender has served one-half of the 20-year sentence. The offender will then need to serve the remainder of the 20-year sentence before being released.

# Sentencing Models

A **model of criminal sentencing** is a strategy or system for imposing criminal sanctions. Sentencing models vary widely (Table 2–2). Over the past 100 years, a shift has occurred from what might be called a judicial model of sentencing to an administrative model. Judges generally have far less discretion in sentencing decisions today than they previously did. The majority of sentences imposed in American courts today follow legislative and administrative guidelines.

Sentencing in nineteenth century-America involved mostly fines, probation, and "flat" prison sentences. **Flat sentences** specify a given amount of time to be served in custody and allow little or no variation from the time specified. A typical flat sentence might be stated as "five years in prison." Flat sentences generally meant that an offender had to complete the sentence imposed and could not earn an early release.

## Indeterminate Sentence

By the close of the nineteenth century, sentencing reform in the United States began replacing the flat sentence with indeterminate sentences.[14] At the time, the criminal justice system was coping with a rapidly expanding and increasingly diverse prison population, the increased efficiency of the police and courts, and other factors. Overcrowded prisons and the warehousing of inmates resulted.[15]

**TABLE 2–2**

**Sentencing Models**

■ **Determinate Sentencing**

Sentencing to a fixed term of incarceration that may be reduced by good time. Usually, explicit standards specify the amount of punishment and a set release date, with no review by a parole board or other administrative agency. Postincarceration supervision may be part of the sentence.

■ **Indeterminate Sentencing**

Sentencing in which an administrative agency, generally a parole board, has the authority to release an incarcerated offender and to determine whether an offender's parole will be revoked for violation of the conditions of release. In one form of indeterminate sentencing, the judge specifies only the maximum sentence length (a fixed term); the associated minimum is automatically implied but is not within the judge's discretion. In the more traditional form of indeterminate sentencing, the judge specifies maximum and minimum durations within limits set by statute. The judge has discretion over the minimum and maximum sentences.

■ **Presumptive Guidelines Sentencing**

Sentencing that meets all the following conditions: (1) The appropriate sentence for an offender in a specific case is presumed to fall within a range authorized by guidelines adopted by a legislatively created sentencing body, usually a sentencing commission; (2) judges are expected to sentence within the range or provide written justification for departure; and (3) the guidelines provide for review of the departure, usually by appeal to a higher court. Presumptive guidelines may employ determinate or indeterminate sentencing structures.

■ **Voluntary/Advisory Guidelines Sentencing**

Recommended sentencing policies that are not required by law. They serve as a guide and are based on past sentencing practices. The legislature has not mandated their use. Voluntary/advisory guidelines may use determinate or indeterminate sentencing structures.

■ **Mandatory Minimum Sentencing**

A minimum sentence that is specified by statute for all offenders convicted of a particular crime or a particular crime with special circumstances (e.g., robbery with a firearm or selling drugs to a minor within 1000 feet of a school). Mandatory minimums can be used in both determinate and indeterminate sentencing structures. Within an indeterminate sentencing structure, the mandatory minimum requires the inmate to serve a fixed amount of time in prison before being eligible for release with the approval of a parole board. Under a determinate sentence, the offender is required to serve a fixed amount of time in prison before being eligible for release.

In an **indeterminate sentence**, the judge specifies a maximum length and a minimum length, within limits set by statute, and a parole board determines the actual time of release. The parole board's determination depends on the board's judgment of whether the prisoner has been reformed, has been cured, or has simply served enough time. An example of an indeterminate sentence is "five to ten years in prison." A second form of indeterminate sentencing requires the judge to specify only the maximum sentence length, with the associated minimum set by statute. Some states, for example, require an offender to serve as little as one-quarter of the sentence before becoming eligible for parole.

**indeterminate sentence**

A sentence in which a judge specifies a maximum length and a minimum length, and an administrative agency, generally a parole board, determines the actual time of release.

**good time** The number of days or months prison authorities deduct from a sentence for good behavior and for other reasons.

With an indeterminate sentence, discretion is distributed, not only among the prosecutor, defense counsel, and judge, but also to prison officials and the parole board, which have considerable influence over an offender's length of stay. Prison officials have discretion over the amount of **good time** an inmate earns, which can affect parole eligibility, the discharge date, or both. The parole board decides the actual release date for most inmates. The result is a system of sentencing in which few people understand or can predict who will be imprisoned and for how long.

Under indeterminate sentencing, punishments are made to fit the criminal rather than the crime. Proponents of indeterminate sentences assume that crime is a product of individual deviation from the norm and that rehabilitation can be achieved within a prison system designed to punish and not treat inmates. They also assume that prison personnel have the knowledge to impose treatment or to predict recidivism accurately enough to justify discretion over when an inmate should be released. The use of indeterminate sentences has prompted numerous accusations of disparity in sentencing as well as protests from inmate groups, penologists, and other critics of the penal system. These protests spurred a movement for sentencing reform.

## Determinate Sentence

**determinate sentence** (also called *fixed sentence*) A sentence to a fixed term of incarceration, which can be reduced by good time. Under determinate sentencing, for example, all offenders convicted of the same degree of burglary are sentenced to the same length of time behind bars.

A **determinate sentence** (also known as a *fixed sentence*) specifies a fixed period of incarceration, which can be reduced for "good time" served. The term is generally used to refer to the sentencing reforms of the late 1970s. Determinate sentences are generally based on the incapacitation and deterrence goals of sentencing. The theory behind determinate sentencing is that criminals will be off the streets for longer periods of time. The other advantage, supporters say, is that prisoners know when they will be released. In most determinate sentencing models, parole is limited or is replaced by the use of good-time credits. With good time, inmates are able to reduce their sentences by earning credits. The amount of the reduction depends on the number of credits earned. Good time credits can be earned by demonstrating good behavior and not being "written up" for violating prison rules. It can also be earned by participating in educational programs, community service projects, or medical experiments. The procedure for earning credits and the number that can be earned vary from state to state. Prison administrators generally favor determinate sentencing and good time credits because they aid in controlling prison populations.

## Guideline Sentencing

As we have seen, the sentences that judges impose are regulated by law. As part of the movement to eliminate sentencing disparities, some states, as well as the federal government, have enacted sentencing guidelines for judges to follow. The guidelines fall into two categories.

**Voluntary/Advisory Sentencing Guidelines** Among the earliest guided-sentencing innovations in the United States was the experiment with voluntary guidelines, also called advisory guidelines. These are recommended sentencing policies that are not required by law. Usually they are based on past sentencing practices and serve as a guide to judges. Voluntary or advisory guidelines have had disappointing results, often because they are not enforced and are sometimes ignored. In some instances, insufficient time has been allowed for the guidelines to take hold. More important, the guidelines are voluntary; judges can simply ignore them. A review of all the major studies conducted on voluntary and advisory guidelines reveals low compliance by judges and, hence, little reduction in disparity.[16]

**Presumptive Sentencing Guidelines**   By the early 1980s, states had begun to experiment with the use of presumptive sentencing guidelines. (See Table 2–3 for a summary of sentencing practices by state.) These models differ from determinate sentences and voluntary or advisory guidelines in three respects. First, the guidelines are developed, not by the legislature, but by a **sentencing commission** that often represents diverse interests, including private citizens as well as all segments of the criminal justice system. Second, the guidelines are explicit and highly structured, relying on a quantitative scoring instrument. Third, the guidelines are not voluntary or advisory. Judges must adhere to the sentencing system or provide a written rationale for departure.

The forces stimulating presumptive sentencing guidelines were the same as those that had driven the moves to determinate sentencing and voluntary or advisory guidelines: issues of fairness and prison crowding. These concerns provided the impetus for states to adopt guidelines, replace indeterminate sentencing with determinate sentencing, and abolish or reduce discretionary parole release.

The first four states to adopt presumptive sentencing guidelines were Minnesota (1980), Pennsylvania (1982), Washington (1983), and Florida (1983). The Minnesota model, in particular, with its focus on controlling prison population growth, has often been cited as an example of the successful control of disparity and rising corrections costs through sentencing guidelines. Like those of most other states, the Minnesota model uses a sentencing matrix of offense severity and offender's prior criminal history to indicate the sentence is appropriate in any given case. The matrix provides ranges for specified offenses within which judges can impose sentence.

**Federal Sentencing Guidelines**   In the early 1980s, the U.S. Congress focused its attention on disparity in sentencing.[17] Congress concluded that the sentencing discretion of federal trial judges needed boundaries. The resulting legislation, termed the Sentencing Reform Act of 1984,[18] created the U.S. Sentencing Commission. The nine-member commission, first organized in October 1985, is a permanent body charged with formulating and amending national sentencing guidelines. The commission's guidelines apply to all federal criminal offenses committed on or after November 1, 1987. Congress has mandated that federal trial judges must follow the guidelines in their sentencing decisions.

The commission may submit guideline amendments to Congress each year between the beginning of the regular congressional session and May 1. Suggested amendments automatically take effect 180 days after submission unless Congress rejects them.

**sentencing commission**
A group assigned to create a schedule of sentences that reflect the gravity of the offenses committed and the prior record of the criminal offender. The commission often includes private citizens as well as representatives of the criminal justice system, including law enforcement, courts, and corrections.

**TABLE 2–3**

### Sentencing Practices by State, 1996

| State | Determinate Sentencing | Indeterminate Sentencing | Guideline Sentencing by Type | Mandatory Minimum Sentencing |
|---|:---:|:---:|:---:|:---:|
| Alabama | | ◆ | | ◆ |
| Alaska | | ◆ | | ◆ |
| Arizona | ◆ | | | ◆ |
| Arkansas | | ◆ | Voluntary/Advisory | ◆ |
| California | ◆ | | | ◆ |
| Colorado | | ◆ | | ◆ |
| Connecticut | | ◆ | | ◆ |
| Delaware | ◆ | | Presumptive | ◆ |
| District of Columbia | | ◆ | | ◆ |
| Florida | ◆ | | Presumptive | ◆ |
| Georgia | | ◆ | | ◆ |
| Hawaii | | ◆ | | ◆ |
| Idaho | | ◆ | | ◆ |
| Illinois | ◆ | | | ◆ |
| Indiana | | ◆ | | ◆ |
| Iowa | | ◆ | | ◆ |
| Kansas | | ◆ | Presumptive | ◆ |
| Kentucky | | ◆ | | ◆ |
| Louisiana | | ◆ | Voluntary/Advisory | ◆ |
| Maine | ◆ | | | ◆ |
| Maryland | | ◆ | Voluntary/Advisory | ◆ |
| Massachusetts | | ◆ | Under Study | ◆ |
| Michigan | | ◆ | Under Study | ◆ |
| Minnesota | ◆ | | Presumptive | ◆ |
| Mississippi | ◆ | | | ◆ |
| Missouri | | ◆ | Voluntary | ◆ |
| Montana | | ◆ | Under Study | ◆ |

TABLE 2–3 (continued)

## Sentencing Practices by State, 1996

| State | Determinate Sentencing | Indeterminate Sentencing | Guideline Sentencing by Type | Mandatory Minimum Sentencing |
|---|---|---|---|---|
| Nebraska | | ◆ | | ◆ |
| Nevada | | ◆ | | ◆ |
| New Hampshire | | ◆ | | ◆ |
| New Jersey | | ◆ | | ◆ |
| New Mexico | ◆ | | | ◆ |
| New York | | ◆ | | ◆ |
| North Carolina | ◆ | | Presumptive | ◆ |
| North Dakota | | ◆ | | ◆ |
| Ohio | ◆ | | Presumptive | ◆ |
| Oklahoma | | ◆ | Voluntary/Advisory | ◆ |
| Oregon | ◆ | | Presumptive | ◆ |
| Pennsylvania | | ◆ | Presumptive | ◆ |
| Rhode Island | | ◆ | | ◆ |
| South Carolina | | ◆ | | ◆ |
| South Dakota | | ◆ | | ◆ |
| Tennessee[1] | | ◆ | Presumptive | ◆ |
| Texas | | ◆ | | ◆ |
| Utah | | ◆ | Voluntary/Advisory | ◆ |
| Vermont | | ◆ | | ◆ |
| Virginia | ◆ | | Voluntary/Advisory | ◆ |
| Washington | ◆ | | Presumptive | ◆ |
| West Virginia | | ◆ | | ◆ |
| Wisconsin[1] | | ◆ | | ◆ |
| Wyoming | | ◆ | | ◆ |
| TOTAL | 14 | 37 | 17 | 51 |

1. Tennessee and Wisconsin continue to have sentencing guidelines; the sentencing commissions were abolished in 1996.

*Source:* Prepared by National Council on Crime and Delinquency. Published in Bureau of Justice Assistance, *1996 National Survey of State Sentencing Structures* (Washington: U.S. Department of Justice, September 1998) NCJ169270.

**mandatory minimum sentencing** The imposition of sentences required by statute on those convicted of a particular crime or a particular crime with special circumstances, such as robbery with a firearm or selling drugs to a minor within 1000 feet of a school, or on those with a particular type of criminal history.

Federal sentencing guidelines take into account the defendant's criminal history, the nature of the criminal conduct, and the particular circumstances surrounding the offense. Ordinarily, a judge must choose a sentence within a range set forth in the guidelines. Deviations from that range must be explained in writing.

In addition to creating the Sentencing Commission, the Sentencing Reform Act abolished parole for federal offenders sentenced under the guidelines. The sentence imposed is essentially the sentence served. Under the law, inmates may earn up to 54 days of credit (time off their sentences) each year for good behavior.

## Mandatory Minimum Sentencing

**Mandatory minimum sentencing** refers to the imposition of sentences required by statute for those convicted of a particular crime or a particular crime with special circumstances, such as robbery with a firearm or selling drugs to a minor within 1000 feet of a school, or on those with a particular type of criminal history. By 1994, all 50 states had enacted one or more mandatory minimum sentencing laws,[19] and Congress had enacted numerous mandatory sentencing laws for federal offenders. Mandatory minimum sentencing rationales dominated the 1980s and early 1990s.

Recently, many states have adopted *sentence enhancements,* usually the mandating of longer prison terms for violent offenders with records of serious crimes. Mandatory sentence enhancements aim to deter known and potentially violent offenders and to incapacitate convicted criminals through long-term incarceration.[20] These sentence enhancements have come to be known as *three-strikes laws* (and, in some jurisdictions, two-strikes laws).

Three-strikes laws vary in breadth. Some stipulate that both the prior convictions and the current offense must be violent felonies; others require only that the prior felonies be violent. Some three-strikes laws count only prior adult convictions; others permit consideration of juvenile adjudications for violent crimes. Under California's three-strikes law, an offender who is convicted of a qualifying felony and has two prior qualifying felony convictions must serve a minimum of 25 years. The law also doubles prison terms for offenders convicted of a second violent felony.[21]

**Rationales** Mandatory sentences have two goals—deterrence and incapacitation. The primary purposes of modest mandatory prison terms (e.g., three years for armed robbery) are specific deterrence, for already-punished offenders, and general deterrence, for prospective offenders. If the law increases the imprisonment rate, it also serves the goal of incapacitation, leaving fewer offenders free to victimize the population at large. The intent of three-strikes (and even two-strikes) laws is to incapacitate selected violent offenders for very long terms—25 years or even life. Mandatory sentencing laws have become highly politicized. By passing mandatory sentencing laws, legislators can convey that they deem certain crimes especially grave and that people who commit these crimes deserve, and can expect, harsh sanc-

*Mandatory sentencing laws are often passed in reaction to public outcries against especially violent or well-publicized criminal acts. Does mandatory sentencing fulfill the goals of deterrence and incapacitation?*

tions. Such laws typically are a rapid and visible response to public outcries following heinous or well-publicized crimes.

**Impact**    Mandatory sentencing has had significant consequences that deserve close attention. Among them are its impact on crime and the operations of the criminal justice system. The possibility that the consequences will be different for different groups of people also bears examination.

*Crime*    Evaluations of mandatory minimum sentencing have focused on two types of crimes—those committed with handguns and those related to drugs (the offenses most commonly subject to mandatory minimum penalties in state and federal courts). An evaluation of the Massachusetts law that imposed mandatory jail terms for possession of an unlicensed handgun concluded that the law was an effective deterrent of gun crime, at least in the short term.[22]

However, studies of similar laws in Michigan[23] and Florida[24] found no evidence that crimes committed with firearms had been prevented. An evaluation of mandatory sentence enhancements for gun use in six large cities (Detroit, Jacksonville, Tampa, Miami, Philadelphia, and Pittsburgh) indicated that the laws deterred homicide but not other violent crimes.[25] An assessment of New York's Rockefeller drug laws was unable to support their claimed efficacy in deterring drug crime in New York City.[26]

*The Criminal Justice System*    The criminal courts rely on a high rate of guilty pleas to speed case processing and thus avoid logjams. Officials can offer inducements to defendants to obtain these pleas. At least in the short term, mandatory sentencing laws may disrupt established plea-bargaining patterns by preventing a prosecutor from offering a short prison term (less than the new minimum) in exchange for a guilty plea. However, unless policy makers enact the same mandatory sentences for several related crimes, prosecutors can usually shift strategies and bargain on charges rather than on sentences.

*Sentencing: To Punish or To Reform?*    CHAPTER 2    51

Michael Tonry, a criminal justice scholar, has summarized the findings of research on the impact of mandatory sentencing laws on the criminal justice system.[27] He concluded that mandatory sentencing laws:

- Do not achieve certainty and predictability because officials circumvent them if they believe the results are unduly harsh.
- Are redundant in requiring imprisonment for serious cases because the offenders in such cases are generally sentenced to prison anyway.
- Are arbitrary in the sentences they require for minor cases.
- May occasionally result in an unduly harsh punishment for a marginal offender.[28]

Most two- and three-strikes laws leave judges no discretion to deviate from the sentences dictated by legislatures. Another central feature of such laws is the extraordinary length of the prison terms they require. Offenders serving life sentences in California and North Carolina under such legislation, for example, become eligible for parole only after serving 25 years, those in New Mexico after 30 years, and those in Colorado after 40 years. Three-strikes laws in some states mandate life without the possibility of parole. Two- and three-strikes laws came about in response to public concerns about crime and the growing belief that many serious offenders were being released from prison too soon.[29] Proponents view such legislation as the best way to deal with the persistent, serious violent offender—the proverbial three-time loser.

**habitual offender statute** A law that (1) allows a person's criminal history to be considered at sentencing or (2) allows a person convicted of a given offense, and previously convicted of another specified offense, to receive a more severe penalty than that for the current offense alone.

Two- and three-strikes laws are a form of **habitual offender statute.** Although habitual offender laws have been on the books in a number of jurisdictions since the 1940s or earlier, the older laws were often geared to specific types of prior offenses, such as crimes of violence, sex offenses, or crimes perpetrated with guns. Moreover, most early habitual offender laws allowed enhanced sentences, but did not make them mandatory as do two- and three-strikes legislation.[30]

# Three-Strikes Models— Washington and California

Between 1993 and 1995, 24 states and the federal government enacted new habitual offender laws that fell into the three-strikes category.[31] Washington state was the first of those to do so.[32] California soon followed with a considerably broader version of the three-strikes law. As those laws were being implemented, the impact they would have on the criminal justice systems of those states was debated. Proponents predicted the laws would curb crime and protect society by warehousing the worst offenders for a long time. Opponents argued that defendants facing lengthy mandatory sentences would be more likely to demand trials, slowing the processing of cases, and that more offenders would serve long terms of incarceration, ballooning prison populations, already at crisis levels in many states.[33]

Although they were enacted within months of each other, amid the same "three strikes and you're out" rallying cry, and they include many of the same offenses as strikes, the Washington and California laws differ in three important ways. First, in Washington all three strikes must be for felonies specifically listed in the legislation. Under the California law, only the first two convictions must be from the state's list of "strikeable" offenses; any subsequent felony can count as the third strike. Second, the California law contains a two-strikes provision, by which a person convicted of any felony after one prior conviction for a strikeable offense is to be sentenced to twice the term he or she would otherwise receive. There is no two-strikes provision in the Washington law. Third, the sanctions for a third strike differ. The Washington statute requires a life term in prison without the possibility of parole for a person convicted for the third time of any of the "most serious offenses" listed in the law. In California a "third-striker" has at least the possibility of being released after 25 years.[34]

## Impact on Local Courts and Jails

When three-strikes laws were first passed in Washington and California, some analysts projected a much greater impact on local criminal justice systems in California, because the California law had a much broader scope.[35] They predicted that California courts would be overwhelmed as defendants facing enhanced penalties demanded jury trials. The added time to process cases through trials and the reluctance of courts to grant pretrial release to defendants facing long prison terms, they said, would cause jail populations to explode as the number of jail admissions and the length of jail stays grew.[36]

Early evidence from California supported these predictions. A review of 12,600 two- and three-strikes cases from Los Angeles, for example, showed that two-strikes cases took 16 percent longer to process, and three-strikes cases 41 percent longer, than nonstrike cases.[37] In addition, strikes cases were three times as likely to go to trial as nonstrike felonies, and four times as likely as the same types of cases before the law took effect. This effect led to a 25 percent increase in jury trials, as well as an 11 percentage-point rise in the proportion of the jail population awaiting trial, from 59 percent before the law was enacted to 70 percent. Furthermore, a survey of sheriff's departments showed that the pretrial detainee population in the state had grown from 51 percent of the average daily population before the three-strikes law to 61 percent by January 1, 1995.[38]

According to more recent data, however, at least some California counties are learning to handle the changes brought about by the law. A survey of eight California counties with populations of more than 1 million identified several that were successfully disposing of two- and three-strikes cases early in the process.[39] In addition, data from the Los Angeles County Sheriff's Department suggest that the pace of strikes cases coming into that system may be slowing.[40]

## Impact on State Prison Systems

The impact of the Washington and California laws on state corrections departments has not been as severe as projected. Planners in Washington

I am a Director and Regional Administrator for the state prison system, and I supervise nursing students in a locked ward with criminally insane clients. In addition, I'm a researcher for the National Commission on Correctional Health Care. The Commission surveys prisons, jails, juvenile facilities, and immigration facilities all over the United States. I have directed teams in 29 states, in facilities ranging from 38 to 1000 beds. Part of my job in prison is to consult and transport clients to other countries, which have in the past included Spain, Portugal, Canada, Panama, and Venezuela.

I love this field and encourage students who want a challenge and a career that is interesting to give corrections, especially work with the criminally insane, a look. Every day and every interaction with our clients is different. No two days are alike, and no two situations are similar.

*Dr. Roger Childers*
*Supervisor, Psychiatric Unit for Criminally*
*   Insane*
*Bryce Hospital*
*Tuscaloosa, Alabama*

had expected that 40 to 75 persons would be sentenced under three-strikes provisions each year. The actual numbers, however, have been much lower. During the first three years the law was in effect, only 85 offenders—not the 120-225 projected—were admitted to the state prison system under the three-strikes law.[41]

A similar overestimate was made of the impact the California law would have on prisons there. As of January 1, 1997, a total of 26,074 offenders had been admitted to the California Department of Corrections (CDC) for two- or three-strikes sentences.[42] Of this number, nearly 90 percent were sentenced under the two-strikes provision. Although the sheer number of cases affected by the law is significantly higher than for any other state, the numbers are not as great as originally projected.

## Issues in Sentencing

Many sentencing reforms have been an attempt to reduce disparity in sentencing and make the process more fair. The term **fair sentencing** or *fairness in sentencing* has become popular in recent years. Although fair sentencing today often refers to fairness for *victims,* many suggest that any truly

**fair sentencing**
Sentencing practices that incorporate fairness for both victims and offenders. Fairness is said to be achieved by implementing principles of proportionality, equity, social debt, and truth in sentencing.

*Joseph L. Hackett*
*Correctional Case*
*Analyst*
*Neuse Correctional*
*Institution*
*Wayne County, NC*

*"I think 90 percent of them [offenders] came from a dysfunctional family and encountered drug abuse or alcohol abuse. Yes, they made the decisions to do the crimes they committed, but if we, as a great society and a great state, can provide support and education to some of these individuals, we can make a difference, which could lead some of them to productive lives. It really gives me great pleasure to be part of that enterprise."*

Joseph L. Hackett is a correctional case analyst with Neuse Correctional Institution in Wayne County, North Carolina. He joined the department as a correctional officer in 1993, three months before earning his associate's degree from a local community college. Over the next three years, he worked third shift at a medium-custody penitentiary and attended college to complete his four-year degree. After graduation, he had many job interviews throughout the North Carolina Department of Corrections and, finally, after the ninth one, was offered his current position.

Joseph now conducts mental health screenings and makes custody classification recommendations for inmates at a state intake center. Part of his job is to investigate the backgrounds of inmates before he makes recommendations. On a typical workday, Joseph might contact a law enforcement agency, the district attorney's office, and several parole agencies to learn about an inmate. "My job? I love it. I never thought I'd be happy about coming to work. I liked being a CO, but sometimes there was a little too much danger lurking around the yard."

---

fair sentencing scheme must incorporate fairness for both victims and offenders. Issues related to fairness in sentencing are:

- proportionality
- equity
- social debt
- truth in sentencing

## Proportionality

**Proportionality** is the sentencing principle that the severity of punishment should match the seriousness of the crime for which the sentence is imposed. To most people today, the death penalty would seem grossly disproportional to the offense of larceny—even if the offender had a history of such violations. (This, however, has not always been the case. Larceny *was* punishable by death in medieval England.) On the other hand, probation would seem disproportional to the crime of murder—although it is occasionally imposed in homicide cases.

**proportionality** The sentencing principle that the severity of punishment should match the seriousness of the crime for which the sentence is imposed.

## Equity

**Equity** is the sentencing principle that similar crimes and similar criminals should be treated alike. The alternative to equity is disparity, in which similar crimes are associated with different punishments in different jurisdictions or in which offenders with similar criminal histories receive widely differing sentences. Disparity can also result from judicial discretion when judges hold widely different sentencing philosophies. In a jurisdiction with wide leeway for judges to determine sentences, one judge might treat offenders very harshly while another is lenient. Under such circumstances, now largely eliminated by sentencing reform, one burglar, for example, might receive a sentence of 30 years in prison upon conviction while his partner in crime is put on probation simply because he appears before a more lenient judge.

## Social Debt

**Social debt** is the sentencing principle that the severity of punishment should take into account the offender's prior criminal behavior. As we have seen, a number of laws designed to recognize social debt have recently been passed. Among them are three-strikes and two-strikes laws. Although there is considerable variation in such laws between states, the primary characteristic of these laws is that they "call for enhanced penalties for offenders with one or more prior felony convictions."[43] They require a repeat offender to serve several years in prison in addition to the penalty imposed for the current offense.

### FIGURE 2–2

### Time Served in State Prisons Compared With Court Sentences

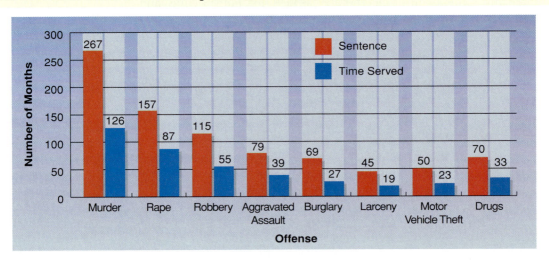

*Source:* Patrick A. Langan and Jodi M. Brown, *Felony Sentences in the United States, 1994* (Washington: Bureau of Justice Statistics, 1997).

# Truth in Sentencing

Until the sentencing reforms of the 1970s, the laws of many states enabled convicted offenders to be released from prison long before they had served their full sentences. Inmates frequently had good time deducted from their sentences, or time off for good behavior. *Gain time* could be earned for going to school, learning a trade, or doing volunteer work. Moreover, many states mandated routine parole eligibility after inmates had served one-quarter, or even one-fifth, of their sentences.

Recent truth-in-sentencing laws have changed such practices by requiring offenders to complete sentences very close to the ones they are given. **Truth in sentencing** requires an offender to serve a substantial portion of the sentence and reduces the discrepancy between the sentence imposed and actual time spent in prison. The results of a recent study, comparing actual time served in prison with sentences imposed, can be seen in Figure 2–2 on page 56. The Violent Crime Control and Law Enforcement Act of 1994 includes a truth-in-sentencing provision. To qualify for federal aid under the act, a state must amend its laws so that an imprisoned offender serves at least 85 percent of his or her sentence before being released. Parole eligibility and good-time credits are generally restricted or eliminated in truth-in-sentencing laws.

As you can see, the purposes of sentencing are diverse, and the issues surrounding it are many and complex.

**truth in sentencing**
The sentencing principle that requires an offender to serve a substantial portion of the sentence and reduces the discrepancy between the sentence imposed and actual time spent in prison.

## SUMMARY BY CHAPTER OBJECTIVES

### CHAPTER OBJECTIVE 1

The philosophy underlying criminal sentencing is that people must be held accountable for their actions and the harm they cause. Western society has a long tradition of sentencing criminal offenders to some form of punishment. Many social scientists suggest that the central purpose of criminal punishment is to maintain social order.

### CHAPTER OBJECTIVE 2

The goals of criminal sentencing today are (1) retribution, (2) deterrence, (3) incapacitation, (4) rehabilitation or reformation, and (5) restoration.

### CHAPTER OBJECTIVE 3

Sentencing options in use today include fines and other monetary sanctions, probation, alternative or intermediate sentences, incarceration, and capital punishment.

### CHAPTER OBJECTIVE 4

A model of criminal sentencing is a strategy or system for imposing criminal sanctions. Sentencing models vary widely among the jurisdictions in the United States. These models include indeterminate sentences, determinate sentences, voluntary or advisory sentencing guidelines, presumptive sentencing guidelines, and mandatory minimum sentencing.

### CHAPTER OBJECTIVE 5

Recent laws have increased penalties for criminal offenses, particularly violent crimes, and for repeat offenders. Many such laws are three-strikes laws. The rationale for such laws is simple: Offenders convicted repeatedly of serious offenses should be removed from society for long periods of time. Many three-strikes laws mandate a life sentence for the third violent-felony conviction. Analysts of three-strikes laws predicted that courts would be overwhelmed as more defendants, facing enhanced penalties, demanded jury trials. The added time to process cases and the reluctance to grant pretrial release to defendants facing long prison terms, said analysts, would cause jail populations to explode as the number of admissions and the length of jail stays grew. The actual effects of the laws have been similar to the effects predicted, but not as great.

### CHAPTER OBJECTIVE 6

Fair sentencing often refers to fairness for *victims*. Fair sentencing advocates, however, suggest that any truly fair sentencing scheme must incorporate fairness for both victims and offenders. Issues related to fairness in sentencing are proportionality, equity, social debt, and truth in sentencing.

## KEY TERMS

sentencing, p. 34
sentence, p. 34
social order, p. 35
retribution, p.36
just deserts, p. 37
deterrence, p. 37
specific deterrence, p. 37

general deterrence, p. 37
pleasure-pain principle, p. 37
incapacitation, p. 40
correctional econometrics, p. 41
rehabilitation, p. 41
reintegration, p. 41
restoration, p. 42

## QUESTIONS FOR REVIEW

1. Define *sentencing*.
2. What are the modern goals of criminal sentencing?
3. Define *retribution*.
4. Describe the two forms of deterrence.
5. Define *incapacitation*.
6. What is *correctional econometrics?*
7. When has rehabilitation been accomplished?
8. Restorative justice is based on what belief?
9. What are the five sentencing options in wide use in the United States today?
10. Differentiate between fines and restitution.
11. Give some examples of alternative sentencing.
12. How have American models of criminal sentencing changed over the past 100 years?
13. What are three-strikes (and two-strikes) laws? Why have such laws been enacted? What consequences might they have for the criminal justice system and for the corrections subsystem?
14. What is fair sentencing? What issues are involved in fair sentencing?

## CRITICAL THINKING EXERCISES

### ON-THE-JOB ISSUE

In recreation yard conversation, Manuel learns that Jack, who committed essentially the same crime as Manuel, is serving a much shorter sentence. Manuel becomes sullen and hostile and complains bitterly to you about injustices and prejudice in the criminal justice system. What is the best way to calm Manuel so that an emotionally charged incident does not occur?

### CORRECTIONS ISSUE

Edgardo Rotman says, "Rehabilitation . . . can be defined tentatively and broadly as a right to an opportunity to return to (or remain in) society with an improved chance of being a useful citizen and staying out of prison."[44] Do you agree that rehabilitation is the right of an offender? Why or why not?

## CORRECTIONS ON THE WEB

1. Access the Sentencing Project at **http://www.sentencingproject. org.** Determine whether the group is prosecution- or defense-based. Then read the information you find about the Sentencing Project and the National Association of Sentencing Advocates. Write a paragraph summarizing the information.

2. Visit the United States Sentencing Commission at **http://www.ussc.gov.** Explore the areas of interest to you. Then use the link to the state sentencing commissions and go to the NASC Contact List. If your state is listed, contact its commission to find out who serves on the commission and what the basic sentencing philosophy of the commission is.

## ADDITIONAL READINGS

Bazemore, Gordon, and Mark Umbreit. *Balanced and Restorative Justice: Program Summary.* Washington: U.S. Department of Justice, Office of Juvenile Justice and Delinquency Prevention, 1994.

Briggs, John, Christopher Harrison, and Angus McInnes. *Crime and Punishment in England: An Introductory History.* New York: St. Martin's Press, 1996.

Galaway, Burt, and Joe Hudson (eds.). *Criminal Justice, Restitution, and Reconciliation.* Monsey, NY: Criminal Justice Press, 1990.

Greenwood, P. W., et al. *Three Strikes and You're Out: Estimated Benefits and Costs of California's New Mandatory Sentencing Law.* Santa Monica, CA: RAND, 1994).

Hudson, Joe, and Burt Galaway (eds.). *Victims, Offenders, and Alternative Sanctions.* Lexington, MA: Lexington Books, 1980.

Rotman, Edgardo. *Beyond Punishment: A New View of the Rehabilitation of Criminal Offenders.* Westport, CT: Greenwood Press, 1990.

Umbreit, Mark. *Victim Meets Offender: The Impact of Restorative Justice and Mediation.* Monsey, NY: Criminal Justice Press, 1994.

## ENDNOTES

1. "*Au Pair* Faces Life in Prison," *USA Today* Online, http://www.usatoday.com, posted October 30, 1997.

2. The South Carolina case was unusual because courts in at least 30 other states have refused to treat a viable fetus as a person under child abuse laws (although they may for other legal purposes). State supreme courts in Florida, Kentucky, Nevada, Ohio, and Wisconsin have issued rulings contrary to that in the South Carolina case.

3. John P. Conrad, "The Pessimistic Reflections of a Chronic Optimist," *Federal Probation*, Vol. 55, No. 2, 1991, p. 7.

4. Sigmund Freud, *Totem and Taboo*, trans. and ed. by James Strachey (New York: W. W. Norton, 1990).

5. Jackie Cooperman, "AIDS Scare Triples in Scope," ABCNEWS.com, Oct. 28, 1997.

6. Conrad, p. 7.

7. Morgan O. Reynolds, *The Reynolds Report: Crime and Punishment in the U.S., NCPA Policy Report No. 209* (Dallas: National Center for Policy Analysis, 1997). Online, available: http://www.public-policy.org/~ncpa/studies/s209/s209.html.

8. Edwin Zedlewski, *Making Confinement Decisions*, Research in Brief (Washington: National Institute of Justice, 1987).

9. John J. DiIulio, "Crime and Punishment in Wisconsin," *Wisconsin Policy Research Institute Report*, Vol. 3, No. 7, 1990, pp. 1–56. See also William Barr, *The Case for More Incarceration* (Washington: U.S. Department of Justice, Office of Policy Development, 1992).

10. See, for example, Zedlewski.

11. Edgardo Rotman, *Beyond Punishment: A New View on the Rehabilitation of Criminal Offenders* (Westport, CT: Greenwood Press, 1990), p. 11.

12. Graeme Newman, *The Punishment Response* (Philadelphia: Lippincott, 1978), p. 104.

13. See, for example, Andrew R. Klein, *Alternative Sentencing: A Practitioner's Guide* (Cincinnati: Anderson, 1988).

14. Much of what follows is derived from Bureau of Justice Assistance *National Assessment of Structured Sentencing* (Washington: Bureau of Justice Assistance, 1996), NCJ153853.

15. S. A. Shane-DuBow, A. P. Brown, and E. Olsen, *Sentencing Reform in the U.S.: History, Content and Effect* (Washington: U.S. Department of Justice, 1985).

16. J. Cohen and M. H. Tonry, "Sentencing Reforms and Their Impacts," in A. Blumstein, et al. (eds.), *Research on Sentencing: The Search for Reform* (Washington: National Academy Press, 1983), pp. 305–459.

17. The materials in this section are derived from the Web site of the Federal Sentencing Commission, http://www.ussc.gov.

18. Title II of the Comprehensive Crime Control Act of 1984; 18 U.S.C. § 3551–3626 and 28 U.S.C. § 991–998.

19. M. Tonry, *Sentencing Matters* (Oxford, England: Oxford University Press, 1995).

20. U.S. Department of Justice, *Mandatory Sentencing* (Washington: Office of Justice Programs, 1997).

21. In mid-1996 the California Supreme Court ruled the state's three-strikes law an undue intrusion on judges' sentencing discretion, and gave judges greater leeway in deciding when the law applies. In 1998, however, the same court held that cases falling "within the spirit of the law" must be sentenced as the law requires. In 1999,

California's three-strikes law was upheld by the U.S. Supreme Court in the case of *Riggs v. California* (No. 98-5021).

22. G. L. Pierce and W. J. Bowers, "The Bartley-Fox Gun Law's Short-Term Impact on Crime in Boston," *Annals of the American Academy of Political and Social Science,* Vol. 455 (1981), pp. 120–132.

23. C. Loftin, M. Heumann, and D. McDowall, "Mandatory Sentencing and Firearms Violence: Evaluating an Alternative to Gun Control," *Law and Society Review,* Vol. 17 (1983), pp. 287–318.

24. C. Loftin and D. McDowall, "The Deterrent Effects of the Florida Felony Firearm Law," *Journal of Criminal Law and Criminology,* Vol. 75 (1984), pp. 250–259.

25. D. McDowall, C. Loftin, and B. Wierseman, "A Comparative Study of the Preventive Effects of Mandatory Sentencing Laws for Gun Crimes," *Journal of Criminal Law and Criminology,* Vol. 83, No. 2 (Summer 1992), pp. 378–394.

26. Joint Committee on New York Drug Law Evaluation, *The Nation's Toughest Drug Law: Evaluating the New York Experience,* a project of the Association of the Bar of the City of New York, the City of New York, and the Drug Abuse Council, Inc. (Washington: U.S. Government Printing Office, 1978).

27. M. Tonry, *Sentencing Reform Impacts* (Washington: U.S. Department of Justice, National Institute of Justice, 1987).

28. Ibid.

29. Much of what follows is taken from John Clark, James Austin, and D. Alan Henry, *Three Strikes and You're Out: A Review of State Legislation* (Washington: National Institute of Justice, 1997), NCJ165369.

30. Bureau of Justice Assistance, *National Assessment of Structured Sentencing* (Washington: U.S. Department of Justice, February 1996).

31. Donna Lyons, " 'Three Strikes' Legislation Update" (paper presented at the National Conference of State Legislatures, December 1995).

32. Several states have had such laws on the books for many years. For example, South Dakota has had three-strikes-type legislation since 1877.

33. James Austin, " 'Three Strikes and You're Out': The Likely Consequences on the Courts, Prisons, and Crime in California and Washington State," *St. Louis University Public Law Review,* Vol. 14, No. 1 (1994).

34. The Washington law does permit the governor to grant a pardon or clemency, but it also recommends that no person sentenced under this law to life in prison without parole be granted clemency until he or she has reached 60 years of age and is judged no longer a threat to society.

35. Austin.

36. Ibid.

37. Countywide Criminal Justice Coordination Committee, *Impact of the "Three Strikes Law" on the Criminal Justice System in Los Angeles County,* (Los Angeles: November 15, 1995). The number of inmates the jail system can house is limited by a federal court order and the sheriff's budget. Therefore, the use of early-release mechanisms for lower-risk offenders has been accelerated to make room for the growing number of two- and three-strikes cases. This policy has not increased the size of the jail population, but it has changed its composition.

38. California Sheriff's Association, *Three Strikes Jail Population Report* (Sacramento, CA: CSA, 1995).

39. Center for Urban Analysis, Santa Clara County Office of the County Executive, *Comparing Administration of the "Three-Strikes Law" in the County of Los Angeles With Other Large California Counties* (Santa Clara, CA: May 1996).

40. Los Angeles County Sheriff's Department, *"Three Strikes" Law—Impact on Jail: Summary Analysis* (Los Angeles: August 31, 1996).

41. John Clark et al., *Three Strikes and You're Out: A Review of State Legislation* (Washington: National Institute of Justice, 1997).

42. Ibid.

43. Edith E. Flynn et al., "Three-Strikes Legislation: Prevalence and Definitions," in National Institute of Justice, *Task Force Reports From the American Society of Criminology* (Washington: NIJ, 1997).

44. Edgardo Rotman, *Beyond Punishment: A New View on the Rehabilitation of Criminal Offenders* (Westport, CT: Greenwood Press, 1990), p. 3.

# Punishments
## A Brief History

### CHAPTER OBJECTIVES

After completing this chapter you should be able to:

1.  Describe the types of punishment prevalent in ancient times.
2.  List and describe the major criminal punishments used throughout history.
3.  Explain the ideas that led to the use of incarceration as a criminal punishment—and as an alternative to earlier punishments.
4.  Explain the role of correctional reformers in changing the nature of criminal punishment.

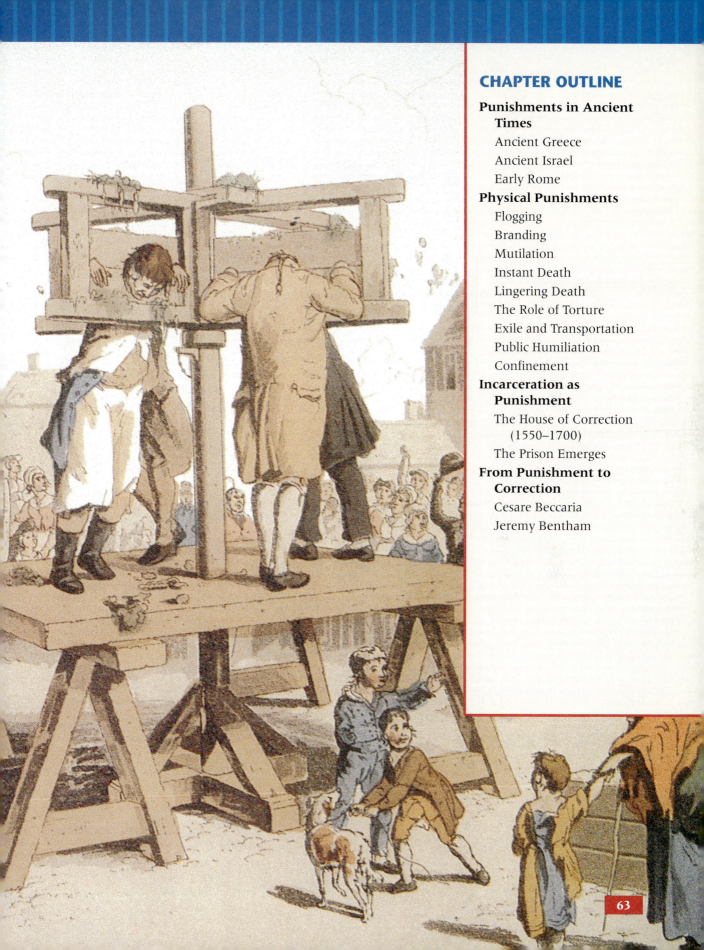

*No man shall be forced by Torture to confesse any Crime against himselfe nor any other unlesse it be in some Capitall case, where he is first fullie convicted by cleare and suffitient evidence to be guilty. After which if the cause be of that nature, That it is very apparent there be other conspiratours, or confederates with him, Then he may be tortured, yet not with such Tortures as be Barbarous and inhumane.*

—Massachusetts Body of Liberties of 1641, Section 45

**corporal punishments**

Physical punishments, or those involving the body.

Before the advent of prisons, **corporal punishments** were often imposed for serious crimes. Some, although not regularly administered, were especially gruesome. In 1757 Robert-François Damiens was sentenced to be publicly quartered in Paris for attempting to kill King Louis XV. As the executioners took their places, it was announced that "the flesh will be torn from his breasts, arms, thighs and calves with red-hot pincers, his right hand, holding the knife with which he committed said [homicide], burnt with sulphur, and, on those places where the flesh will be torn away, poured molten lead, boiling oil, burning resin, wax and sulphur melted together and then his body drawn and quartered by four horses and his limbs and body consumed by fire, reduced to ashes and his ashes thrown to the winds."[1] As it turned out, however, Damiens was a very muscular man. He remained conscious throughout the tortures, although a report tells us that he "uttered horrible cries." When it came time for him to be quartered, the four horses were unable to pull him apart—even after repeated attempts. Finally, six horses were used and, when they were still unable to disjoint the prisoner, his muscles had to be "cut through with knives."

Gruesome as this story may be, it illustrates the relative newness of our present system of corrections, which depends largely on the use of fines, probation, imprisonment, and parole. Corrections has evolved over time into the system we know today. This chapter traces the historical and cultural roots of our present system.

# Punishments in Ancient Times

Before the large-scale building of prisons began in seventeenth-century Europe, a variety of punishments, based on the law and justice concepts of certain cultural groups, sought to punish wrongdoers and maintain civil order. We will briefly highlight some of these developments and the traditions that have influenced modern correctional practices.

## Ancient Greece

In the cultural history of punishments, the Greek city-states provide the earliest evidence that public punishment is part of the Western tradition—and that its roots are in ideas of law and justice. Of all the city-states,

Athens is the best documented. This documentation ranges from the writings of orators and philosophers to plays and poetry. These writings tell us that many early crimes were punished by execution, banishment, or exile. Greek poets described stoning to death, throwing from high cliffs, stake-binding (similar to crucifixion), and ritual cursing as punishments inflicted on convicted criminals. In many cases, the bodies of executed criminals were regarded as dishonored and could not be buried. Their bodies were left to scavengers and the elements—and served as a warning to anyone contemplating similar crimes.

Other punishments in ancient Athens included "confiscation of property, fines, and the destruction of the condemned offenders' houses."[2] Public denunciation, shaming *(atimia)*, imprisonment, and public display of the offender were also used. Criminal punishments in ancient Greece sometimes included civil penalties, such as loss of the ability to transfer property, to vote, and to marry.

## Ancient Israel

The chief record of ancient Hebrew history is the Bible. It describes the law and civilization of the ancient Hebrews, including their criminal law and penology. Punishments used by the Hebrews and mentioned in the Old Testament included cursing, banishment, beating, beheading, blinding, branding and burning, crushing, confiscation of property, crucifixion, cutting asunder, exile, drowning, exposure to wild beasts, fining, flaying, hanging, imprisonment, mutilation, plucking of the hair, casting down from a high place, sawing asunder, scourging with thorns, slavery, slaying by spear or sword, use of the stocks, stoning, strangulation, stripes, and suffocation.[3] Michel Foucault, the French historian, says that the purpose of physical punishments was primarily revenge. "It was as if the punishment was thought to equal, if not to exceed, in savagery the crime itself," he writes.[4]

## Early Rome

The Twelve Tables, the first written laws of Rome, were issued in 451 B.C. Conviction of some offenses required payment of compensation, but the most frequent penalty was death. Among the forms of capital punishment were burning (for arson), throwing from a cliff (for perjury), clubbing to death (for writing insulting songs about a citizen), hanging (for stealing others' crops), and decapitation. Not mentioned in the Twelve Tables were several other forms of capital punishment in vogue in ancient Rome. For killing a close relative, the offender was subjected to the *culleus*. That is, the offender was confined in a sack with an ape, a dog, and a serpent, and the sack was thrown into the sea. Vestal virgins who had violated their vows of chastity were buried alive. As an alternative to execution, offenders might choose exile. Offenders who went into exile lost their citizenship, freedom, and immovable property. If they returned to Rome, they could be killed by any citizen.[5]

**Fugitive Apprehension Officer**
Responsible for locating felons who have escaped or absconded from department of corrections institutions, work crews, or other supervised community programs within the state. Duties also include preparing cases for prosecution and testifying in criminal proceedings. Position may involve use of firearms or other means of physical force. Requirements: two years of recent investigative experience, either in the field or in a correctional institution; college-level courses in law enforcement, criminal justice, law, or a closely related field.

I believe the United States can reduce the rise of violent crime by giving convicted first time offenders the option of either making their punishment more painful or joining the military. People have to get rid of their energy, and one place where it will be all used up is the military.

Also, one reason so many young people become criminals is that they learn the behavior from others. They are exposed to more people with attitudes and definitions favorable to a certain type of crime than with attitudes opposed to it. Even in here, model inmates are those with friends whose attitudes lean more toward doing clean time than doing hard time. For me, clean time means I get to have time with my wife and kids every so often. [Attica allowed conjugal visits at the time these remarks were made.]

*Derrick Stroud 89T2999*
*Attica Penitentiary, NY*

# Physical Punishments

The practice of corporal punishment carried over into the Christian era. Physical punishments were imposed for a wide variety of offenses during the Middle Ages. Physical punishments also flourished in the American colonies. "It is common knowledge that the whole baggage of corporal punishments, as they existed in England, were brought to this country, and flourished, especially in New England where the precepts of Calvinism adorned them with pious sanctions."[6] The Puritans, for example, sometimes burned witches and unruly slaves; made wide use of the stocks, the pillory, and the ducking stool; branded criminal offenders; and forced women convicted of adultery to wear "scarlet letters."

As justice historian Pieter Spierenburg notes, many physical punishments during the Middle Ages and in "early modern Europe" were *theatrical punishments*.[7] That is, they were corporal punishments carried out in public. "Punishments that were both physical and public can be divided into five degrees of severity:" (1) whipping or flogging, (2) burning of the skin, (3) mutilation, or "more serious encroachments on bodily integrity," (4) a merciful instant death, and (5) a torturous and prolonged death.[8]

## Flogging

Flogging (or whipping) has been the most common physical punishment through the ages.[9] The Mosaic code, for example, authorized flogging, and Roman law specified flogging as a punishment for certain forms of theft. Flogging was common in England during the Middle Ages as chastisement for a wide variety of crimes. In England, women were flogged in private, while men were whipped publicly.[10]

The construction of flogging whips varied greatly, from simple leather straps or willow branches to heavy, complicated instruments designed to inflict a maximum of pain. A traditional form of whip was the cat-o'-nine-tails, consisting of nine knotted cords fastened to a wooden handle. The "cat" got its name from the marks it left on the body, which were like the scratches of a cat. One especially cruel form of the whip, the Russian knout, was made of leather strips fitted with fishhooks. When a prisoner was whipped, the hooks would dig into the body, ripping away the proverbial "pound of flesh" with each stroke. A thorough whipping with the knout could result in death from blood loss.

Flogging was also widely used in the American colonies to enforce discipline, punish offenders, and make an example of "ne'er-do-wells" (shiftless and irresponsible individuals). As a mechanism for gaining compliance with prison rules, flogging survived into the twentieth century. As late as 1959, Harry Elmer Barnes and Negley K. Teeters were able to write, "Floggings have been prison practice down to our own times, and deaths have occurred due to over-severe whippings in southern prison camps and chain-gangs. Tying prisoners up by their hands and allowing them to hang

## CAREER PROFILE

*Zaira Tena*
*Correctional Officer*
*New Mexico Women's*
*Correctional Facility*
*Grants, New Mexico*

*"I like my job. I like working with people. What I learned and what I'd tell someone is, Be very professional, firm, fair, and consistent at all times, and be able to work under a lot of pressure."*

Zaira Tena is employed by Corrections Corporation of America (CCA) as a correctional officer at the New Mexico Women's Correctional Facility in Grants, New Mexico. She started working there 16 months ago. This is Zaira's first job in corrections. Zaira was attracted to CCA and a career in corrections because of the benefits that CCA offered her.

Zaira attended Laramie County Community College in Laramie, Wyoming, before joining CCA. The company provided additional training in interpersonal communication, special-needs inmates, crisis intervention, infectious diseases, suicide prevention, first aid, CPR, and firearms, giving her the skills she needs to ensure the health, welfare, and safety of prison employees and inmates. Since Zaira especially enjoys recreation, she also coordinates the institution's recreation activities.

Zaira's enthusiasm for her own career and professional development shows in her advice (quoted above) to persons thinking about a career in corrections. Wisely, Zaira is taking her own advice. She plans to stay in corrections and hopes one day soon to become assistant shift commander at the Grants women's facility.

suspended with their toes barely touching the floor or ground has been a common method of enforcing discipline."[11]

## Branding

Branding, a type of mutilation, was practiced by Roman society. It was used in England until 1829. Criminals were branded with a mark or letter signifying their crimes. Brands, which were often placed on the forehead or another part of the face, served to warn others of an offender's criminal history. The last documented incident of facial branding of English criminals was in 1699.[12] After that year offenders were branded on the hand, since it was feared that more obvious marks would reduce employment possibilities. Branding was abolished in England during the last half of the eighteenth century. The French branded criminals with the royal emblem on the shoulder. They later switched to burning onto the shoulder a letter signifying the crime of which the offender had been convicted.

Branding was also practiced in the early American colonies. The East Jersey Codes of 1668 and 1675, for example, ordered that burglars be branded on the hand with the letter *T* (for *thief*). After a second offense, the letter *R* (for *rogue*) was burned into the forehead. Maryland branded blasphemers with the letter *B* on the forehead. Women, in deference to their beauty, had to wear letters on their clothing, rather than being branded.

## Mutilation

Mutilation was another type of corporal punishment used in ancient and medieval societies. Archaeological evidence shows that the pharaohs of ancient Egypt, and their representatives, often ordered mutilation.[13] In ancient Rome offenders who were mutilated suffered a kind of poetic justice according to the law of retaliation, or *lex talionis*. *Lex talionis*, as a punishment philosophy, resembles the biblical principle of "an eye for an eye and a tooth for a tooth."

Medieval justice frequently insisted that a punishment should fit the crime. Hence, "thieves and counterfeiters had their hands cut off, liars and perjurers had their tongues torn out, spies had their eyes gouged out, sex criminals had their genitals removed, and so forth."[14] Blasphemers sometimes had their tongues pierced or cut out and their upper lips cut away.[15]

Mutilation had a deterrent effect because the permanently scarred and disfigured offenders served as warnings to others of what might happen to criminals. Sometimes, however, mutilation served merely as a prelude to execution. The right hand of a murderer, for example, was sometimes cut off before he was hanged.[16]

## Instant Death

According to Spierenburg, beheading, hanging, and garroting (strangulation by a tightened iron collar) were the most common means of merciful or instant death.[17] Instant death was frequently reserved for members of the nobility who had received capital sentences (usually from the King) or

A 1786 German woodcut depicts a public execution by burning. What purpose did such public dispensing of justice serve for government authorities?

for previously honorable men and women who ran afoul of the law. Decapitation, especially when done by the sword, was regarded as the most honorable form of capital punishment—since a sword was a symbol that was both noble and aristocratic. Hanging, says Spierenburg, "was the standard nonhonorable form of the death penalty." For women, however, hanging was considered indecent. Garroting tended to replace hanging as a capital punishment for women.

## Lingering Death

The worst fate a criminal offender—especially one convicted of heinous crimes—might meet in medieval Europe was a slow or lingering death, often preceded by torture. Some offenders were burned alive, while others were "broken on the wheel." Breaking on the wheel was a procedure that broke all of the major bones in the body. A person who had been broken on the wheel and was still alive was often killed by an executioner's blow to the heart.

Offenders who were to be hanged sometimes had their arms and legs broken first, while others were whipped or burned. Burning alive, a practice used in France until the eighteenth century, was undoubtedly one of the period's cruelest forms of capital punishment.

## The Role of Torture

A variety of other corporal punishments were employed, some of which involved torture. Although pain was central to punishments intended to exact revenge, pain was also used to extract confessions and get information. "Torture," said one source, "is the twisting (torsion) from its subjects of guilty secrets."[18] The use of torture in medieval England was based on a theory that knowledge of one's own guilt, or of the guilt of others, was an offense in itself. Moreover, the theory went, such knowledge was a kind of property that rightly belonged to the state. Hence, forcing an offender to relinquish such "property," by any means necessary, was a right of the government.

Tortures of all kinds were also used during the Middle Ages in an effort to gain confessions from heretics. Heresy was considered a crime against the church and against God. At the time, there was no separation between church and state in many Western societies, and church courts were free to impose punishment as they saw fit. Believers were sure that the heretic's soul was condemned to eternal damnation and that confession would lead to salvation. As a result, torture flourished as a technique for saving souls. Some saw the suffering induced by corporal punishments as spiritually cleansing. Others compared it to the suffering of Christ on the cross. They argued that physical pain and suffering might free the soul from the clutches of crime and evil.

A common medieval torture was to be put on the rack—a machine that slowly stretched a prisoner until his or her joints separated. On other prisoners, red-hot pincers called *hooks* were used to pull the flesh away, or thumbscrews were used as their name implies. Some prisoners underwent *cording*, in which the thumbs were tied tightly together behind the back by a rope that passed through a support in the ceiling. Weights were then tied to the ankles, and the prisoner was hoisted into the air by his thumbs. Stones were also used to crush confessions out of prisoners, who were first covered with boards and then forced to suffer as one stone after another was placed on top of them.

## Exile and Transportation

In a number of early societies, exile, or banishment, sometimes took the place of corporal and capital punishment. The ancient Greeks permitted offenders to voluntarily leave the Greek state and travel to Rome, where they might gain citizenship. Early Roman law also established the punishment of exile. Exile was regarded as akin to a death sentence, since the banished person could no longer depend on his former community for support and protection. He or she could generally be killed with impunity on attempting to reenter the area.

Exile was practiced in some European communities into the 1800s. One historical study, for example, revealed that between 1650 and 1750, 97 percent of the noncapital sentences handed down in Amsterdam included banishment.[19] Sentences of banishment drove petty offenders out of a municipality and kept known offenders out of town. But banished criminals

*A variety of medieval corporal punishments are illustrated in this German woodcut from 1509. Were some forms of punishment considered more honorable than others?*

resurfaced quickly in neighboring towns, and many communities in Europe confronted a floating population of criminals—especially petty thieves.

Though it was rarely practical to banish offenders from an entire province or nation, England practiced for more than 200 years a form of criminal exile known as *transportation*. An English law authorizing the transportation of convicts to newly discovered lands was passed in 1597. The law was intended primarily to provide galley slaves for a burgeoning English merchant fleet. Soon, however, public support grew for the transportation system as a way of ridding England of felons. As a result, large numbers of convicts were sent to America and other English colonies. One writer[20] estimates that by the beginning of the American Revolution, 50,000 prisoners had been sent to the New World. Most of them "were sold as indentured servants in the southern colonies, where their market value was greater than in New England."

After the American Revolution, convicted felons began piling up in English jails with no place to go. Legislation was soon passed authorizing prisoners to be housed aboard floating prison ships called *hulks*. Many of these vessels were abandoned merchant ships or broken-down warships. Hulks were anchored in rivers and harbors throughout England. They were unsanitary, rat-infested, and unventilated, and the keepers flogged the inmates to force them to work. Disease ran rampant in the hulks, sometimes wiping out all the prisoners on a ship, and the crew and nearby citizens as well. This "temporary" solution lasted about 80 years.

The system of hulks eventually proved impractical, and England soon began shifting its convict population to Australia, which had been discovered by Captain Cook in 1770. Convict transportation to Australia began in earnest in 1787,[21] with English convicts being transported to New South Wales, Norfolk Island, and Van Diemen's Land—now known as Tasmania. The journey was long and demanding, and conditions on prison ships were

*In the late eighteenth century, the English government began turning broken-down war vessels and abandoned transport ships into hulks to house prisoners. What event caused the overcrowding in prisons that made these hulks necessary?*

often ghastly. Many convicts did not survive the trip. Those who did were put to work at heavy labor when they reached their destinations, helping to develop the growing region.

Soon convicts who had served their sentences began to receive land grants. In 1791 the governor of New South Wales initiated a program to give released convicts up to 30 acres of land each, along with enough tools, seeds, and rations to last 18 months.

English transportation of criminals began to wane in 1853, when Parliament abolished transportation for prisoners with sentences of less than 14 years. Opposition to transportation was especially strong among the free settlers who had begun to populate Australia and nearby regions. In 1867 the practice of transportation officially ended, although England continued to send inmates from India to its penal colony in the Andaman Islands until World War II.

Other countries also had favorite places of exile for convicted prisoners. Beginning in 1791, French authorities sent prisoners in large numbers to Madagascar, New Caledonia, the Marquesas Islands, and French Guiana. Off the coast of French Guiana, Devil's Island, named for the horrors associated with imprisonment there, continued to function as a prison until 1951. Spanish and Portuguese prisoners went to Africa; Russian exiles were sent to Siberia, a desolate region in central and eastern Russia.

## Public Humiliation

Many corporal punishments were carried out in public, primarily to deter other potential lawbreakers. Some forms of punishment, however, depended on public ridicule for their effect. They included the stocks and the pillory.

Stocks held a prisoner in a sitting position, with feet and hands locked in a frame. A prisoner in the pillory was made to stand with the head and hands locked in place. Both devices exposed the prisoner to public scorn.

While confined in place, prisoners were frequently pelted with eggs and rotten fruit. Sometimes they were whipped or branded. Those confined to the pillory occasionally had their ears nailed to the wood, and had to rip them free when released. England abolished the pillory in 1834, but according to at least one source, the pillory was still in use in Delaware in 1905.[22]

## Confinement

Confinement by chaining or jailing has been a punishment since ancient times. Sometimes confinement served functions other than punishment for crimes. In early Greece, for example, prisons were used to punish convicted offenders, to coerce the payment of debts, to hold those awaiting other punishments, and to detain foreigners who might otherwise flee before their cases could be heard.[23] Until the 1600s, and the development of prisons as primary places of punishment, prisons were used to detain people before trial; to hold prisoners awaiting other punishments, such as death or corporal punishment; to force payment of debts and fines; and to hold and punish slaves.

Early European prisons were rarely called prisons. They went by such names as *dungeon, tower,* and *gaol* (from which we get the modern term *jail*). Some places used as prisons had been built for other purposes. The Tower of London, for example, was originally a fortified palace that had been used as an arsenal. The French Bastille began as a fortified city gate leading into Paris. Judicial proceedings were not necessary before imprisonment, nor was a formal sentence. Anyone thrown into a dungeon at the behest of authorities was likely to stay there until granted clemency or until death.

*Found guilty of the offense of impiety in Athens in 399 B.C., instead of imprisonment, Socrates chose the penalty of drinking poison, a form of execution in ancient Athens. What was the goal of most early penalties for crimes?*

# Incarceration as Punishment

According to Pieter Spierenburg, a Dutch justice historian, a new form of punishment that emerged around the year 1500 was *penal bondage,* which included all forms of incarceration.[24] "Courts came to use it almost as frequently as physical sanctions. Instead of being flogged or hanged, some offenders were incarcerated in workhouses or forced to perform labor in some other setting." According to Spierenburg, the word *bondage* means "any punishment that puts severe restrictions on the condemned person's freedom of action and movement, including but not limited to imprisonment."

Among the forms of penal bondage imposed on criminals, vagrants, debtors, social misfits, and others were forced labor on public works projects and forced conscription into military campaigns. Later, houses of correction subjected inmates to strict routines.

One early form of incarceration developed in France. For at least 200 years, prisoners were regularly assigned to French warships as galley slaves. The naval importance of galleys steadily declined, but French naval officials continued to have custody of convicted offenders. By the mid-1700s, they had begun to put convicts to work in the shipyards of Toulon, Brest, and Rochefort. At night these prisoners were sheltered in arsenals, where they slept chained to their beds. As Spierenburg notes, "the arsenals were in fact labor camps where convicts had to remain within an enclosed space, so the penalty was more akin to imprisonment than to public works."

The public-works penalty, sometimes called *penal servitude,* became especially popular in Germany and Switzerland in the 1600s and 1700s. According to Spierenburg, "convicts dug ore in mines, repaired ramparts, built roads or houses, or went from door to door collecting human waste."[25]

## The House of Correction (1550–1700)

Midway between corporal punishments and modern imprisonment stands the workhouse or the house of correction. The development of workhouses was originally a humanitarian move intended to cope with the unsettling social conditions of the late sixteenth and early seventeenth centuries in England. The feudal system had offered mutual protection for landowning nobles and for serfs, who were tied to the land. By 1550 that system was breaking down in Europe. Hordes of former serfs roamed the countryside, unable to earn a living. Many flocked to the cities, where they hoped to find work in the newly developing industries. This change from an agrarian economy to an industrial one displaced many persons, resulted in growing poverty, and increased the numbers of beggars and vagrants.

**bridewell**   A workhouse. The word came from the name of the first workhouse in England.

Vagrancy became a crime, and soon anyone unable to prove some means of support was imprisoned in a workhouse. The first workhouse in England was called Bridewell because it was at St. Bridget's Well, near the town of Blackfriars. Soon, the word **bridewell** entered the language as a term for a workhouse, and the English Parliament ordered workhouses to be created throughout England. Parliament intended that those housed in workhouses should be taught habits of industry and frugality, and that they should learn a trade.

Better to Work than Stand thus

Bridewells were penal institutions for social outcasts—ranging from vagrants to petty criminals—who were forced to work under strict discipline. What social conditions prompted governments to establish such houses of correction?

At first, prisoners in workhouses were paid for the work they did. Work included spinning, weaving, clothmaking, the milling of grains, and baking. Soon, however, as the numbers of prisoners grew, the workhouse system deteriorated. As workhouses spread through Europe, they became catchall institutions that held the idle, the unemployed, the poor, debtors, the insane, and even unruly individuals whose families could not cope with them. According to one writer, imprisonment in a workhouse could serve "as a tool of private discipline… The family drew up a petition explaining why the individual should be imprisoned, and the authorities decided whether or not to consent. Usually, private offenders were confined because of conduct considered immoral."[26]

Hence, workhouses served as informal repositories for people the community regarded as "inconvenient," irresponsible, or deviant—even if their behavior did not violate the criminal law. In the midst of this large population of misfits and unwanted persons, however, could be found a core group of criminal offenders. In 1706 the British Parliament passed legislation "permitting judges to sentence felons to the house of correction for up to two years."[27]

By the end of the seventeenth century, houses of correction had become mere holding cells with little reformative purpose. Nonetheless, because workhouses relied primarily on incarceration rather than corporal punishments, they provided a model for prison reformers bent on more humanitarian correctional practices.

# The Prison Emerges

Two main elements fueled the development of prisons as we know them today. The first element was a philosophical shift away from punishment of the body, toward punishment of the soul or human spirit. By the late 1700s in Europe and America, a powerful movement was underway to replace traditional corporal punishments with deprivation of personal liberty as the main thrust of criminal sentencing. Michel Foucault explains the shift this way: "The punishment-body relation [was no longer] the same as it was in the torture during public executions. The body now serves as an instrument or intermediary: if one intervenes upon it to imprison it, or to make it work, it is in order to deprive the individual of a liberty that is regarded both as a right and as property. The body, according to this penalty, is caught up in a system of constraints and privations, obligations and prohibitions. Physical pain, the pain of the body itself, is no longer the constituent element of the penalty."[28]

The transition from corporal punishments to denial of liberties found its clearest expression in the work of the Philadelphia Society for Alleviating the Miseries of Public Prisons. The society, established by the Pennsylvania Quakers in 1787, had as its purpose the renovation of existing prisons and jails and the establishment of the prison as the basic form of criminal punishment. Thanks largely to the widely publicized works of the society, Pennsylvania became in April 1794 the first state to permanently abolish the death penalty for all crimes except first-degree murder, and it adopted a system of fines and imprisonment in place of corporal punishments.[29] The new Pennsylvania criminal code was important because it "marked the first permanent American break with contemporary juristic savagery, was the forerunner of the reform codes of other American states, and was the essential basis of Pennsylvania criminal jurisprudence until the next systematic revision in 1860."[30]

The second element fueling the development of modern prisons was the passage of laws preventing the imprisonment of anyone except criminals. Civil commitments to prison ended, and a huge class of social misfits were removed from prisons and dealt with elsewhere. Primary among this group were debtors, who historically had been cast into jails as a result of civil rulings against them. John Howard's study of English jails found 2,437 debtors among the 4,084 prisoners he encountered.[31] Many others were vagrants who had committed no "intentional" crime.

According to Pieter Spierenburg, the Dutch were the first Europeans to segregate serious criminals from vagrants and minor delinquents, and Dutch courts were the first European courts to begin substituting imprisonment for corporal punishments.[32] The workhouse in Amsterdam, which opened in 1654, "represented the first criminal prison in Europe," says Spierenburg. By the start of the 1700s, Dutch "courts frequently imposed sentences of imprisonment. During the third quarter of the seventeenth century, the Amsterdam court did so in one-fifth of its criminal cases; a century later, it did so in three-fifths. By the 1670s the court of Groningen-City imposed imprisonment in two-fifths of criminal cases." Even so, the imprisonment of debtors persisted in Holland for another hundred years, and Dutch prisons of the period held both criminal and civil "convicts."

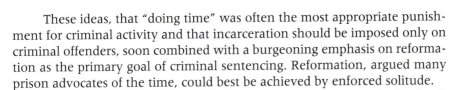

I am a psychologist for the New Hampshire Department of Corrections working in a mental health unit at a correctional institution. My job is to lead a treatment program for offenders with moderate to severe Axis 1 (illness-type) mental disorders. Correctional counselors, nurses, or other mental health employees refer inmates to my supervisor, the Chief of Mental Health. If he thinks the inmate may have a serious illness-type mental disorder, he gives the case to me. Then either I or one of my team members carefully reads the inmate's offender record and medical chart, does a thorough interview, and, with the client's written permission, writes for information from mental health professionals who have worked with the client. Usually, the psychiatrist on the team will see the inmate also. If we think the person does have a disorder appropriate for us to treat, we develop a treatment plan and schedule the individual for a treatment team meeting, attended by a nurse, the correctional counselor, the psychiatrist, my team members, and myself. We talk with the client about goals and interventions. These may include nonaddictive psychotropic medications, psychotherapy (individual and group), case management, and monitoring. When it's appropriate, we refer clients to other programs at the prison, for example, the sexual offender program, or the substance abuse program. As the clients approach release, we do our best to set them up with mental health and other resources in the community, so they will remain in good mental health, and so that a worsening of their mental disorder does not contribute to their re-offending.

*Laura Magzis*
*Psychologist*
*Mental Health Unit*
*New Hampshire State Prison for Men*

These ideas, that "doing time" was often the most appropriate punishment for criminal activity and that incarceration should be imposed only on criminal offenders, soon combined with a burgeoning emphasis on reformation as the primary goal of criminal sentencing. Reformation, argued many prison advocates of the time, could best be achieved by enforced solitude.

In 1776 the British philanthropist Jonas Hanway published a book entitled *Solitude in Imprisonment*. Hanway's work appears to have had a significant influence on prison advocates. Hanway argued that the interruption of transportation provided a much-needed opportunity to reexamine prevailing policies for dealing with prisoners. He suggested that reformation should be the primary goal of criminal sentencing and said that it was plainly not being met by sentencing practices then in existence. Solitary confinement, said Hanway, would force the prisoner to face his conscience—leading to reformation. Hanway wrote, "The walls of his prison will preach peace to his soul, and he will confess the goodness of his Maker, and the wisdom of the laws of his country."[33]

# From Punishment to Correction

Prisons, as institutions in which convicted offenders spend time as punishment for crimes, are relatively modern. They came about largely as a result of growing intellectualism in Europe and America and as a reaction to the barbarities of corporal punishment.

The period of Western social thought that began in the seventeenth century and lasted until the dawn of the nineteenth century is known as the Age of Enlightenment. "The phrase was frequently employed by writers of the period itself, convinced that they were emerging from centuries of darkness and ignorance into a new age enlightened by reason, science, and a respect for humanity."[34] The Enlightenment, also known as the Age of Reason, was more than a set of fixed ideas. Enlightenment thought implied an attitude, a method of knowing based on observation, experience, and reason.

One of the earliest representatives of the Enlightenment was the French social philosopher and jurist Charles de Montesquieu (1689–1755). His masterwork, *The Spirit of Laws,* was published in 1748. Montesquieu wrote that governmental powers should be separated and balanced in order to guarantee individual rights and freedom. Montesquieu also strongly believed in the rights of individuals. His ideas influenced leaders of both the American Revolution and the French Revolution.[35] Another celebrated philosopher of the Enlightenment was the French writer Voltaire. He satirized both the government and the religious establishment of France. Voltaire twice served time in the Bastille and chose exile in England over prison for additional offenses. Voltaire deeply admired the English atmosphere of political and religious freedom.

The Enlightenment influenced the justice systems of Western nations. It strongly influenced the directions the correctional enterprise would take over the next two hundred years. Much of its influence was due to a number of important thinkers who adopted the principles of the Enlightenment. We now turn our attention to those individuals.

## Cesare Beccaria

Cesare Beccaria (1738–1794) was born in Italy, the eldest son of an aristocratic family. By the time he reached his mid-twenties, Beccaria had formed, with his close friends Pietro and Alessandro Verri, an intellectual circle called the Academy of Fists.[36] The academy took as its purpose the reform of the criminal justice system. Through the Verri brothers, Beccaria became acquainted with the work of French and British political writers such as Montesquieu, Thomas Hobbes (1588–1679), Denis Diderot (1713–1784), Claude-Adrien Helvetius (1715–1771), and David Hume (1711–1776).

In 1764 Beccaria published an essay titled *On Crimes and Punishments.* Although the work was brief, it was, perhaps, the most exciting essay on law of the eighteenth century. In the essay, Beccaria outlined a utilitarian approach to punishment, suggesting that some punishments can never be justified because they are more evil than any "good" they might produce. The use of torture to obtain confessions falls into that category, said Beccaria. Beccaria also protested punishment of the insane, a common practice of the times, saying it could do no good because insane people cannot accurately assess the consequences of their actions. Beccaria said that *ex post facto* laws, or laws passed after the fact, imposed punishment unfairly, since a person could not calculate the risk of acting before the law was passed. He also argued against the use of secret accusations, the discretionary power of judges, the inconsistency and inequality of sentencing, the use of personal connections to obtain sentencing reductions, and the imposition of capital punishment for minor offenses.

Beccaria proposed that punishment could be justified only if it was imposed to defend the social contract—the tacit allegiance that individuals owe their society, and the obligations of government to individuals. It is the social contract, said Beccaria, that gives society the right to punish its members.

Beccaria also argued that punishment should be swift, since swift punishment offers the greatest deterrence. When punishment quickly follows a crime, said Beccaria, the ideas of crime and punishment are more closely associated in a person's mind. He also suggested that the link between crime and punishment would be stronger if the punishment somehow related to the crime.

Finally, said Beccaria, punishments should not be unnecessarily severe. The severity of punishment, he argued, should be proportional to the degree of social damage caused by the crime. Treason, Beccaria said, is the worst crime, since it most harms the social contract. Below treason, Beccaria listed crimes in order of declining severity, including violence against a person or his property, public disruption, and crimes against property. Crimes against property, he said, should be punished by fines.

When his essay was translated into French and English, Beccaria became famous throughout much of Europe. Philosophers of the time hailed his ideas, and several European rulers vowed to follow his lead in the reform of their justice systems.

*Cesare Beccaria (1738–1794), an Italian jurist and criminologist, was one of the first to argue against capital punishment and inhumane treatment of prisoners. What writing by Beccaria influenced the criminal justice systems of Western Europe?*

## Jeremy Bentham

The English philosopher and jurist Jeremy Bentham (1748–1832) was born in London. As a young child, he was considered a prodigy, having been found, at the age of 2, sitting at his father's desk reading a multivolume history of England.[37] He began to study Latin at the age of 3. When Bentham was 12, his father, a wealthy attorney, sent him to Queen's College, Oxford, hoping that he would enter the field of law.

After hearing lectures by the leading legal scholar of the day, Sir William Blackstone (1723–1780), young Bentham became disillusioned with the law. Instead of practicing law, he decided to criticize it, and spent the rest of his life analyzing the legal practices of the day, writing about them, and suggesting improvements.

**utilitarianism** The principle that the highest objective of public policy is the greatest happiness for the largest number of people.

Bentham advocated **utilitarianism**, the principle that the highest objective of public policy is the greatest happiness for the largest number of people. Utilitarianism provided the starting point for Bentham's social analysis, in which he tried to measure the usefulness of existing institutions, practices, and beliefs against a common standard. Bentham believed that human behavior is determined largely by the amount of pleasure or pain associated with a given activity. Hence, he suggested, the purpose of law should be to make socially undesirable activities painful enough to keep people from engaging in them. In this way, said Bentham, "good" can be achieved.

**hedonistic calculus** The idea that people are motivated by pleasure and pain and that the proper amount of punishment can deter crime.

Bentham's idea, that people are motivated by pleasure and pain and that the proper amount of punishment can deter crime, became known as **hedonistic calculus**. Bentham's hedonistic calculus made four assumptions:

1. People by nature choose pleasure and avoid pain.
2. Each individual, either consciously or intuitively, calculates the degree of pleasure or pain to be derived from a given course of action.
3. Lawmakers can determine the degree of punishment necessary to deter criminal behavior.
4. Such punishment can be effectively and rationally built into a system of criminal sentencing.

Bentham is also known as the inventor of the panopticon (from a Greek word meaning "all-seeing")—a type of prison he proposed building in England as early as 1787. The panopticon was intended to be a means for putting utilitarian ideas to work in the field of penology.

Key to the proposed panopticon was its unique architecture, which consisted of a circular tiered design with a glass roof and with a window on the outside wall of each cell.[38] The design made it easy for prison staff, in a tower in the center of the structure, to observe each cell (and its occupants). Within the wheel-like structure, walls separated the cells to prevent any communication between prisoners. Speaking tubes linked cells with the observation platform so that officers could listen to inmates.

The panopticon, also called an *inspection house*, was intended to be a progressive and humanitarian penitentiary. Bentham thought of it as a social experiment. The design was touted as consistent with the ideals of utilitarianism because only a few officers would be subject to the risks and unpleasantness of the inspection role, while many prisoners would benefit from this enlightened means of institutional management.

After years of personally promoting the concept, Bentham saw his idea for an innovative penitentiary die. The panopticon was never built in England, and in 1820 government officials formally disavowed it. The concept may have fallen victim to the growing emphasis on transportation, which delayed all prison construction in England. Another significant factor in the demise of the panopticon ideal, however, was Bentham's insistence that panopticons be built near cities to deter crime among the general popu-

*Jeremy Bentham (1748–1832), an English philosopher and social reformer, spent his life trying to reform the law. His innovative plan for a prison, called the panopticon, consisted of a huge structure covered by a glass roof. A central tower allowed guards to see into the cells, which were arranged in a circle. Although the British government did not use Bentham's plan, several U.S. prisons did, including one in Stateville, Illinois. What is the name given to Bentham's principle that the highest object of public policy is the greatest happiness for the greatest number of people?*

lation. Although a number of sites were chosen for construction, nearby residents always protested plans to build any sort of prison in their neighborhoods. Despite Bentham's failure ever to construct a facility completely true to his panopticon plan, he will always be remembered for his idea that order and reform could be achieved in a prison through architectural design.

## SUMMARY BY CHAPTER OBJECTIVES

### CHAPTER OBJECTIVE 1
Corporal, or physical, punishments were the most common response to crime for centuries before criminals began to be incarcerated.

### CHAPTER OBJECTIVE 2
Criminal punishments of the past generally consisted of flogging, branding, mutilation, exile, transportation, and public humiliation.

### CHAPTER OBJECTIVE 3
Many reformist thinkers based their ideas on Enlightenment principles, including the use of rea-son and deductive logic to solve problems. They laid the groundwork for the use of imprisonment as an alternative to traditional punishments.

### CHAPTER OBJECTIVE 4
Beginning in the mid-1700s, a number of correctional reformers fought the use of corporal punishments and sought to introduce more humane forms of criminal punishment. Among those reformers were Cesare Beccaria and Jeremy Bentham.

## KEY TERMS

corporal punishments, p. 64
bridewell, p. 74

utilitarianism, p. 80
hedonistic calculus, p. 80

## QUESTIONS FOR REVIEW

1. What are corporal punishments? What has been the purpose of corporal punishments throughout history?
2. Which ancient civilization provided the earliest evidence that physical punishment is part of Western society tradition?
3. What were the Twelve Tables?
4. List and describe at least four corporal punishments used in the past for criminal offenders.
5. What were *theatrical punishments?*
6. What role did torture play in the application of corporal punishments? How was the use of torture justified?
7. What purpose did the branding of criminals serve?

8. What two important thinkers discussed in this chapter adapted principles born of the Enlightenment, and applied them to the field of law and corrections? Describe the contributions each made to the field.
9. What was the original intent of a 1597 English law authorizing transportation of criminals to the New World?
10. What factors led to the abolition of transportation to Australia?
11. Describe the house-of-correction movement. How did it develop? What kinds of "offenders" were housed in such institutions?
12. What two elements contributed to the development of modern prisons?

# CRITICAL THINKING EXERCISES

## ON-THE-JOB ISSUE

You're a parole officer for the state corrections system. You are so burdened with paperwork that you rarely get out of the office to see any of your 200 clients—even though you are supposed to make regular home visits.

While you are shuffling papers one day, one of your clients, Bob Boynton, knocks at your door. It is time for him to make his monthly report. You tell him to have a seat, and you ask him the usual questions: "Have you been in trouble with the law since I saw you last?" "Are you still working?" "Are you paying your bills on time?"

Before you finish the interview, Boynton says, "You know, I'm never going to get anywhere this way. I need a better education. The time I spent in prison was wasted. They didn't teach me anything. I need to learn a skill so that I can make more money. If I can't earn better money I won't be able to pay my bills—and I'm afraid that I'll be tempted to get into the drug business again. I don't want to do that!"

You tell Boynton that there are a number of training schools in the area that can teach him a skill. Some of the computer classes offered at the local community college, you've heard, can lead to jobs paying decent wages. But, Boynton says, "I don't have a high school diploma. I can't get into the college. I'll never learn computers. I'm just too old. Besides, I need to work with my hands."

You go through the list of schools and training centers in the area, but Boynton raises an objection to each one. You sense that Boynton is trying to transfer responsibility for his success or failure to you. What should you do to get him to take responsibility for himself, yet provide support and guidance for his efforts?

## CORRECTIONS ISSUE

In 1994 Michael Fay, an American teenager convicted of spray-painting parked cars, was flogged in Singapore. The flogging (called "caning" because it was done with a bamboo rod) caused an international outcry from opponents of corporal punishment. In this country, however, it also led to a rebirth of interest in physical punishments—especially for teenagers and vandals.

The last official flogging of a criminal offender in the United States took place in Delaware on June 16, 1952, when a burglar was tied to a whipping post in the state's central prison and was given 20 lashes. Since then, no sentencing authority in this country has imposed whipping as a criminal punishment, and most jurisdictions have removed all corporal punishments from their statutes. Amnesty International, however, reports that whipping is still in use in parts of the world for certain kinds of prisoners.

After the Fay flogging, lawmakers in eight states introduced legislation to institute whipping or paddling as a criminal sanction. Mississippi legislators proposed paddling graffitists and petty thieves, Tennessee lawmakers considered punishing vandals and burglars by public caning on courthouse steps, the New Mexico Senate Judiciary Committee examined the feasibility of caning graffiti vandals, and Louisiana looked into the possibility of ordering parents (or a correctional officer if the parents refused) to spank their children in judicial chambers. So far, none of the proposals have become law.

1. Would a return to corporal punishments, in the form of whipping or paddling, be justified for some offenders? Why or why not?
2. Might paddling be appropriate for some juvenile offenders? Why or why not?
3. Do you think that any state legislatures will eventually pass legislation to paddle or whip criminal offenders? Why or why not?

## CORRECTIONS ON THE WEB

Visit the Web site of the British Home Office, and read about the history of prisons in Britain (**http://www.homeoffice.gov.uk/prishist.htm**).

Learn how British prisons developed during the 1800s and 1900s. Be sure to read about the Gladstone and Mountbatten Reports, the May Inquiry, and the development of the Borstal system.

## ADDITIONAL READINGS

Barnes, Harry Elmer, and Negley K. Teeters. *New Horizons in Criminology,* 3d ed. Englewood Cliffs, NJ: Prentice Hall, 1959.

Beccaria, Cesare. *On Crimes and Punishments.* 1764. Reprint, Indianapolis: Hackett Publishing, 1986.

Howard, John. *The State of Prisons.* New York: Everyman's Library, 1929.

Ives, George. *A History of Penal Methods.* London: Stanley Paul, 1914.

Morris, Norval, and David J. Rothman. *The Oxford History of the Prison.* New York: Oxford University Press, 1995.

Newman, Graeme R. *Just and Painful: A Case for the Corporal Punishment of Criminals.* New York: Macmillan, 1983.

Newman, Graeme. *The Punishment Response.* Philadelphia: Lippincott, 1978.

Phillipson, Coleman. *Three Criminal Law Reformers: Beccaria, Bentham, Romilly.* London: Patterson Smith, 1970.

Scott, George Ryley. *The History of Corporal Punishment: A Survey of Flagellation in Its Historical, Anthropological, and Sociological Aspects.* Detroit: Gale Research, 1974.

Solzhenitsyn, Aleksandr. *The Gulag Archipelago, 1918–1956: An Experiment in Literary Investigation.* 3 vols. Translated by Thomas P. Whitney. Vol. 3 translated by H. Willetts. New York: Harper & Row, 1974–1978.

Von Hentig, Hans. *Punishment: Its Origin, Purpose, and Psychology.* London: Patterson Smith, 1937.

Wines, Frederick Howard. *Punishment and Reformation.* New York: AMS Press, 1919.

## ENDNOTES

1. *Gazette d' Amsterdam,* April 1, 1757, cited by Michel Foucault, *Discipline & Punish: The Birth of the Prison,* trans. Alan Sheridan (New York: Vintage Books, 1995).

2. Edward M. Peters, "Prison Before the Prison: The Ancient and Medieval Worlds," in Norval Morris and David J. Rothman (eds.), *The Oxford History of the Prison* (New York: Oxford University Press, 1995), p. 6.

3. James Hastings, et al. *Dictionary of the Bible* (New York: Charles Scribner and Sons, 1905), Vol. I, pp. 523 ff., cited in Arthur Evans Wood and John Barker Waite, *Crime and Its Treatment: Social and Legal Aspects of Criminology* (New York: American Book Company, 1941), p. 462.

4. Foucault, p. 8.

5. See Peters, pp. 14–15.

6. Wood and Waite, p. 462.

7. Pieter Spierenburg, "The Body and the State: Early Modern Europe," in Norval Morris and David J. Rothman (eds.), *The Oxford History of the Prison* (New York: Oxford University Press, 1995), pp. 52–53.

8. Ibid., p. 53.

9. Harry Elmer Barnes and Negley K. Teeters, *New Horizons in Criminology,* 3d ed. (Englewood Cliffs, NJ: Prentice Hall, 1959), p. 290.

10. Some of the information in this section comes from Harry Elmer Barnes, *Story of Punishment,* and George Ives, *A History of Penal Methods* (London: Stanley Paul, 1914).

11. Barnes and Teeters, p. 349.

12. Ives, p. 53.

13. Henry Burns, Jr., *Corrections: Organization and Administration* (St. Paul, MN: West, 1975), p. 86.

14. Barnes and Teeters, p. 292.

15. Ives, p. 56.

16. John Howard, *The State of the Prisons* (London: J. M. Dent, 1929).

17. Spierenburg, p. 53.

18. Burns, p. 87.
19. Spierenburg, p. 62.
20. See Abbott Emerson Smith, *Colonists in Bondage* (Chapel Hill: University of North Carolina Press, 1947).
21. For a good account of the practice, see Robert Hughes, *The Fatal Shore: The Epic of Australia's Founding* (Vintage Books, 1988).
22. Barnes and Teeters, p. 293.
23. Peters, p. 7.
24. Spierenburg, pp. 49–77.
25. Ibid., p. 67.
26. Spierenburg, p. 72.
27. Randall McGowen, "The Well-Ordered Prison," in Norval Morris and David J. Rothman (eds.), *The Oxford History of the Prison* (New York: Oxford University Press, 1995), p. 83.
28. Foucault, p. 11.
29. See Wood and Waite, p. 463.
30. Harry Elmer Barnes, *The Repression of Crime* (New York: Doran, 1926), p. 101.
31. John Howard, *The State of the Prisons* (London: J. M. Dent and Sons, Ltd., 1929).
32. Spierenburg, pp. 49-77.
33. McGowen, p. 86.
34. "Enlightenment, Age of," *Microsoft Encarta '96, CD-ROM* (Redmond, WA: Microsoft, 1995).
35. Ibid.
36. Some of the information in this section comes from *The Internet Encyclopedia of Philosophy,* June 26, 1999: http://www.utm.edu/research/iep/.
37. Some of the information in this section comes from the Bentham Project at University College, London, June 25, 1999: http://www.ucl.ac.uk/Bentham-Project/jb.htm.
38. For further information, see Frank E. Hagan, "Panopticon," in Marilyn D. McShane and Frank P. Williams III (eds.), *Encyclopedia of American Prisons* (New York: Garland, 1996), pp. 341–342.

# Restorative Justice

## What Is Restorative Justice?

In restorative justice, crime is seen as something done against victims and the community, not just against the state. Restorative justice is concerned with repairing the harm to the victim and the community. The harm is repaired through negotiation, mediation, and empowerment, rather than through retribution, deterrence, and punishment.

The efforts of the criminal justice system as a whole, and corrections in particular, are beginning to broaden from an exclusive focus on the offender to a concern for the victim and the community harmed by an offense. When criminal justice agencies seek *restorative justice*—or as some agencies refer to it, *community justice* or *reparative justice*—they hope to repair some of the harm to the victim, through service and support. An important part of restorative justice is having offenders actively address the harm they have caused. The system accomplishes that both by holding offenders directly accountable and by helping them become productive, law-abiding members of their community.[1]

## Methods of Restorative Justice

States and localities that wish to implement the restorative justice philosophy rely on broad-based citizen involvement to develop appropriate strategies. Restorative justice is based on the premise that since crime occurs in the context of the community, the community should be involved in addressing it. In a restorative- or community-justice model, you might find any of the following:

- victim-offender mediation
- victim-offender reconciliation
- victim-impact (or empathy) panels
- restorative-justice panels
- community reparative boards
- community-based courts
- family-group conferences
- circle sentencing
- court diversion programs
- peer mediation

Restorative-justice programs try to personalize crime by showing offenders the human consequences of their behavior. Such programs also give victims (who are often ignored by the criminal justice system) the opportunity to release their feelings and speak frankly to offenders. Proponents of restorative justice believe that bringing victim and offender together through such processes as mediation can contribute to a healing process that would not otherwise occur for victims and survivors. The question from a restorative-justice perspective is, "Who has been harmed, what losses did they suffer, and—to the extent that it is possible—how can we make them whole again?"

## Restorative Justice and Corrections

Correctional agencies are uniquely situated to hold offenders accountable to their victims and to the community. As a result, more and more correctional agencies are initiating victim-offender programs and are renewing their emphasis on traditional practices, such as restitution, that exemplify the restorative ideal of holding offenders accountable. Correctional agencies now provide a variety of victim services as well as programs to make offenders more aware of and responsible for the consequences of their crimes. Many agencies regularly incorporate victim-impact information into presentence investigation reports, collect and disburse restitution, notify victims of parole hearings, and allow them to participate in those hearings.

Much more needs to be done to involve victims and the community in the correctional process. A recent Department of Justice plan to improve the treatment of crime victims recommended specific steps.[2]

- Every state department of corrections and every parole authority should establish an advisory committee of victims and service providers to guide and support victim-related policies, programs, and services.
- Correctional agencies should designate staff to provide information, assistance, and referrals to victims of crime.
- Mission statements of correctional agencies should recognize victims as an important constituency and should address victims' rights and services.
- A correctional agency should notify victims of any change in the offender's status that would allow the offender access to the community or to the victims.
- A correctional agency should place a high priority on ensuring victims' safety from intimidation, threats, or harm by offenders.
- Information about offender status and victims' rights should be accessible in several languages through toll-free numbers and printed materials.
- Correctional agencies should collect and distribute restitution payments as ordered by the court, and wage-earning opportunities should be increased for inmates, wards, and parolees who owe restitution.
- Victims' input should be sought for all decisions affecting the release of adult and juvenile offenders.
- Victim-impact awareness should be a basic component of the education and treatment programs of correctional agencies.
- Protected, supported, mediated dialogue between victim and offender should be available upon the victim's request.

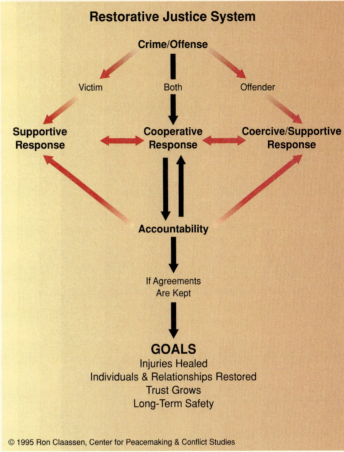

## Restorative Justice System

**Restorative Justice System**

**Crime/Offense**

Victim — Both — Offender

**Supportive Response** ⟷ **Cooperative Response** ⟷ **Coercive/Supportive Response**

**Accountability**

If Agreements Are Kept

**GOALS**
Injuries Healed
Individuals & Relationships Restored
Trust Grows
Long-Term Safety

© 1995 Ron Claassen, Center for Peacemaking & Conflict Studies

- A crime victim should be notified of any violation of the conditions of the offender's probation or parole and should be allowed to comment before or during the violation hearing.
- Uniform practices should be developed and implemented for notification of a sex offender's release.

1. Marty Price, "Crime and Punishment: Can Mediation Produce Restorative Justice for Victims and Offenders?" Online: http://www.vorp.com/articles/crime.html, access: February 9, 1999.
2. Office of Justice Programs, *New Directions from the Field: Victims' Rights and Services for the 21st Century* (Washington: U.S. Department of Justice, 1998).

# 4 Jails
## Way Stations Along the Justice Highway

### CHAPTER OBJECTIVES

After completing this chapter you should be able to:

1. List the purposes of jails.
2. Trace briefly the development of jails in history.
3. Explain how first-, second-, and third-generation jails differ in design and in method of inmate management.
4. Outline the characteristics of jail inmates, and explain what special-needs inmates are.
5. Describe how jail vocational and educational programs affect inmate behavior and recidivism.
6. Discuss how religion and a jail chaplain can influence jail inmates and help jail staff.
7. Discuss why jail accreditation is important.
8. Explain why it is important for jail staff to conduct themselves as professionals.

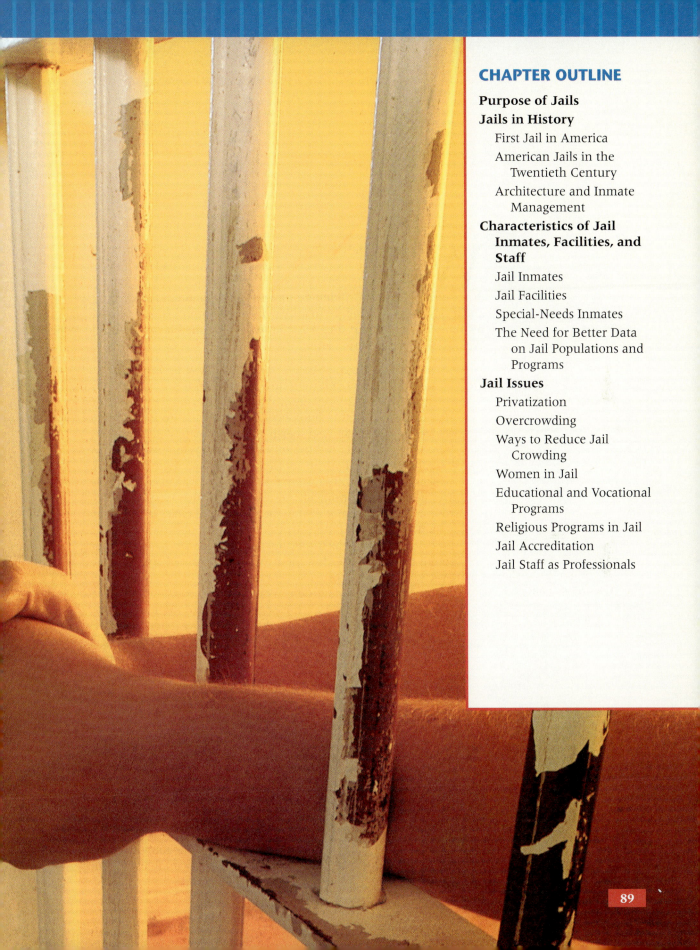

## CHAPTER OUTLINE

*It is with the unfortunate, above all, that humane conduct is necessary.*

—*Fyodor Dostoyevski*

When R. J. Hawkins was 26 years old, he served a six-month sentence in the Story County Jail in Iowa. He had been convicted of an aggravated misdemeanor (proprietorship of a property where drugs were sold), a class C felony (possession with intent to deliver cocaine), and a class D felony (failure to affix a drug tax stamp). He kept a daily log of his time in jail. He sent it to a friend, who published it on the World Wide Web. Here's his first day's entry:

Well, here I am. Story County Jail, Nevada, Iowa. It could be worse I suppose, but right now I think this is pretty bad. I now call home a 10' x 20' cell that I share with 5 other people. On one wall there are 2 sets of bunk beds which stretch from the front of the cell to the back. Each berth is approximately 36" x 9". Two bunks, a shelf unit, and the toilet on the opposite wall. The two bunk beds are at the front of the cell followed by the shelf unit, which is permanently fastened to the wall, and then the toilet. The bunks at the front of the cell have a nice view of the day room. The day room is a large room with two tables, a phone and a TV. The TV is the center of attention and is on from lock-out to lock-down. During lock-out, my "house" door is open to the day room. We share the day room with another cell that is set up exactly the same as ours. So, during the day, twelve of us cohabitate and share the day room. Wake-up is at 6:00 AM. Breakfast is served at 6:30 AM. Lunch is served at 11:30 AM, and dinner is served at 5:00 PM. Between those times we have absolutely nothing to do. People watch TV, play cards, read books, or sleep. Actually, sleep is the big hobby, especially between lunch and dinner. Every once in a while a guard will walk the hall outside the day room. This or a heated disagreement helps break the monotony of the droning television and constant bitching of the inmates.

Like I said, I've been here one day now and already I know my biggest enemy is going to be boredom. This is county, not the pen, so I don't have to worry about being beaten, bullied, or buggered. Things are audio and video monitored at all times so there is a general feeling of safety. I'm in with short-timers. These are men who are awaiting trial or serving time for drunk driving or other minor alcohol or drug offenses. Average stay is 7–30 days. I, on the other hand, have 180 days to serve. I'm going to be seeing people coming and going and sometimes coming back again.

Right now I'm trying to adjust to my new surroundings, the only experience I have ever had with jail is vicariously through television. In terms, where I am at is no Mayberry, but it's closer to Mayberry than Shawshank, thank God. And for me, for the life of me, I never would have thought I'd end up here, however, I know where I went wrong and why and later I'll get into it. For now, though, I am going to concern myself with the current situation of adjusting to my environment. I know this is just a morsel but more is to come. As I am told, "Just a day at a time."[1]

Hawkins's first-day journal entry includes many topics this chapter will address—the design and purpose of jails, inmate characteristics, and jail programs.

# Purpose of Jails

**Jails** are locally operated correctional facilities that confine persons before or after conviction. On June 30, 1998, local jail authorities held or supervised 664,847 offenders, an increase of almost 4.5 percent from midyear 1997.[2]

Inmates sentenced to jail usually receive a sentence of a year or less, but jails also serve other purposes in the correctional system.

Jails are used to:

- Receive persons awaiting arraignment and hold them pending trial, conviction, or sentencing.
- Readmit probation and parole violators and bail-bond absconders.
- Detain juveniles until custody is transferred to juvenile authorities.
- Hold mentally ill persons until they are moved to appropriate health facilities.
- Hold individuals for the military.
- Provide protective custody.
- Confine persons found in contempt.
- Hold witnesses for the courts.
- Hold inmates about to be released after completing a prison sentence.
- Transfer inmates to federal, state, or other authorities.
- House inmates for federal, state, or other authorities because of crowding of their facilities.
- Operate some community-based programs as alternatives to incarceration.
- Hold inmates sentenced to short terms (generally under one year) of incarceration.

For all their important roles and responsibilities, however, jails have been a disgrace to every generation.[3] Many of the nation's 3,304 locally operated jails are old, overcrowded, poorly funded, scantily staffed by underpaid and poorly trained employees, and given low priority in local budgets. Yet, a strong groundswell of progress is rising for the nation's jails. Tomorrow's jail professionals have tremendous opportunities to continue

**jails** Locally operated correctional facilities that confine persons before or after conviction. Persons sentenced to jail usually receive a sentence of a year or less.

EXHIBIT 4-1

## American Jail Association

### Mission Statement

To band together all those concerned with or interested in the custody and care of persons awaiting trial, serving sentences, or otherwise locally confined; to improve the conditions and systems under which such persons are detained.

To advance professionalism through training, information exchange, technical assistance, publications, and conferences.

To provide leadership in the development of professional standards, pertinent legislation, management practices, programs, and services.

To present and advance the interests, needs, concerns, and proficiency of the profession as deemed appropriate by the membership and their representatives.

that momentum. Progress is being made because of new emphases on jail education, staff selection and training, professional associations, standards, technology, accountability, and laws, among other reasons. Groups like the American Jail Association (AJA) are advancing jail professionalism through training, information exchange, technical assistance, publications, and conferences. Members of the AJA include sheriffs, jail administrators, judges, attorneys, educators, correctional staff, jail inspection officials, health care providers, and clergy. The AJA mission statement is shown in Exhibit 4–1. This chapter will explore the problems of the past and present and discuss direction for the twenty-first century.

# Jails in History

It is believed that King Henry II of England ordered the first jail built, in 1166. The purpose of that jail was to detain offenders until they could be brought before a court, tried, and sentenced. From that beginning, jails spread through Europe but changed in scope and size over time.

With the development of workhouses and poorhouses in the fifteenth and sixteenth centuries in England, sheriffs took on the added responsibility of supervising vagrants, the poor, and the mentally ill. In practice, however, these institutions were indistinguishable from jails. Their squalid, unhealthy conditions and the sheriffs' practice of demanding money from persons under their charge caught the attention of eighteenth-century Enlightenment reformers. One such reformer was the English sheriff John

Howard. In 1779, England's Parliament passed the four jail reforms that Howard proposed: secure and sanitary structures, jail inspections, elimination of fees, and an emphasis on reforming prisoners. To this day, the John Howard Association and *Howard Journal* carry Howard's ideas forward.

## First Jail in America

The first jail in America was the Walnut Street Jail in Philadelphia, built in 1776. The jail housed offenders without regard to sex, age, or offense. Conditions at the jail quickly deteriorated. According to some, the jail became a "promiscuous scene of unrestricted intercourse, universal riot, and debauchery."[4] The Philadelphia Quakers had wanted the Walnut Street Jail to be a place where inmates reformed themselves through reflection and remorse. In 1790 the Philadelphia Society for Alleviating the Miseries of Public Prisons and the General Assembly of Pennsylvania designated the Walnut Street Jail a penitentiary. Implementing Quaker beliefs, the penitentiary emphasized prisoner reform through reflection and penitence, and rehabilitation through good conduct. Sixteen solitary cells were added to the facility. Workshops were built; alcohol and prostitution were prohibited; prisoners were segregated by sex, age, and offense; diets were monitored; guardians were appointed to care for minors; religious, health care, and educational services were provided. Debtors, however, were housed separate from the general inmate population and had no such privileges. Their prison conditions were pitiful, and many debtors starved.[5]

In 1798 a fire destroyed the workshops. The destruction brought about disillusionment and idleness. Rising costs crippled the jail's budget. Disciplinary problems rose with overcrowding, and escapes and violence increased. The number of inmates who were destitute vagrants or debtors soared, as did the incidence of disease. There were political conflicts between the religious Quakers and the non-Quaker prison board members. Prisoners

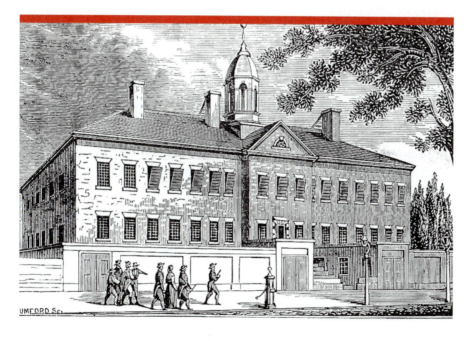

UMFORD Sc.

*Unlike the workhouses, prisons, and jails previously in existence, the Walnut Street Jail, started in Philadelphia in 1776, was used exclusively to house convicted felons. Which religious group's principles influenced correctional institutions in Pennsylvania?*

rioted on March 27, 1820. On October 5, 1835, the Walnut Street Jail closed. State prisoners were transferred to the new Eastern State Penitentiary in Philadelphia, the first institution of its kind in the world. County inmates and those awaiting trial were transferred to a new county jail.

By the close of the nineteenth century, most cities across the United States had jails to hold persons awaiting trial and to punish convicted felons. The sheriff became the person in charge of the jail. As crime increased and urban centers expanded, jails grew in importance, as did the sheriffs' control over jails.

## American Jails in the Twentieth Century

On any given day, America's jails serve a variety of functions. They detain persons awaiting arraignment or trial. They confine offenders serving short sentences for less serious offenses. Jails also serve as surrogate mental hospitals. They frequently detain persons with drug or alcohol dependency. They are the first stop on the social services highway for the homeless, street people, and some with extremely poor physical health, especially those with HIV, AIDS, and tuberculosis (TB).

Historians refer to America's jails as the "poorhouse of the twentieth century," the dumping grounds for society's problems.[6] Jails in twentieth-century America evolved into institutions of social control, not only for persons who committed criminal acts, but also for those who made up the underclass in American society. Such persons have been called society's rabble.

**rabble management**

The control of persons whose noncriminal behavior is offensive to the community (for example, public nuisances, derelicts, junkies, drunks, vagrants, the mentally ill, and street people). According to John Irwin, rabble management is the purpose of jails.

John Irwin (in 1986) called the purpose of jails **rabble management,** that is, control of persons whose noncriminal behavior is offensive to their communities.[7] The central purpose of jail was to detain the most disconnected and disreputable persons, who were arrested more because they were offensive than because they had committed crimes. They were individuals of whom all were aware, yet whom society ignored: public nuisances, derelicts, junkies, drunks, vagrants, the mentally ill, and street people. Moreover, since jails housed such persons, there was no incentive to improve jail conditions. The purpose of America's twentieth-century jails must, therefore, be understood in relation to the composition of the jail population. Jails not only confine persons before and after conviction, but also hold those who do not fit into the mainstream of American society.

## Architecture and Inmate Management

In an attempt to better manage and control inmate behavior, jails have progressed through three phases of architectural design. Each design is based on a particular philosophy of inmate management and control.

**first-generation jail**

A jail with multiple-occupancy cells or dormitories that line corridors arranged in spokes. Inmate supervision is sporadic or intermittent; staff must patrol the corridors to observe inmates in their cells. This linear design dates back to the eighteenth century.

**First-Generation Jails** First-generation jails were built in a linear design that dates back to the eighteenth century. In a typical **first-generation jail,** inmates live in multiple-occupancy cells or dormitories. The cells line corridors that are arranged like spokes. Inmate supervision is sporadic or intermittent; staff must patrol the corridors to observe inmates in their cells. Contact between jailers and inmates is slight unless there is an incident to which jailers must react. See Figure 4–1.

**FIGURE 4–1**

**First-Generation Jail—Intermittent Surveillance**

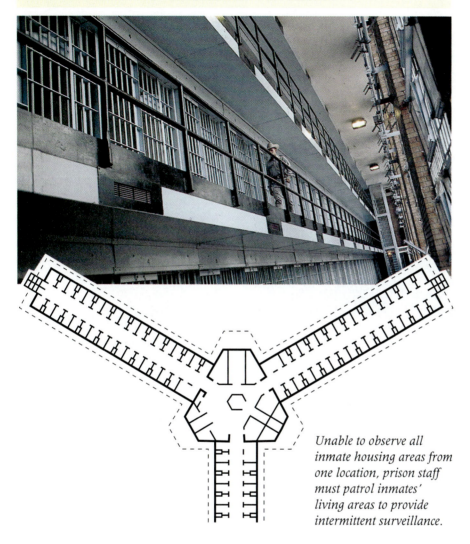

Unable to observe all inmate housing areas from one location, prison staff must patrol inmates' living areas to provide intermittent surveillance.

The design of a linear jail reflects the assumption that inmates are violent and destructive and will assault staff, destroy jail property, and try to escape. The facility is designed to prevent these behaviors. Heavy metal bars separate staff from inmates. Reinforced metal beds, sinks, and toilets are bolted to the ground or wall. Reinforced concrete and razor wire surround the facility.

**Second-Generation Jails** Second-generation jails emerged in the 1960s to replace old, run-down linear jails. They used a different philosophical approach to construction and inmate management. In a **second-generation jail,** staff remain in a secure control booth overlooking inmate housing

**second-generation jail**
A jail where staff remain in a secure control booth surrounded by inmate housing areas called pods. Bars are replaced with reinforced glass. Although visual surveillance increases, verbal interaction with inmates is reduced. This design emerged in the 1960s.

# FIGURE 4–2
## Second-Generation Jail—Remote Surveillance

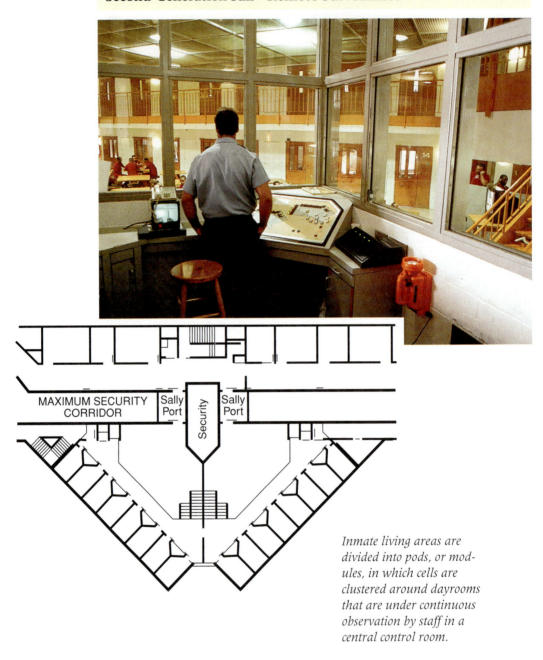

*Inmate living areas are divided into pods, or modules, in which cells are clustered around dayrooms that are under continuous observation by staff in a central control room.*

areas called pods (see Figure 4–2). Bars are replaced by reinforced glass. Although visual surveillance increases, surveillance is remote, and verbal interaction with inmates is even less frequent. Property destruction is minimized because steel and cement continue to define the living areas. Outside, fences and razor wire continue to discourage escapes as well as unauthorized entry.

**Third-Generation Jails** Third-generation jails emerged in the 1970s. Their design combines continual observation with staff-inmate interaction. In a **third-generation jail,** inmates are separated into small groups and housed in pods. The pods are staffed 24 hours a day by specially trained officers (see Figure 4–3). Pods are self-contained to reduce inmate movement. They are designed to enhance officers' interaction with and observation of inmates. Soft furnishings are used to reduce inmate stress from crowding, excessive noise, lack of privacy, and isolation from the outside world. Bars and metal doors are absent, reducing noise and the dehumanization common in first- and second-generation jails.

**third-generation jail,** sometimes called **direct-supervision jail** A jail where inmates are housed in small groups in pods staffed 24 hours a day by specially trained officers. Officers interact with inmates to help change behavior. Bars and metal doors are absent, reducing noise and dehumanization. This approach to jail construction and inmate management emerged in the 1970s.

## FIGURE 4–3

### Third-Generation Jail—Direct Supervision

*Cells are grouped in housing units, or pods. Each pod has a central dayroom. Prison staff are stationed* inside *the housing unit to encourage direct interaction between inmates and staff.*

I n 1993 I received my transfer to the direct-supervision Oxbow Jail Facility. I sensed the painful uneasiness over the anticipated challenges of direct inmate supervision.

It is nearing three years since that transition, and—I must admit—these have been the most rewarding three years I have experienced. All of my pre- conceived concerns about direct inmate supervision were quickly put to rest, and I can think of no better way to manage a population of offenders.

*Sergeant Rocky Finocchio*
*Oxbow Jail Division*
*Salt Lake City, Utah*

Third-generation jails, sometimes called direct-supervision jails, maximize staff interaction with inmates by having staff inside each inmate housing unit. Staff movement and interaction encourage officers to view the pods as space they control and in which they exercise leadership. By supervising activities directly, the staff can help change inmate behavior patterns, rather than simply react to them.

Researchers tell us that pods and direct supervision provide a safer and more positive environment for inmates and staff than do first- and second-generation jails.[8] Today, more than 100 facilities in 24 states use direct supervision.

# Characteristics of Jail Inmates, Facilities, and Staff

Who is in jail? Why are they there? What do we know about the operation and administration of jail facilities? To these and related questions we now turn our attention.

## Jail Inmates

At midyear 1998, local jail authorities held or supervised 664,847 offenders—an increase of 4.5 percent from midyear 1997. Almost 11 percent of these offenders (72,385) were supervised outside jail facilities (see Figure 4–4). Of those offenders supervised outside jail facilities, almost 50 percent were involved in community service or weekender programs. The remaining 89 percent (592,462) were held in local jails.

**FIGURE 4–4**

Persons Under Jail Supervision

## How Many Are Under Jail Supervision?

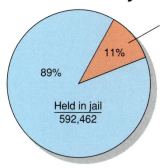

11%

89%

Held in jail
592,462

Supervised outside a jail facility 72,385

Electronic monitoring 10,827
Home detention without electronic monitoring 370
Day reporting 3,089
Community service 17,518
Weekender programs 17,249
Other pretrial supervision 6,048
Workcrews, workgangs and other work alternatives 7,089
Drug, alcohol, mental health and other treatment programs 5,702
Other 4,493

## Who Is Under Jail Supervision?

### Status

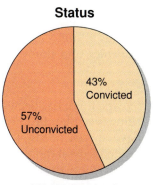

43%
Convicted

57%
Unconvicted

252,600 Convicted
331,800 Unconvicted

### Gender

11%
Female

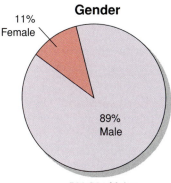

89%
Male

520,581 Males
63,791 Females

## Why Are They Under Jail Supervision?

### Offense

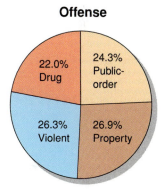

22.0%
Drug

24.3%
Public-order

26.3%
Violent

26.9%
Property

### Race/Ethnicity

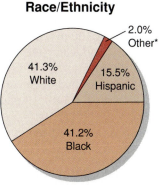

2.0%
Other*

41.3%
White

15.5%
Hispanic

41.2%
Black

244,900 White
244,000 Black
91,000 Hispanic
11,800 Other*

### Age

1.4%
Juveniles

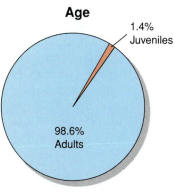

98.6%
Adults

584,372 Adults
8,090 Juveniles
6,542 Held as adults
1,548 Held as juveniles

*Asians, Pacific Islanders, American Indians, Alaska Natives

*Source:* Darrell K. Gilliard and Allen J. Beck, *Prison and Jail Inmates at Midyear 1998,* Bureau of Justice Statistics Bulletin (Washington: Office of Justice Programs, March 1999). Caroline Wolf Harlow, *Profile of Jail Inmates, 1996* (Washington: Bureau of Justice Statistics, April 1998).

Since 1970, when the first national jail statistics were collected, the number of inmates held in locally operated jails has almost quadrupled. During the 1970s the growth was very modest—13 percent—but during the 1980s it was more than 120 percent—more than 220,000 inmates. Since 1990 the nation's jail population has increased by an average of 4.9 percent a year.

**Gender and Jail Populations**   Near the close of the twentieth century, we have seen a slow rise in the proportion of adult female jail inmates. In 1985 there were 19,077 adult female jail inmates—7.4 percent of the jail population. By midyear 1998 that figure had risen to 63,791—11 percent of the jail population. Since 1990 the average annual rate of growth has been 7 percent for the female jail population but only 4.5 percent for the male population.

**Ethnicity and Jail Populations**   From 1990 through midyear 1998, the majority of local jail inmates were black or Hispanic. At midyear 1998 whites made up 41.3 percent of the jail population; blacks, 41.2 percent; Hispanics, 15.5 percent; and other races (Asians, Pacific Islanders, American Indians, and Alaska Natives), 2 percent (see Figure 4–4). Relative to percentages of the U.S. population, the proportion of blacks in local jails at midyear 1998 was 6 times that of whites, nearly 2½ times that of Hispanics, and almost 7½ times that of persons of other races.

**Juveniles and Jail Populations**   Over the past 25 years, there has been a dramatic reversal in the theory and practice of punishing juveniles. In 1974, for example, juvenile offenders were deemed to have special needs. The Juvenile Justice and Delinquency Prevention Act provided federal money to states and cities that agreed not to hold juveniles in jails where they might have regular contact with adults. By 1996, however, in the face of pressure for more punishment of juvenile offenders, new legislation allowed cities and states to detain juvenile offenders for up to 12 hours in an adult jail before a court appearance and made it easier to house juveniles in separate wings of adult jails. That shift in philosophy and policy has increased the number of juveniles held in adult jails. At midyear 1993, 4,300 juveniles, or 0.9 percent of the jail population, were held in jail. By midyear 1998 that number and percentage had increased to 8,090 and 1.4 percent, respectively. At midyear 1998, 81 percent (6,542) of these young inmates had been convicted or were being held for trial as adults. The remaining 1,548 (19 percent) were held as juveniles (see Figure 4–4).

The Bureau of Justice Statistics has compiled a profile of inmates in local jails. That profile is shown in Table 4–1. Note that at the time of arrest:

- More than half of the inmates were under supervision by the courts or corrections.
- Almost one-third were on probation and almost one-eighth were on parole.
- Seven of every ten had prior sentences.
- Almost two-thirds used drugs regularly.
- More than one-third were disabled.

*Jails: Way Stations Along the Justice Highway*

**TABLE 4–1**

## Profile of Jail Inmates

| Categories | Percentage of jail inmates 1996 | Categories | Percentage of jail inmates 1996 |
|---|---|---|---|
| **Criminal Justice Status At Arrest** | | **Reported Disability,** *continued* | |
| None | 46.4% | Difficulty seeing newsprint | 9.2% |
| Status[1] | 53.6% | Learning disability | 9.1% |
| On probation | 31.7% | Difficulty hearing | 6.1% |
| On parole | 13.7% | Speech disability | 3.7% |
| On bail/bond | 12.7% | **Physical Or Sexual Abuse Of Females** | |
| On other pretrial release | 4.4% | Ever | 47.5% |
| **Criminal History** | | Before age 18 | 36.6% |
| None | 27.3% | Age 18 or after | 26.7% |
| Priors[1] | 72.7% | Physically abused | 37.2% |
| Probation | 63.0% | Sexually abused | 37.1% |
| Jail/prison | 58.4% | Raped | 32.2% |
| **Prior Drug Use** | | **Employment Status** | |
| Never | 17.6% | Employed | 64.3% |
| Ever[1] | 82.4% | Full-time | 49.3% |
| Regularly | 64.2% | Part-time | 10.4% |
| In month before the offense[2] | 55.0% | Occasionally | 4.6% |
| At time of the offense[2] | 35.6% | Not employed | 35.8% |
| **Under The Influence Of Alcohol At Time Of The Offense[2]** | | **Person(s) Lived With Most Of The Time** | |
| No | 59.5% | Both parents | 39.7% |
| Yes | 40.5% | Mother only | 43.3% |
| **Substance Abuse Treatment** | | Father only | 4.9% |
| Never | 57.7% | Grandparents | 7.0% |
| Ever[1] | 42.3% | Other | 5.2% |
| Since admission | 10.3% | **Perceived Safety Of Jail Compared To That Of The Streets** | |
| **Reported Disability** | | Jail safer | 20.9% |
| Any disability | 36.5% | Streets safer | 43.3% |
| Physical, mental, or other health | 20.7% | About the same | 35.8% |

1. Detail may add to more than total; inmates may fit more than one category.

2. Based on convicted jail inmates only.

*Source:* Caroline Wolf Harlow, *Profile of Jail Inmates, 1996* (Washington: Bureau of Justice Statistics, April 1998).

- One-third of the women had been physically or sexually abused or raped.
- One-third were unemployed at the time of arrest.
- Two-thirds grew up in homes without both parents.
- Four of every ten believed that the streets were safer than jails.

Another way to look at the nation's jail population is to consider the rate of incarceration. Jail populations give us a count of the total number incarcerated (e.g., 664,847 held in local jails at midyear 1998). Because of differences in total population, however, such counts do not allow accurate comparison of jurisdictions. Rates of jail incarceration, expressed as the number of jail inmates per 100,000 residents aged 18 and older, allow a more meaningful and useful analysis of trends in incarceration. With rate data, we can compare changes over time. Figure 4–5 shows changes in the

### FIGURE 4–5

**Jail Incarceration Rate, 1985–1998**

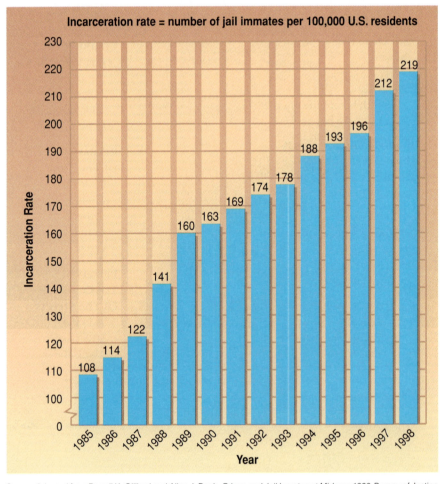

*Source:* Adapted from Darrell K. Gilliard and Allen J. Beck, *Prison and Jail Inmates at Midyear 1998,* Bureau of Justice Statistics Bulletin (Washington: Office of Justice Programs, March 1999).

*Jails: Way Stations Along the Justice Highway*

jail incarceration rate from 1985 through 1998. Note that the incarceration rate almost doubled, from 108 jail inmates per 100,000 adults in 1985 to 219 jail inmates per 100,000 adults in 1998.

## Jail Facilities

The capacity to house jail inmates has kept pace with the jail population. Between July 1, 1994, and June 30, 1998, the occupied percentage of capacity has remained below 100 percent. As of midyear 1998, 97 percent of local jail capacity was occupied, down from a peak of 108 percent, reached in 1989. The jurisdictions with the largest average daily jail populations reported the highest rates of occupancy. In 1998, the nation's 25 largest jail jurisdictions accounted for 27 percent of all inmates. These jurisdictions were in 12 states—7 in California, 5 in Florida, 4 in Texas, and 1 each in New York, Illinois, Arizona, Louisiana, Pennsylvania, Tennessee, Georgia, Maryland, and Wisconsin.[9] (See Table 4–2 on page 104.)

## Special-Needs Inmates

Increasingly, jails are dealing with large percentages of special-needs inmates. **Special-needs inmates** require special treatment or care because they suffer from mental illness, chemical dependency (drug or alcohol), or communicable disease (especially HIV/AIDS and TB). Such jail inmates present substantial operational and administrative problems for jail staff. It is often difficult for the staff to know what they are observing or—once they recognize an inmate's special needs—how to address the situation.

Statewide research on jail management in New Mexico indicated that special-needs inmates require extra attention from jail staff.[10] They must be watched closely for possible suicide. Almost nine out of ten disrupt normal jail activities. Seven out of ten require an excess of scarce medical resources. Four out of ten engage in acts of violence. Almost three out of ten are abused by other inmates. The characteristics of special-needs inmates, the treatment programs offered, and the policies for dealing with those inmates depend on the type of special need.

**Substance Abuse Inmates**    Drug arrests have been a primary factor in increasing the jail population. In fact, the majority of jail inmates—in some jails 70 to 80 percent—have a substance abuse problem at the time of incarceration.[11] Some are arrested for offenses connected with drugs and alcohol (drug sales, DWI, etc.). Others are under the influence of drugs or alcohol when they are arrested for other offenses. Many used drugs or alcohol within the 24 hours preceding their arrests. The National Institute of Justice (NIJ) indicates that 55 percent of convicted jail inmates used illegal drugs the month before the offense, and about 1 in 4 used a major drug (cocaine, crack, heroin) in that month. Thirty-six percent said they were using drugs at the time of their offense (with about 1 in 4 using a major drug), and 41 percent said they had been drinking alcohol. Almost 25 percent of convicted jail inmates drank quantities that, combined with their weight and metabolism, amounted to blood alcohol concentration of 10 gr/ml or higher, the definition of alcoholic impairment in many states.[12] Only a small fraction of

**special-needs inmates**
Prisoners who require special treatment or care because they suffer from mental illness, chemical dependency (drug or alcohol abuse), or communicable disease (especially HIV/AIDS and TB).

**TABLE 4–2**

### The 25 Largest Local Jail Jurisdictions, Midyear 1998

| Jurisdiction | Number of Inmates Held | Average Daily Population[1] | Rated Capacity[2] | Percentage of Capacity Occupied Midyear[3] |
|---|---|---|---|---|
| Los Angeles County, CA | 21,268 | 21,136 | 21,366 | 100% |
| New York City, NY | 17,680 | 17,524 | 22,584 | 78% |
| Cook County, IL | 9,321 | 9,297 | 9,776 | 95% |
| Dade County, FL | 7,036 | 7,836 | 6,005 | 117% |
| Harris County, TX | 7,587 | 7,781 | 8,657 | 88% |
| Dallas County, TX | 6,941 | 7,000 | 8,182 | 85% |
| Maricopa County, AZ | 7,019 | 6,910 | 6,252 | 112% |
| Orleans Parish, LA | 6,670 | 6,398 | 7,174 | 93% |
| Philadelphia County, PA | 5,990 | 5,753 | 6,179 | 97% |
| San Diego County, CA | 6,040 | 5,745 | 5,815 | 104% |
| Shelby County, TN | 5,808 | 5,627 | 6,583 | 88% |
| Orange County, CA | 5,546 | 5,374 | 3,821 | 145% |
| San Bernardino County, CA | 5,713 | 5,103 | 5,000 | 114% |
| Santa Clara County, CA | 4,658 | 4,722 | 3,774 | 123% |
| Broward County, FL | 4,640 | 4,289 | 3,756 | 124% |
| Fulton County, GA | 3,827 | 4,276 | 2,987 | 128% |
| Alameda County, CA | 4,164 | 3,823 | 4,590 | 91% |
| Baltimore City, MD | 3,881 | 3,791 | 2,966 | 131% |
| Orange County, FL | 3,865 | 3,547 | 3,234 | 120% |
| Tarrant County, TX | 3,572 | 3,529 | 4,739 | 75% |
| Sacramento County, CA | 3,654 | 3,507 | 3,871 | 94% |
| Bexar County, TX | 3,368 | 3,398 | 3,670 | 92% |
| Hillsborough County, FL | 3,101 | 3,062 | 2,909 | 107% |
| Milwaukee County, WI | 2,850 | 2,918 | 2,466 | 116% |
| Duval County, FL | 2,899 | 2,755 | 3,000 | 97% |

*Note:* Jurisdictions are ordered by their average daily population in 1998.

1. For the year ending June 30. The average daily population is the sum of the number of inmates in jail each day for a year, divided by the number of days in the year.
2. Rated capacity is the number of beds or inmates assigned by a rating official to all the facilities within a jurisdiction.
3. The number of inmates, divided by the rated capacity and multiplied by 100.

*Source:* Darrell K. Gilliard and Allen J. Beck, *Prison and Jail Inmates at Midyear 1998* (Washington: Bureau of Justice Statistics, March 1999).

the jail inmates who need substance abuse treatment actually receive it. The absence of drug treatment programs is particularly common in small jails.

Drug treatment programs for jail inmates are important, not only because evidence suggests that rehabilitation is more likely for those offenders who complete drug treatment programs, but also because reducing drug-seeking behavior aids in managing the jail facility. A recent NIJ-sponsored research study found that the greatest benefit of drug treatment programs in jails was that they provided a "behavioral management tool" that controlled inmates' behavior and helped lower the incidence of inmate violence.[13]

The study evaluated five drug treatment programs in California and New York. At all five sites, substance abuse inmates in drug treatment programs had lower rates of serious physical violence and other behavioral problems (e.g., insubordination and possession of nondrug contraband) than those not in the programs. As for recidivism, 17 percent of the inmates in drug treatment and 23 percent of the control group were convicted again at least once during a one-year follow-up. Since offenders seldom voluntarily seek substance abuse treatment, jail is an opportunity to introduce treatment and encourage effective aftercare upon release.

**HIV-Positive Inmates**   In a 1995–96 survey of local jail inmates, 2.2 percent of tested inmates who responded were HIV positive.[14] Among jail inmates who said they had been tested for HIV/AIDS, those held for drug offenses were the most likely to be HIV-positive (3.3 percent).

# THE OFFENDER SPEAKS

I didn't want to participate in any programs, but that was the only way I could get out of 33rd Street [the main facility] into one of the buildings that have open spaces, only two guys to a cell, and good visitation rights. So I wouldn't have taken MRT [Moral Reconation Therapy, a substance abuse treatment program] if I didn't have to, but I'm glad I did. I learned about myself: I used to blame drugs as the source of my problems, but I learned it's my own attitudes and behavior that are responsible. Once you learn that, other things fall into place. Drug classes I had taken before never did this for me. In the life skills classes, I learned how to write a résumé and how to present myself at a job interview—by sitting up straight and so on. But you have to obey the rules in the program facilities if you want to stay. I've seen guys get busted back to 33rd Street because of shouting matches between inmates, for example. A few come back here again, and then they're careful to behave, because the other facility stinks. There's a loud noise that keeps you from sleeping, it's cold, and there's no carpeting, so they like it here much better.

*An inmate in the Orange
County (Florida) Jail*

Cost-effective management of inmates with HIV or AIDS has at least five essential elements:

1.  Early detection and diagnosis through medical and mental health screening of each new jail inmate upon admission.
2.  Medical management and treatment by health specialists, including regular reevaluation and assessment.
3.  Inmate classification and housing to discourage intravenous drug use and homosexual intercourse or to provide private rooms for terminally ill inmates.
4.  Education and training of staff and inmates in the cause of AIDS, the stages of the disease, transmission methods, preventive measures, available treatment and therapies, testing issues and policies, confidentiality issues and policies, classification and program assignment policies, and supervision issues, including transportation and inmate movement.
5.  Adequate funds to provide increasingly costly treatment to inmates with HIV or AIDS.

Tomorrow's jail professionals will need a network of medical experts—university medical school faculty, state health department staff, federal health officials, and local health care providers—to consult. Such consultation will give corrections professionals reliable information and familiarize the noncorrectional medical community with the problems facing jails.

**Mentally Ill Inmates**  Every day, our nation's 3,304 local jails face another challenge—dealing with offenders who are mentally ill and require close monitoring, medication, and other services. The percentage of jail inmates with mental disorders significantly outweighs the percentage in the general population.[15] Yet 2 out of 10 jails have no access to mental health

*Because of funding deficiencies and the relatively short period of jail confinement, treatment options for mentally ill persons are often inadequate. What other special needs inmates do local jails sometimes supervise?*

*Jails: Way Stations Along the Justice Highway*

services and 8 out of 10 jail officers receive little or no training in mental health issues.

The NIJ recently sponsored a survey and visits to selected sites to identify successful policies and practices for meeting the needs of jail inmates with mental disorders. Practices included screening, evaluation, and classification of booked detainees; case management services at intake, consisting of crisis intervention services and short-term treatment programs; discharge planning with treatment referrals; mechanisms for dealing with the courts in regard to offenders with mental disorders; and pre- and postbooking programs to divert offenders with mental disorders from jail by working with the courts, the families, and the police.[16]

Because understanding of mental illness is limited, it is unrealistic to expect jail staff to cure these illnesses. The best one can hope for is to help mentally ill detainees achieve some stability in their lives and begin to live independently in the community. Doing so is also likely to lessen a detainee's criminal behavior—mostly thefts, assaults, and involvement with illicit drugs.

**Inmates With Tuberculosis**   Jails are at great risk for the spread of tuberculosis (TB).[17] This is due to the very close living quarters, overcrowding, poor sanitation, and the large number of inmates with a high risk of having TB, such as HIV-positive detainees, intravenous drug users, and immigrants. When a person who has TB coughs, sneezes, or laughs, tiny droplets of fluid containing TB bacteria are released into the air, which are then inhaled by others. Therefore, a jail inmate who has TB is most likely to spread the disease to those with whom he or she has the most contact.

Experts concerned about TB in jails have indicated that the most important issues for jail professionals are to understand the causes and control of TB, to implement an appropriate and cost-effective screening program, and to develop a close working relationship with local health authorities.

## The Need for Better Data on Jail Populations and Programs

The challenge for jail professionals in the twenty-first century will be to manage a growing inmate population with multiple problems. Ken Kerle, managing editor of the American Jail Association, tells us it's time to replace jail ignorance with jail knowledge.[18] Better data can help us decide what works and what doesn't. Then we can improve our programs to better serve our offenders. As taxpayers, we should insist that our jail managers set realistic goals for their jails, their employees, and the inmates, and that they collect performance data toward those goals. Most states do not publish monthly reports on the number of inmates in each jail and those inmates' destinations. All of us should be able to find out easily how our jail system stacks up against other jails in cost, performance, and compliance with standards.

# Jail Issues

Jail administration and staffs face many important issues for the twenty-first century. We will now consider some of these issues and their effects on corrections professionals.

## Privatization

Jails can be privatized in whole or in part. Jails can be financed, built, and operated by private groups, or jails can contract out some of their services (e.g., food service, mental health care, and programming).

One of the most hotly debated issues about privatization deals with the limits of governmental delegation of power and liability. Opponents of privatization believe that the administration of justice is a basic function of government and a symbol of state authority and should not be delegated.

Opponents also fear that if we privatize jails, we risk letting private corporations use their political influence to continue programs not in the public interest. For example, would private contractors keep jail occupancy rates high to maintain profit? Might private contractors accept only the best inmates, leaving the most troublesome for public facilities to handle?

Turning a jail over to a private corporation also raises questions about accountability. Who is responsible for monitoring the performance of the private contractor? Who will see that local laws and regulations are followed? As jail incarceration rates continue to rise, the debate over privatizing jails and the competition for new contracts will continue.

## Overcrowding

Overcrowding is a problem that all jails, especially large urban jails, have to deal with. The number of persons held in local jails grew 4.5 percent from 1997 to 1998. The increase in the rate of jail incarceration is staggering. Between 1985 and 1998, the rate doubled—from 108 per 100,000 adults to 219. Overcrowding has a number of causes, including mandatory arrests and sentences, overcrowding at state and federal prisons, and an overall increase in the arrest rate as politicians "get tough" on crime. Crowded jails have serious health and safety consequences for staff and inmates, including decreased quality of life; overloaded educational, vocational, and recreational programs; insufficient medical services and supplies; increased discipline problems; spread of disease; and staff and inmate assaults.

## Ways to Reduce Jail Crowding

Practices that can reduce crowding include financial and nonfinancial pretrial release, diversion, and new jail construction.

**release on bail** The release of a person upon that person's financial guarantee to appear in court.

**Financial Pretrial Release** Financial pretrial release programs are one alternative to the pretrial detention of accused offenders. Releasing a person upon that person's financial guarantee to appear in court is known as **release on bail.** The Eighth Amendment to the United States Constitution reads, "Excessive bail shall not be required, nor excessive fines imposed, nor

*Quentin X. Escott
Deputy Sheriff
Jefferson County
Birmingham, Alabama*

*"When I work with an inmate and help him change his life, it's extremely gratifying. But the inmate has to want to change. He has to want help. I can't force it. A lot of prisoners want to know you'll help them and give them a chance. That's all."*

Quentin X. Escott has been a deputy sheriff for 1½ years. He is currently assigned to the county jail booking area. His responsibilities include searching incoming prisoners, using the computer imaging system to take inmate photographs and fingerprints, recording personal property, exchanging civilian clothes for jail clothes, and assigning prisoners to housing areas based on their charge classifications.

Deputy Escott has completed almost two years at Lawson State Community College. He is transferring to the University of Alabama at Birmingham, where he will major in criminal justice.

His advice to persons interested in working in a jail? "Treat people like you want to be treated. Yeah, they're prisoners and they broke the law. For that they're in here for punishment. But if I'm going to like my job I have to get along with everybody, prisoners and staff. That means treating everyone with respect and hopefully getting it back in return." For Deputy Escott, the most gratifying part of the job is helping an inmate who really wants help.

---

cruel and unusual punishments inflicted." The Constitution does not guarantee defendants an automatic right to bail, only protection from excessive bail. The defendant may post the full amount of the bail, secure the amount privately through a bail bondsman, or deposit a percentage (usually 10 percent) with the court.

**Nonfinancial Pretrial Release**  An alternative form of pretrial release requires only the defendant's promise to appear in court as required. This release without a cash guarantee is called **release on own recognizance (ROR).** Generally, information about defendants is gathered and verified to determine the appropriateness of nonfinancial pretrial release.

Another type of nonfinancial pretrial release is a **citation.** Similar to traffic tickets, citations are issued by police in some jurisdictions for misdemeanors such as disorderly conduct. A citation binds the defendant to appear in court on a future date. It places no conditions on the released person's behavior and requires no payment to guarantee the court appearance.

In the 1960s and 1970s, a new form of nonfinancial pretrial release emerged. Called **supervised pretrial release,** it imposes more restrictive conditions on defendants. The conditions often include participating in therapeutic or rehabilitative programs, reporting to a pretrial officer, checking in regularly, and so forth. During the same period, a third-party release option developed. A third party—such as the defendant's lawyer, family, or

**release on own recognizance (ROR)**  Pretrial release on the defendant's promise to appear for trial. It requires no cash guarantee.

**citation**  A type of nonfinancial pretrial release similar to a traffic ticket. It binds the defendant to appear in court on a future date.

**supervised pretrial release**  Nonfinancial pretrial release with more restrictive conditions (for example, participating in therapeutic or rehabilitative programs, reporting to a pretrial officer, and checking in regularly).

**conditional release**
Pretrial release under minimal or moderately restrictive conditions with little monitoring of compliance. It includes ROR, supervised pretrial release, and third-party release.

**diversion** Referring defendants to non-criminal-justice agencies for services instead of processing them through the courts.

employer, or a social service agency—assumes responsibility for the defendant's appearance in court. Programs such as ROR, supervised pretrial release, and third-party release are all forms of **conditional release.** They impose minimal or moderately restrictive conditions with little monitoring of compliance. In a number of jurisdictions across the United States today, electronic monitoring is also being used as part of conditional release.

**Diversion** Another way jail crowding can be reduced is through the expanded use of **diversion.** Diversion means referring defendants to non-criminal-justice agencies for services instead of processing them through the criminal justice system. For example, persons with substance abuse problems can be diverted to treatment centers, thus relieving jail crowding. Jail inmates with mental disorders can be referred to mental health clinics, where they receive both treatment and custodial supervision. After accepting diversion, a defendant is required to cooperate and participate in treatment, whether or not he or she feels it is necessary. Failure to show progress may lead to reinstatement of charges.

**New Construction** Finally, new construction is another way to reduce jail crowding. Proponents of new construction argue that jail incarceration is here to stay. Because the public supports jails, we have a responsibility to build them. Opponents argue that if we continue to add new beds to the nation's jails, we will fill up all the space we create. In other words, some believe that availability drives up occupancy. They also claim that most non-violent pretrial detainees and convicted offenders do not need to be in jail and that it wastes resources to house them there.

## Women in Jail

In mid-1998, there were 63,791 female jail inmates. That was 11 percent of the entire jail population. Two-thirds of the women in jail are mothers with children under age 18. Before incarceration 40 percent used drugs daily. Forty percent had had members of their immediate families sentenced to prison. One out of three grew up in a home where one or both parents abused drugs, alcohol, or both. And one out of three had been physically or sexually abused before she was 18 years old. This profile raises troubling concerns about the children of jailed mothers. See Table 4–1.

When mothers go to jail, children become silent victims. The children may already be victims if their mothers used drugs during pregnancy. Young children, not yet capable of understanding why their mother is gone, where she has gone, and if or when she will return, may develop depression and feelings of abandonment. Even children who are fortunate enough to be placed with emotionally supportive caregivers must cope with seeing their mother only through a glass barrier and hearing her voice only over the phone. Studies have shown that children of incarcerated mothers have more behavioral problems at home and in school and are four times as likely to become juvenile delinquents as children from similar socioeconomic backgrounds with parents at home.

Recognizing that children should not be made to suffer for the poor choices of their parents, jails have established a number of successful par-

enting programs. Through such programs, jail administrators have the opportunity to become leaders in preserving families and reducing crime.

## Educational and Vocational Programs

Many jail inmates have poor reading skills. National studies show that more than 40 percent of all jail inmates have less than a ninth-grade education.[19] They also have substance abuse problems and few job skills. They frequently cannot find jobs after they are released or can find only low-paid or temporary work. Partly as a result, they often return to a life of crime.

Too many jails simply warehouse inmates and care little about education or job skills. Yes, it does cost taxpayers money to provide educational services to jail inmates—the same people who already have financially and psychologically burdened society through their crimes. Education does not guarantee that an offender will remain free of crime upon release. But consider the alternative: More than 40 percent of defendants on pretrial release have one or more prior convictions. The cost of keeping one inmate in jail for one year ranges from $20,000 to $40,000. And studies also show that inmates who earn their GEDs while incarcerated are far less likely to return to crime. Educational and vocational programs help offenders help themselves, they boost self-esteem, and they encourage legitimate occupations upon release. Overall, it costs less to educate offenders and teach them job skills than to do nothing to change their attitudes, abilities, and outlooks. Ignoring an offender's educational and vocational deficiencies leaves the offender with fewer marketable skills or qualifications when released, increasing the chance of a return to crime.

Recently, the Orange County, Florida, Jail—one of the largest in the nation, with 3,300 beds—began an innovative strategy.[20] The entire jail—the operation, budget, and architecture—now revolves around its educational and vocational programs. The jail offers inmates a wide range of structured educational and vocational programs designed to fit inmates' short stays. The jail provides job readiness and placement services. It offers inmates valuable incentives to participate in programs and to avoid misconduct. And it uses the design and philosophy of third-generation jails, discussed earlier in this chapter, to manage inmates in a way that contains costs, promotes inmate responsibility, and allows open areas that can be used as classrooms. According to the National Institute of Justice, "Each of these features is part of a comprehensive corrections strategy that enables programming to flourish at the same time that it saves the county money, keeps inmates occupied and out of trouble, and (it is hoped) reduces recidivism."[21]

The principal steps in the Orange County Jail's educational and vocational programs are presented in Figure 4–6. The jail provides unusually intensive educational and vocational opportunities to most of its inmates. Five features are very important to the success of the programs: incentives for participation, direct supervision, active support by corrections officers, cooperation from schools, and programs tailored to short jail stays.

## Religious Programs in Jail

Very little is written about the use and effects of religion in jail. Too often the topic is looked at skeptically by outsiders, who believe that inmates "find God" as a convenient reason for release or forgiveness but really don't mean it. We do not enter that debate. What we present is a view grounded in the experiences of those who minister to jail inmates.

There are at least five benefits of jail chaplaincy. First, most jail chaplains believe that the cycle of crime can only be broken one life at a time. Jail inmates must experience an inner conversion before they change their behavior. Jail chaplains can assist in that conversion. Second, jail chaplains can help jail staff with their emotional and family problems. An on-site chaplain can help staff deal with problems daily, as they develop. Third, jail chaplains are in a unique position to mediate and moderate tensions and conflicts between inmates and staff before they get serious. Pleading for nonviolence is a chaplain's strong tool. Inmates usually see a jail chaplain as neutral—not as "one of them." The chaplain has the unique opportunity to speak his or her mind and be seen as someone who cares enough to confront and comfort. Fourth, ministering to the disadvantaged is legitimate in the eye of the public and helps the community remember those they would just as soon forget (recall the concept of inmates as "rabble," discussed earlier in this chapter). Involving the public as jail volunteers is an added benefit. And fifth, jail chaplains can help inmates confront the truth about themselves and reverse the "everything is relative" attitude that offenders develop to justify their crimes.

In the following excerpt, a chaplain shares some thoughts about his two years on the job:[22]

> A chaplain occupies a unique place in an inmate's thinking. She or he is not seen as "one of them;" we are not associated so much with the institution or judicial system. That gives us unique

**FIGURE 4–6**

## Orange County, Florida, Jail Educational and Vocational Programs

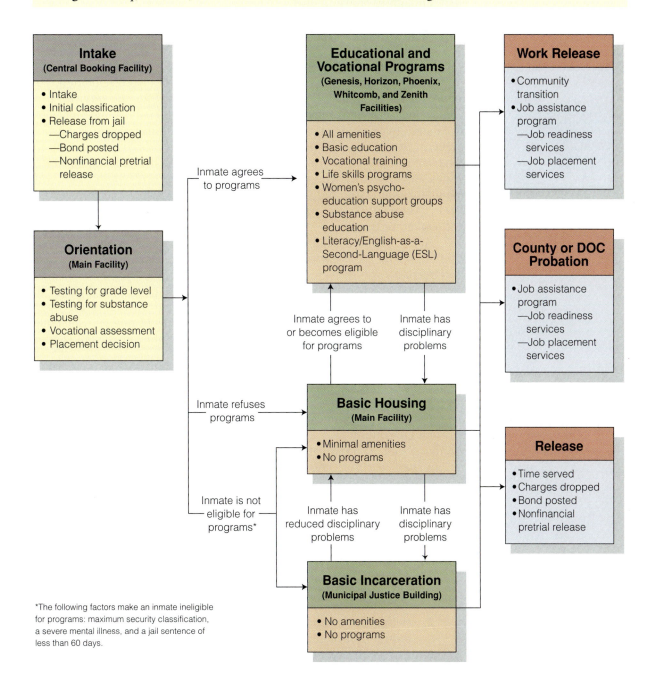

**Intake**
(Central Booking Facility)

- Intake
- Initial classification
- Release from jail
  —Charges dropped
  —Bond posted
  —Nonfinancial pretrial release

**Orientation**
(Main Facility)

- Testing for grade level
- Testing for substance abuse
- Vocational assessment
- Placement decision

**Educational and Vocational Programs**
(Genesis, Horizon, Phoenix, Whitcomb, and Zenith Facilities)

- All amenities
- Basic education
- Vocational training
- Life skills programs
- Women's psycho-education support groups
- Substance abuse education
- Literacy/English-as-a-Second-Language (ESL) program

**Work Release**

- Community transition
- Job assistance program
  —Job readiness services
  —Job placement services

**County or DOC Probation**

- Job assistance program
  —Job readiness services
  —Job placement services

**Basic Housing**
(Main Facility)

- Minimal amenities
- No programs

**Release**

- Time served
- Charges dropped
- Bond posted
- Nonfinancial pretrial release

**Basic Incarceration**
(Municipal Justice Building)

- No amenities
- No programs

Inmate agrees to programs

Inmate agrees to or becomes eligible for programs

Inmate has disciplinary problems

Inmate refuses programs

Inmate is not eligible for programs*

Inmate has reduced disciplinary problems

Inmate has disciplinary problems

*The following factors make an inmate ineligible for programs: maximum security classification, a severe mental illness, and a jail sentence of less than 60 days.

*Source:* National Institute of Justice, *The Orange County, Florida, Jail Educational and Vocational Programs* (Washington: U.S. Department of Justice, 1997).

opportunities to speak openly and be viewed not as someone who has a sinister hidden agenda, but as someone who cares enough to confront.

## Jail Accreditation

**jail accreditation** The formal approval of a jail by a national accrediting body such as the American Correctional Association and the Commission on Accreditation.

**Jail accreditation** is the formal approval of a jail by the American Correctional Association (ACA) and the Commission on Accreditation. The ACA and the commission have developed standards for the services, programs, and operations they consider essential to good jail management. The standards cover administrative and fiscal concerns, staff training and development, the physical plant, safety and emergency procedures, sanitation, food service, and rules and discipline. Standards are divided into two categories. To be accredited, a jail must have 100 percent compliance with mandatory standards and 90 percent compliance with nonmandatory standards. As of 1995, approximately 125 jails had received some form of national accreditation.

Accreditation is valid for three years. Then the jail may apply for reaccreditation and receive another on-site audit by ACA staff and an accreditation hearing.

Very few jails followed established standards or policies before the 1960s. Several reasons for this have been suggested, including the traditional independence of sheriffs, who operate the jails in most jurisdictions, and the tendency of most sheriffs to focus on law enforcement rather than on corrections.

Although jails were slow to respond to the standards movement, their response has picked up in recent years. There are several reasons jails have been slow to adopt national standards or seek national accreditation. First, accreditation is expensive and time-consuming. Many jails do not have the resources to commit to it. This is especially true of small jails that are already overburdened. Approximately 2,000 U.S. jails are designed to hold less than 50 inmates. Second, jails hold relatively few long-term inmates. Few inmates are in a jail long enough to file a successful legal action regarding poor conditions in the jail. Knowing this, some jail administrators may not be willing to undergo the expense and burden of seeking accreditation. Third, some states have their own standards that jails must meet.

There are at least four reasons for jails to have national accreditation:

1. Accreditation by the ACA and the Commission on Accreditation indicates that a jail adheres to strict standards to protect the health and safety of staff and inmates.
2. Being accredited may help a jail defend against lawsuits over conditions of incarceration.
3. In preparing for the accreditation review, the sheriff's office may evaluate all operations, procedures, and policies, leading to better management practices.
4. With accreditation come professional recognition and status, greater appreciation by the community, and a sense of pride in the achievement and in the hard work that went into it.

The Arlington County, Virginia, Jail is a case in point. The sheriff aspired to accreditation for the jail and instilled that goal in all staff. The jail staff spent eight months assembling the documentation needed to comply with specific standards. The staff also conducted a self-evaluation, looking closely at their policies, procedures, and operational practices. After the self-evaluation, the Arlington County Jail enlisted two professionals from nearby accredited jails to conduct a mock audit. The input of the mock auditors helped the jail further refine its documentation and prepare for the site visit of the national accrediting team.

When the national accrediting team arrived, its members toured the jail, interviewed approximately 25 staff members and 30 inmates, and read all the documentation the staff had prepared. The jail had 100 percent compliance with the mandatory standards and 98.6 percent compliance with the nonmandatory standards. The jail's scores were extremely high, reflecting the effort and time of the staff in meeting the standards, as well as the excellence of the jail's policies and procedures and of the accreditation files the staff had prepared.

Today, the Arlington County Jail displays its national award in the lobby of the jail. The staff takes pride in telling everyone that the jail has been accredited. Here is how some of the staff responded to the question "What does accreditation mean to you individually and as a member of this office?"[23]

**Deputy Sheriff 1**
Employees receive full salary and benefits while attending the Reiger Academy, where, upon successful completion, they will receive certification in corrections. Employees will perform a variety of duties in corrections, inmate transportation, service of legal process, or courtroom/courthouse security. Initial assignment will be in our state-of-the-art direct-supervision detention facility. The County Sheriff's Office is accredited by the American Correctional Association's Commission on Accreditation for Corrections. Qualifications: H.S. graduate or equivalent; age 21 at time of appointment; U.S. citizenship at time of application; valid driver's license.

> **Deputy Charles Monroe,** currently assigned to the Intake Housing Unit: "Being accredited means to me that the sheriff's office is always striving to meet and go beyond state and national standards and guidelines. By going beyond and meeting these guidelines, it creates a professional attitude among staff members and creates a cleaner and safer environment for staff. It shows that the sheriff's office takes pride in being one of a few offices which meets accreditation standards. It also shows the dedication of the sheriff's office to providing Arlington County residents with the best service it can."

> **Deputy Jeffrey Tolen,** currently assigned to the general population housing unit for women and a member of our emergency response team: "Coming from the old jail system, I feel that being accredited holds me to a higher standard. Having had an opportunity to see the accreditation process, I understand that my department has met standards that not every department can meet."

> **Deputy Charles Silcox,** currently assigned to oversee the community work program: "As with any job, it is a good feeling to know that you are recognized for something that not everyone else in your field has been able to achieve. It's like setting a standard for others to follow."

# Jail Staff as Professionals

As this chapter has shown, jail staff assume enormous responsibility, and we expect them to conduct themselves as professionals. Before 1970, training and education for jail officers were virtually nonexistent, for several reasons. Jail officers often aspired to be law enforcement officers or some other occupation, or they were using jail work as their last stop on the road to retirement. Many people also believed that education and training for jail staff were unnecessary because the work was unsophisticated and could be learned on the job.

Since 1970, however, the image of jail staff has changed. Thanks to organizations like the American Jail Association and the American Correctional Association; national, state, and local commissions on jail issues; and studies by practitioners, consultants, and academic researchers, jail work is now recognized not only as difficult but also as a career path that is different from law enforcement and requires different attitudes and skills. Jail staff perform work that is vital, complex, and potentially hazardous, even under the best of circumstances.

To conduct themselves as professionals, jail staff must have strong communication skills, knowledge of the psychology of behavior, multicultural sophistication, ethnic and racial tolerance, human management expertise, endurance, and fitness. Even more important, they must, for their own mental well-being, be able to understand and tolerate the stress of a potentially explosive environment. The American Jail Association's Code of Ethics for Jail Officers is shown in Exhibit 4–2.

The trend toward better educated and trained jail staff is evident across the United States. There are tougher entrance requirements. Applicants must have a higher level of education, increased basic training, more experience, other related skills, and the appropriate personality. Jail staff also learn to conduct themselves as professionals.

Many departments require applicants to have completed a correctional officer training and education program. There are a number of advantages to the policy. First, a department can hire certified correctional officers without paying for training. Second, the department can ask training program staff about applicants' abilities, reliability, and other relevant issues. And third, new jail officers will have the needed skills and an essential understanding of the job.

EXHIBIT 4–2

# American Jail Association

## Code of Ethics for Jail Officers

As an officer employed in a detention/correctional capacity, I swear (or affirm) to be a good citizen and a credit to my community, state, and nation at all times. I will abstain from questionable behavior which might bring disrepute to the agency for which I work, my family, my community, and my associates. My lifestyle will be above and beyond reproach and I will constantly strive to set an example of a professional who performs his/her duties according to the laws of our country, state, and community and the policies, procedures, written and verbal orders, and regulations of the agency for which I work.

On the job I promise to:

**KEEP** The institution secure so as to safeguard my community and the lives of the staff, inmates, and visitors on the premises.

**WORK** With each individual firmly and fairly without regard to rank, status, or condition.

**MAINTAIN** A positive demeanor when confronted with stressful situations of scorn, ridicule, danger, and/or chaos.

**REPORT** Either in writing or by word of mouth to the proper authorities those things which should be reported, and keep silent about matters which are to remain confidential according to the laws and rules of the agency and government.

**MANAGE** And supervise the inmates in an evenhanded and courteous manner.

**REFRAIN** At all times from becoming personally involved in the lives of the inmates and their families.

**TREAT** All visitors to the jail with politeness and respect and do my utmost to ensure that they observe the jail regulations.

**TAKE** Advantage of all education and training opportunities designed to assist me to become a more competent officer.

**COMMUNICATE** With people in or outside of the jail, whether by phone, written word, or word of mouth, in such a way so as not to reflect in a negative manner upon my agency.

**CONTRIBUTE** To a jail environment which will keep the inmate involved in activities designed to improve his/her attitude and character.

**SUPPORT** All activities of a professional nature through membership and participation that will continue to elevate the status of those who operate our nation's jails. Do my best through word and deed to present an image to the public at large of a jail professional, committed to progress for an improved and enlightened criminal justice system.

Adopted by the American Jail Association Board of Directors on November 10, 1991. Revised May 19, 1993.

## SUMMARY BY CHAPTER OBJECTIVES

### CHAPTER OBJECTIVE 1

Jails serve a number of purposes besides incarcerating persons who have sentences of a year or less. They hold persons awaiting trial, probation and parole violators, adults and juveniles awaiting transfer, and prison inmates about to be released. Sometimes they operate community-based programs.

### CHAPTER OBJECTIVE 2

Jails emerged in Europe in the twelfth century to detain offenders for trial. In the fifteenth and sixteenth centuries, the poor and unemployed were detained alongside criminals. The first jail in America was the Walnut Street Jail. Quakers planned it based on the principles of religious reflection and penance. It fell short of reaching its goals and closed in 1835.

### CHAPTER OBJECTIVE 3

American jails have progressed through three phases of architecture and inmate management: first-generation jails (linear design and indirect supervision), second-generation jails (pod design and indirect supervision), and third-generation jails (pod design and direct supervision).

### CHAPTER OBJECTIVE 4

At midyear 1998, jails held 664,847 offenders, an increase of 4.5 percent from midyear 1997. An estimated 252,600 (43 percent) are convicted offenders. Women represent 11 percent of the jail population; nonwhites, almost 60 percent; and juveniles, 1.4 percent. Special-needs inmates are persons suffering from mental illness, chemical dependency (drug and alcohol abuse), or disease (especially HIV/AIDS or TB).

### CHAPTER OBJECTIVE 5

Jail vocational and educational programs are important techniques for managing inmates and reducing recidivism. They keep inmates occupied, they boost self-esteem, and they help inmates find jobs after release.

### CHAPTER OBJECTIVE 6

Religion and jail chaplaincy can influence jail inmates in five ways. First, they can help inmates with the inner conversion needed to break the cycle of crime. Second, a jail chaplain can help staff deal with day-to-day problems. Third, a jail chaplain can mediate and moderate tensions and conflicts between inmates and staff. Fourth, jail chaplaincy can involve the public as jail volunteers and remind people that inmates exist. And fifth, chaplains can help inmates confront the truth about themselves.

### CHAPTER OBJECTIVE 7

Jail accreditation is important for four reasons. First, accreditation indicates that a jail adheres to strict standards. Second, accreditation may help a jail defend against lawsuits over conditions of incarceration. Third, through accreditation, the sheriff's office may evaluate all operations, procedures, and policies, leading to better management practices. And fourth, accreditation means professional recognition and status, greater appreciation by the community, and a sense of pride.

### CHAPTER OBJECTIVE 8

It is important for jail staff to conduct themselves as professionals because jail work is difficult and carries enormous responsibility. It requires a special attitude, communication skills, knowledge of the psychology of behavior, multicultural sophistication, endurance, and fitness. Together, college education and jail training prepare jail staff to work as professionals.

# QUESTIONS FOR REVIEW

1. What are the main purposes of jails?
2. When and where was the first jail built? What was the purpose of this jail?
3. Who was John Howard?
4. What was the first jail in America, and when was it built?
5. Explain what John Irwin meant by *rabble management.*
6. Describe how first-, second-, and third-generation jails differ.
7. As of 1998, which ethnic groups make up the majority of jail populations in the United States?
8. What are special-needs inmates? What problems do they pose for jail personnel?
9. List some arguments against jail privatization.
10. Outline some strategies to reduce jail crowding.
11. Why is it important to promote positive relationships between incarcerated mothers and their children?
12. Why are educational and vocational programs for inmates important for jail management?
13. How can religion and jail chaplaincy be positive forces in the jail environment?
14. What are the advantages and disadvantages of jail accreditation?
15. List some characteristics of a professional jail employee.

# CRITICAL THINKING EXERCISES

## ON-THE-JOB ISSUE

You are the administrator of a new county jail with the architecture and philosophy of direct supervision. The new jail replaced the old jail, built in 1912. Some of the senior staff have begun complaining to you about direct supervision. They say they don't like to interact with inmates. They talk about "the good old days" when inmates were "on the other side" of the reinforced glass and steel bars. There's even been a letter to the editor in the local newspaper complaining that the new jail doesn't "look like a jail."

1. What could you tell the senior staff about third-generation philosophy and architecture that might ease their concerns?

2. What strategies might you use to educate the public about the benefits of direct supervision?

## CORRECTIONS ISSUES

1. When deciding whether to grant pretrial release, a judge looks at the offense, the evidence, and the defendant's family ties, employment, financial resources, character, mental condition, length of residence in the community, and criminal record. To which of these do you think the judge should give the greatest weight? Why?

2. A major advantage of financial and nonfinancial pretrial release programs is that they keep the jail population down. That means

less money is spent on jails. Without pretrial release, the number of persons in jail would be higher, and more money would be needed for new jails—money that local communities do not have. When pretrial release programs are properly developed and implemented, defendants appear in court as promised. One criticism of pretrial release programs is that some may coerce defendants, before trial, to participate in therapy, education, or vocational training. Critics argue that such coercion is wrong for defendants who are later acquitted. They also argue that defendants who are convicted are often ordered to repeat the same therapy, education, or vocational training. Do you favor or oppose pretrial release? Explain.

3. The accreditation process can take up to 18 months. When achieved, accreditation lasts three years. Facilities are encouraged to reapply early to prevent a break in accreditation. The process of self-evaluation is almost continuous. Do you think a three-year period of accreditation is too short, too long, or just right? Explain.

4. Correctional facilities seek accreditation to ensure compliance with national standards, to demonstrate to legislators acceptable performance, and to comply with court orders. Which of these reasons do you think should be given the most importance, and why?

## CORRECTIONS ON THE WEB

1. Carefully read the mission statement on the Niagara County Sheriff's Department Web page (**http://www.ncsd.com**). What emphasis does the mission statement give to jail operations? If possible, look at the Web pages of other jail facilities and review their mission statements. What do you think the ideal mission statement should say about jail operations?

2. Visit the Web site of the American Correctional Association at **http://www. corrections.com/aca/.** Click on Accreditation to go to the Standards and Accreditation Online Resource Center. Choose among the topics to learn more about the accreditation process.

## ADDITIONAL READINGS

Irwin, John. *The Jail: Managing the Underclass in American Society.* Berkeley: University of California Press, 1986.

Kerle, Kenneth E. *American Jails: Looking to the Future.* Boston: Butterworth Heinemann, 1998.

Welsh, Wayne N. *Counties in Court: Jail Overcrowding and Court-Ordered Reform.* Philadelphia: Temple University Press, 1995.

Zupan, Linda L. *Jails: Reform and the New Generation Philosophy.* Cincinnati: Anderson, 1991.

# ENDNOTES

1. R. J. Hawkins, "My Own Private Iowa," available: http://www.captivated.com/hawkins/bottom.html.
2. Darrell K. Gilliard and Allen J. Beck, *Prison and Jail Inmates at Midyear 1998* (Washington: Bureau of Justice Statistics, March 1999).
3. National Advisory Commission on Criminal Justice Standards and Goals, *Corrections* (Washington: U.S. Government Printing Office, 1973) p. 273.
4. Marilyn D. McShane and Frank P. Williams III (eds.), *Encyclopedia of American Prisons* (New York: Garland, 1996), p. 494.
5. Ibid., p. 496.
6. Ronald L. Goldfarb, *Jails: The Ultimate Ghetto* (Garden City, NY: Doubleday, 1975), p. 29.
7. John Irwin, *The Jail: Managing the Underclass in American Society* (Berkeley: University of California Press, 1986).
8. Linda Zupan, *Jails: Reform and the New Generation Philosophy* (Cincinnati: Anderson, 1991).
9. Gilliard and Beck, pp. 7–8.
10. G. Larry Mays and Daniel L. Judiscak, "Special Needs Inmates in New Mexico Jails," *American Jails*, Vol. 10, No. 2 (1996), pp. 32–41.
11. Sally Chandler Halford, "Drug Offender Treatment," *American Jails*, Vol. 10, No. 3, July/Aug. 1996, p. 4.
12. Caroline Wolf Harlow, *Profile of Jail Inmates 1996* (Washington: Bureau of Justice Statistics, April 1998), pp. 8–9.
13. Sandra Tunis, et al., *Evaluation of Drug Treatment in Local Corrections* (Washington: U.S. Department of Justice, 1997).
14. Laura Maruschak, *HIV in Prisons and Jails, 1995* (Washington: U. S. Department of Justice, 1997).
15. L. A. Teplin, "Psychiatric and Substance Abuse Disorders Among Male Urban Jail Detainees," *American Journal of Public Health*, Vol. 84, No. 2 (1994), pp. 290–293.
16. Henry J. Steadman and Bonita M. Veysey, *Providing Services for Jail Inmates with Mental Disorders* (Washington: National Institute of Justice, Office of Justice Programs, January 1997).
17. Mason R. Goodman, "An Overview of Tuberculosis in Jails in the United States for Health Care and Administrative Corrections Professionals," *American Jails*, Vol. 10, No. 4 (1996), pp. 45–50.
18. Ken Kerle, "Statistics and Jails," *American Jails*, Vol. 10, No. 6 (1997), p. 5.
19. Harlow, p. 3.
20. National Institute of Justice, *The Orange County, Florida, Jail Educational and Vocational Programs* (Washington: U.S. Department of Justice, 1997).
21. Ibid., p. 3.
22. Sheldon Crapo, "Breaking the Cycle of Crime . . . One Life at a Time," *American Jails*, Vol. 11, No. 1 (March/April 1997), p. 24.
23. Michael Pinson, "Accreditation Is Worth the Effort," *Corrections Today*, Vol. 58, No. 7 (December 1996), p. 73. Reprinted with permission.

# 5 Diversion and Probation
## Alternatives to Imprisonment

**CHAPTER OBJECTIVES**

After completing this chapter you should be able to:

1. Define *diversion* and know its objectives.
2. Explain the rationales for diversion.
3. Give examples of stages at which diversion occurs in the criminal justice process.
4. Discuss diversion policy issues.
5. Define *probation* and know its goals.
6. Explain the reasons for using probation.
7. Describe some of the characteristics of adults on probation.
8. Explain the different ways that probation is administered.
9. Describe the investigation and supervision functions of probation officers.
10. Describe the measures used to evaluate probation.
11. Discuss the issues facing probation in the 21st century.

123

*If all law violations were processed officially as the arrest-conviction-imprisonment model calls for, the system obviously would collapse from its voluminous caseloads and from community opposition.*

—National Advisory Commission on Criminal Justice Standards and Goals

On December 31, 1998, 3.4 million people were on probation in the United States—1 out of every 60 adults. The number of people on probation is equivalent to the population of Oklahoma.

The typical probationer is a Southern white male who has never married and has either completed high school or earned a GED. He was convicted of a felony and has at least one prior sentence, to probation or confinement. He has five or more probation conditions, including payment of monetary restitution to his victim. At least 40 percent of probationers are ordered to undergo substance abuse treatment.

However, the face of probation is changing. Under the authority of federal sentencing guidelines, federal judges are increasingly ordering probation for *corporations* found guilty of violations of federal law. In 1993, 48 U.S. companies were on probation. By 1996, the number had increased to 96.

As a condition of probation, judges order monitoring of a corporation's activities. They assign a monitor to each corporation put on probation. The role of the independent monitor is to investigate any acts, conditions, or problems brought to the attention of the court or the monitor. The monitor conducts an investigation and then files a report with the judge.

Despite federal judges' increasing use of probation for corporations, probation is imposed most often by local judges on individuals convicted of criminal offenses. This chapter introduces you to two areas of corrections that most offenders first experience—diversion and probation. Diversion

## FIGURE 5–1

### Case Flow Model for Diversion and Probation

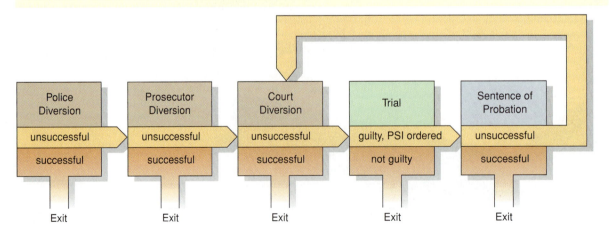

*Diversion and Probation: Alternatives to Imprisonment*

occurs *before* trial. Probation occurs *after* a person has been convicted. Figure 5–1 shows how these two processes can occur in the criminal justice system. Because offenders can be diverted one or more times before they are tried, convicted, and sentenced to probation, we will discuss diversion first.

# Diversion

**Diversion** has been defined as "the halting or suspension, before conviction, of formal criminal proceedings against a person, [often] conditioned on some form of counter performance by the defendant,"[1] and this is the definition we will use. **Counter performance** is the defendant's participation, in exchange for diversion, in a treatment, counseling, or educational program aimed at changing his or her behavior. The candidate for diversion is a person who has been or could be arrested for an alleged offense and who is or could become the defendant in a criminal prosecution. Suspending the prosecution of a case is the hallmark of the diversion process.

In the criminal justice system, diversion is used in two ways. First, it can keep an offender out of the system and avoid formal prosecution and labeling. This is called **true diversion.** For example, a person accused of public drunkenness could be required to attend an alcohol abuse program in lieu of arrest and prosecution. The referral agency, generally the police, may stipulate that if the person successfully completes the alcohol abuse program, no further action will be taken. If the person does not successfully complete the alcohol abuse program, the police might file the initial charge.

The second way of using diversion is to keep an offender from going further into the system. This is called **minimization of penetration.** For example, a man charged with battering his girlfriend could be asked by the prosecutor to attend a batterer's treatment program in lieu of trial, conviction, and sentence. If the accused batterer completes the treatment program, the charge is dropped. If he does not complete the program, the prosecutor may prosecute him for the crime.

Most diversion programs share three objectives:

1. Prevent future criminal activity by diverting certain defendants from criminal justice processing into community supervision and service. This goal is based on the belief that diversion programs are more effective ways to control criminal behavior than taking offenders to court and getting them convicted and sentenced.
2. Save prosecution and judicial resources for serious crimes by offering alternatives to the usual prosecution process for less serious ones. Defendants eligible for diversion are given the opportunity to avoid arrest or prosecution and to obtain medical services, counseling, and educational and vocational training.
3. Provide, where appropriate, a vehicle for restitution to communities and victims of crime.

## Rationales for Diversion

Diversion has four rationales. First, the experience and the stigma of being formally arrested, tried, and convicted can actually encourage more

**diversion** Formal efforts to use alternatives to processing through the justice system; also, "the halting or suspension, before conviction, of formal criminal proceedings against a person, conditioned on some form of counter performance by the defendant."

**counter performance** The defendant's participation, in exchange for diversion, in a treatment, counseling, or educational program aimed at changing his or her behavior.

**true diversion** A form of diversion that keeps an offender out of the system and avoids formal prosecution and labeling.

**minimization of penetration** A form of diversion that keeps an offender from going further into the system.

criminal behavior. For example, having a criminal record might restrict a person's educational, vocational, and social opportunities, making the person more apt to turn to crime to survive. In addition, as a result of time spent in jail or prison, an offender may be more likely to associate with other offenders.

A second rationale for using diversion is that it is less expensive than formally processing an offender through the criminal justice system. The expense of arrest, trial, conviction, and sentence is easily justified for serious crimes. In most cities and counties across the United States today, however, the police are overworked, the courts are overloaded, the jails and prisons are overcrowded, and probation and parole officers have caseloads that are unmanageable. Diversion is a way to reduce or at least contain these burdens, reserving formal criminal justice processing for the cases that need it the most.

A third rationale for diversion is that the public may think formal processing through the criminal justice system is inappropriate for crimes without perceived victims. These offenses involve a willing and private exchange of illegal goods or services. Examples include prostitution, certain forms of sexual behavior, gambling, and drug sales. Such offenses are called victimless crimes because the participants do not feel they are being harmed. Prosecution is justified on the grounds that these offenses harm society as a whole by threatening the moral fabric of the community. Since formal prosecution of these offenses is costly, however, offenders are often diverted to health clinics and treatment programs.

A final rationale for using diversion is to give the typical diversion client a better chance in life. Our nation's jails, lockups, prisons, and probation and parole caseloads are filled with people who are economically disadvantaged, belong to minority groups, and are young, undereducated, and chronically unemployed or underemployed. Diversion offers such persons help with some of the challenges they face, without adding to their difficulties the stigma of formal arrest, trial, and conviction.

## How Does Diversion Occur?

Diversion may occur at any point in the criminal justice process after a criminal complaint has been filed or police have observed a crime. The police, a prosecutor, or a judge may use it. The accused participates voluntarily and has access to defense counsel before deciding whether to participate.

The overall goal of diversion is to reduce recidivism through rehabilitation. Most diversion programs use an assessment process to determine a defendant's needs. Then an intervention plan for that defendant is developed. The diversion program then contracts with the defendant, agreeing on the requirements of the plan and the criminal justice consequences of succeeding or failing in the plan. Figure 5–2 shows the conditions of pretrial diversion used by the Treatment Alternatives to Street Crime (TASC) program in Alabama. Similar conditions are used by diversion programs in many other states. In some states, the diversion process is established by law; in other states, local agreements with prosecutors are the basis for the process.

Diversion programs offer a variety of remedial responses to defendants' problems. Such responses can include drug and alcohol treatment, mental

**FIGURE 5–2**

**Pretrial Release Bond Agreement**

STATE OF ALABAMA

      vs

_Brett Gould_

- STATE OF ALABAMA
- JEFFERSON COUNTY
- _District_ COURT
- BOND $ _$5,000.00_
- CASE NO. _DC99-6342.917_

### CONDITIONS OF RELEASE

1. Defendant must appear to answer and must submit to the orders and process of the court having jurisdiction of this case as directed.

2. Defendant must refrain from committing any criminal offense.

3. Defendant must refrain from any contact with prosecutor's witness(s) /the complainant's victim(s). Specifically: _____ Karen Koch _____.

4. Defendant must continue to reside at _____ 2055 2nd Ave., Birmingham _____ with _____ son _____, and may not leave the state of Alabama or change residence without written permission of the Court having jurisdiction of this case.

5. Defendant must obtain and/or maintain full-time employment or schooling. Written verification of employment attendance or attempts to secure employment/enrollment will be presented to the TASC case manager.

6. Defendant must report to the TASC Office within 72 hours after release, at 401 Beacon Parkway West, for an evaluation by a case manager.

7. Defendant must submit to random urinalysis for drug screening. Defendant must pay the $20 fee for each month. If drug abuse is indicated, appropriate treatment will be required.

8. Defendant must attend AA/NA/CA meetings _3_ times per week and provide case manager with written verification of that attendance.

9. Defendant must abide by a curfew requiring presence in house of residence between hours of _6_ p.m. and _7_ a.m.

10. Defendant must seek and accept drug and/or alcohol treatment within _7_ days of release date.

11. Defendant must appear in this court on the next scheduled court date, _March 20, 2000_.

Done this _13th_ day of _____ March _____, 20 _00_

_____ Carl Stephan _____
               Judge

### INSTRUCTION TO DEFENDANT

You have agreed to appear in court whenever ordered. Your responsibility to the above conditions is to remain until either the case is ended or you are released. If you do not appear whenever ordered, you may be required to pay the bond amount.

_Brett Gould_
DEFENDANT

_Terry Williams_
WITNESSED

health services, employment counseling, and education and training. They may involve agencies in or outside the criminal justice system. The variety of responses often reflects a community's unique criminal justice population.

Diversion is also used for persons who are classified as mentally ill or incompetent and either are not equipped to stand trial or need a form of incarceration and treatment other than imprisonment. Such persons may be referred to an agency for voluntary treatment or civil commitment to an institution in lieu of prosecution and a prison sentence.

## Diversion Policy Issues

Diversion has its supporters and critics. Supporters believe diversion is the first opportunity to give offenders individualized assistance before they get too far down the path of crime. In such cases, diversion resolves problems that lead to offending behavior. Critics argue that diversion tends to force people to give up some of their freedom without being tried and convicted. They argue that it violates the safeguard of due process. Other critics believe that diversion is "nonpunishment" and might actually produce more crime. To these and other issues about diversion we now turn our attention.

**Legal and Ethical Issues**   There is agreement that a diversion program should protect a defendant's rights. Protections include requiring an informed waiver of the right to a speedy trial, the right to a trial by jury, the right to confront one's accusers, and the privilege against self-incrimination, and informed consent to the conditions of a diversion program. For supporters, the risk of violating rights is outweighed by the chance diversion gives defendants to avoid the stigma of a criminal record and by the possibility of resolving problems that might result in future criminal behavior.

**unconditional diversion**

The termination of criminal processing at any point before adjudication with no threat of later prosecution. It generally means that treatment, counseling, and other services are offered voluntarily.

**conditional diversion**

Diversion in which charges are dismissed if the defendant satisfactorily completes treatment, counseling, or other programs ordered by the justice system.

**Unconditional diversion** is the termination of criminal processing at any point before adjudication with no threat of later prosecution. It affords the best protection for a defendant's legal rights because dismissal of charges does not require any counter performance. In effect, the defendant has everything to gain and nothing to lose. In unconditional diversion, treatment, counseling, and other services are offered voluntarily. In addition, the use of any services is voluntary. Many corrections leaders regard voluntary treatment as more likely than coerced treatment to have beneficial effects.

**Conditional diversion** means that charges are dismissed if the defendant satisfactorily completes treatment, counseling, or other programs ordered by the justice system. Conditional diversion at or after arraignment, with judicial participation, affords greater protection against prosecutorial overreach and more assurance of informed voluntary decisions by the defendant than diversion by the police or the prosecutor. In diversion programs run by the police and prosecutor, some persons diverted might not have been prosecuted at all or would have been exonerated (cleared of blame). Conditional diversion does not, however, avoid the prospect of more severe penalties for divertees who fail the program.

**Law Enforcement Issues**   Does diversion weaken law enforcement? Does diversion invite more widespread violation of laws by allowing offenders to avoid conviction? There is no particular evidence one way or the

*Diversion programs often provide counseling for substance abuse offenders to help them overcome the problem that led to the offending behavior. What other obstacles might counseling help divertees overcome?*

other. Certainly, if unconditional diversion were practiced extensively, there might be increases in violations. However, if such diversion is limited to the first charge, or the second, there is a ceiling on such increases. Conditional diversion requiring supervision and counter performance does not seem more likely to encourage crime than the dispositions it most often replaces—fines, suspended sentences, and probation.

**Economic Issues**   How cost-effective is diversion? What is the least costly method of diversion that will yield acceptable results? What are the tradeoffs in using different kinds of diversion programs? How does diversion compare in cost and effectiveness with traditional prosecution and sentencing practices?

Some argue that in the long run, diversion can protect the community better than traditional processing. Treatment starts promptly after the criminal events. The social handicap of a criminal record is avoided. Exposure to criminal influences is minimized. And diversion is presumably less conducive to recidivism than traditional processing.

Evidence to support these assertions is anything but conclusive. Most diversion programs have shown good results, but efforts to compare them with what would have happened without diversion have been unsuccessful. However, it seems safe to say the community protection that diversion affords is at least comparable to the traditional measures that would most likely be used if prosecution were not suspended. The economic question, then, is, Which approach costs less?

The costs of both diversion and its alternatives include the costs of arriving at a decision; the costs of implementing decisions; and the costs of undesired consequences of decisions, such as reinstatement of prosecution, new charges, or revocation of probation or parole because of a new charge or violation.

Diversion is not always the appropriate response to criminal behavior. When diversion is not used or when it fails to bring about the desired changes in an offender's behavior, probation is often the next step in the corrections process.

# Probation

Probation has long been one of the most popular and most frequently used forms of punishment (see Figure 5–3). It is a way to keep the offender at home in the community, avoid incarceration, and carry out sanctions imposed by the court or the probation agency. **Probation** is the conditional release of a convicted offender into the community, under the supervision of a probation officer. It is conditional because it can be revoked if certain conditions are not met. The judge or the probation department usually imposes a set of restrictions on the offender's freedom. Almost all probationers have at least one special condition on their release.[2] Among them are paying fines or restitution; submitting to electronic monitoring, house arrest, or drug tests; obeying a curfew; and keeping a log of daily activities. More than 80 percent of probationers have three or more conditions on their sentences. The most common condition (84%) is the payment of fees, fines, or court costs. If the probationer violates any of the technical conditions of her or his probation, or commits a new crime, the judge may order that the entire sentence be served in prison.

Under probation, the offender lives at home but is monitored in some way, such as meeting with a probation officer a specified number of times

**probation** The conditional release of a convicted offender into the community, under the supervision of a probation officer. It is conditional because it can be revoked if certain conditions are not met. The judge or the probation department usually imposes a set of restrictions on the offender's freedom.

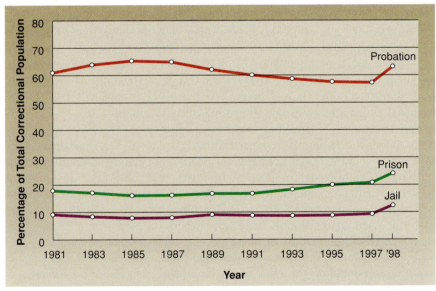

**FIGURE 5–3**

**Adults on Probation, in Jail, or in Prison**

*Source:* Adapted from *Sourcebook of Criminal Justice Statistics, 1997,* Bureau of Justice Statistics (October 1998), p. 464 and Bureau of Justice Statistics, *Probation and Parole in the United States, 1998* (Washington: U.S. Department of Justice, August 1999).

*Diversion and Probation: Alternatives to Imprisonment*

per month. According to a 1998 report by the Bureau of Justice Statistics, more than three-quarters of probationers maintain regular contact with a probation agency.[3] The rest are not required to have regular contact or cannot be located.

## Reasons for and Goals of Probation

Probation is used for at least four reasons. First, probation permits the offender to remain in the community for reintegration purposes. Offender reintegration is more likely to occur if social and family ties are not broken by incarceration.

Second, probation avoids prison institutionalization and the stigma of incarceration. Prison institutionalization is the process of learning the norms and culture of institutional living. It is an artificial environment and not helpful to teaching prisoners how to adjust to the free world. Probationers never experience prison institutionalization, nor do they have to worry about the negative labeling effects of being treated like a prisoner, which decreases even further a prisoner's ability to function as a law-abiding citizen when released.

The third reason to have probation is that it is less expensive than incarceration, more humanitarian, and at least as effective in reducing future criminal activity as is incarceration.

The final reason in favor of probation is that it is fair and appropriate sentencing for offenders whose crime does not merit incarceration. Furthermore, probation is the base from which more severe punishments can be built. Not all crimes deserve incarceration, nor do all crimes deserve probation. Probation is preferred when the offender poses no threat to community safety, when community correctional resources are available, and when probation does not unduly deprecate the seriousness of the offense. The probation risk-needs assessment and statutory sentencing guidelines help identify which offenders deserve community or institutional punishment.

The goals of probation reflect society's values. In the 1960s, when society showed a strong interest in social welfare and offender rehabilitation, probation work reflected that emphasis. Today, probation emphasizes offender control. Most probation programs share five objectives:

1. Protect the community by preparing the presentence investigation (PSI) report to assist judges in sentencing and supervising offenders. The PSI indicates the degree of risk an offender poses to the community. It also identifies the offender's special needs. Offenders posing a threat to the community are then given secure placement, usually incarceration. Offenders who do not pose a threat to the community are given probation supervision. We will return to the PSI later in this chapter.
2. Carry out sanctions imposed by the court. Probation officers accomplish this by educating offenders about the orders of the court, supervising offenders, and removing them from the community when they violate the conditions of their probation.
3. Conduct a risk-needs assessment to identify the level of supervision and the services probationers need.

**EXHIBIT 5-1**

## American Correctional Association

**ACA**

### Policy on Probation

Probation is a frequently used and cost-effective sanction of the court for enhancing social order and public safety. Probation may be used as a sanction by itself or, where necessary and appropriate, be combined with other sanctions such as fines, restitution, community service, residential care, or confinement. Agencies responsible for probation should:

**A.** Prepare disposition assessments to assist the court in arriving at appropriate sanctions. The least restrictive disposition consistent with public safety should be recommended;

**B.** Establish a case management system for allocating supervisory resources through a standardized classification process;

**C.** Provide supervision to probationers and, with their input, develop a realistic plan to ensure compliance with orders of the court;

**D.** Monitor and evaluate, on an ongoing basis, the probationer's adherence to the plan of supervision and, when necessary, modify the plan of supervision according to the changing needs of the offender and the best interests of society;

**E.** Provide access to a wide range of services to meet identifiable needs, all of which are directed toward promoting law-abiding behavior;

**F.** Assure any intervention in an offender's life will not exceed the minimal amount needed to assure compliance with the orders of the court;

**G.** Initiate appropriate court proceedings, when necessary, if the probationer fails to comply with orders of the court, supervision plan, or other requirements, so the court may consider other alternatives for the protection and well-being of the community;

**H.** Oppose use of the probation sanction for status offenders, neglected or dependent children, or any other individuals who are neither accused nor charged with delinquent or criminal behavior;

**I.** Establish an educational program for sharing information about probation with the public and other agencies; and

**J.** Evaluate program efficiency, effectiveness, and overall system accountability consistent with recognized correctional standards.

4. Support crime victims by collecting information about the impact the criminal offense had on the victim. This information, reported in a **victim-impact statement,** is presented to the court. The judge considers it when sentencing the offender. The information is particularly valuable for sentences that include restitution.

5. Coordinate and promote the use of community resources. Probation officers refer offenders to community agencies and programs that serve the offenders' needs. Such programs include drug and alcohol treatment, job training, vocational education, anger management, and life skills training.

Not all probation agencies achieve these objectives in the same way. A probation department's orientation is a function of many things, including department philosophy, leadership, the community served, and the offenders supervised. Some departments lean more toward treating the offender; others lean more toward offender control. Probably the majority of probation departments do both, depending on the need and the situation. The American Correctional Association Policy on Probation is found in Exhibit 5–1.

## History of Probation

Probation in America developed during the nineteenth century. Its origins, though, stem from English practices.

**English Origins** Beginning in the thirteenth century, **benefit of clergy** was used to give lesser sentences to clergymen and women from capital punishment and other severe sentences. To receive benefit of clergy, the accused were required to prove their literacy by reading in court the text of the Fifty-first Psalm. Soon the benefit of clergy was extended to anyone who could read (mostly the upper social classes). When the illiterate memorized the "neck verse," as it came to be called, and pretended to read it in court, use of the benefit declined. The practice was abolished by statute in 1827. It never really took hold in the American colonies.

**Judicial reprieve** became widespread in England in the nineteenth century. At first, judicial reprieve was a temporary suspension of sentence to allow a defendant to appeal to the king for a pardon. However, it developed into a *suspended sentence,* whereby punishment was never imposed. The suspended sentence was adopted in the United States, as early as 1830 in Boston. It became widespread in U.S. courts until the Supreme Court found it unconstitutional in 1916.[4] In that decision, which applied to federal courts only, the Court ruled that judges did not have the power to suspend sentences. The Court stated that Congress could authorize by law the temporary or indefinite suspension of sentences. That opinion gave rise to federal and state statutes authorizing probation.

**Probation Begins in America** It was in the Boston courtroom of Municipal Court Judge Peter Oxenbridge Thatcher, in 1830, that the groundwork for probation was laid. Searching for a new way to exercise leniency and to humanize the criminal law—sentencing goals that still dominate corrections—Judge Thatcher made the first recorded use of release on recognizance in America, in sentencing Jerusa Chase.

**victim-impact statement** A report to the court about the effects the offense had on the victim and/or survivors. The judge considers it when sentencing the offender.

**benefit of clergy** Practiced in England from the thirteenth century through the early nineteenth century, the release of clergymen and women from capital punishment when they proved their literacy by reading in court the text of the Fifty-first Psalm.

**judicial reprieve** A nineteenth-century English forerunner of probation; a temporary suspension, or delay, of sentence. The suspended sentence was adopted in the United States and was used frequently until the Supreme Court found it unconstitutional in 1916.

# THE STAFF SPEAKS

When I started as a probation officer in West Virginia, Martinson's "Nothing Works" study supported the philosophy that since rehabilitation and probation failed, the real answer to crime control was to "lock 'em up" for long periods of time. Nothing-works philosophy translated to the "truth in sentencing" perspective and widespread spending in the construction of new federal, state, and local prisons and jails. Probation and rehabilitation advocates were afraid that if they challenged the new philosophy, they would find themselves unemployed. In the 1970s, I helped develop the West Virginia Association of Probation Officers to improve the professionalism of probation in West Virginia. One of our aims was to consolidate probation under the West Virginia Supreme Court instead of having it under the Department of Welfare, the Department of Corrections, and the local courts. Today, probation comes under the West Virginia Supreme Court. Nationally, the American Probation and Parole Association has enhanced probation and community-based programs that have proved to be successful.

Juvenile programs administered by our department include mediation and arbitration for juveniles in which volunteers help resolve conflicts between juvenile offenders, their families, victims, and others. Alternative Learning Center programs provide education for violent juvenile offenders in off-school settings. Volunteers in Probation programs provide a mentor for every juvenile placed on probation. Adult programs include community probation officers for supervision and treatment and the supervision of community service work by offenders. I can honestly say that after 27 years as a probation officer, I am more energized than I have ever been, thanks to our success in the community. And, I know that the 21st century will confirm that probation and its community-based programs are an effective way to reduce crime, rehabilitate offenders, and bring peace to many households and communities.

*James R. Lee*
*Chief Probation Officer*
*First Judicial Circuit*
*Wellsburg, WV*

The indictment against Jerusa Chase was found at the January term of the court. . . . She pleaded guilty to the same and would have been pronounced at that time, but upon the application of her friends, and with the consent of the attorney of the Commonwealth, she was permitted, upon her recognizance for her appearance in this Court whenever she should be called for, to go at large.[5]

That release had many of the characteristics of present-day probation: suspension of sentence, freedom to stay in the community, conditions on that freedom, and the possibility of revocation of freedom for violation of the conditions.

In 1841—when John Augustus, a Boston shoemaker, became interested in the operation of the courts—the practice of probation began to emerge. Augustus was particularly sensitive to the problems of persons charged with alcohol-related offenses. By posting bail in selected cases, he had the offenders released to his care and supervision. Augustus carefully screened the offenders he sought to help. Here is an entry from his journal:

> In the month of August, 1841, I was in court one morning . . . in which [a] man was charged with being a common drunkard. The case was clearly made out, but before sentence was passed, I conversed with him for a few moments, and found that he was not yet past all hope of reformation. . . . He told me that if he could be saved from the House of Corrections, he never again would taste intoxicating liquors; there was such an earnestness in that one, and a look of firm resolve, that I determined to aid him; I bailed him, by permission of the Court. He was ordered to appear for sentence in three weeks; at the expiration of this period of probation, I accompanied him into the courtroom. . . . The Judge expressed himself much pleased with the account we gave of the man, and instead of the usual penalty—imprisonment in the House of Correction—he fined him one cent and costs, amounting in all to $3.76, which was immediately paid. The man continued industrious and sober, and without doubt has been by this treatment, saved from a drunkard's grave.[6]

So began the work of the nation's first probation officer, an unpaid volunteer.

By the time of his death in 1859, John Augustus had won probation for almost 2,000 adults and several thousand children. Several aspects of his probation system are still common. Augustus investigated the age, character, and work habits of each offender. He identified persons he thought redeemable. He made probation recommendations to the court. He developed conditions of probation. And he supervised offenders during their probation, which lasted, on the average, about 30 days. Until 1878, probation continued to be the work of volunteers—individuals and agencies.

**Early Probation Statutes**   In 1878 the Massachusetts legislature passed the first statute authorizing probation. The law applied only to Suffolk County (Boston). It required the mayor of Boston to appoint a probation officer from the police department or citizenry. In 1880 a new law authorized probation as an option in all cities and towns in Massachusetts. But because the law remained voluntary and the probation concept was still new, few cities and towns exercised the power. In 1891 the power to appoint probation officers was transferred from the mayor to the court, in response to criticism that the mayor's appointments were influenced by political considerations. The second state to pass a probation statute was Vermont, in 1898.

**HELP WANTED**

**Probation Officer Presentence Investigation Unit**

Processes referrals for psychological evaluation, physical examination, and drug/alcohol assessment as required. Collects all court-ordered information and reports in a timely manner. Composes an objective, comprehensive social-background report, completes a risk-needs assessment, attaches all relevant documents, and distributes the report. Requirements: Bachelor's degree in corrections, criminology, criminal justice, or a related field and two years' experience working in probation. Successful candidate will complete a 120-day orientation.

*Kurt Robak
Probation Officer
State of Minnesota*

*"This is the first job I have had that on Sunday nights I don't mind going to work Monday mornings."*

Kurt Robak has been a probation and parole officer for Kandiyohi County Community Corrections in Minnesota for five years. He supervises juvenile and adult offenders on probation and parole. His duties include enforcing court orders, conducting presentence investigations and bail studies, referring offenders for psychological evaluation and treatment, conducting random urinalysis, visiting offenders at home or work, monitoring offenders' restitution and fine payments, and reporting to the court on offenders' progress and compliance with court orders. Previously, he worked as a halfway house case manager for adult male felons and as a juvenile detention officer.

Kurt earned his bachelor's degree in corrections from Mankato State University. When he was a student, classes in probation and parole influenced him the most. He decided to work in corrections because he believed there would be something different to do each day. In his present job, his work schedule is flexible, leading, he says, to less job stress and more time with his family.

For Kurt, the best part about being a probation and parole officer is twofold: referring offenders to community agencies that help them with their problems—for example, domestic violence and alcohol and drug abuse—and holding them accountable for their behavior. He advises students who are thinking about making corrections a career to volunteer in a corrections agency while they're still in school and to do an internship as part of their studies. He believes that those experiences are effective on a résumé and also provide valuable preparation for paid work in the field. Furthermore, he recommends that after graduation students keep up with changes in their state's criminal code because criminal laws are always changing.

As more and more states passed laws authorizing probation, probation became a national institution. On March 4, 1925, probation in the federal courts was signed into law by President Coolidge.[7] The early laws had little in common. Some allowed probation for adults only. Others allowed it for juveniles only. (In fact, the spread of probation was accelerated by the juvenile court movement.) Some laws restricted the crimes for which probation could be granted. Still others provided for the hiring of probation officers, but neglected to provide for paying them. Training for probation officers was brief or nonexistent. Appointments were often based on politics rather than merit, and salaries were typically even lower than those of unskilled laborers. By 1925, probation was available for juveniles in every state; by 1956, it was available for adults in every state.

# Characteristics of Adults on Probation

On December 31, 1998, 3,417,613 adults were on federal, state, or local probation, an increase of 120,845 over 1997.[8] One out of every 60 persons age 18 or older is on probation. The average length of probation is 40 months. Figure 5–4 presents selected characteristics of adults on probation in 1998. For example, women made up 21 percent of the probation population. That is almost twice the percentage of women in jail (11%) and more than three times the percentage of women in prison (6.5%). Blacks represented more than a third of probationers, while Hispanics, who may be of any race, made up 15 percent of probationers. Other interesting findings about probationers are that more than half were sentenced for felony convictions, and 17 percent received sentences that included incarceration as well as probation. Such an arrangement is sometimes called a *split sentence.* As Figure 5–4 shows, almost two-thirds of probationers in 1998 successfully completed their probation.

Probationers who violate the conditions of their probation, or who are arrested for new offenses, may face disciplinary hearings. Such a disciplinary hearing, called a revocation hearing, may result in the issuance of an arrest warrant (if the probationer does not appear at the hearing), a sentence of incarceration, or reinstatement of probation with or without conditions.

Probationers who were unemployed were more likely to have had a disciplinary hearing (23%) than those who were employed (16%). Probationers who had a prior sentence were also more likely to have had a disciplinary hearing than those with no prior sentence (23% compared with

## FIGURE 5–4

### Selected Characteristics of Adults on Probation, 1998

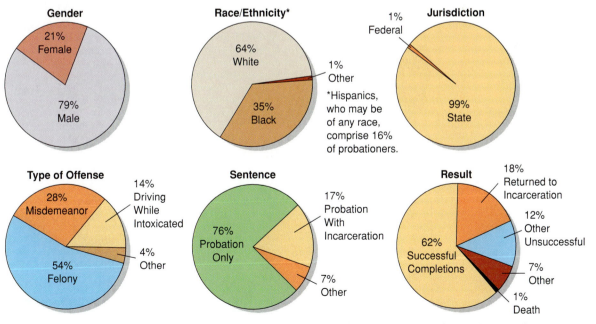

Source: Bureau of Justice Statistics, *Probation and Parole in the United States, 1998* (Washington: U.S. Department of Justice, August 1999).

15%). Of those probationers who had experienced a disciplinary hearing, the most frequent reason was absconding (hiding or leaving the jurisdiction) or failing to contact the probation officer (41%). The next most common reasons were arrest or conviction for a new offense (38%), failure to pay fines or restitution (38%), and failure to complete an alcohol or drug treatment program (22%).[9]

## Who Administers Probation?

As probation spread throughout the United States in the late nineteenth and early twentieth centuries, its organization and administration depended on local and state customs and politics. Currently, probation in the 50 states is administered by more than 2,000 separate agencies,[10] reflecting the decentralized and fragmented character of contemporary corrections. The agencies have a lot of common ground, but because they developed in different contexts, they also have a lot of differences in goals, policies, funding, staffing, salaries, and operation.

Probation is commonly considered a part of the correctional system, although it is technically a function of the court system. Figure 5–5 gives a state-by-state breakdown of how probation is administered. The map shows that in most states (31) the responsibility for adult probation rests with the state department of corrections. This means that one statewide agency administers a central probation system for adult offenders and provides ser-

### FIGURE 5–5

### Administration of Adult Probation in the States

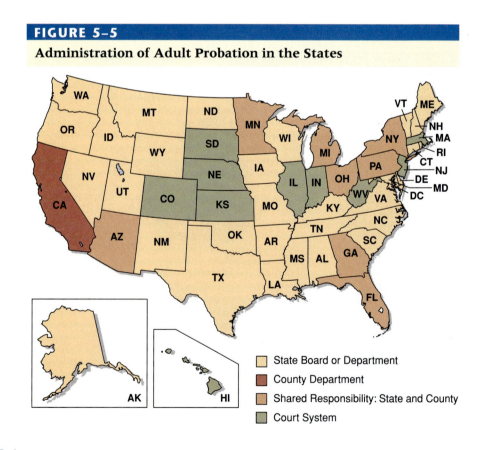

State Board or Department
County Department
Shared Responsibility: State and County
Court System

*Diversion and Probation: Alternatives to Imprisonment*

vices throughout the state. The second most common way of administering adult probation is through the court system. In ten states and the District of Columbia the responsibility for adult probation lies with the state judiciary. In eight states, the responsibility is shared by the state and the counties. In one state, counties provide adult probation services.

## What Probation Officers Do

Probation officers are more extensively involved with offenders and their cases—often starting at arrest—than any other criminal justice professionals. On January 1, 1998, there were 21,878 probation officers employed in the United States. There were more female employees (53%) than male employees.[11] Probation officers interact with many criminal justice agencies and influence many decisions affecting offenders. They do this in two major roles: case investigation and client supervision.

**Case Investigation** Investigation includes the preparation of a **presentence investigation report (PSI),** which the judge uses in sentencing an offender. The PSI is a report on the charge, conviction, and sentence recommendation, the offender's background and personal attributes, and statements from victims. It has two main purposes. First, it provides information to help the judge choose an appropriate sentence. That information concerns the offender's personal and social circumstances, motivations, and characteristics. The information is crucial because the judge's knowledge of the defendant is limited to what is presented at trial and what is contained in the presentence report. The judge uses the PSI to fashion a punishment that serves the purposes of offender rehabilitation and community protection. Research shows that judges follow the recommendation in the PSI 70 to 90 percent of the time.[12]

The second purpose of the PSI is to outline a treatment plan for the offender. During the investigation, besides determining the degree of risk the offender poses to the community, the probation officer identifies treatment needs so that the offender can receive appropriate services (counseling, treatment, education, community service, restitution, employment, and some form of supervision) during probation or in jail or prison.

In most cases, the court orders the PSI after conviction but before sentencing. The defendant reports to the probation department if released on bond pending sentencing. Otherwise, the probation officer visits the defendant in jail.

In addition to the PSI ordered by the court, the defendant or defense counsel may hire a private agency to prepare a PSI. A privately prepared PSI is sometimes called a **client-specific plan (CSP).** CSPs accomplish three things. First, they are an alternative source of information to judges. Second, they generally favor the defendant, encouraging greater use of treatment, counseling, education, community service, restitution, employment, and supervision. They may, however, call for the offender to pay a greater share of the cost of treatment. Third, they balance the PSIs prepared by government agencies.

**presentence investigation report (PSI)** A report on an offender's background and personal attributes. The purposes of the PSI are to help the court choose the most appropriate sentence and to outline a treatment plan.

**client-specific plan (CSP)** A privately prepared presentence investigation report that supplements the PSI prepared by the probation department.

The PSI starts with an interview between the probation officer (PO) and the defendant. The interview follows a structured format for obtaining information on the offense and the offender. The PO is expected to verify, clarify, and explore any information to be presented in the PSI. The PO may also talk with the victim. The PO is also expected to estimate the offender's degree of risk to the community. The estimate is based on the offender's lifestyle, prior criminal involvement, and experience with the criminal justice system. The PO summarizes the information gathered and, in most jurisdictions, makes a sentence recommendation. If the sentence recommended is incarceration, in most jurisdictions the length must be within guidelines set by statute (see Chapter 2). However, if the sentence recommended is probation or some other intermediate sanction (see Chapter 6), few jurisdictions have guidelines for sentence length. Only recently have states (for example, Delaware, North Carolina, and Pennsylvania) begun to design sentencing guidelines for nonprison sentences like probation. Copies of the PSI are filed with the court and made available to the judge, the prosecutor, and the defense attorney. Figure 5–6 is an example of a short-form federal PSI.

The quality of a PSI depends on the ability of the person who prepared it. In 1997, about 3,500 federal adult probation officers wrote 52,174 PSIs; on the state level, about 12,000 adult probation officers wrote 674,838 PSIs.[13] Judges give varying weight to different facts in the PSI when making the sentencing decision.

Today software packages can generate PSIs after probation officers enter data from official records and interviews.[14] The software programs can also calculate risk assessment scores. A PO can edit the report before submitting it to the court. Other computer programs help POs track fine and probation payments, alert them when their clients are behind on payments, and help them track whether probationers have satisfied the conditions of their sentences.

*Case investigation is one of a probation officer's major roles. What questions would you ask a crime victim as part of the investigation?*

**FIGURE 5-6**

Sample Presentence Investigation Report

IN THE UNITED STATES DISTRICT COURT
FOR THE NORTHERN DISTRICT OF ALABAMA

| | | |
|---|---|---|
| UNITED STATES OF AMERICA | ) | |
| | ) | PRESENTENCE INVESTIGATION |
| v. | ) | REPORT |
| | ) | |
| EDDIE PALMER | ) | Docket No. CR-98-H-248-S |

Prepared For:     Honorable Casandra Phillips
                  U. S. District Judge

Prepared By:      Noelle Koval
                  U. S. Probation Officer
                  Birmingham, AL
                  (205)555-0923

Offense:          Count One:          Possession With Intent to Distribute a
                                      Schedule II Controlled Substance (Cocaine
                                      Base), not less than 10 Years and not more
                                      than Life and/or $4,000,000 Fine. With
                                      Enhancement, Mandatory Life and/or
                                      $8,000,000 Fine.

Release Status:                       Released on $25,000 unsecured bond on 8/26/98.
                                      Remanded to custody on 12/14/98.

Identifying Data:

Date of Birth:    1/9/67
Age:              31
Race:             B
Sex:              M

Charge(s) and Conviction(s)

Eddie Palmer was indicted on two counts by the September 1995 Grand Jury for the Northern District of Alabama. Count One charged that on June 12, 1998, the defendant unlawfully possessed with intent to distribute approximately 500 grams of a mixture or substance containing a detectable amount of cocaine, Schedule II controlled substances, in violation of 21 USC § 841(a)(1). Count Two charged that on June 12, 1998, the defendant carried a firearm during the commission of a drug trafficking crime in violation of 18 USC § 924(c)(1). The October 1998 Grand Jury returned a superseding indictment in which the defendant was charged in two counts. Count One charges that

**FIGURE 5–6 (continued)**

Sample Presentence Investigation Report

on June 12, 1998, the defendant intentionally possessed with intent to distribute approximately 100 grams of a mixture or substance containing a detectable amount of cocaine base and approximately 240 grams of a mixture or substance containing a detectable amount of cocaine, Schedule II controlled substances, in violation of 21 USC § 841(a)(1). Count II charges that on June 12, 1998, the defendant carried a firearm during the commission of a drug trafficking crime in violation of 18 USC § 924(c)(1). On December 14, 1998, Palmer pled guilty to Count One, and Count Two was dismissed on motion of the government. Sentencing was continued generally to a later date.

Pretrial Adjustment

Mr. Palmer was released on a $25,000 unsecured bond on 8/26/98 with special conditions. One drug urinalysis was taken which was negative. Mr. Palmer ceased reporting in person on 10/6/98. He stated that people were looking for him and he was afraid to go out. The defendant had given information on a public corruption case. He was allowed to telephone report. On 12/14/98 Palmer was taken into custody following his plea of guilty pursuant to 18 USC § 3143.

Substance Abuse

Mr. Palmer relates that he started using marijuana around the age of 19. He quit using it for one year while he was in the TASC program. He then started back and quit when he got indicted on this case. He was smoking approximately two marijuana cigarettes per day. He first experimented with cocaine at the age of 20. He used cocaine a few times at the age of 22. Although he states that he did not use it again, test reports from TASC indicate that he had a positive for cocaine in June 1997 and again in July 1997. He went to TASC as a special condition of state probation from 1/3/97 to 2/14/98. He was considered to be making minimal effort to comply with TASC and was terminated after he completed his probation term. He also attended UAB Drug Free but was terminated on 9/13/97 for failure to comply. Additionally, Mr. Palmer previously reported to the state probation office that he had used LSD about ten times in 1987.

Education and Vocational Skills

Mr. Palmer attended El Camino Community College, Torrance, California, from 2/7/89 to 6/15/90. His scholastic standing was average. He was in the Vocational School and took courses in Cosmetology.

Employment Record

Mr. Palmer states that he opened SimplyClean Auto Salon, Inc., in 1993. He is the owner and has a monthly gross income of from $1,200 to $2,000 per month. This company washes, details, and repairs automobiles. Mr. Palmer lists his home address as the address of the company.

Mr. Palmer reports that when he initially moved to Alabama from L.A., he worked as a hairdresser out of his mother's home and was paid in cash. While in L.A., he worked for Simply Raw Beauty Salon in 1990 for approximately six months as a cosmetologist. He states that he worked for the

– 2 –

**FIGURE 5–6 (continued)**

**Sample Presentence Investigation Report**

L.A. County Art Museum, Beverly Hills, California, as a laborer earning minimum wage from April through July 1988. The Art Museum could find no record of Mr. Palmer ever working for them. Mr. Palmer states that he often did odd jobs and fixed hair to earn an income.

Mr. Palmer joined the U.S. Army on 9/30/86. He was discharged under honorable conditions on 1/13/88 as a Private, 2nd Class. The discharge was for misconduct which included frequent incidents of a discreditable nature with civil or military authorities.

Financial Condition: Ability to Pay

The following information was verified through a credit report, the Tax Assessor's office, reviewing some household bills, and DEA, who verified values of automobiles and other equipment and is proceeding on forfeiture.

Assets:

    Unencumbered Assets

        1985 FJ1100 Yamaha motorcycle, fair market value:   $ 1,500.00

    Equity in Other Assets

        Residence   21,000.00
        1988 Honda Accord   2,000.00

    Total Assets:   $24,500.00

Unsecured Debt:

    Attorney Fees   $10,000.00
    Medical Center East   4,000.00

    Total Unsecured Debt:   $14,000.00

NET WORTH:   $10,500.00

Monthly Cash Flow:

    Income:

        Net Profit From Business   $ 1,200.00
        Spouse's Salary   400.00

    Total Income:   $ 1,600.00

– 3 –

**FIGURE 5–6 (continued)**

Sample Presentence Investigation Report

Necessary Monthly Living Expenses:

| | |
|---|---:|
| Mortgage | $ 634.00 |
| Electricity | 80.00 |
| Gas | 50.00 |
| Water | 14.00 |
| Telephone | 150.00 |
| Groceries and Supplies | 200.00 |
| Life Insurance | 50.00 |
| Transportation | 50.00 |
| Medical | 300.00 |
| Clothing | 200.00 |
| Child Support | 400.00 |
| Monthly Installment Payments | 250.00 |
| | |
| Total Expenses: | $ 2,378.00 |
| | |
| Monthly Cash Flow: | $ -778.00 |

The above information represents the defendant's version of income and expenses. The mortgage payment and utilities were verified. Other expenses and income were not verified although verification was requested. The defendant claims to have filed income tax returns and stated that the information was with his attorney, Warren Skinner. Mr. Skinner was contacted about financial information but was not forthcoming. In fact, he prohibited the family from talking with me after the defendant pled guilty. Therefore, information may not be complete and is possibly inaccurate based on this lack of cooperation.

The bottom line is that it is very difficult to give an accurate reflection of the defendant's financial status. Based on his purported income from illegal activity, it is quite likely that there are other assets available to him. This cannot be stated as fact because it is frankly unknown.

Respectfully submitted,

*Noelle Koval*

Noelle Koval
U.S. Probation Officer

Approved:

*Frank Medina*  12/23/98

Frank Medina                    DATE
Supervising U.S. Probation Officer

– 4 –

**FIGURE 5-6 (continued)**

**Sample Presentence Investigation Report**

SENTENCING RECOMMENDATION

UNITED STATES DISTRICT COURT
FOR THE NORTHERN DISTRICT OF ALABAMA

UNITED STATES V. EDDIE PALMER      DOCKET NO. CR-98-H-248-S

TOTAL OFFENSE LEVEL:              29
CRIMINAL HISTORY CATEGORY:        III

|  | Statutory Provision | Guideline Provisions | Recommended Sentence |
|---|---|---|---|
| CUSTODY: | Mandatory Life | Mandatory Life | Life |
| PROBATION: | N/A | N/A | N/A |
| SUPERVISED RELEASE: | Not Less Than 10 Years | 10 Years | 10 Years |
| FINE: | $8,000,000 | $15,000 to $8,000,000 | $15,000 |
| RESTITUTION: | N/A | N/A | N/A |
| SPECIAL ASSESSMENT: | $50 | $50 | $50 |

Justification

The sentence of life is mandatory. Supervised release must be ten years. A $15,000 fine is recommended because it is incumbent upon the defendant to demonstrate that he does not have the financial ability to pay a fine. He and his attorney have not cooperated in providing information, and it appears that he does have the ability to pay the minimum fine based on his purported monthly income from trafficking in illegal drugs.

Voluntary Surrender

The defendant is in custody.

Respectfully submitted,

*Noelle Koval*

Noelle Koval
U.S. Probation Officer

– 5 –

## FIGURE 5–7

### Extent of Supervision by Assessed Risk Level

| High Risk Supervision | Close Risk Supervision | Intermediate Risk Supervision | Reduced Risk Supervision |
|---|---|---|---|
| 2 face-to-face contacts each day | 1 face-to-face contact each day | 1 face-to-face contact each week | 1 face-to-face contact each month |
| 2 drug tests each week | 2 drug tests each week | 1 drug test each week | no drug tests |

**supervision** The second major role of probation officers, consisting of intervention, surveillance, and enforcement.

**Supervision**   The second major role of probation officers is client supervision. Probation **supervision** has three main elements: intervention, surveillance, and enforcement. *Intervention* means providing offenders access to a wide variety of services, such as counseling, employment, and education. *Surveillance* means monitoring the activities of probationers through office meetings, home and work visits, drug and alcohol testing, and contact with family, friends, and employers. *Enforcement* means making probationers accountable for their behavior and making sure they understand the consequences of violating the conditions of probation. The average PO in the United States supervises approximately 175 offenders. In California, POs have caseloads of 900, and as many as 60 percent of probationers are tracked solely by computer, having no contact with a PO. In Atlanta, some POs supervise as many as 650 men and women. Such large caseloads do not allow probation officers time for adequate intervention, surveillance, or enforcement.

Even in average caseloads, not all offenders are supervised. Rather, probation officers use a variety of risk classification instruments to determine the level of supervision a probationer needs. A typical risk assessment might use four levels: high risk, close risk, intermediate risk, and reduced risk. The nature and amount of supervision are matched to the risk level. Figure 5–7 shows typical supervision plans matched to risk level.

### Does Probation Work?

**recidivism** The repetition of criminal behavior; generally defined as re-arrest. The primary outcome measure for probation, as it is for all corrections programs.

The most common question asked about probation is, Does it work? In other words, Do persons granted probation refrain from further crime? **Recidivism**—generally defined as re-arrest—continues to be the primary outcome measure for probation, as it is for all corrections programs. Summaries of probation effectiveness usually report the recidivism rates of felons as if felons represented the total adult probation population, instead of 55 percent of it.[15] Failure to distinguish between felons and misdemeanants explains the differing opinions about whether probation "works."

Recidivism rates vary greatly from place to place, depending on the seriousness of offenses, average length of probation, and the amount and quality of intervention, surveillance, and enforcement. A summary of 17 studies of adult felony probationers found that felony re-arrest rates ranged from 12 to 65 percent.

The American Probation and Parole Association (APPA), representing U.S. probation officers nationwide, argues that recidivism rates measure just

*At probation automated monitoring kiosks, probationers check in by handprint or ID card to answer questions about their progress. These machines are used in some areas to supervise low-risk offenders who do not require face-to-face contact with a probation officer. What advantages and disadvantages do you see in this approach?*

one probation task while ignoring others. The APPA has urged its member agencies to collect data on other outcomes, such as the following:

- amount of restitution collected
- number of offenders employed
- amounts of fines and fees collected
- hours of community service performed
- number of treatment sessions attended
- percentage of financial obligations collected
- rate of enrollment in school
- number of days of employment
- educational attainment
- number of days drug-free

Advocates of measures other than recidivism tell us that probation should be measured by what offenders do while they are in probation programs, not by what they do after they leave.

## Probation in the 21st Century

The American public understands that not all criminals can be locked up. Doubts are being raised about allocating a significant proportion of tax dollars to prisons. Pouring billions of dollars into operating costs and new prison construction ($24.5 billion in 1996) and seeing no reduction in crime will slowly move the public to reassess attitudes toward punishment.

Research also shows that citizens are less punishment-oriented than many political leaders believe. For example, in surveys conducted in Pennsylvania, Delaware, and Alabama, the Public Agenda Foundation of New York City found that "when the public is made aware of the possible range of punishments, and given information about how and with whom they are used, they support alternatives to incarceration—including punishments administered in the community—for offenders considered nonviolent and low risk."[16]

Policymakers are urging probation departments to implement credible and effective community-based sentencing options. But how can such options be made credible and effective? We conclude this chapter with five suggestions.

**Implement High-Quality Programs and Enforce Them**   Over the past few decades, many jurisdictions have added new kinds of probation sanctions, such as house arrest, electronic monitoring, boot camp, and intensive supervision. These sanctions are designed to be tougher than regular probation but less severe and less expensive than prison. To work, the new conditions must be backed up by mechanisms to ensure compliance.

**Invest Adequate Resources in Treatment and Surveillance**   When probationers receive *both* surveillance (e.g., unannounced contact and random drug tests) and treatment, recidivism can decline by one-third.[17] However, treatment and surveillance cost money. Adequate funding will be available only if the public believes that new supervision conditions are punitive as well as effective in reducing crime.

**Demonstrate That Probation Is Tough on Crime**   Policymakers say they send large numbers of persons to prison because the public wants to be tough on crime. But there is a groundswell of evidence that tough punishment may no longer equate with prison.[18] Some offenders see probation as more punitive and restrictive than prison. For example, researchers in Texas and Oregon gave offenders the choice of serving a prison term or serving probation with mandatory drug testing, community service, employment, counseling, and frequent visits with a probation officer. In Oregon, 25 percent of those eligible for probation chose prison. In Texas, many offenders described common prison terms as less punitive than even three to five years on probation. Prison was more attractive than the pressures of close supervision. The public must be convinced that probation sanctions can be just as punitive as prison. And the choice of probation or prison should be for the judge to make, not the offender.

**Target Drug Offenders**   Drug offenders are prime candidates for tough probation programs. Research has revealed the different risks and needs of traffickers, addicts, and low-level users.[19] The new knowledge is resulting in different laws and punishment strategies for different kinds of drug offenders. Many Americans prefer prison sentences for drug traffickers but are willing to accept something other than prison for other drug offenders.

**technical violation**
A failure to fulfill the conditions of probation—attending counseling, paying restitution, contacting the probation officer—rather than the commission of a new offense.

**Make Probation Research a Priority**   With over 3.4 million adults under probation supervision today, probation research should be a priority. It would be useful for probation research to assess the value of revoking probation for persons who commit technical violations. A **technical violation** is a failure to fulfill the conditions of probation—attending counseling, pay-

*Diversion and Probation: Alternatives to Imprisonment*

My first PO was a man who had years of experience. He was cynical. He took his job too seriously. I cooperated and soon he trusted me. His requirements were few. I was rarely asked to report at his office, and he would call to let me know he was coming to my home for a visit.

After several months, I was assigned a female PO. I was required to give urine samples under her observation. That bothered me, because I had no history of substance abuse. The purpose of these samples seems to have been to humiliate me. I wondered why the feds wanted to be in the business of humiliating people!

Being on supervised release was no big deal, as long as I sent in my monthly reports and got permission to travel outside the district (which meant ten miles to the north and twelve miles to the west). At my request, my second PO processed the forms for my release from supervision one year ahead of schedule. My cooperation paid off.

I don't know if federal probation reduces crime. But I do think that probation should be used more often, instead of incarceration, with community service. I think most prison sentences are too long and disruptive to families. I also think that all efforts should be made to support an offender's attempts to straighten out his or her life. The entire "justice" system needs to become caring and compassionate, putting more people into treatment and job programs than into prison.

Did probation disrupt my life? Yes. But I committed a crime and accepted probation willingly. Still, I think that it was wasteful, since once the feds realized that I had paid my fine off early, had no drug problems, kept a stable work record, and was cooperative, they might have saved us all some money by letting me off even sooner than they did.

*Anonymous female,*
*previously on federal probation*

ing restitution, contacting the probation officer—rather than the commission of a new offense.

Technical violations are a serious matter. Judges need assurance that probationers will be held accountable for their behavior, and the public needs assurance that probation sanctions are punitive. More research is needed, however, on the relationship of technical violations to criminal behavior. For example, what types of conditions are imposed? How do those conditions manage offenders, encourage rehabilitation, and protect the community? What are the trends in the number of technical violators and the effect on jails and prisons? What innovative programs, policies, and statutes have emerged in other jurisdictions to deal with technical violators?

# 5

# Review and Applications

## SUMMARY BY CHAPTER OBJECTIVE

### CHAPTER OBJECTIVE 1

Diversion is the official halting or suspension, before conviction, of formal criminal proceedings against a person, often conditioned on some form of counter performance, such as participation in a treatment, counseling, or educational program. Diversion is intended to (1) prevent future criminal activity by diverting certain defendants from criminal justice processing into community supervision and service, (2) save prosecution and judicial resources for serious crimes by offering alternatives to the usual prosecution process for less serious ones, and (3) provide, where appropriate, a vehicle for restitution to communities and victims of crime.

### CHAPTER OBJECTIVE 2

There are four rationales for diversion: (1) Formal processing can encourage more criminal behavior. (2) Diversion is cheaper than formally processing an offender through the criminal justice system. (3) Formal processing may seem inappropriate for crimes without perceived victims. (4) Formal arrest, trial, and conviction add to the burdens of certain disadvantaged groups.

### CHAPTER OBJECTIVE 3

Diversion may occur at any stage in the criminal justice process after a criminal complaint has been filed or police have observed a crime. Common diversion programs involve offenses related to drugs or alcohol.

### CHAPTER OBJECTIVE 4

Issues concerning diversion include (1) the legal and ethical issues of protecting a defendant's rights; (2) the law enforcement question whether diversion encourages violation of the law; and (3) the economic question of diversion's cost-effectiveness.

### CHAPTER OBJECTIVE 5

Probation is the conditional release of a convicted offender into the community, under the supervision of a probation officer. Most probation programs are designed to (1) protect the community by assisting judges in sentencing and supervising offenders, (2) carry out sanctions imposed by the court, (3) help offenders change, (4) support crime victims, and (5) coordinate and promote the use of community resources.

### CHAPTER OBJECTIVE 6

Probation is used for four reasons: (1) It permits offenders to be reintegrated into the community. (2) It avoids institutionalization and the stigma of incarceration. (3) It is less expensive than incarceration and more humanitarian. (4) It is appropriate for offenders whose crimes do not necessarily merit incarceration.

### CHAPTER OBJECTIVE 7

On December 31, 1998, federal, state, and local probation agencies supervised 3.4 million adult U.S. residents, with felony convictions accounting for more than half (54%). Twenty-one percent of all probationers were women, and 64 percent of probationers were white. Seventy-six percent of adults received sentences of probation only.

### CHAPTER OBJECTIVE 8

In 31 states, adult probation services are administered by the state department of corrections. In 10 states and the District of Columbia, the responsibility for adult probation lies with the state judiciary. In 8 states, the responsibility is shared by the state and the counties. In 1 state, counties provide adult probation services.

### CHAPTER OBJECTIVE 9

Probation investigation and supervision are the two major roles of probation officers. Investigation includes the preparation of a presentence investigation report (PSI), which the judge uses in sentencing an offender. Supervision includes the functions of intervention, surveillance, and enforcement.

## CHAPTER OBJECTIVE 10

Recidivism rates are low for adults on probation for misdemeanors. However, recidivism rates are high for felony probationers, particularly in jurisdictions that use probation extensively, offer probation for serious offenses, and provide minimal supervision because of high caseloads. Corrections professionals urge evaluators to collect data on outcomes other than recidivism, such as amount of restitution collected, number of offenders employed, amounts of fines and fees collected, hours of community service, number of treatment sessions, percentage of financial obligations collected, rate of enrollment in school, number of days employed, educational attainment, and number of days drug-free.

## CHAPTER OBJECTIVE 11

A number of issues face probation in the twenty-first century. One is the challenge of implementing credible and effective community-based sentencing options. Our suggestions for meeting that challenge are as follows: (1) Implement high-quality programs and enforce them. (2) Invest adequate resources in treatment and surveillance. (3) Demonstrate that probation is tough on crime. (4) Target drug offenders. (5) Make probation research a priority.

## KEY TERMS

diversion, p. 125
counter performance, p. 125
true diversion, p. 125
minimization of penetration, p. 125
unconditional diversion, p. 128
conditional diversion, p. 128
probation, p. 130
victim-impact statement, p. 133

benefit of clergy, p. 133
judicial reprieve, p. 133
presentence investigation report (PSI), p. 139
client-specific plan (CSP), p. 139
supervision, p. 146
recidivism, p. 146
technical violation, p. 148

## QUESTIONS FOR REVIEW

1. What is *diversion*?
2. Describe the different types of diversion and the stages at which they occur.
3. What are three objectives of diversion?
4. What are the four rationales for diversion?
5. At what stage of the criminal justice process does diversion occur?
6. Discuss three diversion policy issues.
7. What is *probation*?
8. Trace the English origins of probation.
9. How did probation originate in the United States?
10. When did federal probation begin?
11. What were some of the characteristics of adults on probation in 1998?
12. What are the four ways adult probation is administered? Which is the most common?
13. What are the two most important roles of probation officers for adults?
14. What is the presentence investigation? What is its purpose?
15. List the elements of probation supervision.
16. What do we know about probation recidivism for misdemeanants? For felons?
17. What measures are there of probation effectiveness, besides recidivism?
18. What issues face adult probation in the United States in the twenty-first century?

# CRITICAL THINKING EXERCISES

## ON-THE-JOB ISSUES

1. The new diversion program in your county was developed to help first-time misdemeanor drug offenders avoid incarceration and seek help in controlling their dependency. Your job as the new diversion officer is to set the conditions of the diversion program and then monitor and enforce compliance. One of your first clients fails the required weekly drug test. Should you immediately remove that person from the program?

2. While you are conducting an interview for a PSI, the defendant reveals details of the offense that did not come out during the trial. The defendant also implicates others, who have not been charged with the crime. What should you do?

3. At a recent staff meeting, the chief probation officer reports that the department's recidivism rate exceeded the national average by five percent. The chief asks what can be done about it. You speak up and say, "Look at other measures." The chief asks you to explain.

## CORRECTIONS ISSUES

1. Critics of PSIs claim that the information in them is not always verified or reliable. Actually, much of the information in a PSI is hearsay. Although defendants or victims may object to the contents of a PSI or the way it characterizes their behavior, they have no right to have the PSI reflect their views. As a probation officer, how would you respond to these criticisms?

2. Recidivism is one current measure of probation effectiveness. Others include the amount of restitution collected, the number of offenders employed, the amounts of fines and fees collected, the number of hours of community service performed, the number of treatment sessions completed, the percentage of financial obligations collected, the rate of school enrollment, the level of educational attainment, the number of days employed, and the number of days drug-free.

   a. In comparison with other measures, how important to you, as a taxpayer, is recidivism as a measure of program success?

   b. Do you believe probation officers can really keep offenders from committing new crimes or violating the conditions of their probation?

   c. If you were a probation officer today, by which outcome measures would you want to be judged? Why?

   d. If recidivism is used as a measure of probation's effectiveness, how should it be defined?

# CORRECTIONS ON THE WEB

1. Most probation agencies—whether administered by the state, a county, the state and a county, or the court system—have Web pages. Using the information in Figure 5–5, try to find the Web page of one probation agency for each of the four methods of administration. What difference, if any, does the type of administration make in philosophy, mission, goals, structure, resources, and so forth? Look at the Web page of the Los Angeles County Probation Department (**http://www.co.la.ca. us/probation**) as an example to get started.

2. In 1994 the Consolidated Edison Company (Con Ed) of New York entered a guilty plea in federal court to charges that it had covered up the release of 200 pounds of asbestos by a steam pipe explosion in New York City on August 19, 1989. Con Ed was sentenced to a $2 million fine plus three years' probation. As a condition of probation, Judge Martin required Con Ed to submit to an ongoing review. Access **http://www.essential.org/ monitor/hyper/mm1097.04.html**. Read the reports and determine whether Con Ed has fulfilled the judge's requirements.

## ADDITIONAL READINGS

Abadinsky, Howard. *Probation and Parole: Theory and Practice*. Englewood Cliffs, NJ: Prentice-Hall, 1994.

Boswell, Gwyneth. *Contemporary Probation Practice*. Aldershot, England: Avebury, 1993.

Carter, Robert M., Daniel Glaser, and Leslie T. Wilkins (eds.). *Probation, Parole, and Community Corrections*. New York: Wiley, 1984.

Ellsworth, Thomas (ed.). *Contemporary Community Corrections*. Prospect Heights, IL: Waveland Press, 1992.

Petersilia, Joan. *Granting Felons Probation: Public Risks and Alternatives*. Santa Monica, CA: Rand Corp., 1985.

## ENDNOTES

1. B. J. George, "Screening, Diversion and Mediation in the United States," *New York Law School Law Review*, Vol. 29 (1984), pp. 1–38.

2. Thomas P. Bonczar, *Characteristics of Adults on Probation, 1995* (Washington: U.S. Department of Justice, Bureau of Justice Statistics, 1997). Online, available: http://www.ojp.usdoj.gov/bjs/pub/ascii/cap95.txt.

3. Bureau of Justice Statistics, *Nation's Probation and Parole Population Reached New High Last Year* (Washington: BJS, August 16, 1998).

4. *Ex parte United States*, 242 U.S. 27 (1916).

5. John Augustus, *A Report of the Labors of John Augustus, For the Last Ten Years, In Aid of the Unfortunate* (Boston: Wright and Hasty, 1852); reprinted as *John Augustus, First Probation Officer* (New York: National Probation Association, 1939), p. 26.

6. Ibid., pp. 4–5.

7. Sanford Bates, "The Establishment and Early Years of the Federal Probation System," *Federal Probation*, Vol. 14 (1950), pp. 16–21; Joel R. Moore, "Early Reminiscences," *Federal Probation*, Vol. 14 (1950), pp. 21–29; and Richard A. Chappell, "The Federal Probation System Today," *Federal Probation*, Vol. 14 (1950), pp. 30–40.

8. All the data in this section are from Bonczar, and Bureau of Justice Statistics, *Probation and Parole in the United States, 1998* (Washington: U.S. Dept. of Justice, Bureau of Justice Statistics, August 1999).

9. Bonczar, pp. 9–10.

10. Howard Abadinsky, *Probation and Parole: Theory and Practice* (Englewood Cliffs, NJ: Prentice-Hall, 1987), p. 21.

11. Camille Graham Camp and George M. Camp, "Categories of Probation and Parole Employees on 1/1/98," in *The Corrections Yearbook, 1998* (Middle-town, CT: Criminal Justice Institute, 1998), pp. 199–200.

12. Comptroller General of the United States, *State and Local Probation: Systems in Crisis* (Washington: U.S. Government Printing Office, 1976).

13. Camp and Camp, p. 179.

14. Jon'a Meyer, "Tradition and Technology: Computers in Criminal Justice," in Laura J. Moriarty and David L. Carter (eds.), *Criminal Justice Technology in the 21st Century* (Springfield, IL: Charles C. Thomas, 1999), pp. 3–16.

15. Bureau of Justice Statistics.

16. William H. DiMascio, *Seeking Justice: Crime and Punishment in America* (New York: Edna McConnell Clark Foundation, 1997), p. 43.

17. Paul Gendreau, "The Principles of Effective Intervention With Offenders," in Alan Harland (ed.), *Choosing Correctional Options That Work: Defining the Demand and Evaluating the Supply* (Thousand Oaks, CA: Sage, 1996).

18. See, for example, Joan Petersilia and Susan Turner, *Evaluating Intensive Supervision Probation/Parole: Results of a Nationwide Experiment* (Washington: National Institute of Justice, 1993); Ben Crouch, "Is Incarceration Really Worse? Analysis of Offenders' Preferences for Prison Over Probation," *Justice Quarterly*, Vol. 10 (1993), pp. 67–88; Joan Petersilia and Elizabeth Piper Deschenes, "Perceptions of Punishment: Inmates and Staff Rank the Severity of Prison Versus Intermediate Sanctions," *The Prison Journal*, Vol. 74 (1994), pp. 304–328.

19. Stanley W. Hodge and Victor E. Kappler, "Can We Continue to Lock Up the Nonviolent Drug Offender?" in Charles B. Fields, *Controversial Issues in Corrections* (Boston: Allyn & Bacon, 1999), pp. 137–151.

# 6 Intermediate Sanctions
## Corrections in the Community

> *Crime and bad lives are the measure of a State's failure; all crime in the end is the crime of the community.*
>
> —H. G. Wells

**intermediate sanctions**
New punishment options developed to fill the gap between traditional probation and traditional jail or prison sentences and to better match the severity of punishment to the seriousness of the crime.

**community corrections**
A philosophy of correctional treatment that embraces (1) decentralization of authority, (2) citizen participation, (3) redefinition of the population of offenders for whom incarceration is most appropriate, and (4) emphasis on rehabilitation through community programs.

It has been estimated that someday as many as 1 million adult and juvenile offenders in the United States will be under some form of electronic house arrest. This projection is not unthinkable. In 1984 there were no offenders in the United States under electronic home confinement. In 1992 there were 45,000! If that rate continues, 90,000 offenders may be under electronic home detention in 2000 and over 200,000 in 2025.

Electronic home detention is quickly taking a place on the growing continuum of sanctions between probation and jail or prison. Called **intermediate sanctions,** the new options fill the gap between traditional probation and traditional jail or prison sentences and better match the severity of punishment to the seriousness of the crime. Intermediate sanctions fulfill all the goals of sentencing: retribution, deterrence, incapacitation, rehabilitation, and restoration. Because intermediate sanctions are administered outside prison or jail, and generally in the offender's community, they are a form of **community corrections.** After looking at the principal intermediate sanctions in use in the United States, we will turn our attention to community corrections in general.

# Intermediate Sanctions

Sanctions less restrictive than prison but more restrictive than probation are not new. Variations of restitution, fines, and community service were used as sentences in ancient Israel, Greece, and Rome.[1] More recent intermediate sanctions—such as electronic house arrest, boot camps, and day fines—started in the 1980s. What is new today is the effort to bring all

## FIGURE 6–1

### Intermediate Sanctions

| | Intensive Supervision Probation (ISP) | Restitution, Fines, and Day Fines | Community Service | Day Reporting |
|---|---|---|---|---|
| **Probation** | Control of offenders in the community under strict conditions, through frequent reporting to a probation officer with a limited caseload. | Regular payments to crime victims or to the courts. Used alone or in conjunction with probation or ISP. | Completion of a set number of hours of work in and for the community. Used alone or in conjunction with probation or ISP. | Reporting to a central location every day to file a schedule with the supervision officer, showing how each hour will be spent. |

*Source:* Adapted from William M. DiMascio, *Seeking Justice: Crime and Punishment in America* (New York: Edna McConnell Clark Foundation, 1997), pp. 32–33.

*Intermediate Sanctions: Corrections in the Community*

of these sanctions together into a comprehensive sentencing system like the one suggested in Figure 6–1 that provides judges with an expanded menu of corrections options.

Advocates for more effective sentencing practices include the American Jail Association (see Exhibit 6–1 on page 158). They call for a range or continuum of sanctions with graduated levels of supervision and harshness. Simple probation is at one end, traditional incarceration is at the other, and a variety of intermediate sanctions bridge the middle ground. This type of sentencing enables criminal justice officials to reserve expensive prison and jail space for violent offenders. It gives nonviolent offenders less restrictive intermediate sanctions and restitution-focused sentences while teaching them accountability for their actions and heightening their chances for rehabilitation. This approach to sentencing treats prisons as the backstop, not the backbone, of the corrections system.

Intermediate sanctions are most often used for offenders considered nonviolent and of low risk. They usually require the offender to lead a productive life in the community by working, finding work if unemployed, or learning new job skills; to do unpaid community service; to pay restitution to victims; to enroll in a treatment or educational program—or sometimes to do all of these.

Intermediate sanctions are sometimes referred to as *front-end* programs or strategies. **Front-end programs** are options for initial sentences that are more restrictive than traditional probation but less restrictive than jail or prison. They are usually designed to limit the number of persons who go to prison. In front-end programs, judges commonly sentence offenders directly to one or a combination of intermediate sanctions. **Back-end programs** are reduced restrictions for offenders who have made progress in compliance and treatment. In back-end programs, offenders are moved from higher to lower levels of control to complete the final phase of their sentences. For example, the state department of corrections may move an offender from prison to electronic house arrest.

**front-end programs**
Punishment options for initial sentences more restrictive than traditional probation but less restrictive than jail or prison.

**back-end programs**
Sanctions that move offenders from higher levels of control to lower ones for the final phase of their sentences.

## FIGURE 6–1 (continued)

### Intermediate Sanctions

| House Arrest and Electronic Monitoring | Residential Community Centers | Boot Camp | Jail or Prison |
|---|---|---|---|
| Restriction of offender to home except when at work, school, or treatment. Used in conjunction with ISP. | Residential settings for selected offenders as a supplement to probation. Usually linked with community service or substance abuse treatment. | Rigorous military-style regimen for younger offenders, designed to accelerate punishment while instilling discipline. Often with an educational component. | |

EXHIBIT 6–1

## American Jail Association Resolution

### Intermediate Punishments

WHEREAS, the American Jail Association (AJA) recognizes the detrimental impact that crowding places on local jails; and

WHEREAS, many of those who are incarcerated in jails do not pose a known danger to themselves or to society;

THEREFORE BE IT RESOLVED THAT AJA supports the expansion of intermediate punishments in states and localities throughout America for offenders who do not pose a known danger to public safety. AJA believes that intermediate punishments address real concerns of constituents.

**net-widening** Increasing the number of offenders sentenced to a greater level of restriction. It results in the sentencing of offenders to more restrictive sanctions than their offenses and characteristics warrant.

Front-end programs tend to draw more heavily from offenders who would otherwise receive less restrictive sentences than from those who would otherwise go to jail or prison. In that way, they contribute to **net-widening**. Net-widening means increasing the number of offenders sentenced to a greater level of restriction. As a result, many offenders may receive more restrictive sentences than their offenses and characteristics warrant. Community service, for instance, might be added to probation. Net-widening happens because judges have more alternatives to confinement for offenders that, in earlier times, they would have put on simple probation. The seductiveness of intermediate sanctions, especially those that provide discipline and structure for disruptive individuals, creates a real threat that large numbers of persons will receive intermediate sanctions, whether or not those sanctions are suitable.

## Value of Intermediate Sanctions

From 1985 through 1998, the number of persons confined in state and federal prisons and local jails skyrocketed 164 percent, from 744,208 in 1985 to 1,966,506 in 1998. This unprecedented growth in the nation's prisons and jails has placed a heavy economic burden on taxpayers. That burden includes the cost of building, maintaining, and operating prisons and jails, as well as the loss of offenders' contributions and the cost of caring for the destabilized families left behind. In addition, overcrowded jails and prisons are hard to manage and staff, and they invite disorder.

During the same period, new intermediate-sanction programs expanded rapidly across the United States, and the number of persons sentenced to them increased. The result has been an explosion in the number of persons under correctional supervision. Many intermediate sanctions were started with the goal of reducing the prison population. Though there has been no decline in the number of persons sentenced to prison since these new intermediate sanctions appeared, proponents argue that without the new programs, the number would be even larger. Other supporters say that by increasing the surveillance, punishment, and treatment of offenders under community supervision, intermediate sanctions achieve other correctional goals.

Intermediate sanctions are valuable for a number of reasons. First, they provide a means for offenders who are not dangerous to repay their victims and their communities. Second, intermediate sanctions promote rehabilitation—which most citizens want, but most prisons and jails find difficult to provide—and the reintegration of the offender into the community. And third, once the programs are in place, they can do these things at a comparatively low cost. Compare the lower costs of intermediate sanctions with jail and prison in Table 6–1.

Intermediate sanctions should not be haphazardly planned or implemented. High-quality intermediate sanctions must be thoughtfully conceived, effectively targeted, well planned, and well staffed. Intermediate sanctions bring the added difficulty of controlling an offender's behavior in the less restrictive setting of the free community. That is why one of the popular approaches to counseling in intermediate sanctions programs is behavior modification.

## TABLE 6–1

### Average Annual Cost of Correctional Options

| Correctional Options | Cost per Year per Participant |
| --- | --- |
| Prison | $20,261 |
| Boot Camp | 20,025 |
| Jail | 19,903 |
| Halfway House | 16,790 |
| Electronic Monitoring | 3,402 |
| Intensive Supervision | 3,270 |
| Day Reporting | 2,781 |
| Community Service | 2,759 |
| Parole | 1,690 |
| Probation | 1,153 |
| House Arrest | 402 |

Source: Adapted from *Seeking Justice: Crime and Punishment in America* (New York: Edna McConnell-Clark Foundation, 1997), p. 34 and Camille Graham Camp and George M. Camp, *The Corrections Yearbook, 1998* (Middletown, CT: Criminal Justice Institute, 1998), pp. 90–91, 248–249.

## Varieties of Intermediate Sanctions

The specific varieties of intermediate sanctions discussed in the following subsections include intensive-supervision probation, day fines, community service orders, day reporting centers, house arrest and electronic monitoring, residential community centers, and boot camps.

**intensive-supervision probation (ISP)** Control of offenders in the community, under strict conditions, by means of frequent reporting to a probation officer, whose caseload is generally limited to 30 offenders.

**Intensive-Supervision Probation** Intensive-supervision probation **(ISP)** is probation with frequent contact between offender and probation officer, strict enforcement of conditions, random drug and alcohol testing, and other requirements. As a technique for increasing control over offenders in the community, ISP has gained wide popularity. It allows offenders to live at home, but under more severe and more punitive restrictions than those of conventional probation. Requirements of ISP usually include performing community service, attending school or treatment programs, working or looking for employment, meeting with a probation officer (or team of officers) as often as five times a week, and submitting to curfews, employment checks, and tests for drug and alcohol use. Because of the frequency of contact, subjection to unannounced drug tests, and rigorous enforcement of restitution, community service, and other conditions, ISP is thought more appropriate for higher-risk offenders.

ISP was initially the most popular intermediate sanction. It has the longest history and has been the most extensively evaluated. Intensive-supervision programs exist in every state. They may be state or county programs and may be administered by parole, probation, or prison departments. As a result, it not easy to estimate the number of ISP programs in the United States.

In general, evaluators of ISP have concluded that offenders sentenced to ISP commit new crimes at about the same rate as comparable offenders receiving different sentences. Also, technical violation and revocation rates are typically higher for ISP participants because more frequent contact makes misconduct more likely to be discovered. Early proponents of ISP argued that ISP would reduce recidivism rates, rehabilitate offenders, and save money and prison resources. However, most evaluations suggest that the combination of net-widening, high revocation rates, and costs of processing revocations makes savings unlikely.[2]

There is one tantalizing positive finding about ISP: it increases participants' involvement in counseling and treatment programs. There is evidence that re-arrests are reduced when offenders receive treatment in addition to the increased surveillance and control of ISP programs. The literature demonstrates that participation in drug treatment, whether voluntary or compelled, can reduce both drug use and crime by drug-using offenders. Data indicate that in many cities, one-half to three-fourths of arrested felons are drug abusers; ISP holds promise as a device for getting addicted offenders into treatment and keeping them there.[3]

*Intensive-supervision probation officers conduct random drug tests on offenders at home and at work. What other controls are used to monitor offenders on ISP?*

*Intermediate Sanctions: Corrections in the Community*

I was so grateful my sentence was probation because I got three kids. Electronic monitoring meant I could stay home with them. It meant that they wouldn't be put into a foster home or something like that. It meant I could be sure they won't wind up like me. But when I need money, I can't just leave to get it. I can't leave to visit a friend or my mama. Can't visit my man, and he can't come here cause he's off limits for me. He's a violation like my brother. I hate that, but the alternatives are jail time and kids without their mama. It gets bad sometimes because I want to go out and have a good time. I got needs. But that ain't going to happen yet. I take in other kids to watch—washing and ironing, too. Chump money! But I was given a chance and for that I'm grateful. But those feds think they own me. My PO is cool, but he thinks he owns my life, too. Owns my time. Lost my man because of him. But I get to do what's right for my kids and me, and once this is over—I ain't gettin' a parking ticket! I hate being tied down. Hate the drug testing all the time. Hate the questions. But at night— I've got my kids and they got me.

*Anonymous*

Evaluation of the Florida Community Control Program (FCCP) by the National Council on Crime and Delinquency concluded that ISP graduates commit new crimes at a lower rate than a comparable group of offenders released from prison and that each FCCP participant saved the state $2750.[4]

To reap the benefits of ISP, what must be done is straightforward. Because recidivism rates for new crimes are no higher for ISP participants than for comparable imprisoned offenders, ISP is a cost-effective alternative to prison for offenders who do not present unacceptable risks to public safety. Cost savings are likely to depend, however, on using ISP only for offenders who would have received appreciable prison time. And technical violations require a range of responses, not a rush to incarcerate the violator. Incarcerating all violators cancels out the initial savings of ISP.

**Day Fines**   A **fine** is a financial sanction requiring a convicted person to pay a specified sum of money. The fine is one of the oldest forms of punishment. It is, in practice, the criminal justice tool for punishing minor misdemeanors, traffic offenses, and ordinance violations. To be effective, fines should be proportionate to the seriousness of an offense and should have roughly similar economic impacts on persons with differing financial resources who are convicted of the same offense. In the United States, fines are rarely regarded as a tough criminal sanction. They are not taken seriously, for at least four reasons. First, judicial, legislative, and prosecutorial attitudes restrict their use to traffic offenses, minor misdemeanors, and ordi-

**fine** A financial penalty used as a criminal sanction.

nance violations. Second, a judge seldom has enough reliable information on an offender's personal wealth to impose a just fine. Third, mechanisms for collecting fines are often ineffective. Far too often the responsibility for collecting fines has been left to probation officers, who were already overburdened and had no interest in fine collection. As a result, fines were seldom paid. Fourth, many believe that fines work hardship on the poor, while affluent offenders feel no sting.

In contrast, many northern and western European countries have made fines the sanction of choice in a high proportion of criminal cases, including many involving serious crimes. In the Netherlands, a fine is legally presumed to be the preferred sentence for every crime, either alone or in conjunction with another penalty. Judges there are required to provide a statement of reasons in every case in which a fine is *not* imposed. In Germany, since the mid-1980s, a large percentage (sometimes over 80 percent) of all adult criminals sentenced have been ordered to pay fines. In some years, almost 75 percent of those convicted of crimes of violence were ordered to pay fines. In Sweden, fines constitute about 90 percent of all sentences. In England, fines are included in about 50 percent of cases of those individuals convicted of indictable offenses (roughly equivalent to U.S. felonies).[5]

**day fine** A financial penalty scaled both to the defendant's ability to pay and to the seriousness of the crime.

A **day fine** is a financial penalty based on the seriousness of the crime and the defendant's ability to pay. It is called a day fine because it is based on the offender's daily income.

Day fines, also called *structured fines*, have been common in some northern and western European countries for many years. They were introduced in Sweden in the 1920s and were quickly incorporated into the penal codes of other Scandinavian counties. West Germany adopted day fines as a sentencing option in the early 1970s. Today these countries have made day fines the preferred punishment for most criminal cases, including those involving serious crimes. In Germany, for example, day fines are the only punishment for three-quarters of all offenders convicted of property crimes and two-thirds of offenders convicted of assaults.[6]

Day fines have been tried experimentally in some areas of the United States, including New York, Arizona, Connecticut, Iowa, and Oregon. Figure 6–2 is a sample notification of a structured fine program. The notice may be mailed to a defendant along with the summons or handed to the defendant when he or she appears in court.

To be effective, a day fine program must have the support of a cross-section of criminal justice professionals in a jurisdiction, as well as others who have a stake in the operation of the criminal justice system. According to a Bureau of Justice Assistance report[7] on day fines, the following officials should be involved in planning a county day fine program:

- the presiding judges of the general- and limited-jurisdiction courts
- a prosecutor
- a public defender
- a representative of the private defense bar
- a court administrator
- the director of a pretrial services agency
- the chief probation officer or the director of a community corrections agency

**FIGURE 6–2**

Sample Notification of a Structured Fine Program

## A PRELIMINARY COMPLAINT HAS BEEN FILED CHARGING YOU WITH AN INDICTABLE OFFENSE

IF CONVICTED, THE COURT <u>MAY</u> IMPOSE ONE OR MORE OF THE FOLLOWING SANCTIONS:

1. JAIL OR PRISON
2. PROBATION
3. A FINE

If a fine is imposed, the Court may <u>structure</u> the level of the fine partly according to the seriousness of the offense and partly in relation to your means or ability to pay the fine. This method of computing the amount of a "structured fine" is an effort by the Court and the Polk County Attorney's Office to <u>equalize</u> the impact of criminal sanctions and to <u>reduce</u> the number of persons who are sentenced to prison, jail, or formal probation.

In order for the County Attorney's Office to consider recommending a structured fine to the Court at the time of sentencing, you or your attorney must schedule an interview with a Structured Fines Officer at 555-1234, IMMEDIATELY. If you intend to secure an attorney to represent you on this charge, please make these arrangements prior to calling the Structured Fines Program.

Your ability to pay a structured fine, as well as the length of time needed to pay the fine, is based on the information you provide in the attached AFFIDAVIT OF FINANCIAL CONDITION. It is required that you and/or your attorney complete this form prior to meeting with a Structured Fines Officer. It is also required that you take to your meeting with the Structured Fines Officer verification of your income in the form of paycheck stubs, income tax returns, etc.

POLK COUNTY ATTORNEY'S OFFICE
STRUCTURED FINES PROGRAM
POLK COUNTY COURTHOUSE, ROOM B-40
DES MOINES, IOWA 50309
555-1234

Appointments with a Structured Fines Officer are available
Monday through Friday, from 1:30 p.m. - 4:30 p.m.

- the sheriff or another jail administrator
- representatives of county government

The planning process for introducing day fines will be unique for each jurisdiction, depending on its organizational structure, traditions, personalities, and local legal culture. Every jurisdiction, however, will have to address similar issues: current sentencing patterns, current fine collection operations and their effectiveness, goals and priorities for the day fine program, and potential legal challenges to the program.

Once a system for imposing day fines has been put in place, the next step is to develop a structured process for setting fines. This structured process is the feature that distinguishes day fines from traditional fines. The process usually has two parts: (1) a unit scale that ranks offenses by seriousness and severity and (2) a valuation scale for determining the dollar amount per unit for a given offender.

The first step in setting a day fine is to determine the number of fine units to be imposed. A portion of the unit scale used in a Staten Island, New York, day fine experiment is shown in Figure 6–3. The number of units ranges from a low of 5 to a high of 120, for the most serious misdemeanors handled by the court. For example, the presumptive number of units for the offense of assault with minor injury and aggravating factors is 70; the range is from 59 to 81 units. The presumptive number is the starting point. Negotiation and consideration of individual circumstances may raise or lower the number. There is no magic in the unit scale established. What is important is to establish a scale broad enough to cover the full range of offenses handled by the courts that will use structured fines.

Once the unit scale is established, the second step is to create a valuation table. The purpose of the valuation table is to establish the dollar amount of each fine. A portion of the valuation table used in the Staten Island experiment is shown in Figure 6–4. Net daily incomes run down the left side, and numbers of dependents run across the top. Net daily income is the offender's income (after-tax wages, welfare allowance, unemployment compensation, etc.) divided by the number of days in a payment period. Staten Island planners also adjusted the net daily income downward to account for subsistence needs, family responsibilities, and incomes below the poverty line.

Suppose a defendant convicted of assault, with minor injury and aggravating factors, has a net daily income of $15 and supports 4 persons, including herself. Find the row for her net daily income. Move across the row to the column for the number of dependents. The figure there is the value of one structured fine unit for that defendant. Multiply the number of fine units to be imposed (70) by the value of a single fine unit (3.38). The product, $236.60, is the amount of the day fine to be imposed.

The National Institute of Justice sponsored an evaluation of the Staten Island experiment. That evaluation showed that judges used day fines for many offenses for which they had formerly used fixed fine amounts—including some property crimes, drug possession, and assault.[8] Most judges cooperated with the new, voluntary scheme throughout the year-long experiment. Research showed that the average fine increased by 25 percent, from $206 before the experiment to $258 during the year day fines were

**FIGURE 6–3**

Example of Day Fine Unit Scale

### Staten Island Day Fine Unit Scale
### (Selected Offense Categories)

| Penal Law Charge* | Type of Offense** | Number of Day Fine Units Discount – PRESUMPTIVE - Premium |
|---|---|---|
| 120.00 AM | Assault 3: Range of 20-95 DF | |
| | A. Substantial Injury | 81 - **95** - 109 |
| | *Stranger-to-stranger; or where victim is known to assailant, he/she is weaker, vulnerable* | |
| | B. Minor Injury | 59 - **70** - 81 |
| | *Stranger-to-stranger; or where victim is known to assailant, he/she is weaker, vulnerable; or altercations involving use of a weapon* | |
| | C. Substantial Injury | 38 - **45** - 52 |
| | *Altercations among acquaintances; brawls* | |
| | D. Minor Injury | 17 - **20** - 23 |
| 110/120.00 BM | Attempted Assault 3: Range of 15-45 DF | |
| | A. Substantial Injury | 38 - **45** - 52 |
| | *Stranger-to-stranger; or where victim is known to assailant, he/she is weaker, vulnerable* | |
| | B. Minor Injury | 30 - **35** - 40 |
| | *Stranger-to-stranger; or where victim is known to assailant, he/she is weaker, vulnerable; or altercations involving use of a weapon* | |
| | C. Substantial Injury | 17 - **20** - 23 |
| | *Altercations among acquaintances; brawls* | |
| | D. Minor Injury | 13 - **15** - 17 |
| | *Altercations among acquaintances; brawls* | |

*AM = Class A Misdemeanor; BM = Class B Misdemeanor
**DF = Day Fines

*Source:* Bureau of Justice Assistance, *How to Use Structured Fines (Day Fines) as an Intermediate Sanction* (Washington: Bureau of Justice Assistance, 1996), p. 59.

used. If day fines had not been held low by state law, the average day fine would have been $440. The news on collections was also good. Eighty-five percent of the defendants in the day fine program paid their fines in full, compared with 71 percent in a control program using routine collection

## FIGURE 6–4

**Example of Day Fine Valuation Table**

### Staten Island, New York, Valuation Table
### Dollar Value of One Day Fine Unit, by Net Daily Income
### and Number of Dependents

| Net Daily Income($) | Number of Dependents (Including Self) | | | | | | | |
|---|---|---|---|---|---|---|---|---|
| | 1 | 2 | 3 | 4 | 5 | 6 | 7 | 8 |
| 3 | | 1.05 | 0.83 | 0.68 | 0.53 | 0.45 | 0.37 | 0.30 |
| 4 | 1.70 | 1.40 | 1.10 | 0.90 | 0.70 | 0.60 | 0.50 | 0.40 |
| 5 | 2.13 | 1.75 | 1.38 | 1.13 | 0.88 | 0.75 | 0.62 | 0.50 |
| 6 | 2.55 | 2.10 | 1.65 | 1.35 | 1.05 | 0.90 | 0.75 | 0.60 |
| 7 | 2.98 | 2.45 | 1.93 | 1.58 | 1.23 | 1.05 | 0.87 | 0.70 |
| 8 | 3.40 | 2.80 | 2.20 | 1.80 | 1.40 | 1.20 | 1.00 | 0.80 |
| 9 | 3.83 | 3.15 | 2.48 | 2.03 | 1.58 | 1.35 | 1.12 | 0.90 |
| 10 | 4.25 | 3.50 | 2.75 | 2.25 | 1.75 | 1.50 | 1.25 | 1.00 |
| 11 | 4.68 | 3.85 | 3.03 | 2.47 | 1.93 | 1.65 | 1.37 | 1.10 |
| 12 | 5.10 | 4.20 | 3.30 | 2.70 | 2.10 | 1.80 | 1.50 | 1.20 |
| 13 | 5.53 | 4.55 | 3.58 | 2.93 | 2.28 | 1.95 | 1.62 | 1.30 |
| 14 | 7.85 | 4.90 | 3.85 | 3.15 | 2.45 | 2.10 | 1.75 | 1.40 |
| 15 | 8.42 | 5.25 | 4.13 | 3.38 | 2.63 | 2.25 | 1.87 | 1.50 |

*Source:* Bureau of Justice Assistance, *How to Use Structured Fines (Day Fines) as an Intermediate Sanction* (Washington: Bureau of Justice Assistance, 1996), p. 64.

processes. Furthermore, when full payment was not made, partial payment was much more likely in the day fine cases than in cases from before the experiment or in the control group. Thus, the higher fines levied in the day fine cases did not make collection more difficult, and the new enforcement procedures independently improved collection rates.

There has been little research on the effectiveness of fines in reducing recidivism rates. However, since the use of fines could reduce the costs of courts and corrections, and since day fines address problems of inequality, fines are a promising intermediate sanction. At present, most Western justice systems, except the United States, rely heavily on financial penalties. In the next century, U.S. jurisdictions are likely to continue their experiments with monetary penalties and to assign them even greater importance.

**community service**

A sentence to serve a specified number of hours working in unpaid positions with nonprofit or tax-supported agencies.

**Community Service**  Community service is a sentence to serve a specified number of hours working in unpaid positions with nonprofit or tax-supported agencies.[9] Community service is punishment that takes away an offender's time and energy. Community service is sometimes called a "fine of time." Requiring offenders to compensate victims with their time or money was customary in ancient civilizations. The desire for compensation in time or money was probably at least as common then as the urge to retaliate.

Community service as a criminal sanction began in the United States in 1966 in Alameda County, California. Municipal judges there devised a community service sentencing program for indigent women who violated traffic and parking laws. Too poor to pay fines, these women were likely to be sentenced to jail. But putting them behind bars imposed a hardship on their families. Community service orders (CSOs) increased sentencing options, punished the offenders, lightened the suffering of innocent families, avoided the cost of imprisonment, and provided valuable services to the community. As Alameda judges gained experience with the new sentencing option, they broadened the program to include male offenders, juveniles, and persons convicted of crimes more serious than traffic or parking violations.

The Alameda County community service program received international attention. England and Wales developed pilot projects in the 1970s, using community service as a midlevel sanction between probation and prison and as an alternative to prison sentences up to six months. By 1975, community service had become a central feature of English sentencing. The approach swept throughout Europe, Australia, New Zealand, and Canada.

However, what had begun as an American innovation atrophied in the United States.[10] Today in the United States, community service is seldom used as a separate sentence. Instead, it may be one of many conditions of a probation sentence. Nor is it viewed as an alternative to imprisonment in the United States, as it is in other countries. Generally speaking, in the United States, public officials do not consider any sanction other than imprisonment punitive enough. Substituting community service for short prison sentences is not accepted. This is unfortunate because community service is a burdensome penalty that meets with widespread public approval,[11] is inexpensive to administer, and produces public value. Also, it can largely be scaled to the seriousness of the crime.

Community service can be an intermediate sanction by itself or with other penalties and requirements, including substance abuse treatment, restitution, or probation.[12] Offenders sentenced to community service are usually assigned to work for government or private nonprofit agencies. They paint churches; maintain parks; clean roadways, public parks, and county fairgrounds; remove snow around public buildings; perform land and river reclamation; and renovate schools and nursing homes. Offenders who are doctors may be ordered to give medical service to persons who might otherwise lack medical attention. Traffic offenders may be ordered to serve in hospital emergency rooms to learn about the injuries they risk for themselves and others. Drug offenders who are prominent sports figures may be ordered to lecture in high schools on the dangers of drugs. The service options are limited only by the imagination of the sentencing judge and the availability of personnel to ensure that the offender fulfills the terms of the sentence. To become and remain a tough criminal sanction, community service must have credible and efficient enforcement mechanisms.

By the late 1980s, some form of community service sanction was in use in all 50 states. The Bureau of Justice Statistics estimates conservatively that 6 percent of all felons in the United States are sentenced to perform community service, often in conjunction with other sanctions.[13] The state of

*Community service as a criminal sanction is valuable to the community, the victim, and the offender. How does each benefit?*

Washington has made the most extensive use of community service. At least one-third of its convicted felons receive sentences that include community service. Washington state sentencing guidelines permit substitution of community service for incarceration at a rate of 8 hours of work for 1 day of incarceration, with a limit of 30 days. Most jurisdictions recognize 240 hours as the upper limit for community service. Washington State is breaking new ground in sentencing reform with the idea of *interchangeable sentences* for nonviolent or not very violent crimes against strangers. The actual sentence depends on the offender and the purposes to be served. For those with little or no income, community service may substitute for a fine. Before offenders are sentenced to community service in Washington, they complete a community service order questionnaire (see Figure 6–5 on page 169). The questionnaire helps the state Department of Corrections match the offender's abilities and limitations with community service work. A community corrections officer then makes sure the offender performs the required community service.

For offenders who do not present unacceptable risks of future violent crimes, a punitive intermediate sanction like community service—which costs much less than prison, promises comparable recidivism rates, and presents negligible risks of violence by those who would otherwise be confined—has much to commend it.

**FIGURE 6-5**

**Sample Community Service Order Questionnaire**

STATE OF WASHINGTON
DEPARTMENT OF CORRECTIONS

**COMMUNITY SERVICE WORKER QUESTIONNAIRE
AND RELEASE OF INFORMATION**

_____

Name

_____

DOC Number

By action of the Superior Court, or an administrative Department of Corrections action, you have been ordered to perform community service work. This work must be performed within an approved unit of government or non-profit agency. To help us find the best assignment for you, and ensure reasonable accommodation for any sensory, physical or mental limitations or disabilities that you may have, please supply the following information. You are not obligated to disclose conditions that do not relate to your ability to perform community service.

1. List your job skills.

2. Do you have a preference for a certain agency or a particular type of work that you would like to perform?
   If yes, describe:

3. List the hours and days you are available for work.
   Monday _____ Wednesday_____ Friday _____ Sunday _____
   Tuesday _____ Thursday _____ Saturday _____

4. What means of transportation do you have to get to and from the work site?

5. Do you wear contacts or glasses?           Yes       No       N/A       (circle one)

6. Are you pregnant?           Yes       No       N/A       (circle one)

7. Are you currently taking any prescription medications that have side effects that may affect your ability to perform community service work (i.e., drowsiness, slurred speech, etc.)?       Yes       No       (circle one)
   If "Yes," describe side effects:

8. Note whether you have been diagnosed as having any of the following problems:

| | Yes | No | | Yes | No | | Yes | No |
|---|---|---|---|---|---|---|---|---|
| Severe Allergy Reactions | | | Heart Problems | | | Epilepsy | | |
| Breathing Disorders | | | Hearing Loss | | | Uncorrected Vision Problems | | |
| Balance Problems | | | Diabetes | | | Other | | |

   If "Yes," please describe:

9. Is there any activity or motion that is difficult for you to do (i.e., crawling, climbing, bending, lifting, etc.)?
   Yes       No       (circle one)       If "Yes," please describe:

10. Do you have any other sensory, physical and/or mental limitations or disabilities that may affect your ability to do community service?       Yes       No       (circle one)       If "Yes," please describe:

11. You are required to provide to your Community Corrections Officer, a clearance from your health care provider, documenting any sensory/physical/mental limitations or disabilities which impact your ability to perform community service hours. This documentation is required within 30 days of today's date, and will be at your expense. Release of information is on the reverse side.

Distributions: ORIGINAL-Community Service Worker, COPY-Worksite, Community Service Coordinator, File

DOC 05-103 (REV 10/97) OCO

COMMUNITY SERVICE PROGRAM

**day reporting center (DRC)** A community correctional center where an offender reports each day to file a daily schedule with a supervision officer, showing how each hour will be spent.

**Day Reporting Centers**   A **day reporting center (DRC)** is a community correctional center where an offender reports each day to file a daily schedule with a supervision officer. The schedule shows how each hour will be spent—at work or looking for work, in class, at a support group meeting, etc.[14] Aiming primarily to provide treatment and reduce prison crowding, DRCs typically offer numerous services to address offenders' problems, and they strictly supervise offenders who otherwise would be confined.

Day reporting centers first developed in Great Britain in 1972. British officials noted that many offenders were imprisoned, not because they posed a risk to the public, but because they lacked basic skills to survive lawfully. Frequently, such offenders were dependent on drugs and alcohol. In 1985, officials in Connecticut's Department of Corrections learned about British day reporting centers and believed that such centers might alleviate the state's prison crowding problem. A National Institute of Justice survey conducted in mid-1994 identified 114 DRCs in 22 states.[15] Most opened after 1990. Many of the programs are concentrated in just a few states, including Connecticut, Texas, Wisconsin, Oregon, and Kansas.

DRCs commonly require offenders to obey a curfew, perform community service, and undergo drug testing twice a week. Participants check in at the center in person once a day and telephone periodically. They are responsible for following a full-time schedule that includes a combination of work, school, and substance abuse or mental health treatment. Programs range in duration from 40 days to 9 months, and program content differs. Most programs require hour-by-hour schedules of participants' activities. Some are highly intensive, with 10 or more supervision contacts per day, and a few include 24-hour electronic monitoring.[16] Some centers refer clients to service agencies; others provide services directly. Some focus on monitoring; others emphasize support. The 1994 survey showed generally high failure rates, averaging 50 percent. Unfortunately, no substantial evaluations have yet been published.

As DRCs move into the twenty-first century, a number of policy issues will influence their development and implementation. Those issues are (1) ensuring offenders' access to services, (2) responding to violations of DRC regulations in ways that will not add to jail and prison crowding, and (3) conducting evaluation of DRC programs.

**house arrest** A sanction that requires an offender to remain in his or her home except for approved absences, such as work, school, or treatment programs.

**electronic monitoring (EM)** The tracking of an offender's location by means of electronic signals from a small transmitter on the offender's wrist or ankle to a monitoring unit.

**House Arrest and Electronic Monitoring**   **House arrest** is an intermediate sanction that requires an offender to remain in his or her home except for approved absences, such as work, school, or treatment programs. **Electronic monitoring (EM)** is the tracking of an offender's location by means of electronic signals from a small transmitter on the offender's wrist or ankle to a monitoring unit. When used together, the two are sometimes referred to as *electronic house arrest.*

Electronic monitoring units may be active or passive. An active unit sends a continuous signal. The receiving computer notes any break in the signal and alerts the officer monitoring the offender. For example, the offender wears a bracelet fitted to the wrist or ankle. The bracelet has a wire running through it. If the wire is broken or the offender moves outside the signal range, the receiving computer notes a break in the signal. Passive units respond only to inquiries. Most commonly, the offender receives an

*Intermediate Sanctions: Corrections in the Community*

*Megan Hill*
*Case Manager*
*Day Reporting Center*
*Boston, Massachusetts*

*"Probably the best part about my job is working with individuals who are truly dedicated to their recovery and reintegration back into society. The feeling you get from seeing a client start with all the frustrations of job rejections and discrimination to seeing them attain their first legal job and actually enjoy it is pretty satisfying. I am actually helping people put their lives back together."*

While an undergraduate at Northeastern University, Megan Hill participated in several co-op programs, including six months at a day reporting center in Boston. Shortly after her co-op ended, the day reporting center advertised for a case manager and hired Megan for the job. Megan credits Northeastern's co-op program with giving her the qualifications to be hired full-time before earning her degree and with providing her the opportunity to explore different aspects of the criminal justice field.

Each day, Megan's responsibilities include approving day reporting clients' daily itineraries, monitoring clients' call-in times, and visiting her clients at home and work. Daily contact, she says, helps her know her clients better, understand what they're going through, and know how to assist them. She also believes it's important to respect clients. "The more respect you give your clients, the more respect and honesty you get in return."

Megan's advice to persons interested in working in corrections is to do an internship or a co-op to find out if they like the work. For Megan Hill, the most important thing is to be happy with your job and to feel that you're making a difference.

---

automated telephone call from the probation office and is told to place the bracelet on an identification unit attached to the telephone. Another method of passive EM is voice verification by means of digitized voice templates. For offenders with alcohol and drug problems, breath testing may be used. The offender blows into the unit, which records drugs or alcohol in the offender's breath. The instrument is often accompanied by a video display that gives visual proof that the subject performing the alcohol or drug test is actually the offender.

Electronic monitoring sometimes, but not necessarily, backs up house arrest. House arrest can stand alone as a sanction or can be coupled with fines and other obligations. The term of the sentence can range from several days to several years.

In theory, electronic house arrest satisfies three correctional goals. First, it incapacitates the offender by restricting him or her to a single location. Second, it is punitive because it forces the offender to stay home when not at work, school, counseling, or community service. And third, it contributes to rehabilitation by allowing the offender to remain with his or her family and continue employment, education, or vocational training.

The growing popularity of electronic house arrest is due in large part to prison and jail overcrowding, increasing demands to supervise more offenders, and concerns over the ability of standard probation to protect the community. Electronic house arrest is seen as a cost-effective, humane intervention that allows offenders to maintain or establish ties to the community, which are important to rehabilitation, and to avoid the negative influences of incarceration. Yet, it is also more punitive than standard probation, which provides little supervision to offenders.

Advocates of electronic house arrest point to a number of advantages: the equipment has evolved to a point where it is fairly reliable. It usually pays for itself, since the offender often pays to use the system; it often generates profits for the supervising agency. It's tougher than routine probation. And since offenders can remain at home and keep working, it is more humane. The American Probation and Parole Association supports electronic house arrest.

Critics say that the requirement to have a telephone and pay for the monitoring equipment keeps electronic house arrest out of reach for many offenders who would benefit from it. In addition, electronic house arrest does not guarantee that crimes will not occur in the house. Vice crimes, domestic violence, and assaults—to name a few—occur during electronic house arrest. And electronic monitors intrude on the privacy of the family and increase family stress.

Despite these concerns, electronic house arrest has grown enormously throughout the United States since electronic surveillance technology was introduced in 1969. Not only is the number of offenders on electronic house arrest increasing, but also the offenders are becoming more diverse. Initially, electronic house arrest targeted only the traditional clients of house arrest: low-risk probationers, such as those convicted of driving while intoxicated. More recently, however, it has expanded to include persons awaiting trial or sentencing, offenders released from institutional and community corrections facilities, and juvenile offenders. Furthermore, whereas electronic house arrest initially gained acceptance as a response to property crimes, it is used more and more with selected offenders whose crimes are not very violent. New technology also makes it possible to track an offender's movements throughout the world. Using a network of 24 satellites called Global Positioning System (GPS) orbiting 12,000 miles above earth's surface, a monitoring system called SMART (Satellite Monitoring and Remote Tracking System) can track an offender's bracelet and notify police, victims, and others when the offender enters a prohibited area.

**residential community center (RCC)** A medium-security correctional setting that resident offenders are permitted to leave regularly—unaccompanied by staff—for work, for educational or vocational programs, or for treatment in the community.

**Residential Community Centers**  A **residential community center (RCC)** is a medium-security correctional setting that resident offenders are permitted to leave regularly—unaccompanied by staff—for work, for educational or vocational programs, or for treatment in the community. Initially such centers were called *halfway houses* and were for offenders who either were about to be released from an institution or were in the first stages of return to the community. However, as the number of halfway houses grew,

Tippecanoe County Community Corrections, through its Home Detention Program, provides punitive sentencing alternatives for Class B, C, and D felons, Class A misdemeanants, and nonviolent habitual offenders in lieu of DOC commitment to state prison. These offenders, who are classified as high-risk probationers, are those assessed as nonviolent who could benefit from up to 24-hour supervision complemented by a personalized treatment plan designed around employment, education, family, and substance abuse needs. The offenders also pay fees to be in the program. These fees are used to offset operating costs.

Tippecanoe County Community Corrections currently has 7 surveillance officers to monitor between 200 and 250 clients sentenced to home detention. The surveillance officers use both electronic monitoring and daily visits to the client's residence and place of employment.

Electronic monitoring is accomplished by utilizing Suretrac monitoring equipment. The equipment consists of an ankle unit (PIU) and a receiving unit (PRU). The PRU is placed in the client's residence when the client enters the Home Detention Program. The PIU is attached to the client's ankle. The equipment is used to monitor the client whenever he or she leaves or enters the residence. Each client is entered into a main computer and given time frames when authorized to be away from home for employment or appointments (probation, court, counseling, doctor, etc.). The Suretrac equipment uses the client's existing telephone line to communicate with the main computer

as well as with the surveillance officer. Whenever a client leaves or enters the range of the monitoring equipment, the PRU will automatically call the main computer. The main computer will then check the client's curfew, and if there is a violation, it will then call the surveillance officer, using an alphanumeric pager, and state whether the client has entered or left the residence. The equipment will also automatically page the surveillance officer if the client tampers with the PIU, if the power is cut off to the PRU, if the telephone line is disconnected, or if any other problem occurs. With this system, the surveillance officer can react quickly to a given situation.

Visits to the clients' residences take place daily. The purpose of these visits is (1) to determine whether the clients are at home when they are supposed to be; (2) to ensure the clients are not using alcohol or drugs (breathalyzers and random monthly drug screens are performed); (3) to check on the clients' employment status (verify time cards, work hours, etc.); and (4) to check on the clients' well-being and family situation and just to see how they are doing while on home detention.

Clients who violate home detention rules are dealt with immediately. Clients may lose all privileges, may be given road crew hours to complete, or may be sent back to jail to complete their sentences.

*David Kuebler*
*Executive Director*
*Tippecanoe County, Indiana,*
*Community Corrections*

and new client groups (divertees, pretrial releasees, and probationers) were added, the umbrella term *residential community center* was adopted.

Halfway houses, prerelease and work release centers, and restitution centers are examples of RCCs. Some RCCs specialize in a type of client or treatment—for example, in drug and alcohol abuse, violent and sex offenders, women, abused women, or prerelease federal prisoners. The type of population served varies from community to community and from RCC to RCC. According to the latest figures from the National Institute of Corrections, there are more than 1200 RCCs in the United States,[17] and there is substantial diversity among them.[18] Some are public, and some private. There are RCCs at all levels of government. The largest number of programs (about 40 percent) are operated by private nonprofit agencies. The next largest group (about 35 percent) are run by state government. Then come those run by county government (almost 20 percent), for-profit corporations (less than 10 percent), and other agencies (less than 5 percent). RCCs range from fewer than 10 beds to more than 200 beds. More than half are small, with fewer than 50 beds; almost 30 percent are classified as medium in size, with 50 to 100 beds; and 20 percent are large, with over 100 beds. More than half of RCCs serve only men, 40 percent serve both men and women, and fewer than 10 percent serve only women. According to the American Correctional Association, in 1997 there were more than 35,000 RCC residents.[19]

The objectives of RCCs are community protection and offender reintegration. Community protection is achieved by screening offenders, setting curfews, administering drug or polygraph tests, confirming that when residents leave the center they go directly to work, school or treatment, and by providing a medium-security correctional setting. Reintegration is achieved by giving residents opportunities to learn and use legitimate skills, thereby reducing their reliance on criminal behavior. Staff determine the obstacles to each resident's reintegration, plan a program to overcome those obstacles, and provide a supportive environment to help the resident test, use, and refine the skills needed.

The benefits of RCCs are many. RCCs benefit offenders by providing them with the basic necessities of food, clothing, and shelter while they find housing and employment. RCCs also offer residents emotional support to deal with the pressures of readjustment and help them obtain community services. Benefits to the community include a moderately secure correctional setting in which residents' behavior is monitored and controlled, as well as an expectation that opportunities for offenders to get on their feet will reduce post-release adjustment problems and criminal behavior. For the criminal justice system, an RCC offers a low-cost housing alternative to incarceration for nonviolent offenders. An RCC can control offenders in the community at less cost than building and operating more secure facilities. It may also serve as an enhancement to probation and an option for dealing with probation and parole violators.

There has not been much research on the effectiveness of RCCs. An early General Accounting Office (GAO) report proposed that extensive planning and coordination of information were greatly needed for halfway houses to reach their objectives.[20]

Recently, researchers have concluded that, "Adopting more realistic outcome measures may make it possible to bridge the wide gap between public expectations for the justice system and what most practitioners recognize as the system's actual capability to control crime. By documenting what corrections programs can accomplish, we can move toward integrating programs like work release [as part of a residential community center program] into a more balanced corrections strategy. Such a strategy would successfully return low-risk inmates to the community, thereby making room to incarcerate the truly violent offenders."[21]

**Boot Camps**   In 1983, in an effort to alleviate prison crowding and reduce recidivism, the departments of corrections in Oklahoma and Georgia opened the first adult prison programs modeled after military boot camps. Since then, boot camp, or *shock incarceration*, has become an increasingly popular intermediate sanction.

**Boot camp** is a short institutional term of confinement, usually followed by probation, that includes a physical regimen designed to develop self-discipline, respect for authority, responsibility, and a sense of accomplishment. According to the National Institute of Justice, four characteristics distinguish boot camps from other correctional programs: (1) military drill and ceremony, (2) a rigorous daily schedule of hard labor and physical training, (3) separation of boot camp participants from the general prison population, and (4) the idea that boot camps are an alternative to long-term confinement.[22]

Although all boot camps involve a short period of imprisonment in a military atmosphere, the specific components of boot camp programs vary widely. Boot camps differ in whether their activities include work, community services, education, and counseling and whether they provide aftercare support and monitoring for community reintegration. There is some consistency, however, in their goals: reducing prison crowding and changing offenders' behavior and thus their future involvement in crime.

Most boot camps target young, first-time offenders who have been convicted of such nonviolent crimes as drug possession, burglary, or theft and seem more open to changing their attitudes and behavior than older offenders. Most participants are males who do not have extensive criminal histories and are physically and psychologically able to complete the strict military exercise requirements. Disabled offenders or those with nondisabling medical conditions that limit their physical performance (for example, being overweight) are typically excluded.

States differ in their age requirements for boot camp eligibility. For example, in California, participants must be 40 or younger; in Illinois, 17 to 29; in Kansas, 18 to 25; in Maryland, under 32; in New York, 30 or younger; in Oklahoma, under 25; and in Tennessee, 17 to 29.

Several researchers have examined boot camp programs for women.[23] In some programs, women were integrated with male inmates. Others were completely separate female programs. The researchers found that when boot camps combined men and women, few women were in the camps, and those women faced serious problems. They were supervised more intensely

**boot camp** A short institutional term of confinement, usually followed by probation, that includes a physical regimen designed to develop self-discipline, respect for authority, responsibility, and a sense of accomplishment.

than the men and their activities were restricted to protect them from abuse, harassment, and sexual relations with male drill instructors. Combined programs did not take into consideration women inmates' physical stamina, nor did they offer therapeutic programs for the problems that many of these women faced, such as how to survive sexual assault or battering, make a successful transition into the community, or obtain job skills. Combined programs also failed to take into consideration the importance of children to women in boot camps.

Women in separate programs fared better. The separate camps were more likely to offer therapeutic programs suited to women's needs. Visitation policies were less restrictive, and the women had more opportunities to see their children while in boot camp. The researchers concluded that women should not be combined with men in boot camps designed for men. If boot camps are developed for women, they should be compatible with the needs and characteristics of women offenders.

On January 1, 1998, 84 boot camps involving more than 12,000 adult inmates were in operation by state departments of corrections, jails, and probation and parole agencies.[24] The Violent Crime Control and Law Enforcement Act of 1994 allocated $25 million for the development of boot camp programs, virtually ensuring their continued growth.

Critics have raised questions about using boot camps as a correctional tool. They note that correctional boot camp programs are built on a model of military basic training that the military itself has found lacking and in some cases has revised.[25] Critics also argue that the military model was designed to produce a cohesive fighting unit. That is not a goal of corrections. One analyst wrote, "If an offender can't read [or] write and is drug-involved,

*The military-style training and drill of boot camps is sometimes supplemented with substance abuse education and vocational training. What aftercare programs might contribute to the effectiveness of boot camp strategies?*

sending him to a 90-day boot camp that does not address his job or literacy needs will only have a short-term effect, if any, on his behavior."[26]

There is reason for both optimism and skepticism about boot camps. Although boot camps are promoted as a means of reducing recidivism rates, there is no evidence that they significantly reduce recidivism or promote socially desirable activities. When behavior during the first year back in the community is examined, there is no evidence that boot camp participants perform any better than those who stayed longer in prison. Some researchers have reported that boot camp graduates have higher self-esteem, have better attitudes toward family, are less likely to see themselves as victims of circumstances, and are more likely to feel in control of their future. However, the research does not always compare boot camp graduates with other groups. Research into what boot camp participants say they'll do is less conclusive than research into what they've actually done.

Also disappointing is that the recidivism rates of boot camp graduates are very similar to those of other parolees.[27] In front-end boot camp programs, one-third to one-half of the participants fail to complete the program and are sent to prison as a result. In most programs, close surveillance of graduates after release leads to technical-violation and revocation rates that are higher than those of comparable offenders in less intensive programs.

Boot camps are also promoted as a means of reducing prison crowding and corrections costs. Here the news is not all bad. Back-end programs, to which imprisoned offenders are transferred by corrections officials, do save money and prison space. Although they too often experience high failure, technical violation, and revocation rates, those rates are no higher than for offenders who have been kept in prison longer. If enough offenders complete boot camp and are released early from prison, the programs can reduce prison crowding. However, many boot camp programs select participants from those who would otherwise be sentenced to probation. Those programs widen the net, including more offenders in prison and requiring additional beds. A number of researchers have found that most boot camps have not reduced prison crowding, because the programs are designed for offenders who would otherwise be on probation, not those who would otherwise have received prison terms.[28] Crowding can be reduced only if boot camp participants are selected from inmates already incarcerated and only if their participation substantially reduces their overall sentence lengths.

## Policy-Centered Approach to Developing Intermediate Sanctions

A policy is a statement of intent. It expresses *why* we are engaging in a particular set of activities. It also tells *how* we are to carry out these activities. Policy can be very general, very specific, or in between.

In recent decades sanction options have proliferated, increasing the choices available to judges at sentencing and to governmental agencies moving offenders from higher levels of control to lower ones. As we take stock of the contributions and limitations of the movement toward intermediate

**Drill Instructor**

The Polk County Sheriff's Office operates a boot camp program for male and female offenders ages 14 to 19. Our program provides an aftercare component directly supervised by the same DIs who monitored the offenders during the in-residence phase of the program. We are looking for DIs who can participate in and lead the physical training as well as provide positive role models. Requirements: Graduation from a two-year associate's program in a human services field and one year of experience as an assistant drill instructor; skill in motivating trainees in a military boot camp environment.

sanctions, it is important to think about intermediate sanctions, not as punishments developed in isolation from one another, but rather as parts of a system of policy-driven responses to criminal behavior.

Unfortunately, most intermediate sanctions are discrete local programs, devised and implemented without the participation of the decision makers who will use them. In this **program-centered approach**, planning for an intermediate-sanction program (e.g., electronic house arrest) is usually undertaken by a single agency, which develops and funds the program. The program staff then tries to inform judges, prosecutors, defense counsel, and other corrections agencies about the program, its potential benefits, and the target population for which it is best suited.

The program-centered approach has serious limitations and often results in disappointment. It makes nationwide comparison and evaluation difficult because there is no coordination between the programs of different jurisdictions. Programs that are established this way are seldom evaluated, because most local agencies lack the resources and the understanding of evaluation research. The program-centered approach often leads to many new programs that pursue multiple goals, sometimes even conflicting ones. When that happens, ambiguous and inconsistent operating policies develop. Finally, the program-centered approach tells us very little about how intermediate sanctions affect a jurisdiction's overall sentencing and imprisonment practices, very important information for most intermediate-sanction programs.

The **policy-centered approach** to intermediate sanctions, however, emphasizes the *policy* that spells out the sentencing scheme and the place of each sentencing option as much as the sanctions and programs themselves. This approach draws together stakeholders from inside and outside the corrections agency that will implement the proposed sanction. The planning group often includes decision makers from all three branches of government

**program-centered approach** A method of planning intermediate sanctions in which planning for a program is usually undertaken by a single agency, which develops and funds the program.

**policy-centered approach** A method of thinking about and planning for intermediate sanctions that draws together key stakeholders from inside and outside the corrections agency that will implement the sanction.

*In Anoka County, Minnesota, a policy team of key stakeholders inside and outside the corrections agency developed a day reporting center for high-risk probationers as one of six intermediate sanctions designed to save jail space for serious offenders. What are the advantages of using a policy-centered approach to devise intermediate sanctions?*

(judicial, executive, and legislative) and all three subsystems of criminal justice (police, courts, and corrections). The group examines the overall context within which the proposed new sanction will be used and analyzes data on offenses and offenders to form sound policy. Public hearings may also be held. The policy that emerges is a statement of intent. It expresses why the group has decided to provide a particular set of sanctions and explains how those sanctions should be implemented.

# Community Corrections

So far in this chapter we have been discussing intermediate sanctions as strategies to control crime. Now we turn our attention from the *strategies* to the *goal* they are designed to achieve. That goal is community corrections. There is no consensus in the field of criminal justice on the definition of community corrections. Sometimes the term refers to noninstitutional programs. Sometimes it refers to programs administered by local government rather than the state. Other times, it indicates citizen involvement.

We define community corrections as a philosophy of correctional treatment that embraces (1) decentralization of authority from state to local levels, (2) citizen participation in program planning, design, implementation, and evaluation, (3) redefinition of the population of offenders for whom incarceration is most appropriate, and (4) emphasis on rehabilitation through community programs.

Community corrections recognizes the importance of partnership with the community in responding to crime. In short, our communities not only have a *right* to safe streets and homes, but also bear *responsibility* for making them safe. All the major components of the criminal justice system have alliances today with the community. Examples include the following:

- *Community policing* A law enforcement strategy to get residents involved in making their neighborhoods safer by focusing on crime prevention, nonemergency services, public accountability, and decentralized decision making that includes the public.
- *Community-based prosecution* A prosecution strategy that uses a combination of criminal and civil tactics and the legal expertise, resources, and clout of the prosecuting attorney's office to find innovative solutions to a neighborhood's specific problems.
- *Community-based defender services* A defender strategy that provides continuity in representation of indigent defendants and helps defendants with personal and family problems that can lead to legal troubles.
- *Community courts* A judicial strategy of hearing a criminal case in the community that is most affected by the case and including that community in case disposition.

## Community Corrections Acts

This spirit of correctional collaboration and community partnership has led 28 states to pass **community corrections acts (CCAs)** (see Figure 6–6 on page 180). CCAs are state laws that give economic grants to local com-

**community corrections acts (CCAs)** State laws that give economic grants to local communities to establish community corrections goals and policies and to develop and operate community corrections programs.

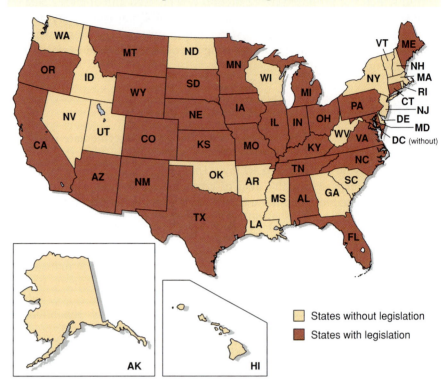

## FIGURE 6-6

### States With Community Corrections Legislation

States without legislation
States with legislation

Source: William M. DiMascio, *Seeking Justice: Crime and Punishment in America* (New York: Edna McConnell Clark Foundation, 1997), p. 38. Data on map is as of January 1996.

munities to establish community corrections goals and policies and to develop and operate community corrections programs. Most CCAs transfer some state functions to local communities, decentralizing services and engaging communities in the process of reintegrating offenders. Along with the transfer of correctional responsibility from the state to the community, CCAs provide financial incentives for counties, private citizens' groups, and private agencies to participate. The financial incentives help communities manage more of their own correctional cases rather than ask the state to manage them. With the money, local communities design, implement, and evaluate a complete range of local sentencing options. (The intermediate sanctions discussed earlier in this chapter, for example, can be funded through a CCA.) Locally designed sanctions have a better chance of succeeding because they are based in the community where offenders' families, friends, and other social supports are. Although CCAs authorize and allow funding for a range of sanctions, including intermediate sanctions, they do more than that. CCAs implement community corrections philosophy by providing statewide structures that specify government and citizen roles and responsibilities in the planning, development, implementation, and funding of community sanctions.

*Intermediate Sanctions: Corrections in the Community*

In 1973, Minnesota became the first state to adopt a CCA. Minnesota officials wanted to reduce fragmentation in criminal justice service delivery, to control costs, and to redefine the population of offenders for whom state incarceration was most appropriate. Communities throughout Minnesota were willing to assume greater correctional responsibility for less serious offenders, as long as the communities were also given state subsidies and significant control over planning and service delivery. The huge success of Minnesota's CCA can be seen in Minnesota's incarceration rate, one of the lowest in the United States today. While the crime rate is not much different from those of other states, the incarceration rate is only 117 persons for every 100,000 residents. The U.S. average on December 31, 1998, was 461 per 100,000 residents. The majority of Minnesota's offenders are handled under the CCA.

There are tremendous differences in the CCAs in the United States. The most common goal, held in 14 states, is expansion of sanction choices. Twelve states cite the promotion of state and community partnerships as the goal. Some CCAs focus on nonviolent offenders; others merely include them. Some CCAs help communities move offenders out of local jails and into correctional programs that are less expensive and offer reasonable community protection. Simply having correctional programs in a community does not mean that a community corrections program exists. Consistent goals and consistent approaches to achieving those goals are the backbone of successful community corrections. Community corrections legislation can help accomplish that consistency.

## SUMMARY BY CHAPTER OBJECTIVES

### CHAPTER OBJECTIVE 1
Intermediate sanctions is the term given to the range of new sentencing options developed to fill the gap between traditional probation and traditional jail or prison sentences, better match the severity of punishment to the seriousness of the crime, reduce institutional crowding, and control correctional costs. Punishments typically identified as intermediate sanctions include intensive-supervision probation (ISP), fines, community service, day reporting centers, house arrest, residential community centers, and boot camp.

### CHAPTER OBJECTIVE 2
Net-widening means increasing the number of offenders sentenced to a greater level of restriction. As a result, many offenders receive more restrictive sentences than their offenses and characteristics warrant.

### CHAPTER OBJECTIVE 3
Intensive-supervision probation (ISP) is control of offenders in the community through strict enforcement of conditions and frequent reporting to a probation officer with a reduced caseload. ISP programs exist in all 50 states. They may be state or county programs and may be administered by parole, probation, or prison departments.

### CHAPTER OBJECTIVE 4
A day fine is a financial punishment scaled to the seriousness of the offense and the offender's ability to pay. A traditional fine is based on a fixed amount, without regard to the offender's ability to pay.

### CHAPTER OBJECTIVE 5
Community service is a sentence to serve a specified number of hours working in unpaid positions with nonprofit or tax-supported agencies. Research suggests that for offenders who do not present unacceptable risks of future violent crimes, community service costs much less than prison, has comparable recidivism rates, and presents negligible risks of violence by those who would otherwise be confined.

### CHAPTER OBJECTIVE 6
A day reporting center (DRC) is a community correctional center where an offender reports each day to file a daily schedule with a supervision officer, showing how each hour will be spent. DRCs aim to provide strict surveillance over offenders and, depending on their resources, provide treatment services, refer offenders to community social service agencies, or arrange to have community agencies offer services on site.

### CHAPTER OBJECTIVE 7
House arrest is a sanction that requires an offender to remain in his or her home except for approved absences such as work, school, or treatment programs. Electronic monitoring sometimes helps enforce the offender's compliance with house arrest.

### CHAPTER OBJECTIVE 8
Residential community centers are medium security correctional settings that resident offenders are permitted to leave regularly—unaccompanied by staff—for work, for educational or vocational programs, or for treatment in the community.

### CHAPTER OBJECTIVE 9
Boot camp is a short institutional term, usually followed by probation, that includes a physical regimen designed to develop self-discipline, respect for authority, responsibility, and a sense of accomplishment.

### CHAPTER OBJECTIVE 10
In a program-centered approach, the planning of an intermediate-sanction program (e.g., electronic house arrest) is usually undertaken by a

single agency, which develops and funds the program in isolation from other programs. A policy-centered approach, on the other hand, draws together diverse stakeholders to think about and plan for an intermediate sanction.

## CHAPTER OBJECTIVE 11

Community corrections is a philosophy of correctional treatment that embraces decentralization of authority from state to local levels; citizen participation in program planning, design, implementation, and evaluation; redefinition of the population of offenders for whom incarceration is most appropriate; and emphasis on rehabilitation through community programs.

## CHAPTER OBJECTIVE 12

Community corrections acts (CCAs) are state laws that give economic grants to local communities to establish community corrections goals and policies and to develop and operate community corrections programs. CCAs decentralize services and engage communities in the process of reintegrating offenders by transferring correctional responsibility from the state to the community and by providing financial incentives for communities to manage more of their own correctional cases rather than ask the state to manage them.

## KEY TERMS

intermediate sanctions, p. 156
community corrections, p. 156
front-end programs, p. 157
back-end programs, p. 157
net-widening, p. 158
intensive-supervision probation (ISP), p. 160
fine, p. 161
day fine, p. 162
community service, p. 166

day reporting center (DRC), p. 170
house arrest, p. 170
electronic monitoring (EM), p. 170
residential community center (RCC) p. 172
boot camp, p. 175
program-centered approach, p. 178
policy-centered approach, p. 178
community corrections acts (CCAs), p. 179

## QUESTIONS FOR REVIEW

1. What are intermediate sanctions?
2. What are the purposes of intermediate sanctions?
3. Define *front-end programs, back-end programs,* and *net-widening.* How do these three terms relate to intermediate sanctions?
4. What is ISP? How is it more punitive than standard probation?
5. What are four reasons fines are not taken seriously as punishment in the United States? Might enforced collection change that perception?
6. Distinguish between *fixed fines* and *day fines.*
7. Describe community service. Where, when, and why were community service orders first used in the United States?

8. What is a *day reporting center* (DRC), and how widespread is the use of DRCs in the United States?
9. What is electronic house arrest? What correctional goals does it satisfy?
10. What are boot camps? How are they different from other correctional programs? What features vary among boot camps?
11. What problems do boot camps pose for women offenders?
12. Describe the differences between a program-centered approach and a policy-centered approach to the development and implementation of intermediate sanctions.
13. What is community corrections?
14. What are community corrections acts?

# CRITICAL THINKING EXERCISES

## ON-THE-JOB ISSUE

Your state legislature recently passed a bill authorizing day fines as an intermediate sanction. Part of the bill requires each probation department to send one or more probation officers to a workshop to prepare for implementing the bill. The chief probation officer designates you. Before the workshop, you are given two questions: (1) Why are day fines a good idea? (2) What would you do with offenders who don't pay? You are to write a response to bring to the workshop.

## CORRECTIONS ISSUES

1. Summarizing the results of a national survey of judges' attitudes toward fines, researchers noted that "at present, judges do not regard the fine alone as a meaningful alternative to incarceration or probation."[29] What could you tell such judges to convince them that day fines, or structured fines, are a viable sentencing option?

2. Supporters of the policy-centered approach to devising intermediate sanctions cite three advantages: (1) It avoids wasting scarce resources on the wrong category of offender, (2) it draws the support of judges, prosecutors, and defense counsel outside the sponsoring agency, and (3) it helps develop consensus on specific goals for a program. Do you agree that these are advantages of the approach? Explain.

# CORRECTIONS ON THE WEB

 The National Institute of Corrections (NIC) provides training, technical assistance, information services, and assistance in policy and program development to federal, state, and local corrections agencies. NIC's Web page at **http://www.nicic.org** provides full-text articles on community corrections issues. Click on Publications and then on Community Corrections. Choose an article that interests you. Prepare a one-page report to present in class.

# ADDITIONAL READINGS

Ellsworth, Thomas (ed.). *Contemporary Community Corrections,* 2d ed. Prospect Heights, IL: Waveland Press, 1997.

Morris, Norval, and Michael Tonry. *Between Prison and Probation: Intermediate Punishments in a Rational Sentencing System.* New York: Oxford University Press, 1990.

Smykla, John Ortiz, and William L. Selke (eds.). *Intermediate Sanctions: Sentencing in the 1990s.* Cincinnati: Anderson, 1995.

Tonry, Michael. "Parochialism in U.S. Sentencing Policy." *Crime and Delinquency,* Vol. 45, No. 1, January 1999, pp. 48–65.

# ENDNOTES

1. Herbert A. Johnson, *History of Criminal Justice* (Cincinnati: Anderson, 1988).

2. Joan Petersilia, Arthur J. Lurigio, and James M. Byrne, "Introduction," in James M. Byrne, Arthur J. Lurigio, and Joan Petersilia (eds.), *Smart Sentencing: The Emergence of Intermediate Sanctions* (Newbury Park, CA: Sage, 1992), pp. ix–x.; see also Elizabeth Deschenes, Susan Turner, and Joan Petersilia, *Intensive Community Supervision in Minnesota: A Dual Experiment in Prison Diversion and Enhanced Supervised Release* (Washington: National Institute of Justice, 1995).

3. Doris Layton MacKenzie and J. W. Shaw, "Inmate Adjustment and Change During Shock Incarceration: The Impact of Correctional Boot Camp Programs," *Justice Quarterly,* Vol. 7 (1990), pp. 125–150; Joan Petersilia and Susan Turner, "Intensive Probation and Parole," in Michael

Tonry (ed.), *Crime and Justice: A Review of Research, Volume 17* (Chicago: University of Chicago Press, 1993), pp. 281–335.

4. William M. DiMascio, *Seeking Justice: Crime and Punishment in America* (New York: Edna McConnell Clark Foundation, 1997), p. 36.

5. Sally Hillsman and Judith Greene, "The Use of Fines as an Intermediate Sanction," in Byrne, Lurigio, and Petersilia; Peter P. Tak, "Sentencing in the Netherlands," *Acta Criminologica*, Vol. 7, 1994, pp. 7–17; Norval Morris and Michael Tonry, *Between Prison and Probation: Intermediate Punishments in a Rational Sentencing System* (New York: Oxford University Press, 1990).

6. Bureau of Justice Assistance, *How to Use Structured Fines (Day Fines) as an Intermediate Sanction* (Washington: Department of Justice, November 1996).

7. Ibid.

8. Ibid.

9. Morris and Tonry, p. 152.

10. Michael Tonry, "Parochialism in U.S. Sentencing Policy," *Crime and Delinquency*, Vol. 45, No. 1 (1999), p. 58.

11. DiMascio, pp. 43–45.

12. Warren Young, *Community Service Orders* (London: Heinemann, 1979); Gill McIvor, *Sentenced to Serve: The Operation and Impact of Community Service by Offenders* (Aldershot, England: Avebury, 1992); Peter J. O. Tak, "Netherlands Successfully Implements Community Service Orders," *Overcrowded Times*, Vol. 6 (1995), pp. 16–17.

13. DiMascio, p. 37.

14. Dale G. Parent, "Day Reporting Centers: An Evolving Intermediate Sanction," *Federal Probation*, Vol. 60, No. 4 (December 1996), pp. 51–54 and George Mair, "Day Centres in England and Wales," *Overcrowded Times*, Vol. 4 (1993), pp. 5–7.

15. Dale G. Parent, Jim Byrne, Vered Tsarfaty, and Julie Esselman, *Day Reporting Centers* (Washington: National Institute of Justice, 1995).

16. Dale Parent, "Day Reporting Centers: An Emerging Intermediate Sanction," *Overcrowded Times*, Vol. 2 (1991), pp. 6, 8; Jack McDevitt and Robyn Miliano, "Day Reporting Centers: An Innovative Concept in Intermediate Sanctions," in Byrne, Lurigio, and Petersilia.

17. National Institute of Corrections, *1989 Directory of Residential Community Corrections Facilities in the United States* (Longmont, CA: National Institute of Corrections, 1989).

18. Kay Knapp, Peggy Burke, and Mimi Carter, *Residential Community Corrections Facilities: Current Practice and Policy Issues* (Longmont, CA: National Institute of Corrections, August 1992).

19. American Correctional Association, *1997 Directory of Juvenile and Adult Correctional Departments, Institutions, Agencies and Paroling Authorities* (Lanham, MD: American Correctional Association, 1997).

20. General Accounting Office, *Federal Guidance Needed if Halfway Houses Are to Be a Viable Alternative to Prison* (Washington: U.S. Government Printing Office, 1975).

21. Ibid, p. 12.

22. Doris L. MacKenzie and Eugene E. Hebert (eds.), *Correctional Boot Camps: A Tough Intermediate Sanction* (Washington: National Institute of Justice, 1996).

23. Doris Layton MacKenzie, et al., "Boot Camps as an Alternative for Women," in Mackenzie and Hebert, ibid.

24. Camille Graham Camp and George M. Camp, *The Corrections Yearbook 1998* (Middletown, CT: Criminal Justice Institute, 1998), pp. 118–121, 194, 250.

25. Merry Morash and Lila Rucker, "Critical Look at the Ideal of Boot Camp as Correctional Reform," *Crime and Delinquency*, Vol. 36 (1990), pp. 204–222.

26. DiMascio, p. 41.

27. Dale Parent, "Boot Camps Failing to Achieve Goals," *Overcrowded Times*, Vol. 5 (1994), pp. 8–11; Doris Layton MacKenzie, "Boot Camps: A National Assessment," *Overcrowded Times*, Vol. 5 (1994), pp. 14–18; and Philip A. Ethridge and Jonathan R. Sorensen, "An Analysis of Attitudinal Change and Community Adjustment Among Probationers in a County Boot Camp," *Journal of Contemporary Criminal Justice*, Vol. 13, No. 2 (May 1992), pp. 139–154.

28. W. J. Dickey, *Evaluating Boot Camp Prisons* (Washington: National Institute of Justice, 1994); Peter Katel and Melinda Liu, "The Bust in Boot Camps," *Newsweek*, February 21, 1994, p. 26; Dale Parent, "Boot Camps Failing to Achieve Goals."

29. George F. Cole, Barry Mahoney, Marlene Thornton, and Roger A. Hanson, *The Practice and Attitudes of Trial Court Judges Regarding Fines as a Criminal Sanction* (Washington: National Institute of Justice, 1987).

# Technology in Corrections

## Communication

Information is crucial to a well-run correctional system. Knowing what is happening gives correctional administrators the power not only to react to problems promptly, but also to anticipate and prevent them. In recent decades, communication technology has undergone significant changes. Correctional officers can now keep in touch by e-mail and can share information in electronic databases and on Web pages on the Internet.

Videoconferencing is another way to share thoughts and ideas in the correctional community. Meetings and lectures that once required expensive travel can now be "attended" from the comfort of one's office or from a local teleconference site. In addition, satellite TV and video technology have enhanced distance learning for both officers and inmates. Correctional facilities are also starting to use videoconferencing for arraignments, interrogations, and visitation. Friends and family can now save on travel and avoid standing in line by scheduling videoconferences with inmates.

*Telemedicine allows medical personnel in prisons to consult with physicians to determine treatment for inmates.*

Telemedicine, one of the newest and most exciting advances in medicine, could provide prisoners with adequate, cost-effective health care in the future. Taking a prisoner to a specialist outside the prison poses a danger to correctional officers and the community by giving the prisoner an opportunity to escape or to have contact with other persons in a less controlled environment. Telemedicine allows physicians to consult with on-site medical personnel through videoconferencing and compatible medical devices, such as medical microcameras. It can improve health care in correctional settings, and the substantial savings on in-prison consultations and on trips to local providers can offset the costs of introducing this technology.

## Offender and Officer Tracking

Automated kiosks are on the way to replacing routine visits to parole officers. Offenders are instructed to report to a kiosk at a specified location. There they are electronically interviewed, and in some cases tested for alcohol by means of a breath analysis attachment. Using the kiosks, offenders can also e-mail their parole officers to schedule personal meetings. The system identifies the offender by reading a magnetic card and using a biometric fingerprint scanner. Besides fingerprint scanners, other biometric devices are making their way onto the market. One such device is called IriScan. The device scans the eye and identifies the person from the unique patterns in the iris.

Electronic monitoring technology is steadily improving and is likely to be used far more in the future. Fairly new in the field of corrections is the global positioning system (GPS). Already used in airplanes and automobiles, GPS is now also used for monitoring parolees. The GPS tracking unit worn by a parolee allows computers to pinpoint the parolee's location at any time to the precise street address. In the field of inmate monitoring, there is also some discussion about implanting chips in offenders' bodies that would alert officials to undesirable behavior. In some cases, when criminal activity was detected, the chip might even give an electric shock that would temporarily shut down the offender's central nervous system.

Administrators are also relying on new telecommunications technology to help track inmates and former inmates. Speaker ID technology identifies a speaker even if he or she has a cold, just awoke from a deep sleep, or has a poor telephone connection. Systems using Speaker ID can be used to keep track of who calls inmates in prison and to monitor criminal activity such as escape plans, gang activity, and smuggling of contraband. Speaker ID can also be used for low-risk offenders granted early parole as an alternative to incarceration. The system can make random calls and positively identify the speaker from his or her response. The offenders never know when or how they will receive calls. When no one answers the phone or the speaker is not identified, the system alerts authorities to a possible violation.

To increase the efficiency of inmate monitoring and cut administrative costs, a smart card, a plastic card embedded with a computer chip, can be used to store all types of information about the inmate, from medical care to meals eaten.

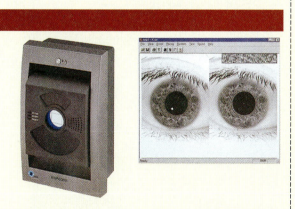

*An IriScan device can capture the unique features of the human iris with a camera lens from a distance of 10 to 12 inches, and absolute identification can be accomplished in less than 2 seconds.*

*Surveillance technology allows correctional staff to view several areas of a prison at the same time.*

Electronic monitoring isn't just for inmates. Correctional officers can also wear personal alarm and location units that allow a computer to track their locations and respond to distress signals by sending the closest officers to the site of the emergency.

## Detection Technology

To maintain prison security, researchers have developed new detection technologies. One is ground-penetrating radar (GPR), which can be used to locate underground escape tunnels. Another is heartbeat monitoring, which can detect the heartbeat of an inmate trying to escape in a laundry or trash truck leaving the prison. Devices that use X rays to scan the body for concealed weapons and noninvasive skin tests for drugs are also part of the wave of the future.

## Implementation

Despite the growth of this technology, there are still obstacles to be overcome. Corrections personnel can be resistant to drastic changes. Another reason for hesitancy to adopt new technology is the cost. Ethical concerns about the rights of offenders might be another barrier to implementing new technology. There is no question, however, that new systems and devices will play an increasing part in the work of correctional agencies.

# 7 Prisons Today
## Change Stations or Warehouses?

### CHAPTER OBJECTIVES

After completing this chapter you should be able to:

1. Explain the differences between the Pennsylvania and Auburn prison systems.
2. Outline the nine eras of prison development.
3. Explain prisoner classification and its purposes.
4. Report on the availability of programs for prisoners.
5. Describe the characteristics of today's prisoners.
6. Compare state and federal prison organization and administration.

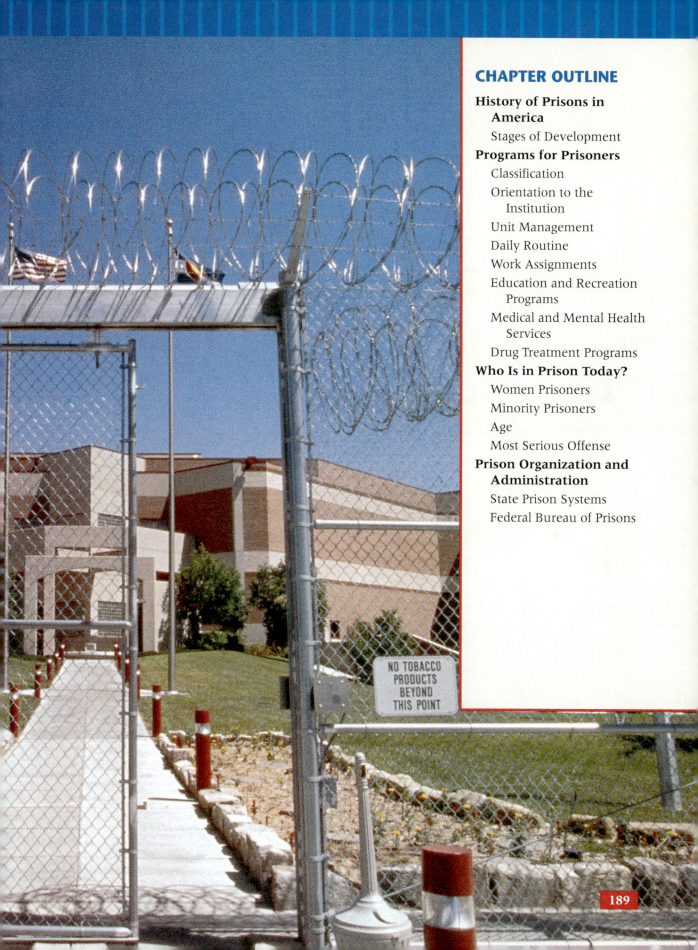

NO TOBACCO PRODUCTS BEYOND THIS POINT

189

*Men copied the realities of their hearts when they built prisons.*

—Richard Wright, *The Outsider*, 1953

It's 6 o'clock on Monday morning, still dark outside, when the alarm goes off and Delbert Morris struggles out of bed. He's in and out of the shower in a minute and then nearly cuts himself shaving, he's in such a hurry. He promised a couple of the other guys on the company softball team that he'd meet them for breakfast, but he's already running behind and can't afford to be late for work. It'll have to be just coffee and a quick doughnut on the run.

Just after Delbert punches in at 7, Denise Loftus, the Section 3 supervisor, calls him and the other members of his work team together to go over the day's production schedule. Northern Telecom just put in a rush order for a thousand coaxial cables. The team will have to work with Section 5 if they're going to make the Friday shipping date.

After the meeting, Delbert sets up the work team's hand tools and production boards while some of his crew rush off with the bill of materials to get the parts they need for the job. As soon as they get back, the whole team will start assembling the cables. They want to get started by 7:30.

By 8 the shop is humming, and it stays that way until noon, when everyone breaks for lunch. After lunch, an industrial engineer from the company's main plant stops by to ask the work team what they think about the design for a new IBM cable the company is bidding on. Roberto Kelly, the team's quality control specialist, recommends a change that will allow the cable to fit the team's hand tools more easily. The engineer agrees and alters the design. That's one of the things that Delbert likes about the company—they listen.

Delbert knows he'll be tired when the final whistle blows at 3, but he figures that comes with the job—that and taxes. With taxes, rent, and child support payments, there isn't much left for the car he's been saving for. He gets paroled next month and will need a car for commuting to the Myrtle Beach plant.

At the end of the day, Delbert shows the new man on the team how to do his final inspection and product count, while the other men clean up their work area. After they punch out, they wait in line to go through the metal detector before leaving the shop and walking across the prison yard to their cells.

Delbert (a fictitious name for a real inmate) and the other inmate-workers who assemble wire harnesses for Escod Industries are part of an innovative joint venture inside the Evans Correctional Institution in South Carolina, a maximum-to-medium-security prison holding more than 1,000 prisoners.[1] When prison work programs are mentioned, most people still think of one product and one customer—license plates for state governments. However, a small but growing number of private companies like Escod are paying inmates to produce a wide variety of products and services while in prison.

*Prisons Today: Change Stations or Warehouses?*

Joint ventures between a private company and a prison, like the partnership in South Carolina that employs Delbert, are not yet common. In the past decade, however, company executives in an increasing number of states have formed joint ventures with prison officials eager to branch out from their traditional state-use prison industries to produce goods and services for the private sector. Later in this chapter, we'll learn more about prison industries. We'll begin the chapter with a look at the history of American prisons. Then we'll discuss programs for prisoners, the composition of the prison population, and the way America's prisons are organized and administered.

# History of Prisons in America

The development of prisons was distinctively American. It reflected and fueled a shift from the assumption that offenders were inherently criminal to a belief that they were simply not properly trained to resist temptation and corruption. The two prison systems that emerged in the United States—the Pennsylvania system and the Auburn system—were copied throughout the world.

The Pennsylvania and Auburn prison systems emerged in the United States at the turn of the nineteenth century. Pennsylvania Quakers advocated a method of punishment more humane than the public corporal punishment used at the time. The Quakers shifted the emphasis from punishing the body to reforming the mind and soul. Together with an elite group of eighteenth-century Philadelphians, they ushered in the first **penitentiary**, a place for reform of offenders through repentance and rehabilitation. They believed prisoners needed to be isolated from each other in silence to repent, to accept God's guidance, and to avoid having a harmful influence on each other. Known as the **Pennsylvania system** or the separate system, this method was first used at the Walnut Street Jail, which the Quakers reorganized in 1789 as the country's first institution for punishment. The construction of the

**penitentiary** A place for reform of offenders through repentance and rehabilitation. The earliest form of large-scale incarceration, it punished criminals by isolating them so that they could reflect on their misdeeds, repent, and reform.

**Pennsylvania system** The first style of prison discipline, begun at the Walnut Street Jail to punish offenders with confinement instead of corporal punishment. Conceived by the American Quakers in 1790, it emphasized solitary confinement in silence.

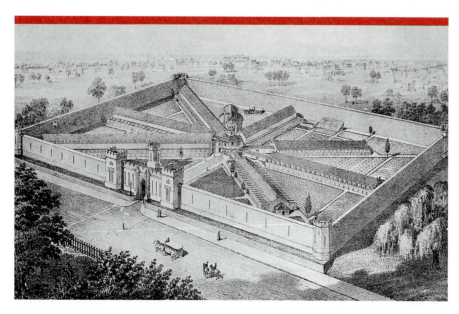

*The Eastern State Penitentiary, completed in 1829, was designed for solitary confinement, with instruction in labor, morals, and religion. What name was given to this separate system of prisoner management?*

Eastern State Penitentiary in 1829 was also based on these principles. The prison was designed for solitary confinement at labor, with instruction in labor, morals, and religion. For the first time in American history, rehabilitation and deterrence emerged as goals of corrections.

The solitary confinement of the Pennsylvania system was expensive, and it reportedly drove prisoners insane and further hardened criminal tendencies. Reformers responded with what has been termed the **Auburn system:** regimentation, silence unless conversation was required in workshops, congregate working and eating, separation of prisoners into small individual cells at night, harsh discipline, shaved heads, black and white striped uniforms, and industrial workshops that contracted with private businesses to help pay for the institution. The first prison to use this system opened in Auburn, New York, in 1819. The Auburn system, congregate by day and separate by night, eventually gave way to congregate cells at night and removal of the restrictions against talking.

Prison reform in the United States caught the attention of prison officials around the world. The Pennsylvania system of isolation and silence became popular in Europe. In the United States, the two competing philosophies of prison life clashed, and the debate over which system was superior raged on for decades. Supporters of the Pennsylvania system argued that their system made it easier to control prisoners and prevented prisoners from learning bad habits from each other. Supporters of the Auburn system claimed that prisoners' spirits needed to be broken before true reform could begin and that their system of harsh discipline and congregate but silent labor accomplished that. Auburn supporters also argued that their prison system was cheaper to build and the use of contract labor would keep costs down.

A system that was congregate by day (and eventually by night as well) seemed more compatible with the political and economic tone of the time. The Pennsylvania system represented a traditional approach to production: handcraft labor in solitary cells. In contrast, the Auburn system reflected the emerging Industrial Revolution, using power machinery, factory production, and division of labor. The attractiveness of the Auburn system's perceived economic benefits, as well as belief in the rehabilitative value of hard work, settled the debate. Thus, the congregate system became the preferred model of incarceration in the United States. In 1913, Eastern State Penitentiary, the epitome of the Pennsylvania system, changed to the Auburn system, ending the great debate. Congregate prisons have been the mode ever since. Today, however, new voices are calling for a return to long-term solitary confinement.

## Stages of Development

Prisons in America have progressed through nine stages of development (see Figure 7–1 on pages 194–195). Many of these changes were influenced by cultural movements in society. As you review the historical stages, think about how the goals of imprisonment changed in each era.

**Penitentiary Era (1790–1825)**   The first of nine eras in prison history was the penitentiary era. It included the emergence of the Pennsylvania and

---

**Auburn system** The congregate style of prison discipline that began with the opening of the prison at Auburn, New York, in 1819. This system allowed inmates to work silently together during the day. At night, however, prisoners were isolated in small sleeping cells. With time, even sleeping cells became congregate.

*Prisons Today: Change Stations or Warehouses?*

Auburn prisons, the demise of the Pennsylvania system of separate and silent, and the building of 30 state prisons on the Auburn pattern of congregate by day and separate by night, which eventually became congregate both day and night.

**Mass Prison Era (1825–1876)**  The second era was the mass prison era. During that period, the idea of prison as a place for punishment flourished across the United States. As a result, 35 more Auburn-system prisons were built, including Sing Sing, in New York state, in 1825 and San Quentin, in California, in 1852.

**Reformatory Era (1876–1890)**  The third era was the reformatory era. Influenced by the Progressive Era beliefs that education and science were vehicles to control crime, the first reformatory for young men opened at Elmira, New York, in 1876. The reformatory, whose prisoners had indeterminate sentences, used a grading system that led to early release on parole, and offered academic education, vocational training, individual rehabilitation, and military instruction and discipline. During this era, 20 reformatories opened for men, as well as the first prison for women, Mount Pleasant in Ossining, New York, and the first reformatory for women, the Indiana Reformatory for Women and Girls in Indianapolis.

**Industrial Era (1890–1935)**  Fourth was the industrial era. During this time, inmates worked in prison industries. The first prisons used the **public-accounts system**. The warden at the Walnut Street Jail determined the product, purchased materials and equipment, and oversaw the manufacture, marketing, and sale of the prison-made items. At Auburn, prison industries expanded to include copper, weaving, tailor, blacksmith, and shoemaking shops. However, as more states adopted the Auburn model, the **contract system** replaced the public accounts system. Under the contract system, the prison advertised for bids for the employment of prisoners, whose labor was sold to the highest bidder. The desire to increase profits for the prison and the private contractor often led to exploitation of the prisoners.

During the industrial era, prisons progressed from the public-accounts and contract systems of the Pennsylvania and Auburn prisons, respectively, to *state-use, convict lease,* and *public-works* systems. The system used in a state depended on the region the state was in and the period in which the transition was made. At the turn of the twentieth century, many prisons adopted the state-use system. Under the **state-use system**, prisoners manufactured products for use by state governments and their agencies, departments, and institutions. The **convict lease system** was prevalent in the post–Civil War South. Many Southern prisons had been destroyed during the war. Southern states found it easier to relinquish supervision of their prisoners to a lessee. The lessee either employed prisoners within a state institution or transported them anywhere in the state. Railway, lumber, and coal mining companies leased the greatest numbers of inmates. Lessees housed, fed, clothed, and disciplined inmates. The inmates' labor provided revenue to state treasuries. As the Western states developed, a **public-works system** emerged. This system used inmates to build public buildings, roads, and parks.

**public-accounts system**
The earliest form of prison industry, in which the warden was responsible for purchasing materials and equipment and for the manufacture, marketing, and sale of prison-made items.

**contract system**  A system of prison industry in which the prison advertised for bids for the employment of prisoners, whose labor was sold to the highest bidder.

**state-use system**  A system of prison industry that employs prisoners to manufacture products consumed by state governments and their agencies, departments, and institutions.

**convict lease system**
A system of prison industry in which a prison temporarily relinquished supervision of its prisoners to a lessee. The lessee either employed the prisoners within the institution or transported them anywhere in the state.

**public-works system**
A system of prison industry in which prisoners were employed in the construction of public buildings, roads, and parks.

**FIGURE 7–1**

**Stages of Prison History in the United States**

| Stage | Penitentiary Era | Mass Prison Era | Reformatory Era | Industrial Era |
|---|---|---|---|---|
| **Years** | 1790–1825 | 1825–1876 | 1876–1890 | 1890–1935 |
| **Goal** | Rehabilitation and deterrence | Incapacitation and deterrence | Rehabilitation | Incapacitation |
| **Characteristics** | Separate and silent Congregate and silent | Congregate labor and living spaces without silence Contract prison labor | Indeterminate sentencing Parole | Public-accounts industries Contract labor State-use labor Convict lease Public-works labor |
| **Examples of Institutions** | Walnut Street Penitentiary Philadelphia, PA Eastern State Penitentiary Cherry Hill, PA Auburn Prison, Auburn, NY | Sing Sing Prison Ossining, NY San Quentin State Prison, San Quentin, CA | Elmira, NY Indiana Reformatory for Women and Girls, Indianapolis | Most major prisons |

In time, national labor organizations saw prison industries as unfair competition and lobbied Congress to regulate prison industry. In 1929, the Hawes-Cooper Act banned the interstate shipment of prison-made goods. The Ashurst-Sumners Act of 1935 prohibited carriers from accepting prison-made goods for transportation. Ashurst-Sumners also mandated the labeling of prison-made goods. In 1940, Congress passed the Sumners-Ashurst Act, forbidding the interstate transportation of prison-made goods for private use regardless of whether a state banned importation of prison goods (products manufactured for the federal government or other state governments were exempt). Thus, much of the private market was closed to goods made by inmates.

**Punitive Era (1935–1945)**   The closing of prison industries ushered in the punitive era, with its emphasis on strict punishment and custody. The

FIGURE 7–1 (continued)

## Stages of Prison History in the United States

| Punitive Era | Treatment Era | Community-Based Era | Warehousing Era | Just-Deserts Era |
|---|---|---|---|---|
| 1935–1945 | 1945–1967 | 1967–1980 | 1980–1995 | 1995–Present |
| Retribution | Rehabilitation | Reintegration | Incapacitation | Retribution |
| Strict punishment and custody | Medical model Emerging prisoner unrest | Intermediate sanctions: halfway houses, work release centers, group homes, fines, restitution, community service | Sentencing guidelines End of discretionary parole release Serious crowding More prison riots | Just deserts Determinate sentencing Truth in sentencing Three-strikes laws Serious crowding |
| U.S. Penitentiary Alcatraz, CA | Patuxent Institution Jessup, MD | Major prison riots (Attica, NY; Santa Fe, NM) | Most major prisons | Rapidly spreading through the United States |

holding of prisoners in the Big House, in complete idleness, monotony, and frustration, characterized this era. The "escape-proof" federal prison on the island of Alcatraz in San Francisco Bay opened on the eve of this era.

**Treatment Era (1945–1967)**   The sixth era, treatment, emerged in response to prison riots across the United States. After World War II, the prison population exploded. Overcrowding, idleness, poor food, and other deprivations led prisoners to take matters into their own hands. Prison riots erupted in California, Colorado, Georgia, Illinois, Louisiana, Massachusetts, Michigan, Minnesota, New Jersey, New Mexico, Ohio, Oregon, Pennsylvania, Utah, and Washington. The riots aroused public support for prisoner rehabilitation. Reform through classification, therapy, and increased use of the indeterminate sentence was the focus of the **medical model**, in which criminal behavior was regarded as a disease to be treated.

**medical model**   A philosophy of prisoner reform in which criminal behavior is regarded as a disease to be treated with appropriate therapy.

Maryland's Patuxent Institution, with legions of mental health experts, promised to predict dangerousness accurately and to release only those prisoners who were no longer a threat to the community. However, Patuxent failed to keep that promise. Scholars and advocacy groups were also finding fault with the medical model. In addition, the social and political unrest of the 1960s had found its way into the nation's prisons. A race riot broke out at San Quentin in 1967, and protests, riots, and killings occurred in other prisons. Corrections experts believed that a new approach was needed—one in which offenders were supervised in the community rather than imprisoned in fortresslike institutions.

**Community-Based Era (1967–1980)**   What emerged in the seventh era was community-based corrections. President Johnson's 1967 crime commission came to the conclusion that the community was a source of offenders' problems. Therefore, they thought it best to rehabilitate offenders by using community resources. Halfway houses, community corrections centers, intensive-supervision probation, work release centers, and the like quickly spread across the United States. However, observers discovered that the approach did not lower the crime rate, reduce the prison population, or make the community safer. The stage was set for more prison riots. In 1969, there were 39 riots in the nation's prisons. In 1970, there were 59 more. After four days of rioting in September 1971, 43 people were dead at Attica prison in New York, the largest number ever killed in a United States prison riot. With the goals of community corrections unmet, the community-based era gave way to the warehousing era.

**Warehousing Era (1980–1995)**   During the warehousing era, indeterminate sentencing gave way to determinate sentencing in all states. Parole release was abolished in a number of states and the federal government, and the pendulum swung from rehabilitation to incapacitation. Within 15 years, the number of persons under correctional supervision jumped from 1.8 million to almost 6 million. Prisons were over capacity, and controlling prisoners in such an environment was difficult. For staff and inmates alike, the nation's prisons were dangerous places to be. Extreme crowding resulted in violent disturbances, which further hardened the attitudes of correctional policy makers and caused them to crack down even more.

**Just-Deserts Era (1995–Present)**   The philosophy of just deserts, popular in the 18th century, returned. Under that philosophy, offenders are punished because they deserve it, and the sanction used depends on the seriousness of the offense. Just deserts is not concerned with inmate rehabilitation, treatment, or reform. It separates treatment from punishment. Prisons today provide opportunities for inmates to improve themselves, but participation is not mandatory, nor is it a condition of release, as it was for most of this century. Change is facilitated, not coerced. Determinate sentencing, capital punishment, truth in sentencing, and three-strikes laws have grown in popularity. As we move into the twenty-first century, "supermax" and no-frills prisons are becoming the trend.

# Programs for Prisoners

Among the most important elements of an inmate's institutional experience, whether in federal or state prison, are the programs and services available. The American Correctional Association's policy on conditions of confinement advocates strong programs that meet offenders' needs (see Exhibit 7–1). The programs described in this section are classification, orientation, unit management, a daily routine, work assignments, education and recreation, medical and mental health services, and drug and alcohol treatment.

**EXHIBIT 7–1**

## American Correctional Association Conditions of Confinement

### Policy Statement

Maintaining acceptable conditions of confinement requires adequate resources and effective management of the physical plant, operational procedures, programs, and staff. To provide acceptable conditions agencies should:

**A.** Establish and maintain a safe and humane population limit for each institution based upon recognized professional standards;

**B.** Provide an environment that will support the health and safety of staff, confined persons, and citizens participating in programs. Such an environment results from appropriate design, construction, and maintenance of the physical plant as well as the effective operation of the facility and programming of offenders;

**C.** Maintain a professional and accountable work environment for staff that includes necessary training and supervision as well as sufficient staffing to carry out the mission of the facility;

**D.** Maintain a fair and disciplined environment that provides a range of programs and services appropriate to the needs and requirements of offenders, in a climate that encourages responsible behavior.

# Classification

Prisoner classification is the process of subdividing the inmate population into meaningful categories to match offender needs with correctional resources. It is based on the premise that there are wide differences among prisoners. Its purpose is to assign inmates to appropriate prison housing and to help staff understand, treat, predict, and manage prisoner behavior. One hundred years ago, the Elmira Reformatory in Elmira, New York, classified offenders as "specimens" and labeled them "Mathematical Dullards," "Those Deficient in Self-Control," and "Stupid."[2] Today the classifications are more sophisticated. Still, the belief is that "somewhere between the extremes of 'all offenders are alike' and 'each offender is unique' lies a system (or systems) of categorization along pertinent dimensions that will prove to be of value in reaching correctional goals."[3] That is why not all persons who have killed others are in high-security prisons or on death row. Persons convicted of manslaughter generally are not placed under high security and are not sentenced to die. Proper prisoner classification considers the type of institution and the level of security that an offender needs.

The two broad goals of classification are: (1) to assign prisoners to institutions that match their security and program needs and (2) to enhance prison security. In reaching those goals, a clear, objective classification system offers at least four advantages over less systematic assignment.[4] First, separating inmates by risk level and program needs puts extremely aggressive inmates in high security while those who require less security or are at risk of being victimized are kept in low security. Within those levels of security, prisoners' needs can also be considered. Does the facility offer drug and alcohol treatment? Sex offender treatment? Anger management training? GED preparation? Such classification offers prisoners a chance for counseling,

*Classification of incoming inmates is based on many factors, including medical and health-care needs, custody needs and institutional risk, work skills, and educational needs. Classification serves the custody goals of a prison but tends to label prisoners. Is such labeling appropriate?*

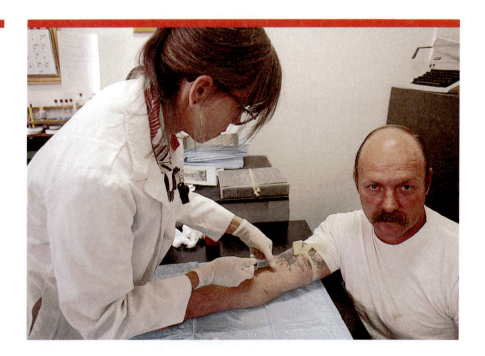

education, or vocational training, and it may keep aggressive inmates from assaulting passive inmates.

The second advantage of a good classification system is that it minimizes misclassification, thus promoting a safe environment for inmates and staff. For example, when prisons are over capacity, as they are today, staff feel pressure to classify inmates quickly. This results in misclassification. A good classification system will include safeguards against misclassification. For example, when there is not enough space in maximum-security facilities, the system will direct staff to house only the lowest-risk high-security inmates in medium-security facilities and never to house high-risk inmates in minimum-security units.

The third advantage a good classification system has for enhancing prison security is that it more accurately places inmates and more effectively deploys staff. Without good classification, the tendency is to place inmates in more secure, more expensive prisons than necessary. Good classification controls the inmate population, assigns inmates to appropriate security levels, and allows better deployment of staff. That results in better use of all resources.

The final way a clear classification system enhances prison security is by reducing tension in prison. For example, misclassification can jeopardize a prison's security and increase violence and escapes. Whether high-risk offenders are housed in low-risk prisons not capable of controlling their behavior or low-risk prisoners are housed in high-risk prisons not capable of protecting them, tension, violence, and the number of escapes mount. Good classification helps to reduce these problems. A review of the major developments and trends in prisoner classification over a recent 20-year period found significant improvement in classification technology (for example, computer software to help collect, store, and manage the data) and more sophisticated assessment of risk and of such needs as medical and mental health treatment and education.[5]

Factors commonly used in inmate classification include offense severity, history of escape or violence, expected length of incarceration, and types of prior commitments to correctional facilities. In a number of jurisdictions, including the federal Bureau of Prisons (BOP), additional public safety considerations require increased security measures to ensure the protection of society from certain offenders. These include sex offenders and offenders convicted of the most brutal crimes.

**Corrections Officer**

Medium-security adult correctional facility is seeking qualified individuals for several positions. Shift work. Degree or 2 years' experience in corrections, criminal justice, probation, parole, or law enforcement required. Must be at least 21 years old, possess a valid driver's license, and pass a criminal background check. Duties include monitoring client activities, report writing, filing. Computer skills and prior experience working with offender population desirable. Pay based on experience and education.

## Orientation to the Institution

State and federal prison systems use a standard approach to managing offenders after they are committed to the correctional institution by the court. For the first week or two at an institution, inmates participate in an admission and orientation program. It provides an introduction to all aspects of the institution and includes screening by staff from the case management, medical, and mental health units. Inmates receive copies of the institution's rules and regulations, including the inmate discipline policy, and they are introduced to the programs, services, policies, and procedures of the facility.

## Unit Management

**unit management system** A method of controlling prisoners in self-contained living areas that include office space for unit staff, making staff and inmates accessible to each other. A unit team—typically composed of the unit manager, one or more case managers, two or more correctional counselors, and a unit secretary—is responsible for the inmates living in that unit.

After orientation, each inmate is assigned living quarters. The institution's security level and the inmate's custody status determine whether the inmate will be housed in a single or double cell, a dormitory, or some other multiple-occupant room. In the federal system and in a number of states, prisons use a **unit management system**. A unit is a self-contained inmate living area that includes office space for unit staff, so staff and inmates are accessible to each other. The unit team—typically composed of the unit manager, one or more case managers, two or more correctional counselors, and a unit secretary—is directly responsible for the inmates living in that unit.

After the initial orientation, each inmate meets with the unit team to formulate a program plan, which may include drug treatment, education, and vocational training as well as institution maintenance jobs or other work assignments. The unit team reviews the inmate's progress and makes changes in the program plan as needed. Unit management emphasizes candid, open communication between staff and inmates. Direct and frequent communication helps staff know inmates, understand their needs, and respond appropriately to those needs. In prison systems without unit management, program planning and staff and inmate interaction are not encouraged.

## Daily Routine

A typical prison day begins with breakfast at 6:30 A.M. For inmates with prison jobs, work begins about 7:30. By this time, inmates are expected to have cleaned their personal living areas and made their beds. After work and the evening meal, inmates may participate in organized or individual recreation, watch television, or engage in personal hobbies. In most prisons, inmates must remain in their quarters after the 10 P.M. count. The weekend and holiday routines are somewhat more relaxed for all inmates.

Prisons regularly count inmates to ensure that all are where they are supposed to be. How often inmates are counted varies considerably. In some prisons, formal inmate counts are taken five times a day, including a morning count at 6, an afternoon count at 4, and three counts between 10 P.M. and morning. Informal counts may be conducted in program areas at various times during the day, to ensure that inmates are in the proper place. Emergency counts may be held at any time. On weekends and holidays, when routines are more relaxed, counts are still made.

## Work Assignments

Work is a very important part of institutional management and offender programs. Meaningful work programs are the most powerful tool prison administrators have in managing crowding and idleness, which can lead to disorder and violence.

Many states operate prison industries to employ and train inmates. Prison administrators believe the training-oriented work helps inmates return to society as useful, productive citizens. The prison industries provide a variety of goods and services for the prisons, thereby reducing the costs of

PRIDE Enterprises of Florida is a unique business. Its mission is to train inmate workers and create job opportunities, which will be strengthened by the establishment of a variety of industries under the Prison Industry Enhancement (PIE) program. PRIDE is chartering a process to ensure the integrity of the present PRIDE operation, while at the same time providing a structure to expand PIE industries. In 1998, PRIDE trained a total of 4,870 inmate workers, surpassing the previous year's total. With 4,321,548 hours worked, this nontraditional workforce is helping to increase productivity and keep jobs in America that might otherwise go offshore. Inmate workers represent a skilled and dependable workforce in today's tight labor market and a ready human resource for private-sector partners. PRIDE alone, with sales of $81.2 million in fiscal 1998, contributed $1.5 million to the state of Florida, including $300,000 for victim restitution and $900,00 for on-the-job training and post-release job placement. An additional $1.9 million was paid in inmate compensation. Under the PIE program, PRIDE paid an additional $74,600 to help offset the myriad costs of crime and incarceration. Now in its eighteenth year of operation, PRIDE is also encouraged by the current national focus on the potential of inmate workers to become an asset to America's economy.

*Pamela J. Davis*
*President and CEO*
*PRIDE Enterprises of Florida*

prison operation, and offer high-quality products and services to businesses and individuals at substantial savings. Some U.S. corporations have entered partnerships with prisons to use inmate labor to manufacture products or to deliver information services. Inmates generally must undergo training after qualifying to participate in the employment program. Once employed, they must meet performance standards, just as they would if employed on the outside. In many instances, success in working while in prison leads to continued employment with the company after release.

Prison-based industries today include agriculture (29 states), manufacturing (49 states), public works (34 states), prison construction (14 states), and prison maintenance (all states).[6] Private companies generally take one of three approaches when partnering with prisons. The first is the **manpower model**, in which the prison's role is similar to that of a temporary personnel service. The company leases rather than employs the prison workforce. The second approach is the **employer model**. In this approach, the prison provides the company space in which to operate and a labor pool of inmates from which to hire. The company supervises employees and makes all decisions related to personnel, products, wages, and market sales. This is the most common model. The third approach is the **customer**

**manpower model**
An approach to private business partnerships with prisons in which the prison's role is similar to that of a temporary personnel service.

**employer model**  The most common approach to private business partnerships with prisons. The prison provides a company space in which to operate and a labor pool from which to hire. The company supervises its inmate employees and makes all decisions.

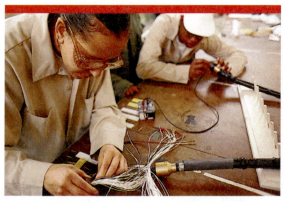 

*Joint ventures between private companies and correctional agencies to operate prison industries offer opportunities for offenders to become gainfully employed and learn salable skills. Left: Female inmates at a correctional facility in Connecticut assemble electronic components. Right: An inmate at a correctional facility in Texas assembles parts for a computer firm. What valuable work habits does joint venture prison employment develop?*

**customer model** An approach to private business partnerships with prisons. In this model, a company contracts with a correctional institution to provide a finished product at an agreed-upon price. The correctional institution owns and operates the business that employs the inmate workforce.

**model**, in which a company contracts with a correctional institution to provide a finished product at an agreed-upon price. In the customer model, the correctional institution owns and operates the business that employs the inmate workforce. For example, the Hennepin County Adult Correctional Facility in Minnesota operates a job shop employing 50 inmates. The shop provides a variety of light assembly, sorting, packaging, and warranty repair services for dozens of private firms in the Minneapolis–St. Paul area.

The benefits of prison industries are many. For companies, inmates represent a readily available and dependable source of entry-level labor, a cost-effective alternative to foreign work forces. Corrections administrators report that joint ventures provide meaningful, productive employment that helps reduce inmate idleness, a common cause of prison disruptions. Prison employment can also motivate positive inmate behavior and good work habits. Inmates benefit by developing valuable work habits, which may reduce the chances of returning to a life of crime. Many others benefit from inmate employment. Deductions from inmates' wages offset the cost of the inmates' incarceration, increase federal and state tax revenues, fund victim compensation, and support inmates' families.

In the federal prison system, Federal Prison Industries, Inc., employs approximately 15 percent (18,000) of the inmate population. Better known by its trade name, UNICOR, it is a self-supporting corporation owned by the federal government and overseen by a governing board appointed by the President. Its mission is to employ and train inmates by operating factories. In 1998, its gross sales were $534.3 million, and its net profit was $2.4 million.[7] UNICOR products include electronic cable assemblies, executive and systems furniture (it ranks ninth in the United States), metal pallet racks, stainless steel food service equipment, mattresses, towels, utility bags, and brooms. UNICOR also provides services, such as data entry, sign making, and printing. To ensure that UNICOR does not compete unfairly with the private sector, product guidelines require a public announcement and a hearing process for any new product it proposes.

Inmates employed by UNICOR start out earning 23 cents per hour. The maximum wage is $1.15 per hour. Although wages are low in most prison industry programs, most inmates who work in them are more interested in doing something meaningful that keeps them busy and makes serving time seem to go faster. In many cases, prisoners also learn job skills and have a better chance of staying crime-free after release.

*Many state correctional systems channel prison labor into industrial and commercial programs. One such program is the Prison Blues® brand of jeans, tee shirts, work shirts, and yard coats manufactured by Inside Oregon Enterprises, a division of the Oregon Department of Corrections. What benefits to inmates do such work programs provide?*

## Education and Recreation Programs

The majority of prisoners cannot read or write well enough to function in society. In fact, the illiteracy rate among prisoners is 3½ times that in the U.S. adult population. Only 38 percent of the 1.3 million state and federal prisoners have completed high school, GED, or above.[8] That's a prisoner illiteracy rate of 62 percent! In comparison, 82 percent of the U.S. adult population have completed high school, GED, or above, and only 18 percent cannot read or write at the high school level.[9] States vary considerably in the education and recreation programs they provide for prisoners. For inmates without a high school diploma, some states provide adult basic education or GED classes. Some states offer academic and life skills programs. Other states form alliances with colleges to provide college-level educational opportunities for inmates.

Each federal prison has an education department which is responsible for providing literacy programs and other education programs for prisoners. Generally, at minimum-security federal institutions, only literacy programs are offered. At higher-security facilities, a broader range of programs is usually provided. Literacy is the only mandatory education program in the fed-

eral prison system. It is required by statute for all federal prisoners who are functionally illiterate. Non-English-speaking inmates are required to participate in an English-as-a-second-language program until they are able to function at the eighth-grade level. Inmates who do not have a GED or a high school diploma are required by BOP policy to enroll in an adult literacy program for 120 days.

Occupational training is also provided in a wide variety of areas but is often limited to a few inmates. In addition to the occupational training that inmates receive by working in prison industries, some inmates receive training in building construction, heating and air-conditioning, auto mechanics, computer-assisted drafting, electronics, food preparation, and business education.

Although the number of inmates who can participate in occupational training is limited, all inmates are entitled to some form of recreation. Recreation and organized sports can make doing time more bearable and, as a result, make the jobs of correctional officers easier. They can also be used as an incentive for good behavior, and by reducing tension, they can cut the number of prison assaults. Physical and mental health experts tell us that recreation programs can be a vehicle for teaching ways to promote health and prevent disease. Inmates who play hard are more likely to stay fit, possibly reducing health costs. Nutrition experts know that eating healthful food, having a regular exercise program, and stopping smoking are central to maintaining good health in prison. They also reduce the cost of prison medical care.

## Medical and Mental Health Services

Prisons vary in the way they provide medical and mental health services. In Oregon, for example, prison medical and mental health professionals are state employees. Georgia, on the other hand, contracts for services with local medical and mental health care providers. Interest in contracting for individual services is growing.

Ordinarily, inmates who are sick are required to make an appointment and get an appointment slip. If an illness occurs after hours, prison staff evaluate the situation and decide whether to seek emergency care. In most prisons, medication is dispensed at a specific location during specified periods. Staff watch while inmates take their medication, to guard against the hoarding of medication for sale or for a possible suicide attempt and to make sure prisoners are taking the medication they need.

Inmates with special health care needs (such as aging and HIV/AIDS) are treated differently in different jurisdictions. Some states segregate HIV-positive prisoners. The federal system provides treatment for HIV-positive inmates through outpatient clinics, inpatient hospitals, and prison hospice programs, emphasizing education, not segregation.

Typical mental health services include initial testing and evaluation, crisis intervention counseling, individual and group therapy, drug and alcohol dependency counseling and awareness, psychological and psychiatric counseling, employment counseling, life skills and community adjustment

I was on my unit doing nothing—gambling and talking slick and hustling inside the institution—the same things I did on the outside, and I got tired of it. So when my friend enrolled in the Life Skills Program, which teaches reading, math, anger management, ways to reduce violence, and life skills like credit and banking, job search, and legal and family responsibilities, I decided to enroll. It broke the monotony of prison—gave me structure. The *Cage Your Rage* book and videos and acting out prison scenes—for example, someone knocking over your cup of coffee—helped me deal with my anger. I used to get angry if someone on the basketball court called a foul. The program taught me a different perspective: considering the consequences of my actions.

*A released program graduate*
*Life Skills Program*
*Delaware Department of Correction*

counseling, parent training, and suicide prevention. Inmates judged criminally insane and those suffering from severe mental illness are sometimes cared for in specialized facilities.

Providing inmates adequate health care is of concern to the courts and professional associations. In 1976, the U.S. Supreme Court ruled in *Estelle v. Gamble*[10] that inmates have a constitutional right to reasonable, adequate health services for serious medical needs. However, the Court also made clear that such a right did not mean that prisoners have unqualified access to health care. Lower courts have held that the Constitution does not require the medical care provided prisoners to be perfect, the best obtainable, or even very good.[11] According to an excellent review of legal health care standards and the legal remedies available to prisoners, the courts support the **principle of least eligibility**: that prison conditions—including the delivery of health care—must be a step below those of the working class and people on welfare. As a result, prisoners are denied access to medical specialists, second opinions, prompt delivery of medical services, technologically advanced diagnostic techniques, the latest medications, and up-to-date medical procedures. In addition, prisoners do not have the right to sue physicians for malpractice, or if they do, the damages are lower than those awarded to persons outside prison. Still, health care professionals and inmate advocates—such as the American Medical Association and the American Correctional Health Services Association—insist on alleviating the pain and suffering of all persons, regardless of their status. They believe that no distinction should be made between inmates and free citizens.

**principle of least eligibility**   The requirement that prison conditions—including the delivery of health care—must be a step below those of the working class and people on welfare.

## Drug Treatment Programs

In most prisons today, the percentage of prisoners who are drug offenders is increasing significantly. Officials estimate that 70 to 85 percent of prison inmates need some sort of substance abuse treatment.[12] Drug and alcohol treatment should be particularly important in prison because it is generally accepted that it reduces recidivism. Drug treatment is not guaranteed, and when offered, it is not always of high quality. Most state institutions do not have the staff or the resources to provide treatment to every inmate who needs it. In 1996, only 13 percent of state inmates and 10 percent of federal inmates were in treatment. It is estimated that of the 60 percent of prisoners serving sentences for drug offenses, about one-third have moderate to severe substance abuse problems that urgently need care. Furthermore, as the number of inmates in need of treatment has risen, the proportion receiving treatment has declined.[13]

Recently the BOP evaluated its drug abuse treatment program. The inmates in the evaluation had been released into the community for 6 to 12 months after completing a three-stage treatment program. In the first stage, inmates participated in a residential drug abuse treatment program for 9 or 12 months. Inmates continued the treatment up to 12 more months after they returned to the general prison population. Treatment continued with community drug treatment providers in a community residential center during a transition from prison to parole. The offenders who had completed the program were found less likely to be re-arrested or to be caught using drugs again than were similar offenders who had not participated in the program.[14] Because previous research had indicated that the first 6 to 12 months after release are often a critical period for an offender, the results of this evaluation suggest that drug treatment can improve the lives of offenders and reduce recidivism.

# Who Is in Prison Today?

On January 1, 1999, 1,302,019 adults were in the custody of state and federal prison authorities—123,041 in federal prisons, 1,178,978 in state prisons.[15] This is an increase of 4.8 percent from one year earlier, less than the average annual increase of 6.9 percent for every year since 1990. At the start of 1999, approximately 461 persons per 100,000 U.S. residents were incarcerated in a state or federal prison. California had the most inmates (161,904); North Dakota had the fewest (915). See Table 7–1.

States with almost identical populations and crime rates have widely different rates of incarceration. For example, in 1998, Alabama had a population of 4.3 million residents, a crime rate of 4,889 offenses per 100,000 population,[16] and an incarceration rate of 519 per 100,000. Minnesota had 4.3 million residents, a crime rate of 4,413 offenses per 100,000 population, and an incarceration rate of only 117 per 100,000 population. With similar population and crime rates, Alabama's incarceration rate was four times Minnesota's! The difference in rates reflects differences in the way the states use prison. It shows that a state's prison population is not related to the size of its total population or to its crime rate. Rather, a large prison population is a result of a conscious choice to use prison to punish offenders.

TABLE 7–1

## Prison Statistics Among the States and the Federal Government in 1998

| | Number of Inmates | | Incarceration Rate per 100,000 State Residents | | Number of Female Prisoners | |
|---|---|---|---|---|---|---|
| **Ten Highest** | California | 161,904 | Louisiana | 736 | California | 11,694 |
| | Texas | 144,510 | Texas | 724 | Texas | 10,343 |
| | Federal | 123,041 | Oklahoma | 622 | Federal | 9,186 |
| | New York | 72,638 | Mississippi | 574 | New York | 3,631 |
| | Florida | 67,224 | South Carolina | 550 | Florida | 3,526 |
| | Ohio | 48,450 | Nevada | 542 | Ohio | 2,912 |
| | Michigan | 45,879 | Alabama | 519 | Illinois | 2,646 |
| | Illinois | 43,051 | Arizona | 507 | Georgia | 2,474 |
| | Georgia | 39,252 | Georgia | 502 | Louisiana | 2,126 |
| | Pennsylvania | 36,377 | California | 483 | Oklahoma | 2,091 |
| **Ten Lowest** | North Dakota | 915 | Minnesota | 117 | Vermont | 45 |
| | Vermont | 1,426 | Maine | 125 | Maine | 63 |
| | Wyoming | 1,571 | North Dakota | 128 | North Dakota | 69 |
| | Maine | 1,612 | New Hampshire | 182 | New Hampshire | 116 |
| | New Hampshire | 2,169 | Vermont | 188 | Wyoming | 131 |
| | South Dakota | 2,435 | West Virginia | 192 | South Dakota | 202 |
| | Montana | 2,734 | Utah | 205 | West Virginia | 211 |
| | West Virginia | 3,445 | Nebraska | 215 | Rhode Island | 235 |
| | Rhode Island | 3,478 | Rhode Island | 220 | Montana | 248 |
| | Nebraska | 3,676 | Washington | 247 | Nebraska | 254 |

*Source:* Adapted from Allen J. Beck and Christopher J. Mumola, *Prisoners in 1998* (Washington: Bureau of Justice Statistics, August 1999).

## Women Prisoners

Over the past decade, the number of women in prison has tripled while the number of men has doubled. On January 1, 1999, women prisoners constituted 6.5 percent (84,631) of the U.S. prison population. (See Figure 7–2.) The rate of incarceration for women was 57 per 100,000 female residents, compared with 885 males per 100,000 male residents. See Table 7–1 for the states with the highest and lowest female prison populations.

## Minority Prisoners

The percentage of state and federal prisoners that belong to minority groups has been increasing. From 1990 to 1997, the percentage of black, Hispanic (of any race), American Indian, Alaska Native, and Asian/Pacific Islander inmates increased from 50 percent to 52 percent. If recent incarceration rates remain unchanged, it is estimated that 1 person out of every 20 will serve time in prison during his or her lifetime. The lifetime chances are

## FIGURE 7–2

### Persons Held in State or Federal Prisons

## How Many Are in Prison?

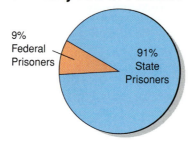

9%
Federal
Prisoners

91%
State
Prisoners

1,178,978 State Prisoners
123,041 Federal Prisoners
1,302,019 Total

## Who Is in Prison?

### Gender

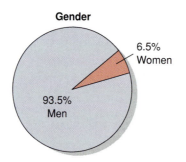

6.5%
Women

93.5%
Men

### Race/Ethnicity*

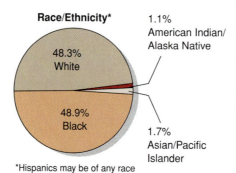

48.3%
White

48.9%
Black

1.1%
American Indian/
Alaska Native

1.7%
Asian/Pacific
Islander

*Hispanics may be of any race

### Age

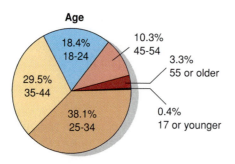

18.4%
18-24

29.5%
35-44

38.1%
25-34

10.3%
45-54

3.3%
55 or older

0.4%
17 or younger

## Why Are They in Prison?

### State Prisoners

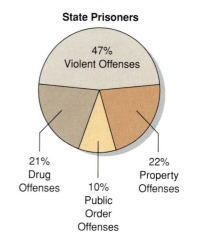

47%
Violent Offenses

21%
Drug
Offenses

10%
Public
Order
Offenses

22%
Property
Offenses

### Federal Prisoners

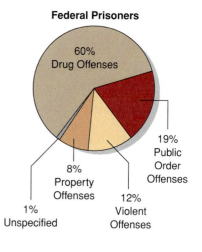

60%
Drug Offenses

19%
Public
Order
Offenses

8%
Property
Offenses

12%
Violent
Offenses

1%
Unspecified

*Source:* Allen J. Beck and Christopher J. Mumola, *Prisoners in 1998* (Washington: Bureau of Justice Statistics, August 1999).

*Prisons Today: Change Stations or Warehouses?*

higher for men (9%) than for women (1%) and higher for blacks (16%) and Hispanics (9%) than for whites (2%). Newborn black males in the United States have a chance greater than 1 in 4 of going to prison during their lifetimes, while Hispanic males have a 1-in-6 chance, and white males have a 1-in-23 chance.[17]

## Age

The nation's population is aging, and this is reflected in the prison population. Middle-aged inmates make up a growing portion of the prison population. In 1991, 65.2 percent of the nation's prisoners were between 18 and 34 years old, and 23 percent were between 35 and 44. In 1998, 18-to-34-year-olds had decreased to 56.5 percent while 35-to-44-year-olds had increased to 29.5 percent. The percentage of inmates 55 and older remained about 3 percent. (See Figure 7–2).

## Most Serious Offense

Another characteristic to compare is the most serious offense of which a prisoner was convicted. Most state inmates (47%) are in prison for violent offenses; most federal inmates (60%), for drug offenses. Figure 7–2 shows the breakdown for other offenses.

# Prison Organization and Administration

All 50 states and the BOP operate prisons. In addition, four local jurisdictions in the United States operate prison systems: Cook County (Chicago), Illinois; Philadelphia; New York City; and Washington, D.C. In 1995, the last year for which data are available, there were 1196 state and federal prisons.[18] Of those, 1008 housed only males, 104 housed only females, and 84 housed both.

Jurisdictions use a variety of capacity measures to reflect both the space available to house inmates and the ability to staff and operate an institution. Some use **rated capacity**, the number of beds or inmates a rating official has assigned to an institution. Some use **operational capacity**, the number of inmates that a facility's staff, existing programs, and services can accommodate. Others use **design capacity**, the number of inmates that planners or architects intended for the facility. For instance, an architect might design a prison for 1100 inmates. Administrators might add more staff, programs, and services to be able to confine 1300 in the same space. The design capacity was 1100, but the operational and rated capacities are 1300. The institution is operating 18 percent above design capacity.

**rated capacity** A measure of prison capacity. It is the number of beds or inmates a rating official has assigned to a prison.

**operational capacity** A measure of prison capacity. It is the number of inmates that a facility's staff, existing programs, and services can accommodate.

**design capacity** A measure of prison capacity. It is the number of inmates that planners or architects intended for the facility.

## State Prison Systems

The administration of state prisons today is a function of the executive branch of government. The governor appoints the director of corrections, who in turn appoints the wardens of the state prisons. A change in governors often means a change in state prison leadership and administration. The organizational structure of the Ohio Department of Rehabilitation and Corrections, which is similar to the structure of corrections departments in other states, is shown in Figure 7–3.

The organization of most state prison systems, like Ohio's, is around a central authority, based in the state capital. Local communities, private contractors, or the state itself may provide prison services (from treatment and education to maintenance and repair). This method of organizational structure and delivery of services across wide geographical areas is often criticized for its fragmentation; duplication of structure, effort, and services; lack of coordination; and ambiguous goals. Still, for legal control and for maintaining an equitable distribution of resources, a centralized model has been maintained, while in other areas of corrections (for example, community corrections and probation) services are often decentralized.

There is no correct way to organize corrections. Any arrangement that helps corrections reach its goals is appropriate. The organizational styles found across the United States developed over time and are the result of political interaction and accommodation among government agencies and interest groups. Today, prisons borrow consumer-oriented management techniques from private businesses. They periodically survey staff and inmates to identify problems and avoid confrontations. Technological improvements allow prison administrators access to more information for decision making, and management training is more popular.

State prison organizations vary in size.[19] The smallest is North Dakota's, with slightly more than 200 employees and an annual budget of $732.4 million for all adult corrections (including probation, intermediate sanctions, prison, and parole). The largest is California's, with almost 35,000 employees and an annual operating budget of $3.6 billion.

Prisons are classified by the level of security they provide. A **maximum-security prison** is designed, organized, and staffed to confine the most violent and dangerous offenders for long periods. It imposes strict controls on the movement of inmates and their visitors, and custody and security are constant concerns. The prison has a highly secure perimeter with watchtowers and high walls. Inmates live in single- or multiple-occupancy barred cells. The staff-to-inmate ratio is high, routines are highly regimented, and prisoner counts are frequent. Programs, amenities, and privileges are few. More than half of the 298 maximum security prisons in the United States held 1,000 inmates or more apiece in 1995.

A **minimum-security prison** confines the least dangerous offenders for both short and long periods. It allows as much freedom of movement and as many privileges and amenities as are consistent with the goals of the facility, while still following procedures to avoid escape, violence, and disturbance. The staff-to-inmate ratio is low, and inmates live in dormitory housing or private rooms. Some leave the institution for programming in the community. About 80 percent of the 440 minimum-security prisons in the United States held fewer than 500 prisoners each in 1995. Prison farms and camps are minimum-security institutions. They are sometimes referred to as **open institutions** because they have no fences or walls surrounding them.

**maximum-security prison** A prison designed, organized, and staffed to confine the most dangerous offenders for long periods. It has a highly secure perimeter, barred cells, and a high staff-to-inmate ratio. It imposes strict controls on the movement of inmates and visitors, and it offers few programs, amenities, or privileges.

**minimum-security prison** A prison that confines the least dangerous offenders for both short and long periods. It allows as much freedom of movement and as many privileges and amenities as are consistent with the goals of the facility, while still following procedures to avoid escape, violence, and disturbance. It may have dormitory housing, and the staff-to-inmate ratio is relatively low.

**open institution** A minimum-security facility that has no fences or walls surrounding it.

**FIGURE 7–3**

## Ohio Department of Rehabilitation and Corrections

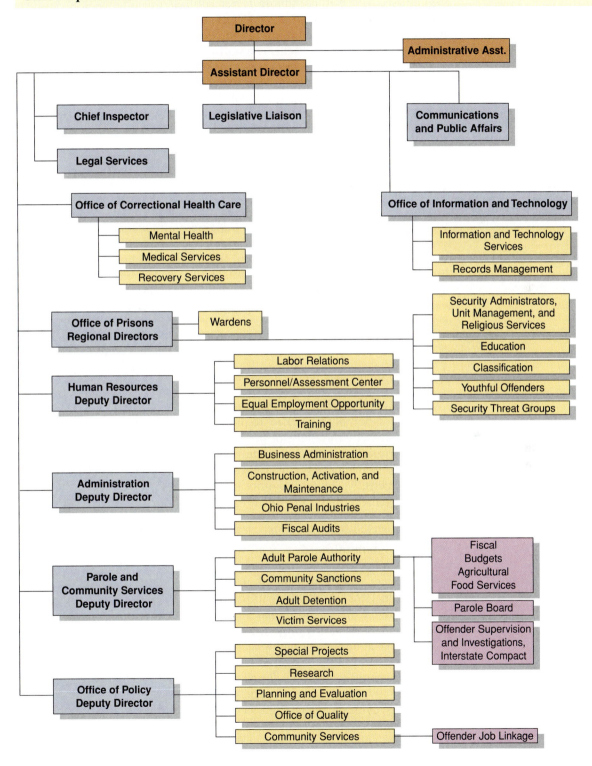

medium-security
prison A prison that
confines offenders considered less dangerous than
those in maximum secu-
rity, for both short and
long periods. It is also
designed, organized, and
staffed to prevent vio-
lence, escape, and disturbance but places fewer
controls on inmates' and
visitors' freedom of movement than a maximum-
security facility. It, too, has
barred cells and a fortified
perimeter. The staff-to-
inmate ratio is generally
lower than in a maxi-
mum-security facility, and
the level of amenities and
privileges is slightly
higher.

Inmates in a **medium-security prison** are considered less dangerous than those in maximum security and may serve short or long sentences. Medium-security prisons impose fewer controls on inmates' and visitors' freedom of movement than maximum-security facilities. Outwardly, medium-security prisons often resemble maximum-security institutions, and they, too, have barred cells. The staff-to-inmate ratio is higher than minimum-security facilities. Medium-security prisons place more emphasis on treatment and work programs than maximum-security prisons, and the level of amenities and privileges is slightly higher. In 1995, 25 percent of the men's prisons were maximum-security. The rest was split between medium- and minimum-security. There are fewer maximum-security and more minimum-security prisons for women: 19 percent maximum-security, 35 percent medium-security, and 46 percent minimum-security.

Prisons are expensive. Besides the cost of building a prison, there are also annual operating costs. In the same way it took money to build the classroom you're in, it takes money each year to operate it (pay for electricity, heat, air conditioning, supplies, building maintenance and upgrading, teachers' salaries, etc.). In 1996, the states spent $22 billion for adult prisons—to build, staff, and maintain the facilities and to house the prisoners. The federal BOP spent an additional $2.5 billion.[20] Approximately $20.7 billion, or 96 percent of state prison expenditures in 1996, went for salaries, wages, benefits, and other operating expenses. Average inmate cost in 1996 was $20,100.

## Federal Bureau of Prisons

The BOP is an entirely separate system from state and local prison systems. The mission of the BOP is "to protect society by confining offenders in the controlled environments of prison and community-based facilities that are safe, humane, and appropriately secure, and that provide work and other self-improvement opportunities to assist offenders in becoming law-abiding citizens."[21] The central office in Washington, D.C., 6 regional offices, 2 training centers, and 93 correctional institutions carry out the BOP mission. The BOP also houses the National Institute of Corrections (NIC) which advises and assists state and local correctional agencies throughout the country, primarily through technical assistance, training, and information services. The Attorney General appoints the director of the BOP. Kathleen Hawk Sawyer, the first woman to hold the position of director, was appointed in 1992. The BOP organizational chart is shown in Figure 7–4.

The BOP employs more than 30,900 people nationwide. Its budget for 1999 was $3.3 billion. The largest portion, $1.48 billion, was for institution security and administration, including the costs of facility maintenance, motor pool operations, powerhouse operations, institution security, and other administrative functions for all BOP facilities. The second-highest cost was $1.18 billion for inmate care and programs. This included all food, medical supplies, clothing, welfare services, release clothing, transportation, staff salaries, and the costs of academic courses, social and occupational education courses, religious programs, psychological services, and drug abuse treatment.

## FIGURE 7–4

**Organization of Federal Bureau of Prisons**

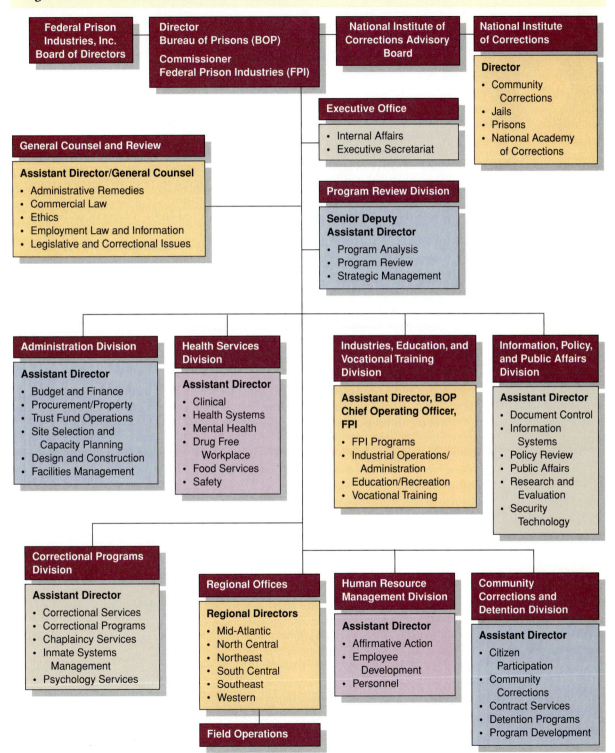

*Rachel Beverly*
*Staff Training Officer*
*Arizona Department of*
*Corrections*

*"You have to be very inquisitive. You have to know a lot about people. You have to be a good communicator. You especially have to be a good listener and develop training programs that adapt to the evolving challenges in the field."*

Rachel Beverly is Staff Training Officer for the Arizona Department of Corrections. She plans the statewide corrections staff training curriculum and coordinates staff training at the Arizona State Prison in Yuma. She joined the department in 1996. Previously, she had worked as an adult probation officer and a jail case manager.

Rachel received her bachelor's degree in criminal justice from California State University at San Bernardino. She feels that a number of undergraduate courses helped her succeed in the corrections field. Constitutional law gave her an appreciation for the ethical issues in corrections. Procedural law gave her an understanding of offenders' due process safeguards. And criminological theory led her to understand that the causes of criminal behavior are complex. She says that criminological theory was "a real challenge."

Rachel believes that careers in corrections can really make a difference in offenders' lives. As a corrections training officer, she believes that her work has additional influences, because she has the opportunity to develop a curriculum that influences the way staff throughout the state interact with inmates.

In the future, Rachel hopes to move forward in corrections administration, possibly doing corrections research and influencing correctional policy.

**Institutions and Security Level** At the start of 1999, the BOP held 123,041 inmates (of whom approximately 14,500 were held in privately managed prisons or facilities under contract with the BOP). The BOP operates institutions of several different security levels to appropriately confine a broad range of federal offenders. The classification of facilities by security level is based on such factors as the presence of gun towers, security barriers, or detection devices; the types of housing within the institution; internal security features; and the staff-to-inmate ratio. Each facility is placed in one of five groups—minimum-security, low-security, medium-security, high-security, and administrative.

■ Minimum-security institutions, also known as federal prison camps (FPCs), have dormitory housing, a relatively low staff-to-inmate ratio, and no fences. These institutions are work- and program-oriented. Many are adjacent to larger institutions or on military bases, where inmates help serve the labor needs of the institution or the base. There are 12 FPCs. Approximately 28 percent (30,391) of BOP inmates are in minimum-security facilities.

- Low-security federal correctional institutions (FCIs) have double-fenced perimeters, mostly dormitory housing, and strong work and program components. The staff-to-inmate ratio in these institutions is higher than in minimum-security facilities.
- Medium-security FCIs have fortified perimeters (often double fences with electronic detection systems), cell housing, and a wide variety of work and treatment programs. They have an even higher staff-to-inmate ratio than low-security FCIs, providing even greater internal controls. There are 47 low- and medium-security FCIs.
- High-security institutions, known as U.S. penitentiaries (USPs), have highly secure perimeters (featuring walls or reinforced fences), multiple- and single-occupancy cell housing, close staff supervision, and strict movement controls. There are 8 USPs.
- Administrative institutions have special missions, such as detention of noncitizens or pretrial offenders, treatment of inmates with serious or chronic medical problems, or containment of extremely dangerous or escape-prone inmates. There are 26 administrative institutions, holding inmates of all security categories. Figure 7–5 shows the locations of all BOP facilities.

As it moves into the twenty-first century, the BOP is planning 11 new facilities, including 5 low- and medium-security FCIs, 4 camps, 1 penitentiary, and 1 metropolitan detention center, to accommodate the expected growth in the federal inmate population.

## FIGURE 7–5

### Institutions of the Federal Bureau of Prisons

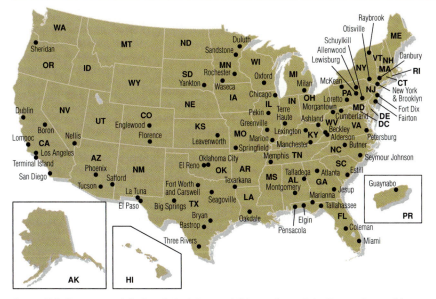

Kathleen Hawk Sawyer,
Director, Bureau of Prisons

*Source:* U.S. Department of Justice, Federal Bureau of Prisons, *State of the Bureau: Accomplishments and Goals, Year-End, 1998* (Washington: U.S. Department of Justice, 1999), p. 23. Some locations have more than one institution.

*Prisons Today: Change Stations or Warehouses?*  CHAPTER 7   215

# 7

## Review and Applications

## SUMMARY BY CHAPTER OBJECTIVES

### CHAPTER OBJECTIVE 1

The Pennsylvania and Auburn prison systems emerged in the United States at the turn of the nineteenth century. The Pennsylvania system isolated prisoners from each other to avoid harmful influences and to allow prisoners to repent. The Auburn system allowed inmates to work together during the day under strict silence. At night, however, prisoners were isolated in small sleeping cells. With time, even sleeping cells became congregate.

### CHAPTER OBJECTIVE 2

There have been nine eras in U.S. prison history:
- The Penitentiary Era (1790–1825)
- The Mass Prison Era (1825–1876)
- The Reformatory Era (1876–1890)
- The Industrial Era (1890–1935)
- The Punitive Era (1935–1945)
- The Treatment Era (1945–1967)
- The Community-Based Era (1967–1980)
- The Warehousing Era (1980–1995)
- The Just-Deserts Era (1995–Present)

### CHAPTER OBJECTIVE 3

Offenders sentenced to prison are first classified into groups based on offense severity, expected length of incarceration, security risk, and program needs. The purpose is to assign inmates to appropriate prison housing and to help staff understand, treat, predict, and manage prisoner behavior.

### CHAPTER OBJECTIVE 4

Programs for prisoners vary among state and federal systems. Prison systems generally offer education and recreation, medical and mental health services, drug abuse treatment, classification, orientation, unit management, daily routines, and work assignments.

### CHAPTER OBJECTIVE 5

On January 1, 1999, 1,178,978 persons were in state prisons; 123,041 were in federal prisons. Of these state and federal inmates, 93.5 percent were male, 48.3 percent were white, and 48.9 percent were black.

### CHAPTER OBJECTIVE 6

All 50 states, the Federal Bureau of Prisons (BOP), and four local jurisdictions operate prison systems. State prison administration, a function of the executive branch of government, is most often organized around a central authority, operating from the state capital. There are three levels of prison security: maximum, for the most dangerous offenders serving long sentences; medium, for less dangerous offenders serving long or short sentences; and minimum, for the least dangerous offenders. Most prisons are either medium- or minimum-security. The BOP operates 93 federal prisons. The BOP operates minimum-security prisons known as federal prison camps, low- and medium-security facilities known as federal correctional institutions, high-security institutions known as U.S. penitentiaries, and administrative institutions with special missions, such as detention of illegal immigrants, treatment of persons with chronic medical problems, and containment of extremely dangerous or escape-prone inmates. The majority of federal prisoners are confined in low- and medium-security facilities.

penitentiary, p. 191
Pennsylvania system, p. 191
Auburn system, p. 192
public-accounts system, p. 193
contract system, p. 193
state-use system, p. 193
convict lease system, p. 193
public-works system, p. 193
medical model, p. 195
unit management system, p. 200
manpower model, p. 201

employer model, p. 201
customer model, p. 202
principle of least eligibility, p. 205
rated capacity, p. 209
operational capacity, p. 209
design capacity, p. 209
maximum-security prison, p. 210
minimum-security prison, p. 210
open institution, p. 210
medium-security prison, p. 212

## QUESTIONS FOR REVIEW

1. Distinguish between the Pennsylvania and Auburn prison systems.
2. How and why did the penitentiary era begin?
3. What was the mass prison era?
4. Why did reformatories develop?
5. What were the characteristics of the first reformatories?
6. Why did industrial prisons develop?
7. Distinguish among the five models used to employ prisoners during the industrial era.
8. What caused the decline in prison industry?
9. What caused the punitive era to evolve?
10. Why did the treatment era begin?
11. What is the medical model?
12. What caused the end of the treatment era?
13. What was the reasoning behind the community-based approach?
14. Describe the warehousing era.

15. What is meant by *just deserts?*
16. What is classification, and what are the advantages of a clear, objective classification system?
17. What is unit management?
18. How are prisons partnering with private companies?
19. What purpose does recreation play in prison?
20. What is the principle of least eligibility? How does it affect prisoners?
21. Are drug treatment programs necessary in prisons? Why or why not?
22. Describe state and federal prison organization and administration.
23. Distinguish among maximum-, medium-, and minimum-security prisons.
24. What is the role of the federal Bureau of Prisons?

## CRITICAL THINKING EXERCISES

### ON-THE-JOB ISSUES

1. According to the Department of Corrections of the state of Washington, the operational capacity of its prisons is 12,966 prisoners.[22] (Recall that *operational capacity* means the number of inmates a facility's staff, programs, and services can accommodate.) If Washington currently incarcerates 14,454 prisoners, what percentage of operational capacity is the inmate population?

2. The state prison where you work as prison industry supervisor contracted with a pharmaceutical company to open an AIDS testing lab and employ 30 prisoners as laboratory technicians. Prisoners will be paid a maximum of one dollar an hour. The local newspaper is running a series of articles on prison industry and wants to interview you. What will you tell them about the advantages of prison industry?

## CORRECTIONS ISSUES

1. Charles Dickens, the English novelist, visited Eastern State Penitentiary in 1842. After witnessing solitary confinement, he wrote that "very few men are capable of estimating the immense amount of torture and agony which this dreadful punishment, prolonged for years, inflicts upon the sufferers."[23] He added, "I hold this slow and daily tampering with the mysteries of the brain to be immeasurably worse than any torture of the body; and because its ghastly signs and tokens are not so palpable to the eye and sense of touch as scars upon the flesh . . . , I denounce it as secret punishment." Do you think Dickens's writing may have influenced reformers to seek other systems of punishment?

2. For 200 years prisons have tried to change inmates' negative behaviors. Recently, the BOP has said that prison is not the ideal setting to do that, nor is such change realistic in prison, considering prisoners' resistance and the failure of previous attempts. What realistic goals of prisons would you devise? What measures of outcome would you propose to tell if prisons are meeting those goals?

## CORRECTIONS ON THE WEB

1. Go to the Justice Information Center at **www.ncjrs.org** or the Bureau of Justice Statistics at **www.ojp.usdoj.gov/bjs**. Review the documents to obtain sources of prisoner data from your state (for example, number and percentage of offenders in jail; numbers and percentages of women, minorities, and so on). Use the data to construct a pie-chart profile of the current prison population in your state.

2. Access the Web site of a state department of corrections. For example, the North Carolina Department of Correction has a site at **www.doc.state.nc.us/**. Review the topics available at the site. Possible topics include prisoners, programs, industries, employment, and administration. Select several topics related to the chapter content, and review the information provided. Then write a summary of what you learn.

## ADDITIONAL READINGS

Branham, Lynn. *The Use of Incarceration in the United States: A Look at the Present and the Future*. Washington: American Bar Association, 1992.

Clements, Carl B. *Offender Needs Assessments*. College Park, MD: American Correctional Association, 1986.

McShane, Marilyn D., and Frank P. Williams III. *The Management of Correctional Institutions*. New York: Garland, 1993.

Sexton, George E. *Work in American Prisons: Joint Ventures with the Private Sector*. Washington: National Institute of Justice, 1995.

Sullivan, Larry E. *The Prison Reform Movement: Forlorn Hope*. Boston: Twayne, 1990.

Zimring, Franklin E., and Gordon Hawkins. *The Scale of Imprisonment*. Chicago: University of Chicago Press, 1991.

# ENDNOTES

1. George E. Sexton, *Work in American Prisons: Joint Ventures with the Private Sector* (Washington: National Institute of Justice, 1995), pp. 2–3. Online, available: http://www. ncjrs.org/txtfiles/workampr.txt.

2. Carl B. Clements, "The Future of Offender Classification: Some Cautions and Prospects," *Criminal Justice and Behavior*, Vol. 8 (1981), pp. 15–16.

3. Carl B. Clements, "Offender Classification: Two Decades of Progress," *Criminal Justice and Behavior*, Vol. 23 (1996), p. 123.

4. James Austin, "Managing Facilities: Objective Offender Classification Is Key to Proper Housing Decisions," *Corrections Today*, Vol. 56, No. 4 (1994), pp. 94–97.

5. Carl B. Clements, "Offender Classification."

6. American Correctional Association, *Correctional Industries Information: Correctional Industries Survey Final Report* (Lanham, MD: American Correctional Association, 1992).

7. Cited in *Hoover's Online* at http://www.hoovers.com/capsules/43053.html on September 29, 1999.

8. Bureau of Justice Statistics, *National Corrections Reporting Programs* (Washington: U.S. Department of Justice, 1994), p. 12.

9. Bureau of the Census, *Statistical Abstract of the United States*, 1997 (Washington: U.S. Department of Commerce, 1997), p. 159.

10. *Estelle* v. *Gamble* 429 U.S. 97 (1976).

11. Michael S. Vaughn and Leo Carroll, "Separate and Unequal: Prison Versus Free-World Medical Care," *Justice Quarterly*, Vol. 15 (1998), pp. 3–40.

12. Center on Addiction and Substance Abuse, *Behind Bars: Substance Abuse and America's Prison Population* (New York: Columbia University, 1998). Online, available: http://www.casacolumbia.org.

13. Ibid.

14. Federal Bureau of Prisons, *Triad Drug Treatment Evaluation, Six-Month Report, Executive Summary* (Washington: Federal Bureau of Prisons, no date. Online, available: http://www.bop.gov/triad.html.

15. Allen J. Beck and Christopher J. Mumola, *Prisoners in 1998* (Washington: Bureau of Justice Statistics, August 1999).

16. Federal Bureau of Investigation, *Crime in the United States 1997* (Washington: Federal Bureau of Investigation, 1998).

17. Thomas P. Bonczar and Allen J. Beck, *Lifetime Likelihood of Going to State or Federal Prison* (Washington: Bureau of Justice Statistics, 1997).

18. James J. Stephan, *Census of State and Federal Correctional Facilities*, 1995 (Washington: Bureau of Justice Statistics, August 1997).

19. For a complete listing of organization names, sizes, budgets, personnel, responsibilities and appointments, and list of all correctional facilities, see American Correctional Association, *1999 Directory of Juvenile and Adult Correctional Departments, Institutions, Agencies and Paroling Authorities* (Lanham, MD: American Correctional Association, 1999).

20. James J. Stephan, *State Prison Expenditures*, 1996 (Washington: Bureau of Justice Statistics, August 1999).

21. Federal Bureau of Prisons, "Monday Morning Highlights" (Washington: Federal Bureau of Prisons, October 18, 1999).

22. Online at http://www.wa.gov/doc/.

23. Charles Dickens, *American Notes and Pictures From Italy* (London: Chapman & Hall, 1842), Vol. I, p. 238.

# 8

# The Staff World
## Managing the Prison Population

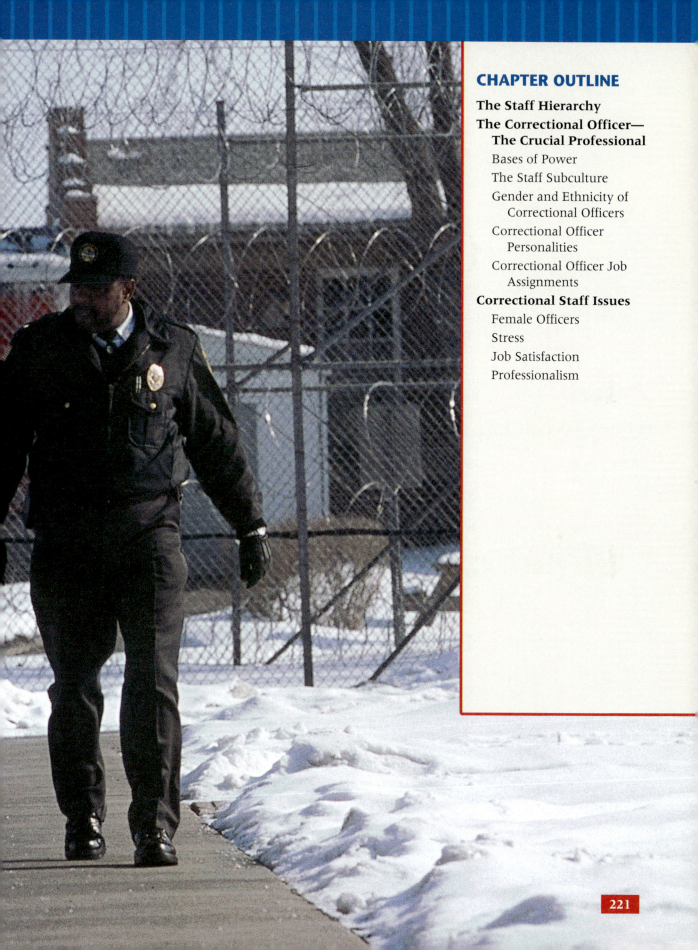

221

*Corrections is not a business where only one sex, race, religion, or type of person can succeed. It takes men and women of all races, religions, and color to create a dynamic and effective workforce to manage diverse inmates and solve the problems we face.*

—Dora Schriro, former Missouri Director of Corrections

On a calm Saturday afternoon in April 1998 at the Everglades Correctional Institute, a maximum-security prison in Florida, correctional officers staffing guard towers were shocked to see a big-rig truck heading toward prison fences and beginning to accelerate.[1] The truck rammed through four security fences and stopped in the middle of the prison yard. The driver, later identified as 31-year-old John Beaston, pulled out a shotgun and started firing at officers in the towers and the yard. Two officers were injured. Other officers returned fire.

A car, allegedly driven by 58-year-old Sandra Sigler, then drove through the hole the truck had ripped in the prison fences, picked up Beaston and inmate Jay Junior Sigler, 31, and sped away. Jay Sigler, son of Sandra Sigler, had served 8 years of a 20-year sentence for armed robbery.

Prison superintendent Joe T. Butler spoke to reporters shortly after the prison break. "I guess we were blessed, but my officers did respond appropriately and got the inmates to their respective dormitories," he said. "This happened in the daytime and there are a lot of activities in the prison at that time, both recreation and visitation."

The Everglades Correctional Institute is a state-of-the art facility, incorporating a number of high-technology security systems. The institution houses more than 1500 prisoners. Butler said the breakout did not raise new security concerns. "I think anyone would think this was a very unusual situation," he noted. "How often do you hear about a semi truck . . . crashing through your security system?"

# The Staff Hierarchy

Although planned escapes with outside help are rare, correctional personnel must be constantly alert for possible threats to institutional security. Ever since prisons began, one observer after another has noted that security is the number one concern of correctional staff. Barnes and Teeters, for example, wrote more than half a century ago: "Above all else, the main purpose of the prison is to keep the prisoners from escaping."[2]

Practically speaking, a prison of any size has a number of different staff roles—each with its own unique set of tasks. **Roles** are the normal patterns of behavior expected of those holding particular social positions. **Staff roles** are the patterns of behavior expected of correctional staff members in particular jobs. Eventually, many people internalize the expectations others have of them, and such expectations can play an important part in their self-perceptions.

**roles**  The normal patterns of behavior expected of those holding particular social positions.

**staff roles**  The patterns of behavior expected of correctional staff members in particular jobs.

Ideally, today's correctional staff members have four main goals:

1. To provide for the security of the community by incarcerating those who break the law.
2. To promote the smooth and effective functioning of the institution.
3. To ensure that incarceration is secure but humane.
4. To give inmates the opportunity to develop a positive lifestyle while incarcerated and to gain the personal and employment skills they need for a positive lifestyle after release.[3]

Prison staff are organized into a hierarchy, or multilevel categorization, according to responsibilities. An institution's hierarchy generally has the warden or superintendent at the top and includes a level for correctional officers. A typical correctional staff hierarchy includes:

- Administrative staff (wardens, superintendents, assistant superintendents, and others charged with running the institution and its programs and with setting policy)
- Clerical personnel (record keepers and administrative assistants)
- Treatment and educational staff (psychologists, psychiatrists, medical doctors, nurses, medical aides, teachers, counselors, caseworkers, and ministers—many of whom contract with the institution to provide services)
- Custodial staff (majors, captains, lieutenants, sergeants, and correctional officers charged primarily with maintaining order and security)
- Service and maintenance staff (kitchen supervisors, physical plant personnel, and many outside contractors)
- Volunteers (prison ministry, speakers, and other volunteers in corrections)

Organizational charts graphically represent the staff structure and the chain of command within an institution. An organizational chart for a typical medium-to-large correctional institution is shown in Figure 8–1. **Custodial staff** are most directly involved in managing the inmate population, through daily contact with inmates. Their role is to control prisoners within the institution. **Program staff**, on the other hand, are concerned with encouraging prisoners to participate in educational, vocational, and treatment programs. Custodial staff, who make up over 60 percent of prison personnel, are generally organized in a military-style hierarchy, from assistant or deputy warden down to correctional officer (see Figure 8–1). Program staff generally operate through a separate organizational structure and have little in common with custodial staff.

Prison management involves to a great extent managing relationships—among employees, between employees and inmates, and between inmates. Prisons are unique in that most of the people in them (the inmates) are forced to live there according to the terms of their sentence; they really do not want to be there. Such a situation presents tremendous challenges. The people on the front lines dealing around the clock with such challenges are the correctional officers.

**custodial staff** Those staff members most directly involved in managing the inmate population.

**program staff** Those staff members concerned with encouraging prisoners to participate in educational, vocational, and treatment programs.

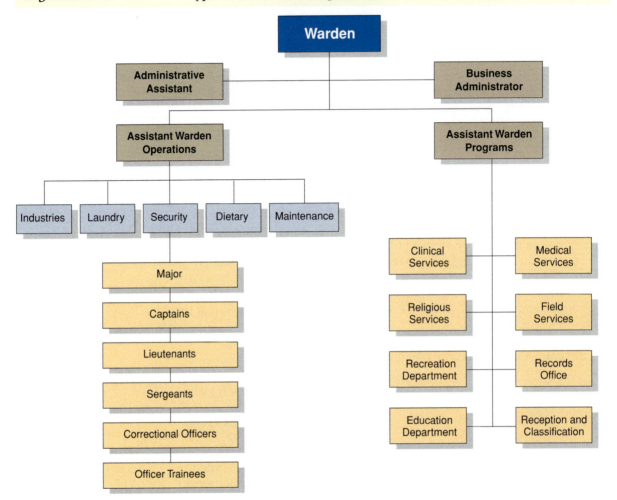

# The Correctional Officer— The Crucial Professional

Although security is still the major concern, correctional officers today are expected to perform a variety of other tasks. As one commentator has said,

> Correctional officers have more responsibilities [now] than in the past and their duty is no longer to merely watch over the prisoners. They now have to play several roles in keeping prisoners in line. They have to be "psychiatrists" when prisoners come to them with their problems and they have to be "arbitrators and protectors" when inmates have complaints or problems with each other, while still watching out for their own safety. In these

situations, the wrong decision could offend someone and start a riot. This makes correctional officers "prisoners" of the daily emotional and physical moods of the inmates.[4]

Don Josi and Dale Sechrest explain it this way:

> Correctional officers today must find a balance between their security role and their responsibility to use relationships with inmates to change their behavior constructively. They routinely assume numerous essential yet sometimes contradictory roles (e.g., counselor, diplomat, caretaker, disciplinarian, supervisor, crisis manager), often under stressful and dangerous conditions."[5]

Josi and Sechrest then go on to say, "These divergent and often incompatible goals can prove problematic; role conflict, role diffusion, and role ambiguity may be difficult if not impossible to avoid."[6]

## Bases of Power

Correctional officers rely on a variety of strategies to manage inmate behavior. After surveying correctional officers in five prisons, John Hepburn identified five bases of officers' power: legitimate power, coercive power, reward power, expert power, and referent power.

**Legitimate Power**   Correctional officers have power by virtue of their positions within the organization. That is, they have formal authority to command. As Hepburn says, "the prison guard has the right to exercise control over prisoners by virtue of the structural relationship between the position of the guard and the position of the prisoner."[7]

**Coercive Power**   Inmates' beliefs that a correctional officer can and will punish disobedience give the officer coercive power. Many correctional officers use coercive power as a primary method of control.

**Reward Power**   Correctional officers dispense both formal and informal rewards to induce cooperation among inmates. Formal rewards include assignment of desirable jobs, housing, and other inmate privileges. Correctional officers are also in a position to influence parole decisions and to assign good-time credit and **gain time** to inmates. Informal rewards correctional officers use include granting special favors and overlooking minor infractions of rules.

**Expert Power**   Expert power results from inmates' perceptions that certain correctional officers have valuable skills. For example, inmates seeking treatment may value treatment-oriented officers. Inmates who need help with ongoing interpersonal conflicts may value officers who have conflict-resolution skills. Such officers may be able to exert influence on inmates who want their help.

**HELP WANTED**

**Business Manager— High-Custody Institution**

Works in a Class 1 institution housing more than 1000 inmates. Is responsible for the administration of business and personnel activities; preparation of operating budgets; procurement, storage, and distribution of materials, supplies, and equipment; the food service program; powerhouse control; and maintenance of buildings and grounds. Requirements include six years of financial experience in a medical, educational, correctional, or training facility; master's degree in business, public administration, accounting, or finance.

**gain time**   Time taken off an inmate's sentence for participating in certain activities such as going to school, learning a trade, working in prison, etc.

*Correctional officers need to obtain inmates' cooperation to carry out their custodial duties. What are some techniques officers might use?*

**Referent Power**   Referent power flows from "persuasive diplomacy." Officers who win the respect and admiration of prisoners—officers who are fair and not abusive—may achieve a kind of natural leadership position over inmates.

Some years before Hepburn's study, Gresham Sykes wrote that correctional officers' power can be corrupted through inappropriate relationships with inmates.[8] Friendships with prisoners, as well as indebtedness to them, can corrupt. According to Sykes, staff members who get too close to inmates and establish friendships are likely to find their "friends" asking for special favors. Similarly, officers who accept help from inmates may one day find that it's "payback time." In difficult or dangerous situations, help may be difficult to decline. In such cases, staff members must be careful not to let any perceived indebtedness to inmates influence their future behavior.

## The Staff Subculture

Prison life is characterized by duality. An enormous gap separates those who work in prisons from those who live in them. This gap has a number of dimensions. One is that staff members officially control the institution and enforce the rules by which inmates live. Other formal and informal differences exist, including differences in background, values, and culture. Primarily, however, the relationship between correctional officers and inmates can be described as one of structured conflict.[9]

**Structured conflict** is a term that describes the tensions between prison staff members and inmates that arise out of the correctional setting. In one sense, the prison is one large society—in which the worlds of inmates

**structured conflict**   The tensions between prison staff members and inmates that arise out of the correctional setting.

*Effective communication is one way of overcoming the differences in beliefs, values, and behaviors between inmates and prison staff. What barriers to communication might such differences create?*

and staff bump up against one another and intermingle. In another sense, however, the two groups keep their distance from each other—a distance imposed by both formal and informal rules. Conflict arises because staff members have control over the lives of inmates while inmates often have little say over important aspects of their own lives. The conflict is structured because it occurs within the confines of an organized institution and because, to some extent, it follows the rules—formal and informal—that govern institutional life.

Both worlds—inmate and staff—have their own cultures. Those cultures are generally called *subcultures* to indicate that both are contained within and surrounded by a larger culture. One writer has defined **subculture** as the beliefs, values, behavior, and material objects shared by a particular group of people within a larger society.[10] That is the definition we will use. The subcultures of inmates and correctional officers exist simultaneously in any prison institution. The beliefs, values, and behavior that make up the **staff subculture** differ greatly from the inmate subculture. Additionally, staff members possess material objects of control, such as keys, vehicles, weapons, and security systems.

Kauffman has identified a distinct correctional-officer subculture within prisons.[11] This set of beliefs, values, and behaviors sets correctional officers apart from other prison staff and from inmates. Their beliefs and values form an "officer code," which includes the following:

- Always go to the aid of an officer in distress.
- Don't "lug" drugs (bring them in for inmate use).
- Don't rat on other officers.

**subculture** The beliefs, values, behavior, and material objects shared by a particular group of people within a larger society.

**staff subculture** The beliefs, values, and behavior of staff. They differ greatly from those of the inmate subculture.

- Never make a fellow officer look bad in front of inmates.
- Always support an officer in a dispute with an inmate.
- Always support officer sanctions against inmates.
- Don't be a "white hat" or a "goody two-shoes."
- Maintain officer solidarity in dealings with all outside groups.
- Show positive concern for fellow officers.

# Gender and Ethnicity of Correctional Officers

According to the American Correctional Association (ACA), state and local adult correctional facilities employed 337,736 custodial and administrative staff members as of September 30, 1997.[12] According to the ACA, most correctional personnel at state and local levels are white males. Of 105,975 female staff members, almost two-thirds (64.5%) are white (see Figure 8–2). Thirty percent of corrections personnel are members of minority groups. Of these, most are black (20%).

Ideally, the ethnic breakdown of correctional staff should closely approximate the ethnic breakdown of the population of the United States. According to the U.S. Census Bureau,[13] out of a 1995 population of about 265 million people, 33 million persons (12.7%) were black, 22.8 million (8.9%) were Hispanic, and 9.5 million (4%) were members of other minor-

## FIGURE 8–2

### Profile of Correctional Personnel in Adult State and Local Correctional Facilities

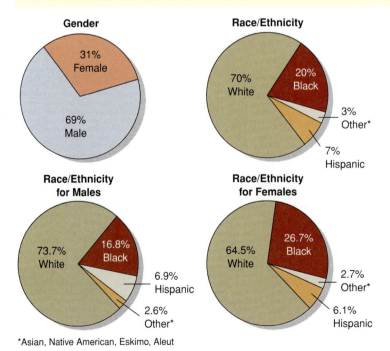

*Asian, Native American, Eskimo, Aleut

*Source:* Preliminary data (1996) from the table "Personnel in Adult and Juvenile Corrections," American Correctional Association, *Vital Statistics in Corrections.* Courtesy of the American Correctional Association.

*The Staff World: Managing the Prison Population*

## FIGURE 8–3

**Ethnic Groups as a Proportion of the U.S. Population and as a Proportion of Prison Staff**

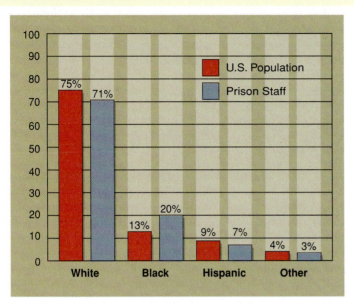

*Sources:* Staff statistics provided by David M. Wakefield, American Correctional Association, fax transmission June 12, 1998; preliminary data for the table "Personnel in Adult and Juvenile Corrections," American Correctional Association, *Vital Statistics in Corrections* (forthcoming). Population statistics derived from U.S. Bureau of the Census, *Population Profile of the United States:1995,* Current Population Reports, Series P23–189 (Washington: U.S. Government Printing Office, 1995); available online: http://www.census.gov/prod/1/pop/profile/95, access: July 20, 1998.

ity groups. Figure 8–3 above compares ethnic groups as a proportion of prison personnel and as a proportion of the U.S. population.

From Figure 8–3, it is easy to see that blacks are overrepresented among correctional personnel. While only 12.7 percent of the U.S. population, they account for 20 percent of the correctional workforce. Hispanics are slightly underrepresented (accounting for 8.9 percent of the country's population and 7 percent of the correctional workforce), as are other minorities (4 percent of the population, 3 percent of correctional staff). Whites, on the other hand, are almost evenly represented.

In addition, the federal Bureau of Prisons employs another 15,239 administrative and custodial personnel, of which 5,118 (33%) are female.[14] About 30 percent of correctional staff members in federal institutions are black. In juvenile facilities, females make up slightly more than 40 percent of a correctional workforce of 30,825.[15]

The American Correctional Association also says that approximately 10 percent of all correctional staff positions are supervisory (i.e., above the level of sergeant). Females hold 22.5 percent of all supervisory positions but only 18 percent of those at the level of warden or superintendent. Blacks fill approximately 21 percent of positions at the level of warden or superintendent. Members of other minority groups hold 5 percent of the top-level positions.[16]

# Correctional Officer Personalities

**correctional officer personalities** The personal characteristics of officers as well as their modes of adaptation to their jobs, institutional conditions, the requirements of staff subculture, and institutional expectations.

The staff subculture contributes to the development of **correctional officer personalities**. Those personalities reflect the personal characteristics of the officers as well as their modes of adaptation to their jobs, institutional conditions, the requirements of staff subculture, and institutional expectations.[17] Common personality types that have been identified include those described in the following paragraphs.[18]

**The Dictator** The dictator likes to give orders and seems to enjoy the feeling of power that comes from ordering inmates around. Correctional officers with dictator personalities are often strongly disliked by prisoners and may face special difficulties if taken hostage during a prison uprising.

**The Friend** The correctional officer who tries to befriend inmates is often a quiet, retiring, but kind individual who believes that close friendships with inmates will make it easier to control the inmates and the work environment. Inmates, however, usually try to capitalize on friendships by asking for special treatment, contraband, and the like.

**The Merchant** Merchant-personality correctional officers set themselves up as commodity providers to the inmate population. If an inmate needs something not easily obtained in prison, the merchant will usually procure it—at a cost. Often, such behavior is a violation of institutional rules, and it can lead to serious violations of the law as the merchant–correctional officer smuggles contraband into the institution for the "right price."

**The Turnkey** Turnkey officers do little beyond the basic requirements of their position. A turnkey usually interacts little with other officers and does the minimum necessary to get through the workday. Unmotivated and bored, the turnkey may be seeking other employment. Some turnkey officers have become disillusioned with their jobs. Others are close to retirement.

**The Climber** The correctional officer who is a climber is set on advancement. He or she may want to be warden or superintendent one day, and is probably seeking rapid promotion. Climbers are often diligent officers who perform their jobs well and respect the corrections profession. Climbers who look down on other officers, however, or attempt to look good by making coworkers look bad, can cause many problems within the institution.

**The Reformer** The reformer constantly finds problems with the way the institution is run or with existing policies and rules. He or she always seems to know better than anyone else and frequently complains about working conditions or supervisors.

**The Do-Gooder** The do-gooder is another type of reformer—one with a personal agenda. A devoutly religious do-gooder may try to convert other correctional officers and inmates to his or her faith. Other do-gooders actively seek to counsel inmates, using personal techniques and philosophies that are not integrated into the prison's official treatment program.

*Charles D. Walston*
*Correctional Trainer*
*North Carolina*
*Department of*
*Correction*

*"Looking back, the majority of what I did was to guide people (offenders) and deal with unacceptable behavior. Even though I tried to be a positive influence on the inmates, the decision to change was all theirs. Now, I am in a position to encourage and motivate new employees. It is extremely rewarding to see students come into a training program with limited knowledge and leave as Certified Correctional Officers, beaming with confidence and professionalism."*

Charles D. Walston is a Correctional Trainer with the North Carolina Department of Correction, Office of Staff Development and Training. He spent almost 12 years working in a close-custody state prison facility with 540 prisoners. Prior to leaving that facility, Charles was the Assistant Commander of the Institutional Prison Emergency Response Team and the First Shift Commander.

His duties currently include the development and delivery of certification training to new correctional employees throughout the state. In North Carolina, successful completion of a four-week basic training results in participants being certified as State Correctional Officers by the state Criminal Justice Training and Standards Commission.

Charles recently received an Associate Degree from a local community college and is currently working to complete a B.S. degree in criminal justice. He enjoys training new employees and helping them get their careers off the ground.

Although the personalities described may be exaggerated, their variety suggests that correctional officer personalities result from many influences, including:

- General life experiences
- Biological propensities
- Upbringing
- Staff subculture
- Working conditions
- Institutional expectations and rules

## Correctional Officer Job Assignments

Seven different correctional officer roles or job assignments have been identified.[19] They are classified by their location within the institution, the duties required, and the nature of the contact with inmates.

**block officers**  Those responsible for supervising inmates in housing areas.

**Block Officers**  Block officers are responsible for supervising inmates in housing areas. Housing areas include dormitories, cell blocks, modular living units, and even tents in some overcrowded prisons. Safety and security are the primary concerns of block officers. Conducting counts, ensuring the orderly movement of prisoners, inspecting personal property, overseeing inmate activity, and searching prisoners are all part of the block officer's job. Block officers also lock and unlock cells and handle problems that arise within the living area. Block officers are greatly outnumbered by the inmates they supervise. Hence, if disturbances occur, block officers usually withdraw quickly to defensible positions within the institution.

**work detail supervisors**  Those that oversee the work of individual inmates and inmate work crews.

**Work Detail Supervisors**  Work detail supervisors oversee the work of individual inmates and inmate work crews assigned to jobs within the institution or outside it. Jobs assigned to inmates may include laundry, kitchen, and farm duties, as well as yard work and building maintenance. Work detail supervisors must also keep track of supplies and tools and maintain inventories of materials. Prison buildings are sometimes constructed almost exclusively with the use of inmate labor—creating the need for large inmate work details. On such large projects, supervising officers usually work in conjunction with outside contractors.

**industrial shop and school officers**  Those that ensure efficient use of training and educational resources within the prison.

**Industrial Shop and School Officers**  Industrial shop and school officers work to ensure efficient use of training and educational resources within the prison. Such resources include workshops, schools, classroom facilities, and associated equipment and tools. These officers oversee inmates who are learning trades, such as welding, woodworking, or automobile mechanics, or who are attending academic classes. Ensuring that students are present and on time for classes to begin, protecting the school and voca-

## THE OFFENDER SPEAKS

Ms. Eagle, a teacher in the Delaware Prison Life Skills Program, invited family members twice to come to the prison. On one occasion, she had the family members and students break into small groups—I wasn't in the same group with my mom—to discuss what various family members should do when someone comes home very late at night. Then each group reported its solutions to the whole class. In my group, a mom actually had a son who was going through this problem. The groups help each family to see how other families would solve the problem, and they also help everyone to see that everyone has the same problems.

*An inmate in the Life Skills Program*

tional instructors, and securing the tools and facilities used in instruction are all part of the job of these officers. The officers work with civilian instructors, teachers, and counselors.

**Yard Officers**   Yard officers supervise inmates in the prison yard. They also take charge of inmates who are (1) moving from place to place, (2) eating, or (3) involved in recreational activities. Like other officers, yard officers are primarily concerned with security and order maintenance.

**Administrative Officers**   Administrative officers are assigned to staff activities within the institution's management center. They control keys and weapons. Some administrative officers oversee visitation. As a result, they have more contact with the public than other officers do. Many administrative officers have little, if any, contact with inmates.

**Perimeter Security Officers**   Perimeter security officers (also called *wall post officers*) are assigned to security (or gun) towers, wall posts, and perimeter patrols. They are charged with preventing escapes and detecting and preventing intrusions (such as packages of drugs or weapons thrown over fences or walls from *outside*). Perimeter security can become a routine job because it involves little interaction with other officers or inmates and because relatively few escape attempts occur. Newer institutions depend more heavily on technological innovations to maintain secure perimeters, requiring fewer officers for day-long perimeter observation.

**Relief Officers**   Relief officers are experienced correctional officers who know and can perform almost any custody role in the institution. They are used to temporarily replace officers who are sick or on vacation or to meet staffing shortages.

# Correctional Staff Issues

## Female Officers

On a pleasant Sunday morning a few years ago, a high-custody female inmate at the Chillicothe (Missouri) Correctional Center was sitting in a dormitory, drinking her morning coffee. Having a good time, surrounded by friends, the inmate began laughing. Soon, however, the laughter turned to choking. Unable to breathe, she turned blue. Correctional officer Lisa Albin rushed to her side, and found her hanging onto her bed, unable to speak. Albin remained calm as she applied the Heimlich maneuver to the inmate. After three attempts, the trapped coffee cleared the inmate's windpipe and she began breathing again. After the incident, the inmate wrote a letter of thanks to the superintendent, saying, "If it had not been for Mrs. Albin I could have very well died in that room. She literally saved my life and I will be forever grateful to her and for the training she received."[20]

Literature and films almost invariably portray correctional officers as "tobacco-chewin', reflective-sunglass-wearin', chain-gang-runnin', good ol' boys."[21] Today's officer generally defies this stereotype, and women working in corrections have helped erode this otherwise persistent myth.

**yard officers**   Those that supervise inmates in the prison yard.

**administrative officers**   Those that control keys and weapons and sometimes oversee visitation.

**perimeter security officers**   Those assigned to security (or gun) towers, wall posts, and perimeter patrols. These officers are charged with preventing escapes and detecting and preventing intrusions.

**relief officers**   Experienced correctional officers who know and can perform almost any custody role within the institution, used to temporarily replace officers who are sick or on vacation or to meet staffing shortages.

Like most women working in male-dominated professions, female correctional officers face special problems and barriers—many of which are rooted in sexism. Prisons are nontraditional workplaces for women. As a consequence, female correctional officers—especially those working in men's prisons—often find themselves in a confusing position. As one author explains it: "On the one hand, to be female is to be different, an outsider. On the other hand, female guards have much in common with, and are sympathetic to, their male peers as a result of their shared job experience."[22]

According to studies, female correctional officers typically say that they perform their job with a less aggressive style than men.[23] This difference in style seems due mostly to differences in life experiences and to physical limitations associated with women's size and strength. Life experiences prepare most women for helping roles rather than aggressive ones. As a consequence, women are more likely to rely heavily on verbal skills and intuition. Female correctional officers use communication rather than threats or force to gain inmate cooperation. They tend to talk out problems. Studies have also found that female correctional officers rely more heavily than male correctional officers on established disciplinary rules when problems arise. Male staff members, on the other hand, are more likely to bully or threaten inmates to resolve problems.

According to research, 55 percent of female officers indicate that their primary reason for taking a job in corrections was an interest in human service work or in inmate rehabilitation.[24] In striking contrast, only 20 percent of male officers give this as their primary reason for working in corrections.

Perhaps as a result of such attitudes, gender makes a dramatic difference in the number of assaults on correctional officers. One national survey of maximum-security prisons in 48 states, the District of Columbia, and the federal Bureau of Prisons showed that female officers were assaulted only 27.6 percent as often as male officers.[25]

Though female correctional officers may take a different approach to their work, the skills they use complement those of male staff members. "Women may humanize the workplace in small ways by establishing less aggressive relationships with inmates."[26]

Studies also show that male officers, by and large, believe that female officers competently

*As the number of women who work in corrections increases, more men must confront the unfamiliar situation of a female authority figure. What kinds of skills do female correctional officers tend to rely on to resolve problems?*

perform day-to-day custodial tasks. Most male staff members are "pro-woman," meaning that they applaud the entry of women into the corrections profession.[27] Many male correctional officers do express concerns about women's ability to provide adequate backup in a crisis. It is important to note, however, that the need to use force in prison is relatively rare and that officers generally do not respond to dangerous situations alone. Nonetheless, some female correctional officers report that in emergencies some male officers adopt a protective, chivalrous attitude toward them. Women generally report that they resent such "special treatment," because it makes them feel more like a liability than an asset in an emergency.

Another issue concerning women in today's workplace is personal and sexual harassment. Studies show that few female correctional officers personally experience unwanted touching or other forms of sexual harassment. The forms of harassment women most commonly experience are physical (nonsexual) assaults, threats, unfounded graphic sexual rumors about them, and demeaning remarks from peers, inmates, and supervisors.[28]

A fair amount of harassment is tolerated in the correctional officer subculture. It is viewed as customary and is often accorded little significance. The response to any form of harassment, however, is up to the officer experiencing it. He or she can tolerate it, resist it, or report it. Female correctional officers, however, express a real fear of being ostracized if they complain.

One writer has made the following recommendations for improving the acceptance of women as correctional officers:[29]

1. Require managers and guards to undergo training to sensitize them to the concerns of women working in prisons.

Female correctional officers competently perform day-to-day custodial tasks. Are there any areas of a male prison that female correctional officers should be barred from supervising?

2. Establish a strong policy prohibiting sexual and personal harassment, with significant consequences for harassers.
3. Screen male job candidates for their ability and willingness to develop relationships of mutual respect with female colleagues.

## Stress

**stress** Tension in a person's body or mind, resulting from physical, chemical, or emotional factors.

In all occupational categories, employers estimate that more than 25 percent of all reported sick time is due to stress.[30] **Stress**—tension in a person's body or mind, resulting from physical, chemical, or emotional factors—appears to be more commonplace in prison work than in many other jobs. Nonetheless, it is often denied. As one early writer on correctional officers' stress observed, "Most officers . . . try to disguise the toll taken by the job and make the best of what is often a frustrating situation. Though not immune to the pressures of the workplace these officers project a tough, steady image which precludes sharing frustrations with other co-workers or family members. Some of these officers may be particularly vulnerable to stress."[31]

Correctional officers frequently deny that they are under stress. Many resort to self-medication or other tactics to deal with feelings that they may not readily admit, even to themselves. Unfortunately, ineffective methods of dealing with stress do not alleviate the pressure, but may instead make it worse.

Stress among correctional officers has a number of sources. Feelings of powerlessness, meaninglessness, social isolation, and self-estrangement all contribute to stress. Some authors have identified job alienation as the major source of stress among correctional officers.[32] Correctional officers rarely participate in setting the rules they work under and the policies they enforce; as a result, they may feel alienated from those policies and rules, and from those who create them.

Other factors that create stress include:

- Work overload
- Family conflict
- Lack of autonomy or control over one's life
- Threat of job loss
- Role conflict or role ambiguity
- Conflicts with coworkers
- Conflicts with supervisors
- The organizational culture
- The working environment
- Insufficient resources to reach one's goals
- Inadequate job training
- Overqualification for one's current position
- Supervisors' attitudes
- Changes in the work environment

Symptoms of stress can be psychological, behavioral, and physical. Psychological symptoms of stress include anxiety, irritability, mood swings, sadness or depression, low self-esteem, emotional withdrawal, and hypersensitivity (to others and to what others say). Behavioral symptoms of stress

*The Staff World: Managing the Prison Population*

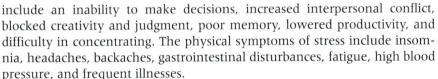

Always read the supervision file or pretrial services bond report before making a field contact. If possible, talk to the prior supervision officer before any contact. If the Bureau of Prisons or another district does not provide sufficient background material, make them do their job by requiring this information before making any field contact.

After reviewing the material, determine what precautions need to be taken. Decide whether to make contact at a certain place or time of day, to take a partner, or to make some other arrangement. If you find you are still not comfortable, and no precaution can assuage this feeling, don't make the contact.

Consciously consider possible risks and what actions to take before making a field contact. After you have done this, there is still the unexpected. For this possibility, all you can do is be aware, have your safety equipment, and heed your sixth sense.

1. Things happen fast. Have a plan, and mentally rehearse various scenarios in advance.
2. Have a plan that includes immediate rapid movement to a place of cover.
3. Don't think you can talk yourself out of every situation. Sometimes immediate action is called for.
4. Listen to your instincts. If things don't feel right, leave.
5. Most of the time acting firmly helps you to control the situation. It creates the impression you are not an easy target.
6. Remain professional, but act firm. (Note: May not be the best course in a very few mental health cases.)

*Ben Bridgman*
*Federal Supervision Probation Officer*
*Middle District of Florida*

include an inability to make decisions, increased interpersonal conflict, blocked creativity and judgment, poor memory, lowered productivity, and difficulty in concentrating. The physical symptoms of stress include insomnia, headaches, backaches, gastrointestinal disturbances, fatigue, high blood pressure, and frequent illnesses.

Poorer job performance and exhaustion are the results of stress. When stress reaches an unbearable level, burnout can occur. Burnout, a severe reaction to stress, "describes a state of physical and emotional depletion that results from the conditions of one's occupation."[33]

Studies have shown that a person's ability to tolerate stress depends on the frequency, severity, and types of stressors confronted.[34] Stress tolerance also depends on a number of personal aspects, including past experiences, personal values and attitudes, sense of control, personality, residual stress level, and general state of health.

Authorities suggest a number of techniques for avoiding or reducing job stress. Among them are the following:[35]

1. Communicate openly. Tell people how you feel.
2. Learn not to harbor resentment, not to gossip, and to complain less often.
3. Learn to feel confident in your skills, your values and beliefs, and yourself.
4. Develop a support system. Close friends, pets, social activities, and a happy extended family can all help alleviate stress.
5. Be a good and conscientious worker, but don't become a workaholic.
6. Learn to manage your time, and do not procrastinate.
7. Make it a habit to get a good night's sleep.
8. Exercise regularly.
9. Watch your diet. Avoid excessive fat, sugars, salt, red meat, and caffeine.
10. Learn some relaxation exercises such as self-affirmation, mental imaging, deep breathing, stretching, massage, or yoga.
11. Try to have fun. Laughter can combat stress quite effectively.
12. Spend time cultivating self-understanding. Analyze your feelings and your problems—and recognize your accomplishments.
13. Set goals and make plans. Both bring order and direction to your life.

One especially effective strategy for coping with job stress is to develop clear and favorable role definitions. According to J. T. Dignam and coauthors, "officers who have more opportunities for receiving assistance and goal clarification from supervisors and coworkers [are] less likely to experi-

As more and more prison staff develop a professional perspective, the structural organization of prisons and interactions among staff and inmates may significantly change. What characteristics may help correctional officers adjust to a changing environment?

*The Staff World: Managing the Prison Population*

ence role ambiguity than those for whom such support is not available or sought. Further, the risk of burnout or other deleterious consequences of occupational stress may be reduced for those who are 'insulated' by social support."[36]

Similarly, another group of researchers found that "support from colleagues or supervisors may be one of the most important factors ameliorating stress in the workplace."[37] The same researchers also found that when correctional officers felt "rewarding companionship" with fellow correctional officers, they reported fewer stressful events (even when objective measures showed an actual rise in such events). Most researchers agree that officers need more extensive and thorough training to prepare them for the psychological and sociological consequences of becoming a correctional officer.

## Job Satisfaction

High levels of stress reduce the satisfaction correctional officers get from their jobs. In a sad indictment of the corrections field, a 1996 study found that correctional officers were significantly different from most other groups of correctional employees. "They showed the lowest levels of organizational commitment, possessed the highest levels of skepticism about organizational change, were the least positive about careers in corrections and the rehabilitation of offenders, possessed the lowest levels of job satisfaction, were the least involved in their jobs, and were described as having the poorest work habits and overall job performance."[38] In a separate study, correctional supervisors and managers were found to have much higher levels of job satisfaction and professionalism.[39]

One reason for the difference in job satisfaction between supervisory personnel and those on the front lines of corrections work is that correctional officers often feel alienated from policy making.[40] As one writer puts it, "when looking at the atmosphere and environment of a state or federal prison, it would seem obvious what correction personnel like least about working there: surveys of personnel who resign or quit show that their biggest problems are with supervisory personnel rather than inmates."[41]

Correctional officers' job satisfaction appears to be tied to the amount of influence they feel they have over administrative decisions and policies. Officers who feel they have some control over the institution and over their jobs seem much more satisfied than officers who believe they have no control. Hence, it appears that correctional officers' job satisfaction can be greatly enhanced by caring administrators who involve the officers in policy making.

There is evidence that job satisfaction among correctional officers is rising. The rise may be partly due to increasing awareness of what correctional officers find most important in the work environment. Recent studies have identified the most important determinants of job satisfaction among correctional officers as (1) working conditions, (2) the level of work-related stress, (3) the quality of working relationships with fellow officers, and (4) length of service.[42]

In one of the most significant studies to date, treatment-oriented correctional staff reported far higher levels of job satisfaction than custody-oriented staff.[43] The study was of survey data collected from 428 Arizona correctional service officers (CSOs) and 118 correctional program officers (CPOs). Job satisfaction was significantly greater among the human-services-oriented CPOs than among the traditional-custody-oriented CSOs. The findings suggest that additional attention should be given to enhancing and enriching the duties of correctional officers, extending their control over and involvement in prisoners' activities, and redefining their roles more as service workers than as control agents.

Determinants of job satisfaction appear to differ for male and female correctional officers. One study found that the quality of working relationships with other officers, the amount of stress experienced at work, the length of service as a correctional officer, and educational level were all positively related to job satisfaction for males.[44] Women officers, on the other hand, appeared to place more emphasis on the quality of working relationships with all other correctional officers (not just the ones with whom they worked) and tended to be happier in prisons at lower security levels. Other studies have related higher job satisfaction among white female officers to the officers' positive evaluation of the quality of supervision. In other words, white female correctional officers tend to be happier in prisons that they believe are well run.[45]

## Professionalism

On October 29, 1994, correctional officer Ken Davis was instantly catapulted to the forefront of national attention when he tackled White House shooter Francisco Martin Duran. Without warning, Duran had leveled a Chinese-made AK-47 assault rifle at the White House from outside the iron gates and had begun firing. While most other bystanders either fled or stood stunned, Davis ran toward Duran and wrestled him to the ground, holding him until police and White House security officers arrived. Duran was later sentenced to 40 years in prison with no chance of parole on charges of attempting to assassinate President Clinton.

Davis, a correctional officer at the Victor Cullins Academy[46] in Maryland, was honored for his quick actions. During the ceremony, he noted a few lifestyle principles that could benefit all correctional officers. "Correctional officers serve and survive better," said Davis, "if they adopt the capacity for balance as a personal philosophy."[47] Balance means understanding themselves, knowing when they can handle a situation and when they cannot, and admitting when they need help. It also means having a clear sense of their roles and keeping a clear view of their purpose and their career goals. A good sense of balance, said Davis, reduces job stress and "improves officer-officer relations" by leading to good teamwork and by ensuring that correctional officers understand the importance of positive peer relationships in maintaining high morale. Officer Davis observed that inmates look for correctional officers without a personal sense of balance and "systematically and continuously work to manipulate the human frailties of correctional officers."

"There is danger in ignorance," Davis said. "Learning is a lifelong process. True knowledge is knowing what you do not know! Don't worry about sounding stupid. Know when to call for help. Don't be afraid to say, 'I need help,' 'I don't understand this duty post,' or 'This approach seems wrong.'"

Davis also noted that "listening is the heart of communication. Good listening practices shape a successful officer. Effective officers strive to perfect both active and passive listening skills, by exploring innovative ways to improve communication with peers and supervisors, inmates, visitors, and the public."

"One way for officers to accomplish the achievement of their personal career goals," noted Davis, "is to constantly groom themselves early in their career for higher rank and responsibility by learning from their experienced supervisors and by keeping a journal of lessons learned. This process will provide dividends for years to come. It will give you a bank of positive experiences to draw on in future times of career decisions and in times of crisis."

The International Association of Correctional Officers has published a Correctional Officer's Creed (see Exhibit 8–1), which summarizes the duties and responsibilities of a correctional officer.

**EXHIBIT 8–1**

## International Association of Correctional Officers

### The Correctional Officer's Creed

To speak sparingly...to act, not argue...to be in authority through personal presence...to correct without nagging...to speak with the calm voice of certainty...to see everything, and to know what is significant and what not to notice...to be neither insensitive to distress nor so distracted by pity as to miss what must elsewhere be seen...

To do neither that which is unkind nor self-indulgent in its misplaced charity...never to obey the impulse to tongue slash that silent insolence which in time past could receive the lash...to be both firm and fair...to know I cannot be fair simply by being firm, nor firm simply by being fair...

To support the reputations of associates and confront them without anger should they stand short of professional conduct...to reach for knowledge of the continuing mysteries of human motivation...to think; always to think...to be dependable...to be dependable first to my charges and associates, and thereafter to my duty as employee and citizen...to keep fit...to keep forever alert...to listen to what is meant as well as what is said with words and with silences.

To expect respect from my charges and my superiors yet never to abuse the one for abuses from the other...for eight hours each working day to be an example of the person I could be at all times...to acquiesce in no dishonest act...to cultivate patience under boredom and calm during confusion...to understand the why of every order I take or give...

To hold freedom among the highest values though I deny it to those I guard...to deny it with dignity that in my example they find no reason to lose their dignity...to be prompt...to be honest with all who practice deceit that they not find in me excuse for themselves...to privately face down my fear that I not signal it...to privately cool my anger that I not displace it on others...to hold in confidence what I see and hear, which by telling could harm or humiliate to no good purpose...to keep my outside problems outside...to leave inside that which should stay inside...to do my duty.

## 8 Review and Applications

### CHAPTER OBJECTIVE 1
There is a hierarchy of staff positions, from warden (or superintendent) at the top, down to correctional officer and correctional officer trainee. A typical correctional staff includes (1) administrative staff, (2) clerical personnel, (3) treatment and educational staff, (4) custodial staff, (5) service and maintenance staff, and (6) volunteers.

### CHAPTER OBJECTIVE 2
The custodial staff consists of correctional officers only—not correctional administrators, treatment or educational staff, or other staff members.

### CHAPTER OBJECTIVE 3
The types of power available to correctional officers are legitimate power, coercive power, reward power, expert power, and referent power.

### CHAPTER OBJECTIVE 4
In correctional institutions, structured conflict refers to the tensions between prison staff members and inmates that arise out of institutional arrangements.

### CHAPTER OBJECTIVE 5
A subculture is the beliefs, values, behavior, and material objects shared by a particular group of people within a larger society. The subculture of correctional officers reinforces group solidarity and cohesion among correctional personnel.

### CHAPTER OBJECTIVE 6
State prisons and local jails employed 337,736 corrections personnel (including administrative staff) in late 1997. One-third were women. About 30 percent were minorities.

### CHAPTER OBJECTIVE 7
Common correctional officer personality types include (1) the dictator, (2) the friend, (3) the merchant, (4) the turnkey, (5) the climber, (6) the reformer, and (7) the do-gooder.

### CHAPTER OBJECTIVE 8
The seven correctional officer assignments are (1) block officers, (2) work detail supervisors, (3) industrial shop and school officers, (4) yard officers, (5) administrative officers, (6) perimeter security officers (also called wall post officers), and (7) relief officers.

### CHAPTER OBJECTIVE 9
Female correctional officers tend to differ from male ones in their approach to workplace problem solving because they are generally less aggressive than male officers. They are more likely to resolve disputes through nonconfrontational means and tend to rely more heavily on verbal skills and interpersonal communication than do male officers. Studies have also found that female correctional officers depend more on established disciplinary rules when problems arise.

### CHAPTER OBJECTIVE 10
Feelings of powerlessness, meaninglessness, social isolation, self-estrangement, and alienation are all sources of correctional officer stress. Techniques for reducing stress include open communication, self-confidence, a support system, conscientious work performance, effective time management, adequate sleep, exercise, a wholesome diet, relaxation techniques, laughter, self-understanding, realistic goals and plans, and avoidance of resentment.

## QUESTIONS FOR REVIEW

1. What staff roles does the hierarchy of a typical correctional institution include?
2. What is the role of a prison's custodial staff?
3. According to John Hepburn, what are five bases of the power correctional officers have to gain inmate compliance?
4. What is meant by *structured conflict*?
5. What elements make up the staff subculture?
6. According to the ACA, what percentage of corrections personnel are members of minority groups?
7. List common personality types of correctional officers.
8. What are the seven correctional officer job assignments?
9. List and explain some challenges facing women who work as correctional officers.
10. What are some sources of stress for correctional officers?

## CRITICAL THINKING EXERCISES

### ON-THE-JOB ISSUE

You are an experienced correctional officer, assigned to yard duty. As you patrol the prison yard, watching inmates milling around and talking, a fellow officer named Renée approaches you. Renée was hired only a week ago, and she has gained a reputation for being inquisitive—asking experienced correctional officers about prison work.

Renée walks up and says, "You know, I'm wondering what I should do. Yesterday I saw an officer push an inmate around because the guy didn't do what he asked. I don't know if the inmate didn't hear what was being said, or if he was just ignoring the officer."

Renée looks at the ground. "What am I supposed to do in a situation like that? Should I have said something right then? Should I talk to the officer privately? Should I suggest to the officer that maybe the inmate didn't hear him? He knows we aren't supposed to use force on inmates unless it's really necessary. If I see him do this kind of thing again, should I report him?" Looking up, Renée says, "I know we're supposed to support each other in here. But what would you do?" How should you respond to Renée's questions?

### CORRECTIONS ISSUE

The staff culture is generally instilled in correctional officer trainees by more experienced officers and by work experiences. Socialization into the staff subculture begins on the first day of academy training or the first day of work (whichever comes first). One of the most important beliefs of the staff subculture is that officers should support one another.

Some people argue that the staff subculture is dangerous because it can sustain improper and even illegal behavior, while forcing correctional officers to keep to themselves what they know about such behavior. Others, however, suggest that the staff subculture is a positive element in the correctional world. It is important to correctional officer morale, they claim. They also suggest that it "fills the gaps" in formal training by establishing informal rules to guide staff behavior and decision making in difficult situations. The staff subculture can provide informal "workarounds" when the formal requirements of a correctional officer's position seem unrealistic.

1. Do you think the staff subculture contributes to or detracts from meeting the goals of institutional corrections? Why?
2. Do you think the staff subculture benefits or harms the lives and working environment of correctional officers? Explain.
3. What functions of the staff subculture can you identify? Rate each of those functions as positive or negative for its role in meeting the goals of institutional corrections.

## CORRECTIONS ON THE WEB

 Access the Arizona Peace Officer Standards and Training Board at **http://www.azpost.state.az.us/**. Click on "Correctional Officer Rules," and then read all eight sections of the state code relating to correctional officers. After reading the state code sections, write a short paragraph summarizing the expectations the state of Arizona has of its correctional officers.

## ADDITIONAL READINGS

American Correctional Association. *The State of Corrections: Proceedings—ACA Annual Conferences 1995.* Lanham, MD: ACA, 1996.

Farkas, Mary Ann, and P. K. Manning. "The Occupational Culture of Corrections and Police Officers." *Journal of Crime and Justice*, Vol. 20, No. 2 (1997), pp. 51–68.

Josi, Don A., and Dale K. Sechrest. *The Changing Career of the Correctional Officer: Policy Implications for the 21st Century.* Boston: Butterworth-Heinemann, 1998.

Kantrowitz, Nathan. *Close Control: Managing a Maximum Security Prison.* Guilderland, NY: Harrow and Heston, 1996.

Price, Barbara Raffel, and Natalie J. Sokoloff. *The Criminal Justice System and Women: Offenders, Victims, and Workers,* 2d ed. New York: McGraw-Hill, 1995.

## ENDNOTES

1. CNN Online, "Truck Rams Prison Fence in Florida Breakout," Web posted April 11, 1998.
2. Harry Elmer Barnes and Negley K. Teeters, *New Horizons in Criminology*, 3d ed. (Englewood Cliffs, NJ: Prentice Hall, 1959), p. 463.
3. See Sylvia G. McCollum, "Excellence or Mediocrity: Training Correctional Officers and Administrators," *The Keeper's Voice*, Vol. 17, No. 4 (Fall 1996).
4. Anthony R. Martinez, "Corrections Officer: The 'Other' Prisoner," *The Keeper's Voice*, Vol. 18, No. 1 (Spring 1997).
5. Don A. Josi and Dale K. Sechrest, *The Changing Career of the Correctional Officer: Policy Implications for the 21st Century* (Boston: Butterworth-Heinemann, 1998), p. 11.
6. Ibid., p. 12.
7. John Hepburn, "The Exercise of Power in Coercive Organizations: A Study of Prison Guards," *Criminology*, Vol. 23, No. 1 (1985), pp. 145–164.
8. Gresham Sykes, *The Society of Captives* (Princeton, NJ: Princeton University Press, 1958).
9. See, for example, James B. Jacobs and Lawrence J. Kraft, "Integrating the Keepers: A Comparison of Black and White Prison Guards in Illinois," *Social Problems*, Vol. 25, No. 3 (1978), pp. 304–318.
10. Adapted from John J. Macionis, *Society: The Basics*, 2d ed (Englewood Cliffs, NJ: Prentice Hall, 1994), p. 405.
11. Kauffman, Kelsey, *Prison Officers and Their World* (Cambridge, MA: Harvard University Press, 1988), pp. 85–86.
12. David M. Wakefield, American Correctional Association, fax transmission June 12, 1998. Preliminary data for the table "Personnel in Adult and Juvenile Corrections," in ACA, *Vital Statistics in Corrections* (forthcoming).
13. U.S. Bureau of the Census, *Population Profile of the United States: 1995*, Current Population Reports,

Series P23–189 (Washington: U.S. Government Printing Office, 1995); available online: http://www.census.gov/prod/1/pop/profile/95, access: July 20, 1998.

14. Preliminary data for ACA, *Vital Statistics in Corrections*.

15. Ibid.

16. Ibid.

17. See, for example, E. Poole and R. M. Regoli, "Work Relations and Cynicism Among Prison Guards," *Criminal Justice and Behavior*, Vol. 7 (1980), pp. 303–314.

18. Adapted from Frank Schmalleger, *Criminal Justice Today: An Introductory Text for the 21st Century*, 5th ed. (Upper Saddle River, NJ: Prentice Hall, 1999).

19. Lucien X. Lombardo, *Guards Imprisoned: Correctional Officers at Work*, 2d ed. (Cincinnati, OH: Anderson, 1989).

20. Adapted from Dora B. Schriro, "Women in Prison: Keeping the Peace," *The Keeper's Voice*, Vol. 16, No. 2 (Spring 1995).

21. Ibid.

22. M. I. Cadwaladr, "Women Working in a Men's Jail," *FORUM*, Vol. 6, No. 1 (1994).

23. Ibid.

24. N. C. Jurik and J. Halemba, "Gender, Working Conditions, and the Job Satisfaction of Women in a Non-Traditional Occupation: Female Correctional Officers in Men's Prisons," *Sociological Quarterly*, Vol. 25 (1984), pp. 551–66.

25. Joseph R. Rowan, "Who Is Safer in Male Maximum Security Prisons?" *The Keeper's Voice*, Vol. 17, No. 3 (Summer 1996).

26. Ibid.

27. See, for example, Stephen Walters, "Changing the Guard: Male Correctional Officers' Attitudes Toward Women as Co-workers," *Journal of Offender Rehabilitation*, Vol. 20, No. 1 (1993), pp. 47–60.

28. Cadwaladr.

29. Ibid.

30. Public Service Commission (of Canada), "Stress and Executive Burnout," *FORUM*, Vol. 4, No. 1 (1992). Much of the material in this section is taken from this work.

31. B. M. Crouch, "The Guard in a Changing Prison World," in B. M. Crouch (ed.), *The Keepers: Prison Guards and Contemporary Corrections* (Springfield, IL: Charles C. Thomas, 1980).

32. Lombardo.

33. Public Service Commission.

34. Ibid.

35. "Not Stressed Enough?" *FORUM*, Vol. 4, No. 1 (1992). Adapted from C. C. W. Hines and W. C. Wilson, "A No-Nonsense Guide to Being Stressed," *Management Solutions*, October 1986, pp. 27–29.

36. J. T. Dignam, M. Barrera, and S. G. West, "Occupational Stress, Social Support, and Burnout Among Correctional Officers," *American Journal of Community Psychology*, Vol. 14, No. 2 (1986), pp. 177–193.

37. M. C. W. Peeters, B. P. Buunk, and W. B. Schaufeli, "Social Interactions and Feelings of Inferiority Among Correctional Officers: A Daily Event-Recording Approach," *Journal of Applied Social Psychology*, Vol. 25, No. 12 (1995), pp. 1073–1089.

38. David Robinson, Frank Porporino, and Linda Simourd, "Do Different Occupational Groups Vary on Attitudes and Work Adjustment in Corrections?" *Federal Probation*, Vol. 60, No. 3 (1996), pp. 45–53. See also Francis T. Cullen et al., "How Satisfying Is Prison Work? A Comparative Occupational Approach," *The Journal of Offender Counseling Services and Rehabilitation*, Vol. 14, No. 2 (1989), pp. 89–108.

39. Timothy J. Flanagan, Wesley Johnson, and Katherine Bennett, "Job Satisfaction Among Correctional Executives: A Contemporary Portrait of Wardens of State Prisons for Adults," *Prison Journal*, Vol. 76, No. 4 (1996), pp. 385–397.

40. Lombardo.

41. Martinez.

42. Stephen Walters, "The Determinants of Job Satisfaction Among Canadian and American Correctional Officers," *Journal of Crime and Justice*, Vol. 19, No. 2 (1996), pp. 145–158.

43. John R. Hepburn and Paul E. Knepper, "Correctional Officers as Human Services Workers: The Effect on Job Satisfaction," *Justice Quarterly*, Vol. 10, No. 2 (1993), pp. 315–337.

44. Stephen Walters, "Gender, Job Satisfaction, and Correctional Officers: A Comparative Analysis," *The Justice Professional*, Vol. 7, No. 2 (1993), pp. 23–33.

45. Dana M. Britton, "Perceptions of the Work Environment Among Correctional Officers: Do Race and Sex Matter?" *Criminology*, Vol. 35, No. 1 (1997), pp. 85–105.

46. The Victor Cullins Academy is a facility operating under contract with the Youth Services Division of the state of Maryland.

47. The material in this section comes from Jess Maghan, "Ken Davis: The Complete Correctional Officer," *The Keeper's Voice*, Vol. 16, No. 2 (Spring 1995).

# 9 The Inmate World

## Living Behind Bars

247

*In prison, those things withheld from and denied to the prisoner become precisely what he wants most of all.*

— Eldridge Cleaver

In 1997, Rebecca Lynn Thornton pulled open a section of the chain link fence surrounding the prison in Florence, South Carolina, and opened fire. Her husband, a death row inmate, was working in a prison vegetable garden. A hail of gunfire followed, as correctional officers staffing prison towers returned fire. When the smoke cleared, Thornton, 38, and her husband, Floyd Bennet Thornton, Jr., 36, were both dead. Officials were unsure whether the woman meant to kill her husband or was trying to spring him from the institution. Floyd Thornton had been sentenced to die for the 1993 slaying of a 74-year-old man. Thornton was a fugitive at the time. He had escaped from Arizona's Cochise County Jail while awaiting trial for a 1991 slaying.[1]

As this story shows, prison inmates are not as isolated as they may sometimes seem in popular culture. Not only do inmates interact with one another, but they also have relationships that extend beyond prison walls. This chapter will describe prison life, the inmate subculture, and the prison experience in general.

# Characteristics of State Inmates

As we have already seen, most state inmates are male, belong to racial or ethnic minority groups, are relatively young, and have been incarcerated for a violent offense. A recent Bureau of Justice Statistics study examined the social, economic, and other characteristics of all state inmates.[2] Highlights of that study are shown in Figure 9–1.

# Men in Prison

**total institution** A place where the same people work, play, eat, sleep, and recreate together on a continuous basis. The term was developed by the sociologist Erving Goffman to describe prisons and other facilities.

In his classic work *Asylums*, Erving Goffman used the phrase **total institution** to describe a place where the same people work, eat, sleep, and engage in recreation together day after day.[3] Prisons, concentration camps, mental hospitals, and seminaries are all total institutions, said Goffman. They share many of the same characteristics—even though they exist for different purposes and house different kinds of populations. His words were echoed years later by Hans Toch, who noted that "prisons are 24-hour-a-day, year-in-and-year-out environments in which people are sequestered with little outside contact."[4]

Prisons and other total institutions are small, self-contained societies with their own social structures, norms, and rules. Physically, emotionally, and socially, prison inmates are almost completely cut off from the larger society. As a consequence, they develop their own distinctive lifestyles, roles, and behavioral norms.

## FIGURE 9-1

### Profile of State Prison Inmates

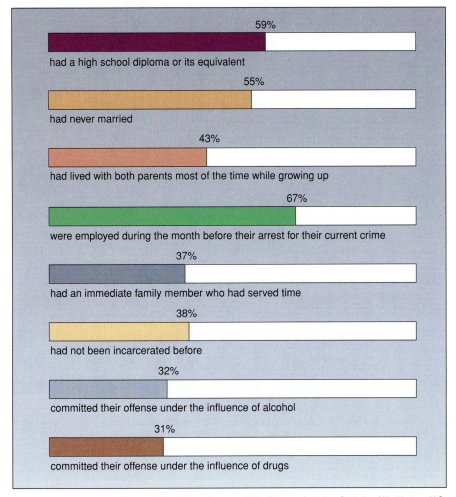

59%
had a high school diploma or its equivalent

55%
had never married

43%
had lived with both parents most of the time while growing up

67%
were employed during the month before their arrest for their current crime

37%
had an immediate family member who had served time

38%
had not been incarcerated before

32%
committed their offense under the influence of alcohol

31%
committed their offense under the influence of drugs

*Source:* Allen Beck, et al., *Survey of State Prison Inmates*, 1991, Bureau of Justice Statistics (Washington: U.S. Department of Justice, March 1993).

## What Is the Inmate Subculture?

Although any prison has its own unique way of life or culture, it is possible to describe a general inmate subculture that characterizes the lives of inmates in correctional institutions nationwide. The **inmate subculture** (also called the *prisoner subculture*) can be defined as "the habits, customs, mores, values, beliefs, or superstitions of the body of inmates incarcerated in correctional institutions."[5]

Prisoners are socialized into the inmate subculture through a process known as prisonization. The concept of **prisonization** was developed by Donald Clemmer in his book *The Prison Community*.[6] Clemmer defined prisonization as the process by which inmates adapt to prison society, and he described it as "the taking on of the ways, mores, customs, and general cul-

**inmate subculture**
(also *prisoner subculture*)
The habits, customs, mores, values, beliefs, or superstitions of the body of inmates incarcerated in correctional institutions; also, the inmate social world.

**prisonization**
The process by which inmates adapt to prison society; the taking on of the ways, mores, customs, and general culture of the penitentiary.

ture of the penitentiary." When the process of prisonization is complete, Clemmer noted, prisoners have become "cons."

In a further study of prisonization, Stanton Wheeler examined how prisoners adapted to life at the Washington State Reformatory.[7] Wheeler found that prisonization has greater impact with the passage of time. The prisonization of inmates, said Wheeler, can be described by a U-shaped curve. When an inmate first enters prison, the conventional values of the outside society still hold sway in his life. As time passes, however, he increasingly adopts the prison lifestyle. Wheeler also found that within the half-year before release, most inmates begin to demonstrate a renewed appreciation for conventional values.

**pains of imprisonment**
Major problems new inmates face, such as loss of liberty and personal autonomy, lack of material possessions, loss of heterosexual relationships, and reduced personal security.

In *The Society of Captives*,[8] Gresham Sykes described what he called the **pains of imprisonment**. According to Sykes, new inmates face major problems, including the loss of liberty, a lack of material possessions, deprivation of goods and services, the loss of heterosexual relationships, the loss of personal autonomy, and a reduction in personal security. These deficits, Sykes noted, lead to self-doubts and reduced self-esteem. Prison society compensates for such feelings and reduces the pains of imprisonment for the prison population as a whole. It also meets the personal and social needs induced in inmates by the pains of imprisonment. In short, said Sykes, inmate society compensates for the losses caused by imprisonment, and it offers varying degrees of comfort to those who successfully adjust to it.

# THE OFFENDER SPEAKS

When I was in school and didn't have any homework, my parents would give me some. I was always encouraged and questioned about current events by them. It was a must that we watch the news instead of cartoons on television, and then they would quiz me about what I saw. My parents would come up to school uninvited to check things out. It was embarrassing. My behavior was perfect. Then I joined a gang! They had no control over me after that. I did as I wished. That's why I think that families have little impact on the behavior of a kid. They could be great parents, but once the kid is running the streets with a gang, anything goes.

I'll get out in the year 2002, I think. When I do and I'm with my own kids, there ain't no way they'll run with a gang. I don't care if I gotta quit my job and watch 'em day and night. If the gang don't corrupt 'em, the cops will, 'cause they see the boy with the gang and they think he's bad. They arrest him. They rough him up. They set him up to fail. Prison life? Hell is better. Here it's fight, push, and violate—that's the code. Those who don't keep it can die a thousand different ways.

*Michael L. Johnson, N71961*
*Joliet Correctional Institution*
*Illinois Department of Corrections*

*The Inmate World: Living Behind Bars*

The inmate subculture can vary from one institution to another. Variations are due to differences in the organizational structure of prisons. Maximum-security institutions, for example, are decidedly more painful for inmates because security considerations require greater restriction of inmate freedoms and access to material items. As a result, the subcultures in maximum-security institutions may be much more rigid in their demands on prisoners than those in less secure institutions.

## How Does an Inmate Subculture Form?

Early students of inmate subcultures, particularly Clemmer and Sykes, believed that such subcultures developed in response to the deprivations in prison life. This perspective is called **deprivation theory**. It suggests that inmates' values arise in response to the prison environment and its deprivations. Shared deprivation gives inmates a basis for solidarity.[9]

A more recent perspective is that an inmate subculture does not develop in prison, but is brought into prison from the outside world. Known as **importation theory**, this point of view was popularized by John Irwin and Donald R. Cressey.[10] It was further supported by the work of James Jacobs.[11] Importation theory holds that inmate society is shaped by factors outside prison—specifically, preprison life experiences and socialization patterns. Inmates who lived violent lives outside tend to associate with other violent inmates and often engage in similar behavior in prison.[12]

More realistic is the **integration model**, which acknowledges that both theories have some validity. According to the integration model, people undergo early socialization experiences. In childhood, some persons develop leanings toward delinquent and criminal activity, acquiring—from peer groups, parents and other significant adults, television, movies, other mass media, and even computer and video games—values that support law-

**deprivation theory**
The belief that inmate subcultures develop in response to the deprivations in prison life.

**importation theory**
The belief that inmate subcultures are brought into prisons from the outside world.

**integration model**   A combination of importation theory and deprivation theory. The belief that in childhood, some inmates acquired, usually from peers, values that support law-violating behavior, but that the norms and standards in a prison also affect an inmate.

*In some prisons, the inmate subculture is being fragmented as inmates form competing gangs and other groups along ethnic, racial, and geographic lines. How could the differences among such groups affect the order and stability of a prison?*

*The Inmate World: Living Behind Bars*

violating behavior. Those who become inmates are also likely to have experienced juvenile court proceedings and may have been institutionalized as juveniles. As a consequence, such persons are likely to have acquired many of the values, much of the language, and the general behavioral patterns of deviant or criminal subcultures before entering adult prison.

The integration model also recognizes, however, the effects that the norms and behavioral standards of inmates in a particular prison have on those who are imprisoned. If a new inmate has already been socialized into a criminal lifestyle, the transition into the inmate subculture is likely to be easy. For some persons, however—especially white-collar offenders with little previous exposure to criminal subcultures—the transition can be very difficult. The language, social expectations, and norms of prison society are likely to be foreign to them.

## Norms and Values of Prison Society

**prison code** A set of norms and values among prison inmates. It is generally antagonistic to the official administration and rehabilitation programs of the prison.

Central to prison society is a code of behavior for all inmates. The **prison code** is a set of inmate rules antagonistic to the official administration and rehabilitation programs.[13] Violations of the code result in inmate-imposed sanctions, ranging from ostracism to homicide. Sykes and Messinger have identified five main elements of the prison code:[14]

1. Don't interfere with the interests of other inmates. Never rat on a con. Don't have loose lips.
2. Don't lose your head. Don't quarrel with other inmates. Play it cool. Do your own time.
3. Don't exploit other inmates. Don't steal. Don't break your word. Pay your debts.
4. Don't whine. Be tough. Be a man.
5. Don't be a sucker. Don't trust the guards or staff. Remember that prison officials are wrong and inmates are right.

## Prison Argot—The Language of Confinement

**prison argot** The special language of the inmate subculture.

**Prison argot** is the special language of the inmate subculture. *Argot* is a French word meaning "slang." Prison society has always had its own unique language, illustrated by the following argot-laden paragraph:

> The new con, considered fresh meat by the screws and other prisoners, was sent to the cross-bar hotel to do his bit. He soon picked up the reputation through the yard grapevine as a canary-bird. While he was at the big house, the goon squad put him in the freezer for his protection. Eventually, he was released from the ice-box and ordered to make little ones out of big ones until he was released to the free world. Upon release he received $100 in gate money, vowing never to be thrown in the hole or be thought of as a stool-pigeon again.[15]

Prison argot originated partly as a form of secret communication. Gresham Sykes, however, believes that it serves primarily as "an illustrative symbol of the prison community"—or as a way for inmates to mark themselves as outlaws and social outcasts.[16] Sykes's work brought prison argot to the attention of sociologists and criminologists. Since Sykes's time other authors have identified a number of words, terms, and acronyms in prison argot. Some of these terms are presented in Table 9–1 on page 254.

## Social Structure in Men's Prisons

Inmate societies, like other societies, have a hierarchy of positions. Inmates assume or are forced into specific social roles, and some inmates—by virtue of the roles they assume—have more status and power than others.

Early writers often classified prisoners by the crimes they had committed or their criminal histories. Irwin, for example, divided prisoners into such categories as thieves (those with a culture of criminal values), convicts (time doers), square johns (inmates unfamiliar with criminal subcultures), and dope fiends (drug-involved inmates).[17]

Other writers have identified **inmate roles**, defining them as prison lifestyles or as forms of ongoing social accommodation to prison life. Each role has a position in the pecking order, indicating its status in the prison society.

**inmate roles**   Prison lifestyles; also, forms of ongoing social accommodation to prison life.

Frank Schmalleger recently developed a contemporary typology of male inmate roles.[18] It is based on actual social roles found among inmates in prison, and it uses contemporary prison argot to name or describe each type. Each type can be viewed as a prison lifestyle either chosen by inmates or forced on them. Some of the types were previously identified by other writers. The twelve inmate types are discussed in the following paragraphs.

**The Real Man**   Real men do their own time, don't complain, and don't cause problems for other inmates. They see confinement as a natural consequence of criminal activity, and view time spent in prison as an unfortunate cost of doing business. Real men know the inmate code and abide by it. They are well regarded within the institution and rarely run into problems with other inmates. If they do, they solve their problems on their own. They never seek the help of correctional officers or the prison administration. Although they generally avoid trouble within the institution, they usually continue lives of crime once released.

**The Mean Dude**   Some inmates are notorious for resorting quickly to physical power. They are quick to fight and, when fighting, give no quarter. They are callous, cold, and uncaring. Mean dudes control those around them through force or the threat of force. The fear they inspire usually gives them a great deal of power in inmate society. At the very least, other inmates are likely to leave the mean dude alone.

**The Bully**   A variation of the mean dude is the bully. Bullies use intimidation to get what they want. Unlike mean dudes, they are far more likely to use threats than to use actual physical force. A bully may make his threats in public so that others see the victim's compliance.

**The Agitator**   The agitator, sometimes called a "wise guy," is constantly trying to stir things up. He responds to the boredom of prison life by causing

**TABLE 9–1**

### Prison Argot: The Language of Confinement

#### Argot in Men's Prisons

**ace duce:** best friend

**badge (or bull, hack, "the man," or screw):** a correctional officer

**ball busters:** violent inmates

**banger (or burner, shank, sticker):** a knife

**billys:** white men

**boneyard:** conjugal visiting area

**cat-J (or J-cat):** a prisoner in need of psychological or psychiatric therapy or medication

**cellie:** cellmate

**center men:** inmates who are close to the staff

**chester:** child molester

**dog:** homeboy or friend

**fag:** a male inmate believed to be a natural (preprison) homosexual

**featherwood:** a peckerwood's "woman"

**fish:** a newly arrived inmate

**gorilla:** an inmate who uses force to take what he wants from others

**hipsters:** young, drug-involved inmates

**homeboy:** a prisoner from one's hometown or neighborhood

**ink:** tattoos

**lemon squeezer:** an inmate who has an unattractive "girlfriend"

**man walking:** phrase used to signal that a guard is coming

**merchant (or peddler):** one who sells when he should give; or one who sells goods and services to other inmates illegally

**nimby:** not in my back yard

**peckerwood (or wood):** a white prisoner

**punk:** male inmate who is forced into a submissive or feminine role during homosexual relations

**rat (or snitch):** an inmate who squeals (provides information about other inmates to the prison administration)

**real men:** inmates respected by other inmates

**schooled:** knowledgeable in the ways of prison life

**shakedown:** search of a cell or a work area

**shu** (pronounced shoe)**:** special housing unit

**toughs:** those with a preprison history of violent crimes

**tree jumper:** rapist

**turn out:** to rape or make into a punk

**wolf:** a male inmate who assumes an aggressive masculine role during homosexual relations

#### Argot in Women's Prisons

**cherry (or cherrie):** an inmate not yet introduced to lesbian activities

**fay broad:** a white inmate

**femme (or mommy):** an inmate who plays the feminine role during lesbian relations

**safe:** the vagina, especially when used for hiding contraband

**stud broad (or daddy):** an inmate who assumes the role of a male during lesbian relations

*Sources:* Gresham Sykes, *The Society of Captives* (Princeton, NJ: Princeton University Press, 1958); Rose Giallombardo, *Society of Women: A Study of Women's Prison* (New York: John Wiley, 1966); Richard A. Cloward et al., *Theoretical Studies in Social Organization of the Prison* (New York: Social Science Research Council, 1960). For a more contemporary listing of prison slang terms, see Reinhold Aman, *Hillary Clinton's Pen Pal: A Guide to Life and Lingo in Federal Prison* (Santa Rosa, CA: Maledicta Press, 1996); Jerome Washington, *Iron House: Stories from the Yard* (Ann Arbor, MI: QED Press, 1994); Morrie Camhi, *The Prison Experience* (Boston: Charles Tuttle Co., 1989); Harold Long, *Survival In Prison* (Port Townsend, WA: Loompanics Unlimited, 1990).

problems for others. An agitator may point out, for example, how a powerful inmate has been wronged by another inmate or that an inmate seen talking to a "rat" must be a snitch himself.

**The Hedonist**   The hedonist adapts to prison by exploiting the minimal pleasures it offers. Hedonists always seek the easy path, and they plot to win the "cushiest" jobs. They may also stockpile goods to barter for services of various kinds. Hedonists live only in the now, with little concern for the future. Their lives revolve around such activities as gambling, drug running, smuggling contraband, and exploiting homosexual opportunities.

**The Opportunist**   The opportunist sees prison as an opportunity for personal advancement. He takes advantage of the formal self-improvement opportunities of the prison, such as schooling, trade training, and counseling. Other inmates generally dislike opportunists, seeing them as selfish "do-gooders." Staff members, however, often see opportunists as model prisoners.

**The Retreatist**   Some inmates, unable to cope with the realities of prison life, withdraw psychologically from the world around them. Depression, neurosis, and even psychosis may result. Some retreatists lose themselves in drugs or alcohol. Others attempt suicide. Isolation from the general prison population, combined with counseling or psychiatric treatment, may offer the best hope for retreatists to survive the prison experience.

**The Legalist**   Legalists are known as "jailhouse lawyers," or simply "lawyers," in prison argot. They are usually among the better-educated prisoners, although some legalists have little formal education. Legalists fight confinement through the system of laws, rules, and court precedent. Legalists file writs with the courts, seeking hearings on a wide variety of issues. Although many legalists work to better the conditions of their own confinement or to achieve early release, most also file pleas on behalf of other prisoners.

**The Radical**   Radicals see themselves as political prisoners of an unfair society. They believe that a discriminatory world has denied them the education and skills needed to succeed in a socially acceptable way. Most of the beliefs held by radical inmates are rationalizations that shift the blame for personal failure onto society. The radical inmate is likely to be familiar with contemporary countercultural figures.

**The Colonist**   Colonists, also referred to as "convicts," turn prison into home. Colonists know the ropes of prison, have many "friends" on the inside, and often feel more comfortable in prison than outside it. They may not look forward to leaving prison. Some may even commit additional offenses to extend their stay. Colonists are generally well regarded by other prisoners. Many are old-timers. Colonists have learned to take advantage of the informal opportunity structure in prisons, and they are well versed in the inmate code.

**The Religious Inmate**    Religious inmates profess a strong religious faith and may attempt to convert both inmates and staff. Religious inmates frequently form prayer groups, request special meeting facilities and special diets, and may ask for frequent visits from religious leaders. Religious inmates are often under a great deal of suspicion from inmates and staff, who tend to think they are faking religious commitment to gain special treatment. Those judged sincere in their faith may win early release, removal from death row, or any number of other special considerations.

**The Punk**    The punk is a young inmate, often small, who has been forced into a sexual relationship with an aggressive, well-respected prisoner. Punks are generally "turned out" through homosexual rape. A punk usually finds a protector among the more powerful inmates. Punks keep their protectors happy by providing them with sexual services.

Violence and victimization occur in men's prisons. A good deal of prison violence has sexual overtones. One person who has contributed significantly to the study of sexual violence in men's prisons is Daniel Lockwood.[19] Using interviews and background data from prison files, Lockwood identified and studied 107 "targets" of aggressive sexual threats and 45 inmate "aggressors" in New York state male prisons. He also conducted a general survey, which revealed that 28 percent of all male prisoners had been targets of sexual aggressors in prison at least once. Lockwood found that only one of the inmates he interviewed had actually been raped—an indication that the incidence of prison rape is quite low relative

## CAREER PROFILE

*Jack Osborn*
*Custody Utility Officer*
*Jefferson City*
*Correctional Center*
*Jefferson City, MO*

*"What makes a good custody officer? Being firm, fair, and consistent—clear, concise actions with the inmates and the other prison staff. Being honest goes far. If you don't know the answer, say so. If you say you will find out, do it. Learn to say no, too. You can change it to a yes easier than changing a yes to a no."*

Jack Osborn is a custody utility officer at the Jefferson City Correctional Center in Missouri. As a utility officer, he may be assigned to any area or department that needs an additional staff member. Before becoming a correctional officer, Jack was a deputy sheriff for 10 years. He has completed two years of community college coursework.

Jack advises knowing the inmates and being able to interpret behavioral changes. "Know what silence means. Communicate—listen," says Jack. "Learn who runs drugs and gambling, who the punks are. That's where your trouble will come from." Jack believes that if you follow this advice and know the mechanics of the job, you should have a great career in corrections.

to other types of harm that may accompany sexual incidents, such as physical abuse, verbal abuse, threatening gestures, and threatening propositions.

Targets, when compared with nontargets, were found to be physically slight, young, white, nonviolent offenders from nonurban areas. They generally had a higher rate of psychological disturbance than other inmates and were more apt to attempt suicide while in prison. Shown here is a note found by a new inmate in his cell at a New York state prison unit. The new inmate was young and not prison-wise. After discovering the note, the inmate asked to be moved to the prison's isolation area. His request was granted.[20]

The typical incident of sexual aggression, Lockwood found, is carried out by a group. About half the incidents Lockwood identified included physical violence, and another third involved threats. The incidents studied showed patterns of escalation from verbal abuse to physical violence.

Lockwood also found that prison rapes generally occur when gangs of aggressors circumvent security arrangements and physically control their victims. Fear, anxiety, suicidal thoughts, social disruption, and attitude changes develop in many victims of homosexual rape.

Yo S
Check this out if you don't give me a peace of your ass I am going to take you off the count and that is my word.
I be down a very long time So I need It very Bad I will give you 5 Pack's of Smokes If you do it OK That is my word So if you want to live you Better do it and get it over with there are Three of us who need it.
OK . . . .

# Women in Prison

In America today, there are far fewer women's prisons than men's prisons, and men in prison outnumber women in prison 16 to 1.[21] A state usually has one women's prison, housing a few hundred women. The size of a women's prison generally depends on the population of the state. Some small states house women prisoners in special areas of what are otherwise institutions for men.

Women's prisons are generally quite different from men's. Here's how one writer describes them:

> Often, there are no gun towers, no armed guards and no stone walls or fences strung on top with concertina wire. Neatly pruned hedges, well-kept flower gardens, attractive brick buildings and wide paved walkways greet the visitor's eye at women's prisons in many states. Often these institutions are located in rural, pastoral settings which may suggest tranquility and well-being to the casual observer.[22]

Such rural settings, however, make it hard for female inmates to maintain contact with their families, who may live far from the correctional facility.

Many prisons for women are built on a cottage plan. Cottages dot the grounds of such institutions, often arranged in pods. A group of six or so cottages constitutes a pod. Each cottage is much like a traditional house, with individual bedrooms; a day room with a television, chairs, couches, and tables; and small personal or shared bathrooms.

**FIGURE 9–2**

**Sample Regulations at a Women's Prison**

## RULES AND REGULATIONS
### SYBIL BRAND INSTITUTE FOR WOMEN
### LOS ANGELES, CALIFORNIA

Appearance—Cleanliness—Neatness

*Cells and Dormitories.* Each inmate is required to keep her own cell or bed area and surrounding area neat and clean at all times.

*Lockers.* Only cup and ashtray on outside locker shelf in Dorms. There are to be no liners on the inside locker shelves. Locker contents must be orderly and not excessive. Any amount over five (5) of each cosmetic item is considered excessive and will NOT be returned to you. Dresses, etc. to be hung on rack inside locker. Do NOT hang anything on doors of locker.

*Beds.* Must be made prior to breakfast and kept neat during the day.

*Floors and Walls.* Nothing is to be left on the floor during the night except one (1) pair of shoes or thongs per person. Do NOT deface or paste pictures on walls or lockers. No blankets or pillows on floor.

*Trash.* All trash which will burn is to be placed in the trash can. There are to be NO individual trash receptacles (boxes, paper bags, etc.) in bed areas or lockers. Soiled napkins must be wrapped securely in newspaper and placed in trash cans. Glass and metal are to be turned in to the officer.

*Personal Appearance.* Each inmate is required to keep herself neat and clean at all times. You must be fully dressed and presentable when leaving your housing area for any reason: do NOT walk around in stocking feet or barefooted.

*Showers.* Shower is to be taken daily. You are allowed ten (10) minutes to shower. No showers one-half hour prior to any meal line or after lights out.

*Headscarves or Pin Curls.* Headscarves or pin curls are not permitted from 7:00 A.M. to 5:30 P.M. unless special permission is granted.

*Nightcaps.* May be worn after 5:30 P.M. only if hair is in curlers. May be worn from bedtime to 7:00 A.M. whether or not hair is in curlers. Are to be worn above eyebrows.

*Source:* Kathryn Watterson, *Women in Prison* (Boston, MA: Northeastern University Press, 1996), appendix (p. 365).

Security in women's prisons is generally more relaxed than in men's, and female inmates may have more freedom within the institution than their male counterparts. Practically speaking, women—even those in prison—are seen as less dangerous than men and less prone to violence or escape. Despite the more relaxed nature of women's prisons, certain rules govern the behavior of inmates (see Figure 9–2 on page 258 for sample regulations at a women's prison).

Treatment, education, recreation, and other programs in women's prisons have often been criticized as inferior to those in men's prisons. Recent research has uncovered continuing disparities in many areas.[23] For example, men's institutions often have a much wider range of vocational and educational training programs and services, and larger and better-equipped law libraries. Similarly, exercise facilities—including weight rooms, jogging areas, and basketball courts—are often better equipped and larger in men's institutions today than in women's.

Prison administrators have often found it impractical to develop and fund programs at the same level in women's and men's prisons, because of differences in interest, participation, space, and so on. Nonetheless, it is important to strive for parity of opportunity as an ideal. The American Correctional Association, for example, through its Guidelines for Women's Prison Construction and Programming,[24] insists that the same level of services and opportunities be available in women's prisons as in men's prisons in the same jurisdiction.

In some instances, women may be placed in an institution housing inmates with a range of security levels. Consequently, women who are low security risks may have less personal freedom than their male counterparts. Women may also not have the opportunity to transfer to a less secure institution as they become safer risks.

## Characteristics of Women Inmates

Many of our conceptions of female inmates derive more from myth than reality. Two recent BJS surveys provide a more realistic picture of female inmates.[25] In 1998, women were 6.5 percent of the prisoners in the nation. Female prisoners largely resembled male prisoners in race, ethnic background, and age. However, they were substantially more likely to be serving time for a drug offense and less likely to have been sentenced for a violent crime. Women were also more likely than men to be serving time for larceny or fraud.

Female inmates had shorter criminal records than male inmates. They generally had shorter maximum sentences than men. Half of all women had a maximum sentence of 60 months or less, while half of all men had a sentence of 120 months or less. Significantly, more than 4 in 10 of the women prisoners responding to the BJS survey reported prior physical or sexual abuse. One of the major factors distinguishing male inmates from female is that the women have experienced far more sexual and physical abuse than the men. Figure 9–3 is a comparison of selected characteristics of female and male state prisoners.

## FIGURE 9-3

### Characteristics of Women and Men in State Prisons

## Women in Prison

**Criminal Offense**
35% were in prison for drug offenses
28% were in prison for violent offenses
27% were in prison for property offenses

**Criminal History**
46% were nonviolent recidivists
28% had no previous sentence
26% were violent recidivists

**Family Characteristics**
78% had children
42% had lived with both parents most of time growing up
33% had a parent/guardian who abused alcohol or drugs
17% were married at the time they committed the offense for which they were incarcerated
45% had never married
47% had a family member who had been incarcerated

**Drug and Alcohol Use**
41% had used drugs daily in the month before the current offense
36% were under the influence of drugs at the time of the offense
12% were under the influence of alcohol at the time of the offense

## Men in Prison

**Criminal Offense**
48% were in prison for violent offenses
22% were in prison for property offenses
20% were in prison for drug offenses

**Criminal History**
50% were violent recidivists
31% were nonviolent recidivists
19% had no previous sentence

**Family Characteristics**
64% had children
43% had lived with both parents most of time growing up
26% had a parent/guardian who abused alcohol or drugs
18% were married at the time they committed the offense for which they were incarcerated
56% had never married
37% had a family member who had been incarcerated

**Drug and Alcohol Use**
36% had used drugs daily in the month before the current offense
31% were under the influence of drugs at the time of the offense
18% were under the influence of alcohol at the time of the offense

*Source:* Allen J. Beck and Christopher J. Mumola, *Prisoners in 1998,* Bureau of Justice Statistics (Washington: U.S. Department of Justice, August 1999) and Allen Beck et al., *Survey of State Prison Inmates, 1991,* Bureau of Justice Statistics (Washington: U.S. Department of Justice, March 1993).

# Offenses of Incarcerated Women

Drug offenses account for a large percentage of the women behind bars. Two-thirds of all women in federal prisons, for example, are serving time on drug charges.[26] Some sources estimate that, together, drug crimes and other crimes indirectly related to drug activities account for the imprisonment of around 95 percent of today's women inmates. In short, drug use and abuse, or crimes stimulated by the desire for drugs and drug money, are what send most women to prison. (See Figure 9–4.) This has been true for at least a decade. According to an American Correctional Association report, the primary reasons incarcerated women most frequently gave for their arrest were (1) trying to pay for drugs, (2) attempts to relieve economic pressures, and (3) poor judgment.[27]

According to the BJS, before arrest, women in prison used more drugs than men and used those drugs more frequently.[28] About 54 percent of imprisoned women had used drugs in the month before the offense for which they were arrested, compared with 50 percent of the men. Female inmates were also more likely than male inmates to have used drugs regularly (65 percent versus 62 percent), to have used drugs daily in the month preceding their offense (41 percent versus 36 percent), and to have been under the influence at the time of the offense (36 percent versus 31 percent). Nearly 1 in 4 female inmates surveyed reported committing the offense to get money to buy drugs, compared with 1 in 6 males.

Female inmates who used drugs differed from those who did not in the types of crimes they committed. Regardless of the amount of drug use, users were less likely than nonusers to be serving a sentence for a violent offense.

## FIGURE 9–4

### Imprisoned Inmates by Offense Category and Gender

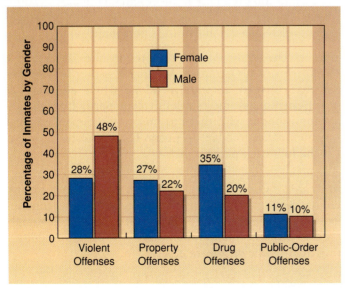

Source: Allen J. Beck and Christopher J. Mumola, *Prisoners in 1998*, Bureau of Justice Statistics (Washington: U.S. Department of Justice, August 1999).

# Social Structure in Women's Prisons

As might be expected, the social structure and the subcultural norms and expectations in women's prisons are quite different from those in men's prisons. Unfortunately, however, relatively few studies of inmate life have been conducted in institutions for women.

One early study, of women at the Federal Reformatory for Women in Alderson, West Virginia, was an effort to compare subcultural aspects of women's prisons with those of men's. Rose Giallombardo reached the conclusion that "many of the subcultural features of the institution are imported from the larger society."[29] Giallombardo believed that male and female inmate subcultures are actually quite similar, except that women's prisons develop "a substitute universe," a world "in which inmates may preserve an identity which is relevant to life outside the prison."

Giallombardo was unable to find in the women's prison some of the values inherent in a male inmate subculture, such as "Do your own time." The inmate subculture in a women's prison, she said, tended to encourage relationships rather than isolation. Hence, women were expected to share their problems with other inmates and to offer at least some support and encouragement to others. On the other hand, she observed, women prisoners tend to see each other as conniving, self-centered, and scheming. Hence, a basic tenet of the inmate subculture in a women's prison is "You can't trust other women." As Giallombardo put it, women prisoners tend to believe that "every woman is a sneaking, lying bitch."

Giallombardo concluded that the social structure of women's prisons and the social role assumed by each inmate were based on three elements:

1. The individual woman's level of personal dependence and her status needs (which were said to be based upon cultural expectations of the female role).
2. The individual's needs arising from incarceration, combined with the institution's inability to meet female inmates' emotional needs.
3. Needs related to the individual's personality.

A more recent study was of inmates in the District of Columbia Women's Reformatory at Occoquan, Virginia.[30] Esther Heffernan identified three roles that women commonly adopt when adjusting to prison. According to Heffernan, women's roles evolved partly from the characteristics the women brought with them to prison and depended partly on the ways the women chose to adapt to prison life. The roles she described are discussed in the following paragraphs:

**The Cool Inmate**   Cool women usually had previous records, were in the know, were street-wise, and did not cause trouble for other inmates while in prison. Cool women were seen as professional or semiprofessional criminals who worked to win the maximum number of prison amenities without endangering their parole or release dates.

**The Square Inmate**   Square women were not familiar with criminal lifestyles and had few, if any, criminal experiences other than the one for

Oftentimes, my prison clients tell me that prison rehab providers like myself have few clues about the needs of people in prison rehabilitation programs. I think that many prisoners believe that educated people who have never used drugs have difficulty in developing and implementing drug rehab programs that really work. Many of my clients say they would design the program differently. I usually listen to their ideas, and sometimes I incorporate some of their thoughts in my work. But I realize that they would water a program down so much that other inmates who want to save themselves wouldn't have an opportunity to do so. Sometimes these clients argue that drug rehab providers should be former addicts—as if any knowledge gained in school, many years of experience, and dedication to helping others are worthless. I don't say that to them, but I do remind them that dentists don't need rotten teeth to be good dentists.

*John McNerney*
*Correctional Counselor*
*Willard-Cybulski Correctional Institution*
*Enfield, CT*

which they were imprisoned. They tended to hold the values and roles of conventional society.

**The Life Inmate**   Life inmates were habitual or career offenders, and were generally well socialized into lives of crime. They supported inmate values and subculture. Life inmates typically were in and out of prison from an early age and had developed criminal lifestyles dedicated to meeting their political, economic, familial, and social needs outside conventional society.

One writer, summarizing the results of studies such as those discussed here, found two features that distinguish women's prisons from men's prisons:[31]

1. The social roles in women's prisons place greater emphasis on homosexual relations as a mode of adaptation to prison life.
2. The mode of adaptation a female inmate selects is best assessed by studying the inmate's preinstitutional experiences.

## Pseudofamilies and Sexual Liaisons

One of the most serious deprivations women in prison experience is isolation from family and loss of contact with loved ones, especially children.

A BJS study of women in prison showed that two-thirds of imprisoned women had at least one child younger than 18.[32] The children usually stayed with their maternal grandmothers or with other relatives, although some were placed in foster homes. Worry about children affects female inmates' physical and emotional well-being.

A unique feature of women's prisons is pseudofamilies. **Pseudofamilies** are familylike structures, common in women's prisons, in which inmates assume roles similar to those families in free society. Pseudofamilies appear to provide emotional and social support for the women who belong to them. Courtship, marriage, and kinship ties formed with other women inmates provide a means of coping with the rigors of imprisonment. One inmate has explained pseudofamilies this way: "It just happens. Just like on the outside, you get close to certain people. It's the same in here— but we probably get even closer than a lot of families because of how lonely it is otherwise."[33]

Some authors suggest that pseudofamilies are to women's prisons what gangs are to men's.[34] Men establish social relationships largely through power, and gang structure effectively expresses such relationships. Women relate to one another more expressively and emotionally. Hence, family structures are one of the most effective reflections of women's relationships in prison, just as they are in the wider society. At least one study of prison coping behavior found that new female inmates, especially those most in need of support, advice, and assistance in adjusting to the conditions of incarceration, are the women most likely to become members of prison pseudofamilies.[35]

**pseudofamilies**
Familylike structures, common in women's prisons, in which inmates assume roles similar to those in families in free society.

The kinship of substitute families plays a major role in the lives of many female inmates, who take the relationships very seriously. How might these relationships supplant values such as "do your own time" commonly found in the subculture of men's prisons?

*The Inmate World: Living Behind Bars*

To a large extent, the social and behavioral patterns of family relationships in prison mirror their traditional counterparts in the community. Moreover, homosexual relationships, marriage alliances, and the larger informal familylike groupings that emerge within the social structure of women's prisons fulfill women's social and emotional needs during incarceration.

Families in women's prisons come in all sizes and colors. They can be virtual melting pots of ethnicity and age. A member of a family may be young or old and may be black, white, or Hispanic. As in families in free society, there are roles for husbands and wives, sisters, brothers, grandmothers, and children. Roles for aunts and uncles don't exist, however.

"Stud broads," in prison argot, assume any male role, including husband and brother. Other inmates think of them as men. "Men" often assume traditional roles in women's prisons, ordering women around, demanding to be waited on, expecting to have their rooms cleaned and their laundry done, and so forth. Most women who assume masculine roles within prison are said to be "playing" and are sometimes called "players." Once they leave, they usually revert to feminine roles. A "femme" or "mommy" is a woman who assumes a female role in a family, and during homosexual activity.

Most women in prison, including those playing masculine roles, were generally not lesbians before entering prison. They resort to lesbian relations within prison because relationships with men are unavailable. The lesbian, in contrast, prefers homosexual relationships to heterosexual ones, even in the outside world.

Though gender roles and family relationships within women's prisons appear to have an enduring quality, women can and sometimes do change gender. When a woman playing a masculine role, for example, reverts to a feminine one, she is said to have "dropped her belt." A stud broad who drops her belt may wreak havoc on relationships within her own family and in families related to it.

## Special Needs of Female Inmates

Rarely are the special needs of imprisoned women fully recognized—and even less frequently are they addressed. Many of today's prison administrators and correctional officers still treat women as if they were men. Nicole Hahn Rafter, for example, says that many prisons have an attitude akin to "just add women and stir."[36]

Susan Cranford is division director of the Community Justice Assistance Division of the Texas Department of Criminal Justice. Rose Williams is warden of Pulaski State Prison in Hawkinsville, Georgia. Cranford and Williams wrote in a 1998 article that "correctional staff should keep the unique needs of women offenders in mind."[37] They say that the effective running of a women's prison requires consideration of those needs.

A critical difference between male and female prisoners, say Cranford and Williams, is "the manner in which they communicate." Female offenders, they note, are usually much more open, more verbal, more emotional,

**HELP WANTED**

### Food Services Coordinator

This position is responsible for all matters relating to a seven-day-a-week, 365-days-a-year institutional food service operation: diet planning; menu publication; food ordering and purchasing; inventory control; scheduling, supervising, training, directing, and evaluating full- and part-time food service staff. Qualified candidates must possess a degree in food service, dietetics, or other related field or at least five years' work experience in food service, with a minimum of two years' supervisory or management experience preferred.

*Most children of incarcerated mothers have little contact with their mothers. The lack of contact often upsets their emotional development. How might prisons contribute to the development of positive relationships between incarcerated mothers and their children?*

and more willing to share the intimacies of their lives than men are. Male prisoners, like most men in free society, are guarded about the information they share and the manner in which they share it. "For men, information is power. For women, talking helps establish a common ground, a way to relate to others."

Gender-specific training is vital for COs who work in women's prisons, say Cranford and Williams. Proper training, they write, can head off the development of inappropriate relationships (especially by male staff members), which could lead to sexual misconduct. Moreover, staff members who work with women should receive additional training in negotiating and listening skills.

Finally, say Cranford and Williams, it is important to realize that a woman's children are usually very important to her and that many imprisoned women have children on the outside. Even more significant is that children of offenders are about eight times as likely as children of nonoffenders to become criminals. Hence, parenting skills should be taught to imprisoned mothers, since most imprisoned mothers will rejoin their children and will be with the children during critical stages in their development.

# Cocorrectional Facilities

In 1971, a disturbance at the federal women's prison at Alderson, West Virginia, led to calls for ways to expand incarceration options for women. The federal Bureau of Prisons responded by moving low-security female

*The Inmate World: Living Behind Bars*

prisoners from the crowded Alderson institution to a federal minimum-security prison at Morgantown, West Virginia. The Morgantown facility had been built for young males but had not reached its design capacity. With this move, the modern era of coed prisons, or cocorrections, was born.

A **coed prison** is a facility housing both men and women, and **cocorrections** is the incarceration and interaction of female and male offenders under a single institutional administration.[38] It is estimated that as many as 52 adult correctional institutions in the United States are coed and that they confine almost 23,000 men and 7,000 women.[39]

Since its inception, cocorrections has been cited as a potential solution to a wide variety of corrections problems. The rationales in support of cocorrections are that it

1. Reduces the dehumanizing and destructive aspects of incarceration by permitting heterosocial relationships.
2. Reduces problems of institutional control.
3. Creates a more "normal" atmosphere, reducing privation.
4. Allows positive heterosocial skills to emerge.
5. Cushions the shock of release.
6. Increases the number of program offerings and improves program access for all prisoners.
7. Expands career opportunities for women.

An examination of the cocorrections literature from 1970 to 1990, however, found no evidence that cocorrections benefits female prisoners.[40] A former warden of a coed prison contends that "going coed" has often been done to appease male egos and smooth the running of men's prisons. Warden Jacqueline Crawford tells us that most women in prison have generally been exploited by the men in their lives. A coed prison, she says, furthers this experience because male prisoners continue the abuse women have come to expect from men.[41]

Others have found that all too often women's prisons have been turned into coed prisons, thus limiting correctional options for women. Overall, researchers have concluded, "Co-corrections offers women prisoners few, if any, economic, educational, vocational, and social advantages."[42] Whether prisoners released from coed prisons adjust better to the community or experience less recidivism has not been sufficiently studied.

Although the literature on single-sex prisons[43] has repeatedly shown poor overall performance in prisoner rehabilitation and public safety, correctional decision makers, policy makers, legislators, and the public are not calling for an end to one-sex imprisonment. If cocorrections is to become more than window dressing, however, it requires more attention to planning, implementation, and evaluation. Contrary to some early claims, coed prisons are not a quick fix for problems of prison administration.

**coed prison** A prison housing both female and male offenders.

**cocorrections** The incarceration and interaction of female and male offenders under a single institutional administration.

# 9

# Review and Applications

**CHAPTER OBJECTIVE 1**

Most state inmates are male, belong to racial or ethnic minority groups, are relatively young, and have been incarcerated for a violent offense.

**CHAPTER OBJECTIVE 2**

Prison inmates live their daily lives in accordance with the dictates of the inmate subculture. The inmate subculture consists of the customs and beliefs of those incarcerated in correctional institutions.

**CHAPTER OBJECTIVE 3**

Deprivation theory holds that prisoner subcultures develop in response to the pains of imprisonment. Importation theory claims that inmate subcultures are brought into prisons from the outside world. A more realistic approach might be the integration model, which uses both theories to explain prisoner subcultures.

**CHAPTER OBJECTIVE 4**

An important aspect of the male inmate subculture is the prison code. The prison code is a set of norms for the behavior of inmates. Central elements of the code include notions of loyalty (to prison society), control of anger, toughness, and distrust of prison officials. Because the prison code is a part of the inmate subculture, it is mostly opposed to official policies.

**CHAPTER OBJECTIVE 5**

The inmate subculture also has its own language, called prison argot. Examples of prison argot include "fish" (a new inmate), "cellie" (cellmate), and "homeboy" (a prisoner from one's hometown).

**CHAPTER OBJECTIVE 6**

Inmate roles are prison lifestyles. They include the real man, the mean dude, the bully, the agitator, the opportunist, the retreatist, the legalist, and the punk.

**CHAPTER OBJECTIVE 7**

There are far fewer women's prisons than men's in the United States. Women's prisons often have no gun towers or armed guards and no stone walls or fences topped by barbed wire. They tend to be more attractive and are often built on a cottage plan. Security in most women's prisons is more relaxed than in institutions for men, and female inmates may have more freedom within the institution than their male counterparts. Even so, gender-based disparities exist. A lack of funding and inadequate training have been cited to explain why programs available to women inmates are often not on a par with those available to male prisoners.

**CHAPTER OBJECTIVE 8**

Female prisoners largely resemble male prisoners in race, ethnic background, and age. However, they are substantially more likely to be serving time for a drug offense and less likely to have been sentenced for a violent crime.

**CHAPTER OBJECTIVE 9**

While there are many similarities, the social structure and the subcultural norms and expectations in women's prisons differ from those in men's prisons in a number of important ways. One important difference can be found in the fact that the prisoner subculture in a women's prison tends to encourage relationships rather than isolation. As a consequence, pseudofamilies arise, with fully developed familial relationships and roles.

total institution, p. 248
inmate subculture, p. 249
prisonization, p. 249
pains of imprisonment, p. 250
deprivation theory, p. 251
importation theory, p. 251
integration model, p. 251

prison code, p. 252
prison argot, p. 252
inmate roles, p. 253
pseudofamilies, p. 264
coed prison, p. 267
cocorrections, p. 267

## QUESTIONS FOR REVIEW

1. What did Erving Goffman mean when he wrote that prisons are *total institutions*?
2. What is the *inmate subculture*, and how is it central to understanding society in men's prisons?
3. What is *prisonization*?
4. According to Gresham Sykes, what are the pains of imprisonment?
5. Explain how inmate subcultures develop, according to deprivation theory, importation theory, and the integration model.
6. What is the *prison code*? How does it influence behavior in men's prisons?
7. Explain what is meant by inmate roles, and give some examples.
8. Compare female and male inmates by their criminal histories, their family characteristics, and the offenses for which they were incarcerated.
9. In what ways do women's prisons differ from men's prisons?
10. What are *pseudofamilies*, and why are they important to the society of women's prisons?
11. What is the most common type of offense for which women are imprisoned?
12. What are some issues relating to cocorrectional facilities?

## CRITICAL THINKING EXERCISES

### ON-THE-JOB ISSUE

You are a correctional officer assigned to a women's prison. Six months ago, the superintendent of your institution ordered an investigation to determine the proper role of male officers within the facility. The investigation centered on charges by a handful of inmates that they had been sexually harassed by male COs. The alleged harassment included requests for sexual favors in return for special privileges, observation of female inmates in various states of undress while in their rooms and in shower facilities, and inappropriate touching during cell and facility searches (policy allowed only female COs to conduct body searches).

Although the investigation was inconclusive, the activities of male COs have been restricted. They are no longer permitted to have any physical contact with inmates unless an emergency demands that they restrain or search inmates. They have been reassigned to areas of the facility where they cannot view shower and toilet facilities. They are expected to announce their presence in living areas, and they have been ordered to take special classes on staff-inmate interaction.

Unfortunately, however, there are not enough female COs for all of the reassignments required by the recent shift in policy. As a result, the routines of female officers are being significantly disrupted. Female officers are being asked to work shifts that are inconvenient for their personal lives (many are mothers or college students and had come to count on predictable shift work). Most female COs also feel that their work load has increased, since they have to cover areas of the institution and assume tasks that male officers would previously have handled.

A few female COs have already left for jobs elsewhere, citing difficulties created in the work environment by the new policies. The talk among the correctional staff is that many of the remaining female staff members might also soon leave. If more female COs leave the facility, it will be impossible for those who remain to keep the facility running under the new rules.

1. Did the superintendent make the right decision in limiting the activities of male COs? Why or why not?

2. Might there be other ways to resolve the issues raised by the investigation into sexual harassment? If so, what might they be?

### CORRECTIONS ISSUE

A woman who gives birth in prison may lose her child to state authorities or may have her parental rights severely restricted. In most cases, the child is removed from the inmate mother shortly after birth. Do you think this is fair? Why or why not?

## CORRECTIONS ON THE WEB

Access the Bureau of Justice Statistics at **http://www.ojp.usdoj.gov/bjs**, and click on "Criminal offenders." Review the following topics: Lifetime Likelihood of going to state or federal prison, Intimate victimizers, and Use of alcohol by convicted offenders. Write a summary of the information you find under each topic.

## ADDITIONAL READINGS

American Correctional Association. *The Female Offender: What Does the Future Hold?* Washington: St. Mary's, 1990.

Flanagan, Timothy J. (ed.). *Long-Term Imprisonment: Policy, Science, and Correctional Practice.* Thousand Oaks, CA: Sage, 1995.

Johnson, Robert. *Hard Time: Understanding and Reforming the Prison,* 2d ed. Belmont, CA: Wadsworth, 1996.

Morris, Allison, et al. *Managing the Needs of Female Prisoners.* London: Home Office, 1995.

Pollock-Byrne, Joycelyn. *Women, Prison and Crime.* Pacific Grove, CA: Brooks-Cole, 1990.

Rafter, Nicole. *Partial Justice: Women, Prisons and Social Control.* Brunswick, NJ: Transaction, 1990.

Watterson, Kathryn. *Women in Prison: Inside the Concrete Tomb,* 2d ed. Boston: Northeastern University Press, 1996.

## ENDNOTES

1. Adapted from "Inmate, Wife Killed in Prison Shootout," *The Keeper's Voice,* Vol. 18, No. 2–3 (Summer-Fall 1997), citing the *Arizona Tribune,* July 10, 1997.

2. Allen Beck et al., *Survey of State Prison Inmates, 1991* (Washington: U.S. Department of Justice, March 1993) online, available: http://www.ojp.usdoj.gov/bjs/pub/ascii/sospi91.txt.

3. Erving Goffman, *Asylums: Essays on the Social Situation of Mental Patients and Other Inmates* (Garden City, NY: Anchor Books, 1961).

4. Hans Toch, *Living in Prison: The Ecology of Survival,* reprint ed. (Washington: American Psychological Association, 1996), p. xv.

5. "Inmate Subculture," in Virgil L. Williams (ed.), *Dictionary of American Penology: An Introductory Guide* (Westport, CT: Greenwood, 1979).

6. Donald Clemmer, *The Prison Community* (Boston: Holt, Rinehart, Winston, 1940).

7. Stanton Wheeler, "Socialization in Correctional Communities," *American Sociological Review,* Vol. 26 (October 1961), pp. 697–712.

8. Gresham M. Sykes, *The Society of Captives: A Study of a Maximum Security Prison* (Princeton, NJ: Princeton University Press, 1958).

9. Stephen C. Light, *Inmate Assaults on Staff: Challenges to Authority in a Large State Prison System,* dissertation, State University of New York at Albany (Ann

Arbor, MI: University Microfilms International, 1987).

10. John Irwin and Donald R. Cressey, "Thieves, Convicts and the Inmate Culture," *Social Problems,* Fall 1962 (Vol. 10), pp. 142–155.

11. James Jacobs, *Statesville: The Penitentiary in Mass Society* (Chicago: University of Chicago Press, 1977).

12. Miles D. Harer and Darrell J. Steffensmeier, "Race and Prison Violence," *Criminology*, Vol. 34, No. 3 (1996), pp. 323–355.

13. John M. Wilson and Jon D. Snodgrass, "The Prison Code in a Therapeutic Community," *Journal of Criminal Law, Criminology, and Police Science*, Vol. 60, No. 4 (1969), pp. 472–478.

14. Gresham M. Sykes and Sheldon L. Messinger, "The Inmate Social System," in Richard A. Cloward et al. (eds.), *Theoretical Studies in Social Organization of the Prison* (New York: Social Science Research Council, 1960), pp. 5–19.

15. Peter M. Wittenberg, "Language and Communication in Prison," *Federal Probation*, Vol. 60, No. 4 (1996), pp. 45–50.

16. Sykes.

17. John Irwin, *The Felon* (Englewood Cliffs, NJ: Prentice Hall, 1970).

18. Adapted from Frank Schmalleger, *Criminal Justice Today*, 5th ed. (Upper Saddle River, NJ: Prentice Hall, 1999).

19. Daniel Lockwood, *Sexual Aggression Among Male Prisoners*, dissertation, State University of New York at Albany (Ann Arbor, MI: University Microfilms International, 1978); Daniel Lockwood, "Issues in Prison Sexual Violence," *The Prison Journal*, Vol. 58, No. 1 (1983), pp. 73–79.

20. Adapted from Toch, p. 274.

21. See American Correctional Association, Task Force on the Female Offender, *The Female Offender: What Does the Future Hold?* (Washington: St. Mary's, 1990).

22. Phyllis J. Baunach, "Critical Problems of Women in Prison," in Imogene L. Moyer, ed., *The Changing Roles of Women in the Criminal Justice System* (Prospect Heights, IL: Waveland Press, 1985), pp. 95–110.

23. See John W. Palmer, *Constitutional Rights of Prisoners* (Cincinnati: Anderson, 1997).

24. American Corrections Association, *Standards for Adult Correctional Institutions* (Lanham, MD: ACA, 1990).

25. Tracy L. Snell, *Women in Prison*, Bureau of Justice Statistics Bulletin NCJ-145321 (Washington: Bureau of Justice Statistics, March 1994); Allen J. Beck and Christopher J. Mumola, *Prisoners in 1998* (Washington: Bureau of Justice Statistics, August 1999).

26. Bureau of Justice Statistics, "Comparing Federal and State Prisoners," press release, October 2, 1994.

27. American Correctional Association.

28. Bureau of Justice Statistics.

29. Rose Giallombardo, *Society of Women: A Study of a Women's Prison* (New York: John Wiley, 1966).

30. Esther Heffernan, *Making It in Prison: The Square, the Cool, and the Life* (New York: Wiley-Interscience, 1972).

31. Williams, p. 109.

32. Snell, op. cit.

33. Kathryn Watterson, *Women in Prison: Inside the Concrete Tomb*, 2d ed. (Boston: Northeastern University Press, 1996), p. 291.

34. For example, John Gagnon and William Simon, "The Social Meaning of Prison Homosexuality," in David M. Petersen and Charles W. Thomas (eds.), *Corrections: Problems and Prospects* (Englewood Cliffs, NJ: Prentice Hall, 1980).

35. Doris Layton MacKenzie, James Robinson, and Carol Campbell, "Long-Term Incarceration of Female Offenders: Prison Adjustment and Coping," *Criminal Justice and Behavior*, Vol. 16, No. 2 (1989), pp. 223–238.

36. Nicole Hahn Rafter, *Partial Justice: Women, Prisons and Social Control* (New Brunswick, NJ: Transaction, 1990).

37. Susan Cranford and Rose Williams, "Critical Issues in Managing Female Offenders," *Corrections Today*, Vol. 60, No. 7 (December 1998), pp. 130–135.

38. John Ortiz Smykla, "Coed Prison: Should We Try It (Again)?" in Charles B. Fields (ed.), *Controversial Issues in Corrections* (Boston: Allyn and Bacon, 1999), pp. 203–218.

39. John Ortiz Smykla and Jimmy J. Williams, "Co-Corrections in the United States of America, 1970–1990: Two Decades of Disadvantages for Women Prisoners," *Women & Criminal Justice*, Vol. 8, No. 1 (1996), pp. 61–76.

40. Ibid.

41. Jacqueline K. Crawford, "Two Losers Don't Make a Winner: The Case Against the Co-correctional Institution," in John Ortiz Smykla (ed.), *Coed Prison* (New York: Human Sciences Press, 1980), pp. 263–268.

42. Smykla and Williams, p. 61.

43. Lawrence W. Sherman, et al, *Preventing Crime: What Works, What Doesn't, What's Promising* (Washington: NIJ, 1997).

# 10 Legal Aspects
## Prisons and the Courts

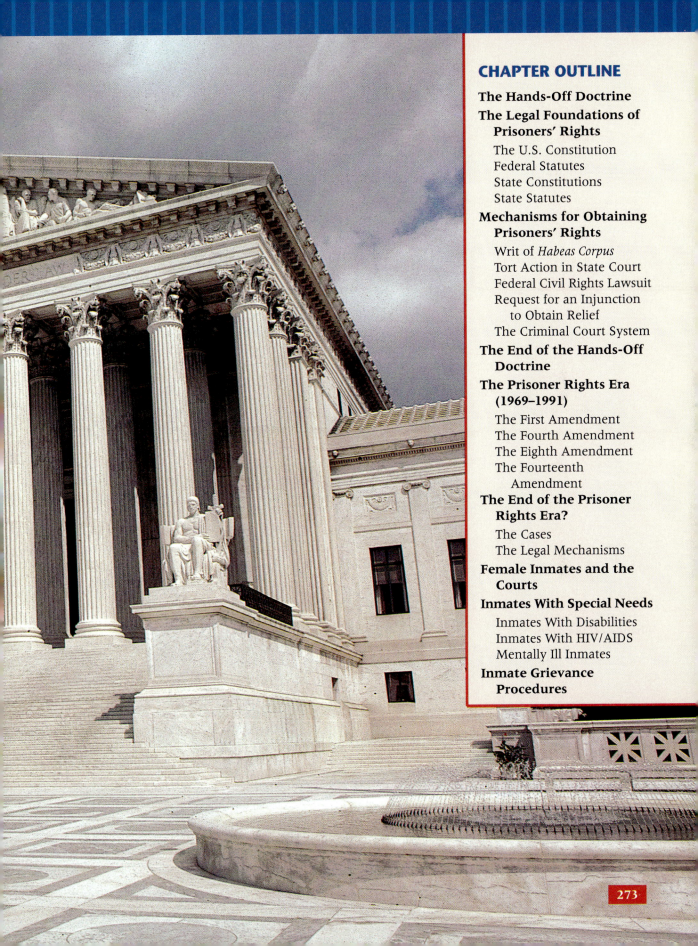

*The federal courts traditionally have adopted a broad hands-off attitude toward problems of prison administration. . . . Suffice it to say that the problems of prisons in America are complex and intractable, and, more to the point, they are not readily susceptible of resolution by decree.*

—*Procunier* v. *Martinez* (1974)

I n 1871, in the case of *Ruffin* v. *Commonwealth*, a Virginia judge declared:

> A convicted felon . . . punished by confinement in the penitentiary instead of with death . . . is in a state of penal servitude to the State. He has, as a consequence of his crime, not only forfeited his liberty, but all his personal rights except those which the law in its humanity accords to him. He is for the time being the slave of the State. He is *civiliter mortuus*; and his estate, if he has any, is administered like that of a dead man. The Bill of Rights is a declaration of general principles to govern a society of freemen, and not of convicted felons and men civilly dead.[1]

The judge in *Ruffin* was voicing what had long been believed: that prisoners had no rights. It was this kind of thinking that long supported a "hands-off" approach to prisoners' rights. If inmates were really civilly dead, the federal government and the federal courts certainly had no cause to tell the states how to run their prisons.

# The Hands-Off Doctrine

**hands-off doctrine**
An historical policy of American courts not to intervene in prison management. Courts tended to follow the doctrine until the late 1960s.

Under the **hands-off doctrine**, American courts for many decades avoided intervening in prison management. The doctrine was based on two rationales: (1) that under the *separation of powers* inherent in the U.S. Constitution, the judicial branch of government should not interfere with the running of correctional facilities by the executive branch and (2) that judges should leave correctional administration to correctional experts.[2] For a very long time in our nation's history, states ran their prisons as they saw fit. Prison inmates were thought of as "nonpersons," and rights were things that only persons had. Pleas from prisoners based on allegations of deprivations of their rights were ignored.

The hands-off doctrine and the philosophy of the prisoner as a slave of the state began to change in the mid-1900s. Public attitudes about punishment versus rehabilitation changed, and more and more people became aware that inmates had *no* rights. As a result, the courts began to scrutinize the correctional enterprise in America.

# The Legal Foundations of Prisoners' Rights

**Prisoners' rights** have four legal foundations: the U.S. Constitution, federal statutes, state constitutions, and state statutes. Most court cases involving prisoners' rights have involved rights claimed under the U.S. Constitution, even though state constitutions generally parallel the U.S. Constitution and sometimes confer additional rights. State legislatures and Congress can also confer additional prisoners' rights.

## The U.S. Constitution

The U.S. Constitution is the supreme law of our land. At the heart of any discussion of prisoners' rights lies one question: What does the Constitution have to say? As scholars began to search the Constitution, they could find no requirement that prisoners give up all of their rights as American citizens (and human beings) after conviction.

It is important to remember, however, that **constitutional rights** are not absolute. Does freedom of speech mean that you have a protected right to stand up in a crowded theater and yell "Fire"? No, it does not (at least, not unless there *is* a fire). That's because the panic that would follow such an exclamation would probably cause injuries and would put members of the public at risk of harm. Hence, the courts have held that although freedom of speech is guaranteed by the Constitution, it is not an absolute right; in other words, there are limits to it.[3]

So the question seems to be, Which constitutional rights do you keep and which rights do you lose when you become a prisoner of the state? Answering that question has become a job of the courts. The results depend on the courts' interpretation of the U.S. Constitution, state constitutions, and federal and state laws. Generally speaking, the courts have recognized four legitimate **institutional needs** that justify some restrictions on the constitutional rights of prisoners:

1. The maintenance of institutional order
2. The maintenance of institutional security
3. The safety of prison inmates and staff and
4. The rehabilitation of inmates

According to the courts, *order* refers to calm and discipline within the institution, *security* is the control of individuals and objects entering or leaving the institution, *safety* means avoidance of physical harm, and *rehabilitation* refers to practices necessary for the health, well-being, and treatment of inmates.[4]

## Federal Statutes

Laws passed by Congress can confer certain rights on inmates in federal prisons. In addition, Congress has passed a number of laws that affect the running of state prisons. The Civil Rights Act of 1871, for example, was enacted after the Civil War to discourage lawless activities by state officials. Section 1983 is as follows:

---

**prisoners' rights**
Constitutional guarantees of free speech, religious practice, due process, and other private and personal rights, as well as constitutional protections against cruel and unusual punishments, made applicable to prison inmates by the federal courts.

**constitutional rights**
The personal and due-process rights guaranteed to individuals by the U.S. Constitution and its amendments, especially the first ten amendments, known as the Bill of Rights. Constitutional rights are the basis of most inmate rights.

**institutional needs**
Prison administration interests recognized by the courts as justifying some restrictions on the constitutional rights of prisoners. Those interests are maintenance of institutional order, maintenance of institutional security, safety of prison inmates and staff, and rehabilitation of inmates.

Every person who, under color of any statute, ordinance, regulation, custom, or usage, of any State or Territory, subjects, or causes to be subjected, any citizen of the United States or other person within the jurisdiction thereof to the deprivation of any rights, privileges, or immunities secured by the Constitution and laws, shall be liable to the party injured in an action at law, suit in equity, or other proper proceeding for redress.

**civil liability** A legal obligation to another person to do, pay, or make good something.

This section imposes **civil liability** (but not criminal blame) on any person who deprives another of rights guaranteed by the U.S. Constitution. The case of *Cooper* v. *Pate* (1964) established that inmates have protections under the Civil Rights Act of 1871. The act allows state prisoners to challenge conditions of their imprisonment in federal court. Most prisoner suits brought under this act allege deprivation of constitutional rights.

## State Constitutions

Most state constitutions are patterned after the U.S. Constitution. However, state constitutions tend to be longer and more detailed than the U.S. Constitution and may contain specific provisions regarding corrections. State constitutions generally do not give prisoners more rights than are granted by the U.S. Constitution, except in a few states such as California and Oregon. Inmates in such a state may challenge the conditions of their confinement in state court under the state's constitutional provision.

## State Statutes

Unlike the federal government, state governments all have inherent police power, which allows them to pass laws to protect the health, safety, welfare, and morals of their citizens. A state legislature can pass statutes to grant specific rights beyond those conferred by the state constitution. Often such legislation specifies duties of corrections officials or standards of treatment for prisoners. Prisoners who can show failure of officials to fulfill state statutory obligations may collect money damages or obtain a court order compelling officials to comply with the law.

# Mechanisms for Obtaining Prisoners' Rights

Today, inmates have five ways to legally challenge prison conditions or the practices of corrections officials: (1) a state *habeas corpus* action, (2) a federal *habeas corpus* action after state remedies have been exhausted, (3) a state tort lawsuit, (4) a federal civil rights lawsuit, and (5) a petition for an injunction to obtain relief.[5]

**writ of *habeas corpus*** An order that directs the person detaining a prisoner to bring him or her before a judge, who will determine the lawfulness of the imprisonment.

## Writ of *Habeas Corpus*

A **writ of *habeas corpus*** is an order from a court to produce a prisoner in court so that the court can determine whether the prisoner is being legally detained. A prisoner, or someone acting for a prisoner, files a *habeas corpus* petition asking a court to determine the lawfulness of the imprisonment. *Habeas corpus* is Latin for "you have the body." The petition for the writ is merely a procedural tool. If a writ is issued, it has no bearing on any issues to be reviewed. It only guarantees a hearing on those issues.

Federal and state prisoners may file *habeas corpus* petitions in federal courts. State prisoners must first, however, exhaust available state *habeas corpus* remedies. In 1995, out of 3,459 petitions that inmates filed in federal courts, 456 (13 percent) were *habeas corpus* actions; out of 11,533 petitions that inmates filed in state courts, 3,939 (34 percent) were *habeas corpus* actions.[6]

## Tort Action in State Court

State inmates can file a tort action in state court. A **tort** is a civil wrong, a wrongful act, or a wrongful breach of duty, other than a breach of contract, whether intentional or accidental, from which injury to another occurs. In tort actions, inmates commonly claim that a correctional employee, such as the warden or a correctional officer, or the correctional facility itself failed to perform a duty required by law regarding the inmate. Compensation for damages is the most common objective. Tort suits often allege such deficiencies as negligence, gross or wanton negligence, or intentional wrong.

## Federal Civil Rights Lawsuit

Federal and state inmates can file suit in federal court alleging civil rights violations by corrections officials. Most of these suits challenge the conditions of confinement, under Section 1983 of the Civil Rights Act of 1871, which is now part of Title 42 of the U.S. Code. Lawsuits may claim that officials have deprived inmates of their constitutional rights, such as adequate medical treatment, protection against excessive force by correctional officers or violence from other inmates, due process in disciplinary hearings, and access to law libraries. According to the Bureau of Justice Statistics, 1 out of 10 civil cases filed in U.S. district courts is Section 1983 litigation, as it is commonly called.

If inmates are successful in their civil suits, in state or federal courts, the courts can award three types of damages. **Nominal damages** are small amounts of money that may be awarded when inmates have sustained no actual damages, but there is clear evidence that their rights have been violated.

**Compensatory damages** are payments for actual losses, which may include out-of-pocket expenses the inmate incurred in filing the suit, other forms of monetary or material loss, and pain, suffering, and mental anguish. Some years ago, for example, a federal appeals court sustained an award of $9300 against a warden and a correctional commissioner. The amount was calculated by awarding each inmate $25 for each day he had spent in solitary confinement (a total of 372 days for all the inmates) under conditions the court found cruel and unusual.[7]

**Punitive damages** are awarded to punish the wrongdoer when the wrongful act was intentional and malicious or was done with reckless disregard for the rights of the inmate.

**tort** A civil wrong, a wrongful act, or a wrongful breach of duty, other than a breach of contract, whether intentional or accidental, from which injury to another occurs.

**nominal damages** Small amounts of money a court may award when inmates have sustained no actual damages, but there is clear evidence that their rights have been violated.

**compensatory damages** Money a court may award as payment for actual losses the inmates suffered, including out-of-pocket expenses the inmate incurred in filing the suit, other forms of monetary or material loss, and pain, suffering, and mental anguish.

**punitive damages** Money a court may award to punish the wrongdoer when a wrongful act was intentional and malicious or was done with reckless disregard for the rights of the inmate.

## Request for an Injunction to Obtain Relief

**injunction** A judicial order to do or refrain from doing a particular act.

An **injunction** is a judicial order to do or refrain from doing a particular act. A request for an injunction might claim adverse effects of a health, safety, or sanitation procedure and might involve the entire correctional facility. It is important for anyone working in corrections to realize that a lack of funds cannot justify failure to comply with an injunction.[8]

## The Criminal Court System

There is a dual court system in the United States: the federal and state court systems coexist. (See Figure 10–1.) The federal court system is nationwide, with one or more federal courts in each state. These courts coexist with state court systems. Whether a defendant is tried in a federal court or a state court depends on which court has jurisdiction over the particular case.

**jurisdiction** The power, right, or authority to interpret and apply the law.

The **jurisdiction** of a court is the power or authority of the court to act with respect to a case before it. The acts involved in the case must have taken place or had an effect in the geographical territory of the court, or a statute must give the court jurisdiction.

### FIGURE 10–1
### Criminal Court Structure

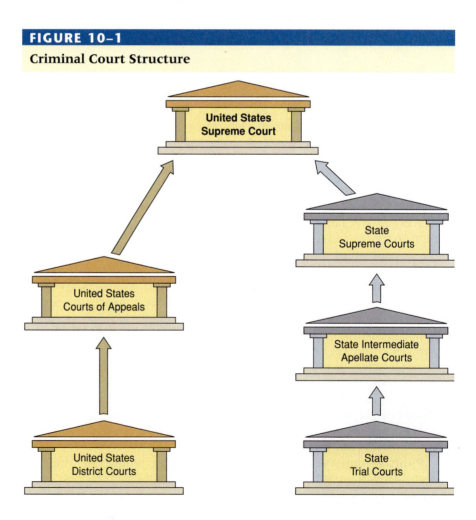

*Legal Aspects: Prisons and the Courts*

District courts are the trial courts of the federal system. They have original jurisdiction over cases charging defendants with violations of federal criminal laws. Each state has at least one United States district court, and some, like New York and California, have as many as four. There are also federal district courts in Puerto Rico, the District of Columbia, and the U.S. territories. There are currently 12 United States courts of appeals, arranged by circuit (11 numbered circuits, a District of Columbia circuit, and one federal circuit—see Table 10–1).

Each state has its own court system. Most state court structures are similar to the federal court structure—trial courts, intermediate appellate courts, and a top appellate court. In most states, the trial courts are organized by county.

## TABLE 10-1

### United States Courts of Appeal

| Court of Appeals | District Courts Included in Circuit |
|---|---|
| Federal Circuit | United States |
| District of Columbia Circuit | District of Columbia |
| First Circuit | Maine, Massachusetts, New Hampshire, Rhode Island, and Puerto Rico |
| Second Circuit | Connecticut, New York, and Vermont |
| Third Circuit | Delaware, New Jersey, Pennsylvania, and the Virgin Islands |
| Fourth Circuit | Maryland, North Carolina, South Carolina, Virginia, and West Virginia |
| Fifth Circuit | Louisiana, Mississippi, and Texas |
| Sixth Circuit | Kentucky, Michigan, Ohio, and Tennessee |
| Seventh Circuit | Illinois, Indiana, and Wisconsin |
| Eighth Circuit | Arkansas, Iowa, Minnesota, Missouri, Nebraska, North Dakota, and South Dakota |
| Ninth Circuit | Alaska, Arizona, California, Hawaii, Idaho, Montana, Nevada, Oregon, Washington, Guam, and the Northern Mariana Islands |
| Tenth Circuit | Colorado, Kansas, New Mexico, Oklahoma, Utah, and Wyoming |
| Eleventh Circuit | Alabama, Florida, and Georgia |

*Source:* Administrative Office of the United States Courts

Though federal offenses are prosecuted in federal court and state offenses are prosecuted in state courts, the federal courts have supervisory jurisdiction over the administration of criminal justice in the state courts. The U.S. Supreme Court has ruled that constitutional requirements for criminal procedure in federal courts also apply to the states. Violation of these constitutional requirements can be the subject of both state appeals and federal suits by prisoners.[9]

# The End of the Hands-Off Doctrine

In 1941, the hands-off doctrine began to wane. *Ex parte Hull*[10] established that no state or its officers may interfere with a prisoner's right to apply to a federal court for a writ of *habeas corpus*. Before that time, it had been common for corrections personnel to screen inmate mail, including prisoner petitions for writs of *habeas corpus*. Corrections officials often confiscated the petitions, claiming they were improperly prepared and not fit to submit to court. In *Ex parte Hull*, the Supreme Court ruled that no state or its officers may interfere with a prisoner's right to apply to a federal court for a writ of *habeas corpus*. Thus, court officials, not corrections officials, have the authority to decide whether such petitions are prepared correctly.

Though this seemed like a small step at the time, it would later enable a major leap in prisoners' rights. Three years later, *Coffin* v. *Reichard* (1944) brought the end of the hands-off era one step closer.[11] In *Coffin*, the Sixth Circuit Court of Appeals extended *habeas corpus* hearings to consideration of the conditions of confinement. Even more important, the *Coffin* case was the first in which a federal appellate court ruled that prisoners do not automatically lose their civil rights when in prison.[12]

Another important development in the abandonment of the hands-off doctrine occurred in 1961, with the Supreme Court's ruling in *Monroe* v. *Pape*.[13] Prior to *Pape*, it was believed that the phrase "under color of state law" in the 1871 statute meant that a Section 1983 suit could only involve actions authorized by state law. In *Pape*, however, the Court held that for activities to take place *under color* of state law, they did not have to be *authorized* by state law. The statute, said the Court, had been intended to protect against "misuse of power, possessed by virtue of state law and made possible only because the wrongdoer is clothed with the authority of state law."[14]

Officials "clothed with the authority of state law" seemed to include state corrections officials. Thus, state corrections officials who violated an inmate's constitutional rights while performing their duties could be held liable for their actions in federal court, regardless of whether state law or policy supported those actions.[15]

A third important case establishing inmates' rights to access to the courts was *Cooper* v. *Pate* (1964).[16] In *Cooper*, a federal circuit court clarified the *Pape* decision, indicating that prisoners could sue a warden or another correctional official under Title 42 of the United States Code, Section 1983, based on the protections of the Civil Rights Act of 1871.

Commenting on the importance of *Cooper*, one observer noted:

> Just by opening a forum in which prisoners' grievances could be heard, the federal courts destroyed the custodian's absolute power and the prisoners' isolation from the larger society. The litigation itself heightened prisoners' consciousness and politicized them.[17]

With prisoners' access to the courts now established, cases challenging nearly every aspect of corrections were filed. The courts, primarily the federal district courts, began to review prisoners' complaints and intervene on prisoners' behalf.

The hands-off era is said to have ended in 1970, when a federal district court, in *Holt* v. *Sarver*, declared the entire Arkansas prison system "so inhumane as to be a violation of the Eighth Amendment bar on cruel and unusual punishment."[18] Robert Sarver, the Arkansas commissioner of cor-

## CAREER PROFILE

*Tammy Waldrop*
*Inspector*
*Correctional Facilities*
*Palm Beach County, FL*

*"In corrections, the words* care, custody, *and* control *are repeatedly stated as your primary tasks. But remember three additional words in your interactions with inmates:* fair, firm, *and* consistent. *If you build your officer reputation on this foundation, you will not have any problems. Treat everyone with respect and the respect will come back to you. And* never, never *lie to an inmate."*

Tammy Waldrop is an inspector with the Palm Beach County (Florida) Sheriff's Office, assigned to Corrections Administration. She's been in the position for almost one year. Quarterly, Tammy inspects all four correctional facilities in Palm Beach County to verify that each one complies with agency, local, state, and American Correctional Association standards. She investigates staff and inmate grievances and works with the Legal Advisors' office to resolve conflicts.

Tammy received her bachelor's degree in criminal justice from Florida Atlantic University in Boca Raton. She remembers that the undergraduate course that influenced her the most was a sociology course titled "Social Conflict." She says, "This course changed my perspective on life and my views on crime. It was the best preparation for my current job. It helped me understand the importance of changing conflict into occasions for problem solving."

In the future, Tammy would like to build on her present career, attend law school, concentrate on corrections law, and work in the Legal Advisors' office.

rections, admitted that, "the physical facilities at both [prison units named in the suit] were inadequate and in a total state of disrepair that could only be described as deplorable." Additionally, he testified that inmates with trustee status, some of them serving life or long-term sentences, constituted 99 percent of the security force of the state's prison system.

Commissioner Sarver continued, testifying that, "trustees sell desirable jobs to prisoners and also traffic in food, liquor and drugs. Prisoners frequently become intoxicated and unruly. The prisoners sleep in dormitories. Prisoners are frequently attacked and raped in the dormitories and injuries and deaths have resulted. Sleep and rest are seriously disrupted. No adequate means exist to protect the prisoners from assaults. There is no satisfactory means of keeping guns, knives and other weapons away from the prison population."

The *Holt* court declared:

> The obligation . . . to eliminate existing unconstitutionalities does not depend upon what the Legislature may do, or upon what the Governor may do. . . . If Arkansas is going to operate a Penitentiary System, it is going to have to be a system that is countenanced by the Constitution of the United States.[19]

Prisoner litigation had brought sad conditions to light, and the court had intervened to institute reforms for the prisoners in Arkansas.

# The Prisoner Rights Era (1969–1991)

Many refer to the era following *Holt* v. *Sarver* as the Prisoner Rights Era. That title might give the impression that during that time, prisoners won virtually every case. That is far from true. Although prisoners won many cases involving their rights during this period, it was the turnaround in court attitudes toward prisoners that was most remarkable. As we shall see, courts went from practically ignoring prison systems to practically running those systems. It might be more appropriate to refer to the period as "the court involvement era." We will now review some of the most important cases won *and* lost by inmates, presented in order of the constitutional amendments on which they were based.

When we speak of prisoners' rights, we are generally speaking of the rights found in four of the amendments to the U.S. Constitution. Three of these—the First, Fourth, and Eighth Amendments—are part of the Bill of Rights (the first ten amendments to the Constitution). The fourth is the Fourteenth Amendment. Keep in mind that what we call inmate rights today are largely the result of federal court decisions that have interpreted constitutional guarantees and applied them to prisons and prison conditions. Often such a case sets a **precedent,** serving as an example or authority for future cases. Rulings in cases that find violations of inmate rights must be implemented by the administrators of affected correctional systems and institutions.

**precedent** A previous judicial decision that judges should consider in deciding future cases.

*Legal Aspects: Prisons and the Courts*

# The First Amendment

*Congress shall make no law respecting an establishment of religion, or prohibiting the free exercise thereof; or abridging the freedom of speech, or of the press; or the right of the people peaceably to assemble, and to petition the government for a redress of grievances.*

First Amendment guarantees are important to members of free society. It is no surprise, then, that some of the early prisoners' rights cases concerned those rights. For example, in 1974, in *Pell* v. *Procunier*,[20] four California prison inmates and three journalists challenged the constitutionality of regulation 415.071 of the California Department of Corrections. That regulation specified that "press and other media interviews with specific individual inmates will not be permitted." The rule had been imposed after a violent prison episode that corrections authorities attributed at least in part to a former policy of free face-to-face prisoner-press interviews. Such interviews had apparently resulted in a relatively small number of inmates gaining disproportionate notoriety and influence among other prisoners.

The U.S. Supreme Court held that "in light of the alternative channels of communication that are open to the inmate appellees, [regulation] 415.071 does not constitute a violation of their rights of free speech." Significantly, the Court went on to say, "A prison inmate retains those first amendment rights that are not inconsistent with his status as prisoner or with the *legitimate penological objectives* of the corrections system." [Emphasis added.] **Legitimate penological objectives** are the permissible aims of a correctional institution and include the realistic concerns that correctional officers and administrators have for the integrity and security of the correctional institution and the safety of staff and inmates. The *Pell* ruling established a **balancing test** that the Supreme Court would continue to use, weighing the rights claimed by inmates against the legitimate needs of prisons.

**Freedom of Speech and Expression**    Visits to inmates by friends and loved ones are forms of expression. But prison visits are not an absolute right. In *Cruz* v. *Beto* (1972),[21] the Supreme Court ruled that all visits can be banned if they threaten security. Although *Cruz* involved short-term confinement facilities, the ruling has also been applied to prisons.

Another form of expression is correspondence. As a result of various court cases, prison officials can (and generally do) impose restrictions on inmate mail. Inmates receive mail, not directly from the hands of postal carriers, but from correctional officers. They place their outgoing mail, not in U.S. Postal Service mailboxes, but only in containers provided by the correctional institution.

Corrections officials often read inmate mail—both incoming and outgoing—in an effort to uncover escape plans. Reading inmate mail, however, is different from censoring it. In 1974, in *Procunier* v. *Martinez*,[22] the U.S. Supreme Court held that the censoring of inmate mail is acceptable only

**legitimate penological objectives** The realistic concerns that correctional officers and administrators have for the integrity and security of the correctional institution and the safety of staff and inmates.

**balancing test** A method the U.S. Supreme Court uses to decide prisoners' rights cases, weighing the rights claimed by inmates against the legitimate needs of prisons.

**TABLE 10–2**

### Selected U.S. Supreme Court Cases Involving Rights of Prisoners

| Case Name | Year | Decision |
|---|---|---|
| *Monroe* v. *Pape* | 1961 | Individuals deprived of their rights by state officers acting under color of state law have a right to bring action in federal court. |
| *Johnson* v. *Avery* | 1968 | Inmates have a right to consult "jailhouse lawyers" when trained legal assistance is not available. |
| *Cruz* v. *Beto* (First Amendment) | 1972 | Inmates have to be given a "reasonable opportunity" to pursue their religious faiths. Also, visits can be banned if such visits constitute threats to security. |
| *Pell* v. *Procunier* (First Amendment) | 1974 | Inmates retain First Amendment rights that are not inconsistent with their status as prisoners, nor with the legitimate penological objectives of the corrections system. |
| *Procunier* v. *Martinez* (First Amendment) | 1974 | Censorship of inmate mail is acceptable only when necessary to protect legitimate governmental interests. |
| *Wolff* v. *McDonnell* (Fourteenth Amendment) | 1974 | Sanctions cannot be levied against inmates without appropriate due process. |
| *Estelle* v. *Gamble* (Eighth Amendment) | 1976 | Prison officials have a duty to provide proper inmate medical care. |
| *Bounds* v. *Smith* | 1977 | Resulted in creation of law libraries in many prisons. |
| *Jones* v. *North Carolina Prisoners' Labor Union, Inc.* (First Amendment) | 1977 | Inmates have no inherent right to publish newspapers or newsletters for use by other inmates. |
| *Cooper* v. *Morin* | 1980 | Neither inconvenience nor cost are acceptable excuses for treating female inmates differently from male inmates. |
| *Rhodes* v. *Chapman* (Eighth Amendment) | 1981 | Double-celling of inmates is not cruel and unusual punishment unless it involves the wanton and unnecessary infliction of pain, or conditions grossly disproportionate to the severity of the crime committed. |

**TABLE 10–2 (continued)**

### Selected U.S. Supreme Court Cases Involving Rights of Prisoners

| Case Name | Year | Decision |
|---|---|---|
| *Block* v. *Rutherford* (First Amendment) | 1984 | State regulations may prohibit inmate union meetings and use of mail to deliver union information within the prison. Prisoners do not have a right to be present during searches of cells. |
| *Hudson* v. *Palmer* (Fourth Amendment) | 1984 | A prisoner has no reasonable expectation of privacy in his prison cell that entitles him to protections against "unreasonable searches." |
| *Ponte* v. *Real* | 1985 | Inmates have certain rights in disciplinary hearings. |
| *Whitley* v. *Albers* (Eighth Amendment) | 1986 | The shooting and wounding of an inmate was not a violation of that inmate's rights, since "the shooting was part and parcel of a good-faith effort to restore prison security." |
| *O'Lone* v. *Estate of Shabazz* (First Amendment) | 1987 | An inmate's right to practice religion was not violated by prison officials who refused to alter his work schedule so that he could attend Friday afternoon services. |
| *Turner* v. *Safley* (First Amendment) | 1987 | A Missouri ban on correspondence between inmates was upheld as "reasonably related to legitimate penological interests." |
| *Washington* v. *Harper* (Eighth Amendment) | 1990 | An inmate who is a danger to self or others as a result of mental illness may be treated with psychoactive drugs against his or her will. |
| *Wilson* v. *Seiter* (Eighth Amendment) | 1991 | Clarified the totality of conditions notion, saying that some conditions of confinement "in combination" may violate prisoners' rights when each would not do so alone. |
| *Sandin* v. *Conner* (Fourteenth Amendment) | 1995 | Perhaps signaling an end to the Prisoner Rights Era, this case rejected the argument that disciplining inmates is a deprivation of constitutional due-process rights. |
| *Lewis* v. *Casey* | 1996 | Earlier cases do not guarantee inmates the wherewithal to file any and every type of legal claim. All that is required is "that they be provided with the tools to attack their sentences." |

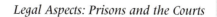

*Inmates have limited rights to send and receive mail. Restrictions on inmates' mail focus on maintaining institutional security. Judicial interpretations of which amendment have led to inmates' rights to send and receive mail?*

when necessary to protect legitimate government interests. The case turned upon First Amendment guarantees of free speech.

Under a 1979 federal appeals court decision, in *McNamara* v. *Moody*, prison officials may not prohibit inmates from writing vulgar letters, or those that make disparaging remarks about the prison staff.[23] Similarly, while correctional administrators have a legitimate interest in curbing inmates' deviant sexual behavior, courts have held that viewing nudity is not deviant sexual behavior. Hence, prison officials may not ban mailed nude pictures of inmates' wives or girlfriends.[24] Nor may they prevent inmates from receiving, by mail direct from publishers, publications depicting nudity unless those publications depict deviant sexual behavior.[25]

In 1989, in the case of *Thornburgh* v. *Abbott*, in an effort to clear up questions raised by lower court rulings concerning mailed publications, the U.S. Supreme Court ruled as follows:

> Publications which may be rejected by a warden include but are not limited to publications which meet one of the following criteria: (1) It depicts or describes procedures for the construction or use of weapons, ammunition, bombs, or incendiary devices; (2) It depicts, encourages or describes methods of escape from correctional facilities, or contains blueprints, drawings, or similar descriptions of Bureau of Prisons institutions; (3) It depicts or describes procedures for the brewing of alcoholic beverages, or the manufacture of drugs; (4) It is written in code; (5) It depicts, describes, or encourages activities which may lead to the use of physical violence or group disruption; (6) It encourages or instructs in the commission of criminal activities; (7) It is sexually explicit material which by its nature or content poses a threat to

the security, good order, or discipline of the institution, or facilitates criminal activity.[26]

Prison officials haven't lost every mail case. In the case of *Turner* v. *Safley*, for example, the Supreme Court upheld a Missouri ban on correspondence between inmates.[27] Such a regulation is valid, the Court said, if it is "reasonably related to legitimate penological interests." *Turner* established that officials had to show only that a regulation was reasonably *related* to a legitimate penological interest. No clear-cut damage to legitimate penological interests had to be shown.

The U.S. Supreme Court sided with corrections officials in its 1977 decision in *Jones* v. *North Carolina Prisoner's Labor Union, Inc.*[28] In *Jones*, the Court upheld regulations established by the North Carolina Department of Correction that prohibited prisoners from soliciting other inmates to join the union and barred union meetings and bulk mailings concerning the union from outside sources. Citing *Pell* v. *Procunier*, the Court went on to say, "The prohibition on inmate-to-inmate solicitation does not unduly abridge inmates' free speech rights. If the prison officials are otherwise entitled to control organized union activity within the confines of a prison the solicitation ban is not impermissible under the First Amendment, for such a prohibition is both reasonable and necessary."[29]

**Freedom of Religion**   Lawsuits involving religious practices in prison have been numerous for at least 40 years. In 1962, for example, the court of appeals for the District of Columbia ruled that the Black Muslim faith must be recognized as a religion, and held that officials may not restrict members of that faith from holding services.[30]

In 1970 the U.S. Supreme Court refused to hear an appeal from inmate Jack Gittlemacker, who wanted the state of Pennsylvania to provide him with a clergyman of his faith.[31] The court held that although states must give inmates the opportunity to practice their religions, they are not required to provide clergy for that purpose.

In *Cruz* v. *Beto* (mentioned earlier), the Supreme Court also decided that inmates had to be given a "reasonable opportunity" to pursue their religious faiths.[32] Later federal court decisions expanded this decision, requiring officials to provide such a "reasonable opportunity" even to inmates whose religious faiths were not traditional.

In 1975, the U.S. Court of Appeals for the Second Circuit ruled in *Kahane* v. *Carlson* that an Orthodox Jewish inmate has the right to a kosher diet unless the government can show good cause for not providing it.[33] Similarly, the courts have held that "Muslims' request for one full-course pork-free diet once a day and coffee three times daily is essentially a plea for a modest degree of official deference to their religious obligations."[34]

On the other hand, courts have determined that some inmate religious demands need not be met. In a 1986 case, for example, Muslim prisoners had requested raw milk, distilled water, and organic fruits, juices, vegetables, and meats. The special diet was so costly that a federal court allowed the prison to deny the inmates' request.[35]

In 1986, a federal court of appeals considered the appeal of Herbert Dettmer, an inmate at Powhatan Correctional Center in Virginia.[36]

Beginning in 1982, Dettmer had studied witchcraft through a correspondence course provided by the Church of Wicca. Within a year, he was holding private ceremonies for meditation as described in the course. Dettmer decided that he needed certain items to aid him in these ceremonies. Those items included a white robe with a hood, sea salt or sulfur to draw a protective circle on the floor around him, and candles and incense to focus his thoughts. Late in 1983, Dettmer requested permission to order the items he felt he needed for meditating. The prison property officer refused permission because the prison rules did not list the items as "authorized personal property." The Supreme Court concluded that "the security officer's concern about inmates' unsupervised possession of candles, salt, and incense is reasonable."

In *O'Lone* v. *Estate of Shabazz* (1987), the U.S. Supreme Court found that a Muslim inmate's right to practice religion was *not* violated by prison officials who refused to alter his work schedule so that he could attend Friday afternoon services.[37] The Court concluded that "even where claims are made under the First Amendment, this Court will not substitute its judgment on difficult and sensitive matters of institutional administration for the determinations of those charged with the formidable task of running a prison."

## The Fourth Amendment

*The right of the people to be secure in their persons, houses, papers, and effects, against unreasonable searches and seizures, shall not be violated, and no Warrants shall issue, but upon probable cause, supported by Oath or affirmation, and particularly describing the place to be searched, and the persons or things to be seized.*

The right to privacy is at the heart of the Fourth Amendment. Clearly, unreasonable searches without warrants are unconstitutional. Does this mean that an inmate has a right to privacy in his or her cell? When is it reasonable to search a cell without a warrant? Some suggest that the needs of institutional security prohibit privacy for inmates. Others argue that a prison cell is the equivalent of an inmate's house. Over the years, the courts have been fairly consistent in deciding that the privacy rights implied in this amendment must be greatly reduced in prisons to maintain institutional security.

In *United States* v. *Hitchcock* (1972), an inmate claimed that his Fourth Amendment rights had been violated by a warrantless search and seizure of documents in his prison cell.[38] Previously, courts had generally held that "constitutionally protected" places—such as homes, motel rooms, safe-deposit boxes, and certain places of business—could not be searched without a warrant. In *Hitchcock*, however, the U.S. Court of Appeals for the Ninth Circuit created a new standard: "first, that a person have exhibited an actual (subjective) expectation of privacy and second, that the expectation be one

*Legal Aspects: Prisons and the Courts*

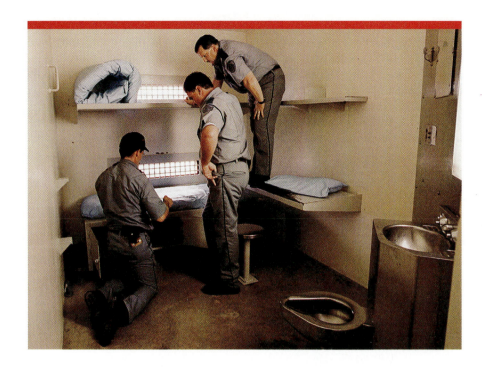

*Prisoners do not retain the right to privacy in their cells or possessions because institutional interests of safety and security supersede constitutional guarantees of privacy. Under which amendment to the Constitution does the right to be free from unreasonable searches and seizures fall?*

that society is prepared to recognize as reasonable." The court concluded that although Hitchcock plainly expected to keep his documents private, his expectation was not reasonable. In the words of the court:

> [It] is obvious that a jail shares none of the attributes of privacy of a home, an automobile, an office, or a hotel room. In prison, official surveillance has traditionally been the order of the day. . . . [Hence], we do not feel that it is reasonable for a prisoner to consider his cell private.

In *Hudson* v. *Palmer* (1984), a Virginia inmate claimed a correctional officer had unreasonably destroyed some of his permitted personal property during a search of his cell.[39] The inmate also claimed that under the Fourth Amendment, the cell search was illegal. Echoing *Hitchcock*, the U.S. Supreme Court ruled that "a prisoner has no reasonable expectation of privacy in his prison cell entitling him to the protection of the Fourth Amendment against unreasonable searches." Similarly, in *Block* v. *Rutherford* (1984), the Court ruled that prisoners do not have the right to be present during searches of their cells.[40]

In 1985, the Ninth Circuit Court of Appeals decided a case involving inmates at San Quentin State Prison.[41] The inmates had brought a class action lawsuit against prison administrators, objecting to the policy of allowing female correctional officers to view nude or partly clothed male inmates. Women officers, complained the inmates, could see male inmates while they were dressing, showering, being strip-searched, or using toilet facilities. Such viewing, said the inmates, violated privacy rights guaranteed by the United States Constitution.

At the time of the suit, approximately 113 of the 720 correctional officers at San Quentin were female. Both female and male correctional officers were assigned to patrol the cell block tiers and gun rails. Both were also assigned to supervise showering from the tiers and from the gun rails, but only male officers were permitted to accompany inmates to the shower cells and lock them inside to disrobe and shower. Female officers were allowed to conduct pat-down searches that included the groin area.

The court found that prison officials had "struck an acceptable balance among the inmates' privacy interests, the institution's security requirements, and the female guards' employment rights." According to the court:

> The female guards are restricted in their contact with the inmates, and the record clearly demonstrates that at all times they have conducted themselves in a professional manner, and have treated the inmates with respect and dignity. . . . Routine pat-down searches, which include the groin area, and which are otherwise justified by security needs, do not violate the Fourteenth Amendment because a correctional officer of the opposite gender conducts such a search.

## The Eighth Amendment

*Excessive bail shall not be required, nor excessive fines imposed, nor cruel and unusual punishments inflicted.*

**cruel and unusual punishment** A penalty that is grossly disproportionate to the offense or that violates today's broad and idealistic concepts of dignity, civilized standards, humanity, and decency. In the area of capital punishment, cruel and unusual punishments are those that involve torture, a lingering death, or unnecessary pain.

**consent decree** A written compact, sanctioned by a court, between parties in a civil case, specifying how disagreements between them are to be resolved.

Many prisoners' rights cases turn upon the issue of **cruel and unusual punishment.** Defining such punishment is not easy. A working definition, however, might be: punishments that are grossly disproportionate to the offense, as well as those that transgress today's broad and idealistic concepts of dignity, civilized standards, humanity, and decency.[42] Cases concerning constitutional prohibition of cruel and unusual punishment have centered on prisoners' need for decent conditions of confinement. In one case, *Ruiz* v. *Estelle* (1980),[43] the conditions of confinement in the Texas prison system were found unconstitutional, and a **consent decree** was imposed on the system. Inmate rights cases involving the Eighth Amendment cover areas as diverse as medical care, prison conditions, physical insecurity, psychological stress, and capital punishment.

**Medical Care**   The right to adequate medical care was one of the issues in *Holt* v. *Sarver* (1970), a case in which the Arkansas prison system was declared inhumane and a violation of the Eighth Amendment ban on cruel and unusual punishment.[44]

In one case, medical personnel in state prisons had given inmates injections of apomorphine without their consent, in a program of "aversive stimuli." The drug caused vomiting, which lasted from fifteen minutes to an hour. The state justified it as "Pavlovian conditioning." The federal courts, however, soon prohibited the practice.[45]

Another decision, that of *Estelle* v. *Gamble* (1976), spelled out the duty of prison officials to provide inmates medical care.[46] The Court held that prison officials could not lawfully demonstrate **deliberate indifference** to the medical needs of prisoners.

**Prison Conditions**   The 1976 federal court case of *Pugh* v. *Locke* introduced the **totality of conditions** as a standard.[47] That standard, said the court, is to be used in evaluating whether prison conditions are cruel and unusual. The *Pugh* court held that "prison conditions [in Alabama] are so debilitating that they necessarily deprive inmates of any opportunity to rehabilitate themselves or even maintain skills already possessed." The totality-of-conditions approach was also applied in a 1977 federal case in which officials in overcrowded Oklahoma prisons had forced inmates to sleep in garages, barbershops, libraries, and stairwells. Oklahoma prison administrators were found in violation of the cruel-and-unusual-punishment clause of the U.S. Constitution.[48]

The U.S. Supreme Court ruled on the use of solitary confinement in *Hutto* v. *Finney* (1978).[49] The Court held that confinement in Arkansas's segregation (solitary-confinement) cells for more than 30 days was cruel and unusual punishment. It then went on to exhort lower courts to consider the totality of the conditions of confinement in future Eighth Amendment cases. Where appropriate, it said, a court should specify the changes needed to remedy the constitutional violation.

In the 1991 case *Wilson* v. *Seiter*, the U.S. Supreme Court clarified the totality-of-conditions standard.[50] The Court noted that:

> Some conditions of confinement may establish an Eighth Amendment violation "in combination" when each would not do so alone, but only when they have a mutually enforcing effect that produces the deprivation of a single, identifiable human

**deliberate indifference**
Intentional and willful indifference. Within the field of correctional practice the term refers to calculated inattention to unconstitutional conditions of confinement.

**totality of conditions**
A standard to be used in evaluating whether prison conditions are cruel and unusual.

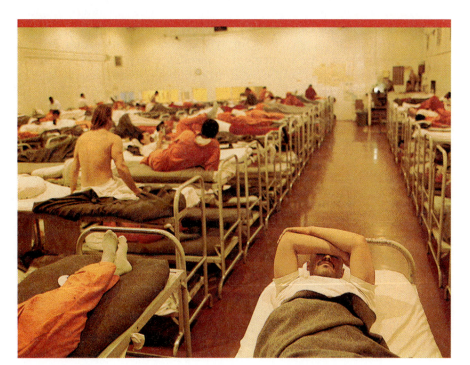

*The Eighth Amendment's prohibition of cruel and unusual punishment has been tied to prisoners' need for decent conditions of confinement. In determining if conditions such as overcrowding and inadequate diet constitute a denial of such protection, courts have used the concept of totality of conditions. What is meant by the totality of conditions?*

need such as food, warmth, or exercise—for example, a low cell temperature at night combined with a failure to issue blankets. . . . To say that some prison conditions may interact in this fashion is a far cry from saying that all prison conditions are a seamless web for Eighth Amendment purposes. Nothing so [shapeless] as "overall conditions" can rise to the level of cruel and unusual punishment when no specific deprivation of a single human need exists.

Several rulings have addressed inmate claims that overcrowding was cruel and unusual punishment. A U.S. Supreme Court case, *Rhodes* v. *Chapman* (1981), decided the issue of double-celling (housing two inmates in a cell designed for one) in long-term correctional facilities.[51] In response to rising prison populations, Ohio authorities had begun double-celling. There was no evidence that Ohio authorities had wantonly inflicted pain through the practice, and double-celling had not resulted in food deprivation, a lower quality of medical care, or a decrease in sanitation standards. For those reasons, the Court denied the inmates' claims.

In *Rhodes*, the Court also emphasized that the Eighth Amendment prohibition of cruel and unusual punishments is a fluid concept that "must draw its meaning from the evolving standards of decency that mark the progress of a maturing society." In other words, what is considered cruel and unusual, changes as society evolves.

In 1982, the U.S. Court of Appeals for the Seventh Circuit ruled, in *Smith* v. *Fairman*, that double-celling in a short-term facility (a jail) was not cruel and unusual punishment.[52] The court said that government officials did not intend to punish inmates by double-celling. The double-celling was innocent overcrowding required by circumstances.

Many conditions of confinement that violate prisoners' Eighth Amendment rights can be remedied by changes in prison rules, by special training for correctional personnel, or by educational programs for prisoners. The remedies can be implemented through everyday administrative policies in the prison, once prisoners' court petitions have brought violations to light. Relief of overcrowding, however, is not always within the power of prison administrators. Prison officials have little control over the sizes of their prisons or the numbers of inmates the courts assign to them. New prison facilities are expensive and take time to build.

## The Fourteenth Amendment

When the Constitution and the Bill of Rights became law, the people of many states thought the document applied only to federal courts and to federal law. This attitude prevailed at least until the end of the Civil War. After the war, to clarify the status of the newly freed slaves and to apply the Bill of Rights to state actions, the Fourteenth Amendment was passed. The portion relevant to our discussion is as follows:

*No State shall make or enforce any law which shall abridge the privileges or immunities of citizens of the United States;*

*nor shall any State deprive any person of life, liberty, or property, without due process of law; nor deny to any person within its jurisdiction the equal protection of the laws.*

Most cases involving prisoners' rights and the Fourteenth Amendment deal with issues of **due process**. Due process requires that laws and legal procedures be reasonable and be applied fairly and equally. The right to due process is a right to be fairly heard before being deprived of life or liberty.

To get their cases to court, prisoners need access to legal materials, and many of them need legal assistance. Without access to the courts, inmates have no due process. What if one inmate understands how to file cases with the court, but a second inmate does not? Does the second inmate have a right to enlist the aid of the first? "Yes," said the U.S. Supreme Court in *Johnson* v. *Avery* (1968).[53] Inmates have a right to consult "jailhouse lawyers" (other inmates knowledgeable in the law) when trained legal advisers are not available.

The case of *Wolff* v. *McDonnell* (1974) expanded the concept of due process by applying it to disciplinary actions within prisons.[54] Prior to *Wolff*, prison administrators had the discretion to discipline inmates who broke prison rules. Disciplinary procedures were often tied to vague or nonexistent rules of conduct and were exercised without challenge. A prisoner might be assigned to solitary confinement or might have good-time credits reduced because of misconduct. Because the prisoner was physically confined and lacked outside communication, there was no opportunity for the prisoner to challenge the charge. The *Wolff* court concluded that sanctions (disciplinary actions) could not be levied against inmates without appropriate due process, saying:

> [The state of Nebraska] asserts that the procedure for disciplining prison inmates for serious misconduct is a matter of policy raising no constitutional issue. If the position implies that prisoners in state institutions are wholly without the protection of the Constitution and the Due Process Clause, it is plainly untenable. Lawful imprisonment necessarily makes unavailable many rights and privileges of the ordinary citizen, a retraction justified by the consideration underlying our penal system. . . . But though his rights may be diminished by the needs and exigencies of the institutional environment, a prisoner is not wholly stripped of constitutional protections when he is imprisoned for a crime.

The *Wolff* Court imposed minimal due-process requirements on prison disciplinary proceedings that could lead to solitary confinement or reduction of good-time credits. The requirements included (1) advance notice by means of a written statement of the claimed violation, (2) a written statement by an impartial fact finder of the evidence relied on and the reasons for imposing punishment, and (3) an opportunity to testify and call witnesses unless the fact finder concluded such proceedings would undermine institutional security.[55]

**due process** A right guaranteed by the Fifth, Sixth, and Fourteenth Amendments to the U.S. Constitution and generally understood, in legal contexts, to mean the expected course of legal proceedings according to the rules and forms established for the protection of persons' rights.

In 1976 inmates lost three due-process appeals. First, in *Baxter* v. *Palmigiano*, the Supreme Court decided that due process for an inmate in a disciplinary hearing does not include a right to counsel, even when the consequences are potentially "serious."[56] In a second opinion issued that year (*Meacham* v. *Fano*), the Court held that prisoners have no right to be in any particular prison and therefore have no due-process protections before being transferred from one prison to another.[57] A third case (*Stone* v. *Powell*) denied prisoners the right in most instances to seek federal review of state court Fourth Amendment search-and-seizure decisions.[58]

Inmates' right to legal materials was formally recognized in 1977, in the U.S. Supreme Court decision in *Bounds* v. *Smith*.[59] In *Bounds* the Court held:

> The fundamental constitutional right of access to the courts requires prison authorities to assist inmates in the preparation and filing of meaningful legal papers by providing prisoners with adequate law libraries or adequate assistance from persons trained in the law.

As a result of the *Bounds* decision, law libraries were created in prisons across the nation.

As we saw in Chapter 8, one challenge facing corrections personnel is to find safe, humane ways to manage inmate populations. Inmates often have grievances regarding conditions of confinement or disciplinary actions for infractions. Those grievances must be dealt with to maintain the safety and security of the institution. The Supreme Court's decision in *Jones* v. *North Carolina Prisoners' Labor Union, Inc.* (1977) required prisons to establish and maintain formal opportunities for the airing of inmate grievances.[60] *Ponte* v. *Real* (1985) required prison officials to explain to inmates why their

*Inmates must be allowed access to the courts and assistance in preparing their cases. Most states stock law libraries in each correctional institution. Under which clause of the Fourteenth Amendment does inmates' access to the courts fall?*

requests to have witnesses appear on their behalf at disciplinary hearings were denied.[61]

The due-process clause protects against unlawful deprivation of life or liberty. When a prisoner sued for damages for injuries (*Daniels* v. *Williams*, 1986), the Supreme Court ruled that prisoners could sue for damages in federal court only if officials had inflicted injury intentionally.[62] According to the Court, "The due process clause is simply not implicated by a negligent act of an official causing unintended loss or injury to life, liberty or property."

As we have seen, federal and state inmates can file suits in federal court alleging civil rights violations by corrections officials. In 1988, the U.S. Supreme Court (in *West* v. *Atkins*) decided that private citizens who contracted to do work for prisons could be sued for civil rights violations against inmates.[63] The Court found that such contractors were acting "under color of state law," as required by Section 1983 of the Civil Rights Act of 1871.

As a result of Supreme Court decisions, most prisons now have rules that provide the due process required when prisoners must appear before disciplinary committees. The makeup of disciplinary committees varies among institutions. The committees may include both inmates and free citizens.

# The End of the Prisoner Rights Era?

By the late 1980s, the Prisoner Rights Era seemed to be drawing to a close. The Justices sitting on the Supreme Court had become less sympathetic to prisoners' claims of denial of civil rights. As indicated in *Daniels* v. *Williams* (1986), discussed in the preceding section, due process was intended only to prevent abuse of power, not to protect against mere carelessness. Further, judicial and legislative officials began to realize that inmates frequently abused their access to the courts. As state costs of defending against **frivolous lawsuits** by inmates began to grow, federal courts began to take a new look at prisoners' rights.

Examples of abuse of the court system by prison inmates abound. One inmate sued the state of Florida because he got only one roll with dinner. He sued two more times because he didn't get a salad with lunch and because prison-provided TV dinners didn't come with drinks. He sued yet again because his cell wasn't equipped with a television. Another inmate claimed prison officials were denying him freedom of religion. His religion, he said, required him to attend prison chapel services in the nude. Still another inmate, afraid that he could get pregnant through homosexual relations, sued because prison officials wouldn't give him birth control pills.

As early as 1977, the U.S. Supreme Court refused to hear an appeal from Henry William Theriault, founder of the Church of the New Song (or CONS).[64] Theriault, an inmate at the federal penitentiary in Atlanta, had a mail-order divinity degree. Members of CONS celebrated communion every Friday night. They claimed that prison officials must supply them with steak and Harvey's Bristol Cream Sherry for the practice. Although "Bishop Theriault" admitted that he had originally created CONS to mock other reli-

**frivolous lawsuits**
Lawsuits with no foundation in fact. They are generally brought for publicity, politics, or other reasons not related to law.

My name is Brian Pierce. I'm an ex-con.

Let me tell you about myself. I grew up in a small southern Minnesota river town. In an effort to bring our family closer together, my parents purchased a small family-run tourist business they hoped we could eventually run as a family. My parents have always been hard workers and Christians. I am not sure what got me started really, but by the time I was 14 I was using drugs heavily and starting to spin the revolving door of Minnesota's illustrious correctional system.

First, I was court-ordered into a drug treatment center called the Cannon Valley Center in Cannon Falls, Minnesota. From there I went to a halfway house in Winona named the East House. When the county ran out of funding, they told me I could leave despite the fact that the counselors did not think I was ready. Not long after getting home I was on the way to the Minnesota Correctional Facility at Red Wing, the end of the line for juveniles in Minnesota.

When I turned 18, I was moving too fast to slow down and was soon on my way to the Minnesota Correctional Facility at St. Cloud. I was sentenced to 38 months for third-degree burglary and received two shorter sentences that ran concurrently for theft charges. Under Minnesota's guidelines, I had to serve two thirds of that sentence inside and the remaining one third on parole.

St. Cloud is relatively old and made predominately out of dark gray granite. The wall is solid granite and somewhere around 20 feet high and several feet thick. It encompasses over 50 acres, including several cell houses, factories, maintenance facilities, and a yard for recreation. There are armed guard towers spaced evenly around the top of the wall.

Like most of my friends there, I got out and quickly got back into the same old routine. An Olmstead County judge gave me the option of pleading guilty to possession of a controlled substance but getting a stay of adjudication pursuant to Minnesota Statute Section 152.18 and being sentenced to treatment rather than a prison term. If I completed the recommended treatment, follow-up, and aftercare, the charge would not appear on my record. Although it sounded good, I had already been in prison once and thought I would screw it up in the treatment program and end up doing the time anyway. I asked to have my sentence executed.

gions, he claimed that he became a serious believer as the religion developed and acquired more followers. The U.S. Supreme Court dismissed that argument and held that the First Amendment does not protect so-called religions that are obvious shams.

## The Cases

In *Wilson* v. *Seiter* (1991),[65] the U.S. Supreme Court again sided with prison officials in a way uncharacteristic of the previous two decades. In *Wilson* the Court found that overcrowding, excessive noise, insufficient

A few months after being released from St. Cloud for the second time in four years, I jumped my parole and began wandering around the country with a group of misfits selling Dunn-EZ, a homemade chemical cleaner, to small businesses. Eventually, we ended up in Atlanta, Georgia, where I met my wife. She was a single mother with two young boys and was as wild as I was. Together, my wife, the boys, and I traveled the country treading water for the next several months until we found ourselves in the Lowndes County, Georgia, jail for credit card fraud. It was the most miserable time I have ever had in jail—first, because the woman I loved was in with me and, second, because the conditions were unbelievable. I slept on the floor of a very small one-man cell with two other guys. At night the guards would come by and for a Little Debbie snack or two, they would sell you a full bottle of Nyquil. One of my cellmates would drink it and get high.

With the help of my parents, my new wife and I rode the Greyhound back to Minnesota. I had to finish up about 30 days' worth of my last Minnesota sentence so that my parole would expire. Because the time left on my sentence was so short, Minnesota refused to extradite me from Georgia for the parole violation (leaving the state), but was ready and willing to incarcerate me for every day I had coming if I returned to Minnesota.

Once released and working odd jobs, I enrolled in the University of Minnesota, Duluth. I received my B.A. *magna cum laude* in criminology, with a minor in psychology, almost four years later. Graduating from college felt so unbelievably good to me. I was energized and committed to going on to law school. I applied to the University of Minnesota's law school, where I received my Juris Doctorate *cum laude*, May 10, 1997. Midway through my first year I hooked up with a law professor interested in computers, as I was. Together we created the Human Rights Library on the World Wide Web.

I completed a one-year judicial clerkship with a judge on the Court of Appeals and I am currently clerking for my second year with the Chief Judge of the Court of Appeals. In addition, I develop Web sites for law firms and nonprofit human-rights organizations, and I am writing a book. I also do public speaking about drugs, crime, corrections, and rehabilitation.

locker space, and similar conditions did not violate the Constitution if the intent of prison officials was not malicious. The Court ruled that the actions of officials did not meet the "deliberate indifference" standard defined in *Estelle* v. *Gamble* (1976).

After *Wilson*, inmates won very few new cases. The courts either reversed themselves or tightened the conditions under which inmates could win favorable decisions. Decisions supporting freedom of religion had been among the earliest and most complete victories during the Prisoner Rights Era. Even in that area, however, things began to change. The courts held that crucifixes and rosaries could legally be denied to inmates because of their possible use as weapons.[66] Although some jurisdictions had previously allowed certain Native American religious items within prisons,[67] the courts now ruled that prohibiting ceremonial pipes, medicine bags, and eagle claws did *not* violate the First Amendment rights of Native American inmates.[68]

The "deliberate indifference" standard was soon interpreted to require both actual knowledge *and* disregard of the risk of harm to inmates or others.[69] This tighter definition allowed federal courts to side more easily with state prison officials in cases where prisoners claimed there was deliberate indifference.

If there was any question that the Prisoner Rights Era had ended, that question was settled in 1995 by the case of *Sandin* v. *Conner*.[70] In *Sandin* the Supreme Court rejected the argument that by disciplining inmates, a state deprived prisoners of their constitutional right not to be deprived of liberty without due process. "The time has come to return to those due process principles that were correctly established and applied in earlier times," said the Court. A year later, the decision in *Lewis* v. *Casey*[71] overturned portions of *Bounds* v. *Smith*. The *Bounds* case had been instrumental in establishing law libraries in prisons. The Court in *Lewis* held, however, that "*Bounds* does not guarantee inmates the wherewithal to file any and every type of legal claim, but requires only that they be provided with the tools to attack their sentences."

## The Legal Mechanisms

Changes in state and federal statutes have also slowed the pace of prisoners' rights cases. In 1980 Congress modified the Civil Rights of Institutionalized Persons Act.[72] It now requires a state inmate to exhaust all state remedies before filing a petition for a writ of *habeas corpus* in federal court. Inmates in federal prisons may still file *habeas corpus* petitions directly in federal court. In their petitions, federal inmates are now required to show (1) that they were deprived of some right to which they were entitled despite the confinement and (2) that the deprivation of this right made the imprisonment more burdensome.

The Prison Litigation Reform Act of 1996[73] (PLRA) was another legislative response to the ballooning number of civil rights lawsuits filed by prisoners. It restricts the filing of lawsuits in federal courts by:

1. Requiring inmates to pay $120 in federal filing fees unless they can claim pauper status.[74]
2. Limiting awards of attorneys' fees in successful lawsuits.
3. Requiring judges to screen all inmate lawsuits and immediately dismiss those they find frivolous.
4. Revoking good-time credit toward early release if inmates file malicious lawsuits.
5. Barring prisoners from suing the federal government for mental or emotional injury unless there is an accompanying physical injury.
6. Allowing court orders to go no further than necessary to correct the particular inmate's civil rights problem.
7. Requiring court orders to be renewed every two years or be lifted.
8. Ensuring that no single judge can order the release of federal inmates for overcrowding.

When inmates bring lawsuits against the Department of Corrections in behalf of their rights, those lawsuits are not a big-bucks undertaking for a lawyer. Most prisoners cannot afford to pay a retainer. When an attorney agrees to a contingency fee, there's always the likelihood that the state or federal government will prevail against the prisoner. After all, government agencies have more lawyers and more money than do prisoners. Also, judges tend to be more sympathetic to their own than to prisoners. It is true that prisoner litigants won more cases 20 years ago, but the political trends since then have resulted in judicial appointments more favorable to the corrections side of the scale. There's also been legislation limiting prisoners' access to the courts. I'm afraid the mood of the courts does not favor prisoners, and I believe that's true across the United States.

*A Texas attorney*

# Female Inmates and the Courts

The prisoners' rights movement has been largely a male phenomenon. While male inmates were petitioning the courts for expansion of their rights, female inmates frequently had to resort to the courts simply to gain rights male inmates already had.

One early state case, *Barefield* v. *Leach* (1974),[75] demonstrated that the opportunities and programs for female inmates were clearly inferior to those for male inmates. In that case a court in New Mexico spelled out one standard for equal treatment of male and female inmates. The court said that the equal-protection clause of the Constitution requires equal treatment of male and female inmates, but not identical treatment. *Barefield*, however, was a state case—not binding on other states or the federal government.

In 1977, the Supreme Court of North Dakota ruled that a lack of funds was not an acceptable justification for unequal treatment of male and female prisoners.[76] Although this decision also came in a state court case, it would later be cited as a legal authority in a similar federal court case.

In *Glover* v. *Johnson* (1979), a U.S. district court case, a group of female prisoners in the Michigan system filed a class action lawsuit claiming that they were denied access to the courts and constitutional rights to equal protection.[77] The prisoners demanded educational and vocational opportunities comparable to those for male inmates. At trial, a prison teacher testified that while men were allowed to take shop courses, women were taught remedial courses at a junior-high-school level because the attitude of those in charge was "Keep it simple, these are only women." The court found that "the educational opportunities available to women prisoners in Michigan were substantially inferior to those available to male prisoners." Consequently, the court ordered a plan to provide higher education and vocational training for female prisoners in the Michigan prison system. *Glover* was a turning point in equal treatment for imprisoned women. Since 1979, female inmates have continued to win the majority of cases seeking equal treatment and the elimination of gender bias.

In the 1980 case of *Cooper* v. *Morin*, the U.S. Supreme Court accepted neither inconvenience nor cost as an excuse for treating female jail inmates differently from male inmates.[78] Female inmates at a county jail in New York had alleged that inadequate medical attention in jail violated their civil rights. Later that same year, a federal district court rejected Virginia's claims that services for female prison inmates could not be provided at the same level as those for male inmates because of cost-effectiveness issues.[79] Virginia authorities said that the much smaller number of women in prison raised the cost of providing each woman with services. The appellate court ordered the state of Virginia to provide equitable services for inmates, regardless of gender.

An action challenging the denial of equal protection and the conditions of confinement in the Kentucky Correctional Institution for Women was the basis of *Canterino* v. *Wilson*, decided in U.S. district court in 1982.[80] The district court held that the "levels system" used to allocate privileges to female prisoners, a system not applied to male prisoners, violated both the equal-protection rights and the due-process rights of female inmates. The court also held that female inmates in Kentucky's prisons must have the same

*Many claims of female inmates have focused on the failure of correctional institutions to provide them with educational opportunities and medical care comparable to those provided male inmates. The equal protection clause of which amendment guarantees female inmates conditions of confinement comparable to those of male inmates?*

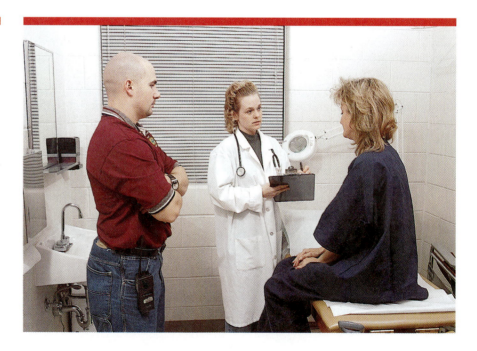

opportunities as men for vocational education, training, recreation, and outdoor activity.

In 1982, a district court in Louisiana ordered an end to the unequal treatment of female inmates in that state's jails.[81] (Recall that the federal courts have supervisory jurisdiction over state courts.) The next year, the Seventh Circuit Court of Appeals found that strip searches of female misdemeanor offenders awaiting bond in a Chicago lockup were unreasonable under the Fourth Amendment.[82] In addition, the court found that a policy of subjecting female arrestees to strip searches while subjecting similarly situated males only to hand searches violated the equal protection clause of the Constitution.

Women inmates have continued to win significant court cases regarding conditions of confinement. In 1994, for example, in a class action suit by female inmates, a federal district court held the District of Columbia Department of Corrections liable under the Eighth Amendment for inadequate gynecological examinations and testing, inadequate testing for sexually transmitted diseases, inadequate health education, inadequate prenatal care, and an inadequate overall prenatal protocol.[83]

# Inmates With Special Needs

Inmates with special needs face numerous difficulties. This section focuses on the legal claims brought by such inmates.

## Inmates With Disabilities

Ronald Yeskey was sentenced to 18 to 36 months in a Pennsylvania correctional facility. Yeskey was recommended for a motivational boot camp, which would have shortened his sentence to 6 months. He was, however, refused admission to the boot camp because of a physical disability—hypertension. He sued, claiming that the Americans with Disabilities Act (ADA) of 1990 prohibits any "public entity" from discriminating against a "qualified individual with a disability" because of that disability.[84] In a unanimous opinion, the U.S. Supreme Court held that state prisons fall squarely within the ADA's definition of a "public entity."[85] As a consequence, it is now recognized that the Americans with Disabilities Act applies to all prisons. Reacting to the decision, Yeskey's attorney noted, "The court's ruling means that prison officials cannot discriminate against prisoners with disabilities, and must make reasonable modifications to prison operations so that these prisoners will have reasonable access to most prison programs."[86]

## Inmates With HIV/AIDS

Most suits by prisoners with HIV/AIDS are claims that officials have violated a prisoner's rights by revealing the condition or by segregating the prisoner because of the condition. In 1988, officials in Erie County, New York, placed an HIV-positive female prisoner in a segregated prison wing reserved for mentally ill inmates. They also placed on her possessions red stickers revealing her HIV-positive status. The inmate sued, claiming denial of her rights to privacy and due process. The district court agreed.[87] In the same year, however, the Eleventh Circuit Court of Appeals held that an Alabama policy of isolating all HIV-positive inmates did not violate the Fourth or Eighth Amendment.[88]

In 1994, the Ninth Circuit Court of Appeals ruled that California correctional officials could continue to bar HIV-positive inmates from working in prison kitchens.[89] The court made it clear that its decision was based more on the anticipated reactions of prisoners receiving the food than on any actual risk of infection. The court agreed that food service "has often been the source of violence or riots" because inmates "are not necessarily motivated by rational thought and frequently have irrational suspicions or phobias that education will not modify" and because prisoners "have no choice of where they eat." Correctional officials had based their policy, the court said, on "legitimate penological concerns."

## Mentally Ill Inmates

The federal courts have recognized the right of mentally ill inmates to treatment. According to a district court in Illinois, this right is triggered when it becomes reasonably certain that (1) the prisoner's symptoms demonstrate a serious mental disease or brain injury, (2) the disease or injury is curable or at least treatable, and (3) delaying or denying care would cause substantially more harm to the inmate.[90]

In 1990, in *Washington* v. *Harper*, the U.S. Supreme Court ruled that an inmate who is dangerous to himself or others as a result of mental illness may be treated with psychoactive drugs against his will.[91] Such involuntary drug treatment, however, has to be in the best interest of the inmate's mental health, not just for the convenience of the correctional institution.

# Inmate Grievance Procedures

Inmate grievance procedures are formal institutional processes for hearing inmate complaints. Grievance procedures are required under a U.S. Supreme Court ruling in 1977 in *Jones* v. *North Carolina Prisoners' Labor Union* (discussed earlier in this chapter). Federal law allows a federal judge to refer a state inmate's lawsuit back to the state correctional system.[92] For such a referral, court precedents require the state correctional agency to have an inmate grievance procedure certified by the U.S. Department of Justice. A referral can save the state correctional agency enormous amounts of time and money. Once the federal judge sends the case back to the state, correctional officials do not have to defend themselves in federal court, transport the inmate to and from federal court, or contend with the publicity that can go along with a court case. Hence, inmate grievance procedures are in the best interest of state correctional officials.

Certification of state grievance procedures by the U.S. Department of Justice requires that:[93]

1. Both inmates and employees of the institution have advisory roles in the development of the procedures.

2. Maximum time limits for responses to grievances be established.
3. Provisions exist for rapid processing of emergency inmate grievances when undue delay could result in harm to an inmate.
4. A mechanism exists for review of decisions by a person or committee not under the direct control of the prison in which the grievance originated.

Today most correctional systems use a three-step process for resolving grievances. First, a staff member or committee in each institution receives complaints, investigates them, and makes decisions. Second, if a prisoner is dissatisfied with that decision, the case may be appealed to the warden. Third, if the prisoner is still dissatisfied, the complaint may be given to the state's commissioner of corrections or the state's corrections board. This three-step procedure satisfies the requirements for U.S. Department of Justice certification.

# 10 Review and Applications

**CHAPTER OBJECTIVE 1**

The hands-off doctrine was a working philosophy of the courts in this country until the 1970s. It allowed corrections officials to run prisons without court intervention. The hands-off doctrine existed because courts were reluctant to interfere with activities of the executive branch and because judges realized that they were not experts in corrections.

**CHAPTER OBJECTIVE 2**

The sources of prisoners' rights are the U.S. Constitution, federal statutes, state constitutions, and state statutes.

**CHAPTER OBJECTIVE 3**

Inmates can challenge the conditions of their confinement through (1) a state *habeas corpus* action, (2) a federal *habeas corpus* action, (3) a state tort lawsuit, (4) a federal civil rights lawsuit, and (5) an injunction to obtain relief.

**CHAPTER OBJECTIVE 4**

During the Prisoner Rights Era (1969–1991), inmates won many court cases based on claims that conditions of their confinement violated their constitutional rights. Court decisions affected inmate rights concerning freedom of expression, including free speech; personal communications; access to the courts and legal services; religious issues; the right to assembly and association; grievances and disciplinary procedures; personal and cell searches; health care, including diet and exercise; protection from violence; the physical conditions of confinement; and rehabilitation.

**CHAPTER OBJECTIVE 5**

Most prisoners' claims focus on denial of constitutional rights guaranteed by the First (freedom of expression and religion), Fourth (freedom from unlawful search and seizure), Eighth (freedom from cruel and unusual punishment), and Fourteenth (due process and equal protection of the law) Amendments.

**CHAPTER OBJECTIVE 6**

The prisoners' rights movement has been largely a male phenomenon. Female inmates have had to petition the courts to gain rights that male inmates already had.

**CHAPTER OBJECTIVE 7**

Claims involving conditions of confinement have been brought by inmates with disabilities, inmates with HIV/AIDS, and mentally ill inmates.

## KEY TERMS

hands-off doctrine, p. 274
prisoners' rights, p. 275
constitutional rights, p. 275
institutional needs, p. 275
civil liability, p. 276
writ of *habeas corpus*, p. 276
tort, p. 277
nominal damages, p. 277
compensatory damages, p. 277
punitive damages, p. 277
injunction, p. 278

jurisdiction, p. 278
precedent, p. 282
legitimate penological objectives, p. 283
balancing test, p. 283
cruel and unusual punishment, p. 290
consent decree, p. 290
deliberate indifference, p. 291
totality of conditions, p. 291
due process, p. 293
frivolous lawsuits, p. 295

1. What constitutional rights were prisoners thought to have a hundred years ago?
2. Why was the hands-off doctrine so named? What was the basis for the doctrine?
3. Which statutes might have a bearing on the rights of prison inmates?
4. What are the legal mechanisms through which inmates have gained access to the courts?
5. To what degree are prison officials liable for their actions toward inmates?
6. What led to the end of the hands-off doctrine?
7. What First Amendment rights have been gained by inmates? What First Amendment rights do inmates *not* have?
8. What Fourth Amendment rights have been gained by inmates? What Fourth Amendment rights do inmates *not* have?
9. What Eighth Amendment rights have been gained by inmates? What Eighth Amendment rights do inmates *not* have?
10. How does the Fourteenth Amendment relate to prisoners' rights? Are there Fourteenth Amendment rights enjoyed by the average citizen but not by inmates? If so, what are they?
11. What caused the relatively recent slowdown in the granting of rights to inmates by the courts?
12. Do the rights of male inmates correspond to the rights of female inmates? Why or why not?
13. Have the courts given any direction to prisons regarding the treatment of inmates with disabilities? If so, what have the courts said?
14. Are there differences in legal status between HIV-negative inmates and HIV-positive inmates? If so, what are the differences?
15. What are the court-required obligations of prisons in their treatment of mentally ill prisoners?
16. What are inmate grievance procedures? Why do they exist? How do they function?

## CRITICAL THINKING EXERCISES

### ON-THE-JOB ISSUE

You are a prison administrator. The prison where you work has a rule that inmates may write letters in English only. This rule seems sensible. After all, if inmates could write in languages not understood by correctional officers, they could discuss plans to escape, riot, or smuggle drugs or weapons into the prison. Even though the courts allow the censoring of outgoing inmate mail, what good is that power if corrections personnel can't read the mail?

It occurs to you, however, that inmates who can't write in English will have difficulty communicating with the outside world and with their families. Inmates unable to write in English won't even be able to write to their attorneys. You also wonder what might happen if an inmate can write in English, but his parents read only a foreign language. If the inmate and his parents can't afford long-distance phone calls, they will not be able to communicate with each other at all. You begin to consider how the English-only rule might be changed to facilitate wholesome communications while still preventing communications that might endanger the safety of the institution and the inmate population.

1. Can the English-only rule be amended to meet the inmate needs discussed here, while still being consistent with legitimate institutional concerns? If so, how?
2. Does an inmate have a constitutionally protected right to communicate with his or her parents? What if that right conflicts with prison policy?

### CORRECTIONS ISSUE

The right to freedom of nonverbal expression is said to be implied in the First Amendment. Hence, how people wear their hair and how they dress are expressions that some believe are protected by the First Amendment. Might there be modes of dress that interfere with a correctional institution's legitimate goals?

## CORRECTIONS ON THE WEB

 In 1996, the state of Ohio passed a law designed to limit frivolous lawsuits by state inmates. The law requires inmates to pay at least a portion of the filing fee from their prison accounts, sets up a process by which a court may declare a lawsuit frivolous, institutes sanctions for inmates whose claims are dismissed as frivolous, and requires screening of new cases by inmates who file multiple cases in one year. Search the Internet for other ways in which states have attempted to limit frivolous inmate lawsuits. Write a report summarizing the techniques and laws that states employ to limit inmates to filing valid lawsuits.

## ADDITIONAL READINGS

del Carmen, Rolando, Susan Ritter, and Betsy Witt. *Briefs of Leading Cases in Corrections*, 2d ed. Cincinnati: Anderson, 1998.

DiIulio, John J., Jr. (ed.). *Courts, Corrections and the Constitution*. New York: Oxford University Press, 1990.

Mushlin, Michael. *The Rights of Prisoners*, 2d ed. Colorado Springs: Shepard's/ McGraw-Hill, 1993.

Palmer, John W. *Constitutional Rights of Prisoners*, 5th ed. Cincinnati: Anderson, 1997.

## ENDNOTES

1. *Ruffin* v. *Commonwealth*, 62 Va. 790 (1871).
2. Frances Cole, "The Impact of *Bell* v. *Wolfish* Upon Prisoners' Rights," *Journal of Crime and Justice*, Vol. 10 (1987), pp. 47-70.
3. *Schenk* v. *United States*, 249 U.S. 47 (1919).
4. Todd Clear and George F. Cole, *American Corrections*, 4th ed. (New York: Wadsworth, 1997).
5. R. Hawkins and G. P. Alpert, *American Prison Systems: Punishment and Justice* (Englewood Cliffs, NJ: Prentice-Hall, 1989).
6. John Scalia, *Prisoner Petitions in the Federal Courts, 1980–96* (Washington: U.S. Department of Justice, October 1997).
7. *Sostre* v. *McGinnis*, 442 F.2d 178 (1971).
8. *Smith* v. *Sullivan*, 553 F.2d 373 (5th Cir. 1977).
9. Adapted from Norman M. Garland and Gilbert B. Stuckey, *Criminal Evidence for the Law Enforcement Officer*, 4th ed. (Columbus: Glencoe/McGraw-Hill, 1999), pp. 14–16.
10. *Ex parte Hull*, 312 U.S. 546 (1941).
11. *Coffin* v. *Reichard*, 143 F.2d 443 (1944).
12. Cole.
13. *Monroe* v. *Pape*, 365 U.S. 167 (1961).
14. Ibid.
15. D. J. Gottlieb, "The Legacy of *Wolfish* and *Chapman*: Some Thoughts About 'Big Prison Case' Litigation in the 1980s," in I. D. Robbins (ed.), *Prisoners and the Law* (New York: Clark Boardman, 1985).
16. *Cooper* v. *Tate*, 382 F.2d 518 (1964).
17. James B. Jacobs, *New Perspectives on Prisons and Imprisonment* (Ithaca, NY: Cornell University Press, 1983).
18. *Holt* v. *Sarver*, 300 F.Supp. 825 (D.C. 1969); see also *Holt* v. *Sarver*, 309 F.Supp. 362 (E.D. Ark. 1970), aff'd, 442 F.2d 304 (8th Cir. 1971).
19. *Holt* v. *Sarver*, 309 F.Supp. 362 (E.D. Ark. 1970).
20. *Pell* v. *Procunier*, 417 U.S. 817 (1974).
21. *Cruz* v. *Beto*, 405 U.S. 319, 321 (1972).
22. *Procunier* v. *Martinez*, 416 U.S. 396 (1974).
23. *McNamara* v. *Moody*, 606 F.Supp.2d 621 (5th Cir., 1979).
24. *Peppering* v. *Crist*, 678 F.Supp.2d 787 (1981).
25. *Mallery* v. *Lewis*, 106 Idaho 227 (1983).
26. *Thornburgh* v. *Abbott*, 490 U.S. 401 (1989).
27. *Turner* v. *Safley*, 482 U.S. 78, 94–99 (1987).
28. *Jones* v. *North Carolina Prisoners' Labor Union, Inc.*, 433 U.S. 119 (1977).
29. *Pell* v. *Procunier*, 417 U.S. 817, 822 (1974).
30. *Fulwood* v. *Clemmer*, 206 F.Supp. 370, 373 (D.D.C., 1962).
31. *Gittlemacker* v. *Prasse*, 428 F.2d 1 (3rd Cir., 1970).
32. *Cruz* v. *Beto*, 405 U.S. 319 (1972).
33. *Kahane* v. *Carlson*, 527 F.2d 492 (2nd Cir., 1975).
34. *Kahane* v. *Carlson*, elaborating on *Barnett* v. *Rodgers*, 133 U.S. App. D.C. 296, 410 F.2d 995 (1969).
35. *Udey* v. *Kastner*, 805 F.2d 1218 (1986).
36. *Dettmer* v. *Landon*, 799 F.2d 929 (1986).

37. *O'Lone* v. *Estate of Shabazz,* 482 U.S. 342 (1987).
38. *United States* v. *Hitchcock,* 467 F.2d 1107 (9th Cir., 1972).
39. *Hudson* v. *Palmer,* 468 U.S. 517 (1984).
40. *Block* v. *Rutherford,* 486 U.S. 576 (1984).
41. *Grummett* v. *Rushen,* 779 F.2d 491 (9th Cir., 1985).
42. See *Estelle* v. *Gamble,* 429 U.S. 97, 102 (1976), and *Hutto* v. *Finney,* 437 U.S. 678, 681 (1978).
43. For a complete history of this case, see *Ruiz* v. *Estelle,* 503 F. Supp. 1265, 1385–1390 (S.D.Tex., 1980), and *Ruiz* v. *Estelle,* 679 F.Supp.2d 1115 (1982).
44. *Holt* v. *Sarver,* 309 F.Supp. 362 (E.D. Ark., 1970). See also, *Holt* v. *Sarver,* 300 F.Supp. 825 (D.C. 1969).
45. *Knecht* v. *Gillman,* 488 F.2d 1136 (8th Cir., 1973).
46. *Estelle* v. *Gamble,* 429 U.S. 27 (1976).
47. *Pugh* v. *Locke,* 406 F.Supp. 318, 332 (M.D.Ala., 1976).
48. *Battle* v. *Anderson,* 564 F.2d 388 (10th Cir., 1977).
49. *Hutto* v. *Finney,* 437 U.S. 678 (1978).
50. *Wilson* v. *Seiter,* 501 U.S. 294 (1991).
51. *Rhodes* v. *Chapman,* 452 U.S. 337 (1981).
52. *Smith* v. *Fairman,* 690 F.2d 122 (7th Cir., 1982).
53. *Johnson* v. *Avery,* 393 U.S. 483 (1968).
54. *Wolff* v. *McDonnell,* 418 U.S. 539 (1974).
55. Ibid.
56. *Baxter* v. *Palmigiano,* 425 U.S. 308 (1976).
57. *Meacham* v. *Fano,* 427 U.S. 215, 228 (1976).
58. *Stone* v. *Powell,* 96 S.Ct. 3037 (1976).
59. *Bounds* v. *Smith,* 430 U.S. 817 (1977).
60. *Jones* v. *North Carolina Prisoners' Labor Union, Inc.,* 433 U.S. 119 (1977).
61. *Ponte* v. *Real,* 471 U.S. 491 (1985).
62. *Daniels* v. *Williams,* 474 U.S. 327 (1986).
63. *West* v. *Atkins,* 487 U.S. 42, 48 (1988).
64. See *Theriault* v. *Carlson,* 339 F.Supp. 375 (N.D.Ga., 1972), vacated, 495 F.2d 390 (5th Cir., 1973), cert. denied 419 U.S. 1003 (1974). In 1977, Theriault's appeal to the U.S. Supreme Court was denied. See 434 U.S. 953 (November 14, 1977).
65. *Wilson* v. *Seiter,* 501 U.S. 294 (1991).
66. See *Mark* v. *Nix,* 983 F.2d 138 (1993), and *Escobar* v. *Landwehr,* 837 F.Supp. 284 (1993).
67. *Sample* v. *Borg,* 675 F.Supp. 574 (E.D. Cal., 1987).
68. *Bettis* v. *Delo,* 14 F.3d 22 (1994).
69. *Hudson* v. *McMillan,* 503 U.S. 1 (1992).
70. *Sandin* v. *Conner,* 515 U.S. 472 (1995).
71. Electronic citation: *Lewis* v. *Casey,* S.Ct. 131 (1996). (http://www.versuslaw.com).
72. Civil Rights of Institutionalized Persons Act, 42 U.S.C. § 1997 et seq. (1976 ed., Supp. IV), as modified 1980 (see especially Sec. 1997e). In section 1997e, Congress created a specific, limited exhaustion requirement for adult prisoners bringing actions pursuant to section 1983.
73. Prison Litigation Reform Act, Pub. L. No. 104-134, 801-10, 110 Stat. 1321 (1996).
74. If a prisoner wishes to proceed as an indigent on appeal, the prisoner must file in the district court, with the notice of appeal, a motion for leave to proceed as an indigent, a certified copy of a prison trust account statement, and Form 4 from the Appendix of Forms found in the *Federal Rules of Appellate Procedure.*
75. *Barefield* v. *Leach,* New Mexico Civil Action No. 10282 (1974).
76. *State, ex rel. Olson* v. *Maxwell,* 259 N.W.2d 621 (Supreme Ct. of N.D., 1977).
77. *Glover* v. *Johnson,* 478 F.Supp. 1075 (1979).
78. *Cooper* v. *Morin,* 446 U.S. 984 (1980).
79. *Bukhari* v. *Hutto,* 487 F.Supp. 1162 (E.D. Va., 1980).
80. *Canterino* v. *Wilson,* 546 F.Supp. 174 (W.D.Ky., 1982).
81. *McMurray* v. *Phelps,* 535 F.Supp. 742 (W.D.La., 1982).
82. *Mary Beth G.* v. *City of Chicago,* 723 F.2d 1263 (7th Cir., 1983).
83. *Women Prisoners of the District of Columbia Department of Corrections* v. *District of Columbia,* 877 F.Supp. 634 (D.D.C., 1994).
84. 42 U.S.C. Section 12132.
85. *Pennsylvania Dept. of Corrections* v. *Yeskey,* U.S. Supreme Court Case No. 97-634 (1998).
86. The Associated Press, "Supreme Court Upholds Rights of Disabled Inmates," June 15, 1998.
87. *Nolley* v. *County of Erie,* 776 F.Supp. 715 (W.D.N.Y., 1991).
88. *Harris* v. *Thigpen,* 941 F.2d 1495 (11th Cir., 1991). See also *Austin* v. *Pennsylvania Dept. of Corr.,* 876 F.Supp. 1437 (11th Cir., 1991).
89. *Gates* v. *Rowland,* 39 F.3d 1439 (9th Cir., 1994).
90. *Parte* v. *Lane,* 528 F.Supp. 1254 (N.D. Ill., 1981).
91. *Washington* v. *Harper,* 494 U.S. 210, 1990.
92. Title 42 U.S.C., Section 1997.
93. Hans Toch, "Democratizing Prisons," *Prison Journal,* Vol. 74 (1995), pp. 62–72.

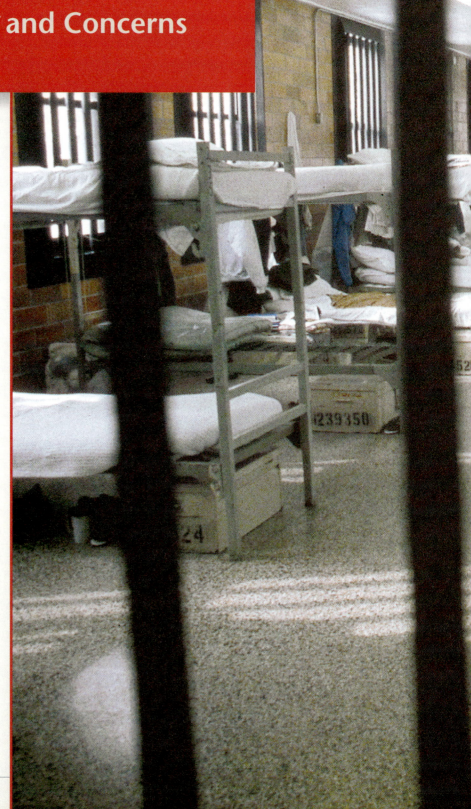

# 11 The Prison Environment

## Issues and Concerns

### CHAPTER OBJECTIVES

After completing this chapter you should be able to:

1. List the three main reasons why prisons are overcrowded.
2. Identify six methods of controlling prison overcrowding.
3. Identify six causes of prison riots.
4. Describe what can be done to prevent prison riots.
5. Outline the emergence of supermax housing and its impact.
6. Describe "no-frills" jails and prisons and their impact on corrections.
7. Summarize the issues that special needs inmates raise for corrections professionals.

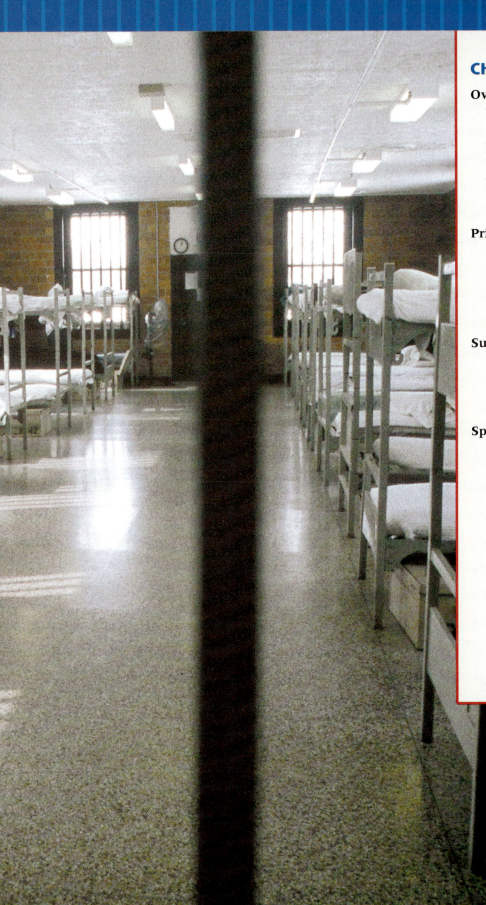

309

> *Those of us on the outside [of prisons] do not like to think of wardens and guards as our servants. Yet they are, and they are intimately locked in a deadly embrace with their human captives behind the prison walls. By extension so are we. A terrible double meaning is thus imparted to the original question of human ethics: Am I my brother's keeper?*
>
> —Jessica Mitford

The Happy Valley Redirection Institution was in the midst of a riot. Warden Batman shook his head in disbelief as he tried to figure out how this had happened. Prison riots, common in the 1980s, were a thing of the past. Maybe, he thought, the robot correctional officers malfunctioned; they were overdue for tune-ups. Robots were so complex. Fortunately, he still had 25 human correctional officers.

One clear mistake was his decision to forego the inmates' serotonin for one night. He wanted them to have a fun night—it didn't occur to him that things might get out of hand. Serotonin—the master chemical of mood, appetite, and memory—controls aggression; he should not have forgotten.

He imagined explaining the riot to his superiors. He would tell them that the riot only proved that land prisons were a thing of the past. The decision in late 2005 to build prisons on the floors of oceans or on orbiting space stations had proven to be the proper direction for corrections. He also knew, regrettably, that the old excuse of riots resulting from improper food would not fly in 2010. All inmates were tested for chemical imbalances that might cause deficiencies, dependencies, or toxicity. Furthermore, vitamin megadoses were standard treatment.

On a positive note, no property damage could occur; all furniture was fireproof and unbreakable. Also, human staff would remain unharmed; inmates had received drug-induced amnesia treatments to forget violent learned behaviors.

Suddenly the solution hit him like a bolt of lightning. He would simply end the riot—which was nothing more than inmates running aimlessly around the institution—by pressing the sound alarm. This modern device produced high intensity sound waves that would render the inmates unconscious for several minutes. He pressed the activator, and the inmates fell to the floor. Fortunately, all the human correctional officers wore riot helmets to protect their eardrums. As a precaution, they sprayed the more aggressive of the unconscious inmates with sticky foam; they would not escape, or move, for that matter.

The riot was over. As the inmates were returned to their temperature-controlled cellular units, he relaxed. Perhaps his career was not over.[1]

Sound far out? It may not be as unimaginable as you think. Imagine reporting a crime to a "software agent" police officer at your local police department via the Internet. Imagine probation officers using electronically transmitted smells to monitor the lifestyles of convicted drug offenders. Imagine virtual courtrooms, digitally displayed evidence, and virtual tours of crime scenes. Don't imagine. They're already here.

*The Prison Environment: Issues and Concerns*

But what are the issues and concerns of the prison environment today? In this chapter we shall consider four aspects of the prison environment: overcrowding; riots and violence; supermax housing and "no-frills" prisons; and special needs inmates.

# Overcrowding

A prison was often referred to as "the big house" in the past. Today, however, a more appropriate description is "the full house." Over the past 25 years prison population has increased six-fold—from 240,000 to 1.3 million. Some say that prisons are "capacity-driven"; that is, cut the ribbon and they're full. Saying exactly how full, though, is difficult, because each state has its own method for measuring prison capacity. Some use **rated capacity** (the number of beds in a facility); others **operational capacity** (the number of inmates that can be accommodated based on a facility's staff and existing programs and services); still others **design capacity** (the number of inmates that planners intended the facility to house). The problem is compounded because some states have their own definitions. In spite of the differences, by any measure, today's prisons are overcrowded.

On January 1, 1999, 36 states and the Federal Bureau of Prisons (BOP) were operating above capacity, most by 15 percent. That would suggest that as many as 195,302 (15%) of the 1,302,019 million adult prisoners on January 1, 1999, were housed in overcrowded facilities. Eliminating the present overcrowding would require building 150 new prisons at a cost of $7.2 billion (assuming that each has a capacity of 1,300 and costs approximately $48 million to build), then staffing and maintaining the new facilities. Even if this were possible, the relief from overcrowding would be short-term; the prisoner population continually grows. The increase in prisoner population in 1998 was 4.8 percent over 1997—58,090 more prisoners in 1998. Based on the forementioned assumptions and averaging 58,000 more prisoners each year, keeping up with the increase would require adding 45 new prisons each year.

**rated capacity**   The number of beds in a facility.

**operational capacity**   The number of inmates that can be accommodated based on a facility's staff and existing programs and services.

**design capacity**   The number of inmates that planners intended the facility to house.

## Why Are Prisons Overcrowded?

There are three main reasons why prisons are crowded. The first is a continuous increase in the number of persons imprisoned. This number increased significantly between 1990 and 1998—almost 64,000 per year; from 743,382 in 1990 to almost 1.3 million in 1998, an increase of almost 75 percent. Nearly 1 of every 150 people in the United States is incarcerated.

The second reason is that offenders are serving a larger portion of their sentences. Sentencing laws changed, reducing the difference between the sentence imposed and the actual time served, and restricting the possibility of early release from prison. Jurisdictions began to depart from the prevailing approach, known as indeterminate sentencing (broad authorized sentencing ranges, parole release, and case-by-case decision making), in the mid-1970s (see Chapter 2). Today the trend in many jurisdictions is toward determinate sentencing—a fixed term of incarceration and no possibility of parole. In addition, most jurisdictions have adopted one or more of the fol-

Do you want to know why Louisiana has the second highest incarceration rate in this country? Our sentences are too long, our sentences are too tough! You're doing more time for every crime than you do in most any other state. The problem with Louisiana? We don't ever let 'em go. Once you break the law, you don't get another chance. If it were up to me I'd say let's not keep dying old men in prison. They're too old to pull an armed robbery or be a ski-mask rapist. They ought to do about twenty years on most any serious crime and when they turn about fifty years old—when those two come together on a graph—they pretty well should have a good shot at going free.

*Burl Cain, Warden*
*Louisiana State Penitentiary*
*at Angola*

lowing sentencing approaches: mandatory minimum sentences, three-strikes laws, or truth-in-sentencing laws requiring offenders to serve mandated percentages of imposed sentences (see Chapter 2). As a result, between 1990 and 1998 the number of offenders held in state prisons grew annually by an average of almost 7 percent.

The goal of sentencing policies such as mandatory minimums or three-strikes laws is to curtail repeat offenses. Research, however, suggests that time spent in prison or jail actually increases the risk of future crime.[2] Thus, while a strong case can be made for lengthier prison sentences, legislators and prison administrators may find little evidence to support the theory that longer sentences deter crime.

The third reason why prisons are overcrowded is that many incoming prisoners are drug users, not the drug dealers the tougher drug laws were designed to capture. Today, more than 400,000 people are behind bars for drug crimes; nearly one-third of these are for simple possession. Nearly 60 percent of all federal prisoners and 22 percent of state prisoners are doing time for drug offenses; triple the percentages of 15 years ago. The goal of tougher drug laws was more convictions, putting more people in jail and prison and reducing the drug-related crime rate. This goal has not been achieved. At least 22 percent of the federal prison population consists of nonviolent drug offenders; their continued incarceration is extremely costly and wasteful of precious prison space.

# How Can Overcrowding Be Controlled?

In most jurisdictions across the United States today we find at least six methods of controlling prison overcrowding:

1. Reduce the number of people going to prison.
2. Release the less dangerous to make room for the more dangerous.
3. Change prison or jail sentences to community-related sentences.
4. Increase the number of releases.
5. Expand existing prison capacity or build new prisons.
6. Implement an overall program of structured sentencing.

The first four methods are referred to as front-end, trap-door, side-door, and back-door strategies, respectively (see Chapter 6).

The fifth method of controlling prison overcrowding is the most commonly considered—in 1996, the United States spent $859 million on prison expansion and $2.5 billion on new prison construction. Prison overcrowding, however, continues to worsen. Some experts believe that legislators will one day have to choose between new prison construction and funding for other areas, such as health care or education.

The sixth method refers to sentencing guidelines that are designed to save prison beds for more serious crimes and violent offenses, using community and intermediate sanctions for lesser offenses. Structured sentencing is a compromise between indeterminate sentencing and mandatory determinate sentencing (see Chapter 2). Under **structured sentencing**, a commission creates a set of guidelines that consider both the offense and a few personal characteristics of the offender (notably, a prior criminal record). The guidelines for the type and duration of sentence are normally determined by deciding what type of punishment a particular crime deserves and calculating the probable cost of the sentence. Under a structured sentencing system, sentences are more uniform and less subject to the individual discretion of judges or parole board members. Structured sentencing makes it possible to anticipate and meet correctional resource needs on an ongoing basis rather than reacting after an overcrowding problem develops.

A jurisdiction establishing structured sentencing might consider implementing non-prison options such as interchangeability of punishments, also called **exchange rates.** A sentencing commission might, for example, decide that three days under house arrest or 40 community service hours is equivalent to one day of incarceration, or that three years under intensive supervision is equivalent to one year in prison.

**structured sentencing** A set of guidelines for determining an offender's sentence.

**exchange rates** An approach to sentencing, implemented by a sentencing commission, that emphasizes interchangeability of punishments; for example, three days under house arrest might be considered equal to one day of incarceration.

# What Are the Consequences of Overcrowding?

Researchers and prison administrators routinely observe the consequences of overcrowding. These include increases in idleness, drug trafficking, predatory sexual behavior, safety risks, gang confrontations, arguments, fights, assaults, murders, suicides, riots, medical and mental health problems, staff turnover, and stress. Other consequences include decreases in program opportunities; inappropriate housing assignments; judicial intervention to counteract illegal conditions; fines by state governments for operating over capacity; excessive wear and tear on prison facilities and equipment; and negative publicity about conditions in overcrowded facilities. Researchers have also linked overcrowding to higher rates of recidivism.[3]

# Prison Security

Prison gang confrontations and riots inspire frightening images. For prisoners, staff, and their families on the outside, nothing is more frightening than a prison gang confrontation or riot, regardless of where it occurs.

## Prison Gangs—Security Threat Groups (STGs)

Prison gangs are one of the most significant developments in American prisons since the existence of the Gypsy Jokers Motorcycle Club was first recorded at the Walla Walla, Washington, penitentiary in 1950. The problem of prison gangs is so pervasive today that experts now refer to them as **security threat groups** (STGs). The American Correctional Association (ACA) reports that there are 1,153 different STGs having over 46,000 members in U.S. prisons.[4] Most STGs are founded along racial and ethnic boundaries. STGs commonly found across the United States are the Aryan Brotherhood, Black Disciples, Black Guerrilla Family, Bloods, Crips, Latin Kings, Mexican Mafia, Nuestra Familia, Skinheads, Texas Syndicate, and Vice Lords. The STGs most tracked because of violent behavior are the Aryan Brotherhood, Black Guerrilla Family, Mexican Mafia, Nuestra Familia, and Texas Syndicate.

STGs have a profound impact on prison security. STG members are five times more likely to incite or be involved in prison violence than nonmembers.[5] In an attempt to control STG influence, some prison administrators transferred known STG members from one institution to another only to find that this practice actually increased STG organization and activity—it extended the STG's influence throughout a state's prison system. Other states enacted "gang enhancement" statutes that imposed severe sentences

**security threat groups (STGs)** *The current term for prison gangs.*

*Correctional institutions may use identifiable tattoos as one of the ways to designate that an inmate is a member of a security threat group. Once an STG member is identified, what restrictions might prison administrators place on such an individual?*

on STG activity. Today, many states are adopting a new strategy—segregate known STG members to highly restrictive supermax housing, correctional facilities that are designed to house the "worst of the worst" prisoners under complete lockdown and total isolation. Advocates of this approach contend that removing STG leaders from the general prison population reduces the amount of control that STG leaders exert. Critics of the approach argue that violence actually may increase because conditions within supermax housing are so harsh that they emotionally damage inmates who may one day be returned to the general prison population or released or paroled into the community.

Two explanations for STG development are deprivation and importation. As we saw in Chapter 9, the basic premise of deprivation theory is that inmates develop a social system as a way to adapt to the pains of imprisonment. Because inmates are deprived of liberty, autonomy, goods and services, sexual relations, and security, they develop a culture that helps them get back what imprisonment has taken. Importation theory, on the other hand, emphasizes that inmates' pre-prison attitudes and values guide their reactions and responses to the internal conditions of prison. Both theories are valid; most major STGs can be traced to pre-prison attitudes and values, but prison conditions influence when and to what extent STG activity and violence occur.

## Prison Riots

Prison disturbances occur in a variety of forms, not all of which are violent. A hunger strike or refusal to work is a disturbance because it is a defiance of prison authority and could disrupt prison routine. A prison **riot** involves seizure of control by inmates over all or part of a correctional facility, violence against staff and/or other prisoners, and demands for administrative changes in the facility.[6]

**riot** Seizure of control by inmates over all or part of a correctional facility with violence against staff and/or other prisoners.

On Wednesday, February 23, 2000, the worst prison riot in more than a decade in California broke out when correctional officers permitted white, Black, and Hispanic inmates in the maximum-security unit at the Pelican Bay State Prison to enter the exercise yard together for the first time since racial tension had flared in August 1999. (The maximum-security unit is one of three units in the Pelican Bay prison complex. The complex also includes a super-maximum housing unit for 1,500 inmates and a minimum-security housing unit for 200 inmates.)

Correctional officers used pepper spray, tear gas, rubber bullets, and lethal force to break up the riot. Sixteen inmates were shot, one was killed, and another was critically wounded. Prisoners stabbed 32 inmates. No correctional officers were injured. Observers believed that the riot was caused by overcrowding (the maximum-security unit was built to house 2,280 prisoners but was overcrowded with 3,326) and mismanagement (in 1995 a federal judge found prison officials had endorsed the use of excessive force). An FBI investigation of alleged civil rights violations followed the disturbance.

There is no agreement on what constitutes a prison riot. What some call a riot, others downplay and call a disturbance. For example, in 1993 there were over 186 disturbances in 21 corrections systems—only 7 were classified as riots.[7] In Connecticut, a gang fight involving over 300 inmates and causing over $100,000 in damage was called a riot. At Leavenworth, a racial fight involving 427 inmates that caused significant damage to the prison's auditorium, chapel, and industry buildings was called a disturbance. Correctional administrators label most incidents disturbances because the term is less sensational.

How many prison riots have there been in the United States? Nobody knows for sure. Not only do we have different opinions as to what constitutes a riot, but wardens and state officials are reluctant to publicize loss of control. Scholars estimate that almost 500 prison riots have taken place in the United States since 1855.[8]

Prison violence and riots are as old as prisons themselves. There were riots and mass escapes at the Walnut Street Jail in Philadelphia, at Newgate Prison in New York, and almost everywhere, from the beginning of prisons in this country.[9] One particularly eventful year was 1952, when riots erupted in 25 of the 152 U.S. prisons. Although no lives were lost, prison staff and inmates were in danger and damage ran into the millions. Reasons for the riots included absence of inmate programs and work, idleness, unqualified staff who were poorly trained and poorly paid, old facilities (one-third were more than 70 years old), absence of policies to hear inmate grievances, crowding, insufficient prison budgets, absence of inmate classification, philosophical conflicts about the nature of prisoners (treat them as human beings who will one day rejoin society or "treat them rough"), and the presence of a new generation of prisoners.[10]

In 1954, reformers advocated overhauling and modernizing prison programs, replacing old prisons, hiring more and better staff, and developing an integrated state system. They advocated the creation of:

- professionally staffed classification centers;
- prisons no larger than 500 beds;
- professionally trained, well-paid correctional officers;
- inmate self-governance;
- procedures that allow inmate grievances to be aired;
- prison work programs with fair wages paid to prisoners;
- periodic review of sentencing patterns and parole board decisions;
- dissemination of statistics on commitments and releases;
- pre-release orientation and job-finding assistance for discharged prisoners; and
- statewide prison leadership headed by nonpolitical, nationally recruited, and professionally trained individuals.[11]

Despite reformers' calls for overhauls of prison programs and management, violence-provoking conditions continue to exist in many prisons. One might wonder if anything has changed since the storm of prison riots in 1952. Three of the bloodiest and most violent prison riots in the United States occurred in severely overcrowded prisons in New York in 1971, in New Mexico in 1980, and in Ohio in 1993.

In the 1971 riot at the Attica Correctional Facility, New York, where 2,225 inmates were incarcerated in a prison designed for 1,200, 43 lives were lost: four inmates were killed during the riot as part of inmate "justice," and when police stormed in to retake the prison, they killed 10 civilian hostages and 29 prisoners. The New York State Special Commission that investigated the riot wrote, "With the exception of Indian massacres in the late 19th century, the State Police assault which ended the four-day prison uprising was the bloodiest one-day encounter between Americans since the Civil War."[12]

In the 1980 riot at the Penitentiary of New Mexico in Santa Fe, where 1,136 inmates were confined in space designed for 900 inmates, the taking of human life was brutal. Thirty-three inmates were tortured, dismembered, decapitated, burned alive, and killed by fellow inmates. Although staff were held hostage, none was killed.

The longest prison riot in United States history occurred at the Southern Ohio Correctional Facility in Lucasville in 1993, where 1,820 inmates were held in a prison built for 1,540. Inmates killed nine of their fellow inmates and one correctional officer in the 11-day siege.

The riot at Lucasville cost an estimated $15 million in property damage. At Santa Fe, the estimate was $28.5 million. At Attica, the cost was more than $3 million.

## Causes of Prison Riots

The causes of prison riots today are no different than they were in the 1950s: overcrowding, racial antagonism, environmental factors, administrative factors, individual factors, and prison social structure.

**Overcrowding**  Overcrowding is the most important cause of heightened prison tension and potential violent disruption. Overcrowding is responsible for curtailing or even eliminating opportunities for education, vocational training, and recreation. When the ratio of correctional officers to inmates becomes too low, something has to give. At Attica, Santa Fe, and Lucasville, overcrowding raised tensions, interfered with prisoner classification, reduced living space, and restricted access to programs. Restlessness and boredom grew.

**Racial Antagonism**  Outside prison the ratio of racial minorities to whites is about one to five. In prison, however, whites are the minority. That disproportion, in addition to overcrowding, close living quarters, and lack of space, adds to racial antagonism. Antagonism is heightened when inmates separate themselves along racial or ethnic lines for self-protection. Researchers have discovered that as inmates' perception of overcrowding increases, their antagonism toward other racial and ethnic groups also increases.[13]

**Environmental Factors**  Environmental factors refer to the ability of the physical structure to withstand a riot situation. At Attica, a faulty weld joint in a metal gate gave way and allowed prisoners access to most areas of the institution. At Santa Fe, "shatter-proof" glass broke. At Lucasville, inmates collected master keys from staff hostages and opened cell doors.

**Administrative Factors**  Poor prison management and administration are linked to prison riots. Poor management can result from frequent staff

**Program Analysts**
Adult Correctional Services Section seeks program analysts to develop, monitor, and evaluate grant projects funded by the agency, including jail and prison-based drug treatment, drug courts, community justice, and local pretrial services. Candidates must have a degree in criminal justice, public administration, or a related field, or equivalent experience. Applicants should have experience with criminal justice intervention strategies, drug treatment programming, and grants administration.

turnover, low correctional officer qualifications, inadequate training, poor staff-inmate communication, and low staff pay. At Attica, Santa Fe, and Lucasville, inmates' complaints about living conditions, lack of programs, and officers' excessive use of force and harassment went unheard by administration. Rumors of riots were not taken seriously.

**Individual Factors** Prisoners at Attica, Santa Fe, and Lucasville were young, violence-prone and poorly classified. Most were undereducated, underemployed, and uncommitted to society's means for achieving social goals. The racial and ethnic minority imbalance, together with these individual factors, prompted many inmates to adopt tough attitudes and join STGs for self-protection.

**Social Structure** The social structure in prison is often cited as a key cause of violence and incidents that may escalate into a riot. The social structure consists of racial, political, and ideological tensions; deprivation of inmate goods and services; confusion over prison goals; and a natural desire by prisoners to challenge authority. Controlling this social structure requires strong and consistent leadership from the prison administration. When inmates sense little likelihood of improvement in prison conditions and inconsistent and unpredictable shifts in administration and prison policies, they may feel as if there is little to lose in inciting a disturbance.

## Preventing Prison Riots

Prison violence provokes more violence. Measures to prevent prison riots must become a national priority, and change must occur. Three years before the Attica riot, the U.S. National Advisory Commission on Civil Disorders (the Kerner Commission) warned that the only effective way to prevent riots, whether in or out of prison, was to eliminate sources of tension by making good "the promises of American democracy to all citizens, urban and rural, white and black, Spanish surname, American Indian, and every minority group."[14] While that change is long-range, corrections officials can implement immediate measures to reduce the likelihood of inmate aggression including:

- formal inmate grievance procedures;
- ombudsmen to mediate disputes;
- an improved classification system;
- smaller institutions;
- meaningful prison school and work programs;
- alternatives to incarceration;
- professional corrections staff who are trained and well paid;
- administrators who are visible and available to staff and inmates; and
- clearly written and understood policies on the use of force when necessary.

To assure that the use of force is appropriate and justifiable, the American Correctional Association recommends establishing polices and procedures that govern its use (see Exhibit 11–1).

**EXHIBIT 11-1**

## American Correctional Association

### Policy on Use of Force

Use of force consists of physical contact with an offender in a confrontational situation to control behavior and enforce order. Use of force includes use of restraints (other than for routine transportation and movement), chemical agents, and weapons. Force is justified only when required to maintain or regain control, or when there is imminent danger of personal injury or serious damage to property. To assure the use of force is appropriate and justifiable, correctional agencies should:

**A.** Establish and maintain policies that require reasonable steps be taken to reduce or prevent the necessity for the use of force, that authorize force only when no reasonable alternative is possible, that permit only the minimum force necessary, and that prohibit the use of force as a retaliatory or disciplinary measure;

**B.** Establish and enforce procedures that define the range of methods for and alternatives to the use of force, and that specify the conditions under which each is permitted. The procedures must assign responsibility for authorizing such force, assure appropriate documentation and supervision of the action;

**C.** Establish and maintain procedures that limit the use of deadly force to those instances where it is legally authorized and where there is an imminent threat to human life or a threat to public safety that cannot reasonably be prevented by other means;

**D.** Maintain operating procedures and regular staff training designed to anticipate, stabilize and defuse situations that might give rise to conflict, confrontation, and violence;

**E.** Provide specialized training to ensure competency in all methods of use of force, especially in methods and equipment requiring special knowledge and skills such as defensive tactics, weapons, restraints, and chemical agents; and

**F.** Establish and maintain procedures that require all incidents involving the use of force be fully documented and independently reviewed by a higher correctional authority. A report of the use of force, including appropriate investigation and any recommendations for preventive and remedial action, shall be submitted for administrative review and implementation of recommendations when appropriate.

# Supermax Housing and "No-Frills" Prisons and Jails

In an effort to control the behavior of violence-prone inmates, two new types of prisons are emerging—supermax housing and "no-frills" prisons. Both alter the conditions of confinement for thousands of U.S. prisoners, raising important issues for the prisoners and staff who must live and work in them and the society that must accept the prisoners when they are released.

## Supermax Housing

Prison systems have always needed a way to deal with inmates whose violent behavior makes it impossible for them to live with the general prison population. Segregation and solitary confinement have been the most widely used methods of dealing with this issue. You may recall from Chapter 4 that in 1829, the Eastern State Penitentiary in Cherry Hill, Pennsylvania, was built on the principle of solitary confinement. However, in 1913 the Pennsylvania legislature dropped "solitary" from sentencing statutes and housing arrangements at Eastern State became congregate. From that point forward, specialized housing units were developed for management and control of troublesome inmates.

The BOP returned to the idea of controlling the most violent and disruptive inmates in indefinite solitary confinement when it opened Alcatraz in 1934. Alcatraz, which had a capacity of 275, did not offer any treatment program; its sole purpose was to incarcerate and punish the federal prison system's most desperate criminals and worst troublemakers. "Alcatraz, it was charged, was America's Devil's Island, it was 'Hellcatraz'—a place where convicts slowly went insane from the tedium and hopelessness of endless years on 'the Rock.'"[15] By 1963, Alcatraz was judged an expensive failure; it symbolized a penal philosophy that was outdated in an era that espoused rehabilitation, not punishment, as the goal of incarceration.[16] Alcatraz closed in the early 1960s under orders from U.S. Attorney General Robert Kennedy. During the era of rehabilitation that followed the Alcatraz closing, prison officials used the *dispersal model*—problem prisoners were distributed to a number of prisons. Prison officials hoped that dispersal among populations of generally law-abiding inmates would dilute the influence of problem prisoners. Inmates from Alcatraz were moved to federal prisons in Atlanta and Leavenworth.

By the 1970s, the goal of incarceration had shifted back to punishment. Disturbances, violence, and riots at state and federal prisons convinced the BOP to try again to control the most troublesome federal inmates in one location. The BOP reverted to the *concentration model*—all problem prisoners are housed together in a separate facility. The federal prison at Marion, Illinois, was chosen for this purpose. The construction features at Marion, however, made it difficult for staff to maintain complete control over recalcitrant inmates. Open cell-fronts were a major limitation in Marion's design to control the toughest prisoners. Through their cell bars, inmates threw trash, urine, and feces at corrections officers; passed contraband; set fires; and verbally harassed and lunged at staff and other prisoners as they walked by. Tension, hostility, violence, and murder were all too common. On October 23, 1983, a state of emergency was declared and the Marion facility was placed on lockdown status. Over the next few years, the BOP conceived plans to build a supermax facility that would implement construction features for controlling difficult inmates.

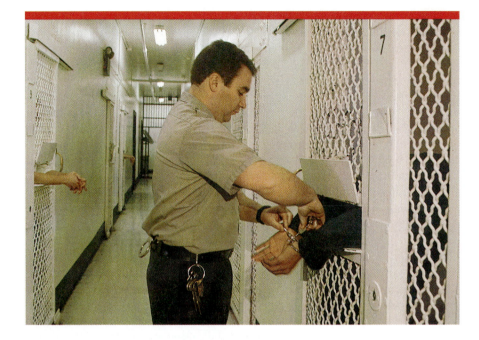

In 1994, the BOP opened its first supermax housing facility at Florence, Colorado, for the 400 most dangerous, violent, escape prone, and STG federal inmate leaders. Construction cost totalled $60 million ($150,000 per cell). Annual operating cost per cell per year may be as much as another $40,000, or $19.2 million total. Cell design resists vandalism. Each prisoner's bed, desk, stool, and bookcase are made of reinforced concrete and anchored in place. Each cell has a shower stall with flood-proof plumbing and a 12-inch black-and-white television set. Cell windows deny prisoners all views of the outside except the sky above. A simple hole-in-the-wall apparatus for lighting cigarettes has replaced matches and cigarette lighters. Meals are dispensed through cell slots in separate heated trays from airline-style carts pulled by small tractors. Cells are staggered so that inmates cannot make eye contact with other inmates. Each cell has a double entry door; an interior barred cage door backed up by a windowed steel door that prevents voice contact among prisoners.

The new prison has 1,400 electronically-controlled gates, 168 television monitors, and two mirrored-glass gun towers. The 400 cells are subdivided into nine units—each unit is self-contained and includes a sick-call room, law library, and barber chair. After three years of good behavior, an inmate gradually regains social contact. "What puts a man in is his behavior, and what gets a man out is his behavior," said John M. Vanyur, the associate warden.[17]

This type of super-controlled environment is taking hold across the United States. California opened Pelican Bay State Prison in Crescent City in 1990. Construction cost was $133,653 per cell. The supermax housing unit of Pelican Bay has a capacity of 1,500 inmates, all of whom are isolated in windowless cells and denied access to prison work and group exercise yards.

Pelican Bay, like the federal supermax housing facility in Florence, Colorado, is entirely automated. Inmates in the supermax housing unit have no face-to-face contact with staff or other inmates. Cell doors are solid stainless steel with slots for food trays. Cell doors open and close electronically. Officers can talk with or listen in on inmates through a speaker system. These inmates do not work. They have no recreational equipment. They don't mix with other inmates. They are not permitted to smoke. They eat all meals in their cells. They leave their cells only for showers and 90 minutes of daily exercise in small cement areas enclosed by 20-foot cement walls. An inmate who leaves his cell to go to the exercise pen must strip naked in front of a control booth; the door to the exercise pen is then opened electronically.

In 1997, the National Institute of Corrections (NIC) conducted a nationwide survey to determine the number of supermax housing facilities and the policies and procedures of each.[18] NIC defined **supermax housing** as a free-standing facility, or a distinct unit within a facility, that provides for the management and secure control of inmates who have been officially designated as exhibiting violent or serious and disruptive behavior while incarcerated. This includes STG leaders. Supermax housing controls inmate behavior through separation, movement restriction, and limited access to staff and other inmates. Supermax housing does not include maximum or close custody facilities that are designated for routine housing of inmates with high custody needs, inmates in disciplinary segregation or protective custody, or other inmates requiring segregation or separation for other routine purposes.

What NIC found is that a common definition of supermax housing is problematic. The many states that provided information had different reasons and needs for supermax housing. They consider different factors in their inmate classification systems and facility operations procedures. What is considered supermax housing in one jurisdiction may not be considered supermax housing in another. NIC's conclusion is, "Supermax as defined in the survey may exist in relatively few agencies."[19]

Criminologists and psychiatrists who have studied the effects of long-term solitary confinement report evidence of acute sensory deprivation, paranoid delusion belief systems, irrational fears of violence, little ability to control rage, and mental breakdowns.[20] The vast majority of inmates in long-term solitary confinement remain anxious, angry, depressed, insecure, and confused. Some commit suicide. Others fail to adjust upon release and become recidivists.

Some inmates in supermax housing facilities have challenged the conditions of their confinement. In 1995, inmates at Pelican Bay's supermax unit challenged the constitutionality of extreme isolation and environmental deprivation. They claimed that the degree of segregation was so extreme and the restrictions so severe, the inmates confined there were psychologically traumatized and, in some cases, deprived of sanity. The federal court agreed. The court ruled that "conditions in security housing units did impose cruel and unusual punishment on mentally ill prisoners"[21] and "those who were at particularly high risk for suffering very serious or severe injury to their mental health."[22] The court declared that the state of California cannot continue to confine inmates who are already mentally ill or those who are at an unreasonably high risk of suffering serious mental illness in the supermax unit. The court also appointed a **special master** (a person appointed to act as the representative of the court) to work with the state of California to

**supermax housing**
A free-standing facility, or a distinct unit within a facility, that provides for management and secure control of inmates who have been officially designated as exhibiting violent or serious and disruptive behavior while incarcerated.

**special master**   A person appointed by the court to act as its representative to oversee remedy of a violation and provide regular progress reports.

develop a satisfactory remedial plan and provide a progress report to the court.

## "No-Frills" Prisons and Jails

The image of prisons and jails as "country clubs" and "mini-resorts" is not new. That description continues to make for great speeches, but it is erroneous. It ignores the harsh realities of imprisonment. Having only the information that appears on television and in newspapers and magazines, the public still believes that inmates are living the good life, lounging on recliners and channel surfing. In 1995, an NBC television poll found that 82 percent of Americans felt that prison life was too easy.[23]

Public perception has influenced reality as corrections reform has focused on the conditions of confinement. **"No-frills" prisons and jails** that take away prisoner amenities and privileges are the latest fad on the corrections landscape. New policies are designed to make jail and prison life as brutal as possible in the belief that such conditions deter even the most hardened criminals. Proponents of "no-frills" jails and prisons believe that criminals will shun future illegal activity to avoid returning. Mississippi representative Mark McInnis said it clearly: "The people who run the prisons want happy prisoners. I want prisoners to be so miserable that they won't even think of coming back."[24] However, that sentiment is not supported by research and may actually be causing a backlash. Violent offenders do not think about the consequences beforehand. They think they'll never get caught.

For the past few years state legislatures, governors, corrections commissioners, and county sheriffs have been eliminating or reducing the availability of certain amenities and privileges that prisoners previously enjoyed. They've justified their positions publicly by arguing that pleasures of any kind contribute to the crime rate by making prison a tolerable way of life and claiming that more austere prison and jail conditions will reduce crime. Others claim that it's what inmates deserve. Skeptics wonder if the driving force behind these new "no-frills" statutes and bills is the belief that they help get legislators and others elected or reelected by offering the impression that they are tough on crime.[25]

The amenities and privileges that have been reduced or eliminated include smoking, weightlifting equipment, long hair and beards, hot meals, personal clothing, recreation, telephone calls, television, family days, funeral furloughs, and unrestricted access to medical care. Proponents of "no-frills" incarceration argue that punishing offenders in "no-frills" environments is not vindictive revenge. They argue that reducing or eliminating amenities and privileges is deserved—the offender committed a serious crime that warrants incarceration, and incarceration is intended to be punitive. The "no-frills" movement is catching on, but not everybody agrees with it.

To date, no court case has been heard on "no-frills" prisons and jails. Unless the eliminated or reduced amenity or privilege results in serious harm to the inmate, the "no-frills" movement will continue.

At present, there is no evidence that making prisons and jails more unpleasant has any effect on crime. Legislators claim that inmates will not want to be incarcerated or reincarcerated under such harsh conditions.

**"no-frills" prisons and jails** Correctional institutions that take away prisoner amenities and privileges.

However, over 200 years of prison history has not proven that making a prison austere deters offenders. In a recent survey, state wardens, corrections experts, and attorneys said that they did not believe that eliminating privileges would reduce crime.[26] Correctional officers, on the other hand, cringe at the idea of trying to maintain civility without amenities and privileges. "What some outside the corrections profession perceive as privileges, we in the profession see as vital prison and jail management tools to insure the safety of the facility," said Bobbie Huskey, former president of the American Correctional Association.[27]

Others have wondered what impact "no-frills" may have on institutional security. "The elimination of privileges theoretically could increase disturbances, either in the short term if inmates react violently to the loss or in the long term if inmates have more idle time, resent the perceived vindictiveness of corrections managers, or conclude they have nothing more to lose by misbehaving."[28] A corrections official in Florida concluded, "From a correctional administrator's standpoint, there is a point at which further reductions create an undue risk to a safe and orderly operation." A 27-year veteran corrections administrator in the New Jersey Department of Corrections fears that the "take-back trend," as he calls it, might result in inmate retaliation on staff.[29] Sufficient time has not passed to study the long-term impact of "no-frills" incarceration. However, there is concern that eliminating privileges (such as weightlifting, television, and recreation) that keep inmates busy may encourage inmates to spend more time planning or causing trouble.

If privileges are eliminated, what positive incentives will correctional staff have with which to motivate appropriate inmate behavior? A July 1995 survey of 823 wardens of state adult prisons indicates that programs and amenities serve a critical control function.[30] Correctional officers can grant access to privileges and amenities in exchange for adherence to rules and restrict access as punishment for rule violation. "The entire prison disciplinary structure is founded on punishments that amount to restriction of privileges," report the survey's authors.[31] Chances are, prison administrators will not completely eliminate or abolish privileges or amenities; they will curtail availability and offer the privileges or amenities as reward for good behavior.

# Special Needs Inmates

Prison inmates have disproportionately high rates of substance abuse, high-risk sexual activity, and other health problems. Because thousands of these inmates return to the general population each month, correctional health and public health are becoming increasingly intertwined. Health care and disease prevention in correctional facilities must become a top priority for correctional managers and all correctional personnel.

## Substance-Abusing Inmates

Substance abuse takes a toll on users, the community, and the criminal justice system. In January 1998, the National Center on Addiction and Substance Abuse at Columbia University (CASA) released its findings from a

3-year study on substance abuse and the prison population.[32] According to this study, 80 percent of America's jail and prison population—some 1.4 million prisoners at year-end 1996—were seriously involved with drug and/or alcohol abuse and addiction and the crimes it spawns. Those 1.4 million offenders had violated drug/alcohol laws, were high at the time they committed their crimes, stole property to buy drugs, had a history of drug/alcohol abuse and addiction, or had some combination of these characteristics.

**Treatment for Offenders**   Research shows that drug/alcohol treatment can result in reduced substance abuse, criminal activity, and associated problems. When substance abusers are incarcerated, the correctional system becomes a potential point of intervention to reduce or eliminate their abuse. What most concerns CASA is the low priority given to dealing with inmates' drug/alcohol addictions. From 1993 to 1996, the number of inmates who needed substance abuse treatment climbed from 688,000 to 840,000. The number of inmates receiving treatment remained the same—about 150,000. From 1995 to 1996, the number of inmates in treatment decreased by 18,360 as the number of inmates who needed treatment rose by 39,578. CASA estimates that states spend 5 percent of their prison budget on drug/alcohol treatment; the BOP spends less than 1 percent.

**Alcohol: The Real Culprit**   According to CASA, alcohol is linked more closely with violent crimes than drugs. More widely available than illegal drugs, alcohol is connected with rape, assault, child and spouse abuse, and most homicides arising from disputes or arguments. Over 20 percent of inmates in state and federal prisons for violent crimes were under the influence of alcohol—and no other substance—when they committed their crimes; in contrast, at the time of their crimes, 4 percent of violent offenders were under the influence of drugs.

CASA also reports a link between alcohol abuse and addiction and property crime. Among state prisoners, 17 percent of property offenders were under the influence of alcohol (and no other substance) at the time of their crime; among federal prisoners, 9 percent.

**Consequences of No Treatment**   Lack of treatment for substance-abusing prisoners endangers the public. Releasing substance abusers from prison without treatment maintains the market for illegal drugs and keeps drug dealers in business; untreated substance abusers are likely to return to substance abuse and crime upon release. As CASA put it, "Release of untreated drug and alcohol addicted inmates is tantamount to visiting criminals on society."[33] Brooklyn, New York, district attorney Charles Hynes calls releasing untreated drug/alcohol-addicted inmates "lunacy."[34]

Recidivism also is related to drug/alcohol abuse. "The more often an individual is imprisoned," CASA wrote, "the likelier that inmate is to be a drug or alcohol addict or abuser."[35] Over 40 percent of first-time offenders have a history of drug use. The proportion increases to over 80 percent for offenders with five or more prior convictions. Regardless of the crimes committed, offenders who test positive for drugs at the time of arrest have longer criminal records and have been imprisoned more often than those who do not. The cost to society of their recidivism is enormous.

**Treatment Works** Why should prisoners receive drug treatment? According to Jeremy Travis, Director of the National Institute of Justice, there are two powerful reasons.[36] First, drug offenders consume a staggering volume of illegal drugs, and any reduction in their drug use represents a significant reduction in the nation's demand for illegal drugs. About 60 percent of the cocaine and heroine consumed by the entire nation in a year is consumed by individuals arrested in that year. Drug treatment has the potential for significantly reducing the nation's demand for illegal drugs.

The second reason we should provide drug treatment to prisoners is we now know that we can reduce drug use in the offender population. In other words, treatment works, with the important corollary that we can reduce the new crimes offenders commit. Treatment programs that start 9 months to a year before prison release, provide community-based aftercare services in the community (housing, education, employment, and health care), attract and retain staff that demonstrate concern for the offender's welfare, and give offenders a clear understanding of the program's rules and the penalties for breaking them provide the greatest chances for success.[37] Such programs have success rates as high as 80–90 percent. Community aftercare services are particularly important for substance abusers because they tend to have medical problems such as cirrhosis of the liver, diabetes, and HIV/AIDS.

One successful prison-based substance treatment program is a therapeutic community. A **therapeutic community (TC)** is a residential treatment program under which inmates are housed in a separate unit within a prison or jail facility, characterized by highly structured treatment involving resocialization, intensive counseling, and an increasing level of responsibility as the inmate progresses through the program. Recent evaluations of prison-based TCs offer solid evidence of their effectiveness. The TC treatment program at the R. J. Donovan Correctional Facility near San Diego, California was recognized by the U.S. Department of Justice as a model program.[38]

Donovan's TC inmates participate in group meetings, seminars, group and individual counseling, video feedback, relapse prevention, and urine testing. Pre-parole planning is also provided to assist inmates in return to their communities. Seminars, workshops, and group meetings are also provided for the TC inmates' families and friends. After release, TC inmates are paroled to a community residential facility where full treatment services and community-based aftercare services are available. The average stay in a community residential facility is 5.3 months; the participant then makes the transition to independent living.

Most treatment programs are successful when offenders attend often and stay in contact with treatment counselors over long periods. Also important to successful program completion is effective aftercare. CASA reports on the success of other prison-based substance abuse programs followed by community aftercare services. For example, the California Department of Corrections operates Forever Free, a prison-based substance abuse treatment program followed by community aftercare for women offenders. Graduates of the prison-based treatment program alone had a 62 percent success rate. When women completed the community aftercare phase, their success rate climbed even higher: 90 percent for women who completed an average of 5 months in the community residential treatment setting versus 72 percent for those who did not. There is ample evidence that offenders who participate in

**therapeutic community (TC)** A highly structured residential treatment program within a prison or jail involving resocialization, intensive counseling, and an increasing level of inmate responsibility.

*The Prison Environment: Issues and Concerns*

in-prison treatment and post-release community aftercare treatment are more likely to remain drug- and arrest-free after release from prison.

**Costs and Benefits of Treatment**  CASA estimates that the cost of proven treatment programs for inmates, accompanied by appropriate education, job training, and health care, averages $6,500 per year per offender. The annual economic benefit to society—in terms of avoided incarceration and health care costs, salary earned, taxes paid, and contribution to the economy—is $68,000 for every prisoner who successfully completes such treatment and becomes a taxpaying, law-abiding person. Excluding over 200,000 drug dealers who don't use drugs, if only 10 percent of the 1.2 million abusers and addicts are successfully treated (120,000), the economic benefit in the first year of work after release would be $8.256 billion. CASA says that's $456 million more than the $7.8 billion cost of providing training and treatment (at a cost of $6,500 each) for the entire 1.2 million inmates with drug and/or alcohol problems.

**Recommendations for Managing Substance-Abusing Offenders**
Controlling the revolving door of drug and alcohol abusers and addicts going in and out of prison is an important aspect of management for corrections officials. In its report, CASA offers pre-prison, prison, and post-prison recommendations designed to cut taxpayer costs and protect the public safety by reducing recidivism:[39]

**Pre-Prison:**
1.  Assess the substance abuse involvement of offenders at the time of arrest—perform drug tests and thoroughly evaluate substance abuse history. This can form the basis for decisions about pretrial supervision, sentencing, and treatment.
2.  Encourage development, implementation, and evaluation of treatment alternatives to prison, such as diversion and drug courts, and expand diversion programs for nonviolent first offenders who are drug/alcohol abusers and addicts.
3.  Provide police, prosecutors, and judges with the training and assistance required to effectively deal with substance-related crime, including counselors and public health experts experienced in evaluating substance abuse and addiction.
4.  Get rid of mandatory sentences that eliminate the possibility of alternative sentencing and/or parole. Judges and prosecutors need the flexibility to divert substance-abusing offenders into treatment, drug courts, coerced abstinence, or other alternatives to prison when appropriate. Corrections officials need every possible carrot and stick to encourage inmates to seek treatment, including the carrot of reduced prison time for substance-abusing inmates who successfully complete treatment and the stick of getting sent back to jail for parolees who fail to participate in required post-release treatment or aftercare.

**In Prison:**
1.  Train corrections officers and other personnel in treating substance abuse and addiction so that they can better prevent the use

of alcohol and drugs in prison and better assist inmates in the recovery process.

2. Keep jails and prisons tobacco-, alcohol-, and drug-free. This means enforcing prohibitions against alcohol and drugs, promoting smoke-free prisons and local jails to enhance inmate health, and eliminating distribution of tobacco products to inmates.

3. Expand random testing of prisoners to corrections officers and deter drug and alcohol use; refer inmates for substance abuse treatment and monitor their progress.

4. Provide treatment in prison for all who need it: every alcohol- or drug-involved offender, including property offenders, violent offenders, and drug sellers. Tailor treatment to the special needs of inmates, such as women or children of alcoholics and drug addicts.

5. Encourage participation in literacy, education, and training programs. Such programs should be widely available, and inmates should be encouraged to enroll in them—participation in these programs will increase inmates' chances of securing gainful employment upon release.

6. Provide substance-abusing prisoners with a range of support services including medical care, mental health services, prevention services (including confidential HIV testing), counseling, and other services they need.

7. Increase the availability of religious and spiritual activity and counseling in prison and provide an environment that encourages such activity.

**Post-Prison:**

1. Provide pre-release planning for treatment and aftercare services for individuals who need them. Help parolees find services they need to remain substance-free after leaving prison, such as drug-free housing, literacy training, job placement, and social services.

2. Train parole and probation officers to deal with alcohol and drug abuse and assist parolees and probationers with locating addiction services and staying in treatment.

## HIV/AIDS in Correctional Facilities

HIV/AIDS continues to be far more prevalent among prison inmates than in the total U.S. population (see Table 11–1). The Northeast region has the highest number and percentage of inmates with HIV/AIDS. Generally, the prevalence of HIV/AIDS is higher among Hispanic and black inmates than among white inmates and higher among female inmates than among males. High-risk behaviors for transmitting HIV—sex, drug use, sharing needles, and tattooing—occur in correctional facilities. Also, some transmission of HIV among inmates has been shown to occur.[40] Thus, prisons and jails are places to reach a large concentration of persons who are HIV-positive or infected with AIDS and provide them treatment, education, and behavior modification techniques prior to release to the community.

## TABLE 11–1

### Percent of Population With Confirmed AIDS

| Year | U.S. General Population | Inmates in State and Federal Prisons |
|------|-------------------------|--------------------------------------|
| 1991 | 0.03% | 0.21% |
| 1992 | 0.03 | 0.33 |
| 1993 | 0.06 | 0.50 |
| 1994 | 0.07 | 0.52 |
| 1995 | 0.08 | 0.51 |
| 1996 | 0.09 | 0.54 |

*Source:* Theodore M. Hammett, Patricia Harmon, and Laura M. Maruschak, *1996–1997 Update: HIV/AIDS, STDs, and TB in Correctional Facilities* (Washington: National Institute of Justice, July 1999), p. 5.

**HIV Testing and Treatment** Most correctional systems test their inmates for HIV, but testing policies vary widely.

- 45 jurisdictions test inmates if they have HIV-related symptoms or if the inmates request a test
- 24 states test inmates after they are involved in an incident
- 15 states test inmates who belong to specific "high-risk groups"
- 16 states test all inmates who enter their facilities
- 3 states and the BOP test inmates upon their release
- 3 states test all inmates currently in custody
- 2 states and the BOP test inmates selected at random

Treating HIV in prison is difficult for at least five reasons. [41] The first is the issue of privacy. Inmates, like other people infected with HIV, do not want to disclose their condition. The therapeutic regimen often involves taking multiple drugs several times a day. Going to the prison medication line often compromises a prisoner's privacy and increases the risk of stigmatization by other inmates and staff. Stigmatization can range from isolation and shunning to more overt forms of abuse. This is true even when high-quality health care is available. Anti-retroviral therapies (ART) can effectively treat HIV, but only if corrections officials help inmates overcome the obstacles to obtaining the treatment.

A second reason focuses on the frequency of taking medication and the prison routine. Some drugs must be taken with food and others in a fasting state. As the therapeutic regimen increases to five or six times a day, it strains the routine of most prisons to dispense medication frequently and to provide food as required.

The third reason is distrust of the medical and legal system. Not surprisingly, many inmates distrust the legal and health care system. This may be especially true for women and minorities who have a documented history of being experimented on without consent and being denied appropriate legal and medical care.

The fourth reason is fear of side effects. The HIV drug regimen is known to make patients feel worse than they already do. Consequently, inmates will be less likely to adhere to the strict dosages and timing.

The final reason it is difficult to treat HIV-infected prisoners is a legal one. The courts have rejected the idea that the level and quality of health care available to prisoners must be the same as is available to society at large.[42] You may recall the *principle of least eligibility* from Chapter 7—the belief that prison conditions, including the delivery of health care, be a step below those of the working class and people on welfare. Thus, prisoners are denied access to medical specialists, timely delivery of medical services, technologically advanced diagnostic techniques, the latest medication and drug therapies, up-to-date surgical procedures, and second opinions.[43]

Overcoming these obstacles will not be easy. The key is developing trust between HIV-infected prisoners and the prison health-care team, extending the regimen when inmates are discharged, and building collaboration between correctional institutions and public health agencies. If an inmate undergoes complex drug therapy in prison but cannot obtain the same therapy upon release, his/her health is threatened and he or she may transmit the virus to others.

Incarceration offers opportunities to provide HIV and sexually-transmitted disease education as well as prevention programs for high-risk inmates. Such programs benefit not only the inmate but also the health and well-being of the community to which the inmate returns. The types of education and prevention programs provided vary among correctional systems and may include instructor-led programs, peer-led programs, pre-/post-test counseling, multi-session prevention counseling, and audiovisual and written materials. Within programs, high-risk inmates may learn basic disease information, safer sex practices, tattooing risks, self-perception of risk, and triggers for behavior relapse. Education and prevention programs are becoming more common in correctional facilities, but only 10 percent of state/federal prison systems offer comprehensive education and prevention programs.[44]

## Older Inmates

Most of us imagine prisoners as young and aggressive. However, elderly and passive describes a significant portion of the prison population. Defining *elderly* is subject to debate. Some define *elderly* as 65 years of age and older, some suggest 60 years, others suggest 55, and still others 50. There are some who do not consider chronological age at all. Rather, they believe that, because of the impact of prison lifestyle, including lower socioeconomic status and limited access to medical care, a prisoner's physiological age may be higher than his or her chronological age. Simply put, the declining health of many prisoners makes them appear old before their time. In addition, some say prison life can age an inmate 10 years beyond chronological age.

*Mark A. Molesworth*
*Substance Abuse Unit*
*Manager*
*North Dakota*

*"My philosophy is that all staff have two important roles regardless of their profession. First, 30 percent of our job is to make sure individuals who are incarcerated do not escape, hurt staff, hurt other inmates or themselves. Second, 70 percent of our role is directed toward rehabilitating inmates who will live in society after they leave our care. It is everyone's responsibility to provide appropriate role modeling and opportunities (treatment, education, employment, social, and cognitive) which permit residents to make the necessary changes which will enable them to live productively in society after their release. We cannot force people to change. But, if we do not provide the opportunity for change, we are a part of the problem."*

Mark A. Molesworth is a unit manager for a long-term residential substance abuse facility for convicted male and female felons in North Dakota. He began his career as a temporary correctional officer during summer vacations. When he graduated from Minot State University with a B.S. degree in criminal justice, he was promoted to the rank of lieutenant and made director of the Adult Services Program at a minimum security unit. Mark is the single custodial father of two young children and is the past president of the board of directors of the Bismarck School of Hope (a nonprofit learning center for disabled preschool-age children). He is currently involved in the MPA program through the University of North Dakota.

Despite the differences in defining *elderly,* it is important to establish a common chronological starting point to define *older* inmates for purposes of comprehensive planning, programming, evaluation, and research within and among prison systems. After careful study of the issue, the NIC recommended that correctional agencies nationwide adopt age 50 as the chronological starting point to define **older inmates**.[45] In 1998, 7.2 percent (almost 84,000) of the 1.2 million state and federal prisoners were over age 50.[46] Experts believe that by the year 2010, inmates over the age of 50 will comprise 33 percent of the total prison population.[47]

**older inmates** Inmates age 50 and older, as defined by the National Institute of Corrections.

**Health Issues** Physical health, mental health, and medical care for older inmates have implications for prison policymakers, administrators, and staff. It is estimated that an elderly prisoner suffers from an average of three chronic illnesses.[48] Incarcerating older prisoners with impaired eyesight, physical handicaps, cancer, arthritis, diabetes, heart disease, hypertension, or Alzheimer's disease and treating these illnesses raises many concerns. For example, providing surgery, physical therapy, and daily medication for elderly prisoners raises ethical questions about providing health care to prisoners when persons outside prison are unable to receive similar medical treatment. In addition, new laws such as the Americans With Disabilities Act

In October 1997, journalist Anne Seidlitz and National Prison Hospice Association representative Nancy Craig spent five days at the Louisiana State Penitentiary (LSP) at Angola, observing training sessions for the inmate volunteers who would be part of the interdisciplinary team of the LSP Hospice. Together with Carol Evans, they interviewed five of the volunteers at the R. J. Barrow Treatment Center. The following excerpt has been edited.

**Anne Seidlitz:** I'd like to know why you decided to join the volunteer group, what your experience has been with this kind of work, and what you expect to get out of it.

**Charles Buie:** The way the hospital used to be here, before they changed it to the Treatment Center, inmates would more or less die alone, with only the hospital staff around. So some of us came up with the idea of doing some kind of hospice work. We used to come over here and visit our friends. The administration used to let us do that, but then they stopped it, and that really worried some of us, because we had friends who were really ill or even dying. So that's how the idea got started. We sent the idea to Warden Cain, and he sent it to someone else and this hospice program came about. This all really came out of love for our fellow inmates. The important thing is that now when we get sick, we won't be afraid to come to the hospital. Some of us were terrified of coming to the hospital because of the perception that if you came here you died. Now we are working on changing that perception in the larger prison population.

**Claude Donald:** This program is really needed here at Angola. I'm an orderly on this ward and for a long time, I've thought about

how wonderful it would be for guys to get involved in this type of program, not only for the patients but for the inmates themselves. You've got to sit back and imagine: how would it be—and this is deep—when a prisoner is dying? You never know what state of mind that prisoner is in. But you do know that he doesn't even have a family member around; he doesn't even have a close friend around. That's where you come in—you be that family member, you be that friend. You know, I've gotten so tied up in this ward, with these guys, that I've often told myself, I'm not going to get involved anymore. I've been through it over and over, with guys dying on me. But it's something you can't avoid; you've got to get attached to these guys and their families. To know that someone is dying, and take care of him like this and he says, "I appreciate that"—well, that's more to me than anything I could get in a material way. In the end it's just a joy to be able to do that.

**AS:** Were there any times when you felt that you could have used some help in dealing with the patients' needs?

**Claude Donald:** Well, I was reading this hospice volunteer manual and I saw things in there that really could have helped me over the year. This morning on the [training video], I saw that when a person is in his last stages and he don't want to eat, you don't force that eating upon him. When he don't want to sleep, you don't force that sleep upon him. That little bit of information right there was a great help. In the past, I've tried to persuade a guy to eat, but I learned today to let them do whatever they want to do, and whatever is comfortable for them. This program is giving us some first-class knowledge.

**David Veal:** I agree that the knowledge of hospice is very important for us to hear. Like Claude said, now we know what to do for the patients. Our desire is to help them, but without the right information we got to figure out things by ourselves. Like the food issue, it would have been easier for Claude to relax and talk to the fellow—to where that brother would have felt comfortable about eating or not eating—rather than trying to convince him to do it.

**Michael Singletary (a patient as well as a volunteer):** The thing about being in prison for any length of time is that you begin to lose family members, or they forget about you. I've got one friend who is dying on the ward right now; he's been my friend for my fifteen years of incarceration, and I can be there for him. My family and friends are now at Angola. I've been over here for twelve days and I've had numerous cards from my friends down the Walk since I have been sick. And that's my strength; that's where it comes from.

**Charles Buie:** "What will happen to me in years to come if I don't get parole or a pardon, when I get old, sick?" That's a question we're asking ourselves. We see so many of our friends, people we are growing old with, getting sick. Who takes care of them? We have to become our own family, and believe me that happens. Even if someone is in one of the outcamps, he's still my friend; I can still send messages and letters to him because we've bonded together. But if he's in the hospital—it used to be that you might not know that for a while. Then you find out and worry about him. Before, there was no way to make contact with him. That set-up is going to change with the hospice program. The volunteers come from every area of the institution, and we can take information back to friends, so it becomes like a big family network. Someone is in the hospice program from every area.

I can tell you this: from attending last night's meeting and from talking to some of the guys in my dormitory that saw us on the Walk and wanted to know what was going on, everybody is excited. The inmates are happy because someone is here who cares about them; the myth and the concept we have about the treatment in the hospital is fading away. That especially goes for the inmates who live where David lives in Camp F, where most of the elderly people live.

**David Veal:** Those guys in Camp F are maybe 74 years old; they haven't seen their families for 25 years or so, and they've got life sentences. This one guy the other day was shooting horseshoes. He was from Baton Rouge, and he started talking about life there in the '50s, way before I was around! I found out that he really needed to share the things that he knew and had experienced. I gave him so much ear play, that it burnt my ears up! But it was a learning experience for me, to help me understand that talking was what he needed to do. And right now, today, with this hospice program, people are being trained to provide just this type of attention and caring. We understand the social workers' position, but we have to come along and make it work for one another. We've got to really do it. It's not that we want to push for the staff to do it, because these folks don't live with you at night. At eleven or twelve at night, they are not there—we are there. We are right there next to one another. This guy sleeping next to me, if he's in a bad way, I've got to wake up and understand.

**AS:** People on the outside think that kind of sensitivity would be very hard to develop in this environment.

**Larry Landry:** I've been in trouble all my life. This is my second time at Angola. In the early seventies, there was no such thing as this program. You had to lead a macho life; no matter how much fear you had, you couldn't show it. You couldn't have compassion for another guy, because they would take it as weakness. Over the years it changed. Now my feeling is that this is my community, this is my life, I want to put something back.

In 1995, I had to come in here and be operated on. I saw a friend I hadn't seen in ten years because he was in an outcamp. He was dying of AIDS. His leg was smaller than my arm, and I just felt so hurt 'cause I couldn't do nothing for him. [Starts to cry.] Even if I could have come back to see him after I left the hospital, I couldn't get to him 'cause he had AIDS. I heard that he would ask for me to come and see him, but I couldn't. I said to myself, "My God, that could be me." I would want somebody to care for me; so now I try to do that, to show that somebody cares. My family gave up on me, and most of the guys in here—nobody cares for them, so who's gonna care for them? This is our community. If we don't take care of each other, who's going to take care of us? I have friends in the infirmary right now. I want them to know that I care. Just to see their faces, I can tell it means a lot to them.

**Charles Buie:** It has a lot to do with our Warden Cain. He genuinely cares about human beings even though his job is to keep us here. If you explain things to him and show him a need, where it makes sense he'll do something. He's changed this penitentiary. Now sometimes people don't like to hear that, but he has changed this institution and I've been here a long time. Some hardened criminals are changing, going to church more. Now security can take you to church almost any time. And that was once unheard of. Now we would like to have a wake service in the chapel when somebody dies. But that's another project.

**Carol Evans:** One of the greatest needs of family is a funeral service of some type, some sort of ritual in which they can say goodbye to their friends, at least at the burial site.

(ADA) affect not only mainstream society but also prisons and jails. Designing prison spaces that are accessible for elderly prisoners, with ramps, handrails, good lighting, and subtle grades is now law under ADA.

**Cost Issues** The economic consequences of incarcerating older prisoners are huge. The estimated national costs per year to confine an inmate over 55 years old is $70,000.[49] In North Carolina it costs $37,000 per year to keep elderly prisoners at the McCain Correctional Facility. In Maryland, it's $69,000 per year. In California, it's $80,000 per year.

Could elderly prisoners who are considered harmless be released early to go back to their families or to independent care living and thereby save prisons money? Systematic research on how elderly prisoners adapt after prison release is sketchy, although it's known that recidivism drops with age. According to the U.S. Parole Commission, older federal prisoners show lower recidivism rates. The U.S. Department of Justice reported that only 2 percent of inmates who are 55 or older when paroled return to prison.[50] It is doubtful that when mandatory sentencing laws, "three-strikes" laws, and "truth-in-sentencing" laws were enacted the economic impact of incarcerating elderly prisoners for long periods of time was actually considered. Unless legislatures give courts and prison administrators more leeway to interchange prison sentences with community sentences, states will find themselves in economic crisis providing for the 33 percent of the inmate population that is projected to be elderly by the year 2010.

**Geriatric Prison Facilities**   An increasing number of states are beginning to house their older prisoner population away from the general population, in nursing-home-like settings. Alabama, Arizona, Georgia, Illinois, Kansas, Kentucky, Maryland, Michigan, Minnesota, Mississippi, North Carolina, New Jersey, Ohio, Pennsylvania, South Carolina, Tennessee, Texas, Virginia, West Virginia, and Wisconsin have special prisons for the elderly, often called "aged/infirm," "medical/geriatric," "disabled," or simply "geriatric." The facility itself accommodates special needs of the elderly. Few stairs, reduced distances, more crafts and leisure activities, and staff trained in gerontological issues make these facilities unique. The majority confine only elderly male prisoners. Older female prisoners, who constitute only a small percentage of the total elderly prisoner population, are generally kept in the state's only women's prison.

A number of states are also opening prison **hospices** as a compassionate way to deal with dying inmates.[51] A hospice is an interdisciplinary, comfort-oriented care facility that allows seriously ill and dying patients to die with dignity and humanity in an environment where they have mental and spiritual preparation for the natural process of dying. Hospice programs provide a wide array of services, including pain management, spiritual support, and psychological counseling, as well as grief counseling for bereaved families.

In 1998, the NIC looked at prison care for terminally ill prisoners across the United States.[52] Of the slightly more than 1,000 inmates diagnosed as terminally ill, 800 were in regular prison hospitals, 150 in formal prison hospice settings, and 100 on parole or another form of compassionate release. The same survey found that 11 states and the BOP have started formal prison hospice programs and 20 states are developing such programs.

Often, one of the challenges in starting a prison hospice is educating the prison staff in caring for the terminally ill and making a psychological adjustment—getting over the resentment that prisoners are getting this level of care. According to Elizabeth Craig, executive director of the National Prison Hospice Association (NPHA) in Boulder, Colorado, "In my view, inmates are being punished by being incarcerated; we don't need to create more suffering for them. It can only be helpful for ill inmates to see that people care for them, which might be the starting point for some kind of transformation."[53]

**hospice**   An interdisciplinary, comfort-oriented care unit that allows seriously ill and dying prisoners to die with dignity and humanity in an environment that provides mental and spiritual preparation for the natural process of dying.

# Mothers in Prison

According to a recent BJS study,[54] an estimated 6.7 percent of black women, 5.9 percent of Hispanic women, and 5.2 percent of white women are pregnant at the time of incarceration.

An estimated 4,000 women prisoners give birth each year, even though most women's prisons have no special facilities for pregnant inmates.[55] Some experts recommend that women's prisons should routinely make counseling available to pregnant inmates, and that they should fully inform these women of the options available to them, including abortion and adoption.[56]

The ACA[57] recommends that institutions provide counseling for pregnant inmates, that "prenatal care" should be offered, and that deliveries should be made at community hospitals.[58] Similarly, the American Public Health Association's standards for health services in correctional institutions say that pregnant inmates should be provided with prenatal care, including medical exams and treatment, and that pregnant prisoners should be allowed a special program of housing, diet, vitamin supplements, and exercise.[59]

Once inmates give birth, other problems arise—including the critical issue of child placement. Some states still have partial civil death statutes, which mean that prisoners lose many of their civil rights upon incarceration. In such states women may lose legal custody of their children. Children either become wards of the state or are placed for adoption.

Although there is some historical precedent for allowing women inmates to keep newborns with them in the institutional setting, very few women's prisons permit this practice. Overcrowded prisons lack space for children, and the prison environment is a decidedly undesirable environment for children. A few women's prisons allow women to keep newborns for a brief period. Most, however, arrange for foster care until the mother is able to find relatives to care for the child or is released. Others work with services which place prison-born infants up for adoption. Some facilities make a special effort to keep mother and child together. Even relatively progressive prisons which allow mother-child contact usually do so only for the first year.

Many women are already mothers when they come to prison. BJS statistics[60] show that more than three-quarters of all women in prison in the United States have young children (i.e., those under the age of 18). Black (69%) and Hispanic (72%) female inmates are more likely than white (62%) women to have young children. Also, black women are more likely than other women to have lived with their young children before being imprisoned.

Twenty-five percent of women inmates with children under age 18 have children living with the other parent. More than a third of white female inmates report that their children are living with their fathers, compared to a quarter of Hispanic women and less than a fifth of black women. Regardless of race, grandparents were the most common caregivers: 57 percent of black mothers, 55 percent of Hispanic mothers, and 41 percent of white mothers. Nearly 10 percent of the inmate mothers reported that their children were in a foster home, agency, or institution.

According to BJS, nearly 90 percent of women with children under age 18 have had contact with their children since entering prison. Half of all women inmates surveyed had been visited by their children, four-fifths had corresponded by mail, and three-quarters had talked with children on the telephone. Female inmates with children under age 18 were more likely than those with adult children to make daily telephone calls to their children.

Understandably, inmate mothers frequently express concern about possible alienation from their children due to the passage of time associated with incarceration. They often worry that their children will develop strong bonds with new caretakers and be unwilling to return to their mothers upon release.[61]

Finally, it is important to note that a number of women's prisons operate programs designed to develop parenting skills among inmates. Included here are the Program for Caring Parents at the Louisiana Correctional Institute for Women; Project HIP (Helping Incarcerated Parents) at the Maine Correctional Center; and Neil J. Houston House, a program for nonviolent female offenders in Massachusetts.[62]

# 11

## Review and Applications

### CHAPTER OBJECTIVE 1

Prisons are overcrowded for three main reasons. First, over the past decade there has been an increase in imprisonment. Second, changes in federal and state sentencing laws require more offenders to serve longer periods. The third is an increase in imprisonment for drug and violent offenses.

### CHAPTER OBJECTIVE 2

This chapter presented six methods of controlling prison overcrowding. First, reduce the number of persons who go to prison by making more use of front-end strategies such as diversion, community corrections, and intermediate sanctions. Second, put a cap or ceiling on the prison population, sometimes called trap-door strategies. Third, use what are called side-door strategies, such as giving sentenced offenders the opportunity to apply to the sentencing court for release to intensive community corrections programs, usually six months after imprisonment. Fourth, use more parole and halfway houses, called back-door strategies. Fifth, build more prisons and/or expand existing facilities. Sixth, use structured sentencing guidelines that are designed to save prison space for serious crimes and violent offenses while using community corrections and intermediate sanctions for lesser offenses.

### CHAPTER OBJECTIVE 3

Prison riots occur for a number of reasons. Sometimes they are a result of spontaneous outburst; others are planned. Most experts believe that the primary causes of prison riots are overcrowding, racial antagonism, environmental factors, weak prison administration, young and violence-prone prisoners, and control of the inmate social structure.

### CHAPTER OBJECTIVE 4

Preventing prison riots requires changes both outside and inside the prison. It is important for other social institutions to reduce sources of tension that contribute to crime. Experts recommend formal inmate grievance procedures, ombudsmen, improved classification systems, smaller institutions, meaningful educational and work programs, alternatives to incarceration, professional prison staff who are well trained and well paid, and clearly written and well-understood policies on the use of force.

### CHAPTER OBJECTIVE 5

A supermax housing facility is a free-standing facility, or a distinct unit within a facility, that provides for management and secure control of inmates who have been officially designated as violent or who exhibit serious and disruptive behavior while incarcerated. It is not yet known what impact conditions of extreme isolation will have on the prisoner or on the public when prisoners released from these facilities return to the community.

### CHAPTER OBJECTIVE 6

"No-frills" prisons and jails eliminate prisoner privileges and amenities in the belief that this process will deter criminals from future criminal activity. It appears, however, that "no-frills" correctional facilities may actually produce the results they were designed to avert. Corrections professionals tell us that what outsiders perceive as privileges and amenities, they consider to be important management tools. They also suggest that eliminating privileges and amenities may increase the number of prison disturbances and make it more difficult for corrections staff to motivate appropriate inmate behavior.

## CHAPTER OBJECTIVE 7

Special needs inmates in prison include substance abusers, HIV-positive and AIDS-infected inmates, elderly prisoners, pregnant inmates, and female prisoners with children. Eighty percent of the U.S. prison and jail population is seriously involved with drug/alcohol abuse and addiction. Comprehensive prison-based treatment programs that provide community-based aftercare services are most likely to succeed. Prison-based treatment, education, and prevention programs can also help reduce the risk of becoming HIV-positive or acquiring AIDS. The rate of confirmed prison AIDS cases is over six times that of the general population, and the AIDS-related death rate in prison is three times higher. Finally, projections indicate that older prisoners will comprise 33 percent of the prison population by the year 2010. The cost of treating older inmates' health problems is enormous—an estimated $70,000 per year per person. States are beginning to confine the oldest prisoners in nursing-home-like facilities and provide a prison hospice environment for those who are dying. Adding to the pain of imprisonment is the frustration and conflict felt by female inmates at being separated from and unable to care for their children. Pregnant inmates are an additional concern for correctional facilities. Few of them offer adequate medical care to fulfill the needs of pregnant inmates.

## KEY TERMS

rated capacity, p. 311
operational capacity, p. 311
design capacity, p. 311
structured sentencing, p. 313
exchange rates, p. 313
security threat groups (STGs), p. 314
riot, p. 315

supermax housing, p. 322
special master, p. 322
"no-frills" prisons and jails, p. 323
therapeutic community (TC), p. 326
older inmates, p. 331
hospices, p. 335

## QUESTIONS FOR REVIEW

1. Explain the differences among *rated capacity*, *operational capacity*, and *design capacity*.
2. How has the increase in convicted offenders affected prisons?
3. What changes in federal and state sentencing laws have affected prison populations?
4. How have arrests for drug offenses affected prison populations?
5. What are the six methods of controlling prison overcrowding?
6. How does *structured sentencing* work?
7. What is meant by *exchange rates*?
8. Compare and contrast the causes of prison riots in the 1950s and the 1990s.
9. What are *security threat groups*?
10. What are some factors that can lead to a prison riot?
11. What are some ways to prevent prison riots?
12. Distinguish between a supermax housing facility and a prison built for maximum-security prisoners.
13. What are some of the psychological effects of long-term solitary confinement?
14. What is a "no-frills" prison or jail and why are they emerging?
15. What impact can we expect "no-frills" prisons and jails to have on recidivism, institutional security, and inmate behavior control?
16. According to the National Center on Addiction and Substance Abuse (CASA), what percentage of America's jail and prison population at yearend 1996 was involved in substance abuse?
17. Why is alcohol more closely linked with violent crimes than drugs?
18. What is a *therapeutic community*?
19. How does lack of treatment for substance-abusing inmates endanger the public?
20. What are some CASA recommendations for managing substance-abusing inmates?
21. What in-prison recommendations does CASA offer?

22. What post-prison recommendations does CASA offer?

23. How does the number of people in the general population with HIV/AIDS compare with the number of prisoners with HIV/AIDS?

24. What are five reasons that it is difficult to treat HIV in prison?

25. Define what is meant by *older inmate*. What are some issues concerning older prisoners?

26. How does a geriatric prison differ from a regular prison?

27. What is a prison *hospice*?

28. What are two issues that corrections officials face in regard to female inmates?

## CRITICAL THINKING EXERCISES

### ON-THE-JOB ISSUES

1. You are the state corrections department's public information officer. Write a press release that explains to an angry public the reasons why the corrections department pays for older prisoners' medical treatment.

2. It's 2010 and you are the director of your state's Department of Corrections and Rehabilitation. Predictions from the year 2000 that older inmates would comprise 33 percent of the state's prison population were wrong. It's actually 42 percent because twice earlier in the decade the state legislature changed the habitual offender law from "three-strikes" to "two-strikes," and mandated that offenders sentenced under the new law serve all their sentence, not just 85 percent. It's difficult to find reliable figures on what it is costing to care for older inmates' health, yet there are signs all around that it's expensive. For example, your state is now building its third geriatric prison. You are currently working on the department's budget for next year. What issues should you consider when determining what monies to request for the incarceration of older offenders?

### CORRECTIONS ISSUES

1. Under the Violent Offender Incarceration and Truth-in-Sentencing Incentive Grants Program passed by Congress in 1994, to qualify for federal funds to build new prisons and jails, states must require persons convicted of a Part I violent offense to serve not less than 85 percent of their prison sentences. Do you think such a requirement is appropriate? Why or why not?

2. In the district court case *Madrid* v. *Gomez*,[63] the court said: "It is clear that confinement in the Pelican Bay SHU severely deprives inmates of normal human contact and substantially reduces their level of environmental stimulation."[64] The court further said, "Based on studies undertaken in this case, and the entirety of the record bearing on this claim, the court finds that many, if not most, inmates in the SHU experience some degree of psychological trauma in reaction to their extreme social isolation and the severely restricted environmental stimulation in the SHU."[65] Do you agree with the court that the conditions in the supermax unit imposed cruel and unusual punishment on mentally ill prisoners? Explain.

## CORRECTIONS ON THE WEB

1. The Publications section of the Centers for Disease Control and Prevention maintains a Web site at **http://www.cdc.gov/nchstp/od/ cccwg/publications.htm** that discusses HIV, AIDS, and TB in correctional institutions. Go to the site and find and report on a document that discusses HIV, AIDS, or TB in corrections.

2. Access the National Prison Hospice Association at **www.npha.org.** Read the Association's Mission Statement. Then access the Newsletter and read one of the articles. Summarize the article in light of the Association's mission statement.

## ADDITIONAL READINGS

Braswell, Michael C., Reid H. Montgomery, and Lucien X. Lombardo. *Prison Violence in America, 2d ed.* Cincinnati, OH: Anderson Publishing Co., 1994.

Finn, Peter. "No-Frills Prisons and Jails: A Movement in Flux," *Federal Probation.* Volume 60, Number 3, September 1996, pp. 35–44.

Hammett, Theodore M. *Public Health/Corrections Collaboration: Prevention and Treatment of HIV/AIDS, STDs, and TB.* Washington, DC: National Institute of Justice Centers for Disease Control and Prevention Research in Brief, NCJ 169590, July 1998.

Irwin, John, and James Austin. *It's About Time: America's Imprisonment Binge, 2d ed.* Belmont, CA: Wadsworth Publishing Company, 1997.

LIS, Inc. *Supermax Housing.* Longmont, CO: National Institute of Corrections, March 1997.

Logan, Charles H. *Private Prisons: Cons and Pros.* New York: Oxford University Press, 1990.

Morton, Joann B. *An Administrative Overview of the Older Inmate.* Washington, DC: National Institute of Corrections, August 1992.

Belenko, Steven. *Behind Bars: Substance Abuse and America's Prison Population.* New York: National Center on Addiction and Substance Abuse, Columbia University, January 1998.

National Institute of Corrections. *Hospice and Palliative Care in Prison.* Longmont, CO: National Institute of Corrections, September 1998.

Shichor, David. *Punishment for Profit: Private Prisons/Public Concerns.* Thousand Oaks, CA: Sage Publications, Inc., March 1995.

## ENDNOTES

1. Adapted from Reid H. Montgomery, "Bringing the Lessons of Prison Riots Into Focus," *Corrections Today,* Volume 59, Number 1 (February 1997), pp. 28–33. Reprinted with permission.

2. James M. Byrne and Linda Kelly, *Restructuring Probation as an Intermediate Sanction, An Evaluation of Massachusetts' Intensive Probation Supervision Program, Final Report,* (Washington, DC: National Institute of Justice, 1989).

3. David P. Farrington and C. P. Nuttal, "Prison Size, Overcrowding, Prison Violence, and Recidivism," *Journal of Criminal Justice,* Volume 8, Number 4 (1980), pp. 221–231.

4. Victoria G. Putnam, *Gangs in Correctional Facilities: A National Assessment,* NCJ 173076. (Washington, DC: National Institute of Justice, 1993).

5. Mary E. Pelz, "Gangs," In Marilyn D. McShane and Frank P Williams III (eds.), *Encyclopedia of American Prisons.* (New York: Garland Publishing, Inc., 1996), p. 213.

6. Bert Useem and Peter Kimball, *States of Siege: U.S. Prison Riots, 1971-1986* (New York: Oxford University Press, 1991).

7. J. Lillis, "Prison Escapes and Violence Remain Down," *Corrections Compendium,* Volume 19, Number 6 (1994), pp. 6–21.

8. Vernon B. Fox, *Violence Behind Bars: An Explosive Report on Prison Riots in the United States,* (New York: Vantage Press, 1956) and Reid H. Montgomery, Jr., "Bringing the Lessons of Prison Riots Into Focus," *Corrections Today.*

9. Negley K. Teeters, "The Dilemma of Prison Riots," *The Prison Journal,* Volume 33, Number 1 (April 1953), p. 14.

10. "Prison Riots. . . Why?" *The Prison Journal,* Volume 33, Number 1 (April 1953) and "Aftermath of Riot," *The Prison Journal,* Volume 34, Number 1 (April 1954).

11. Negley K. Teeters, "The Dilemma of Prison Riots," pp. 19–20.

12. New York State Special Commission on Attica [McKay Commission], *Attica: The Official Report of the New York State Special Commission on Attica* (New York: Bantam Books, 1972), p. xi.

13. Sue Mahan, Richard Lawrence, and Deanna Meyer, "Riots," in Marilyn D. McShane and Frank P. Williams III (eds.), *Encyclopedia of American Prisons* (New York: Garland Publishing, Inc., 1996), pp. 406–412.

14. U.S. National Advisory Commission on Civil Disorders [Kerner Commission], *Report,* (Washington DC: The Commission, 1968), p. 2.

15. David A. Ward and Allen F. Breed, *The U.S. Penitentiary, Marion, Illinois: Consultants' Report Submitted to the Committee on the Judiciary, U.S. House of Representatives, Ninety-Eighth Congress, Second Session,* (Washington, DC: U.S. Government Printing Office, 1985), p. 1.

16. Ibid., pp. 1–2.

17. As quoted in Francis X. Clines, "A Futuristic Prison Awaits the Hard-Core 400," *The New York Times* (October 17, 1994), Section A, p. 1.

18. LIS, Inc., *Supermax Housing*, (Longmont, CO: National Institute of Corrections, March 1997).

19. Ibid., p. 1.

20. Richard H. McCleery, "Authoritarianism and the Belief System of Incorrigibles," in Donald R. Cressy (ed.), *The Prison: Studies in Institutional Organization and Change*, (New York: Holt, Rinehart and Winston, 1961), pp. 260–306 and *Wright* v. *Enomoto* (July 23, 1980), pp. 5, 15.

21. *Madrid* v. *Gomez*, 889 F.Supp. 1146 (N.D. Cal. 1995).

22. Ibid., p. 1151.

23. Mark Curriden, "Hard Time: Chain Gangs Are In and Exercise Rooms Are Out in the Prisons of the 90s," *ABA Journal*, Volume 81 (July 1995), pp. 72–76.

24. As quoted in Garry Boulard, "What's Tough Enough," *State Legislatures*, Volume 21, Number 10 (December 1995), p. 26.

25. Peter Finn, "No-Frills Prisons and Jails: A Movement in Flux," *Federal Probation*, Volume 60, Number 3 (September 1996), pp. 35–44.

26. As quoted in "5 Florida County Jails Make It Real Hard Time: No Television," *The New York Times* (August 14, 1994, Section L), p. 27.

27. As quoted in Brett Pulley, "Always a Good Sound Bite: The 'Good Life' Behind Bars," *The New York Times* (September 22, 1996, Section 13), p. 2.

28. "5 Florida County Jails Make It Real Hard Time: No Television."

29. John J. Rafferty, "Prison Industry: The Next Step," *Corrections Today*, Volume 60, Number 4 (July 1998), p. 22.

30. W. Wesley Johnson, Katherine Bennett, and Timothy J. Flanagan, "Getting Tough on Prisoners: Results From the National Corrections Executive Survey, 1995," *Crime and Delinquency*, Volume 43, Number 1 (January 1997), pp. 24–41.

31. Ibid., p. 38.

32. National Center on Addiction and Substance Abuse, *Behind Bars: Substance Abuse and America's Prison Population*, (New York: National Center on Addiction and Substance Abuse, Columbia University). Online at http://www.casacolumbia.org/pubs/jan98. Accessed August 1998.

33. National Center on Addiction and Substance Abuse, *Behind Bars: Substance Abuse and America's Prison Population*.

34. As quoted in Joseph A. Califano, "Foreword," National Center on Addiction and Substance Abuse, *Behind Bars: Substance Abuse and America's Prison Population* (Columbia University, NY: National Center on Addiction and Substance Abuse, January 1998). Online at http://www.casacolumbia.org/pubs/jan98. Accessed August 1998.

35. Ibid.

36. Jeremy Travis, *Framing the National Agenda: A Research and Policy Perspective. Speech to National Corrections Conference on Substance Abuse*, April 23, 1997.

37. Marcia R. Chaiken, *Prison Programs for Drug-Involved Offenders*, (Washington, DC: National Institute of Justice, October 1989); D. A. Andrews, Ivan Zinger, Robert D. Hoge, James Bonta, Paul Gendreau, and Francis T. Cullen, "Does Correctional Treatment Work? A Clinically Relevant and Psychologically Informed Meta-Analysis," *Criminology*, Volume 28, Number 3 (1990), pp. 369–404; and Donald Lipton and Frank Pearson, "The CDATE Project: Reviewing Research on the Effectiveness of Treatment Programs for Adults and Juvenile Offenders," Paper presented at the annual meeting of the American Society of Criminology, Chicago, IL, 1996.

38. Bureau of Justice Statistics, *Improving the Nation's Criminal Justice System: Findings and Results From State and Local Program Evaluations*, (Washington, DC: Bureau of Justice Statistics, December 1997).

39. National Center on Addiction and Substance Abuse, *Behind Bars: Substance Abuse and America's Prison Population*.

40. Theodore M. Hammett, Patricia Harmon, and Laura M. Maruschak, *1996–1997 Update: HIV/AIDS, STDs, and TB in Correctional Facilities* (Washington, DC: National Institute of Justice, July 1999), pp. xiii–xiv.

41. *Management of the HIV-Positive Prisoner*, (New York: World Health CME), no date.

42. Michael S. Vaughn and Leo Carroll, "Separate and Unequal: Prison Versus Free-World Medical Care," *Justice Quarterly*, Volume 15, Number 1 (March 1998), pp. 3–40.

43. Ibid., pp. 31–32.

44. Hammett, et al., op. cit., pp. 25–44.

45. Joann B. Morton, *An Administrative Overview of the Older Inmate*, (Washington, DC: National Institute of Corrections, August 1992). Online at http://www.nicic.org. Accessed November 1998.

46. Ronald H. Aday, "Responding to the Graying of American Prisons: A National Perspective Update." Paper presented to the annual meeting of the Academy of Criminal Justice Sciences, March 13, 1999, Orlando, FL.

47. Connie L. Neeley, Laura Addison, and Delores Craig-Moreland, "Addressing the Needs of Elderly

Offenders," *Corrections Today,* Volume 59, Number 5 (August 1997), pp. 120–124.

48. Ronald H. Aday, "Golden Years Behind Bars: Special Programs and Facilities for Elderly Inmates," *Federal Probation,* Volume 58, Number 2 (June 1994), pp. 47–54.

49. Jurgen Neffe, "The Old Folks' Slammer: Aging Prison Population in the United States," *World Press Review,* Volume 44, Number 6 (June 1997), pp. 30–32; Irina R. Soderstrom and W. Michael Wheeler, "Is It Practical to Incarcerate the Elderly Offender? Yes and No," in Charles B. Fields, *Controversial Issues in Corrections* (Boston: Allyn and Bacon, 1999), pp. 72–89.

50. Alexandra Pelosi, "Age of Innocence: A Glut of Geriatric Jailbirds," *The New Republic,* Volume 216, Number 18 (May 5, 1997), pp. 15–18.

51. Anne Seidlitz, "National Prison Hospice Association Facilities Deal With Inmate Deaths," *CorrectCare,* Volume 12, Number 1 (Spring 1998), p. 10.

52. National Institute of Corrections, *Hospice and Palliative Care in Prisons,* (Longmont, CO: National Institute of Corrections, September 1998).

53. Seidlitz, op. cit., p. 10.

54. Tracy L. Snell, "Women in Prison," *Bureau of Justice Statistics Bulletin,* NCJ 145321 (March, 1994).

55. As estimated by Vesna Markovic, "Pregnant Women in Prison: A Correctional Dilemma?" *The Keepers' Voice* (Summer 1995).

56. Ibid.

57. American Correctional Association, *Standards for Adult Correctional Institutions,* 3d ed. American Correctional Association, January, 1990.

58. Gerald Austin McHugh, "Protection of the Rights of Pregnant Women in Prison and Detention Facilities," *New England Journal of Prison Law,* Vol. 6, No. 2 (Summer 1980), pp. 231–263.

59. Ibid., p. 246.

60. Snell, op. cit.

61. Phyllis Jo Baunach, "Critical Problems of Women in Prison," in Imogene L. Moyer (ed.), *The Changing Roles of Women in the Criminal Justice System* (Prospect Heights, IL: Waveland Press, 1985), p. 16.

62. John J. Sheridan, "Inmates May Be Parents, Too," *Corrections Today,* Volume 58, Number 5 (August 1996), p. 100.

63. *Madrid* v. *Gomez,* 889 F.Supp. 1146 (N.D. Cal. 1995).

64. Ibid., p. 1232.

65. Ibid., p. 1235.

# 12 Parole
## Early Release and Reintegration

## CHAPTER OBJECTIVES

After completing this chapter you should be able to:

1. Present a brief history of American parole development.
2. Understand the function of parole in the criminal justice system.
3. Define *parole* and explain the parole decision-making process.
4. Describe the characteristics of the parole population.
5. Explain the circumstances under which parole may be revoked.
6. Describe the reentry court concept.
7. List and explain three major U.S. Supreme Court decisions that affected parole.
8. Describe trends in post-release practices.

*Sorry it's taken so long to write, but I do have a good excuse. I'm working 7 days a week, 14 hours a day, driving for an appliance store. I deliver appliances for $15 a trip, and I try to do as much as possible each day. I average about $100 a day, saving every cent for a new truck.*

*When I went for my job interview I told the interviewer up front that I was on parole, but it made no difference at all to him. And for anyone who is interested, Project RIO works. Not only does it help you find a job, they call and talk to the company before you have your interview. Get involved with Project RIO.*

*When I went to the employment office under Project RIO, it made finding a job easy. I went for two interviews and got one job [with the second company]. But the first company I applied with has already called me for a second interview and [also] wants to hire me. It starts out at less money, but within a year I'll be making about $35,000 a year, working 5 days a week, 8 hours a day. Once I get enough money together to buy a new truck I may switch jobs.*

—Peter Finn, Texas' Project RIO (Re-Integration of Offenders)

The letter above, written by a Texas parolee to a friend still in a Texas prison, is indicative of the success of a program designed to help parolees find jobs. Project RIO (Re-Integration of Offenders) is a major initiative the state of Texas has undertaken to help keep parolees from returning to prison. Inmates who find decent jobs soon after release are less likely to return to a life of crime. In 1996, 16,000 Texas parolees participated in Project RIO.

For more than a century, parole has been used for early release from prison—inmates are released from some type of institutional custody but remain in the legal custody of the government. A parolee who violates one or more of the conditions of parole may be returned to custody to serve the remainder of the original sentence plus any additional sentence imposed for the parole violation.

# Parole as Part of the Criminal Justice System

People often confuse parole, probation, and pardon. All three place offenders in the community, but they are very different.

**Parole** is the release of a prison inmate, prior to sentence expiration, with supervision in the community. A parole usually comes from authorities in the correctional system—responsibility for offenders passes from the judicial system to the correctional system upon imprisonment. In those states that permit parole, state laws give correctional officials the authority to change, within certain limits, the length of a sentence. Correctional officials may, therefore, change the conditions under which convicted offenders are supervised—they may release offenders from prison to supervision in the community or in an outside facility.

As we saw in Chapter 5, **probation** is a judge's sentence that allows a convicted offender to continue to live in the community, with restrictions on activities and with supervision for the duration of the sentence.

A **pardon** is an executive act that legally excuses a convicted offender from penalty. It is granted by a governor or the President. Those who are pardoned are excused from any further supervision.

## Historical Overview

The parole concept has its roots in an 18th century English penal practice—banishment. Judges transferred custody of physically fit condemned felons to independent contractors, paying those contractors a fee to transport the prisoners to the American colonies and sell their services, for the duration of their sentences, to the highest bidder. This practice, known as indentured servitude, was similar to today's parole in that the indentured servant had to comply with certain conditions to remain in supervised "freedom." This practice was discontinued in 1787 because of the Revolutionary War—English offenders were joining colonial forces against England.

From 1787 through 1879, English offenders were sent to Norfolk Island, Australia, a British penal colony. In 1840, British Navy Captain Alexander Maconochie was appointed superintendent of the penal colony. He developed a "ticket of leave" system, which moved inmates through stages: imprisonment, conditional release, and complete restoration of liberty. Inmates moved from one stage to the next by earning "marks" for improved conduct, frugality, and work habits.

In 1854, Sir Walter Crofton, director of the Irish prison system, implemented a system that was based on Maconochie's "ticket of leave" system. Crofton's version required that, upon conditional release, a former inmate:

1. Report immediately to the constabulary on arrival and once a week thereafter.
2. Abstain from any violation of the law.
3. Refrain from habitually associating with notoriously bad characters.
4. Refrain from leading an idle and dissolute life, without means of obtaining an honest living.
5. Produce the "ticket of leave" when asked to do so by a magistrate or police officer.
6. Not change locality without reporting to the constabulary.[1]

The former inmate who did not comply with the conditions of release was re-imprisoned. Crofton's system of conditional release is considered the forerunner of modern American parole.

**parole** The conditional release of a prisoner, prior to completion of the imposed sentence, under the supervision of a parole officer.

**probation** The conditional release of a convicted offender into the community under the supervision of a probation officer as a sentence for conviction of a crime.

**pardon** An executive act that legally excuses a convicted offender from a criminal penalty.

Captain Alexander Maconochie, who became superintendent of the British penal colony on Norfolk Island, Australia in 1840, implemented a "ticket of leave" system to ease inmate transition from custody to freedom. Later, Sir Walter Crofton, director of the Irish prison system, implemented a system based on Maconochie's ideas. How did their systems influence current parole procedures?

Use of the term *parole* for early release from prison began with a letter from Dr. S. G. Howe of Boston to the Prison Association of New York in 1846. Howe said, "I believe there are many (prisoners) who might be so trained as to be left upon their parole (a promise made with or confirmed by a pledge of one's honor) during the last period of their imprisonment with safety."[2]

### Early American Parole Development

The first legislation authorizing parole in the United States was enacted in Massachusetts in 1837. However, the Elmira Reformatory in New York, opened in 1876, was the first U.S. correctional institution to implement an extensive parole program. Zebulon Brockway, the institution's first superintendent, implemented a system of upward classification. The first grade was Brockway's personal interview with the new inmate. The second grade was the prison regime that Brockway established for the prisoner: a mix of labor (in the iron foundry or factories, on the farm, or on the maintenance crew), formal schooling, mandatory religious service, and military drill. An inmate who earned three marks each for labor, education, and behavior each month for six months in the second grade was promoted to the third grade. Six months after achieving the third grade promotion, the inmate was granted a parole hearing before Brockway and five other Elmira staff members. Paroled inmates made their own living and work arrangements. Elmira employees and community volunteers provided parole supervision. Failure to comply with conditions of parole meant parole revocation and return to Elmira's second grade.[3]

By 1889, twelve states had implemented parole programs; by 1944 all 48 states had enacted parole legislation.

### Parole Development in the Early 20th Century

The 1920s and early 1930s were turbulent. During Prohibition, organized crime increased, street

*Parole: Early Release and Reintegration*

gang warfare escalated, and the media became obsessed with coverage of notorious criminals. Prison riots became all too familiar. Prisoner idleness, arbitrary rules and punishment, and failure of prison and parole to rehabilitate were recurring themes.

The Wickersham Commission, a commission on law enforcement and observance appointed by President Herbert Hoover, issued a report in 1931 that recommended that states establish a centralized policy-making board to write standards and guidelines for parole practices, advocating uniformity in state parole practices.[4] This report included a list of the "essential elements" of a good parole system:

1. Indeterminate sentence law permitting the offender to be released (conditionally) at the time when he or she is most likely to successfully make the transition back to society.
2. Provision of quality release preparation—in the institution—for the offender who is reentering the community.
3. Familiarity by the parole officer with the home and environmental conditions of the offender before he or she leaves the institution.
4. Sufficient staffing levels to ensure an adequate number of parole officers to supervise parolees.[5]

The Wickersham Commission reported that parole was logical because it was an inexpensive way to supervise offenders. Moreover, the Commission reported, the parolee earns money, whereas the prisoner cannot support him- or herself, and cannot contribute financially to his or her family. Parole advocates advised the public that more parole was the answer. By 1944, all of the states had passed enabling legislation for parole.[6]

Despite the fact that all the states had enacted parole legislation, opposition was strong. The attitude that parole boards were turning hardened criminals loose on society sparked a series of angry attacks, through national and state commissions, investigatory hearings, editorials and cartoons, press releases, and books.[7] Opponents claimed that parole had a dismal performance record, its goals were never realized, parole board members and parole officers were poorly trained, and that parole hearings were little more than hastily conducted, almost unthinking interviews.

In spite of the gap between goals and reality, parole fulfilled important functions for officials in the criminal justice system. Wardens supported parole—the possibility of parole served as an incentive, making it easier to keep peace. Wardens also used parole to control prison overcrowding by keeping the number of persons being released on parole about equal to the number of new prisoner admissions.

Legislators supported parole because it cost less than incarceration. District attorneys supported parole because they felt it helped with plea bargaining. Without parole, district attorneys argued, there was little motivation for defendants, particularly those facing long prison sentences, to plead guilty to lesser crimes. District attorneys also supported parole because parolees could be returned to prison without new trial proceedings.

Together, these groups made a claim to the public that parole actually extended state control over offenders—parolees were supervised. The public accepted the claim that parole was tough on criminals and that abolishing parole ended state control over dangerous persons.

**Parole Development in the Late 20th Century**   Opposition to parole resurfaced in the 1960s and 1970s, this time as part of a larger political debate about crime, the purposes of sanctioning, and the appropriateness of the unlimited discretion afforded various sectors of the criminal justice system (paroling authorities in particular). During this period, the debate on correctional policy addressed both the assumptions of the rehabilitative ideal and the results of indeterminate sentencing and parole.

In the 1970s, research indicated that prison rehabilitation programs had few positive benefits. Parolees were not rehabilitated as parole advocates claimed.[8] This position was supported on all sides of the political spectrum, including those who believed that prisons "coddled" dangerous criminals and those who questioned the ethics of coercing offenders into submitting to unwanted treatment as a condition of release.[9] These research findings led to many of the sentencing reforms of the 1970s and 1980s, when political rhetoric implied that parole meant a "soft" stance on crime. During a time when crime rates and recidivism were up, the public did not want prisoners released on parole.

In 1987, the American Probation and Parole Association (APPA), the nation's largest association of probation and parole professionals, voiced its support of parole and objected to efforts to abolish it. However, in that same year, six states abolished discretionary parole-board release. By the year 2000, 15 states and the federal government had abolished it. The APPA position statement on parole is presented in Exhibit 12–1.

## EXHIBIT 12–1

### American Probation and Parole Association

#### Position Statement on Parole

The mission of parole is to prepare, select, and assist offenders who, after a reasonable period of incarceration, could benefit from an early release while, at the same time, ensuring an appropriate level of public protection through conditions of parole and provision of supervision services. This is accomplished by:

- Assisting the parole authority in decision making and the enforcement of parole conditions;
- Providing pre-release and post-release services and programs that will support offenders in successfully reintegrating into the community;
- Working cooperatively with all sectors of the criminal justice system to ensure the development and attainment of mutual objectives.

# The Parole Process

**Eligibility**   An inmate's eligibility for parole is determined by the sentence received from the court, as set by law. The **parole eligibility date** is the earliest date on which an inmate might be released. State statutes usually dictate parole eligibility dates and specify what portion of a sentence an offender must serve before being considered for release. Generally, state statutes apply formulas to deduct amounts of time from sentences to determine when an inmate might be eligible for release. The state statutes vary but, in general, reduce the sentence based on the number of days the inmate serves without disciplinary problems. The parole eligibility date, then, is determined by subtracting the maximum number of good-time days that could be earned from the length of the sentence. For example, a state statute might allow one day of good-time credit for every five days of good behavior. In this instance, an inmate could be eligible for parole after serving 292 days of a one-year sentence.

Although parole eligibility is ordinarily based on time served, some states have additional requirements, such as maintaining good conduct for a specific time period preceding the parole hearing.

**parole eligibility date**
The earliest date on which an inmate might be paroled.

**Release Preparation**   Most correctional systems recognize the importance of planning for early release. A good institution encourages inmates to participate in an established release preparation program that is designed to ensure successful reintegration into the community.

Release preparation should begin at incarceration and continue through release. A well-designed release preparation program requires participation by parole officers and the institution's staff, as well as various community resources. It may include training and/or information in the following areas:

1. Release—requirements for early release, types of release, the parole hearing, conditions of release, and post-release supervision.
2. Information/Community Resources—finding and using local resources such as social service agencies.
3. Health—mental health counseling, stress management, disease prevention, AIDS awareness, holistic health, nutrition, sexuality, weight management, and physical fitness.
4. Personal Growth and Development—anger management, marriage counseling, parenting classes, drug education, decision-making skills development, speech and communication classes, and general education classes.
5. Employment—basic job readiness, job search techniques, state employment services, interview skills, keeping a job, resume writing techniques, and dressing for interviews.
6. Personal Finance/Consumer Skills—maintaining and balancing checking and savings accounts, managing money and credit, buying a car and/or home, and living on a budget.

**paroling authority**
A person or correctional agency (often called a parole board or parole commission) that has the authority to grant parole, to revoke parole, and to discharge from parole.

**Granting Parole—The Paroling Authority**   Every jurisdiction in the United States has a paroling authority. A **paroling authority** is a correctional agency (often called a parole board or parole commission) that has the authority to grant parole, set conditions of parole, supervise parolees, revoke parole, and discharge from parole.

Parole boards vary in size from 3 members (Alabama, Hawaii, Montana, North Dakota, Washington, and West Virginia) to 10 or more (Connecticut, 11; Illinois,12; Michigan, 10; New York, 19; Ohio, 11; and Texas, 18). Of the 52 jurisdictions—the 50 states, the District of Columbia, and the federal government—34 have full-time salaried parole board members and 18 do not. Minnesota's paroling authority is its Commissioner of Corrections.[10]

The paroling authority's decision to grant or deny parole is partially based on its assessment of potential risk to the community. Risk assessment factors may include: the nature and circumstance of the crime; the offender's criminal record and prison record; and input from court officials, victims, and other interested parties. Some states use scoring instruments for risk assessment—the most commonly used are based on the U.S. Parole Commission's **salient factor score (SFS)**.[11] The salient factors are: (1) number of prior convictions/adjudications, (2) number of prior commitments of more than 30 days, (3) age at current offense, (4) recent commitment-free period (three years), (5) probation/parole/confinement/escape violation at time of current offense or during present confinement, (6) heroin/opiate dependence, and (7) if an older offender. The SFS places the offender in one of four risk categories: very good, good, fair, or poor. Parole officials consider this score in deciding whether parole is to be granted and, if so, what level of supervision will be required.

Policymakers differ on which criteria are the most important, and each parole board member brings to the release decision a variety of assumptions, values, and different views on the purpose of imprisonment (rehabilitation, incapacitation, or deterrence). The information used to make the parole decision varies significantly, depending on the goal or goals of the decision-maker.[12]

State statutes also specify factors that paroling authorities must consider when making their decisions. These considerations generally include likelihood of recidivism, welfare of the community into which the inmate will be released, the inmate's prison conduct, and any treatment or rehabilitation plans developed for the inmate.

Parole plays a key role in criminal justice administration, and that puts a parole board in a powerful position. The majority of state parole boards determine the actual duration of incarceration and exercise discretionary release and revocation powers, specifying conditions of release and terms of supervision. The parole board's release policies can have a direct impact on institutional management. For example, parole boards can help reduce prison population by increasing the number of parolees.

**Granting Parole—The Hearing**   In general, parole hearings are attended by the applicant, the institutional representative, and hearing examiners or parole board members. The final decision to grant or deny parole considers both eligibility guidelines and the interview. If parole is granted, a contract that defines the release plan is executed and the inmate is given a release date. The inmate who is conditionally released to community supervision is called a **parolee**.

**salient factor score (SFS)**   Scale, developed from a risk-screening instrument, used to predict parole outcome.

**parolee**   A person who is conditionally released from prison to community supervision.

*Kenneth Wong*
*State Parole Agent*
*California Department*
*of Corrections*

*"I like being a parole agent because the job allows me to help people who got caught up in the criminal justice system and assist them with a smooth transition from prison back into society by providing a range of services. The most exciting thing about my job is I get to help parolees perform acceptably in the community and remove those who cannot."*

Kenneth Wong is a state parole agent with the California Department of Corrections. Before joining the San Francisco parole office in 1990, Ken worked three and one-half years as a correctional officer at the California State Prison at San Quentin and one and one-half years as an auto mechanic. Ken completed the automotive program at the College of Alameda and later enrolled in courses in human behavior at the University of California at Hayward.

As a parole officer, Ken works closely with police and social service agencies. He conducts anti-narcotic testing, refers parole violators to the State Board of Prison Terms, and helps parolees make a smooth transition from prison to the community. His paramount concern is community protection.

Ken's advice to persons interested in corrections is simple: "If you like working with people who've been in prison and if you have the patience to listen to their problems and make positive referrals and provide advice, then you should apply. The job is challenging and there is always something new."

In 1996, the California Probation, Parole, and Correctional Association recognized Ken Wong as Parole Agent of the Year. The Association said Wong's job performance was exemplary and he made a significant contribution to the field of corrections.

Ken plans to spend his career with the California Department of Corrections. He'd like to pursue management positions, beginning with parole unit supervisor.

---

If parole is denied, the inmate remains in prison and a date is set for the next review. The waiting period between hearings depends on the jurisdiction and the inmate's offense.

**Conditions of Parole**  Paroling authorities set specific conditions for parole, on a case-by-case basis (see Figure 12–1). Parolees must comply with these conditions, which may include restitution, substance abuse aftercare, electronic monitoring, and/or house arrest, among others.

Parole requires supervision. Parole officers, who work closely with the parolee and the paroling authority, carry out this supervision and can return parolees to prison if they threaten community safety or otherwise violate the conditions of release. Depending on the severity of the crime and the risk

## FIGURE 12–1

### Sample Order for Release on Parole

# MARYLAND PAROLE COMMISSION

No 028239

### ORDER FOR RELEASE ON PAROLE

The Parole Commission, by virtue of the authority conferred upon it by the laws of the State of Maryland, does hereby grant parole to:

(True Name) _____ Travis Glen Hardin, #273843, DOB November 24, 1950 _____
(Commitment Name/s)

who was convicted of: _____ Distribution of cocaine; Violation of probation _____

Court:     Talbot County Circuit Court #6903

Sentenced:     May 18, 1996

Term:     6 years;    2 years, 6 months

From:     March 10, 1996;    consecutive

Therefore, the said Commission does hereby order the release on parole of the said prisoner from

_____ Eastern Correctional Institution _____
(Correctional Institution or Jail)

The Parolee, upon release, shall be deemed to remain in legal custody until the expiration of the full, undiminished term and upon violation of any condition of his parole shall be remanded to the authority from which paroled, where a hearing shall be conducted by the Parole Commission. If parole is revoked, the Commission shall determine the amount of time spent on parole, if any, which shall be credited to the parolee.

This order is subject to the rules, regulation, and conditions of this parole as set forth below and on page 2 of this agreement, and such further conditions as the Commission may impose at any time during the period of parole.

Upon being released, report to the Division of Parole and Probation office located at

301 Bay Street, Suite 302, Easton, MD 21601    (410-555-1212)

MARYLAND PAROLE COMMISSION

Parole Expiration Date:    September 2004

By: _____ Patricia K. Cushwa _____
Commissioner

Special Condition(s):   substance abuse therapy,
    subject to curfew as directed by parole agent,
    community service if agent directs, employment within 30 days

March 20, 2000
Date

Home/Employment Plan: _____ live with mother – Lynn Fortney, 2055 Sokol Drive, _____
Tilghman, MD 21671   (410-822-5555)

Anyone serving a sentence for a crime committed on or after May 1, 1991, must pay supervision and/or drug testing fees as prescribed in Article 41, Section 4.519 of the Annotated Code of Maryland.

Date(s) of Offense(s): _____ January 6, 1999 _____

MPC - 14 - (Revised 8/15/96)

WHITE – Parolee • PINK – Parole Commission Copy • YELLOW – Institution Copy • BLUE – Certified Copy • GREEN – Court Copy

presented by the offender, parole supervision can incorporate several types of contact with and "examination" of the parolee, including drug testing, curfew, electronic monitoring, and employment verification.

The conditions under which parolees must live are very similar in form and structure to those for probationers. Sometimes the rules are established by law, but more often they are established by the paroling authority. The paroling authority can require any of the following forms of release: standard parole supervision, parole with enhanced treatment and programming conditions, halfway house placement, intensive supervision, parole with electronic monitoring and/or voice and location tracking, or release with follow-up drug testing and payment of supervision fees and restitution.

Parolees are technically still in state custody. They have been granted the privilege of living in the community rather than in prison. The paroling authority, therefore, has at least three responsibilities:

1. Help a parolee with employment, residence, finances, or other personal issues that often present difficulties for a person trying to readjust to life in the community.
2. Protect the community by helping parolees avoid situations that might encourage recidivism.
3. Expedite parole for those who meet the criteria established by the paroling authority and are unlikely to commit another crime.

**Types of Parole**  Release on parole may be mandatory or discretionary. **Mandatory release** requires that the correctional authority grant parole after a specific period of time, as specified by law—the inmate serves the time that is mandated by the sentence minus good-time credits. Mandatory release is generally associated with determinate sentencing or parole guidelines. **Discretionary release** is at the paroling authority's discretion, within boundaries established by the sentence and by law. Discretionary release, associated with indeterminate sentencing, requires that a paroling authority certify eligibility for release. The effective date of release may be contingent upon completion of a satisfactory plan for parole supervision.

**mandatory release**
Early release after a  time period specified by law.

**discretionary release**
Early release based on the paroling authority's assessment of eligibility.

# Characteristics of Parolees

According to the U.S. Department of Justice, 704,964 American adults were on parole on January 1, 1999—an increase of 1.5 percent over January 1, 1998.[13] Ninety-one percent of those adults were state parolees; the rest were federal. The typical adult parolee was a white, non-Hispanic male, on mandatory parole, and under active parole supervision. Women made up 12 percent of the parole population. The region with the highest number of parolees was the South, followed by the Northeast, West, and Midwest (see Figure 12–2, on page 357).

Not all who are sent to prison are released on parole. Those who are the most serious offenders (those who have life sentences or are facing the death penalty) or have disciplinary problems while incarcerated generally are not paroled. Instead, they live out their lives in prison or are released when they have served their entire sentences.

**FIGURE 12–2**

### Selected Characteristics of Adults on Parole

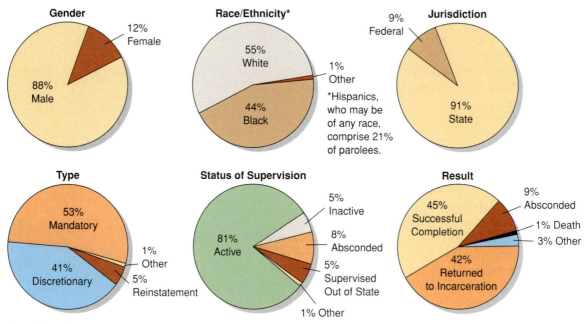

*Source:* Thomas P. Bonczar and Lauren E. Glaze, *Probation and Parole in the United States, 1998* (Washington: Bureau of Justice Statistics), August 1999, revised 10/13/99.

## Trends in the Parole Population

The estimated number of adults under community supervision and incarceration from 1990 through 1998 is shown in Table 12–1. As you can see, except for 1995, the parole population has continually increased.

**TABLE 12–1**

### Adults on Probation, in Jail or Prison, and on Parole, 1990–1998

| | Total Estimated Correctional Population | Probation | Jail | Prison | Parole |
|---|---|---|---|---|---|
| 1990 | 4,348,000 | 2,670,234 | 403,019 | 743,382 | 531,407 |
| 1991 | 4,535,600 | 2,728,472 | 424,129 | 792,535 | 590,442 |
| 1992 | 4,762,600 | 2,811,611 | 441,781 | 850,566 | 658,601 |
| 1993 | 4,944,000 | 2,903,061 | 455,500 | 909,381 | 676,100 |
| 1994 | 5,141,300 | 2,981,022 | 479,800 | 990,147 | 690,371 |
| 1995 | 5,335,100 | 3,077,861 | 499,300 | 1,078,542 | 679,421 |
| 1996 | 5,475,000 | 3,161,996 | 510,400 | 1,127,528 | 679,733 |
| 1997 | 5,726,200 | 3,296,513 | 557,974 | 1,176,922 | 694,787 |
| 1998 | 5,890,300 | 3,417,613 | 584,372 | 1,232,900 | 704,964 |

*Sources: Sourcebook of Criminal Justice Statistics 1998 Online,* Bureau of Justice Statistics (October 1999), p. 462; Thomas P. Bonczar and Lauren E. Glaze, *Probation and Parole in the United States, 1998,* Bureau of Justice Statistics (August 1999), p. 1.

Table 12–2 defines parole populations among the states in 1998. Texas had the largest number of adults on parole, followed by California and Pennsylvania. Pennsylvania also had the highest rate of parole supervision (910 parolees supervised per 100,000 adult residents), which means it used parole more than any other state per capita residents; Maine used parole the least per capita residents (7 per 100,000 adult residents).

**TABLE 12–2**

### Selected Parole Populations Among the States, 1998

| 10 States with the largest parole populations | Number supervised | 10 States with the highest rates of supervision | Persons supervised per 100,000 adult U.S. residents | 10 States with the lowest rates of supervision | Persons supervised per 100,000 adult U.S. residents |
|---|---|---|---|---|---|
| Texas | 112,022 | Pennsylvania | 910 | Maine | 7 |
| California | 110,617 | Texas | 793 | Washington | 9 |
| Pennsylvania | 83,168 | Oregon | 703 | North Dakota | 37 |
| New York | 59,548 | Louisiana | 590 | Connecticut | 48 |
| Illinois | 30,432 | California | 466 | Nebraska | 51 |
| Georgia | 20,482 | New York | 436 | Oklahoma | 62 |
| Louisiana | 18,759 | Maryland | 404 | Rhode Island | 62 |
| Oregon | 17,270 | Georgia | 364 | Florida | 65 |
| Maryland | 15,528 | Illinois | 344 | West Virginia | 69 |
| Michigan | 15,331 | Arkansas | 338 | Mississippi | 75 |

*Source:* Adapted from Thomas P. Bonczar and Lauren E. Glaze, *Probation and Parole in the United States, 1998,* Bureau of Justice Statistics (August 1999), p. 2.

# Parole Revocation

Parole may be revoked for two reasons. A **technical violation** occurs when any of the technical conditions of parole (e.g., find and keep a job, live at home, sign no contracts, pay restitution and fees, perform community service, attend drug and alcohol abuse counseling) are violated. Alaska's standard conditions of parole are presented in Figure 12–3 on page 358. The second type of violation is a **new offense violation**. This involves arrest for the commission of a new crime. A new offense violation might involve a technical violation. For example, an arrest for selling drugs and a positive test for drug use would be a violation for a new offense and a technical violation. When a violation occurs, a revocation hearing date is set. The purpose of a **revocation hearing** is to determine whether the violation warrants the parolee's removal from the community. During a revocation hearing, the parolee has certain rights of due process because he or she could lose conditional freedom; but he or she is not entitled to a full adversary

**technical violation**
Failure to comply with conditions of parole (e.g., nonreporting).

**new offense violation**
Arrest and prosecution for the commission of a new crime by a parolee.

**revocation hearing**
Administrative review to determine whether a violation of the conditions of parole warrants return to prison.

**FIGURE 12–3**

Sample State Conditions of Parole

# STATE OF ALASKA

## STANDARD CONDITIONS OF PAROLE

The following standard conditions of parole apply to all prisoners released on mandatory or discretionary parole, in accordance with AS 33.16.150(a).

1. REPORT UPON RELEASE: I will report in person no later than the next working day after my release to the parole officer located at the PAROLE OFFICE and receive further reporting instructions. I will reside at _____ .

2. MAINTAIN EMPLOYMENT/TRAINING/TREATMENT: I will make a diligent effort to maintain steady employment and support my legal dependents. I will not voluntarily change or terminate employment without receiving permission from my parole officer to do so. If discharged or if employment is terminated (temporarily or permanently) for any reason, I will notify my parole officer the next working day. If I am involved in an education, training, or treatment program, I will continue active participation in the program unless I receive permission from my parole officer to quit. If I am released, removed, or terminated from the program for any reason, I will notify my parole officer the next working day.

3. REPORT MONTHLY: I will report to my parole officer at least monthly in the manner prescribed by my parole officer. I will follow any other reporting instructions established by my parole officer.

4. OBEY LAWS/ORDERS: I will obey all state, federal, and local laws, ordinances, orders, and court orders.

5. PERMISSION BEFORE CHANGING RESIDENCE: I will obtain permission from my parole officer before changing my residence. Remaining away from my approved residence for 24 hours or more constitutes a change in residence for the purpose of this condition.

6. TRAVEL PERMIT BEFORE TRAVEL OUTSIDE ALASKA: I will obtain the prior written permission of my parole officer in the form of an interstate travel agreement before leaving the state of Alaska. Failure to abide by the conditions of the travel agreement is a violation of my order of parole.

*Source:* State of Alaska Board of Parole, *Parole Handbook, Appendix II; Conditions of Parole,* June 1998.

**FIGURE 12–3 (continued)**

Sample State Conditions of Parole

7. NO FIREARMS/WEAPONS: I will not own, possess, have in my custody, handle, purchase, or transport any firearm, ammunition, or explosives. I may not carry any deadly weapon on my person except a pocket knife with a 3" or shorter blade. Carrying any other weapon on my person such as a hunting knife, axe, club, etc. is a violation of my order of parole. I will contact the Alaska Board of Parole if I have any questions about the use of firearms, ammunition, or weapons.

8. NO DRUGS: I will not use, possess, handle, purchase, give, or administer any narcotic, hallucinogenic, (including marijuana/THC), stimulant, depressant, amphetamine, barbiturate, or prescription drug not specifically prescribed by a licensed medical person.

9. REPORT POLICE CONTACT: I will report to my parole officer, no later than the next working day, any contact with a law enforcement officer.

10. DO NOT WORK AS AN INFORMANT: I will not enter into any agreement or other arrangement with any law enforcement agency which will place me in the position of violating any law or any condition of my parole. I understand the Department of Corrections and Parole Board policy prohibits me from working as an informant.

11. NO CONTACT WITH PRISONERS OR FELONS: I may not telephone, correspond with, or visit any person confined in a prison, penitentiary, correctional institution or camp, jail, halfway house, work release center, community residential center, restitution center, juvenile correctional center, etc. Contact with a felon during the course of employment or during corrections-related treatment is not prohibited if approved by my parole officer. Any other knowing contact with a felon is prohibited unless approved by my parole officer. I will notify my parole officer the next working day if I have contact with a prisoner or felon.

12. CANNOT LEAVE AREA: I will receive permission from my parole officer before leaving the area of the state to which my case is assigned. My parole officer will advise me in writing of limits of the area to which I have been assigned.

13. OBEY ALL ORDERS/SPECIAL CONDITIONS: I will obey any special instructions, rules, or order given to me by the Alaska Board of Parole or by my parole officer. I will follow any special conditions imposed by the Alaska Board of Parole or my parole officer.

*Source:* State of Alaska Board of Parole, *Parole Handbook, Appendix II; Conditions of Parole,* June 1998.

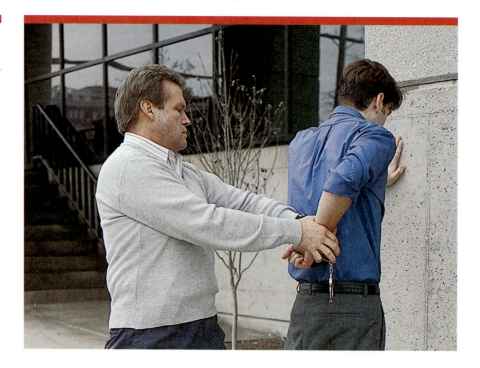

hearing, as would be the case in a new criminal proceeding. If the parolee violates his or her conditions of parole, a revocation hearing could return the offender to prison to serve the remainder of the original sentence, plus any new sentence that might be given because of new violations.[14]

The primary difference between a criminal trial and a revocation hearing is the threshold of evidence that the hearing body needs to convict. In a criminal trial, a conviction may be obtained only if the government proves its facts beyond a reasonable doubt. In a revocation hearing, the panel need only find that a violation is shown by a preponderance of the evidence.[15] In addition, there is a more relaxed rule of what constitutes evidence—a rule that permits letters, affidavits, and reports to be presented in lieu of direct testimony.

# Issues in Parole

Over the past few decades, the face of parole has changed. We conclude this chapter with a discussion of several innovative programs in parole, court rulings that have changed the parole revocation process, and the future of parole.

## Reentry Courts

**reentry court** A court that manages the return to the community of individuals released from prison.

The latest innovation in helping offenders released from prison make a successful adjustment to the community is reentry courts. A **reentry court** manages the return to the community of individuals released from prison, using the authority of the court to apply graduated sanctions and positive reinforcement and to marshal resources to support the prisoner's reintegration. The U.S. Attorney General has proposed that reentry courts operate like drug courts or other problem-solving courts (domestic violence court, community court, family court, gun court, and DWI court).[16] In drug court, for example, a judge is limited to managing a caseload of drug-involved offenders. The judge requires the offender to make regular court appearances and participate in drug treatment and testing. If the drug offender violates the conditions of release, the judge administers a predetermined range of graduated sanctions that do not automatically require return to prison (except for new crimes or egregious violations). The frequent appearances before the court with the offer of assistance, coupled with the knowledge of a predetermined range of sanctions for violations of the conditions of release, assist the offender in getting back on track. Research on drug courts is still new, but already studies show that recidivism among all drug court participants has ranged between 5 and 28 percent and less than 4 percent for program graduates.[17]

The U.S. Department of Justice proposes that a reentry court have six core elements:

**Parole Caseworker**
Helps develop the parole division's day resource centers, which are highly structured, treatment-directed programs providing traditional parole supervision and reporting, employment counseling, and basic adult education. Required qualifications: U.S. citizen, at least 18 years of age, and a bachelor's degree from an accredited college or university. May not be on probation for any criminal offense, have pending charges for any criminal offense, have an outstanding warrant, or conviction for family violence. Mandatory drug testing.

- **Assessment and Planning** Correctional administrators and the reentry judge meet with inmates who are near release to explain the reentry process, assess inmates' needs, and begin building links to a range of social services, family counseling, health and mental health services, housing, job training, and work opportunities that support reintegration.
- **Active Judicial Oversight** The reentry court sees all prisoners released into the community with a high degree of frequency, maybe once or twice a month. Also involved are the parole officer and others responsible for assessing the parolee's progress. In court, offender progress is praised, and offender setbacks are discussed.
- **Case Management of Support Services** The reentry court acts as a service broker and advocates on behalf of parolees for substance abuse treatment, job training, private employment, faith instruction, family member support, housing, and community services.
- **Accountability to the Community** Reentry courts appoint broad-based community advisory boards to develop and maintain accountability to the community. Advisory boards also help courts negotiate the sometimes difficult task of brokering services for parolees and advocating on their behalf.
- **Graduated Sanctions** Reentry courts establish a predetermined range of graduated sanctions for violations of the conditions of release that do not automatically require return to prison.
- **Rewarding Success** Reentry courts incorporate positive judicial reinforcement actions after goals are achieved. Examples include negotiating early release from parole or conducting graduation ceremonies similar to those used in drug courts.

# THE STAFF SPEAKS

I work in a city of 80,000, which currently has no supervised accommodations for parolees who have been serving sentences of two years or more in a federal facility. Currently, there are 30–40 such individuals in unsupervised conditions. There are also many more who are assigned to halfway houses in nearby communities, making life unnecessarily difficult on some of these individuals.

We are trying to bring a 12-bed facility into the community. We are facing strenuous resistance, including death threats—ironic, isn't it—of both the NIMBY (not in my back yard) and the NOPE (not on planet earth) variety. Some of the resistance, I'm sure, is based on fear that we are bringing criminals into the community. One obvious answer is that many of these individuals came from the community in the first place.

One really hard question to answer is whether the local property values will be negatively affected. That's a realistic concern for everyone. Yet, the most recent material that I have been able to find is from the early 1980s. It suggests that there is no clear effect on property values, and that most people on a street are unaware that such accommodations are there, once they have been there a while. Of course, if these former offenders are released into the community without any preparation or socialization, they won't have a chance, let alone a halfway chance, of following the rules and becoming a positive contributor to the very community that denies them.

*Linda Deutschmann*
*Halfway House Worker*
*Brookhaven, KS*

According to the U.S. Department of Justice, "The successful completion of parole should be seen as an important life event for an offender, and the court can help acknowledge that accomplishment. Courts provide powerful public forums for encouraging positive behavior and for acknowledging the individual effort in achieving reentry goals."[18]

Reentry court is still a concept, not a reality. The U.S. Department of Justice is promoting the idea and asking communities to experiment with it, depending upon statutory framework, caseload considerations, administrative flexibility, levels of collaboration among the judiciary, corrections, parole, police, business community, religious institutions, community organizations, and the like. Whichever form a reentry court takes, developing new ways that communities can manage and support offenders after release from prison with assistance in securing employment, housing, substance abuse treatment, family counseling, and other services, is essential to our ability to reduce crime and keep communities safe.

# Reintegration of Offenders

The institution where the offender is incarcerated and the paroling authority play a large part in the parolee's return to society. An important part of reintegration into society is the opportunity to earn a living. Institution and parole personnel must actively seek opportunities to further parolees' chances of securing employment.

Texas' Project RIO (Re-Integration of Offenders) is one of the most ambitious state programs for parolee job placement in the United States. From its beginnings in 1985, RIO has grown to more than 100 staff members, serving 92 Texas cities and towns, and provides job placement services to nearly 16,000 parolees each year. To date, over 12,000 companies throughout Texas have hired RIO participants.[19]

Project RIO involves close collaboration between the Texas Workforce Commission and two divisions of the Texas Department of Criminal Justice—Institutional Division (prisons) and the Parole Division. Project RIO's principal presence in prisons is through the Windham School District, which is a school operating within the state's prisons. The Windham/Project RIO team provides inmates with the following services:

- **Assessment and Testing** A Project RIO assessment specialist evaluates each participant's skills and work history and devises an employability development plan that reflects availability of jobs and occupational demands in the community where the inmate will be released.
- **Documentation** Assessment specialists gather birth certificates, social security cards, diplomas, and school records to provide documentation for employment applications.

# THE OFFENDER SPEAKS

I got out of prison April 22, 1996, after being locked up for 10 years for robbing a bank at gunpoint. For three weeks, I just hung out, reacclimating to society. I got restless the fourth week and tried to get a job, but nobody called me back. My parole officer kept asking me, "Have you gone to RIO yet?" I thought the program would get me only menial jobs, like heavy cleanup work, but finally I went just to appease my parole officer. After I completed RIO's five-day job preparation course I got the first job I interviewed at, a sales agent at a hotel.

*Project RIO Participant*

- **Job Readiness Training** A specialist meets with every RIO enrollee who is within 2 years of release every 90 days to hone the inmate's job interviewing skills.
- **Employability and Life Skills Projects** Inmates work at their own pace to complete a series of skill-building projects under a specialist's supervision.
- **Changes Program** The Windham School offers a life-skills program to RIO participants who are within 6 months of release; the course includes self-concept, family relationships, civic and legal responsibilities, victim awareness, personal health and hygiene, and job preparation.

As you can see, Project RIO works with offenders while they are still in prison, helping them develop the skills and attitudes they need to find and keep a job and giving them a head start in their search for employment. Evaluations of Project RIO have come from several sources and focus on a number of important questions for policymakers, legislators, and the general public. Project RIO has a high placement rate (almost 75%) of participants. Also, Project RIO participants are much more likely to get jobs than ex-offenders who do not participate in the program. Participation in RIO while in prison is a statistically significant predictor of post-release employment. Minority offenders do especially well in RIO: 66 percent of black participants and 66 percent of Hispanic participants found employment, compared with only 30 percent of blacks and 36 percent of Hispanics who were not enrolled in the program. Does Project RIO prevent recidivism? According to a Texas A&M study, the answer is yes. Ex-offenders who found jobs through RIO had lower recidivism rates than unemployed ex-offenders who did not enroll in RIO, with demographic factors and reoffending risk taken into account. These findings suggest that employment and participation in Project RIO have been of greatest benefit to ex-offenders whom prison and parole personnel consider most likely to reoffend.

Can other states duplicate RIO's success? Although other states may not have the same circumstances as Texas, they can implement a Project RIO-type program. Georgia is using aspects of the Project RIO model; local employment security offices and staff provide job placement services for ex-offenders. The state of Washington uses a different model; the state contracts with local community-based organizations throughout the state to provide integration services to offenders.

## Legal Decisions Affecting Parole

As we saw in Chapter 10, numerous challenges to the correctional system have brought about changes in prisoners' rights. You may recall that due process guarantees that a person has a right to be fairly heard before being deprived of liberty. Three of the most widely cited cases affecting parolees' and probationers' rights are *Morrissey* v. *Brewer* (1972), *Gagnon* v. *Scarpelli* (1973), and *Greenholtz* v. *Inmates of the Nebraska Penal and Correctional Complex* (1979).

In *Morrissey* v. *Brewer*, John Morrissey pled guilty to writing bad checks in 1967. He was sentenced to not more than 7 years of confinement in the Iowa State Prison and paroled in June 1968. Seven months later he was arrested for parole violation and incarcerated in the county jail. One week later, at the direction of the parole officer's written report, the Iowa Board of Parole revoked his parole and he was returned to the penitentiary.

Morrissey's complaint stated that he received no counsel and no hearing prior to parole revocation. The Supreme Court agreed and overturned the Iowa parole board's decision. The Court ruled that due process establishes a parolee's right to a preliminary and a final hearing before parole can be revoked. According to the Court, a preliminary hearing must be held at the time of arrest and detention to determine whether there is probable cause to believe that the parolee has violated the conditions of supervision. If probable cause is established, "a more comprehensive hearing prior to making of the final revocation decision" determines guilt or innocence and extends to the parolee certain minimum due process rights: written notification of the alleged violation, disclosure of evidence, opportunity for a hearing to present witnesses and evidence, the right to confront and cross-examine adverse witnesses, a neutral hearing body, and a written statement by the hearing authority as to the evidence relied upon and the reasons for revocation.[20]

*Morrissey* did not extend to parolees the right to legal representation in parole revocation hearings. This issue was addressed one year later, in *Gagnon* v. *Scarpelli*.

In a Wisconsin court in July 1965, Gerald Scarpelli pled guilty to a robbery charge. He was sentenced to 15 years; the judge suspended the sentence and placed him on probation for 7 years. One month later, Scarpelli was arrested and charged with burglary. His probation was revoked. He was sent to the Wisconsin state reformatory to serve a 15-year prison term and was paroled after 3 years. Before he was paroled, however, Scarpelli filed a *habeas corpus* petition. He alleged that his right to due process had been denied—he had no access to counsel and no hearing prior to probation rev-

Daniel Savasta, a U.S. probation officer, demonstrates an alcohol breath analyzer. The technology uses voice verification and allows probation/parole officers to monitor an offender's alcohol use from his or her home. Testing can be scheduled at regular intervals, randomly, or on demand. Voice verification technology reduces the likelihood of an imposter taking the test. What are the advantages of such technology in supervising parolees?

**Parole Officer**

Supervises offenders pursuant to agency policies and procedures. Provides counseling, work referrals, and services related to offender's risk and needs. Works with Common Pleas Court judges, prosecutors, and other law enforcement personnel. Conducts investigations and writes reports. Makes arrests and transports violators. Testifies at violation hearings. Qualifications: Bachelor's degree in criminal justice, law enforcement, or social service; no legal prohibition against carrying firearms; successful project managerial skills.

ocation. The Court ruled in favor of Scarpelli. It applied the fundamental due process and two-stage hearing requirements that it had laid out one year earlier in *Morrissey*, thus equating probation with parole. In *Gagnon*, the Court ruled that state officials may be required to assign counsel at the hearing under "special circumstances" and that decisions should be made on a case-by-case basis, depending on the offender's competence, case complexity, and mitigating evidence.

In *Greenholtz* v. *Inmates of the Nebraska Penal and Correctional Complex* (1979), a case involving a routine parole board hearing, the U.S. Supreme Court ruled that parole is a privilege—the full complement of due process rights need not be afforded at parole hearings. The Court also said that the parole board is not required to specify the evidence used in deciding to deny parole. As a result of this case, states are deciding what inmate privileges are appropriate at parole hearings.

# The Future of Parole

We read earlier in this chapter that there was strong opposition to parole in the 1930s and that opponents wanted to abolish it. They argued that parole boards were turning hardened criminals loose on society, that parole had a dismal performance record, its goals were never realized, parole board members and parole officers were poorly trained, and that parole hearings were little more than hastily conducted, almost unthinking interviews. In spite of the gap between goals and this 1930s reality, parole fulfilled important functions for wardens, legislators, and district attorneys. Parole continued.

The movement to abolish parole resurfaced in the 1970s, when the concept of "just deserts"—the idea that offenders deserve punishment for what they did to society—was being discussed.[21] However, states did not do away with parole; they restructured parole. In a number of states, discretionary release was replaced with mandatory release, with or without supervision, after a certain amount of time served. As the data in Table 12–3 show, discretionary release has been on the decline for some time.

The backdrop for the debate on just deserts was an extraordinary increase in the nation's crime rate that began in the mid-1960s and continued through the 1970s. Legislatures were growing anxious about crime and were willing to try new options in correctional approaches to the crime problem. They felt that rehabilitation and indeterminate sentencing were not working. Hence, their answer was determinate sentencing and abolition of discretionary release.

Why did some states abolish discretionary parole? There are at least four reasons. First, scholars concluded that indeterminate sentencing and discretionary parole did not achieve offender rehabilitation and that was unfair, since it was based solely on parole board judgment, without explicit standards of fairness and equity in sentencing.

TABLE 12–3

## Post-release Practices in States That Have Abolished Parole

| State | Year Discretionary Parole Was Abolished | Post-release Supervision Available After Abolishment of Discretionary Release by Parole Board |
|---|---|---|
| Arizona | 1994 | Community supervision |
| Delaware | 1990 | Administrative supervision, field supervision, intensive supervision, electronic monitoring, and halfway houses |
| Florida | 1983 | Conditional release and controlled release |
| Illinois | 1978 | Mandatory supervised release |
| Maine | 1976 | Probation term can be imposed by the court after prison term is completed |
| Minnesota | 1982 | Supervised release |
| Mississippi | 1995 | Earned release supervision |
| North Carolina | 1994 | Post-release supervision for most serious offenses |
| Ohio | 1996 | Judicial release, shock incarceration, and furlough with judicial approval |
| Oregon | 1989 | Community supervision |
| Virginia | 1995 | Probation term can be imposed by the court after prison term is completed |
| Washington | 1984 | Community custody and community supervision |

Additional jurisdictions that abolished discretionary release include California, Indiana, New Mexico, and the federal government.

*Source: 1996 National Survey of State Sentencing Structures*, Bureau of Justice Assistance (September 1998), p. 15.

Second, eliminating discretionary parole appeared to be tough on crime.

Third, parole boards' lack of openness in the decision-making process—making all their parole decisions on a case-by-case basis without benefit of a written set of policies and procedures—prompted criticism.

Finally, state politicians were able to convince the public that parole was the cause of the rising crime problem and abolition was the solution.

## SUMMARY BY CHAPTER OBJECTIVES

### CHAPTER OBJECTIVE 1

Early English judges spared the lives of condemned felons by exiling them to America as indentured servants. Captain Alexander Maconochie, superintendent of the British penal colony on Norfolk Island, devised a "ticket of leave" system that moved inmates through stages. Sir Walter Crofton used some of Maconochie's ideas for his early release system in Ireland. In the United States, Zebulon Brockway implemented a system of upward classification.

### CHAPTER OBJECTIVE 2

Paroling authorities have powerful roles in the criminal justice system. They determine the length of incarceration for many offenders and can revoke parole. The paroling authority's policies have a direct impact on an institution's population. Paroling authorities use state laws and information from courts and other criminal justice agencies to make release decisions.

### CHAPTER OBJECTIVE 3

Parole is serving part of a sentence under supervision in the community following a period of incarceration. The parole process of release begins in the courtroom when the judge sentences an offender to either a determinate or indeterminate sentence. After serving a certain portion of his or her sentence, an offender is eligible for parole release. That portion varies from state to state. If an inmate does maintain good conduct for a certain amount of time preceding the parole hearing and is granted parole, he or she must live in accordance with specified rules and regulations in the community. If a parolee violates either the technical conditions of parole or commits a new crime, he or she may have parole revoked. For the past few decades, the parole decision-making process has become standardized in most states through the use of parole guidelines. Guidelines ensure that each parole decision is based on limited factors that are considered important to the parole decision.

### CHAPTER OBJECTIVE 4

The majority of the American parole population consists of state parolees in the South. Nine out of ten are male. More than half are white. The parole sector of the correctional population has the highest growth rate. Texas has the largest number of persons on parole. Pennsylvania has the highest rate of parole supervision.

### CHAPTER OBJECTIVE 5

Parole may be revoked for a technical violation (failure to comply with one of the conditions of parole) or for a new offense violation (commission of a crime).

### CHAPTER OBJECTIVE 6

The reentry court concept, designed to manage parolee return to the community, requires that the parolee make regular court appearances for progress assessment.

### CHAPTER OBJECTIVE 7

Three important U.S. Supreme Court decisions significantly affected parole. In *Morrissey* v. *Brewer* (1972), the U.S. Supreme Court said that parole, once granted, becomes a right and that parolees are to have certain due process rights in any revocation hearing. In *Gagnon* v. *Scarpelli* (1973), the U.S. Supreme Court held that a probationer has a limited right to counsel in a revocation hearing and that the hearing body must decide whether counsel should be provided on a case-by-case basis. In *Greenholtz* v. *Inmates of the Nebraska Penal and Correctional Complex* (1979), the U.S. Supreme Court ruled that parole is a privilege; therefore, the full complement of due process rights need not be afforded at parole hearings. As a result, states are deciding what inmate privileges are appropriate at parole hearings.

## CHAPTER OBJECTIVE 8

Between 1976 and February 1996, 15 states and the federal government abolished or restricted parole. Many states added statutes that require mandatory minimum sentences and a mandatory incarceration period for each crime.

## KEY TERMS

parole, p. 347
probation, p. 347
pardon, p. 347
parole eligibility date, p. 351
paroling authority, p. 351
salient factor score (SFS), p. 352
parolee, p. 352

mandatory release, p. 355
discretionary release, p. 355
technical violation, p. 357
new offense violation, p. 357
revocation hearing, p. 357
reentry court, p. 360

## QUESTIONS FOR REVIEW

1. What are the similarities among indenture and parole?
2. Who were Captain Alexander Maconochie and Sir Walter Crofton, and what were their contributions to the parole development?
3. What did the Elmira Reformatory contribute to the history of American parole?
4. What is parole?
5. What is the difference between parole and probation? Between parole and pardon?
6. What is parole eligibility?
7. What is the paroling authority's role in the parole decision-making process?
8. How does parole affect the criminal justice system?
9. What are conditions of parole?
10. Explain the difference between mandatory release and discretionary release.
11. What is a revocation hearing and when is it used?
12. What are the typical parolee's characteristics?
13. Which state has the largest parole population? The highest rate of parole supervision? The lowest?
14 What are reentry courts?
15. What is Project RIO? What results has it achieved?
16. What are three U.S. Supreme Court decisions that affected parole?
17. Why did some states and the federal government abolish or limit discretionary release?

## CRITICAL THINKING EXERCISES

### ON-THE-JOB ISSUE

You have just learned that one of your parolees tested positive in a drug test. The positive drug test, a technical violation of parole, requires a revocation hearing. You have long wished that your state had a set of informal guidelines for responding to such technical violations so that you could handle the violation without waiting for a hearing. In this case, you could immediately place the parolee in a substance abuse program rather than waiting for a decision that might have the same result. Draft a proposal for such a technical violation response policy. First, formulate the basic expectations of the policy (for example, "The least restrictive response to the behavior should be used."). Then determine what components the policy should include (for example, "Define clear goals and understand the agency's concept of supervision.").

### CORRECTIONS ISSUE

1. Paroling authorities generally maintain a low profile, and their work is often known only to the offenders seeking release and the victims of their crimes. This is changing as the public demands to know more about paroling authorities' actions. In some states, legislatures and sentencing commissions replaced

the case-by-case decision-making process with a policy-driven decision-making process. A policy-driven decision-making process implements a written set of policies and procedures in the parole decision-making process. Such a process standardizes the procedure and the information used to make a paroling decision. What are the advantages and disadvantages of a policy-driven decision-making process?

2. In *The Prison Reform Movement* (1990), Larry E. Sullivan suggests that prison reforms have always failed because they never addressed the "carceral problem." That is, is it possible to instill free society values in a caged population? What do you think about Sullivan's premise in terms of preparing prisoners for early release?

## CORRECTIONS ON THE WEB

 The United States Parole Commission maintains a Web site at **http://www.usdoj.gov/uspc/ overview.htm.** It describes the Commission's mission, organization, jurisdiction, and procedures. It gives background information on all the commissioners and lists federal conditions of parole and mandatory release supervi-

sion. It also presents the 54 most frequently asked questions (FAQs) and answers about federal parole procedures. Visit the site and look at the FAQs. Compare federal parole procedures with your state's by asking a member of your state's paroling authority similar questions. Compare and contrast the differences.

## ADDITIONAL READINGS

Abadinsky, Howard. *Probation and Parole: Theory and Practice,* 2d ed. Englewood Cliffs, NJ: Prentice-Hall, 1982.

Burke, Peggy B. *Abolishing Parole: Why the Emperor Has No Clothes.* Lexington, KY: American Probation and Parole Association, 1995.

Hoffman, Peter B. "History of the Federal Parole System, Part I (1910–1972)." *Federal Probation,* Vol.

61, NCJ 172978, September 1997, pp. 23–31, and "History of the Federal Parole System, Part II (1973–1997)," *Federal Probation,* Vol. 61, December 1997, pp. 49–57.

McGarry, Peggy. *Handbook for New Parole Board Members,* Philadelphia: Center for Effective Public Policy, NCJ 124111, 1989.

## ENDNOTES

1. Charles L. Newman, *Sourcebook on Probation, Parole and Pardons,* 3d ed. (Springfield, IL: Charles C. Thomas Publisher Ltd., 1968), 1970, pp. 30–31.

2. Philip Klein, *Prison Methods in New York State* (New York: Columbia University Press), 1920, p. 417. Cited in U.S. Department of Justice, *Attorney General's Survey of Release Procedures, Vol. 4* (Washington: U.S. Government Printing Office), 1939–1940, p. 5.

3. M. W. Calahan, *Historical Corrections Statistics in the United States, 1850–1984* (Washington: Bureau of Justice Statistics), 1986.

4. G. W. Wickersham, *Reports of the United States National Commission on Law Observance and Enforcement: Wickersham Commission, Report on Penal Institutions, Probation and Parole* (Washington: U.S. Government Printing Office), 1930–1931, p. 324.

5. Ibid., p. 325.

6. Edwin H. Sutherland and Donald R. Cressey, *Principles of Criminology* (Chicago: J. B. Lippincott), 1955, p. 568.

7. David J. Rothman, *Conscience and Convenience: The Asylum and Its Alternatives in Progressive America* (Boston: Little, Brown), 1980, pp. 159–161.

8. Douglas R. Lipton, Robert Martinson, and Judith Wilks, *The Effectiveness of Correctional Treatment: A Survey of Treatment Evaluation Studies* (New York: Praeger), 1975.

9. Peggy McGarry, *Handbook for New Parole Board Members* (Philadelphia: Center for Effective Public Policy), NCJ 124111, 1989, p. 4.

10. Camille Graham Camp and George M. Camp, *The Corrections Yearbook 1997* (Middletown, CT: Criminal Justice Institute), 1997, p. 181.

11. Peter B. Hoffman and Lucille K. DeGostin, "Parole Decision-Making: Structuring Discretion," *Federal Probation*, Vol. 38, Issue 4, 1974, NCJ 19232, pp. 24–28.

12. McGarry, op. cit., p. 4.

13. Thomas P. Bonczar and Lauren E. Glaze, Bureau of Justice Statistics, *Probation and Parole in the United States, 1998* (Washington: U.S. Department of Justice), NCJ 178234, October 1999.

14. Peggy B. Burke, *Abolishing Parole: Why the Emperor Has No Clothes* (Lexington, KY: American Probation and Parole Association), 1995.

15. U.S. Parole Commission, *Notes and Procedures Manual* (Chevy Chase, MD: U.S. Government Printing Office), 1989, p. 143.

16. "Reentry Courts: Managing the Transition from Prison to Community" (Washington: Office of Justice Programs), September, 1999.

17. Ibid., p. 5.

18. Ibid., p. 9.

19. Material for this section was extracted from Peter Finn, *Texas' Project RIO (Re-Integration of Offenders)*, (Washington: National Institute of Justice), June 1998 [Online at http://www.ncjrs.org/txtfiles/168637.txt].

20. Edward J. Latessa and Harry E. Allen, *Corrections in the Community*, 2d ed. (Cincinnati, OH: Anderson Publishing Co.), 1999, p. 221.

21. Andrew von Hirsch, *Doing Justice: The Choice of Punishments, Report of the Committee for the Study of Incarceration* (New York: Hill and Wang), 1976.

22. Bureau of Justice Assistance, 1996 National Survey of State Sentencing Structures (Washington: U.S. Department of Justice), NCJ 169270, September 1998 [Online at http://www.ncjrs.org/txtfiles/169270.txt].

# Privatizing Corrections

## Privatization

In 1998 the California Senate's Public Safety Committee killed a bill that would have stopped the growth of private prisons in that state.[1] The bill, which called for an amendment to the state constitution, had the backing of the California Correctional Peace Officers Association (CCPOA), the state's correctional officers' union. Had the bill passed, it would have forbidden most privatization in state and local law enforcement, correctional, and firefighting agencies throughout the state of California. In rejecting the measure by a 5–2 vote, the committee kept alive state Department of Corrections proposals to add 5000 for-profit beds to the system before the year 2000.

At about the same time, Ohio lawmakers were mulling the idea of closing a private prison near Youngstown.[2] Six prisoners had escaped in July 1998 from the Northeast Ohio Correctional Center, run by Corrections Corporation of America (CCA). The 1500-bed facility had been open only since May 1997. Other problems plagued the CCA prison as well. In the 15 months after it opened, 13 stabbings and 2 murders were reported there. An inmate lawsuit in federal court alleged unfit conditions at the facility, and a federal judge had ordered hundreds of inmates removed and had halted transfers into the prison from Washington, D.C.[3]

As these two state examples illustrate, the privatization of jails, prisons, and other correctional programs is and will continue to be controversial. **Privatization**—a term that refers to privately-owned correctional facilities or private operation of government-owned facilities—has increased dramatically as local, state, and federal government agencies have sought ways to cut costs while still meeting their mandated responsibilities. Expected savings and speedy implementation are the most common reasons for privatization.

## Opportunities for Growth

Almost 2 million people are incarcerated in the United States, and the inmate population is growing at about 5 to 7 percent per year. Experts estimate that two 1000-bed facilities must be built each week just to keep up with demand. Contracts with private prison firms cover less than 5 percent of the inmate population, but that percentage is increasing. In April 2000, private corrections in the United States included 158 facilities with a rated capacity of 122,871 inmates. The capacity of pri-

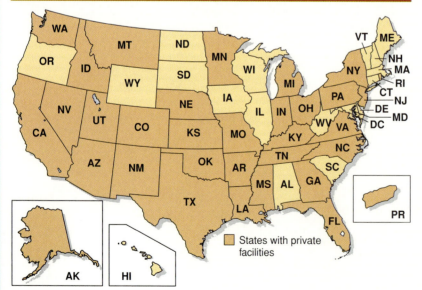

**States With Private Correctional Facilities**

States with private facilities

*Over 65 percent of the states have private correctional facilities.*

vate prisons is expected to more than double within the next few years. Already, 31 states (see map), the District of Columbia, the Federal Bureau of Prisons, the Immigration and Naturalization Service, Puerto Rico, and the U.S. Marshals Service have private correctional facilities.[4] Privatization of prisons and jails is gaining support in other nations, which are closely following the experiences of the United States. In July 1999, private correctional facilities were in operation in Australia, England, the Netherlands Antilles, New Zealand, Scotland, and South Africa.

## Pros and Cons

Largely because there has been no conclusive research, arguments continue to rage over the merits of privately run correctional facilities. Most advocates of privatization rely on information showing that private facilities are less costly to run than public ones. Such arguments are based on budgetary concerns and the results of account audits. Proponents also suggest that privately run correctional facilities can be economic boons for the areas in which they are located, providing many jobs and feeding public coffers with increased tax revenues. Among groups supporting privatization are the American Correctional Association and the President's Commission on Privatization.

Opponents of privatization, on the other hand, build their arguments on mostly philosophical grounds. One writer says that the fundamental issue is a moral one: Should private parties make a profit from inflicting pain on others?[5] Most opponents of privatization argue that the practice is inherently flawed by the profit motive of private corporations. The corporate interest in maximizing profits, they claim, can have numerous negative consequences for inmates, correctional employees, and society. Some claim, for example, that the need to maintain healthy profit margins may preclude the cost of rehabilitation and recreational programs for inmates. Other opponents of privatization say that privately run companies save money by paying lower wages and benefits than states do.[6]

Some critics note that, while the administration of punishment may, in fact, be delegated to the private sector, the government retains ultimate responsibility for it. Among the groups opposing privatization are the American Jail

---

### Privatization

**Arguments For Privatization**

Proponents claim that private companies will:

- Provide better service at lower cost
- Save taxpayers' money
- Use the latest technologies and management techniques
- Reduce costly, time-consuming red tape
- Implement innovative strategies
- Build prisons cheaply and more quickly
- Have greater flexibility in labor policies

---

**Arguments Against Privatization**

Opponents of privatization charge that private companies will:

- Profit from the misery of others
- Lobby for legislation to increase the use of incarceration
- Have no incentive to lower recidivism rates, as doing so would threaten their livelihood
- Reduce the number, quality, and training of personnel
- Abuse inmate civil rights
- Skim the "cream of the crop" inmates, leaving those with behavioral or costly medical problems for publicly operated prisons
- Be more concerned about profit than the well-being of inmates

---

*Source:* Linda L. Zupan, "The State of Knowledge on the Privatization of Prison and Jail Operations," (April 1996), Web posted at: http://codc.nmu.edu/progs/ppjo.html.

Association, the National Sheriffs' Association, and the American Federation of State, County, and Municipal Employees.

Some opponents discount the alleged savings of privatization. Proponents counter that public prisons are not without their problems and that governments almost always renew contracts with private operators—proving such contracts worthwhile. The table on page 373 summarizes the arguments for and against privatization.

## Private Corrections Companies

A number of private companies operate prisons and jails. The pie graph[7] shows the market shares held by the major providers of private prison and jail management. Some are well known and even offer shares of their companies to the public.

### Slicing Up the Market

Wackenhut Corrections Corporation 21.73%

Cornell Corrections, Inc. 5.81%

Management & Training Corporation 7.47%

Correctional Services Corporation 5.30%

9 Other Companies 4.14%

Corrections Corporation of America 55.55%

*Two companies dominate the market. Percentage of market share based on U.S. contracts.*

## Privatizing Community Supervision

We also find movement toward privatization in community corrections, including offender assessment, drug testing and treatment, electronic monitoring, halfway houses, and probation

field services. Two states—Connecticut and Colorado—have successfully privatized community supervision. In both states, the impetus for privatizing community supervision was similar: staffing and resources were not keeping pace with increasing caseloads. Community supervision officials felt they had exhausted the use of interns and volunteers, and funding for new staff was not possible. They used risk management principles to assign staff and resources in direct proportion to the risk level of a case. Both states partnered with the private sector to monitor the low-risk offender population, a group that generally has few needs, whose past records reflect little or no violence, and who successfully complete probation about 90 percent of the time.

In Connecticut, the privatization initiative to monitor low-risk offender populations by the private sector allowed scarce resources to be used to better monitor offenders with higher levels of risk. Private case management responsibilities in Connecticut included sending an introductory letter to the probationer, monitoring restitution payments and compliance with conditions of probation, responding to probationer's inquiries, preparing standardized reports for probation officers, providing verification of condition compliance, and providing statistical reports. Robert J. Bosco, Director of Connecticut's Office of Adult Probation, says that the "success" of this privatization initiative "is in the agency's ability to use its resources to control recidivism of the highest risk offender population."[8]

The situation in Colorado was similar. When Colorado officials adopted risk management and looked at how treatment and supervision were matched with levels of risk, they found more probation officers were needed than the Colorado General Assembly would fund. The result was a directive that allowed probation departments to contract with private agencies for the supervision of low-risk probationers. Thirteen of Colorado's 22 judicial districts have entered into such contracts. The private agencies directly bill the probationers for their supervision services, eliminating public expenditures for community supervision. According to Suzanne Pullen, Management

Analyst with Colorado's Judicial Department, Office of Probation Services, "The diversion of these low-risk offenders allows local probation departments to focus more clearly on the supervision and case management of medium and high risk offenders that are burdening their caseloads."[9]

## Issues

Private companies offer increasingly attractive alternatives for financing and building new correctional facilities. Those alternatives may be less expensive than traditional financing through the selling of government bonds. They can be secured more quickly, thus reducing delays when new facilities are desperately needed. They allow government officials to bypass voters who want tough treatment for criminals but are unwilling to pay for it. A disadvantage is that these alternatives avoid citizen input into decisions that have far-reaching consequences.

According to Reginald A. Wilkinson, Director of the Ohio Department of Rehabilitation and Correction:

> The next ten years will reveal whether the privatization of prisons will succeed. If so, the evolution from public to private management may prove to be painful to correctional traditionalists. Debate on the pros and cons, rights and wrongs, of "punishment for profit" will rage back and forth. In the end, the profit margin and public opinion may

be the determining factors on how much of the corrections profession will be outsourced to for-profit providers.[10]

## Notes

1. See "Effort to Block Private Prisons Dies in Senate," *The Sacramento Bee*, ed., June 17, 1998.
2. Ann Fisher, "Lawmakers Mull Prison's Future," *The Columbus Dispatch*, August 5, 1998.
3. Ibid.
4. Charles W. Thomas, "Frequently Asked Questions," Private Corrections Project, April 23, 2000 (accessed at http://web.crim.ufl.edu/pcp/html/questions.html).
5. David Shichor, *Punishment for Profit: Private Prisons/Public Concerns* (Thousand Oaks, CA: Sage Publications, 1995).
6. Material in this paragraph is adapted from Maeve McMahon, review of *Punishment for Profit: Private Prisons/Public Concerns,* by David Shichor, *Canadian Journal of Criminology,* Vol. 39, No. 1 (January 1997), p. 115.
7. Thomas.
8. Robert J. Bosco, "Connecticut Probation's Partnership with the Private Sector," *Topics in Community Corrections: Privatizing Community Supervision,* p. 12.
9. Suzanne Pullen, "An Evaluation of Private Probation Supervision and Case Management in Colorado," *Topics in Community Corrections: Privatizing Community Supervision,* p. 15.
10. Reginald A. Wilkinson, "The Future of Adult Corrections," *Corrections Management Quarterly,* Vol. 1, Issue 1 (Winter 1997).

# 13 Death
## The Ultimate Sanction

### CHAPTER OBJECTIVES

After completing this chapter you should be able to:

1. Discuss the history of capital punishment in the United States.
2. Describe the characteristics of death row inmates.
3. List and summarize the major U.S. Supreme Court decisions that influenced capital punishment legislation.
4. Summarize the arguments for and against the death penalty.
5. Discuss death penalty issues to be faced in the 21st century.

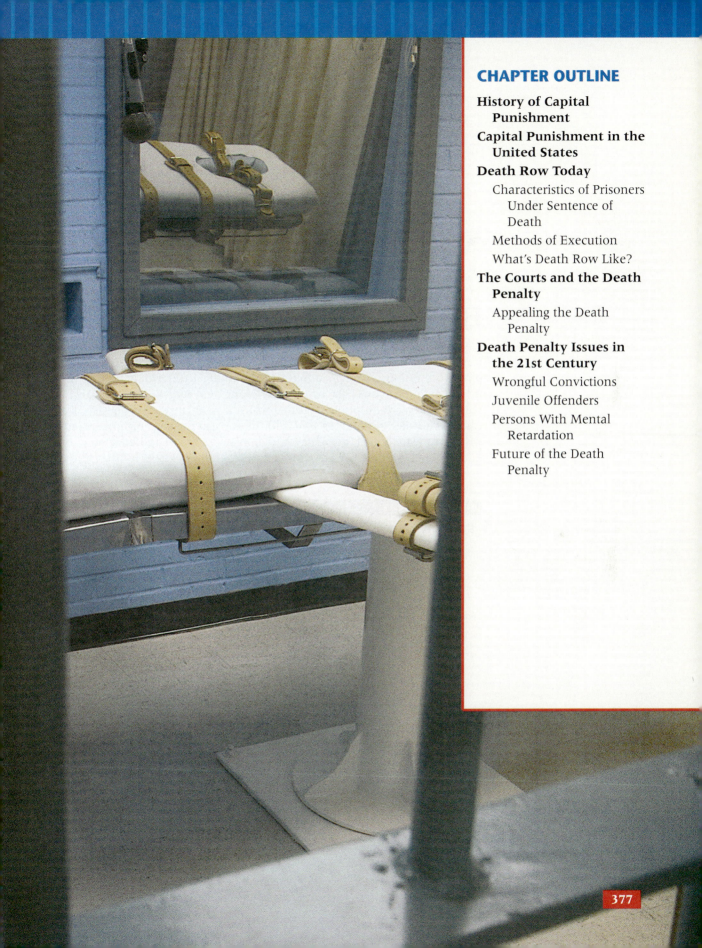

*For centuries the death penalty, often accompanied by barbarous refinements, has been trying to hold crime in check; yet crime persists. Why? Because the instincts that are warring in man are not, as the law claims, constant forces in a state of equilibrium.*

—Albert Camus

**capital punishment**
Legal infliction of the death penalty.

No current corrections issue sparks more passionate debate than **capital punishment**—the death penalty. The debate is a difficult one, with thought-provoking arguments on both sides.

# History of Capital Punishment

Capital punishment was once common throughout the world and imposed for many crimes, including murder, rape, stealing, witchcraft, piracy, desertion, sodomy, adultery, concealing the birth or death of an infant, aiding runaway slaves, counterfeiting, and forgery. Death, however, was not the harshest punishment—torture was. Torture, so cruel that death came as a relief, sometimes lasted for days. Death was a form of leniency. Criminals were boiled, burned, roasted on spits, drawn and quartered, broken on wheels, disemboweled, torn apart by animals, gibbeted (hung from a

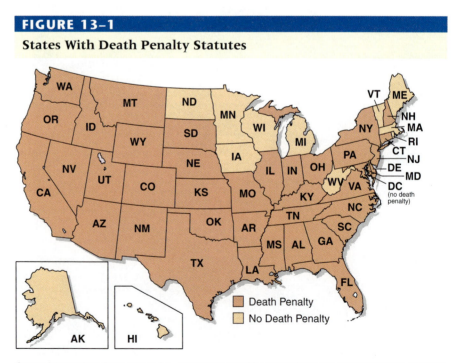

**FIGURE 13–1**

**States With Death Penalty Statutes**

- ■ Death Penalty
- ■ No Death Penalty

DC (no death penalty)

*Source:* Adapted from *Death Row, U.S.A., Winter 2000*, NAACP Legal Defense and Educational Fund, New York, January 1, 2000. Reprinted with permission.

post with a projecting arm and left to die), bludgeoned (beaten to death with sticks, clubs, or rocks), or pressed (crushed under a board and stones).

Capital punishment began changing in the 18th century during the Enlightenment. This philosophical movement led to many new theories on crime and punishment. One of these theories proposed that the punishment fit the crime. Penalties involving torture began to disappear, and the use of the death penalty diminished.

As of January 1, 2000, the majority of countries (106) had abolished the death penalty in law or in practice.[1] In the United States, 40 jurisdictions allowed capital punishment and 13 did not (see Figure 13–1).

# Capital Punishment in the United States

Although research on executions in the United States has been hampered by a lack of official records, almost 15,000 executions, beginning in the 1600s and continuing through 1999, have been confirmed.[2]

Executions stopped in 1968, pending a U.S. Supreme Court decision on the constitutionality of certain aspects of capital punishment. By 1977 the Court ruled that capital punishment itself was not unconstitutional and did not violate the Eighth Amendment to the U.S. Constitution, and executions resumed. The first person to be executed after the moratorium ended was Gary Gilmore, who gave up his right to appeal and was executed by firing squad on January 17, 1977, by the State of Utah.

The number of executions from 1930–1999 is shown in Figure 13–2. Note that in 1999 more inmates were executed than in any other year since the early 1950s.

## FIGURE 13–2

### Persons Executed, 1930–99

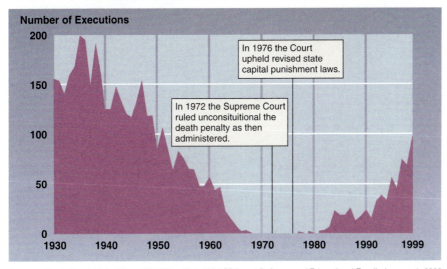

Sources: *Death Row U.S.A., Winter 2000* (New York: NAACP Legal Defense and Educational Fund), January 1, 2000 and Tracy L. Snell, *Capital Punishment 1998*, Bureau of Justice Statistics (Washington: U.S. Department of Justice) December 1999, pp. 7, 11.

**capital crime** A crime for which the death penalty may, but need not necessarily, be imposed.

Today in the United States, what constitutes a **capital crime**—a crime that is punishable by death—is defined by law. This definition varies among jurisdictions. In Louisiana, for example, first-degree murder, aggravated rape of a victim under age 12, and treason are capital crimes; in Nevada, first-degree murder with 13 aggravating circumstances is a capital crime; and in New Jersey, purposeful or knowing murder by one's own conduct, contract murder, or solicitation by command or threat in furtherance of a narcotics conspiracy are capital crimes.[3]

# Death Row Today

## Characteristics of Prisoners Under Sentence of Death

On January 1, 2000, 40 jurisdictions (38 states, the federal government, and the U.S. military) held a total of 3,652 prisoners under sentence of death. Thirty-nine percent of the nation's death row population was in three states: California (561), Texas (462), and Florida (389). Ninety-nine percent of all prisoners sentenced to death were male, with whites predominating (47%).[4] Figure 13–3 shows additional characteristics of inmates under sentence of death.

### FIGURE 13–3

**Characteristics of Prisoners Under Sentence of Death, 2000**

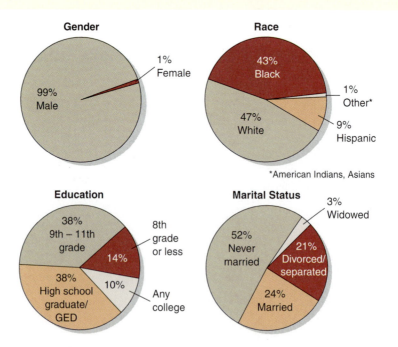

Sources: *Death Row U.S.A., Winter 2000* (New York: NAACP Defense and Education Fund, January 1, 2000), p. 1 and Tracy L. Snell, *Capital Punishment 1998*, Bureau of Justice Statistics (Washington: U.S. Department of Justice), December 1999, p. 8.

*Death: The Ultimate Sanction*

## TABLE 13-1

### Clemency Process by State

**Governor Has Sole Authority (14)**

| | | |
|---|---|---|
| Alabama | New Jersey | South Carolina |
| California | New Mexico | Virginia |
| Colorado | New York | Washington |
| Kansas | North Carolina | Wyoming |
| Kentucky | Oregon | |

**Governor: Must Have Recommendation of Clemency from Board or Advisory Group (9)**

| | | |
|---|---|---|
| Arizona | Indiana | Oklahoma |
| Delaware | Louisiana | Pennsylvania |
| Florida* | Montana | Texas |

**Governor: After Non-binding Recommendation of Clemency from Board or Advisory Group (9)**

| | | |
|---|---|---|
| Arkansas | Mississippi | Ohio |
| Illinois | Missouri | South Dakota |
| Maryland | New Hampshire | Tennessee |

**Board or Advisory Group Makes Determination (3)**

| | | |
|---|---|---|
| Connecticut | Georgia | Idaho |

**Governor Sits on Clemency Board Which Makes the Determination (3)**

| | | |
|---|---|---|
| Nebraska | Nevada | Utah |

*Florida's Governor must have recommendation of Board, on which s/he sits.

For Federal Death Row inmates, the President alone has pardon power.

*Source:* "Executive Clemency Process and Execution Warrant Procedure In Death Penalty Cases," National Coalition to Abolish the Death Penalty (1993), with updates by DPIC through January 2000.

Prisoners spend an average of 10 years and 5 months on death row. They may leave death row by means other than execution—between 1973 and January 1, 2000, 54 persons on death row committed suicide; 157 died of natural causes or were killed; 1,697 had their convictions/sentences reversed;[5] and 90 were granted **clemency** and received a **commutation**. Table 13–1 shows the clemency process by state.

## Methods of Execution

Five methods of execution are used in the United States: (1) lethal injection, (2) electrocution, (3) lethal gas, (4) hanging, and (5) firing squad. As you can see in Table 13–2, lethal injection is the predominant method.

**clemency** Kindness, mercy, forgiveness, or leniency, usually relating to criminal acts.

**commutation** A change of a legal penalty to a lesser one; e.g., from death to life imprisonment.

## TABLE 13–2

### Method of Execution, by Jurisdiction, 2000

| Lethal Injection | | Electrocution | Lethal Gas | Hanging | Firing Squad |
|---|---|---|---|---|---|
| Arizona[a,b] | New Hampshire[a] | Alabama | Arizona[a,b] | Delaware[a,c] | Idaho[a] |
| Arkansas[a,d] | New Jersey | Arkansas[a,d] | California[a] | New Hampshire[a,e] | Oklahoma[f] |
| California[a] | New Mexico | Florida[a] | Maryland[a,j] | Washington[a] | Utah[a] |
| Colorado | New York | Georgia | Missouri[a] | | |
| Connecticut | North Carolina | Kentucky[a,g] | Wyoming[a,h] | | |
| Delaware[a,c] | Ohio[a] | Nebraska | | | |
| Florida[a] | Oklahoma[a] | Ohio[a] | | | |
| Idaho[a,j] | Oregon | Oklahoma[f] | | | |
| Illinois | Pennsylvania | South Carolina[a] | | | |
| Indiana | South Carolina[a] | Tennessee[a,i] | | | |
| Kansas | South Dakota | Virginia[a] | | | |
| Kentucky[a,g] | Tennessee[a,i] | | | | |
| Louisiana | Texas | | | | |
| Maryland[a,k] | Utah[a] | | | | |
| Mississippi | Virginia[a] | | | | |
| Missouri[a] | Washington[a] | | | | |
| Montana | Wyoming[a] | | | | |
| Nevada | U.S. Military | | | | |

Note: The method of execution of Federal prisoners is lethal injection, pursuant to 28 CFR, Part 26. For offenses under the Violent Crime Control and Law Enforcement Act of 1994, the method is that of the State in which the conviction took place, pursuant to 18 U.S.C. 3596. If the state has no death penalty, the inmate will be transferred to another state.

[a]Authorizes 2 methods of execution.

[b]Arizona authorizes lethal injection for persons whose capital sentence was received after 11/15/92; for those sentenced before that date, the condemned may select lethal injection or lethal gas.

[c]Delaware authorizes lethal injection for those whose capital offense occurred after 6/13/86; for those whose offense occurred before that date, the condemned may select lethal injection or hanging.

[d]Arkansas authorizes lethal injection for those whose capital offense occurred on or after 7/4/83; for those whose offense occurred before that date, the condemned may select lethal injection or electrocution.

[e]New Hampshire authorizes hanging only if lethal injection cannot be given.

[f]Oklahoma authorizes electrocution if lethal injection is ever held to be unconstitutional, and firing squad if both lethal injection and electrocution are held unconstitutional.

[g]Kentucky authorizes lethal injection for persons whose capital sentence was received on or after 3/31/98; for those sentenced before that date, the condemned may select lethal injection or electrocution.

[h]Wyoming authorizes lethal gas if lethal injection is ever held to be unconstitutional.

[i]Tennessee authorizes lethal injection for those whose capital offense occurred after 1/1/99; those whose offense occurred before that date may select lethal injection or electrocution.

[j]Idaho authorizes firing squad only if lethal injection is "impractical."

[k]Maryland authorizes lethal injection for those whose capital sentence was received on or after 3/25/94; for those sentenced before that date, the condemned may select lethal injection or lethal gas.

*Sources:* Bureau of Justice Statistics Bulletin NCJ 179012, *Capital Punishment 1998* (U.S. Department of Justice, Office of Justice Programs), December 1999. Update from DPIC online at http://www.essential.org/dpic/methods.html.

Some states authorize more than one method. Arizona, for example, uses lethal injection for persons sentenced after November 15, 1992; those sentenced before that date may select lethal injection or lethal gas. Oklahoma authorizes electrocution if lethal injection is ever held unconstitutional, and firing squad if both lethal injection and electrocution are held unconstitutional. The federal government authorizes a method of execution under two different laws; the method of execution for federal prisoners prosecuted under the *Code of Federal Regulations*, Volume 28, Part 26 is lethal injection; for those offenses prosecuted under the Violent Crime Control and Law Enforcement Act of 1994, the method is that of the state in which the person was convicted. If the state has no death penalty, the inmate will be transferred to another state.

## What's Death Row Like?

Prisoners who are sentenced to death are held on **death row**, a prison within a prison. Death row inmates are segregated from the general prison population; they receive no rehabilitation, treatment, or work programs. Death row existence has been called "living death" to convey a prisoner's loneliness, isolation, boredom, and loss of privacy.[6]

**death row** A prison area housing inmates sentenced to death.

What many people forget is that a death row inmate's living environment is a correctional officer's workplace. The concrete and steel construction materials and furnishings that guarantee security and durability in death row amplify normal sounds within its hard walls. It takes little effort to imagine what effect shouting, flushing toilets, opening and closing steel doors, doing janitorial work, the blaring of televisions and radios, and voices wailing on the bars has not only on those who live there but also on those who work there. In summer the oppressive heat and in winter the freezing cold are trapped in the walls of steel and concrete. The quality of life experienced by inmates depends on the work environment created by the corrections officers who guard them.

Death row cells usually have steel bunks, toilets, and sinks. These are bolted to concrete floors and cinder block walls. Small lockers or wall shelves hold prisoners' personal property, which may include toiletries, books, pictures, a clock, and usually a television. The television is the death row inmate's most valued possession, not only because of its entertainment value, but also because it makes available the world that the death row inmate has lost. Revoking television or telephone privileges is sometimes used by correctional officers as a threat to control behavior on death row. Generally, though, corrections officers say that death row inmates seldom exhibit disciplinary problems. Alabama's death row warden, Charlie Jones, described death row inmates as "the group who causes the least trouble."[7]

Most death row inmates spend 22–23 hours a day in five-by-eight- or six-by-nine-foot cells. They receive their meals through slots in the cell doors. Generally twice a week, they are handcuffed, escorted to, and locked in shower stalls for five- or ten-minute showers. In some jurisdictions, death row inmates may visit the prison library; in others, books are taken to them.

Most death row inmates slowly lose their ties with the outside world. Although some states permit contact visits, most allow only noncontact visits. Every time death row inmates leave death row for visits—whether

I am a 29-year-old death row inmate, and I want to talk to you about death row. I want to tell you that if you look, you will find people! We are small, tall, fat, skinny, and different races living together. I am very happy to say that there is a brotherhood here, but I call it my family, because they know when I am happy or sad.

I get help with schoolwork, law study, hobby crafts, and most of all my feelings. I will not hesitate to speak about my feelings because there are so many people here that are willing to talk about them with me. What I have learned in my five years on the Row is the people here are not mean or crazy like everyone thinks. I see happiness and friendships here.

We do not fight against each other; nor do we disrespect each other. We share birthdays and holidays together. I myself had a birthday party this year. I believe that was the happiest time for me, because all these people sang happy birthday to me. It is the first time so many people did that for me.

I am not going to give an excuse for you to save my life. I am not going to say I am retarded or an ex-drug user or that I was beaten in my childhood. What I will say is, I am a person! An American, of the United States of America. The world looks at America with respect. We go help other countries with food and medicine. We are against violence and aggression. However, having the death penalty does not set a very good example! Executing our people puts a deep scar that will not go away until we stop this madness.

I invite you to visit a state's death row and see for yourself. Meet a death row inmate, talk to him or her, and see what they are like. Society has put an X on our foreheads because they are made to believe that we do not care about the country. That is not true. We do care about this country of ours, and this world, too.

I get really sad when I see news about people starving or dying with AIDS. It really hits home! I am not smart, I did not go to high school or college. But what I do know is street smarts. I know what it feels like to go hungry and not have anything. I know about goals and dreams because I have them too.

I do not want to die in the electric chair. And with your help I will not have to. Violence exists across the world because we want it to be there, just like executions! We can stop all the violence and suffering by pulling together and helping each other. Please come together and stop this madness. Restore the American Dream. Stop executions, help the poor, give medical care to people that need it, go into those cities and neighborhoods, help those families, give them jobs. Let them know you care.

*Mark Allen Jenkins*
*#Z527, Holman Prison*
*Atmore, AL*

contact or noncontact—they are strip-searched before and after the visit. Over the years, visitors and mail are less frequent, and sometimes cease altogether. Corrections officers assigned to death row are instructed not to estab-

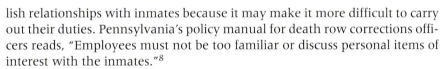

The men in the red jumpsuits—dead men walking! I don't judge them, I don't disrespect them, I just protect them from other inmates and themselves. I work on death row and have for three and a half years. Death row inmates sleep in cell blocks which consist of sixteen individual cells with solid electronic steel doors. Some talk to everybody all the time, some don't talk to anyone and others act as if they have multiple personalities. If they aren't talking, they're playing cards, checkers, or doing push-ups. They get outside two times a day to exercise. Law says they can't work.

Some act like they are your buddies, and some act as if they can't stand you. For the most part, the ones that act like your buddy are usually trying to get you to do something for them.

As a group, they are very manipulative in every exchange they have with everyone, including each other.

Most of the inmates say they are innocent. A few say they actually committed the crime, and others say they were framed. I know a lot about most of their cases and it seems to me that they belong here—on death row. But, a few of the cases seem questionable. That's a private thought and I don't let it change the way I deal with these offenders in red jumpsuits.

*John Juehrs*
*Correctional Officer*
*Death Row*
*Central Prison*
*Raleigh, NC*

lish relationships with inmates because it may make it more difficult to carry out their duties. Pennsylvania's policy manual for death row corrections officers reads, "Employees must not be too familiar or discuss personal items of interest with the inmates."[8]

Preparing for an execution is a correctional officer's toughest job. "We begin to dread electrocutions weeks before they take place," former corrections officer Lynch Alford, Sr., said. "We're almost glad when someone is commuted, regardless of what crime he committed. We just sit around and wait. We drink coffee. We don't talk about anything. We don't talk about the electrocution. We just get it over with as soon as possible and then go home immediately." A death row inmate who refuses to walk to the death chamber is carried by corrections officers, sometimes screaming and kicking. "Guards have been known to go all to pieces during episodes such as these. Their nerves just don't hold up. In my opinion it is something you never become accustomed to. It's the most gruesome job I've come in contact with

EXHIBIT 13–1

## American Correctional Association

### Policy Statement on Capital Punishment

Correctional professionals have a fundamental responsibility to support participation in the public dialogue concerning capital punishment, and to make available to the public and their policymakers the unique perspectives of persons working in the profession. Toward this end, correctional agencies should:

**A.** Support conducting research on capital punishment, to inform the public debate with accurate information about all aspects of capital punishment.

**B.** Support full public discussion of capital punishment, focusing on the morality, purposes, and efficacy of this form of punishment.

**C.** Accept and encourage a diversity of opinion within the field, assuring that employment, promotion, and retention are never affected by the expression of opinion either in support of or opposition to capital punishment.

**D.** Encourage correctional professionals to fully consider this issue, and permit them to present their opinions within the profession and in appropriate public forums.

during my 35 years with the department. The more you see, the more you hate it."[9]

The American Correctional Association (ACA), in its Policy Statement on Capital Punishment (see Exhibit 13–1), encourages corrections professionals to support and participate in the debate about capital punishment.

# The Courts and the Death Penalty

"Death is different [from other punishments]," said U.S. Supreme Court Justice William Brennan. For that reason, every phase of a capital crime proceeding, from jury selection to sentencing instructions, has been influenced by court rulings. The legal history of today's death penalty can be traced through several landmark cases. In the June 29, 1972 decision in *Furman* v. *Georgia*,[10] the U.S. Supreme Court ruled that the death penalty, as imposed and carried out under the laws of Georgia, was cruel and unusual punishment in violation of the Eighth and Fourteenth Amendments. According to the Court, Georgia's death penalty statute gave the sentencing authority (judge or trial jury) complete freedom to impose a death or life imprisonment sentence without standards or guidelines; the death penalty had been imposed arbitrarily, discriminatorily, and selectively against minorities and was therefore "cruel and unusual punishment in violation of the Eighth and Fourteenth Amendments." It is important to note that the Court majority did not rule that the death penalty itself was unconstitutional, only the way in which it was being administered at that time.

About two-thirds of the states responded to the *Furman* decision by rewriting their capital punishment statutes to limit discretion and avoid arbitrary and inconsistent results. The new penalty laws took two forms. Some imposed a **mandatory death penalty** for certain crimes, and others permitted **guided discretion** that sets standards for judges and juries to use when deciding whether to impose the death penalty.

In 1976, the U.S. Supreme Court rejected mandatory death penalty statutes in *Woodson* v. *North Carolina* and *Roberts* v. *Louisiana*, but approved guided discretion statutes in *Gregg* v. *Georgia* and two companion cases.[11]

In *Gregg*, the Court also approved automatic appellate review, a proportionality review whereby state appellate courts compare the sentence with similar cases, and a **bifurcated**, or special two-part, **trial**. The first part, the *guilt phase*, decides the issue of guilt. If the defendant is found guilty, the second part of the trial, the *penalty phase*, takes place. The penalty phase includes presentation of facts that mitigate or aggravate the circumstances of the crime. **Mitigating circumstances** are factors that may be considered as reducing the culpability of the crime. **Aggravating circumstances** are factors that may increase the penalty. A list of mitigating and aggravating circumstances associated with the death penalty in the state of Pennsylvania is shown in Figure 13–4 on the following pages.

## Appealing the Death Penalty

Execution of death row inmates takes an average of 10 years and 5 months. Death penalty cases may pass through up to ten courts, across three stages: trial and direct appeal, state post-conviction appeals, and federal *habeas corpus* appeals.

In stage one, trial and direct appeal, a death sentence is imposed. In a death penalty case, legal issues about the trial and sentence are automatically appealed to the state appellate courts. Some states have a dual level of appellate review; this means that the legal issues may be heard first in the state court of criminal appeals (court 1) before reaching the state supreme court (court 2). These courts evaluate the trial for legal or constitutional errors at trial and determine if the death sentence is consistent with sentences imposed in similar cases. State appellate courts seldom overturn a conviction or change a death sentence. The defendant then petitions the U.S. Supreme Court (court 3) to grant a petition for a **writ of** *certiorari*—

**mandatory death penalty** A death sentence that the legislature has required to be imposed upon persons convicted of certain offenses.

**guided discretion** Decision-making bounded by general guidelines, rules, or laws.

**bifurcated trial** Two separate hearings for different issues in a trial; one for guilt and the other for punishment.

**mitigating circumstances** Factors that, although not justifying or excusing an action, may be considered as reducing the culpability of the offender.

**aggravating circumstances** Factors that may be considered as increasing the culpability of the offender.

**writ of** *certiorari* The written order a superior court issues to a lower court requiring provision of a certified copy of a particular case record.

**FIGURE 13–4**

## Sample Aggravating and Mitigating Circumstances

### Aggravating and Mitigating Circumstances in Pennsylvania

The Commonwealth of Pennsylvania must prove aggravating circumstances beyond a reasonable doubt. Mitigating circumstances must be proved by the defendant by a preponderance of the evidence.

The verdict must be a sentence of death if the jury unanimously finds at least one aggravating circumstance and no mitigating circumstances or if the jury unanimously finds one or more aggravating circumstances which outweigh any mitigating circumstances.

The court shall instruct the jury that if it finds at least one aggravating circumstance and at least one mitigating circumstance, it shall consider, in weighing the aggravating and mitigating circumstances, any evidence presented about the victim and about the impact of the murder on the victim's family. The court shall also instruct the jury on any other matter that may be just and proper under the circumstances.

Aggravating circumstances shall be limited to the following:

1. The victim was a firefighter, peace officer, public servant concerned in official detention, as defined in 18 Pa.C.S. § 5121 (relating to escape), judge of any court in the unified judicial system, the Attorney General of Pennsylvania, a deputy attorney general, district attorney, assistant district attorney, member of the General Assembly, Governor, Lieutenant Governor, Auditor General, State Treasurer, State law enforcement official, local law enforcement official, Federal law enforcement official or person employed to assist or assisting any law enforcement official in the performance of his duties, who was killed in the performance of his duties or as a result of his official position.

2. The defendant paid or was paid by another person or had contracted to pay or be paid by another person or had conspired to pay or be paid by another person for the killing of the victim.

3. The victim was being held by the defendant for ransom or reward, or as a shield or hostage.

4. The death of the victim occurred while the defendant was engaged in the hijacking of an aircraft.

5. The victim was a prosecution witness to a murder or other felony committed by the defendant and was killed for the purpose of preventing his testimony against the defendant in any grand jury or criminal proceeding involving such offenses.

6. The defendant committed a killing while in the perpetration of a felony.

7. In the commission of the offense the defendant knowingly created a grave risk of death to another person in addition to the victim of the offense.

8. The offense was committed by means of torture.

9. The defendant has a significant history of felony convictions involving the use or threat of violence to the person.

10. The defendant has been convicted of another Federal or State offense, committed either before or at the time of the offense at issue, for which a sentence of life imprisonment or death was imposable or the defendant was undergoing a sentence of life imprisonment for any reason at the time of the commission of the offense.

11. The defendant has been convicted of another murder committed in any jurisdiction and committed either before or at the time of the offense at issue.

12. The defendant has been convicted of voluntary manslaughter, as defined in 18 Pa.C.S. § 2503 (relating to voluntary manslaughter), or a substantially equivalent crime in any other jurisdiction, committed either before or at the time of the offense at issue.

*- 1 -*

*Source:* Pennsylvania Consolidated Statutes, Section 9711 (1997).

## FIGURE 13–4 (continued)

### Sample Aggravating and Mitigating Circumstances

13. The defendant committed the killing or was an accomplice in the killing, as defined in 18 Pa.C.S. § 306(c) (relating to liability for conduct of another; complicity), while in the perpetration of a felony under the provisions of the act of April 14, 1972 (P.L.233, No.64), known as The Controlled Substance, Drug, Device, and Cosmetic Act, and punishable under the provisions of 18 Pa.C.S. § 7508 (relating to drug trafficking sentencing and penalties).

14. At the time of the killing, the victim was or had been involved, associated, or in competition with the defendant in the sale, manufacture, distribution, or delivery of any controlled substance or counterfeit controlled substance in violation of The Controlled Substance, Drug, Device, and Cosmetic Act or similar law of any other state, the District of Columbia or the United States, and the defendant committed the killing or was an accomplice to the killing as defined in 18 Pa.C.S. § 306(c), and the killing resulted from or was related to that association, involvement, or competition to promote the defendant's activities in selling, manufacturing, distributing, or delivering controlled substances or counterfeit controlled substances.

15. At the time of the killing, the victim was or had been a nongovernmental informant or had otherwise provided any investigative, law enforcement, or police agency with information concerning criminal activity, and the defendant committed the killing or was an accomplice to the killing as defined in 18 Pa.C.S. § 306(c), and the killing was in retaliation for the victim's activities as a nongovernmental informant or in providing information concerning criminal activity to an investigative, law enforcement, or police agency.

16. The victim was a child under 12 years of age.

17. At the time of the killing, the victim was in her third trimester of pregnancy or the defendant had knowledge of the victim's pregnancy.

18. At the time of the killing, the defendant was subject to a court order restricting in any way the defendant's behavior toward the victim pursuant to 23 Pa.C.S. Ch. 61 (relating to protection from abuse), or any other order of a court of common pleas or of the minor judiciary designed in whole or in part to protect the victim from the defendant.

Mitigating circumstances shall include the following:

1. The defendant has no significant history of prior criminal convictions.

2. The defendant was under the influence of extreme mental or emotional disturbance.

3. The capacity of the defendant to appreciate the criminality of his conduct or to conform his conduct to the requirements of law was substantially impaired.

4. The age of the defendant at the time of the crime.

5. The defendant acted under extreme duress, although not such duress as to constitute a defense to prosecution under 18 Pa.C.S. § 309 (relating to duress), or acted under the substantial domination of another person.

6. The victim was a participant in the defendant's homicidal conduct or consented to the homicidal acts.

7. The defendant's participation in the homicidal act was relatively minor.

8. Any other evidence of mitigation concerning the character and record of the defendant and the circumstances of his offense.

-2-

a written order to the lower court whose decision is being appealed to send the records of the case forward for review.

If the defendant's direct appeals are unsuccessful, stage two—state post-conviction appeals—begins. At this point, many death row inmates allege ineffective or incompetent trial counsel, and new counsel is engaged or appointed. The new counsel petitions the trial court (court 4) with newly discovered evidence; questions about the fairness of the trial; allegations of jury bias, tainted evidence, incompetence of defense counsel, and prosecutorial or police misconduct. If the trial court denies the appeals, they may be filed with the state's appellate courts (either directly to the state supreme court, or, if there exists a dual level of appellate review, a petition first to the state court of criminal appeals (court 5) followed by a petition to the state supreme court (court 6). Most often, the state appellate courts deny the petition. Defendant's counsel then petitions the U.S. Supreme Court (court 7). If the U.S. Supreme Court denies the petition for a writ of *certiorari*, stage two ends and stage three begins.

In stage three, the federal *habeas corpus* stage, a defendant files a petition in U.S. District Court (court 8) alleging violations of constitutional rights. Such rights include the right to due process (Fourteenth Amendment), prohibition against cruel and unusual punishment (Eighth Amendment), and the right to effective assistance of counsel (Sixth Amendment). If the District Court denies the petition, defense counsel submits it to the U.S. Court of Appeals (court 9) for the circuit representing the jurisdiction. If the Court of Appeals denies the petition, defense counsel asks the U.S. Supreme Court (court 10) to grant a writ of *certiorari*. If the U.S. Supreme Court denies *certiorari*, the office of the state attorney general asks the state supreme court to set a date for execution.

In 1996, in an effort to reduce the time persons spent on death row and the number of federal appeals, the U.S. Congress passed the Anti-Terrorism and Effective Death Penalty Act (AEDPA). The AEDPA defines filing deadlines and limits reasons for second, or successive, federal appellate reviews to (1) new constitutional law, (2) new evidence that could not have been discovered at the time of the original trial, or (3) new facts that, if proven, would be sufficient to establish the applicant's innocence. Under the AEDPA, if the U.S. Supreme Court denies the petition for a writ of *certiorari* in the final federal *habeas corpus* appeal, defense counsel may once again petition the federal courts; however, before a second, or successive, application for a writ of *habeas corpus* may be filed in U.S. District Court, defense counsel must petition the appropriate U.S. Court of Appeals for an order authorizing the District Court to consider the application. The petition to the U.S. Court of Appeals is decided by a three-judge panel; the panel must grant or deny the authorization to file the second, or successive, application within 30 days after the petition is filed. If the panel approves the petition, the District Court must render a decision regarding the application within 180 days. If the motion is appealed to the Court of Appeals representing the jurisdiction, the court must render its decision within 120 days. If the petition is filed with the U.S. Supreme Court, the Court may grant the petition for *certiorari* or let the lower court's decision stand.

# Death Penalty Issues in the 21st Century

Current issues on capital punishment include questions about executing the innocent, juveniles, and the mentally retarded.

## Wrongful Convictions

Execution is irreversible. The most extensive safeguards cannot ensure an infallible legal system because human beings are fallible. False testimony, mistaken identification, misinterpretation of evidence, or community prejudices and pressures can result in wrongful conviction and sometimes execution of the innocent. From 1973 through 1999, 84 death row inmates were released as a result of new evidence. Some might consider this statistic as evidence that the legal system's elaborate procedural protections work; others consider it evidence of the likelihood that innocent people have been or will be executed. Most of the new evidence in these 84 cases was not evidence discovered through the normal appeals process, but rather evidence made available as a result of new scientific discoveries such as DNA testing, or investigations by journalists, professors, students, or attorneys. These 84 people sat on death row for an average of six and a half years before their innocence was established and they were released. At least 23 people were not so fortunate; they were executed between 1900 and 1987, before their innocence was proved.[12]

Some professionals and researchers believe that mistakes are more likely in capital cases than in other criminal matters due to the following:[13]

1. Pressure on law enforcement officials to quickly arrest and prosecute the most notorious murders.
2. Lack of eyewitness testimony.
3. Publicity that may influence jurors.
4. Inadvertent conveyance of guilt during jury selection—establishing that jurors can recommend the death penalty may imply that they should.
5. Limited defense resources.
6. Heinousness of the crime—the details of the crime may cause the jury to ignore reasonable doubt and return a guilty verdict.

On January 31, 2000, Governor George Ryan of Illinois announced a temporary halt to executions, saying he had grave concerns about convicting innocent people and putting them on death row. The state of Illinois

*The death penalty issue generates public controversy. In some states, there are movements to end the death penalty, while in others the move is to speed up death row appeals and complete the sentence of execution. Do demonstrations such as these influence the public policy implemented by state legislatures?*

released 13 persons who were wrongfully sentenced to die, outnumbering the 12 who had been executed by lethal injection since the state reinstated the death penalty in 1977. The governor also appointed a special commission to study the state's capital punishment system and determine why 13 persons were wrongfully convicted of capital crimes. Other states are considering similar moratoriums.

## Juvenile Offenders

As youth violence increases, the question of how to deal with juvenile offenders guilty of capital offenses becomes more urgent. International human rights treaties and standards recommend that juveniles not be sentenced to death because they lack adult judgment. Legislators in 24 U.S. jurisdictions disagree (See Table 13–3.): eight do not specify a minimum age

---

**TABLE 13–3**

### Minimum Age Authorized for Capital Punishment, 1998

| Age 16 or less | Age 17 | Age 18 | None specified |
|---|---|---|---|
| Alabama (16) | Georgia | California | Arizona |
| Arkansas (14)[a] | New Hampshire | Colorado | Idaho |
| Delaware (16) | North Carolina[b] | Connecticut[c] | Louisiana |
| Florida (16) | Texas | Federal system | Montana |
| Indiana (16) | | Illinois | Pennsylvania |
| Kentucky (16) | | Kansas | South Carolina |
| Mississippi (16)[d] | | Maryland | South Dakota[e] |
| Missouri (16) | | Nebraska | Utah |
| Nevada (16) | | New Jersey | |
| Oklahoma (16) | | New Mexico | |
| Virginia (14)[f] | | New York | |
| Wyoming (16) | | Ohio | |
| | | Oregon | |
| | | Tennessee | |
| | | Washington | |

Note: Reporting by states reflects interpretations by state attorneys general's offices and may differ from previously reported ages.

[a] See Ark. Code Ann. 9-27-318(b)(2)(Repl. 1991).

[b] Age required is 17 unless the murderer was incarcerated for murder when a subsequent murder occurred; then the age may be 14.

[c] See Conn. Gen. Stat. 53a-46a(g)(1).

[d] The minimum age defined by statute is 13, but the effective age is 16 based on interpretation of U.S. Supreme Court decisions by the Mississippi Supreme Court.

[e] Juveniles may be transferred to adult court. Age can be a mitigating factor.

[f] The minimum age for transfer to adult court by statute is 14, but the effective age is 16 based on interpretation of U.S. Supreme Court decisions by the state attorney general's office.

*Source:* Bureau of Justice Statistics Bulletin NCJ 179012, *Capital Punishment 1998* (U.S. Department of Justice, Office of Justice Programs), December 1999.

for the death sentence; four specify an age of 17; and twelve specify an age between 13 and 17.

From January 1973 through March 2000, 182 convicted juvenile offenders were sentenced to death. Ninety-seven (54%) of these sentences have been reversed; sixteen have been carried out.

Currently there are 69 death row inmates (all males) sentenced as juveniles. All of them were age 16 or 17 when they committed their crimes. One-third (26) of these juveniles are on death row in Texas.

## Persons With Mental Retardation

Most of the opposition to executing mentally ill prisoners is based on the premise that killing people who do not comprehend the nature or purpose of their punishment serves no legitimate purpose. Thirty-four people who were diagnosed as mentally retarded were executed in the United States between 1983 and January 1, 2000. Thirteen of the 40 jurisdictions in the United States that allow the death penalty do not permit execution of the mentally retarded. These states include:

Arkansas
Colorado
Georgia
Indiana
Kansas
Kentucky
Maryland
Nebraska
New Mexico
New York
Tennessee
Washington
the federal government

## Future of the Death Penalty

Capital punishment has always been a subject of debate, and the debate will continue into the 21st century. There are many arguments favoring capital punishment and many arguments opposing it. Some of the arguments—pro and con—are summarized in Table 13–4. The debate over capital punishment is complex and emotional. It has always inspired passionate, partisan feelings and will continue to do so as decisions about how to strike the right balance of justice and social utility are made.

**TABLE 13–4**

### Arguments Favoring and Opposing the Death Penalty

**The Death Penalty Debate**

| PRO | CON |
| --- | --- |
| Deters people from crime through fear of punishment; exerts a positive moral influence by stigmatizing crimes of murder and manslaughter. | Does not deter crime; no evidence exists that the death penalty is more effective than other punishments. |
| Is a just punishment for murder; fulfills "just deserts" principle of a fitting punishment; life in prison is not a tough enough punishment for a capital crime. | Violates human rights; is a barbaric remnant of an uncivilized society; is immoral in principle, and ensures the execution of some innocent people. |
| Is constitutionally appropriate; 8th Amendment prohibits cruel and unusual punishment, yet 5th Amendment implies that with due process of law one may be deprived of life, liberty, or property. | Falls disproportionately on racial minorities; those who murdered whites are more likely to be sentenced to death than those who murdered blacks. |
| Reduces time spent on death row to reduce costs of capital punishment and its attendant costs of post-conviction appeals, investigations, and searches for new evidence and witnesses. | Costs too much; $2 million to $4 million are poured into each execution while other criminal justice components such as police and the courts lack funding. |
| Protects society from the most serious and feared offenders; prevents the reoccurrence of violence. | Boosts the murder rate following an execution; this is known as the *brutalizing effect*; the state is a role model, and when the state carries out an execution, it shows that killing is a way to solve problems. |
| Is more humane than life imprisonment because it is quick; making the prisoner suffer by remaining in prison for the rest of his/her life is more torturous and inhumane than execution. | Not everyone wants vengeance; many people favor alternative sentences such as life without parole. |
| Almost impossible for an innocent person to be executed; slow execution rate results from process of appeals, from sentencing to execution. | Is arbitrary and unfair; offenders who commit similar crimes under similar circumstances receive widely differing sentences; race, social and economic status, location of crime, and pure chance influence sentencing. |

## SUMMARY BY CHAPTER OBJECTIVES

### CHAPTER OBJECTIVE 1

Capital punishment has been imposed throughout history, for crimes ranging from horse stealing and witchcraft to crimes against humanity and murder. Before the 18th century, torture often preceded death. Researchers have confirmed almost 15,000 executions in the United States from 1608 through 1999.

### CHAPTER OBJECTIVE 2

Most death row inmates are male. Only 48 percent of death row inmates completed high school. Only 24 percent of death row inmates were married at the time of incarceration. Whites and minorities are executed in about equal proportion.

### CHAPTER OBJECTIVE 3

Two landmark cases that influenced capital punishment were *Furman* v. *Georgia* (1972) and *Gregg* v. *Georgia* (1976). In *Furman* v. *Georgia*, the U.S. Supreme Court ruled that capital punishment, as imposed by Georgia, constituted cruel and unusual punishment—Georgia's death penalty statute gave the sentencing authority (judge or trial jury) complete freedom to impose a death sentence without standards or guidelines. As a result of the *Furman* ruling, state death penalty statutes took two forms—mandatory death penalty or sentencing based on guided discretion. In *Woodson* v. *North Carolina* and

*Roberts* v. *Louisiana*, the Court rejected mandatory statutes. However, in *Gregg* v. *Georgia*, the Court ruled that Georgia's new guided discretion death penalty legislation was not unconstitutional.

### CHAPTER OBJECTIVE 4

Arguments in favor of the death penalty include the following: it deters rational people from becoming habitual killers; it is "just" punishment for taking someone's life; it is constitutional as long as it is achieved with due process of law; it reduces the amount of time a person spends on death row; it protects society from feared offenders; it is more humane than life imprisonment; and it is almost impossible for an innocent person to be executed. Arguments against the death penalty include the following: it violates human rights; it does not deter violent crime; it is implemented arbitrarily and unfairly; it falls disproportionately on racial minorities; it actually boosts the murder rate by promoting homicides in the months following an execution; not everyone wants vengeance; and it costs too much to support a capital trial, appeals, and execution.

### CHAPTER OBJECTIVE 5

In the 21st century issues that the debate on capital punishment addresses will include execution of the wrongfully convicted, juveniles, and the mentally ill.

## KEY TERMS

capital punishment, p. 378
capital crime, p. 380
clemency, p. 381
commutation, p. 381
death row, p. 383
mandatory death penalty, p. 387

guided discretion, p. 387
bifurcated trial, p. 387
mitigating circumstances, p. 387
aggravating circumstances, p. 387
writ of *certiorari*, p. 387

1. What is *capital punishment*?
2. How many jurisdictions in the United States permit capital punishment? How many do not?
3. What is a *capital crime*?
4. What are the characteristics of death row inmates?
5. What is the average length of time spent on death row?
6. What execution methods are used in the United States today? Which is used most?
7. What are the two landmark U.S. Supreme Court cases that most affected capital punishment legislation? What impact did they have?
8. What is a *bifurcated trial*?
9. What are *aggravating* and *mitigating circumstances*?
10. What is the process for appealing a death sentence?
11. What is the Anti-Terrorism and Effective Death Penalty Act? What is its purpose?
12. List and explain at least four arguments in favor of capital punishment.
13. List and explain at least four arguments against capital punishment.
14. What are the primary causes of wrongful convictions?
15. How many jurisdictions permit execution of juveniles?
16. How many jurisdictions permit execution of the mentally ill?

### ON-THE-JOB ISSUES

1. Capital murder trials are longer and more expensive at every step than other murder trials. The irreversibility of the death sentence requires courts to follow heightened due process in the preparation and course of the trial. Defendants are much more likely to insist on a trial when they are facing a possible death sentence. Crime investigations, pre-trial preparations and motions, expert witness investigations, jury selection, and the necessity for two trials—one on guilt and one on sentencing—makes capital cases extremely costly, even before the appeals process begins. After conviction, there are constitutionally mandated appeals that involve both prosecution and defense costs. In addition, should the jury recommend life over death or end as a hung jury, or if the condemned person's sentence is commuted after he or she has served time on death row, the state has already paid the cost of a capital trial. These are the unsuccessful capital trials in which the death penalty was sought (and paid for) but not achieved. Assume that you are the prosecuting attorney in a rural county of 7,500 people in a southern state. A capital case is coming up for trial. Estimates of costs for the case begin at $500,000. How will you justify paying for the prosecution of the case?

2. According to a study at Kentucky's University of Louisville, blacks who killed whites in Kentucky were more likely to be charged with a capital offense and receive a death penalty than others. As a result of this study, the Kentucky Senate passed the Kentucky Racial Justice Act, which states, in part, "no person shall be subject to or given a death sentence that was sought on the basis of race." This legislation permits introduction of statistical evidence of racial bias in Kentucky's capital sentencing process in cases sentenced after July 15, 1998.[14] What impact do you think this law might have on your life as a corrections professional in Kentucky?

### CORRECTIONS ISSUES

1. Daryl Mease was scheduled to die by lethal injection in Missouri's death chamber on Wednesday, January 27, 1999, at 12:01 A.M. Pope John Paul II, who was visiting St. Louis at the time, called upon Americans to renounce capital punishment and made a personal appeal to Missouri Governor Mel

Carnahan. "The Pope asked me to have mercy on Mr. Daryl Mease," said the Governor. "I continue to support capital punishment, but because of a deep and abiding respect for the pontiff and all that he represents, I decided last night to grant his request." Mease's lawyers were overjoyed and somber. "I'm sort of torn," said Kent Gipson, Mease's lawyer. "I'm happy for Daryl, but it underscores how arbitrary the death penalty is. Daryl gets spared just because his number was up while the Pope was in town. It was the luck of the draw." Do you agree with Mease's lawyer that the death penalty is arbitrary? Why or why not?

2. Ted Bundy's 10-year stay on Florida's death row until he was executed on January 24, 1989, cost in excess of $6 million. Do you think this was an appropriate use of public funds? Why or why not?

3. The majority of death penalty states have higher murder rates than non-death penalty states. The average murder rate among death penalty states was 7.1 per 100,000 population in 1996; for non-death penalty states the rate was 3.6. The South executes the largest percentage of offenders who are convicted of a capital crime (over 80%) and records the highest murder rate (8.4 murders per 100,000 people); the Northeast executes the fewest (less than 1%) and records a murder rate of 4.8. What conclusions might you draw from these data?

4. Research shows that execution costs more than life imprisonment. Do you think there is a point at which the economic consequence of execution outweighs its value to the public? Explain.

## CORRECTIONS ON THE WEB

1. The Death Penalty Information Center, a source of current information on the death penalty, maintains a Web site at **http://www. essential.org/dpic**. Test your knowledge of capital punishment by taking the DPIC "Death Penalty Quiz." Click on "Information Topics," then "Death Penalty Quiz."

2. Use the FindLaw Web site to compare the aggravating and mitigating circumstances different states consider in determining the sentence for a capital crime. See Figure 13–1 on page 378 for the list of jurisdictions that permit the death penalty. For example, if you want to find the aggravating circumstances for the state of Alabama, go to **http://www.findlaw.com/ casecode/state.html**, click on "Alabama," then under "Primary Materials" on "Code." Click "Criminal Code," then "Punishments and Sentences." Scroll down and click the link (Section 13A-5-49) to the left of "aggravating circumstances."

## ADDITIONAL READINGS

Bedau, Hugo Adam. *The Death Penalty in America: Current Controversies*. New York: Oxford University Press, 1997.

Bohm, Robert M. *Deathquest: An Introduction to the Theory and Practice of Capital Punishment in the United States*. Cincinnati: Anderson Publishing Company, 1999.

Costanzo, Mark. *Just Revenge: Costs and Consequences of the Death Penalty*. New York: St. Martin's Press, 1997.

Johnson, Robert. *Death Work: A Study of the Modern Execution Process*, 2d ed. Belmont, CA: Wadsworth Publishing, 1998.

Marquart, James W., Sheldon Ekland-Olson, and Jonathan R. Sorensen. *The Rope, The Chair, and the Needle: Capital Punishment in Texas, 1923–1990*. Austin: University of Texas Press, 1994.

Paternoster, Raymond. *Capital Punishment in America*. New York: Lexington Books, 1991.

## ENDNOTES

1. See the Death Penalty Information Center Web site for current international death information. Online at http://www.essential.org/dpic/dpicintl.html.

2. Victoria Schneider and John Ortiz Smykla, "A Summary Analysis of Executions in the United States, 1608–1987: The Espy File," Robert M. Bohm (ed.), *The Death Penalty in America: Current Research* (Cincinnati: Anderson Publishing Company, 1991), pp. 1–19.

3. Tracy L. Snell, *Capital Punishment 1998*, Bureau of Justice Statistics (Washington: U.S. Department of Justice, NCJ 179012, December 1999), p. 3.

4. *Death Row U.S.A., Winter 2000* (New York: NAACP Defense and Education Fund, January 1, 2000), p. 1.

5. Ibid.

6. Robert Johnson, "Under Sentence of Death, The Psychology of Death Row Confinement," *Law and Psychology Review*, Vol. 5 (Fall 1979), pp. 141–192.

7. As quoted in Bonnie Bartel Latino and Bob Vale, "Welcome to Death Row," *The Birmingham News*, January 16, 2000, pp. 1C, 4C.

8. Mark Costanzo, *Just Revenge: Costs and Consequences of the Death Penalty* (New York: St. Martin's Press, 1997), p. 51.

9. As quoted in John Ortiz Smykla, "The Human Impact of Capital Punishment," *Journal of Criminal Justice*, Vol. 15, Number 4 (1987), pp. 331–347.

10. *Furman* v. *Georgia*, 408 U.S. 238 (1972).

11. *Woodson* v. *North Carolina*, 428 U.S. 280 (1976); *Roberts* v. *Louisiana*, 428 U.S. 325 (1976); *Gregg* v. *Georgia*, 428 U.S. 153 (1976); *Jurek* v. *Texas*, 428 U.S. 262 (1976); and *Proffitt* v. *Florida* 428 U.S. 242 (1976).

12. Hugo Adam Bedau and Michael L. Radelet, "Miscarriages of Justice in Potentially Capital Cases," *Stanford Law Review*, Vol. 40 (1987), pp. 21–179.

13. See, for example, Michael L. Radelet, Hugo Adam Bedau, and Constance E. Putnam, *In Spite of Innocence: Erroneous Convictions in Capital Cases* (Boston: Northeastern University Press, 1992); Samuel Gross, "The Risks of Death: Why Erroneous Convictions are Common in Capital Cases," *Buffalo Law Review*, Vol. 44 (Fall 1996), pp. 469–500; and Richard C. Dieter, *Innocence and the Death Penalty: The Increasing Danger of Executing the Innocent* (Washington: Death Penalty Information Center, 1997).

14. Gennaro F. Vito, "Presidential Address. Research and Relevance: Role of the Academy of Criminal Justice Sciences," *Justice Quarterly*, Vol. 16, Number 1 (March 1999), pp. 10–13.

# 14 Juvenile Corrections

## End of an Era?

## CHAPTER OBJECTIVES

After completing this chapter you should be able to:

1. Explain *parens patriae*.
2. Describe Houses of Refuge, reform schools, and industrial schools.
3. Discuss the history of the juvenile court.
4. Summarize five U.S. Supreme Court cases that changed modern day juvenile court proceedings.
5. Discuss the two types of juvenile crime.
6. List the characteristics of the typical juvenile delinquent.
7. List and explain the three stages of the juvenile justice process.
8. List disposition options for adjudicated juvenile offenders.
9. List and explain four teen court models.
10. Explain how youth gangs affect juvenile correctional institutions.

FRANKLIN COUNTY JUVENILE DETENTION CENTER

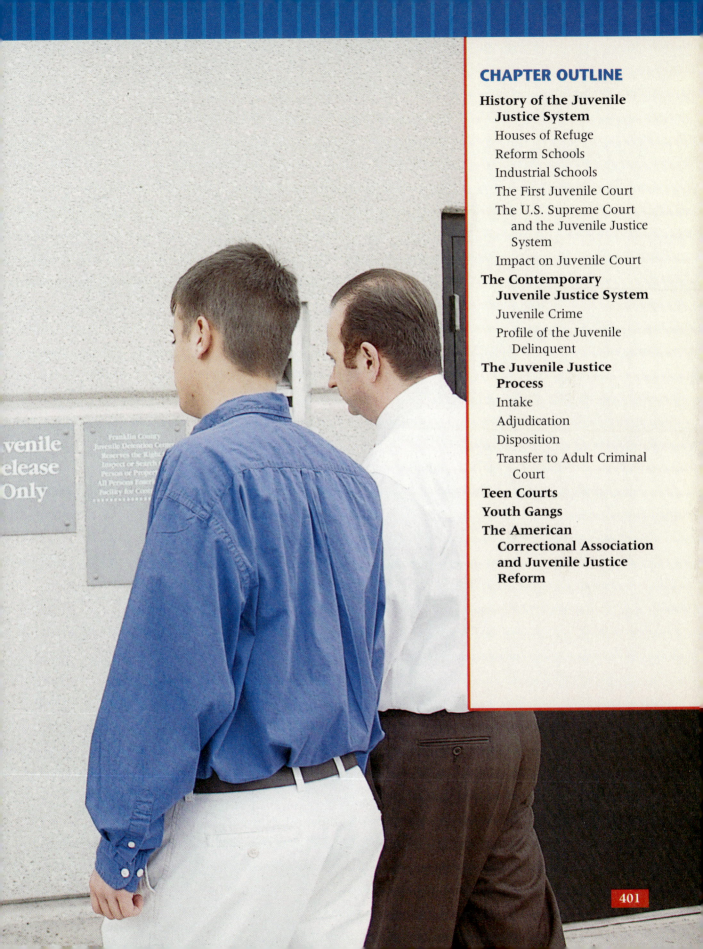

*The vast majority of youth are good citizens who have never been arrested for any type of crime.*

—Shay Bilchik

Here is a portion of a story that recently appeared in a midwestern city newspaper:[1]

A teen-ager accused of killing his father and stepmother disliked his stepmother and used disparaging terms to describe her to his buddies, one of the youth's friends testified yesterday.

"Brandon never really liked Becky," Trevor Howe said during a hearing in Hardin County Juvenile Court. "He also called her the 'B' word."

Howe, 16, testified at a hearing to determine whether Brandon Grigaliunas, 16, should be tried as an adult for the October slayings of his father, Scott, 39, and stepmother, Rebecca, 42, in their home in Kenton, about 50 miles northwest of Columbus.

Grigaliunas is charged with two delinquency counts each of aggravated murder and murder. In juvenile court, the most serious penalty he could face is juvenile detention until age 21. As an adult, he could face life in prison.

He was 15 at the time of the shootings, and County Prosecutor Lora Manon made the request to have him tried as an adult.

Although the majority of juvenile offenders are charged with property offenses rather than violent offenses, the majority of juvenile offenses reported by the media involve violent crime, which overstates the violence issue and unduly alarms the public. High-profile juvenile violence—such as the shootings at Columbine High School on April 20, 1999 and the National Zoo in Washington on April 24, 2000—is changing juvenile corrections from treatment to punishment. As a result, attention and scarce resources focus on a small portion of juvenile offenders, neglecting the vast majority.

Juvenile justice will face other challenges in its second century of existence. The United States Congress, the Department of Justice, the American Bar Association, the NAACP, think-tanks, academic researchers, and others are revealing a juvenile justice system that disproportionately arrests, prosecutes, and sentences minority youth. Data from several sources show that minority youth are more likely than white youth who commit comparable crimes to be arrested, be referred to juvenile court, be detained, face trial as adults, be jailed with adults, and sentenced to correctional institutions.

Some argue that minority youth are victims of racial bias built into the justice system. Others maintain that juvenile justice policies discriminate against low-income youth, who are overwhelmingly minority, from single-parent homes, or in foster care. Still others claim that overrepresentation simply means that minority youth are committing more crimes or more serious crimes. Whatever the explanation, significant change is underway. In 1992, the U.S. Congress strengthened its commitment to end disproportionate juvenile minority confinement by elevating the issue as a core requirement in federal juvenile justice legislation. The Office of Juvenile Justice and Delinquency Prevention (OJJDP) has taken the lead to develop solutions in partnership with the states.

# History of the Juvenile Justice System

The historical origins of America's juvenile justice system can be traced to early England, where bridewells (the first houses of corrections) confined both children and adults until 1704, when John Howard brought to England a model of a Roman institution for juvenile offenders (see Chapter 3). Colonists brought these ideas with them to America, and reformers tailored the ideas to their experiences, creating Houses of Refuge, reform schools, and industrial schools for juveniles. Both the English and American juvenile justice systems utilize the doctrine of *parens patriae*, the state as parent. The first known application of *parens patriae* in America was in 1636. Bridget Fuller was ordered by the governor of Plymouth Colony to take Benjamen Eaton, keep him in school for two years, and keep him employed.[2] By the end of the 19th century, every American state had affirmed its right to act as guardian of minors.

*parens patriae* A Latin term that refers to the state as guardian of minors and incompetent people.

## Houses of Refuge

The New York House of Refuge, the first legally chartered American custodial institution for juvenile offenders, was founded in 1825 by penal reformer Thomas Eddy, educational reformer John Griscom, and the Society for the Prevention of Pauperism. Its purpose was to provide poor, abused, and orphaned youths with food, clothing, and lodging in exchange for hard work, discipline, and study. The concept spread, and Houses of Refuge were established throughout America.

Living conditions in Houses of Refuge were not as generous as the term *refuge* might imply. Administrators of these institutions subjected juveniles to hard physical labor and were known to use corporal punishment. Residents were expected to earn their keep and comply with strict institutional rules. Guards and superintendents, who replaced parents or guardians, exhibited little tolerance or understanding.

Despite the path-breaking role the House of Refuge played in the development of the American juvenile justice system, the original institutions were short-lived. The movement as a whole died out by the middle of the 19th century.

# Reform Schools

**reform school** A penal institution to which especially young or first-time offenders are committed for training and reformation.

The nation's first state-sponsored **reform school** opened in Massachusetts in 1848. Named the Lyman School, for Theodore Lyman, a former mayor of Boston, the institution resembled a prison. The school was designed to house 300 boys. Because of liberal admissions policies and unregulated commitment procedures, the reformatory was filled within a few years. The Massachusetts legislature authorized an addition, doubling the structure's capacity.

In the late 1800s, with the school again becoming overcrowded, a ship in Boston Harbor was designated an annex. Any boy under age 14 could be committed to either Lyman School or its Nautical Branch. Boys who were housed at the Nautical Branch were trained in navigation and the duties of seamen, then transferred to passing vessels that needed cabin boys or young laborers.

Because the Lyman School housed only boys, the Massachusetts legislature voted to create a separate institution for girls. Belief that the physical and emotional make-up of girls was inherently more delicate than that of boys led reformers to focus on a new European model for the girls school.

European-style reform schools introduced a small residential arrangement, breaking down structural barriers so that staff and inmates could interact, providing a more intimate setting for treatment. Advocates of the European-style reform school believed that personal contact with youth was the cornerstone of the rehabilitative effort. Under the new design, as many as thirty inmates with similar personality traits were placed in separate small homes or cottages and supervised by paid "cottage parents." Residents of each house or cottage lived, worked, and attended school together, meeting with inmates in other living quarters only infrequently.

The first of the European-style reform schools was the Lancaster Industrial School for Girls in Massachusetts, established in 1854. The Lancaster cottages had features associated with both school and home, and provided academic classes and domestic training programs. Lancaster's cottage plan gained national attention as prison reform advocates encouraged adoption of this system for youthful offenders throughout the United States.

# Industrial Schools

After the Civil War, state welfare services expanded and began to require that juvenile reform schools and adult penal institutions help pay operating costs by contracting inmate labor to local manufacturers. The use of juvenile contract labor hindered the growth of reform schools. Manufacturers controlled the children during working hours, and exploitation and brutality were common. Some reform schools were converted into housing units to better serve manufacturers' labor needs.

Concerned citizens and elected officials recognized the inadequacies of reform schools. Public efforts were made to improve institutional life and to reduce the number of children being incarcerated. Special state committees investigated abuses in contract labor systems, and reform schools were added to the list of public institutions that were subject to annual inspection by regulatory agencies.

# The First Juvenile Court

The movement toward establishing a separate juvenile court began in 1870, when the Illinois Supreme Court heard *People ex rel O'Connell* v. *Turner*.[3] Daniel O'Connell was committed to the Chicago Reform School for vagrancy. His parents protested the confinement and petitioned the court for Daniel's release. In its decision, which ordered Daniel's release, the Illinois Supreme Court:

- recognized that Daniel's parents genuinely wanted to care for their son;
- held that vagrancy was a matter of misfortune, not a criminal act;
- viewed Daniel's commitment to the Chicago Reform School as a punishment, not merely placement in a school for troubled children; and
- deemed Daniel's incarceration imprisonment—the doctrine of *parens patriae* did not apply and formal due process protections were required.

By the end of the 19th century, debate about juvenile facilities had established the need for differentiating between juveniles and adults in court procedures. Some states had even established children's aid societies to represent juveniles in court and to supervise them in the community.

The first completely separate juvenile court was established in Illinois in 1899. The Illinois legislature passed a law called "An Act to Regulate the Treatment and Control of Dependent, Neglected and Delinquent Children," which established a juvenile court in Cook County that had jurisdiction over any youth who committed an act that would be a crime if committed by an adult. However, young criminal offenders were not the only juveniles who needed help or supervision—the legislation was revised to also give the juvenile court jurisdiction over:

> . . . any child who for any reason is destitute or homeless or abandoned; or dependent on the public for support; or has not proper parental care or guardianship; or who habitually begs or receives alms; or who is found living in any house of ill fame or with any vicious or disreputable person; or whose home, by reason of neglect, cruelty or depravity on part of its parents, guardian or other person in whose care it may be, is an unfit place for such a child; and any child under the age of 8 years who is found peddling or selling any article or singing or playing any musical instrument upon the street or giving any public entertainment.[4]

The intent of the new legislation was to give the juvenile court jurisdiction when the child's best interests would be served.

The Illinois act was a prototype for legislation in other states, and juvenile courts were quickly established in Wisconsin (1901), New York (1901), Ohio (1902), Maryland (1902), and Colorado (1903). By 1945, all states had established separate juvenile courts. New terminology accompanied the establishment of the juvenile court, to differentiate it from adult criminal court. Juvenile offenders are "delinquents" rather than "criminals," they are "taken into custody" rather than "arrested," a "petition" is filed rather than a "charge," juveniles are "held on petition" rather than "indicted," there is an "adjudicatory hearing" rather than a "trial," the court returns a "finding" rather than a "verdict" and imposes a "disposition" rather than a "sentence," the offender is "adjudicated" rather than "convicted," sent to a "training school" rather than a "prison," and put on "aftercare" rather than "parole."

## The U.S. Supreme Court and the Juvenile Justice System

For most of the 20th century, all juvenile hearings were considered civil proceedings—rules of criminal procedure did not apply. Juveniles had no constitutional protections, and there were no challenges to the admissibility of evidence or the validity of testimony.

Five landmark U.S. Supreme Court decisions dramatically changed the juvenile justice system, establishing due process rights for juvenile offenders.

***Kent v. United States* (1966)**[5] In 1959, Morris A. Kent, Jr., age 14, was arrested in Washington, D.C. on charges of burglary and attempted purse snatching. He was placed on juvenile probation and returned to his mother's custody. In September 1961, an intruder entered a woman's apartment, raped her, and stole her wallet. Police found Kent's fingerprints at the crime scene. Kent, now age 16 and still on probation, was arrested and charged with rape and robbery. He confessed to these offenses and several similar incidents. Kent's mother retained an attorney, who, anticipating that the case would be transferred to an adult criminal court, filed a motion to oppose the transfer.

The juvenile court judge did not rule on this motion; instead, he waived jurisdiction and remanded Kent to the jurisdiction of the adult criminal court system. Kent was tried in U.S. District Court, found guilty of six counts of housebreaking, and found "not guilty by reason of insanity" on the rape charge. He received indeterminate sentences of 5 to 15 years on each count of housebreaking.

Kent's lawyer appealed the conviction, citing that the juvenile court judge failed to hear motions filed on Kent's behalf before waiving the case to adult criminal court and that Kent's due process rights had been denied. The U.S. Supreme Court heard the case, and Kent's conviction was reversed.

In *Kent*, the Court ruled that, in a case involving transfer of jurisdiction, the juvenile defendant is entitled to certain essential due process rights: (1) a hearing; (2) representation by an attorney; (3) access to records involved in the transfer; and (4) a written statement of reasons for the transfer.

***In re Gault* (1967)**[6] On June 8, 1964, Gerald F. Gault, age 15, was arrested for making a crank telephone call to an adult neighbor and taken to a detention home by the sheriff of Gila County, Arizona. At the time, Gault was on juvenile probation for involvement in the theft of a lady's wallet in February 1964.

The complainant was not present at the juvenile court hearing on the following day. No one was sworn at the hearing, no transcript or recording of the proceedings was made, and no decision was issued. Gault was

*Juvenile Corrections: End of an Era?*

returned to the detention home—where he remained for several days—then released. At a second hearing, on June 15, the judge committed Gault to the Arizona State Industrial School "for the period of his minority." Gault's attorney filed a petition for a writ of *habeas corpus* that was heard by the U.S. Supreme Court in December 1966.

In its May 1967 *Gault* decision, the U.S. Supreme Court ruled that, in proceedings that might result in commitment to an institution, juveniles have the right to: (1) reasonable notice of charges; (2) counsel; (3) question witnesses; and (4) protection against self-incrimination.

### In re Winship (1970)[7]

Samuel Winship, age 12, was charged with stealing $112 from a woman's purse. Winship's attorney argued that there was "reasonable doubt" of Winship's guilt. The court agreed, but, because New York juvenile courts operated under the civil court standard of "preponderance of the evidence," adjudicated Winship delinquent and committed him to a training school for 18 months.

The U.S. Supreme Court, in *Winship*, ruled that the reasonable doubt standard should be required in all delinquency adjudications.

### McKeiver v. Pennsylvania (1971)[8]

Joseph McKeiver, age 16, was charged with robbery, larceny, and receiving stolen property in Philadelphia, when he and 20 or 30 other juveniles took 25 cents from three boys. McKeiver had no prior arrests, was doing well in school, and was employed. McKeiver's attorney requested a jury trial; his request was denied and McKeiver was adjudicated and put on probation.

McKeiver's attorney appealed to the state supreme court on the grounds that the juvenile court violated the 6th Amendment's guarantee of the right to an impartial jury and the 7th Amendment's guarantee of the right to a trial by jury. The state supreme court affirmed the lower court, arguing that, of all due process rights, a trial by jury is the one most likely to destroy the traditional non-adversarial character of juvenile court proceedings.

The U.S. Supreme Court, in *McKeiver*, held that the due process clause of the 14th Amendment did not require jury trials in juvenile court (although a state could provide a jury trial if it wished), that juries are not necessarily more accurate than judges, and that juries could be disruptive and therefore adversarial to the informal atmosphere of the juvenile court.

### Breed v. Jones (1975)[9]

In February 1971, Gary S. Jones, age 17, was charged with armed robbery and adjudicated delinquent in a Los Angeles juvenile court. The judge deferred sentencing, pending receipt of a predisposition report and a recommendation from the probation department. Jones was returned to detention. When the court reconvened for the disposition hearing, the judge waived jurisdiction to adult criminal court. Counsel for Jones filed a petition for a writ of *habeas corpus*, arguing that waiver to criminal court violated the double jeopardy clause of the 5th Amendment. The U.S. District Court denied the petition, saying that Jones had not been tried twice because juvenile adjudication is not a trial. Jones was tried in adult criminal court, convicted of robbery, and committed to the California Youth Authority for an indeterminate period.

The U.S. Supreme Court, in *Breed*, ruled that juvenile adjudication for violation of a criminal statute is equivalent to a criminal court trial; therefore, the double jeopardy clause applied. The Court ordered that Jones be released or remanded to the original juvenile court for a disposition hearing. Jones, now over 18, was released.

## Impact on Juvenile Court

The U.S. Supreme Court's decisions in these cases affirmed juvenile due process rights. As a result, the "best interests of the child" is no longer the only concern for juvenile courts; they also are required to protect the juvenile's constitutional rights.

# The Contemporary Juvenile Justice System

Age limits for juvenile court jurisdiction are defined by state statutes. In most states, the juvenile court has original jurisdiction over all youths under age 18 at the time of offense, arrest, or referral to court (see Table 14–1).

| TABLE 14–1 | |
|---|---|
| **Oldest Age for Original Juvenile Court Jurisdiction in Delinquency Matters** | |
| **Age** | **State** |
| 15 | Connecticut, New York, North Carolina |
| 16 | Georgia, Illinois, Louisiana, Massachusetts, Michigan, Missouri, New Hampshire, South Carolina, Texas, Wisconsin |
| 17 | Alabama, Alaska, Arizona, Arkansas, California, Colorado, Delaware, District of Columbia, Florida, Hawaii, Idaho, Indiana, Iowa, Kansas, Kentucky, Maine, Maryland, Minnesota, Mississippi, Montana, Nebraska, Nevada, New Jersey, New Mexico, North Dakota, Ohio, Oklahoma, Oregon, Pennsylvania, Rhode Island, South Dakota, Tennessee, Utah, Vermont, Virginia, Washington, West Virginia, Wyoming |

*Juvenile Corrections: End of an Era?*

# Juvenile Crime

U.S. law enforcement agencies arrested approximately 2.6 million juveniles in 1998.[10] According to the Federal Bureau of Investigation (FBI), juveniles accounted for 18 percent of all 1998 arrests, and 17 percent of all 1998 violent crime arrests. Most juvenile arrests were for property crime offenses (see Figure 14–1).

More than 90 percent of the cases handled by juvenile courts are for **delinquent offenses**—acts committed by a juvenile that, if committed by an adult, could result in criminal prosecution. The remaining cases are for **status offenses**—acts that are offenses only when committed by juveniles (e.g., running away, truancy, ungovernability, and liquor law violations). In 1996, liquor law violations accounted for 28 percent of status offense cases; truancy, 24 percent; runaway, 16 percent; ungovernability, 12 percent; and miscellaneous other status offenses, 20 percent.[11]

**delinquent offenses**
Acts committed by juveniles which, if committed by adults, could result in criminal prosecution.

**status offenses**  Acts that are law violations only for juveniles: e.g., running away, truancy, or ungovernability (sometimes referred to as incorrigibility or beyond parental control).

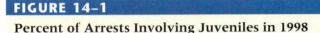

## FIGURE 14–1

### Percent of Arrests Involving Juveniles in 1998

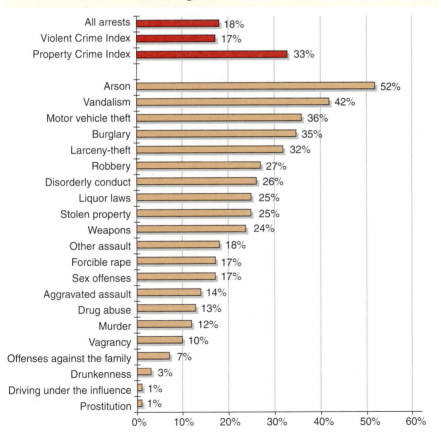

*Source:* Adapted from Federal Bureau of Investigation, *Crime in the United States 1998* (Washington, DC: U.S. Government Printing Office, 1999), table 38.

*Sophia Nelson
Drug Counselor and
Parent Educator
West Palm Beach, FL*

*"Be ready for a roller-coaster ride of emotions. Every day your clients are up and down. Your personality has to be able to adjust to that for you to be successful."*

Sophia Nelson is a drug counselor and parent educator in West Palm Beach, Florida. She's been in her job for four years. As a drug counselor, she carries a caseload of 55 clients and conducts intake assessments and provides treatment. As a parent educator, she facilitates group counseling for children and single mothers. She assists the children in her groups with improving their communication and interaction skills and building confidence techniques. She helps single moms improve their life skills that provide them with the knowledge, skills, and attitudes they need to maintain strong family ties, find and keep good jobs, manage their finances, and lead productive lives.

Sophia graduated from Bethune-Cookman College in Daytona Beach, Florida, with a degree in criminal justice. The courses she recalls enjoying the most were those where there was a lot of classroom discussion, especially courses in prisoners' rights, correctional counseling, and social policy. She says she knew from these courses that she wanted a career working with people. Now that she's a drug counselor and parent educator, she feels she contributes to her community by helping people avoid drugs and develop more healthy lifestyles. She says, "I see lives change each day."

For now, Sophia wants to stay working with drug offenders and teaching life skills to parents and children. But one day she hopes to be a prison warden and influence correctional policy on a large scale.

## Profile of the Juvenile Delinquent

Of the estimated 1.8 million delinquency cases handled by U.S. juvenile courts in 1996:

- Fifty-nine percent involved a juvenile under age 16.
- Seventy-seven percent involved boys.
- Sixty-six percent involved white juveniles, 30 percent black.
- Fifty percent were drug property offenses.

# The Juvenile Justice Process

Juvenile offenders are processed through one or more of three phases of the juvenile justice process: intake, adjudication, and disposition. Figure 14–2 shows that U.S. juvenile courts processed almost 1.8 million delinquency cases in 1996. Juvenile courts also processed 162,000 status offense cases. Fifty-two percent of these status offense cases were adjudicated; the disposition was probation in almost 60 percent of the cases.

FIGURE 14–2

## Juvenile Court Processing of Delinquency Cases, 1996

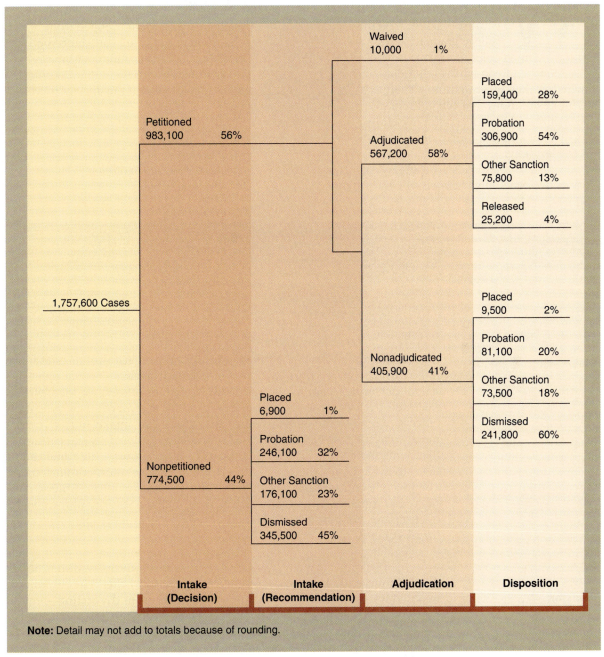

Note: Detail may not add to totals because of rounding.

Source: Anne L. Stahl, Melissa Sickmund, Terrence A. Finnegan, Howard N. Snyder, Rowen S. Poole, and Nancy Tierney, *Juvenile Court Statistics 1996* (Washington, DC: U.S. Department of Justice, Office of Juvenile Justice and Delinquency Prevention, July 1999), p. 9.

**W**orking with teens is especially challenging for me because—being a recent college graduate—I am not that much older than youths who are expected to do what I tell them, whether they want to or not. There are a lot of situations that can get sticky. When they do, I just remind myself to be patient and that I am many of these kids' last hope.

Most of these kids are 180-day expulsion cases from their high schools. If I give up on them, the only alternative is dropping out altogether. Each time I think of giving up I ask myself: "If this student dropped from school today could my conscience be clear that I did everything within my power to work with them?" You know what? I have not had the answer be yes yet.

*Julie Judge*
*Teacher*
*Alternative Learning Center*
*Florissant, Missouri*

## Intake

**intake** The first stage of the juvenile justice process. A court-appointed officer reviews the case and recommends a course of action—dismissal, informal disposition, formal disposition, or transfer to adult criminal court.

In the first phase of the juvenile justice process, **intake**, cases that are referred to juvenile court (by law enforcement agencies, social agencies, school personnel, parents or guardians, probation officers, or victims) are reviewed by a court-appointed officer (usually a prosecutor or probation officer), who recommends a course of action. The intake officer recommends that the case be: (1) dismissed, (2) resolved informally (no petition is filed with the court), (3) resolved formally (a petition for an adjudication hearing is filed with the court), or (4) transferred to adult criminal court. The juvenile court establishes guidelines for the intake officer. Criteria considered in the decision in many jurisdictions include: severity of the alleged offense, any prior history of delinquent behavior, attitude, age, and emotional stability.

**diversion** A non-judicial juvenile sanction.

**Informal Disposition** In cases that are resolved informally, disposition is decided by the intake officer, and the case goes no further. The disposition imposed is usually informal probation or some form of **diversion**—requiring the youth to make restitution or referring the youth to a local social service agency. Diversion is generally an option only for status offenders or low-risk delinquent offenders.

**Formal Disposition**   In cases that are to be resolved formally, the intake officer files a petition for an adjudicatory hearing and decides whether the youth should be confined while awaiting the hearing.

**Detention Hearing**   If the intake officer decides that secure placement is advisable, the youth is taken to a **juvenile detention facility**. In general terms, a juvenile detention facility serves to keep juvenile offenders in secure custody through various stages of the juvenile justice process, to protect the community and the juvenile, and to ensure appearance at scheduled hearings.

A juvenile who is placed in a detention facility by an intake officer must have a **detention hearing**, usually within 48 hours. During this hearing, the court reviews the intake officer's confinement decision and orders either release or continued detention pending adjudication and disposition.

Also during the detention hearing, the court determines whether the youth has legal representation and, if not, appoints defense counsel. The court may also appoint a **guardian *ad litem***, who serves as a special guardian for the youth throughout the court proceedings. In many jurisdictions, defense counsel also serves as guardian.

## Adjudication

In the second phase of the juvenile justice process, **adjudication**, a juvenile court hears the case. A **juvenile court** is any court that has original jurisdiction over matters involving juveniles.

**Adjudicatory Hearing**   During the adjudicatory hearing, attorneys typically present physical evidence, examine and cross-examine witnesses, and argue on behalf of their clients. If, after hearing arguments, the court rules that the evidence supports the allegations, a predisposition report is ordered and a disposition hearing scheduled.

## Disposition

In the third phase of the juvenile justice process, the juvenile court decides on a **disposition**.

**Predisposition Report**   The court's disposition decision is based on its review of the intake report (information regarding the current offense and any previous delinquent behavior—crime severity and prior adjudication greatly influence the decision) and the **predisposition report**, a document, usually prepared by a probation officer, similar to the PSI discussed in Chapter 5. A predisposition report typically includes (1) medical and psychological background; (2) educational history; (3) information gathered from interviews with the juvenile, family members, and other people who know the youth; (4) availability of appropriate placement options; and (5) recommendations for suitable disposition. Any treatment "needs" of the youth are also considered.

---

**juvenile detention facility**   A facility for keeping juvenile offenders in secure custody, as necessary, through various stages of the juvenile justice process.

**detention hearing**   A judicial review of the intake officer's detention decision.

**guardian *ad litem***   A person appointed by the juvenile court, often defense counsel, to serve as a special guardian for the youth being processed through the juvenile justice system.

**adjudication**   The second stage of the juvenile justice process—the court decides whether or not the offender is responsible for (guilty of) the alleged offense.

**juvenile court**   Any court that has jurisdiction over matters involving juveniles.

**disposition**   The third stage of the juvenile justice process—the court decides the disposition (sentence) for a juvenile case.

**predisposition report**   A report that documents: (1) the juvenile's background; (2) educational history; (3) information gathered from interviews with the juvenile, family members, and others; (4) available placement options; and (5) recommended dispositions.

*Juvenile probation officers play an important role in the juvenile justice process, beginning with intake and continuing through the period in which a juvenile is under court supervision. Why is writing the predisposition report such an important part of the probation officer's responsibilities?*

**Disposition Hearing** At the disposition hearing the court imposes the appropriate sanction. In some jurisdictions, the youth is remanded either to the state correctional system or to a social service agency. Many juvenile courts ensure that adjudicated juveniles receive an appropriate disposition by establishing predefined sanctions based on type of offense, past delinquency, effectiveness of previous interventions, and assessment of special treatment, counseling, or training needs. Some of the more widely used sanctions are juvenile probation, group homes, residential treatment centers, boot camps, and commitment to juvenile correctional institutions.

If the sanction imposed is probation, the youth is permitted to remain in the community under the supervision of a court services officer. Figure 14–3 shows a supervision agreement used by the juvenile court of Topeka, Kansas.

If a youth poses a threat to public safety but incarceration is not warranted, the court may impose Intensive Supervised Probation (ISP). The major differences between regular probation and ISP are (1) more rigid conditions, and (2) more frequent contact between the probation officer and the probationer—more face-to-face interaction, closer monitoring of the juvenile's activities, and more frequent evaluation of the juvenile's progress.

**group home** A non-secure residential facility for juveniles.

Another sanction that may be imposed is referral to a **group home**. Group homes are operated by private agencies, under contract with local or state government; or by the public corrections unit, under direction of the juvenile court. Typically, group homes accommodate 15 to 30 residents. They provide living quarters, recreational and leisure areas, kitchen and dining room, and meeting room space. Youths attend school in the community, participate in field trips, and may be granted special passes to visit family, attend religious services, or participate in activities. The range of services provided by the group home often depends on the type of offender usually

## FIGURE 14–3

### Sample Juvenile Court Supervision Agreement

# SUPERVISION AGREEMENT

Name _____Andrea Johnson_____ Case Number _____00JV2751_____

In accordance with authority conferred by the laws of the state of Kansas, you have been placed under the supervision of Court Services. It is the order of the Court that you comply with any special conditions, programs, or counseling as set forth by the supervision Court Services Officer.

The following conditions will apply:

__X__ 1.     You will attend all regularly scheduled appointments with the Court Services Officer and comply with their directions. If you are ill, it is your responsibility to make other arrangements.

__X__ 2.     You will obey all laws of the State and ordinances of the City. You are to immediately report any contacts with law enforcement to your Court Services Officer.

__X__ 3.     You are to obey the rules of your home. Persistent disobedience will be considered a violation of your supervision.

__X__ 4.     You are not to leave the state of Kansas nor change residence without permission of your Court Services Officer. You are to notify the officer of any change in address prior to moving. You will reside in the home of your parent(s) or approved guardian and will not be permitted to spend the night away from home without prior permission of said parent(s) or guardian.

__X__ 5.     You will attend school every day and obey all school regulations. Suspension, truancies, and tardies could result in further court action. If you are home due to illness or school suspensions, you are to consider yourself on a form of house arrest. This means if you are ill, you are only permitted to leave to attend verifiable doctors appointments. If you are on suspension, you are not to leave your home unless you are with a parent or guardian.

_____ 6.     If you have been excused form attending school, you will obtain employment (get a job) and work faithfully at that job in order to maintain it. You will not quit any job without first discussing it with your Court Service Officer. If you are fired or laid off from a job, you are required to report that fact to your Court Service Officer by the end of the next business day.

__X__ 7.     You will neither possess nor carry firearms or other weapons.

__X__ 8.     You will neither use nor possess any alcohol, narcotics, or other controlled substances.

_____ 9.     Your are to submit to chemical tests of blood, breath, or urine.

__X__ 10.   You have a curfew. If you are under the age of 15, your curfew is 9:00 p.m. Sunday through Thursday, and 10:30 p.m. Friday and Saturday. If you are 15 or older, your curfew is 10:00 p.m. Sunday through Thursday, and 12:00 midnight Friday and Saturday. Curfew means that you will be inside your own residence by the stated time. With parent or guardian's permission, you may attend a school or church sponsored function at the school or church you attend, but must be home not later than 30 minutes after the end of the event.

*- 1 -*

## FIGURE 14–3 (continued)

### Sample Juvenile Court Supervision Agreement

_____ 11.      It will be considered a violation of your supervision if you display clothing or insignia indicating membership in a gang, or carry a beeper, pager, or cellular telephone equipment.

__X__ 12.      You will not be discharged from supervision until all costs, fees, and restitution has been paid in full.

| Traffic/City Ordinance | District Court | Guardian Ad Litem | |
|---|---|---|---|
| Fines: _____ | Costs: $25.00 | Fees: _____ | Restitution: $299.95 |

__X__ Payment Plan _____ $54.16/month for 6 months _____

__X__ I will complete __20__ hours Community Service Work ( X ) in addition to, or (  ) in lieu of the above.

SPECIAL CONDITIONS:

__X__ a). Do not go into Electronics Plus for 6 months.

__X__ b). Within two weeks, write a letter of apology to Ms. Valerie Carte, owner of Electronics Plus.

__X__ c). Do not quit your weekend job at Bruno's grocery store until court costs and restitution are paid.

__X__ d). Write a three page paper on why shoplifting is wrong and hand deliver it to Judge Gray in three weeks.

I have read, understood, initialed and agreed to abide by all terms and special conditions of my supervision as explained by the assigned Court Services Officer. I understand fully that my failure to comply could result in the imposition of additional condition, revocation and/or out of home placement.

DATE: _May 17, 2000_             SIGNED: ___*Andrea Johnson*___
                                                       Respondent

                                                    ___*Rosalind Johnson*___
                                                      Parent or Guardian

                                                    ___*Gary Bayens*___
                                                    Court Services Officer

cc: Working File
     Respondent
     Parents or Guardian

- 2 -

referred. Some group homes are treatment-oriented, providing individual and/or group counseling to youths with problems such as substance abuse or lack of self-control.

Another community-based program is the **residential treatment center**. Residential treatment centers often provide long-term care and intensive treatment services.

Today, most states have juvenile boot camps. Boot camp programs vary in size, requirements, and structure. For the most part, juvenile corrections officials have been slow to accept the boot camp concept; they consider the amount of time devoted to military drill, ceremony, and exercise an encroachment on the time available for education or rehabilitation programs.

The most restrictive sanction that a juvenile court may impose is commitment to a juvenile correctional institution. Although the juvenile justice system is different from the adult criminal justice system, many juvenile correctional institutions resemble adult correctional institutions. Access to the facilities is restricted, and perimeter fences are equipped with razor wire. Surveillance cameras, located throughout the complex, are monitored from a central security location. Housing units are austere physical structures that emphasize security.

Characteristics of the estimated 73,000 juvenile offenders confined in juvenile correctional facilities are similar to those of adult prisoners: 90 percent are male, 46 percent are black, 40 percent have committed property offenses (larceny, burglary, auto theft, or vandalism), and 29 percent have committed violent crimes (murder, rape, robbery, or assault).[12] The average age of confined youths is 15.[13] The average time served is eight months.[14]

A few states have responded to violent juvenile crime by enacting **blended sentencing** legislation: the juvenile court may impose both a juvenile sentence and an adult criminal sentence. In 1996, the Kansas legislature passed a blended sentencing law that created a new category, referred to as "extended jurisdiction juvenile prosecution," for serious and violent offenders.[15] Under this legislation, two sentences are imposed, but the adult criminal sentence is waived if the juvenile offender does not violate any of the provisions of the juvenile sentence.

## Transfer to Adult Criminal Court

All states and the District of Columbia allow adult criminal prosecution of juveniles under certain circumstances. Juveniles may be transferred to adult criminal court under one of three provisions: waiver, direct file, or statutory exclusion. Under **waiver provisions**, the juvenile court orders transfer of the case to adult criminal court. In all but four states (Massachusetts, Nebraska, New Mexico, and New York), a juvenile court judge is authorized to waive the juvenile court's original jurisdiction over cases that meet certain criteria and to refer them to criminal court for prosecution. Under **direct file provisions**, the prosecutor determines whether to initiate a case against a juvenile in juvenile court or in adult criminal court. Fifteen states have statutes that specify circumstances in which the prosecutor may make the transfer decision. Under **statutory exclusion provisions**, state law specifies adult criminal court jurisdiction for certain juvenile cases. An increasing number of states (28 in 1996) automatically

**residential treatment center** A residential facility that provides intensive treatment services to juveniles.

**blended sentencing** A two-part (juvenile and adult) sentence—the adult sentence may be waived if the offender complies with all provisions of the juvenile sentence.

**waiver provisions** Provisions under which the juvenile court orders transfer of the case to adult criminal court.

**direct file provisions** Provisions under which the prosecutor determines whether to initiate a case against a juvenile in juvenile court or in adult criminal court.

**statutory exclusion provisions** Provisions under which adult criminal court jurisdiction for certain juvenile cases is established by state law.

exclude from juvenile court any cases that meet specific age and offense criteria. In 1996, 10,000 juvenile cases were transferred to adult criminal court. Of these, 43 percent involved a crime against a person; 37 percent involved property crime; 14 percent involved a drug law violation; and 6 percent involved a public order offense.[16]

# Teen Courts

**teen courts** Courts in which youths adjudicate and impose disposition for a juvenile offense.

**Teen courts**, also called peer and youth courts, have become a popular alternative to the traditional juvenile court for relatively young or first-time offenders. The teen court was first used in Grand Prairie, Texas, in 1976.[17] Since then the number of teen courts has grown, to between 400 and 500 nationwide in 1998.[18] Teen courts handled approximately 65,000 cases in 1998.

Teen courts use one of four models: Adult Judge, Youth Judge, Tribunal, or Peer Jury. In the Adult Judge model, an adult serves as judge, ruling on legal terminology and courtroom procedure, and youth serve as attorneys, jurors, clerks, bailiffs, etc. The Youth Judge model parallels the Adult Judge model, with the exception that a youth serves as judge. In the Tribunal model, youth attorneys present the case to a panel of three youth judges. The Peer Jury model uses no attorneys—the case is presented to a youth jury by

# THE OFFENDER SPEAKS

What about kids? Most juvenile delinquents often show hostile attitudes and are rebellious toward authority because the media shows that it's okay, and these children without adequate supervision will do damn well what they please. A lot of people commit crimes and get away with it, reports the media, and it's cool. The juvenile thinks he can get away with it too, and wants to be cool.

In a broken or poor home, the parent(s) are working all the time so that no one is around the child to give him guidance. Improving family life and enhancing educational systems to make education an exciting and growth-producing experience for juveniles is half the step to crime control.

But is all that what "the man" wants to hear? It's easier to lock those kids up than to put a brake on the media and reduce the opportunities for kids to be alone. When I get out of this hell hole, I hope that somebody will listen! Our children are our future, and if those children are running wild on the streets of Chicago or Columbia, they are going to be here with me, before you know it.

*William Geer*
*Broad River Correctional Institution*
*Columbia, SC*

a youth or adult and the jury questions the defendant directly. Forty-seven percent of teen courts use the Adult Judge model, 12 percent the Peer Jury, 10 percent the Tribunal, and 9 percent the Youth Judge. The remaining 22 percent use more than one model.

Most teen courts require that the defendant plead guilty before participating in the program; only a small number determine guilt or innocence. In teen courts, offenders are sentenced by their peers.

Teen courts are particularly effective in jurisdictions where disposition of misdemeanor offenses is given low priority because of heavy caseloads and focus on more serious offenders. Teen courts also teach young people valuable life skills and provide positive peer influence. Volunteers serve as jurors, attorneys, court clerks, bailiffs, and, in some cases, judges.

According to the Office of Juvenile Justice and Delinquency Prevention (OJJDP), community service was the most common disposition imposed in teen court cases in 1998. Other dispositions included victim apology letters, apology essays, teen court jury duty, drug/alcohol classes, and monetary restitution.

Tammy Hawkins, Teen Court Coordinator for Odessa, Texas, says that teen court makes quite an impact when you give a teenaged jury sole discretion in handing down sentences. "The juvenile defendant receives this sentence from his peers and sees that they are saying, 'We as your peers do not agree with your actions and breaking the law is not acceptable.' A child is more likely to listen to one of their own, as opposed to an adult or the system. After all, as one defendant put it, 'Your peers are the ones that you want to accept you.'"[19]

**Juvenile Detention Officer**

Duties: Maintaining security; Supervising youth; Inspecting for contraband, damage, and repairs; Implementing emergency procedures; Escorting youth to activities; Maintaining an accurate count of residents; Providing non-physical crisis intervention and resolution; Completing logs, security checks, and reports. Requirements: Two years of college in criminology, corrections, law enforcement, or related field. Experience working with youth in a supervised setting.

# Youth Gangs

In a 1999 OJJDP National Youth Gang Center (NYGC) survey, 3,024 law enforcement agencies reported that an estimated 30,818 gangs, with an estimated 846,428 members, were active across the United States.[20] About half of these agencies reported worsening gang problems. All states, and nearly all large cities, reported youth gang problems.[21]

The youth gang problem is one of the most important issues for juvenile corrections today. Many of the youths confined for serious crimes commit violent acts as gang members. For some correctional institutions, a primary housing consideration is a youth's gang affiliation—rival gang members must be housed separately. Juvenile correctional personnel regularly deal with problems that stem from gang-related activity within the institution: extortion, violence, and attempts to smuggle in contraband.

One of the more pressing gang-related issues facing today's juvenile corrections agencies is identification of youth gangs. A **gang** is a group of individuals involved in continuing criminal activity. The group need not wear similar clothing ("colors") or tattoos, have hand signs, initiation rituals, or even a specific name (e.g., "Crips" or "Bloods") to be a gang—participation in criminal activity is what distinguishes community groups or social clubs from gangs.

**gang** A group of individuals involved in continuing criminal activity.

Graffiti is a common method of communication for gangs;[22] the gang "newspaper" or "bulletin board," graffiti communicates many messages, including challenges, warnings, and pronouncements. Juvenile corrections professionals must become familiar with gang language, graffiti, and symbols to be able to deal with gang power and control. A partial listing of gang slang is shown in Table 14–2.

| TABLE 14–2 | |
|---|---|
| **Selected Terms Commonly Associated with Gangs** | |
| **A-K** | An assault rifle |
| **All That** | Something that possesses good qualities |
| **Ay Yo Trip** | To gain another's attention |
| **Bag Up** | To be arrested by the police |
| **Baller** | A gang member who makes money |
| **Bama** | A person who can't dress |
| **Bang** | To fight to kill |
| **Battle** | To compete, i.e., freestyle rapping |
| **Blood** | A member of a Los Angeles gang whose color is red |
| **Blunt** | A marijuana cigarette |
| **Crab** | A derogatory name for a Crip |
| **Crip** | A member of a Los Angeles gang whose color is blue |
| **Cuz** | A greeting, primarily used for Crip members |
| **Down** | To meet expectations |
| **Five-O** | The police |
| **Fly Girl** | A very attractive female |
| **Gangbanging** | To participate in gang activity |
| **Gat** | A gun |
| **Hay Shen** | A term for crack cocaine |
| **Head Up** | To fight one-on-one |
| **Hezee** | A home or house |
| **Highroller** | A Crip term for someone in the gang who makes much money |
| **Homeboy/Homie** | Someone from the neighborhood or gang |
| **Hood** | The neighborhood or turf |
| **Jet** | To go or leave |
| **Jumped In** | To be initiated into a gang, usually by getting beat up |
| **Kickin' It** | To hang out with the gang |
| **Knockin Boots** | To have sex |
| **Loco** | A crazy person |
| **No Diggity** | To accept as the truth |
| **OG** | An original gangster; considered when you have killed someone |
| **Peel** | To kill |
| **Rifa** | To rule |
| **Salty (You)** | To think you know everything |
| **Set** | An individual gang |
| **Smoke** | To kill |
| **Snaps** | A term for money |
| **Whadup Dawg** | A way of greeting friends |
| **Yash** | A greeting used on the telephone to attract attention |

*Source:* Adapted from several online sources [http://www.cus.wayne.edu/u_safety/gang_slang01.html; http://www.leevalley.co.uk/yush/rewind/yush0111/slang.htm]

One reason that gangs successfully recruit members within the correctional setting is that the transition to a confined existence can be traumatic. Residents often challenge new arrivals, usually within the first few days, threatening physical harm to intimidate and exploit the youth. A youth who is the object of such an encounter may believe that joining a gang is the only way to survive.

Another reason that incarcerated juveniles join gangs is boredom. Their typical daily routine includes eating meals, exercise, and schoolwork. Leisure activities, family visitation, social programs, and other special services are intermittent, and are permitted only if the juvenile complies with institution rules. Involvement in gang activity may represent excitement and adventure for confined juveniles.

# The American Correctional Association and Juvenile Justice Reform

Since it was founded in 1870, the American Correctional Association (ACA) has advocated juvenile justice reform. In a 1997 campaign for juvenile justice reform, the ACA called for:

- Legislative and community action to fund and operate early-intervention strategies;
- Support of continued research, and responsible action based on the results of research already available, on prevention programs that work;
- Support of system reforms that allow juvenile justice officials, family, social, educational and other agencies and institutions to relate to a specific child, and to work together for the best interests of the child, including accountability or shared use of confidential information about children at risk;
- Support of programs that address the causes of violent and delinquent activity in communities;
- Opposition to efforts to establish automatic certification of juvenile offenders to adult status for certain offenses;
- Opposition to determinate sentencing for juvenile offenders;
- Support of the use of confidential systems for information-sharing about juvenile offenders.[23]

Juvenile justice officials and the courts rely on the ACA for guidance. The ACA responds to more than 20,000 members, disseminating information, establishing advisory standards for juvenile corrections, providing technical assistance, and training juvenile corrections personnel.

FRANKLIN COUNTY
JUVENILE DETENTION CENTER

Juvenile
Release
Only

## SUMMARY BY CHAPTER OBJECTIVES

### CHAPTER OBJECTIVE 1

*Parens patriae* is a legal philosophy that is used to justify intervention in children's lives when their parents are unwilling or unable to care for them.

### CHAPTER OBJECTIVE 2

Houses of Refuge, the first legally chartered custodial institutions for juvenile offenders, were established in the early 19th century. Reform schools, which were established in the middle of the 19th century, sought to reform rather than punish young offenders through vocational (especially trade and industrial), physical, and military education. Reform schools for girls used "cottage-like" residential units. Industrial schools emerged in the latter part of the 19th century and emphasized vocational training for youthful offenders.

### CHAPTER OBJECTIVE 3

The first completely separate juvenile court in the United States was established in Cook County (Chicago), Illinois, in 1899 and had jurisdiction over youth who committed acts that would be crimes if committed by adults and youth who were in danger of growing up to be paupers or in need of supervision. By 1945, separate juvenile courts had been established in all states.

### CHAPTER OBJECTIVE 4

Five U.S. Supreme Court decisions established due process rights for juvenile offenders:

- *Kent* v. *United States* (1966)—a juvenile who is to be transferred to adult criminal court is entitled to a hearing, representation by an attorney, access to records being considered by the juvenile court, and a statement of reasons for the transfer.
- *In re Gault* (1967)—in a proceeding that might result in commitment to an institution, a juvenile is entitled to: reasonable notice of charges; counsel; question witnesses; and protection against self-incrimination.
- *In re Winship* (1970)—proof beyond a reasonable doubt, not simply a preponderance of the evidence, is required during the adjudicatory stage for a delinquent offense.
- *McKeiver* v. *Pennsylvania* (1971)—trial by jury is not a constitutional requirement for juvenile adjudication.
- *Breed* v. *Jones* (1975)—transfer to adult criminal court after juvenile court adjudication constitutes double jeopardy.

### CHAPTER OBJECTIVE 5

Most cases handled by the juvenile courts are for delinquent offenses—acts committed by a juvenile that, if committed by an adult, could result in criminal prosecution. The remaining cases are for status offenses—acts that are offenses only when committed by juveniles. Such offenses include running away, truancy, ungovernability, and liquor law violations.

### CHAPTER OBJECTIVE 6

Juvenile delinquents are young persons, usually under age 18, who commit acts which, if committed by an adult, could result in criminal prosecution. The typical juvenile offender is a 16-year-old white male property offender.

### CHAPTER OBJECTIVE 7

The three stages of the juvenile justice process are intake, adjudication, and disposition. During the intake stage, a court-appointed officer recommends a course of action—dismissal, informal disposition, formal disposition, or, in some instances, transfer to adult criminal court—for a juvenile who has been referred to the juvenile court. Adjudication is judicial determination of guilt or innocence. Disposition is judicial imposition of the most appropriate sanction.

## CHAPTER OBJECTIVE 8

Disposition for the majority of juvenile offenders is probation. Other dispositions include placement in group homes, residential treatment centers, juvenile boot camps, or juvenile correctional institutions.

## CHAPTER OBJECTIVE 9

Teen court, an alternative to the traditional juvenile court, operates under one of four models: adult judge (an adult serves as judge); youth judge (a youth serves as judge); tribunal (youth attorneys present the case to youth judges); or peer jury (a youth or adult presents the case to a youth jury). Common teen court dispositions are apologies, educational and/or counseling programs, restitution, and community service.

## CHAPTER OBJECTIVE 10

A gang is a group of individuals involved in continuing criminal activity. Youth gangs are a serious problem for juvenile correctional professionals. For some juvenile institutions, gang affiliation is an important consideration in housing arrangements.

## KEY TERMS

*parens patriae*, p. 403
reform school, p. 404
delinquent offenses, p. 409
status offenses, p. 409
intake, p. 412
diversion, p. 412
juvenile detention facility, p. 413
detention hearing, p. 413
guardian *ad litem*, p. 413
adjudication, p. 413
juvenile court, p. 413

disposition, p. 413
predisposition report, p. 413
group home, p. 414
residential treatment center, p. 417
blended sentencing, p. 417
waiver provisions, p. 417
direct file provisions, p. 417
statutory exclusion provisions, p. 417
teen courts, p. 418
gangs, p. 419

## QUESTIONS FOR REVIEW

1. Explain the principle of *parens patriae*.
2. Distinguish among Houses of Refuge, reform schools, and industrial schools.
3. Where and when was the first completely separate juvenile court established?
4. What five U.S. Supreme Court rulings established due process rights for juveniles? What impact did each have on juvenile court proceedings?
5. What is a *delinquent offense*? A *status offense*?
6. What is the typical juvenile delinquent's age? Gender? Race?
7. Identify and explain the three stages of the juvenile justice process.
8. What are the three provisions for transferring juveniles to adult criminal court?
9. What is blended sentencing?
10. What is a guardian *ad litem*?
11. What is a predisposition report? To what does it compare in adult criminal court?
12. What is the most common sanction imposed by a juvenile court?
13. What is a group home? A residential treatment center?
14. What are the characteristics of the typical offender confined in a juvenile correctional institution?
15. What is teen court? How does it operate?
16. What is a gang? What impact do youth gangs have on juvenile correctional institutions?
17. Why is it important for juvenile corrections professionals to stay informed about gang affiliation, membership, and graffiti?
18. What is the American Correctional Association's position on juvenile justice reform?

## ON-THE-JOB ISSUE

Read the following case.

IN THE MATTER OF: BETH LEONARD

CHARGES: Three (3) counts of retail theft. Hoover police were summoned to the Hoover Mall branch store of Fancy This on March 17, 2000, at 11:20 a.m. regarding a shoplifter. Beth Leonard was arrested at 11:52 a.m. for three (3) counts of retail theft.

An employee noticed Beth entering the dressing room with a blue short outfit and a swimsuit. Beth exited the dressing room carrying only her purse. After a quick scan of the room, the attendant, unable to locate the clothes, called security. Beth was led to the manager's office, where she confessed to putting the items on under her clothing and attempting to leave.

When the police arrived, they asked for identification and discovered a bottle of Spring Musk Perfume bearing a new, undamaged sales sticker in Beth's purse. When the officer asked if Beth had a receipt, she stated she had purchased the perfume but upon further prompting admitted that she had taken this item from the Perfumeria, a mall perfume store.

A further search of Beth's purse revealed two pairs of earrings with sales stickers from Carters, a mall accessory shop. Beth admitted to taking these items without purchasing them.

While searching Beth's purse, the officer located her wallet and found $85 in cash. When asked why she didn't just pay for the items, Beth stated she was planning to purchase a gift for her parents' wedding anniversary.

Beth was questioned as to why she had taken these items and she stated she did not know. She was then transported to the Hoover police department and her parents were called.

When Beth's parents arrived, a conference was held between the parents, Beth, and the arresting officer. During this conference, Beth stated that all her girlfriends did this and they never got caught. She was dared by one to bring certain items to her with the sales tags still intact to prove that she had not paid for them. It was dumb, but she did it, and she was sorry.

ITEMS:

| | | | |
|---|---|---|---|
| Tank top | | Perfume | $12 |
| short set | $25 | Two pairs of | |
| Swimsuit | $38 | earrings | $32 |

PERSONAL DATA:

Beth Leonard is 16 years old and resides at 612 Mockingbird Lane in Hoover. She has a younger brother who is in junior high and an older sister who is just ready to start college. Her parents have been married 20 years.

Beth started working at Pizza House after volleyball season. During the school year, she works 20 hours a week; during the summer, she works 35 hours a week.

Beth is a straight A student. She plans to pursue a college degree in teaching Spanish. Beth is an active member of Spanish Club and is a member of Spanish Honor Society. She has played on her high school volleyball team for two years.

If you were the intake officer handling this case, would you recommend that it be handled by a teen court? Why or why not?

## CORRECTIONS ISSUES

1. The Sentencing Project reports that abuse (physical and sexual) and suicide rates are higher for children who serve time in adult correctional institutions than for those held in juvenile correctional institutions—youths held in adult institutions are 7.7 times more likely to commit suicide, 5 times more likely to be sexually assaulted, twice as likely to be beaten by staff, and 50 percent more likely to be attacked with a weapon.[24] What conclusions might you draw from this report?

2. Juvenile court proceedings are becoming more accessible to the public. At least 21 states now permit open juvenile court proceedings for serious or violent crime charges or repeat offenses. In 1995, Georgia passed a law allowing the public admission to adjudicatory hearings for youths who have been charged with delinquent offenses. Do you think juvenile court proceedings should be open to the public? Why or why not?

# CORRECTIONS ON THE WEB

1. Go to the FBI Web page at **http://www.fbi.gov** and in the search box type "gang." Then scroll to the document *Law Enforcement True Story, Gang Alert*. Read the scenarios and decide which the FBI would classify as a gang.

2. Access the National Youth Court Center at its Web site (**http://www.appa-net.org**). Determine the status of teen courts in your state.

## ADDITIONAL READINGS

Leonard, Kimberly Kempf, Carl E. Pope, and William H. Feyerherm (eds.). *Minorities in Juvenile Justice*. Thousand Oaks, CA: Sage Publications, 1995.

Watkins, Jr., John C. *The Juvenile Justice Century: A Socio-Legal Commentary on American Juvenile Courts*. Durham, NC: Carolina Academic Press, 1998.

## ENDNOTES

1. Tom Sheehan, "Buddy testifies teen didn't like his stepmother," *The Columbus Dispatch*, February 2, 2000, p. 1B.
2. Ken Wooden, *Weeping in the Playtime of Others* (New York: McGraw-Hill, 1976), pp. 23–24.
3. *People ex rel. O'Connell* v. *Turner*, 55 Ill.280, 8 Am. Rep. 645.
4. R. M. Mennel, *Thorns and Thistles: Juvenile Delinquency in the United States, 1825-1940* (Hanover, NH: University Press of New England, 1973), p. 131.
5. *Kent* v. *United States*, 383 U.S. 541 (1966).
6. *In re Gault*, 387 U.S. 1, 55 (1967).
7. *In re Winship*, 397 U.S. 358 (1970).
8. *McKeiver* v. *Pennsylvania*, 403 U.S. 528 (1971).
9. *Breed* v. *Jones*, 421 U.S. 519 (1975).
10. Howard N. Snyder, *Juvenile Arrests 1998* (Washington, DC: Office of Juvenile Justice and Delinquency Prevention, December 1999), p. 1.
11. Anne L. Stahl, Melissa Sickmund, Terrence A. Finnegan, Howard N. Snyder, Rowen S. Poole, and Nancy Tierney, *Juvenile Court Statistics 1996* (Washington, DC: Office of Juvenile Justice and Delinquency Prevention, July 1999).
12. S. Rudenstine, *Juvenile Admissions to State Custody, 1993* (Washington, DC: Office of Juvenile Justice and Delinquency Prevention, 1995). American Correctional Association, *1997 Directory, Juvenile and Adult Correctional Departments, Institutions, Agencies, and Paroling Authorities* (Lanham, MD, 1997), p. xxiv.
13. American Correctional Association, op. cit., p. 39.

14. Melissa Sickmund, Howard N. Snyder, and Eileen Poe-Yamagata, *Juvenile Offenders and Victims: 1997 Update on Violence* (Washington DC: Office of Juvenile Justice and Delinquency Prevention, 1997).
15. Gerald Bayens, *Assessing the Impact of Judicial Waiver Laws in Kansas: Implications for Correctional Policy* (Ann Arbor, MI: University Microfilms International, 1998).
16. Anne L. Stahl, *Delinquency Cases Waived to Criminal Court, 1987–1996* (Washington, DC: Office of Juvenile Justice and Delinquency Prevention, April 1999).
17. Tammy Hawkins (personal communication, September 21, 1998).
18. "A Second Chance," *TIME*, August 2, 1999, p. 100.
19. Tammy Hawkins (personal communication, September 21, 1998).
20. *1996 National Youth Gang Survey* (Washington, DC: Office of Juvenile Justice and Delinquency Prevention, 1999).
21. James H. Burch and Betty M. Chemers, *A Comprehensive Response to America's Youth Gang Problem* (Washington, DC: Office of Juvenile Justice and Delinquency Prevention, 1997).
22. Jeff Ferrell, "Criminological Verstehen: Inside the Immediacy of Crime," *Justice Quarterly*, Volume 14, Number 1, 1997, pp. 3–23.
23. James Turpin, "Juvenile Justice in the Spotlight," *Corrections Today*, Volume 59, Number 3, 1997, p. 124.
24. *Briefing Paper: Prosecuting Juveniles in Adult Court* (Washington, DC: The Sentencing Project, 1999).

# The Victim
## Role in the Correctional Process

## CHAPTER OBJECTIVES

After completing this chapter you should be able to:

1. Briefly summarize the history of America's victims' rights movement.
2. Identify and describe important federal victims' rights legislation.
3. Understand why a victims' rights amendment to the U.S. Constitution may be considered necessary.
4. List and describe crime victims' costs.
5. Understand how corrections agencies participate in meeting victims' needs and list victim services provided by correctional agencies.
6. Explain crime victim compensation programs.
7. List the three avenues available to victims to recover financial losses due to crime.
8. Understand the nature of victim impact statements, and explain why they are useful.

*As a victim you're amazed that no one will ask you about the crime, or the effect that it has on you and your family. You took the . . . defendant's blows, heard his threats, listened to him brag that he'd "beat the rap" or "con the judge." No one ever hears these things. They never give you a chance to tell them.*

—A victim

In 1985, Ralph Hubbard's 23-year-old son was shot and killed in New York City. After years of feeling angry, frustrated, and powerless, Hubbard resolved to help himself by helping others work through their suffering. He began to speak out in a New York Victim Services support group for families of homicide victims, telling his story to police, criminal justice officials, social service providers, and the public.

Hubbard started a self-help group for men who had lost family members to violence. He found that telling his story helped him cope with his own pain and anger, and inspired other victims to express their feelings. He also became an adviser to New York's Crime Victims' Board, vice president of Justice For All (a victims' rights advocacy group), and a board member of the National Organization for Victim Assistance (NOVA). A leading spokesperson for victims' rights in New York state, Hubbard felt no less compelled to advocate victims' rights 10 years after his son's murder: "It's something I need to do. This is therapeutic for me."[1]

The efforts that Hubbard and other crime victims have made toward their own recoveries have led to reforms in the criminal justice system and new crime prevention programs.

## A Brief History of America's Victims' Rights Movement

**victim** Someone who suffers direct or threatened physical, emotional, or financial harm as the result of the commission of a crime. The term *victim* also includes the immediate family of a minor or homicide victim.

According to the federal Bureau of Prisons (BOP), a **victim** is "someone who suffers direct or threatened physical, emotional, or financial harm as the result of the commission of a crime. The term 'victim' also includes the immediate family of a minor or homicide victim."[2]

Victims were rarely recognized in the laws and policies that govern our nation until the 1970s. From a legal perspective, crimes were offenses against the state (the state made the law), not against the individual. Victims merely set the wheels of justice in motion (by filing charges), and, if necessary, helped carry out justice (by testifying in court). The victim had little or no status within the justice system, and victims' rights were virtually nonexistent.[3]

**victims' rights** The fundamental rights of victims to be equitably represented throughout the criminal justice process.

Tremendous strides have since been made in **victims' rights** legislation and victims' services. Few movements in American history achieved as much success in prompting legislative response as did victims' rights activists' campaigns through the 1980s and 1990s.

*The Victim: Role in the Correctional Process*

The 1980 enactment of Wisconsin's Victims' Bill of Rights, the nation's first state bill of rights for crime victims, launched an era of dramatic progress in the victims' rights movement.[4] Passage of the federal Victim and Witness Protection Act of 1982[5] (VWPA) and release of the *Final Report* by the President's Task Force on Victims of Crime in the same year, brought national visibility to crime victims' concerns.

The VWPA and the *Final Report* were catalysts for a decade of significant advances in victims' rights. At the date of release of the *Final Report*, four states had legislated victims' basic rights;[6] today, all states have laws, modeled after the VWPA, that establish, protect, and enforce victims' rights. There are now more than 27,000 victim-related state statutes and 29 state victims' rights constitutional amendments.

Although no standard has been defined for victims' rights, most states' victims' bills of rights include basic provisions for treatment with dignity and compassion, ongoing access to information about the status of the case and the offender, notification of hearing and trial dates, attendance at judicial proceedings involving the case, input at sentencing and parole hearings (through victim impact statements), and restitution. (See Figure 15–1.)

Most states have legislated victims' rights to notification of events and proceedings at various stages of the judicial process; 35 have legislated victims' rights to attend criminal justice proceedings, and 24 constitutionally protect these rights.[7] All states permit consideration of victim impact information at sentencing, with most permitting victim presentation of the information during the sentencing hearing. The majority of states require that victim impact information be included in the presentencing report, and at least half require that the court consider this information in its sentencing decision.

## FIGURE 15–1

### Victim's Rights

- THE RIGHT TO INFORMATION about the case as it progresses through the justice system;
- THE RIGHT TO NOTIFICATION of many different types of justice proceedings;
- THE RIGHT TO PARTICIPATE in court proceedings related to the offense;
- THE RIGHT TO BE REASONABLY PROTECTED from the accused offender;
- THE RIGHT TO INFORMATION about the conviction, sentencing, imprisonment, and release of the offender; and
- THE RIGHT TO RECEIVE RESTITUTION from the offender.

*Source:* Office for Victims of Crime

Despite the advances in victims' rights legislation, there remain serious deficiencies, in the laws and in implementation of the laws. Crime victims' rights, which vary significantly at both the federal and state levels, are often ignored, and many victims are still denied the right to participate in the justice process. Implementation of state-enacted constitutional victims' rights is often arbitrary and based on judicial preference. Many states make no provision for victims' rights in cases involving juvenile offenders.

## Legislation

Congressional concern for crime victims was evident in the VWPA; its stated purpose was "to enhance and protect the necessary role of crime victims and witnesses in the criminal justice process; to ensure that the federal government does all that is possible to assist victims and witnesses of crime, within the limits of available resources, without infringing on the constitutional rights of the defendant; and to provide model legislation for state and local governments."[8]

A subsection of the Crime Control Act of 1990,[9] known as the Victims' Rights and Restitution Act of 1990 (Victims' Rights Act), established a Bill of Rights for federal crime victims.[10] The Victims' Rights Act requires that federal law enforcement officials use their "best efforts" to ensure that victims receive basic rights and services, as specified by law, including:

- fair and respectful treatment by authorities,
- reasonable protection from the accused,
- notification of court proceedings,
- presence at public court proceedings unless the court specifies otherwise,
- conference with the prosecutor,
- restitution, and
- updates to information about the offender, including conviction, sentencing, imprisonment, and release.

**best efforts standard**

A requirement of the federal Victims' Rights and Restitution Act of 1990 (also known as the Victims' Rights Act) which mandates that federal law enforcement officers, prosecutors, and corrections officials use their best efforts to ensure that victims receive basic rights and services during their encounter with the criminal justice system.

The **best efforts standard** made the federal law weaker than many state victims' rights laws in which provision for victims' rights and services is mandatory.

The Violent Crime Control and Law Enforcement Act,[11] passed in 1994, established new rights for victims of sexual assault, domestic violence, sexual exploitation, child abuse, and telemarketing fraud. This legislation also designated significant funding for combating domestic violence and sexual assault, placed more than 100,000 community police officers on the street, and launched a number of other crime prevention initiatives.

In 1996, the federal Community Notification Act, known as Megan's Law, was enacted to ensure community notification of the locations of convicted sex offenders.[12]

In the Victims' Rights Clarification Act of 1997, Congress asserted victims' rights to attend proceedings and deliver victim impact statements within the federal system. This act was passed to ensure that victims and survivors of the Alfred P. Murrah Federal Building bombing in Oklahoma City, Oklahoma, could observe the trial and provide input at sentencing.

Table 15–1 summarizes the victims' rights defined by federal legislation.

*The Victim: Role in the Correctional Process*

## TABLE 15-1

### Federal Victims' Rights Legislation

| Legislation | Provisions |
|---|---|
| Victims' Rights Clarification Act, 1997 | Ensured that victims of federal crimes should have the right both to attend proceedings and to deliver or submit a victim impact statement. |
| Mandatory Victim Restitution Act, 1996 | Made restitution mandatory on the federal level in all violent crime cases and in certain other cases. |
| Community Notification Act (also known as Megan's Law), 1996 | Ensured that communities are notified of the release and location of convicted sex offenders. |
| Violent Crime Control and Law Enforcement Act, 1994 | Created new rights for victims of sexual assault, domestic violence, sexual exploitation, child abuse, and telemarketing fraud. |
| Victims' Rights and Restitution Act (also called the Victims' Rights Act), 1990 | Created the first federal bill of rights for victims of crime, and required federal law enforcement officers, prosecutors, and corrections officials to use their *best efforts* to ensure that victims receive basic rights and services. |
| Victims of Crime Act (VOCA), 1984 | Established the federal Office for Victims of Crime (OVC) to provide federal funds in support of victim assistance and compensation programs around the country, and to advocate for the fair treatment of crime victims. Also established the federal Crime Victims' Fund to assist states in paying victim benefits. |
| Victim and Witness Protection Act (VWPA), 1982 | Enacted a set of basic rights for crime victims, and became a national model for state victims' rights laws. |

## The Proposal for a Federal Victims' Rights Constitutional Amendment

The 1982 President's Task Force on Victims of Crime made 68 recommendations for protection of victims' rights, including a recommendation that the Sixth Amendment to the U.S. Constitution be amended to guarantee specific rights to crime victims. Although the recommendation has not yet been implemented, NOVA, Mothers Against Drunk Driving (MADD), the National Center for Victims of Crime (NVC—formerly the National Victim Center), and other national victims' organizations joined together to create, in 1987, the National Victims' Constitutional Amendment Network (NVCAN). NVCAN provides leadership and coordinates ongoing efforts to amend the federal constitution in recognition of victims' rights.[13] NVCAN spent the next decade assisting state legislators in their efforts to pass amendments. Efforts to pass state constitutional amendments produced impressive results. Each of the 29 state victims' rights amendment votes won by an overwhelming majority—80 to 90 percent in most states.[14]

# The Costs and Consequences of Victimization

According to a two-year National Institute of Justice (NIJ) study,[15] personal crimes result in costs of about $105 billion annually in medical expenses, lost earnings, and public victim assistance programs. For victims, crime costs may include: (1) out-of-pocket expenses, such as medical bills and property losses; (2) reduced productivity at work, home, or school; and (3) non-monetary losses, such as fear, pain, suffering, and reduced quality of life.

Unlike **tangible losses** (such as medical expenses or lost wages), **intangible losses** (such as pain, suffering, and reduced quality of life) do not have a market price and cannot be bought or sold. Nevertheless, these losses are real and can be valued in dollars—victims would pay dearly to avoid them.

Tangible losses do not represent the true cost of victimization. Intangible losses, including pain, suffering, and reduced quality of life, place the annual cost of crime at an estimated $450 billion (see Figure 15–2). Violent crime (including drunk driving) accounts for $426 billion of this total; property crime, $24 billion. These estimates exclude several other types of crime such as white collar crime, personal fraud, and drug crime.

The cost of crime victimization is far greater when its impact on society is considered. Such costs include: (1) monies spent by the criminal justice system to find, prosecute, and confine offenders; (2) social costs associated with fear of crime (e.g., changed behavior, the fear of being outside at night, moving to a safer neighborhood, etc.); (3) mental health costs associated with healing "scars" from victimization; (4) private security expenditures by the general population concerned about crime; (5) monies spent by employers to train temporary or new employees; (6) the costs of lost productivity borne by employers; (7) insurance claims processing costs (for example, life insurance claims for fatalities and workers' compensation claims); (8) workers' compensation and disability payments, especially those made to workers

**tangible losses** Costs such as medical expenses, lost wages, and property losses that accrue to crime victims as a result of their victimization.

**intangible losses** Costs such as fear, pain, suffering, and reduced quality of life that accrue to crime victims as a result of their victimization.

**FIGURE 15-2**

**Annual Cost of Crime in the United States**

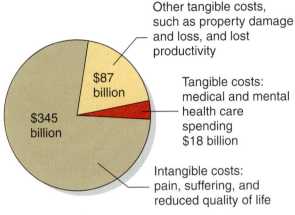

Other tangible costs, such as property damage and loss, and lost productivity

$87 billion

$345 billion

Tangible costs: medical and mental health care spending $18 billion

Intangible costs: pain, suffering, and reduced quality of life

Total = $450 billion

*Source:* Ted R. Miller, Mark A. Cohen, and Brian Wiersema, *Victim Costs and Consequences: A New Look,* U.S. Department of Justice, National Institute of Justice Research Report (Washington, DC: GPO, February 1996), p. 17.

victimized while on the job; and (9) legal expenses incurred in recovering productivity losses from offenders and insurance companies (e.g., drunk drivers and their insurers). The National Crime Victimization Survey (NCVS) data include estimates of the number of hours of work and earnings lost due to medically related problems associated with victimization. Some specifics from the NIJ study show that:

- Violent crime necessitates 3 percent of all U.S. medical spending, and 14 percent of all injury-related medical spending.
- Violent crime results in wage losses equivalent to 1 percent of American earnings.
- Violent crime is a significant factor in mental health care usage. As much as 10 to 20 percent of mental health care expenditures in the United States may be attributable to crime, primarily for victims treated as a result of their victimization.
- Personal crime reduces the average American's quality of life by 1.8 percent. Violence alone causes a 1.7 percent loss. These estimates include only costs to victimized households, ignoring the broader impact of crime-induced fear on our society.

NIJ also reports the estimated total annual cost of crime to victims in the United States, including the value of intangible losses, and victim losses due to crimes.

## Who Pays the Bill?

Victims and their families pay the bill for some crimes, while the public largely pays the bill for others. Insurers pay $45 billion in crime-related claims annually.[16] That's $265 per American adult. Government pays $8 billion annually for restorative and emergency services to victims, plus about one-fourth of the $11 billion in health insurance claim payments.

Taxpayers and insurance purchasers cover almost all the tangible victim costs of arson and drunk driving. They cover $9 billion of the $19 billion in tangible nonservice costs of larceny, burglary, and motor vehicle theft.

Victims pay about $44 billion of the $57 billion in tangible non-service expenses for violent crimes—murder, rape, robbery, assault, and abuse and neglect. Employers pay almost $5 billion because of these crimes, primarily in health insurance bills. (This estimate excludes sick leave and disability insurance costs other than workers' compensation.) Government bears the remaining costs, through lost tax revenues and Medicare/Medicaid payments. Crime victim compensation accounts for 38 percent of homeowner insurance premium costs and 29 percent of automobile insurance premium costs.

Criminologists and public policy researchers are now using crime cost estimates to help assess the desirability of various policy options. Reported costs can be used to assess the wisdom of early offender release and diversion programs.

# The Role of Corrections

In the past, correctional agencies were viewed only as facilities for punishing and rehabilitating offenders. Today, they also serve crime victims—protecting them from intimidation and harassment, notifying them of offender status, providing avenues for victim input into release decisions, and collecting restitution.[17]

Correctional agencies are also beginning to recognize the important role that victims can play in helping them develop policies, procedures, and programs that consider victims as well as correctional staff and offenders. Across the nation, crime victims are being asked to join advisory committees and agency boards, become official members of parole commissions, and serve as teachers in innovative classes that sensitize offenders to the impact of their offenses.

Correctional agencies are beginning to acknowledge victims' needs in their mission statements. In Oregon, for example, the state board of parole recently issued the following statement: "The Board's mission is to work in partnership with the Department of Corrections and local supervisory authorities to protect the public and reduce the risk of repeat criminal behavior through incarceration and community supervision decisions based on applicable laws, victims' interests, public safety, and recognized principles of offender behavioral change." Many state corrections departments have now issued similar mission statements.

Crime victims' involvement with correctional agencies helps ensure priority for victim safety and services within correctional agencies. Victim advisory committees now exist in a number of correctional agencies for that purpose.

## Victim Notification

**victim notification**
Notification to victims of the release or pending release of convicted offenders who have harmed them.

**Victim notification** of the release or pending release of convicted offenders is an important service. Without notification, victims are denied an opportunity to take precautions to ensure their own safety.

The importance of providing offender release information to crime victims has long been recognized. In 1982, it was one of the primary recommendations of the President's Task Force on Victims of Crime. In the *Final Report*, the Task Force recommended that parole boards notify victims and their families in advance of parole hearings if victims provide the paroling authority with their names and addresses. In addition, the Task Force called on parole boards to allow victims of crime, their families, or their representatives to attend parole hearings and to provide information about the impact of the crime. According to the recent National Victim Services Survey, marked improvements have occurred in this area over the last decade or so.[18]

There is, however, no consistent victim notification procedure. Some correctional agencies notify victims of only certain types of inmate releases (such as the release of sex offenders). Others notify victims of changes in offender classification. Some notify victims of an inmate's escape, while others notify victims of an inmate's clemency or death. At the federal level, the BOP has created one of the nation's first comprehensive victim notification programs, which has served as a model to the states for over a decade. The BOP notifies victims of any major change in an inmate's status.

Innovative technologies have emerged in recent years that augment victim access to notification and information. At least 10 state correctional agencies utilize automated voice notification systems that place telephone calls to victims, upon request, and inform them of offenders' pending release or release hearings. Victims can also contact a centralized call center, 24 hours a day, 7 days a week. Call center operators confirm offender status and provide referrals to community-based victim services. Many state correctional agencies are following the example of the Illinois Department of Corrections, which provides current updates on inmate status and location and relevant upcoming hearings to victims and the general public via the Internet.[19]

In most jurisdictions, victims must request certain types of notification. Many victims do not request notification simply because they have not been informed that they have a right to do so.

## Psychologist

Work as a psychologist in a sex offender treatment program for the state. Advise, evaluate, and help with treatment recommendations in conjunction with other sex offender treatment specialists. Moderate travel expected. Required qualifications: a master's degree in psychology from an institution accredited by the Council for Higher Education Accreditation (CHEA). Other requirements: Licensed as a psychological associate by the State Board of Examiners of Psychology or licensed as a marriage and family therapist (preferred).

## Victim and Witness Protection

Every day in the United States, victims and witnesses are harassed, intimidated, and retaliated against by incarcerated offenders, through intimidating phone calls, mail, or threatened visits from friends and associates. Many correctional agencies have responded creatively to this problem. Today, when such problems occur, 37 states revoke an offending inmates' privileges, 36 transfer the inmate to a more restrictive level, 28 allow the filing of a new criminal charge, and 21 allow enhancement of the inmate's sentence. In addition, 40 state correctional agencies document such harassment and threats in the offender's case file, 35 recommend investigation for additional prosecution, and 31 recommend revocation of parole when a

*Karen Taylor George*
*Victim Services*
    *Administrator*
*Department of*
    *Corrections*
*Raleigh, North Carolina*

*"I am often asked how I can handle working with the devastation that offenders leave in the wake of their crimes. What most people don't realize is that victim services allows me the privilege to work with the amazing strength exhibited by survivors and to offer services that support the reconstruction of their emotional and physical lives."*

Upon the governor's recommendation that victims of violent crimes receive information and notification, the North Carolina Post-Release Supervision and Parole Commission hired Karen Taylor George as its first victim services coordinator. To assist victims in understanding the system, she created easily understood educational materials that explained the parole process, and victims' rights and opportunities to be notified and involved. To overcome the long distances that victims had to travel to meet with the Parole Commission, she created a video conferencing program through grant funding by the Governor's Crime Commission.

In 1998, North Carolina had pending legislative requirements for all criminal justice agencies to comply with a new victims' rights amendment to the state's constitution. With 32,000 offenders in prison and 105,000 offenders on probation or parole, Ms. Taylor George recognized the need for additional victim services to meet the upcoming legal mandates. She won two grants to fund three full-time positions to develop and implement victim services and to provide victim training to correctional staffs. The victim services program was expanded from the North Carolina Parole Commission to service all of the North Carolina Department of Corrections, and Ms. Taylor George was named the Victim Services Administrator for the department.

Ms. Taylor George has a bachelor's degree in psychology and is completing her master's degree in social work. She is committed to helping reconstruct the lives of survivors who have suffered at the hands of offenders and to educating those who work to assist them. In addition to her work with the correction department, she has often been called upon to deliver victim sensitivity training to various organizations across the state, such as MADD chapters, Parents of Murdered Children, district attorneys' offices, and the North Carolina Victim Assistance Network. Through her creative vision and innovative approaches, she has made great strides within the department in meeting victims' needs and raising the level of awareness for the importance of ongoing victim services within corrections in North Carolina.

parolee harasses, intimidates, or attempts retaliation.[20] California authorities are using an innovative method to stop the increasing number of instances in which inmates use telephones or letters to threaten and harass victims. The California Department of Corrections has created a program to block victims' phone numbers from inmate access and check inmates' outgoing mail.

In managing offenders who are ordered by the court to community supervision or released early from prison with supervision, probation and parole officers need to ensure the safety of victims and the public. Officers will generally use surveillance to identify offenders who pose a continued threat and make monitoring efforts such as checking with contacts at the offender's home and employment and with neighbors to ensure that he or she is meeting the conditions of probation or parole.

Just as there are special units in law enforcement and prosecutors' offices, probation and parole departments have begun to establish special units, such as sex offender and domestic violence units, to provide intensive probation or parole to reduce the safety risks to victims and society as a whole. Agents in these units have smaller caseloads and have received specialized training in intensive supervision.

Correctional agencies also use intermediate sanctions to ensure victim safety. Such sanctions include electronic monitoring, house arrest, random alcohol and drug testing, parole to a location other than the victim's community, mandatory restitution, and increased surveillance.

## Community Notification

Most states have passed laws that either provide for community notification of sexual offender releases or authorize the general public or certain individuals or organizations to access sexual offender registries. Often referred to as Megan's laws, in memory of seven-year-old Megan Kanka, who was murdered by a twice-convicted sex offender paroled to her New Jersey neighborhood, community notification laws recognize that a community has a compelling interest in being informed of offenders' whereabouts. In 1996, a federal Megan's law was enacted that requires states to release relevant registration information when necessary to protect the public.[21]

To be truly effective, **community notification** laws require coordination among law enforcement officials, courts, correctional agencies, victim service providers, the news media, and other key stakeholders. Correctional agencies play a major role in providing this service by determining when and to where sex offenders will be paroled and by conducting community outreach and public education projects.

A promising practice in planning and implementing community notification programs emerged in 1990 in the state of Washington.[22] The Washington approach considers the rights and interests of victims, the community, and offenders. The strategy incorporates the following elements: establishing requirements for registration, requiring registration information for offenders, implementing guidelines for failure to register, implementing guidelines for a preliminary offender risk assessment, compiling offender information packets for distribution to the county prosecutor where the

**community notification**
Notification to the community of the release or pending release of convicted offenders.

offender plans to reside; distributing special bulletins to law enforcement agencies, developing notification policies, creating guidelines concerning who should have access to sex offender registry information, and conducting community outreach efforts that involve victims and address their rights and needs.

## Crime Impact Classes

Over the past decade, the number of educational programs in correctional institutions that involve both offenders and victims has greatly increased. The purpose of such programs is to help offenders understand the devastating impact their crimes have on victims and their families and friends, on their communities, and on themselves and their own families. For victims, participation in programs with offenders is useful because, although the harm they have suffered cannot be undone, they may prevent others from being victimized. Studies also show that participation in impact panels helps heal victims' emotional scars.[23]

Notable among victim-offender programs is the Impact of Crime on Victims (IOC) program, initiated by the California Youth Authority in 1986. The program has been replicated in more than 20 juvenile and adult correctional agencies and numerous diversion programs. IOC programs include a 40-hour curriculum that is designed to educate offenders about how different crimes affect victims and society.[24]

The U.S. Department of the Navy's Corrections and Programs Division took an important step in integrating victims into its corrections process when it issued guidelines in 1996 instructing U.S. Naval correctional facilities to implement impact-of-crime classes for prisoners before releasing them from custody. Information from inmates and correctional staff indicate that, after completing the classes, offenders have a greater understanding of the impact of their criminal conduct.

## Victim-Offender Dialogue

During the past two decades, a number of victim-offender dialogue programs have been developed in juvenile and criminal justice agencies, predominantly in juvenile probation agencies. These programs, primarily used in property crime cases, give victims an opportunity to engage in a structured dialogue with their offenders, who have already admitted their guilt or been convicted/adjudicated. When conducted with sensitivity to the victim and with care to ensure that participation by both victim and offender is voluntary, the victim-offender dialogue process can be very effective in helping victims overcome feelings of trauma and loss.[25] The program gives victims greater satisfaction with the justice system, increases their likelihood of being compensated, and reduces fear of future victimization.

In recent years, correctional agencies have begun to experiment with victim-offender dialogue in violent crime cases. In 1995, for example, the Texas Department of Criminal Justice initiated a victim-offender mediation/dialogue program for victims of severe violence and their incarcerated offenders. Under this program, the contact is initiated by the victim.

As government has become increasingly centralized, a major source of citizen frustration is the inability to define what is being achieved by the justice system, both on an individual case basis and from the perspective of the community. As the media focus on the spectacular failures and the extremes of the normal spectrum, government is caught between overwhelming caseloads of minor criminals and the need to target resources to protect the public from the dangerous ones. In the rush to efficiency, the government bypasses the most effective agents, the community and the family, instead focusing on the individual cases that squeak the loudest.

In the Reparative Probation program, ordinary citizens of the State of Vermont make sentencing decisions about adult criminal offenders from their community. Board members meet with offenders and victims, resolving their disputes by providing the offenders with the opportunity to acknowledge their wrong-doing, apologize to their victim, and make amends to their community. The offenders are sentenced by the court, having pled guilty to a non-violent crime. The sentence is then suspended, pending their completion of a reparative agreement.

Direct involvement in decision-making about individual cases forces citizens to look at the offenders not as strangers, not as numbers, and not as monsters. The offenders are forced to confront the reality of their offense and its impact on the community and their victims. This confrontation, with a restorative outcome, shifts the paradigm from punishment to reintegration. The offender is held accountable, the victim is restored, and the community is repaired. Perhaps even more important, the dispute is resolved by the community, and the community is empowered.

*John G. Perry*
*Director of Planning*
*Vermont Department of Corrections*

## The Victimization of Correctional Staff

Correctional agencies have begun to recognize the impact of victimization on their employees. Correctional professionals are exposed to a wide range of victimization, including verbal harassment by inmates, sexual harassment by inmates or colleagues, physical or sexual assaults, hostage situations, and murder. To respond to the acute and chronic trauma this violence has on employees, many adult correctional agencies have developed written policies and procedures to respond to staff victimization and critical incidents.[26]

Most institutions have standard procedures for dealing with correctional staff victimization that focus on prevention. Many prison management departments, including California, South Carolina, and Texas have developed procedures for helping victimized staff. Guidelines for response to employee victimization have also been developed, under a national training and technical project funded by the Office for Victims of Crime (OVC).[27] The OVC project provides a comprehensive model for correctional agencies that is based on victims' rights laws, either state or federal.

# Victim Compensation

**victim compensation**

A form of victim assistance in which state-funded payments are made to victims to help them recover financial losses due to crime.

Victims generally have three potential options for recovering crime-related financial losses: (1) state-sponsored compensation programs; (2) court-ordered restitution; and (3) civil remedies. **Victim compensation** programs, which exist in every state, may pay for medical care, mental health counseling, lost wages, funeral expenses, and/or crime scene cleanup.

Restitution can be ordered in juvenile and criminal courts as a way to hold offenders financially accountable for their crimes.[28] The potential financial as well as preventative remedies that crime victims can seek through the civil justice system are not discussed in this text, but you should know that they represent one more avenue that victims can pursue in order to be financially compensated for their injuries. At the very least, correctional offices should consider implementing a policy of informing victims and victim service providers of the legal rights of crime victims to pursue reparations through the civil justice system.

The first victim compensation programs were established in New Zealand and Great Britain in 1964. These programs were based on a concept suggested by British Magistrate Margery Fry in the late 1950s. The first victim compensation program established in the United States was California's, created in 1965. By the time the President's Task Force on Victims of Crime released its *Final Report* in 1982, 36 states had victim compensation programs.[29] Today, all 50 states, the District of Columbia, and the Virgin Islands operate victim compensation programs.[30]

Victim compensation programs provide assistance to victims of almost all types of violent crime: rape, robbery, assault, sexual abuse, drunk driving, and domestic violence. These programs, as a rule, pay expenses but do not pay for lost, stolen, or damaged property. Eligibility and specific benefits vary from state to state.

In a typical year, state compensation programs pay approximately $240 million, to more than 110,000 victims, nationwide.[31] The amounts paid by each state vary considerably. Ten states pay less than $500,000 annually, and about 15 pay more than $3 million. The two states with the largest programs, California and Texas, pay nearly one-half of the total benefits paid in the United States.

Benefit maximums, which also vary from state to state, generally range from $10,000 to $25,000, although maximums are lower or higher for a few states. For example, California, Maryland, Minnesota, Ohio, Texas, and Wisconsin allow benefits of $40,000–$50,000. Some states, New York, for example, set no limit on payment of medical expenses; other states, Washington, for example, pay medical expenses up to a predetermined maximum. Many states also set limits for other types of expense, such as

**440** **CHAPTER 15** | *The Victim: Role in the Correctional Process*

funerals and mental health counseling. Nationally, the average amount paid to each victim applying for compensation is $2,000.

## President's Task Force on Victims of Crime

In 1982 the President's Task Force recommended federal funding to help support state victim compensation programs. It also documented problems in several state victim compensation programs: absence of a system for emergency compensation to cover immediate need for food, shelter, and/or medical assistance; insufficient maximum reimbursement levels; lack of coverage for domestic violence, and differences in residency requirements for eligible crime victims. Many of these problems have since been remedied, through federal and state legislation and increased federal and state funding.

State-operated victim compensation programs have improved dramatically since 1982, in benefits provided and to whom. However, some of the concerns raised by the President's Task Force, such as emergency compensation and insufficient maximums, have not been fully addressed by all states.

## Victims of Crime Act

The Task Force's recommendation for federal support of state victim compensation programs was implemented through the Victims of Crime Act (VOCA),[32] passed in 1984. VOCA established the federal Office for Victims of Crime, which administers the federal Crime Victims' Fund, reimbursing states for up to 40 percent of victim compensation payments and providing technical assistance to state compensation programs.

Victims must apply for compensation in the state where the crime occurs. Prior to VOCA, many states' programs provided compensation only to residents unless a reciprocal agreement had been made with the victim's state of residence. States are now required, by federal law, to cover residents, non-residents, and victims of federal crimes. Two states still restrict eligibility to U.S. citizens.

## Recent Trends

Due to increases in publicity concerning victim compensation programs and new laws mandating that rights, services, and information be provided to victims, the number of victims applying for financial assistance increased. As a result, many victim compensation program budgets were inadequate, and victims did not receive the compensation that they should have. Today, although a few states are still unable to pay all eligible claims, most do.

## Eligibility Requirements

Each state has victim eligibility requirements for compensation benefits. Although states' requirements vary, most programs require that the victim:

- Report the crime promptly, usually within 72 hours. A few states allow more time or less, but most have "good cause exceptions" that apply to children, incapacitated victims, and others with special circumstances.

- Cooperate with law enforcement agencies in investigation and prosecution of the crime.
- Submit a timely application for compensation, generally within one year. Again, a few states allow more time or less, and most may waive the deadline under certain circumstances.
- Provide other information, as needed by the program.
- Not file claims for compensation of victimization that resulted from claimant criminal activity or misconduct.

The VOCA Victim Compensation Final Program Guidelines encourage state compensation program staff members to meet with victims and victim service providers, to review state statutes, program guidelines, and policies for responsiveness to crime victims' needs; and to identify potential barriers to victim cooperation with law enforcement agencies, such as apprehension about personal safety and fear of offender retaliation. Victims tend to be reluctant to cooperate if offenders threaten violence or death. Age and psychological, cultural, or linguistic barriers may also influence the amount of victim cooperation. For instance, a young child, senior citizen, or foreign national may have difficulty communicating. Embarrassment or shame may delay or prevent reporting of a sexual assault.

Compensation programs are the victim's last resort. All other potential sources, such as the offender's insurance or public benefits, must be exhausted before state victims' compensation may be paid. If, however, payment from another source is delayed, the program may provide funds to the victim, which must be repaid if and when the victim receives other payment.

The victim cannot have been engaged in criminal activity. Dependents' eligibility depends largely on the victim's eligibility. Dependents or relatives of a homicide victim, for example, who was committing a crime at the time of death are generally not eligible for benefits.

## Benefit Criteria

All compensation programs cover the same major expenses, although limits vary. The primary costs covered by all states are medical expenses, mental health counseling, wages lost as a result of a crime-related injury, lost support (for dependents of homicide victims), and funeral expenses. Nationwide, medical fees represent well over half of all compensation awards, with lost wage and support payments comprising the next highest payment percentage. In a few states, 20 to 40 percent of awards are for counseling; compensation payment in this area is increasing rapidly throughout the country. Twenty-five to 30 percent of claim payment recipients are children age 17 and under.[33]

Many compensation programs also may pay for:

- Moving or relocation expenses, when a victim may be in danger or relocation becomes medically necessary as a result of victimization.
- Transportation for medical services when the provider is located far from the victim's residence or when other special circumstances exist.

- Services, such as child care and/or housekeeping, that the victim cannot perform due to a crime-related injury.
- Essential lost or damaged personal possessions. Eleven states pay for medically necessary equipment, such as eyeglasses or hearing aids, but only a few cover other such items.
- Crime-scene cleanup—securing or restoring a home to its pre-crime condition.
- Rehabilitation—physical or job therapy, ramps, wheelchairs, and/or home or vehicle modification and/or driving instruction.

## Restitution

**Restitution** is repayment to the victim, by the offender, for losses, damages, or expenses that result from the crime. Restitution is a form of victim compensation that holds the offender liable for the victim's financial losses. Restitution is generally seen not as a punishment or an alternative to fines or sanctions, but as a debt owed.[34]

Criminal courts often order restitution to compensate victims for expenses that are the direct result of a crime. It is most often ordered in cases of property crime, such as a burglary. It may also be ordered to reimburse victims for expenses related to physical and/or mental health recovery, and, for survivors of homicide victims, to make up for loss of support. Restitution is also common for cases of theft of services (e.g., restaurant bills), fraud, forgery, and traffic or vehicle law violation. Judges have also begun to order community restitution in which convicted offenders pay back the community through service.

Restitution, as a significant remedy for crime victims, was first imposed on the federal level in 1982, when the VWPA required federal judges to order full restitution in criminal cases or state their reasons for not doing so on the record.[35] That same year, the *Final Report* of the President's Task Force on Victims of Crime reinforced the VWPA by recommending that judges order restitution in all cases in which the victim suffered financial loss, or state compelling reasons for a contrary ruling in the case record.[36]

The importance of restitution was emphasized in 1994, with enactment of the federal Violent Crime Control and Law Enforcement Act, which made restitution mandatory in cases of sexual assault or domestic violence. The Mandatory Victim Restitution Act made restitution mandatory in all violent crime cases and in certain other cases on the federal level in 1996.[37]

In the decade that followed VWPA, every state enacted statutes that addressed restitution, most following the lead of the federal model. However, states continue to amend their statutes, creating a patchwork of financial reparations for victims across the country. As of 1995, 29 states had mandated restitution in all cases. Some states, however, mandate restitution only in cases involving violent crimes, while others mandate restitution only in cases involving property crimes. A number of states require that offenders be on probation or parole before victims may collect restitution, and many do not require restitution from juvenile offenders. Probationers who fail to make restitution payments may have their probation revoked.

Despite the developments in legislation, restitution remains one of the most underenforced of victims' rights in terms of ordering and in monitoring,

**restitution** The practice of requiring an individual who has harmed another to repay the victim for the harm caused. Also, a court requirement that an alleged or convicted offender pay money or provide services to the victim of the crime or provide services to the community.

collecting, and dispersing payments. A recent BOJ study of recidivism among probationers reported that, of 32 counties surveyed,[38] only half required restitution in at least one-third of all felony probation cases. Of felony probationers who had completed their sentences, only 54 percent had fully satisfied restitution orders.[39] Even so, national research studies indicate that restitution is one of the most significant factors affecting the satisfaction of victims with the criminal justice process.[40]

**Collecting Restitution in Institutions** Many correctional agencies encourage inmates to fulfill restitution obligations. These agencies increase collections by offering incentives (such as increased visitation and prison commissary services or priority enrollment in education programs) for compliance and by denying privileges for failure or refusal to participate.

The California Department of Corrections (CDC) has implemented an Inmate Restitution Fine Collections System, supported by state law, that allows deduction of up to 50 percent of inmate wages for payment of court-ordered restitution. These funds are transferred to the State Board of Control Restitution Fund for disbursement. This system collected over $9 million from its inception in November 1992 through early 1998. CDC's Victim Services Program staff coordinate voluntary inmate and parolee restitution payments as well.

**Community Restitution** Offenders who are truly indigent may be given the option to perform community service in lieu of monetary restitution. According to OVC, however, this option should be offered only with victim consent. Some victims prefer that the monetary restitution order stand until such time, if any, that the offender is able to fulfill it. Other victims may feel somewhat compensated if they participate in the decision about type and location of the service to be performed. Payment of victim restitution does not necessarily preclude an order for community restitution. In many instances the offender has done damage not only to the victim but to the community as well.

## The Office for Victims of Crime

Established by VOCA, OVC's mission is to:[41]

- Help ensure that justice is done and that the victim achieves a sense of personal healing.
- Administer the Crime Victims' Fund. Nearly 90 percent (about $500 million) of the monies collected each year, all from fines and penalties paid by federal criminal offenders, is distributed to state victim assistance and compensation programs, helping to support more than 2,500 local victim services agencies (such as domestic violence shelters, children's advocacy centers, and rape treatment programs) and provide expense reimbursement to victims.
- Advocate fair treatment of crime victims.

- Develop and administer projects for enhancing victims' rights and services.
- Provide training, on a number of victim issues, for many different professions—victim service providers, law enforcement personnel, prosecutors, clergy, and medical and mental health personnel.
- Provide training on victim-witness issues for 70 federal law enforcement agencies, including the Federal Bureau of Investigation (FBI), the Department of Defense (DOD), and the National Park Service.
- Provide services to people victimized on tribal or federal lands, such as military bases and national parks.
- Maintain a fund to provide emergency services such as temporary shelter and travel to court for victims of federal crimes.
- Establish **victim assistance programs** on Indian reservations to recruit and train multidisciplinary teams to handle child sexual abuse cases and provide comprehensive victim services.

# Victim Impact Statements

**Victim impact statements** are assertions—by victims and/or friends or relatives of the victim—about the crime's impact on the victim and the victim's family. Victim impact statements, now permitted at all sentencing hearings,[42] may be verbal or written, depending on the jurisdiction. Many states and the federal government now require that victim impact statements be included in pre-sentencing reports (see Figure 15–3 on page 446). The Crime Control and Law Enforcement Act of 1994 gave federal victims of violent crime or sexual assault a federal **right of allocution**—the right to make a statement at sentencing. Another federal law, the Child Protection Act of 1990, provides that victim impact statements from young children might take the form of drawings or models.

Victim impact statements typically include a tally of the physical, financial, psychological, and emotional impact of crime. As such, they provide information for courts to use in assessing the human and social cost of crime. Of equal significance, they also provide a way for victims to take part in the justice process. In most states, the right to make an impact statement is available to the direct victim, to family members of homicide victims, to the parents or guardians of a victimized minor, and to the guardian or legal representative of an incompetent or incapacitated victim.

According to OVC, the first victim impact statement was made in 1976 in Fresno County, California, by James Rowland,[43] who was then the county's chief probation officer. Mr. Rowland's contributions, which detailed the harm suffered by victims in that case, led Fresno County to make victim impact statements a part of all pre-sentence reports.

In 1991, the U.S. Supreme Court case of *Payne* v. *Tennessee*[44] upheld the constitutionality of victim impact statements. Additionally, the *Payne* decision specifically permitted victim impact statements in cases involving potential application of the death penalty.

Victim impact statements are also frequently provided by victims or their survivors to parole hearing bodies. Statements are sometimes made in

**victim assistance program** An organized program which offers services to victims of crime in the areas of crisis intervention and follow-up counseling, and which helps victims secure their rights under the law.

**victim impact statement** An assertion made by victims (and sometimes by friends or relatives of the victim) about the impact of the crime in question upon the victim and the victim's family. Also, a written document which describes the losses, suffering, and trauma experienced by a crime victim or by the victim's survivors.

**right of allocution** A statutory provision permitting crime victims to speak at the sentencing of convicted offenders. A federal right of allocution was established for victims of federal violent and sex crimes under the Violent Crime Control and Law Enforcement Act of 1994.

**FIGURE 15-3**

Sample Victim Impact Statement

## VICTIM IMPACT STATEMENT

If you need more space to answer any of the following questions, please feel free to use as much paper as you need, and simply attach these sheets of paper to this impact statement. Thank you.

**Your Name**
**Defendant's Name(s)**

1. How has the crime affected you and those close to you? Please feel free to discuss your feelings about what has happened and how it has affected your general well-being. Has this crime affected your relationship with any family members, friends, co-workers, and other people? As a result of this crime, if you or others close to you have sought any type of victim services, such as counseling by either a licensed professional, member of the clergy, or a community-sponsored support group, you may wish to mention this.

2. What physical injuries or symptoms have you or others close to you suffered as a result of this crime? You may want to write about how long the injuries lasted, or how long they are expected to last, and if you sought medical treatment for these injuries. You may also want to discuss what changes you have made in your life as a result of these injuries.

3. Has this crime affected your ability to perform your work, make a living, run a household, go to school, or enjoy any other activities you previously performed or enjoyed? If so, please explain how these activities have been affected by this crime.

person; at other times they are submitted on audiotape or videotape, by teleconferencing, via computerized forms of communication, or in writing. Such statements give the paroling authority crucial information about the financial, physical, and emotional impact of crime upon the individuals most affected by it. In the past two decades, the passage of laws requiring victim input at parole has been seen as one of the greatest advances in victims' rights, with 43 states now providing this right.[45] This right loses its meaning, however, if paroling authorities don't notify victims of crime and their families of hearings in advance, or don't schedule time during the hearing to allow them to describe the impact of crime on their lives.

# The Future of Victims' Rights

The OVC report, *New Directions from the Field*,[46] summarizes hundreds of recommendations from the field and from listening to victims, their advocates, and allied professionals who work with crime victims throughout the nation. In the course of compiling the hundreds of recommendations, certain key recommendations emerged. The following five global challenges for responding to victims of crime in the twenty-first century form the core of the ideas and recommendations presented in the report.

- To enact and enforce consistent, fundamental rights for crime victims in federal, state, juvenile, military, and tribal justice systems, and administrative proceedings.
- To provide crime victims with access to comprehensive, quality services regardless of the nature of their victimization, age, race, religion, gender, ethnicity, sexual orientation, capability, or geographic location.
- To integrate crime victims' issues into all levels of the nation's educational system to ensure that justice and allied professionals and other service providers receive comprehensive training on victims' issues as part of their academic education and continuing training in the field.
- To support, improve, and replicate promising practices in victims' rights and services built upon sound research, advanced technology, and multidisciplinary partnerships.
- To ensure that the voices of crime victims play a central role in the nation's response to violence and those victimized by crime.

# Review and Applications

## SUMMARY BY CHAPTER OBJECTIVES

### CHAPTER OBJECTIVE 1

Victims were rarely recognized in the laws and policies that govern our nation until the 1970s. Since then, tremendous strides have been made in victims' rights legislation and victim services.

### CHAPTER OBJECTIVE 2

The 1980 enactment of Wisconsin's Victims' Bill of Rights, the nation's first state bill of rights for crime victims, began an era of dramatic progress in the victims' rights movement. Passage of the federal Victim and Witness Protection Act (VWPA) of 1982 brought national visibility to crime victims' concerns. In 1990, the Victims' Rights and Restitution Act (Victims' Rights Act) established a bill of rights for federal crime victims. The Violent Crime Control and Law Enforcement Act of 1994 established new rights for victims of sexual assault, domestic violence, sexual exploitation, child abuse, and telemarketing fraud. In 1996, the Community Notification Act, known as Megan's law, was enacted to ensure community notification of the locations of convicted sex offenders. In 1997, The Victims' Rights Clarification Act of 1997 asserted victims' rights to attend proceedings and deliver victim impact statements.

### CHAPTER OBJECTIVE 3

Many believe that a victims' rights amendment to the U.S. Constitution is needed to establish clear rights for crime victims and to protect those rights to the same degree that the rights of criminal suspects are already protected.

### CHAPTER OBJECTIVE 4

The costs that crime victims suffer can be divided into two major categories: (1) tangible losses, including medical bills, lost property, and lost wages; and (2) intangible losses, such as lost quality of life, fear, pain, and suffering.

### CHAPTER OBJECTIVE 5

Correctional agencies play an important role in meeting victims' needs. Services provided by correctional agencies include: (1) victim and community notification of offender release or change in status; (2) victim and witness protection services; (3) classes for offenders on the impact of crime; (4) opportunities for victim-offender dialogue.

### CHAPTER OBJECTIVE 6

Crime victim compensation programs pay for medical and mental health care, lost wages, funeral expenses, and crime-scene cleanup.

### CHAPTER OBJECTIVE 7

The three options available to victims for recovering crime-related financial losses are compensation, restitution, and civil remedies.

### CHAPTER OBJECTIVE 8

Victim impact statements are assertions by victims and/or friends or relatives of victims about the crime's impact on the victim and the victim's family. These statements are considered by judicial authorities in decisions regarding sentencing and parole.

## KEY TERMS

victim, p. 428
victims' rights, p. 428
best efforts standard, p. 430
tangible losses, p. 432
intangible losses, p. 432
victim notification, p. 434

community notification, p. 437
victim compensation, p. 440
restitution, p. 443
victim assistance program, p. 445
victim impact statement, p. 445
right of allocution, p. 445

1. Briefly outline the history of the American victims' rights movement.
2. Explain and date five federal laws that have significantly impacted victims' rights.
3. Why do some people consider a victims' rights amendment to the U.S. Constitution necessary?
4. What costs do crime victims suffer as a result of their victimization?
5. What can correctional agencies do to assist crime victims?
6. What are crime victim compensation programs and what do they do?
7. What three avenues are available to victims to recover financial losses due to crime?
8. Describe victim impact statements. In what ways are they useful?

## CRITICAL THINKING EXERCISES

### ON-THE-JOB ISSUE

You work in a state correctional facility. A month ago you were promoted from yard supervisory work into a program position that tasks you with conducting classes for offenders and their victims. Classes are held within the institution, and usually about 5 or 6 victims show up at each session to confront inmates. Many of the victims come from a local victims' rights group and, although they have all been victims of violent crime, they are not the people who have been victimized by the inmates involved in the class.

Classes usually involve victims telling inmates about the personal impact of their crimes, and about the personal burdens crime places upon victims everywhere. What strategies could you implement to ensure that inmates express true remorse for what they have done and that victims do not use the class as an opportunity to demean inmates?

### CORRECTIONS ISSUES

1. In 1996, resolutions were introduced in the U.S. House and Senate to amend the Constitution to include crime victims' rights. A proposed federal constitutional amendment was reintroduced in modified form in 1999 with bipartisan support. A federal constitutional amendment for victims' rights, say supporters, is needed for many different reasons, including:

   a. to establish consistency in the rights of crime victims in every state and at the federal level;
   b. to ensure that courts engage in careful balancing of the rights of victims and defendants;
   c. to guarantee crime victims the opportunity to participate in criminal justice proceedings;
   d. to further enhance the participation of victims in the criminal justice process.

   Do you agree or disagree that the U.S. Constitution should be amended to include victims' rights? Why?

2. While correctional services for victims exist today in many correctional agencies and institutions across the country, some people believe that correctional agencies have enough to do without worrying about victims. Dealing with offenders is a full-time job, say such critics, and the time and expense required to meet the needs of victims are just not available. Besides, they say, corrections is about controlling and rehabilitating offenders, not about making victims "whole again."

   a. Should correctional agencies and correctional personnel be involved in victims' support programs? Why or why not?
   b. If you were a corrections professional, how would you feel about being called upon to assist crime victims?

## CORRECTIONS ON THE WEB

1. Access the National Center for Victims of Crime at **http://www. nvc.org.** Click on the link to the "Victim Offender Reconciliation Program." Go to "Mediating the Victim-Offender Conflict" and click on "Case Studies." Read the case studies and decide whether or not the victims' needs and concerns were met through the reconciliation process.

2. All 50 states operate victim compensation programs. Some states have crime victim support agencies attached to the office of the state's attorney general. Access the Texas crime victims' page at **http://www.oag.state.tx.us/victims/victims.htm**, then search the Web to see if your state has a similar victim support organization and, if so, what information and services it provides.

## ADDITIONAL READINGS

Alexander, Ellen K. and Janice Harris Lord. *Impact Statements—A Victim's Right to Speak, A Nation's Responsibility to Listen.* (Washington, DC: Office for Victims of Crime), 1994.

Beatty, D.L. Frank, A. J. Lurigio, A. Seymour, M. Paparozzi, and B. Macgargle. *A Guide to Enhancing Victim Services Within Probation and Parole.* (Lexington, KY: American Probation and Parole Association), 1994.

Bureau of Justice Statistics. *Criminal Victimization in the United States,* 1998. (Washington, DC: U.S. Department of Justice), 1999.

National Institute of Justice. *Victim Costs and Consequences: A New Look.* (Washington, DC: NIJ), January 1996.

National Victim Center. *1996 Victims' Rights Sourcebook: A Compilation and Comparison of Victims' Rights Laws.* (Arlington, VA: NVC), 1997.

## ENDNOTES

1. Office for Victims of Crime, *From Pain to Power: Crime Victims Take Action* (Washington, DC: U.S. Department of Justice, 1998).

2. Federal Bureau of Prisons, Program Statement number 1490.03, December 14, 1994.

3. Much of the material in this chapter is adapted from Office for Victims of Crime, *New Directions from the Field: Victims Rights and Services for the 21st Century* (Washington, DC: U.S. Department of Justice, 1998).

4. National Organization for Victim Assistance, *1988 NOVA Legislative Directory* (Washington, DC: National Organization for Victim Assistance, 1988), p. 191.

5. Victim and Witness Protection Act of 1982, Pub. L. No. 97-291.

6. Office of Justice Programs, *President's Task Force on Victims of Crime: Four Years Later* (Washington, DC: U.S. Government Printing Office, May 1986), p. 4.

7. National Victim Center, *1996 Victims' Rights Sourcebook: A Compilation and Comparison of Victims'*

*Rights Laws* (Arlington, VA: National Victim Center, 1997).

8. Victim and Witness Protection Act of 1982, Pub. L. No. 97-291, section 2(b).

9. Crime Control Act of 1990, Pub. L. No. 101-647.

10. Op. cit., Title V, Section 502-503.

11. Violent Crime Control and Law Enforcement Act of 1994, Pub. L. No. 103-322.

12. Megan's Law amendment to the Jacob Wetterling Crimes Against Children and Sexual Violent Offender Act, 42 U.S.C. Section 14071.

13. NVCAN was created following a meeting sponsored by the National Organization for Victim Assistance (NOVA) and Mothers Against Drunk Driving (MADD) in 1985.

14. See the National Victims' Constitutional Amendment Network (NVCAN), *1996 Constitutional Amendment Action Kit.*

15. National Institute of Justice, *Victim Costs and Consequences: A New Look* (Washington, DC: NIJ, January 1996).

16. Ibid.

17. Much of the material in this section comes from Office for Victims of Crime, *New Directions*.

18. A. Seymour, *National Victim Services Survey of Adult and Juvenile Correctional Agencies and Paroling Authorities, 1996* (Arlington, VA: National Victim Center, April 1997).

19. Office for Victims of Crime, *New Directions*.

20. A. Seymour, op. cit., p. 5.

21. Megan's Law, Pub. L. No. 104-145, 110 Stat. 1345.

22. See Office for Victims of Crime, *New Directions*.

23. See Dorothy Mercer, R. Lord, and J. Lord, "Sharing Their Stories: What are the Benefits? Who is Helped?," paper presented at the Annual Meeting of the International Society for Traumatic Stress Studies, Chicago, IL, November 8, 1994.

24. Office for Victims of Crime, *New Directions*.

25. Ibid.

26. A. Seymour, op. cit.

27. A. Seymour, *Promising Practices and Strategies for Victim Services in Corrections* (Washington, DC: Office for Victims of Crime, 1999).

28. Office for Victims of Crime, *New Directions*.

29. President's Task Force on Victims of Crime, *Final Report* (Washington, DC: U.S. Government Printing Office, December 1982), p. 39.

30. National Association of Crime Victim Compensation Boards, *Crime Victim Compensation: An Overview* (Washington, DC: National Association of Crime Victim Compensation Boards, 1997), p. 1.

31. *Nationwide Analysis, Victims of Crime Act: 1996 Victims of Crime Act Performance Report, State Compensation Program* (Washington, DC: U.S. Department of Justice, Office of Justice Programs, Office for Victims of Crime, April 14, 1997).

32. Victims of Crime Act of 1984, Pub. L. No. 104-235.

33. President's Task Force on Victims of Crime, *Final Report*.

34. Much of the material is this section is taken from the Office for Victims of Crime fact sheet on the World Wide Web, http://www.ncjrs.org/ovcfs. htm. Accessed September 1, 1998.

35. Victim and Witness Protection Act of 1982, Pub. L. No. 97-291, Sec. 4.

36. President's Task Force on Victims of Crime, *Final Report* (Washington, DC: U.S. Government Printing Office, December 1982), p. 72.

37. The Mandatory Victim Restitution Act, Title II of the Antiterrorism and Effective Death Penalty Act of 1996, Pub. L. No. 104-132 (1996), 18 U.S.C. Section 3663A (1996).

38. P. A. Langan and M. A. Cunniff, *Recidivism of Felons on Probation, 1986-89* (Washington, DC: U.S. Department of Justice, Bureau of Justice Statistics, February 1992).

39. R. L. Cohen, *Probation and Parole Violators in State Prison, 1991* (Washington, DC: Bureau of Justice Statistics, 1995).

40. Ibid.

41. Much of the material in this section is taken from the office for victims of crime fact sheet, op. cit.

42. The National Victim Center, "INFOLINK: Victim Impact Statements," Web posted at http://www. nvc.org/infolink/info72.htm. Accessed January 2, 1999.

43. See Ellen K. Alexander and Janice Harris Lord, *Impact Statements: A Victim's Right to Speak, A Nation's Responsibility to Listen* (Washington, DC: Office for Victims of Crime, 1994).

44. *Payne v. Tennessee*, 501 U.S. 808, 111 S. Ct. 2597, 115 L. Ed. 2d 720.

45. National Victim Center, *1996 Victims' Rights Sourcebook*.

46. Office for Victims of Crime, *New Directions*.

# 16 Careers
## Your Future in Corrections

**CHAPTER OBJECTIVES**

After completing this chapter you should be able to:

1. List the six steps of career planning.
2. Explain self-assessment.
3. List sources of information on careers and job opportunities.
4. Explain networking.
5. Explain informational interviewing.
6. Explain the purpose of a resume.
7. List and describe the two most widely used resume formats.

*One's philosophy is not best expressed in words: it is expressed in the choices one makes . . . In the long run, we shape our lives and we shape ourselves. The process never ends until we die. And the choices we make are ultimately our responsibility.*

—Eleanor Roosevelt

areer development experts tell us that career development is a life-long process that involves continual and consistent maintenance. Your interests, skills, and preferences change throughout your life. Thus, it is important that you know the steps involved in career planning, developing employability and job readiness, and finding the right job.[1]

# Career Planning

Successful career planning is a continual process of self-assessment, occupational research, decision making, contacting potential employers, working at a job, and reevaluating your situation (see Figure 16–1).

**self-assessment**

A method of enhancing self-understanding— identifying your unique characteristics: what you do well (skills), what is important to you (values), and what you like to do (interests)—clearly and accurately.

## Self-Assessment

Career planning begins with **self-assessment**—learning who you are and what you can and want to do by evaluating your interests, skills, and values. Self-assessment tools, which pose a series of questions and identify potential career choices based on your answers, are available from most col-

**FIGURE 16–1**

**Steps to Career/Life Planning Success**

### STEPS TO CAREER/LIFE PLANNING SUCCESS

Begin at the bottom and work up.
Periodically reevaluate your career/life plans by starting again at step 1.

| | | | | |
|---|---|---|---|---|
| | | | **Planning** | |
| | | | Re-evaluation | |
| | | **Work** | | |
| | | Work Offers/Acceptance | Success at Work | |
| | **Employment Contacts** | | | |
| | Job/Work Search | Resumes/Letters | Job/Work Interviews | |
| **Decision Making** | | | | |
| Career Objectives | Personal Objectives | Community Service | Lifelong Learning | |
| **Occupational Research** | | | | |
| Information Search | Information Interview | Job Shadow | Hands-on Experience | Trends |
| **Self-Assessment** | | | | |
| Personality/Attitudes | Skills/Achievements | Knowledge/Learning Style | Values | Interests | Entrepreneurism |

You may need to move from an upper step to a lower one; e.g., from step 4 to step 2, should a lack of openings in a particular field require research into a different one.

*Source:* Career Services at University of Waterloo

lege and university career counselors, as well as in book stores and on the Internet. The questions involved pertain to: (1) personal information—education, experience, achievements, personality factors, and interest in various activities; (2) skills—abilities in such areas as athletics, analysis, management, communication, and persuasion; and (3) values—ranking work-related issues (such as job location, pressure, security, responsibility, teamwork, and wages) in order of importance.

## Occupational Research

The second step in career planning is research. Make a list of the potential career choices identified by your self-assessment, as well as any additional careers that you would like to know more about. Research job requirements (training, education, certification, licensure), job characteristics, working conditions, duties, employment outlook, salary, and methods of entry for each of the career alternatives: read everything you can find and talk to people.

**Reading** Information on careers and job opportunities is available in libraries (public, school, and special), career development centers, and on the Internet. Among others, three U.S. Department of Labor publications—*Dictionary of Occupational Titles, Occupational Outlook Handbook,* and *Guide for Occupational Exploration*—provide information on more than 20,000 jobs, and cross-reference each career field with others that are similar in nature. The U.S. Department of Labor also publishes two periodicals, *Occupational Outlook Quarterly* and *Monthly Labor Review,* that are excellent sources of information about occupational trends and salaries.

**Talking to People** **Networking** is meeting new people (often through people that you know) who can give you information about careers, the job market, and specific positions. Broadening your acquaintance base to include solid professional contacts, through networking, builds long-term professional relationships that facilitate job hunting and professional development and enhance personal growth.

**networking** An ongoing process of building professional contacts.

Developing a network is an integral part of job hunting; networking is considered the most effective method of job searching and is the number one way people obtain jobs. It has no time limit, nor does it end when you secure a position. Start developing contacts before you begin your career planning, and keep in touch with those contacts—they might hear of a job opening for you. Continue to keep in touch after you get a job—you may need to use your network again.

How do you begin networking? How do you establish contacts if you do not have any? Anyone can be a contact: the student who sits next to you in class, your parents' next-door neighbor, your doctor, your professor, previous supervisors, people with whom you have something in common (attending the same school, working out at the same gym, membership in the same professional association, etc.). Join organizations and participate in local programs that are related to your area of interest.

One of the key elements of networking is talking to people about your career interests and goals. Most people are more than willing to share information; in fact, the majority are flattered by the attention and truly want to help. Talk to the people you meet about what they do, their backgrounds, and their perspectives on the job market for their specialties, and ask if they know anyone else you might speak with. Take advantage of any and every opportunity to build your network—talk to people while you are waiting in line, riding the bus, attending a seminar, playing golf. The other key element is follow-up—keep your contacts apprised of your career status; let them know about your latest career move or your progress in a new job.

**informational interviewing**  A process for obtaining firsthand information about a particular job or career.

**Informational interviewing**, talking to people who are currently employed in a career field that you are interested in exploring, is an excellent means of researching a particular job or position. Introduce yourself to the person you wish to talk to, either by calling or writing, and ask if you might have 30 minutes of time to discuss the job or position. Explain that you're gathering career information, and ask for an appointment. An informational interview can provide:

- An accurate portrayal of the career field you are investigating.
- Specifics about necessary skills, entry level positions, employment trends, etc.
- Information about related volunteer, part-time, or internship opportunities.
- Additional professional contacts.
- Increased confidence in interacting with professionals.
- Information about possible job openings.
- A good chance of "being at the right place at the right time."
- Information about concerns that should not be discussed in a job interview (e.g., salaries, hours, and minority issues).

## Decision Making

The third step in career planning is making your career decision. Carefully review all of the information that you have gathered. For which of the careers that you researched are you best qualified? Which are most appealing? Which are most likely to enhance your career development? List career choices in order of preference, then begin your job search (see Figure 16–2).

# Seeking Employment

Finding a job can be a tough process that requires an overwhelming amount of thought, time, and energy. Make the job search part of your everyday routine; decide how much time you will devote to the search and when, and stick with that decision.

Be creative in your job search; utilize all of the resources available to you—classified ads, Internet ads, professional associations, advisors, employment services (local and Internet), etc.—to identify available positions.

**resume**  A written summary of your education, interests, skills, achievements, and goals.

## Writing Your Resume

A good **resume** may not necessarily get you the job, but a bad resume can ensure that you don't get the job. Your resume is not meant to convey

**FIGURE 16–2**

Job Search Checklist

# JOB SEARCH CHECKLIST

✔ Establish specific goals. Determine two or three potential career areas that are compatible with your values, skills, and interests.

✔ Prepare your search tools. Write a resume and sharpen your interviewing skills. Are you ready for your interview?

✔ Identify and research potential employers by utilizing different resources, such as:
- Career Development Center
- Professional Associations
- Newspaper Classifieds
- Internet Sites
- Deans/Professors/Other Advisors
- Trade Organizations
- Career Library Resources/Texts
- State/County Employment Offices

✔ Conduct informational interviews, which differ from job interviews—they provide you with an excellent opportunity to meet with individuals in a specific career field and obtain up-to-date information on that field. This can help your career decision making and develop a network of contacts.

✔ Initiate contact with employers. Establish a mailing list of potential employers within the targeted fields you identified from your earlier research. Mail your resume with a focused cover letter and then follow up with telephone calls to request interview appointments.

✔ Follow up with each contact. Remember, follow-up is your responsibility.

✔ Get organized, and stay on schedule. Devote at least 20 hours a week to your job search. Develop a schedule and create a list of organizations, contact people, contact dates, and outcomes.

✔ Accept an offer—consider these factors when deciding on which:
- size of the organization
- job security
- travel/relocation requirements
- hours
- formal training arrangements
- people you met with
- advancement potential
- entry level salary
- salary potential
- geographical factors
- education/fringe benefits
- name recognition of employer

your complete life history. Through your resume, you convey your capability for a particular position; it must be clear, directed, and persuasive—its objective is to secure an interview.

Your resume should (1) support a career direction and (2) be selective. Career direction gives the resume focus; all of the information included in the resume should support the career direction that you are trying to convey. Career guidance experts tell us, "You should make yourself as attractive as possible on paper so that the employer feels as though she would be missing out by not interviewing you."[2] Your resume should project you as someone who produces, accomplishes, and is results-oriented. Use active verbs and descriptive terms; i.e., "researched and drafted reports" rather than "responsible for research and reports." What works best today is a conservative style and a focus on key achievements—particularly those that relate to the position for which you are applying; find out as much as you can about the prospective employer, then modify the resume to highlight those items that will most benefit the company or organization. The most effective resume is one that is tailored to a specific job; the results are well worth the extra effort. According to Tom Jackson, "The Perfect Resume is a written communication that clearly demonstrates your ability to produce results in an area of concern to selected employers, in a way that motivates them to meet you."[3]

## FIGURE 16-3

**Tips for Writing Resumes**

### RESUME WRITING–QUICK TIPS

- One Page
- Font Size: 10 (minimum)–12 (preferred)
- Paper Weight: recommended, 24 lb; acceptable, 21 lb.
- Paper Color: white or off-white
- GPA is required dependent upon major
- Margins: .5–1.5 inch, portrait
- Include your objective
- Do not use personal pronouns
- Use action verbs
- Use conventional English, preferably one- or two-syllable words
- Use short paragraphs—preferably no longer than five lines
- Use a chronological or functional format
- Use "bullet" format where appropriate
- Proofread and have others proofread for you
- "References available upon request" ends your resume

When creating your resume, keep the following in mind:

- The "one page rule"—one page is ideal; two is acceptable (however, do not add a second page simply to expand content); three is unacceptable.
- Your resume should be easily scanned: effectively organized to carry the reader's eye from major point to major point (a prospective employer will look for words and phrases that convey the necessary qualifications).
- The eye is drawn to eye-catching type; **bold,** CAPITALIZE, or <u>underscore</u> to emphasize a particular item.
- Bullets break job and skill descriptions into easy-to-read component parts that begin with eye-catching verbs.
- Talents, skills, and experience should be highlighted to some extent, but don't overdo.
- Word processing allows great flexibility in the selection of fonts, but choose something simple. Avoid ornateness, and avoid combining several fonts.
- Employers want employees who can set goals and complete tasks; present yourself as someone who gets things done.
- You must identify your strengths and convey them on paper; this is not arrogance or boasting. The person who is reading your resume wants to know that you are exceptional.
- You should always honestly summarize your work experience and skills, including any technologies you are familiar with (such as computers, calculators, fax machines, telephone systems, word processing, spreadsheet or database software, etc.).
- Personal pronouns should not be used; "I" is implied.
- Complete sentences are not necessary.
- Abbreviations should be avoided.

Your resume is a primary tool in obtaining more attractive positions; thus, extra time spent on its preparation is a good investment. All resumes should be accurate and truthful, but each should highlight different strengths, as they relate to the potential job. The resume should go through several stages of drafting and editing until it is as perfect as it can be.

## Resume Format

The selected resume format should establish a natural flow of information that simplifies the review process, and should incorporate a consistent pattern of information placement, allowing the reader to anticipate where certain information will be found. An employer usually reviews information on the left side first—names of employers, job titles, etc., should be placed on the left. Less important information (dates, locations, etc.) should be placed on the right. No resume format is universally preferred, although the **chronological resume** and the **functional resume** are the most widely used. (See Figures 16–4 and 16–5.)

**Chronological Resume** The chronological resume format is the most widely accepted and preferred resume style. It is most effectively used by

**chronological resume**
An historical resume, in which work experience and personal history are presented, in reverse chronological order.

**functional resume**
A qualitative resume, in which work experience and abilities are presented by major area of involvement, usually with dates.

people who have established or are establishing credentials within a particular field, or whose credentials show career growth and direction within one particular employment environment. To be effective, the chronological resume should project a sense of quality by emphasizing skills and accomplishments, and should be carefully organized (in terms of layout) to most effectively present a particular background. In this format, your education and work experience are presented in reverse time sequence, with the most recent degrees and jobs appearing first. In developing a chronological resume:

- de-emphasize history for the sake of content; place dates and other less relevant information on the right-hand side of the page;
- devote more space to the most recent position;
- fully describe the three or four positions most supportive of the career direction—summarize other work experience unless it is exceptionally meaningful;
- avoid excessive repetition in detail and substance; and
- emphasize career growth.

**Functional Resume**  The functional resume emphasizes abilities over work history by organizing information according to skills, results accomplished, contributions made, or functions successfully performed. It is best used by those who are changing careers or have been out of the work force for some time. In developing a functional resume:

- select functions that describe job-related abilities (versatile abilities, if possible);
- list functions in order of importance and relevance to your career direction, emphasizing accomplishment and achievement while illustrating specific abilities;
- avoid including employment detail (employer names, dates of employment, job titles) within the functional descriptions; include a work history section that sets forth this information.

**What To Include**  Regardless of which resume format you use, your resume should include:

1. Identification—name (first, middle initial, last), address (permanent and/or present), telephone numbers (work and/or home, fax), and e-mail address (if applicable). Accurate information is critical; a prospective employer who is unable to reach you with the information provided is not likely to try to verify contact information. If the information changes, correct your resume and reprint it.
2. Objective/Career Interest—your career objective specifies the type of work you want to do, the position you want, or the skills/attributes you anticipate utilizing, and the employment sector in which you wish to establish a career; a career interest statement is a broader, long-range career direction, which simply lists the field or occupation in which you wish to be employed.

**FIGURE 16–4**

Reverse Chronological Resume Format

**Derrick A. Salyer**
1555 Campus Lake Drive, Richmond, KY 40477
(606) 555-1212

OBJECTIVE

To secure a position as a juvenile court probation officer.

EDUCATION

**Bachelor of Science,** August 1999
Eastern Kentucky University, Richmond, KY
Major: Correctional Services
GPA: 3.20/4.00
Dean's List, Distinguished Undergraduate Award

**Associate of Arts,** December 1995
Houston Community College, Houston, TX
Major: General Studies

Self-financed 50% of education through work, loans, and scholarships

EXPERIENCE

**Intern,** January–May 1999
Kentucky Department of Juvenile Justice, Richmond, KY
– Assisted department staff with hosting of three live national satellite videoconferences
– Served as liaison to downlink sites
– Attended all planning sessions

**Intern,** August–December 1998
Richmond Juvenile Court Services, Richmond, KY
– Assisted intake officer with predisposition investigation and report writing
– Attended detention and adjudication hearings
– Answered questions relating to the predisposition report

**Sales Associate,** March 1996–July 1998
Just For Feet, University Mall, Richmond, KY
– Coordinated sales associates' schedules
– Managed evening cashier sales associates
– Achieved and maintained Best Shift/Least Checkout Errors monthly in 1998

ACTIVITIES

Criminal Justice Student Association, 1998 President, 1997 Vice President
Alpha Phi Sigma (Criminal Justice Honor Society) Spirit Award, 1996

REFERENCES

Available upon request.

**FIGURE 16–5**

**Functional Resume Format**

**Tanisha Williams**

1500 Maplewood Drive, Palmdale, CA 93510

(213) 555-1212

**CAREER INTERESTS:**

Correctional industry managment

**SKILLS:**

**PLANNING/ORGANIZATION**

- Successfully established and operated a T-shirt design shop
- Developed market/trade survey programs to determine customer interest
- Initiated radio T-shirt give-away contests
- Established connection with local homeless shelter to employ the homeless

**ADMINISTRATION/MANAGEMENT/SALES MARKETING**

- Supervised team of 20 sales associates
- Hired and delegated supervision of 18-person T-shirt design shop to two associate managers
- Approved corporate sales contracts
- Increased corporate sales 32%
- Managed commercial sales advertisements—three radio, one television, and one newspaper—averaging $32,000 annually

**EMPLOYMENT EXPERIENCE**

| | |
|---|---|
| **OWNER AND OPERATOR** | **1990–Present** |
| **TANISHA'S SHIRTS AND DESIGNS** | |
| Lancaster, California | |
| | |
| **SALES ASSOCIATE AND MANAGER** | **1987–1990** |
| **HUTTON'S TEES** | |
| Lancaster, California | |

**EDUCATION**

**BACHELOR OF SCIENCE, CRIMINAL JUSTICE ADMINISTRATION, 1999**

California State University

Northridge, California

REFERENCES AVAILABLE UPON REQUEST

3. Education—schools attended, degrees received, dates of graduation, majors and other concentrations of study, and academic achievement (class rank and grade point average for an undergraduate or graduate program). The education section can also include extracurricular activities of particular significance and academic honors and awards.

4. Skills/Accomplishments/Qualifications—descriptions, grouped by major functional skill area. Choose three to five functional skill areas that correspond to your career objective.

5. Experience—for a chronological resume, list experience in reverse chronological order, beginning with your current or most recent position.

6. Optional—Other information that can be included in your resume includes: personal statements (relatively neutral comments about personal interests such as foreign language, community activity, travel, sports, public speaking, unique hobbies, and military experience); honors and awards (academic honors, memberships in national honor societies, scholarships, etc.); curricular and cocurricular activities (those that demonstrate leadership), community activities or volunteer experiences (demonstrates personal work habits, leadership potential, and level of motivation/commitment); professional associations and licenses, and publications.

References should always be listed on a separate page, not on the resume. Do not approach the selection of references casually; your references are critical to the strength of your employment credentials.

The resume copy should be meticulously reviewed before it is forwarded to a potential employer (you might have a friend or a qualified professional critique it):

- Is the resume easily scanned?
- Does the resume immediately project a career direction and provide supporting evidence?
- Is the resume neat, clean, and professional? Is the layout attractive?
- Are the margins wide enough?
- Are there typos? Check and recheck spelling, punctuation, and grammar—proofread by reading the resume backward.
- Is the highlighting (bold, capitalization, underscore) excessive?
- Is the language direct and concise?
- Is the resume action- and results-oriented?
- Is the resume free of jargon that the reader may not understand?
- Are sentences short? Are paragraphs short? Are they vivid and descriptive?
- Is all repetition eliminated?
- Are there time gaps that the employer might question?
- Is all irrelevant information excluded?
- Is the verb tense consistent?
- Are there any personal pronouns?
- Does the resume represent you at your very best?

Many employers and employment services now encourage online job application. Be aware, though, that if you used a word-processing program or desktop publishing program to create your resume, it may not look the same to the online recipient as it did on your computer—a resume that is to be submitted online should be translated to text format. Here are some guidelines:

- Line length—line lengths in excess of 80 characters have a very good chance of wrapping prematurely, creating an annoying double-spaced window.
- Vertical alignment—vertical alignment is achieved by using an equal number of spaces from the left-hand margin; to ensure that all characters are the same size (including spaces), use a fixed-width font such as 10-point Courier and use spaces rather than tabs to indent text.
- Other issues—if your resume design includes columns or bullets, take advantage of ASCII characters such as dashes (-), asterisks (*), and arrows (>).

## The Cover Letter

A cover letter (see Figures 16–6 and 16–7) should always accompany your resume. Like the resume, the cover letter should be direct, persuasive, descriptive, and attractive. Remember, the cover letter is specific to the potential employer; it should emphasize credentials and experience that apply to the position. Your cover letter can differentiate you significantly from others competing for the same position. The following is the basic format for the cover letter:

1. First paragraph—serves to get the attention of the person receiving the letter and answers the question: "Why are you writing?" This can be as simple as stating that you are "a graduating student seeking employment at [name of employer]," or that you are "responding to a job posting from [name of source]." If (in the ideal situation) you are referred by a professional or personal contact, use it to your advantage—begin your letter with "John Smith recommended that I contact you regarding employment."

2. Second paragraph—details your interest in and your fit with the company or organization. Keep in mind that employers are more interested in what you can do for them than in what they can give you. Answer implied questions, such as:

   a. "Why are you interested in working for this firm or organization?" This part need only be a sentence or two, but should include reference to specifics about the organization—its mission, type of work, geographic location, size, reputation in the community, and/or types of positions available. Employers' hiring decisions are often based not only on qualifications, but also on level of interest in the firm or organization. Be genuine. This is an opportunity to show that you researched the employer.

**FIGURE 16–6**

**Tips on Writing Cover Letters**

# WRITING A COVER LETTER

Your Street Address
City, State Zip Code

Today's Date

Contact Person's Name
Contact Person's Title (if applicable)
Company/Organization Name
Street Address
City, State Zip Code

Dear (Contact Person's Name, or Contact Person's Title if name is unknown):

OPENING PARAGRAPH: Clearly state why you are writing, name the position or type of work for which you are applying, and mention how you heard of the opening. If you are writing without prior knowledge of an available opening, say that you are interested in openings that may currently be available.

MIDDLE PARAGRAPH: Explain why you are interested in working for this employer, and/or your reasons for desiring this type of work. Describe applicable experience, achievements, or other qualifications in this environment or type of employment.

MIDDLE PARAGRAPH: Refer the reader to your enclosed resume, which positively illustrates your training, skills, and experience. DO NOT DUPLICATE RESUME INFORMATION IN THE COVER LETTER—"highlight," and elaborate on how you can make a tangible contribution to this company/organization.

CLOSING PARAGRAPH: Use a closing appropriate to acquiring an interview. If you know the contact person's name and telephone number, use a pro-active strategy—say that you will call to request an appointment in the very near future. If you do not know the contact person's name, ending your letter with a question often encourages a response. (e.g., May we meet soon to discuss this matter further?)

Sincerely,

Your signature

Your Full Name (typewritten)

Enclosure

**FIGURE 16–7**

**Sample Cover Letter**

1500 Maplewood Drive
Palmdale, CA 93510
January 12, 2000

Ms. Caroline Butterworth
Human Resources
State of California
Department of Corrections
Sacramento, CA 94283-0001

Dear Ms. Butterworth:

I am applying for the position of Supervisor of Correctional Industries in your Southeast Region. I am a graduate of California State University, Northridge, with a bachelor's degree in criminal justice administration. I believe that my work experience and education make me a strong candidate for this position.

My degree in criminal justice administration has given me an excellent understanding of the criminal justice field, particularly institutional corrections and the corrections industry. I completed a 15-week internship at the Chino, California Institution for Men, where I gained considerable insight into prison industry operations—especially security—and the importance of helping prisoners to develop and maintain job skills prior to release.

My work experience spans 10 years, which includes self-employment (in T-shirt design and sales—I hired and supervised a staff of 20) and industry organization and management.

I look forward to speaking with you about utilizing my business skills and criminal justice qualifications in the position of Supervisor of Correctional Industries. I will contact you next week to arrange an interview. Please call me if you have questions.

Sincerely,

Tanisha Williams

Tanisha Williams

Enclosure

**b.** "Why are you the right person for the job?" In two or three sentences, tell the prospective employer what skills you will bring to the job without reiterating details included in your resume. Give specific examples of skills and accomplishments related to this position that you emphasized in your resume. You might consider a wrap-up sentence commenting on how the organization might benefit from your skills and experience.

**3.** Last paragraph—express appreciation for the prospective employer's time and consideration, and provide details about what you plan to do next—how you will follow up (e.g., a telephone call) and when (either a specific date or within a certain number of weeks; wait at least two weeks). If you do not know whom to call to follow up, you might ask the employer to contact you at a particular telephone number or by e-mail. If a job listing says, "No phone calls, please," state in the cover letter that you look forward to hearing from the employer soon.

## The Job Interview

The **job interview** plays a very important role in your job search. To interview successfully, you must understand the interview process and prepare well. Do not assume that the interview is, or should be, one-sided. During an interview, you must project your most impressive qualities. In other words, you must sell yourself to the prospective employer. As part of the evaluation process, the interviewer will be deciding how you will function as an employee. Therefore, it is essential to demonstrate how your skills, knowledge, and experience match the requirements of the position for which you are interviewing.

It is essential that you speak confidently (not arrogantly) about your skills, knowledge, and experience. In preparing, take time to think about answers to potential interview questions (see Figure 16–8). When the interviewer asks a question for which you are unprepared, think before you speak; take a second or two and organize your thoughts, then answer as best you can.

Reread your resume before every interview—chances are the interviewer did just that, too. In addition, review your resume for possible questions you might be asked. Formulating answers ahead of time will allow you to be more relaxed and articulate during the interview.

Job interview attire can be summed up in two words: "conservative" and "businesslike." Proper dress will give you confidence and enhance your professional image. For most professional-level jobs, the standard dark suit is appropriate for both men and women; less formal clothing may be more appropriate for some jobs. Use common sense. College faculty and career planning counselors can help, as well as someone you may know who is employed in the same field as the position for which you are interviewing. Keep perfume or cologne and jewelry to a minimum. Do not chew gum or other food during the interview.

Take with you to the interview copies of your resume, your list of references (or reference letters), any other relevant papers, and your transcripts(s), as well as a pen or pencil and notebook and a list of questions.

**job interview** A meeting between two or more people for a mutual exchange of information regarding employment.

*Careers: Your Future in Corrections* | CHAPTER 16 | **467**

**FIGURE 16–8**

Sample Interview Questions

## FIFTY QUESTIONS MOST OFTEN ASKED BY EMPLOYERS DURING AN INTERVIEW

1. Tell me about yourself.
2. What personal goals, other than those related to your occupation, have you established for yourself for the next ten years?
3. What do you see yourself doing five years from now?
4. What do you really want to do in life?
5. What are your short-range and long-range career objectives?
6. How do you plan to achieve your career goals?
7. What are the most important rewards you expect in your career?
8. What do you expect to be earning in five years?
9. Why did you choose the career for which you are preparing?
10. Which is more important to you, the money or the type of job?
11. What do you consider your greatest strengths and weaknesses?
12. How would you describe yourself?
13. How do you think a friend or professor who knows you well would describe you?
14. What motivates you to put forth your greatest effort?
15. How has your college experience prepared you for your career?
16. Why should I hire you?
17. What qualifications do you have that makes you think that you will be successful in this environment/setting?
18. How do you determine or evaluate success?
19. What do you think it takes to be successful in an organization like ours?
20. In what ways do you think you can make a contribution to this organization?
21. What qualities should a successful supervisor possess?
22. Describe the relationship that should exist between a supervisor and those reporting to him or her.
23. What two or three accomplishments have given you the most satisfaction? Why?

A typical first job interview usually lasts 30–60 minutes, although it may be longer. Often called a screening interview, the first interview is often used to shorten a long list of candidates. You also may be asked to complete a job-related questionnaire that may serve to shorten the list of candidates (see Figure 16–9). Those who make a positive impression are invited back for second interviews.

Remain alert for indications that you are on track. If the interviewer seems relaxed, is following closely, and encouraging you with comments and nods, you are probably on target. If the interviewer appears puzzled, stop and restate your reply. If the interviewer has obviously lost interest, try getting back on track by asking if you covered the point adequately. Maintain eye contact when answering questions, but do not be afraid to avert your eyes when thinking about an answer.

**FIGURE 16–8 (continued)**

Sample Interview Questions

24. Describe your most rewarding college experience.
25. If you were hiring a graduate for this position, what qualities would you look for?
26. Why did you select your college or university?
27. What led you to choose your field or major?
28. What college subjects did you like best? Why?
29. What college subjects did you like least? Why?
30. If you could do so, how would you plan your academic study differently?
31. What changes would you make in your college or university? Why?
32. Do you have plans for continued study? An advanced degree?
33. Do you think that your grades are a good indication of your academic achievement/ability?
34. What have you learned from participation in extracurricular activities?
35. In what kinds of environments are you most comfortable?
36. How do you work under pressure?
37. In what part-time or summer job have you been most interested? Why?
38. How would you describe the ideal job for you following graduation?
39. Why did you decide to seek a position with this organization?
40. What do you know about this organization?
41. What three things are most important to you in your career/job?
42. Are you seeking employment in an organization of a certain size? Why?
43. What criteria are you using to evaluate the organization/employer for which you hope to work?
44. Do you have a geographical preference? Why?
45. Will you relocate? Do relocations bother you?
46. Are you willing to travel?
47. Are you willing to spend at least six months in training?
48. Why do you think you might like to live in the area in which our organization is located?
49. Describe a major problem you have encountered and how you dealt with it.
50. What have you learned from your mistakes?

A prospective employer may request a second interview, either because initial interviews indicated that more than one of the applicants might qualify for the position or because others are involved in the hiring decision. Keep in mind when preparing for the second interview that you may now be in direct competition with others whose qualifications are as appropriate as yours; prepare carefully:

- Engage in a more extensive study of the organization to gain in-depth knowledge.
- Evaluate your skills, knowledge, and experience and how they are applicable to the position for which you are applying.
- Review general interview skills.
- Gather appropriate documents: resumes, references, transcripts, etc.

## FIGURE 16-9

**Sample Job Screening Questionnaire**

SUPPLEMENTAL QUESTIONNAIRE
SELF-SCREENING
PROBATION AND PAROLE OFFICER I

The following requirements are needed by all candidates for this position. If you answer "yes" to all requirements listed, sign below and return this form with your completed application. If you answer "no" to any of the requirements, do not complete the rest of the form and do not submit an application. An answer "no" in any one area will result in a rating of "not qualified" for this position.

1. Are you willing and able to cope with unmotivated and hostile individuals who have committed all types of crimes?

   Yes _____          No _____

2. Are you willing to do field checks knowing that you will be going into areas where you may be subject to threats or physical danger?

   Yes _____          No _____

3. Are you willing to testify before the court, parole board, and other judicial hearings to answer questions, present progress reports, and make recommendations?

   Yes _____          No _____

4. Are you willing to be trained in the use of firearms and deadly force?

   Yes _____          No _____

5. Are you willing to be trained in the use of defensive tactics which involve physical contact?

   Yes _____          No _____

6. Are you willing to participate in the arrest of criminal offenders?

   Yes _____          No _____

The answers I have given are true and correct to the best of my knowledge, and I understand that I must be willing and able to perform tasks requiring physical strength and agility.

SIGNATURE _____ DATE _____

- Compare your personal agenda with the organization's agenda.
- Make additional copies of pertinent records.
- Prepare a list of questions.

Remember, interviewing is a two-way street. Not only is it an opportunity for the organization to ask questions of you, it is also your opportunity to learn more about the organization. Get answers to your questions; this information will help you decide which of the job offers you receive you should accept, and asking the same question of different individuals will allow you to compare responses. Whatever the outcome of any job interview, bear in mind that the employer is thinking first of organizational needs, not of you. Don't let rejections weaken your self-confidence.

## The Thank-You Letter

A thank-you letter (see Figure 16–10 on page 472) should always immediately follow a job interview; in fact, you should start thinking about the thank-you letter as soon as the interview is over, and mail it within 24 hours of the interview. The thank-you letter is not just "a nice thing to do"; it's also a sales opportunity—another opportunity for you to "sell" yourself. The thank-you letter should be simple; the following is the basic format:

1. First paragraph—Thank the reader for the interview and restate the position for which you are applying and your interest in it.
2. Second paragraph—restate your qualifications and reiterate what you have to offer to the company. Refer to specific points discussed during the interview.
3. Last paragraph—restate the first paragraph.

# Securing Employment

Job offers are not typically made on the spot. However, if an offer is made, you should delay acceptance until you have had an opportunity to evaluate all of your job opportunities. When evaluating your options, be sure to consider all aspects of the position—type of work, location, salary, benefits, opportunity for growth, co-workers. Again, the job hunting process can be tough; choose a job that you will want to keep for a long while.

# Re-evaluation

Because your interests, skills, and preferences change, you should periodically re-evaluate your career choice to determine if you could more effectively utilize your skills, abilities, and talents in a different occupation or at a different organization. Correspond with your contacts on a fairly regular basis and investigate available positions, but be careful not to take steps that may jeopardize your present position—you may find that it is still the best job for you.

**FIGURE 16-10**

**Sample Thank You Letter**

1500 Maplewood Drive
Palmdale, CA 93510
March 16, 2000

Ms. Caroline Butterworth
Human Resources
State of California
Department of Corrections
Sacramento, CA 94283-0001

Dear Ms. Butterworth:

Thank you for taking the time to meet with me on Wednesday and giving me the opportunity to learn more about California's prison industries program. The materials you gave me were very informative and interesting.

As we discussed during our interview, my education and work experience have prepared me for many of the duties of the Supervisor of Correctional Industries, and, based on the additional knowledge that I gained during that interview, I am certain that my performance in this position will exceed the requirements.

As you requested, I have asked the California State University records office to forward a copy of my transcript to your office; you should receive it within a few days.

Thank you again for your time and interest. I look forward to hearing from you.


Sincerely,

*Tanisha Williams*

Tanisha Williams

In the past two years, The Corrections Connection has received thousands of e-mails with questions about getting hired in corrections. So, we thought it would be helpful to get advice from two corrections practitioners in different parts of the country, who frequently conduct job interviews and review applications for employment. We interviewed Warden George F. Wagner from the Hunterdon County Jail in Flemington, New Jersey and Captain Ken E. Richardson from the Licking County Jail in Newark, Ohio.

Both were very willing to share their experiences, the dos and don'ts of interviewing, and the types of interview questions most frequently asked. Although they have two very different styles of interviewing, you can see that they both seek the same type of qualities in an employee: loyalty, dedication, honesty, and integrity. In fact, in an independent survey of 20 other facilities, we found these overall qualities to be important to most corrections employers, even more so than problem solving skills, writing and communication skills. Here is what else we discovered.

**Q: What do you think are the basics that every job applicant should know?**

**Warden George F. Wagner:** Arrive on time and dress appropriately.

**Captain Ken E. Richardson:** Be on time! It shows dependability and that's critical.

**Q: What are you looking for in the interview room?**

**Wagner:** By the time they come in for the interview, I already know everything about them from their application and background checks. Now, I want to know if they can articulate their goals. Why do they want to work in corrections? What I usually find is that the conversation is one-way; I do all the talking. They should be asking me questions, taking an active interest.

**Richardson:** I am looking for people who are able to express themselves. I want people who are proud of where they work. Proud of their employer. Proud of their profession. It makes a difference in their level of performance. I am looking for dedication and, above all, loyalty.

**Q: What is one big mistake applicants should avoid?**

**Wagner:** Don't come too early. Arriving at 8:00 a.m. for a 9:00 a.m. appointment is not good. You are actually impeding the process because now we have to figure out what to do with you while you are here. Being too early is actually a bad decision.

**Q: What should an applicant wear to an interview?**

**Wagner:** You should take the interview seriously and wear something appropriate. I'll tell you a true story. Last summer we were conducting interviews. I looked out into the lobby and saw this guy in shorts, a tee-shirt, flip flops, and a hat with the brim turned to the back. I asked my Lieutenant who he was, and he said, "That's your 10 o'clock. Should I bring him in for the interview?" My response was simple: "He just had his interview!" So sorry I interrupted his day at the beach.

**Richardson:** You should look professional (a suit or sports jacket and tie; a nice tailored dress or suit). You want to make a nice first impression.

**Q: If someone is currently working in law enforcement or is in the armed forces, would you recommend that he or she wear the uniform to the interview?**

**Wagner:** No, I would not. It just reminds me that you are working for someone else while you are looking for another job. I want to know that you're interested in me. Plus, as employers, you can't trust that the uniform is real. I once had a man come in a uniform, saying that he was a veteran. In reality, he

*continued*

had picked up the uniform in a local thrift shop. I'm going to do a thorough background check on you, check your references, meet with you, read your application, so I am going to know all that I have to know about you anyway. I don't need the uniform.

**Q: What should an applicant bring to the interview?**

**Wagner:** You need to look prepared and be prepared. If there are documents that you think we need, bring copies so we don't have to make the copies ourselves. Otherwise, I have to get up, get my secretary, have her make the copies and bring them back to you. Show a little planning on your part. I like it when someone has everything prepared.

**Q: Do you always conduct a background check?**

**Wagner:** We always check background. You can't trust documents, i.e., college records, certificates, etc. We are getting into scannable documents, where you can create anything with a computer and say it's real. An applicant may say he or she has a Ph.D. and have documents and certificates, but they are not authentic. We always do background checks.

**Richardson:** Absolutely. We do a thorough background check on every applicant.

**Q: What kind of information should be included in a background check?**

**Wagner:** We want to know everything. Where you were born, siblings, boyfriends, girlfriends. Financial obligations you have, financial obligations you've had, education, all employers from day 1, any interaction with any law enforcement agency, any judgments of any kind. I have had people come in to the office for an interview who have a criminal record, and they just don't put it on the application. People think if they don't list it, nobody is going to find out. That is simply not true.

**Richardson:** Everything should go on the application. To me, silence is a form of deception.

**Q: What kind of preparation should applicants do prior to the interview?**

**Wagner:** Do a little research on the institution to which they are going for the interview. Contact government authorities and find out how the position being interviewed for fits into the organizational chart. Know a little bit about the facility. It shows initiative to do that. On my end, I like to give them the tour before the interview. They need to know the kind of inmates they are dealing with, as well as our set-up and procedures.

**Q: What about political and moral philosophies? How important is that?**

**Wagner:** Their personal feelings don't matter because their professional behavior is guided by policy. It doesn't matter to me whether they are liberal, conservative, democratic, pro-choice, pro-life, right-wing, left-wing, or pro capital punishment. We formulate their professional conduct via policy and procedure. As long as they are following our procedures, I don't care what their personal views are. I think that's the way it usually is.

**Q: What is the procedure for testing and applying?**

**Wagner:** Well, it is going to depend a lot on the individual requirements of your state. We are a civil service state so applicants test and are ranked according to their scores and by their residence. We run a county jail, so people who live in Hunterdon County would be ranked first; then bordering counties in New Jersey; then state wide; then nationwide. We do give veterans preference. You should find out what your state requires. Of course, we do background checks; conduct oral interviews; require you to provide three references (vouchers) signed by a notary; take a physical which includes a drug test; then take a psychological test. Then you're hired . . . if you pass all that.

**Richardson:** In addition to the tests, the background checks and the interview, we do a writing exercise. We tell applicants to write about the most important day of their life. This serves many purposes. One, we have in their own words what is important to them. Two, it shows us their report writing abilities and how well they can spell, etc. It's just one or two pages, but it gives us great insight into the way they think.

**Q: Does military experience help? What about a B.A.?**

**Wagner:** We are making a 25-year investment in this person, and, based on the pool of applicants we've been seeing, we can afford to be picky. Does military experience count? Is a BA going to help? Absolutely. Not just because the applicant pool is bigger, but because it shows the willingness of the individual to commit and complete things, and that is very important to an employer.

**Q: What kinds of questions do you like to ask?**

**Wagner:** Employees aren't prepared to ask any questions; it always seems to be a one- way conversation. I am going to look at the background packet. I am going to know about you before you come in. Then I want to hear your answers to the following questions:

1. Why do you want to work here?
2. How did you end up in corrections?

I have yet to find anyone who grew up wanting to work in a state jail or a prison. I have no problem with someone being honest and saying "I am graduating from college and I want to work for the FBI, but I saw you had openings and thought this would be a good segue." I would rather know from the employee what his or her career aspirations are.

3. What are your career goals?

Be able to articulate your career aspirations. I find it confounding that people don't know how to interview. You are given the opportunity to sell yourself. Why do I want to pick you as opposed to the other

328 people? Based on turnovers, I have done a lot of interviews. A majority of interviewees now have bachelor's degrees, but they don't know how to interview.

4. What would you do in the event of a riot? How would you prepare for such an event?
5. Are you prepared for the hours of work and varied scheduling?

This place runs 24 hours a day, 7 days a week. You might have to work 8 hours, plus be required to stay and work mandatory overtime when you were planning to go to a family picnic on July 4th.

**Richardson:** Our questions are subjective by some standards, but I think the responses are very useful to determine the person's psychological make up. We are looking for persons with substance to them. I want to know the answers to the following questions:

1. What motivates you?
2. What values are important to you?
3. What is the most significant problem you have ever had to contend with and how did you deal with it?

What is a problem to the interviewee and how he or she perceives it shows problem-solving abilities.

4. What is the most important personal quality you have? What is of value to you? If a person responds "defend myself," that is not really a value. However, responses such as "I have a lot of personal integrity," "I am a compassionate caring person" "People respect me for being honest" show important personal values.
5. Why do you want to work here?

We want to know if this a career to them or just a job. We just started using these kinds of questions in the past year or so. The last bunch of people we hired is about 10 notches above anyone before it.

## CHAPTER OBJECTIVE 1

Successful career planning is a continual process of self-assessment, occupational research, decisionmaking, employment contacts, work, and re-evaluation.

## CHAPTER OBJECTIVE 2

Self-assessment is learning who you are and what you can and want to do by evaluating your interests, skills, and values. Self-assessment tools pose a series of questions and identify potential career choices based on your answers.

## CHAPTER OBJECTIVE 3

Information on careers and job opportunities is available in libraries (public, school, and special), career development centers, and on the Internet.

## CHAPTER OBJECTIVE 4

Networking is meeting new people who can give you information about careers, the job market, and specific positions. Broaden your acquaintance base by networking—talk with people you know, join organizations, and participate in local programs that are related to your area of interest.

## CHAPTER OBJECTIVE 5

Informational interviewing, talking to people who are currently employed in a career field that you are interested in exploring, is an excellent means of researching a particular job or position.

## CHAPTER OBJECTIVE 6

Through your resume, you convey your capability for a particular position. It must be clear, directed, and persuasive—its objective is to secure an interview.

## CHAPTER OBJECTIVE 7

The two most widely used resume formats are the chronological resume and the functional resume. The chronological resume emphasizes skills and accomplishments; the functional resume emphasizes abilities.

## KEY TERMS

self-assessment, p. 454
networking, p. 455
informational interviewing, p. 456
resume, p. 456

chronological resume, p. 459
functional resume, p. 459
job interview, p. 467

## QUESTIONS FOR REVIEW

1. What is self-assessment?
2. What is networking?
3. What is the reason for establishing contacts?
4. What is an informational interview?
5. In what ways does an informational interview differ from a job interview?
6. What is a resume?
7. Describe the chronological resume format.
8. Describe the functional resume format.
9. What information should be included in a resume?
10. What information should be included in a cover letter?
11. What information should be included in a thank-you letter?
12. How do you prepare for a job interview?

## CORRECTIONS ON THE WEB

Access The Corrections Connection's Web site, at **http://www.corrections.com**. Click on "Careers," then "Job Openings." Review several openings for like positions and compare the requirements.

## ADDITIONAL READINGS

Ackerman, Thomas H. *Guide to Careers in Federal Law Enforcement.* Traverse City, MI: Sage Creek Press, 1999.

DeLucia, Robert C., and Thomas J. Doyle. *Career Planning in Criminal Justice,* 2d ed. Cincinnati, OH: Anderson Publishing, 1994.

Harr, J. Scott, and Karen M. Hess. *Seeking Employment in Criminal Justice and Related Fields,* 2d ed. Minneapolis/St. Paul: West Publishing Co., 1996.

Henry, Stuart, ed. *Inside Jobs: A Realistic Guide to Criminal Justice Careers for College Graduates.* Salem, WI: Sheffield Publishing Co., 1994.

Stephens, W. Richard, Jr. *Careers in Criminal Justice.* Needhan Heights, MA: Allyn and Bacon, 1999.

## ENDNOTES

1. John Barker and Jim Kellen, *Career Planning: A Developmental Approach* (Upper Saddle River, NJ: Merrill, 1998).
2. Ibid., p. 75
3. Tom Jackson, *The Perfect Resume* (New York: Doubleday, 1990).

# Glossary

Numbers in parentheses indicate the chapters in which the terms are defined.

## A

**Adjudication** ■ The process by which a court arrives at a final decision in a case. (1)

**Adjudication** ■ The second stage of the juvenile justice process—the court decides whether or not the offender is responsible for (guilty of) the alleged offense. (14)

**Administrative officers** ■ Those that control keys and weapons and sometimes oversee visitation. (8)

**Aggravating circumstances** ■ Factors that may be considered as increasing the culpability of the offender. (13)

**Auburn system** ■ The congregate style of prison discipline that began with the opening of the prison at Auburn, New York, in 1819. This system allowed inmates to work silently together during the day. At night, however, prisoners were isolated in small sleeping cells. With time, even sleeping cells became congregate. (7)

## B

**Back-end programs** ■ Sanctions that move offenders from higher levels of control to lower ones for the final phase of their sentences. (6)

**Balancing test** ■ A method the U.S. Supreme Court uses to decide prisoners' rights cases, weighing the rights claimed by inmates against the legitimate needs of prisons. (10)

**Benefit of clergy** ■ Practiced in England from the thirteenth century through the early nineteenth century, the release of clergymen and women from capital punishment when they proved their literacy by reading in court the text of the Fifty-first Psalm. (5)

**Best efforts standard** ■ A requirement of the federal Victims' Rights and Restitution Act of 1990 (also known as the Victims' Rights Act) which mandates that federal law enforcement officers, prosecutors, and corrections officials use their best efforts to ensure that victims receive basic rights and services during their encounter with the criminal justice system. (15)

**Bifurcated trial** ■ Two separate hearings for different issues in a trial; one for guilt and the other for punishment. (13)

**Blended sentencing** ■ A two-part (juvenile and adult) sentence—the adult sentence may be waived if the offender complies with all provisions of the juvenile sentence. (14)

**Block officers** ■ Those responsible for supervising inmates in housing areas. (8)

**Boot camp** ■ A short institutional term of confinement, usually followed by probation, that includes a physical regimen designed to develop self-discipline, respect for authority, responsibility, and a sense of accomplishment. (6)

**Bridewell** ■ A workhouse. The word came from the name of the first workhouse in England. (3)

## C

**Capital crime** ■ A crime for which the death penalty may, but need not necessarily, be imposed. (13)

**Capital punishment** ■ Legal infliction of the death penalty. (13)

**Chronological resume** ■ An historical resume, in which work experience and personal history are presented, in reverse chronological order. (16)

**Citation** ■ A type of nonfinancial pretrial release similar to a traffic ticket. It binds the defendant to appear in court on a future date. (4)

**Civil liability** ■ A legal obligation to another person to do, pay, or make good something. (10)

**Clemency** ■ Kindness, mercy, forgiveness, or leniency, usually relating to criminal acts. (13)

**Client-specific plan (CSP)** ■ A privately prepared presentence investigation report that supplements the PSI prepared by the probation department. (5)

**Cocorrections** ■ The incarceration and interaction of female and male offenders under a single institutional administration. (9)

**Coed prison** ■ A prison housing both female and male offenders. (9)

**Community corrections acts (CCAs)** ■ State laws that give economic grants to local communities to establish community corrections goals and policies and to develop and operate community corrections programs. (6)

**Community corrections** ■ A philosophy of correctional treatment that embraces (1) decentralization of authority, (2) citizen participation, (3) redefinition of the population of offenders for whom incarceration is most appropriate, and (4) emphasis on rehabilitation through community programs. (6)

**Community notification** ■ Notification to the community of the release or pending release of convicted offenders. (15)

**Community service** ■ A sentence to serve a specified number of hours working in unpaid positions with nonprofit or tax-supported agencies. (6)

**Commutation** ■ A change of a legal penalty to a lesser one; e.g., from death to life imprisonment. (13)

**Compensatory damages** ■ Money a court may award as payment for actual losses the inmates suffered, including out-of-pocket expenses the inmate incurred in filing the suit, other forms of monetary or material loss, and pain, suffering, and mental anguish. (10)

**Concurrent sentences** ■ Sentences served together. (2)

**Conditional diversion** ■ Diversion in which charges are dismissed if the defendant satisfactorily completes treatment, counseling, or other programs ordered by the justice system. (5)

**Conditional release** ■ Pretrial release under minimal or moderately restrictive conditions with little monitoring of compliance. It includes ROR, supervised pretrial release, and third-party release. (4)

**Consecutive sentences** ■ Sentences served one after the other. (2)

**Consent decree** ■ A written compact, sanctioned by a court, between parties in a civil case, specifying how disagreements between them are to be resolved. (10)

**Constitutional rights** ■ The personal and due-process rights guaranteed to individuals by the U.S. Constitution and its amendments, especially the first ten amendments, known as the Bill of Rights. Constitutional rights are the basis of most inmate rights. (10)

**Contract system** ■ A system of prison industry in which the prison advertised for bids for the employment of prisoners, whose labor was sold to the highest bidder. (7)

**Convict lease system** ■ A system of prison industry in which a prison temporarily relinquished supervision of its prisoners to a lessee. The lessee either employed the prisoners within the institution or transported them anywhere in the state. (7)

**Corporal punishments** ■ Physical punishments, or those involving the body. (3)

**Correctional clients** ■ Prison inmates, probationers, parolees, offenders assigned to alternative sentencing programs, and those held in jails. (1)

**Correctional econometrics** ■ The study of the cost-effectiveness of various correctional programs and related reductions in the incidence of crime. (2)

**Correctional officer personalities** ■ The personal characteristics of officers as well as their modes of adaptation to their jobs, institutional conditions, the requirements of staff subculture, and institutional expectations. (8)

**Corrections professional** ■ A dedicated person of high moral character and personal integrity who is employed in the field of corrections and takes professionalism to heart. (1)

**Corrections** ■ All the various aspects of the pretrial and postconviction management of individuals accused or convicted of crimes. (1)

**Counter performance** ■ The defendant's participation, in exchange for diversion, in a treatment, counseling, or educational program aimed at changing his or her behavior. (5)

**Crime index** ■ An annual statistical tally of major crimes known to law enforcement agencies in the United States. (1)

**Crime rate** ■ The number of index offenses reported for each unit of population. (1)

**Criminal justice system** ■ The collection of all the agencies that perform criminal justice functions, whether operations or administration or technical support. The basic divisions of the criminal justice system are police, courts, and corrections. (1)

**Criminal justice** ■ The process of achieving justice through the application of the criminal law and through the workings of the criminal justice system. Also, the study of the field of criminal justice. (1)

**Criminal law** (also called penal law) ■ That portion of the law that defines crimes and specifies criminal punishments. (1)

**Cruel and unusual punishment** ■ A penalty that is grossly disproportionate to the offense or that violates today's broad and idealistic concepts of dignity, civilized standards, humanity, and decency. In the area of capital punishment, cruel and unusual punishments are those that involve torture, a lingering death, or unnecessary pain. (10)

**Custodial staff** ■ Those staff members most directly involved in managing the inmate population. (8)

**Customer model** ■ An approach to private business partnerships with prisons. In this model, a company contracts with a correctional institution to provide a finished product at an agreed-upon price. The correctional institution owns and operates the business that employs the inmate workforce. (7)

## D

**Day fine** ■ A financial penalty scaled both to the defendant's ability to pay and to the seriousness of the crime. (6)

**Day reporting center (DRC)** ■ A community correctional center where an offender reports each day to file a daily schedule with a supervision officer, showing how each hour will be spent. (6)

**Death row** ■ A prison area housing inmates sentenced to death. (13)

**Deliberate indifference** ■ Intentional and willful indifference. Within the field of correctional practice the term refers to calculated inatten-

tion to unconstitutional conditions of confinement. (10)

**Delinquent offenses** ■ Acts committed by juveniles which, if committed by adults, could result in criminal prosecution. (14)

**Deprivation theory** ■ The belief that inmate subcultures develop in response to the deprivations in prison life. (9)

**Design capacity** ■ A measure of prison capacity. It is the number of inmates that planners or architects intended for the facility. (7) (11)

**Detention hearing** ■ A judicial review of the intake officer's detention decision. (14)

**Determinate sentence** (also called fixed sentence) ■ A sentence to a fixed term of incarceration, which can be reduced by good time. Under determinate sentencing, for example, all offenders convicted of the same degree of burglary are sentenced to the same length of time behind bars. (2)

**Deterrence** ■ The discouragement or prevention of crimes similar to the one for which an offender is being sentenced; a goal of criminal sentencing. (2)

**Direct file provisions** ■ Provisions under which the prosecutor determines whether to initiate a case against a juvenile in juvenile court or in adult criminal court. (14)

**Discretionary release** ■ Early release based on the paroling authority's assessment of eligibility. (12)

**Disposition** ■ The third stage of the juvenile justice process—the court decides the disposition (sentence) for a juvenile case. (14)

**Diversion** ■ Referring defendants to noncriminal-justice agencies for services instead of processing them through the courts; also, "the halting or suspension, before conviction, of formal criminal proceedings against a person, conditioned on some form of counter performance by the defendant." (4) (5)

**Diversion** ■ A non-judicial juvenile sanction. (14)

**Due process** ■ A right guaranteed by the Fifth, Sixth, and Fourteenth Amendments to the U.S. Constitution and generally understood, in legal contexts, to mean the expected course of legal proceedings according to the rules and forms established for the protection of persons' rights. (10)

## E

**Electronic monitoring (EM)** ■ The tracking of an offender's location by means of electronic signals from a small transmitter on the offender's wrist or ankle to a monitoring unit. (6)

**Employer model** ■ The most common approach to private business partnerships with prisons. The prison provides a company space in which to operate and a labor pool from which to hire. The company supervises its inmate employees and makes all decisions. (7)

**Equity** ■ The sentencing principle that similar crimes and similar criminals should be treated alike. (2)

**Exchange rates** ■ An approach to sentencing, implemented by a sentencing commission, that emphasizes interchangeability of punishments; for example, three days under house arrest might be considered equal to one day of incarceration. (11)

## F

**Fair sentencing** ■ Sentencing practices that incorporate fairness for both victims and offenders. Fairness is said to be achieved by implementing principles of proportionality, equity, social debt, and truth in sentencing. (2)

**Felony** ■ A serious criminal offense; specifically, one punishable by death or by incarceration in a prison facility for more than a year. (1)

**Fine** ■ A financial penalty used as a criminal sanction. (6)

**First-generation jail** ■ A jail with multiple-occupancy cells or dormitories that line corridors arranged in spokes. Inmate supervision is sporadic or intermittent; staff must patrol the corridors to observe inmates in their cells. This linear design dates back to the eighteenth century. (4)

**Flat sentences** ■ Those that specify a given amount of time to be served in custody and allow little or no variation from the time specified. (2)

**Folkways** ■ Time-honored ways of doing things. Although they carry the force of tradition, their violation is unlikely to threaten the survival of the social group. (1)

**Frivolous lawsuits** ■ Lawsuits with no foundation in fact. They are generally brought for publicity, politics, or other reasons not related to law. (10)

**Front-end programs** ■ Punishment options for initial sentences more restrictive than traditional probation but less restrictive than jail or prison. (6)

**Functional resume** ■ A qualitative resume, in which work experience and abilities are presented by major area of involvement, usually with dates. (16)

## G

**Gain time** ■ Time taken off an inmate's sentence for participating in certain activities such as going to school, learning a trade, working in prison, etc. (8)

**Gang** ■ A group of individuals involved in continuing criminal activity. (14)

**General deterrence** ■ The use of the example of individual punishment to dissuade others from committing crimes. (2)

**Good time** ■ The number of days or months prison authorities deduct from a sentence for good behavior and for other reasons. (2)

**Group home** ■ A non-secure residential facility for juveniles. (14)

**Guardian *ad litem*** ■ A person appointed by the juvenile court, often defense counsel, to serve as a special guardian for the youth being processed through the juvenile justice system. (14)

**Guided discretion** ■ Decision-making bounded by general guidelines, rules, or laws. (13)

## H

**Habitual offender statute** ■ A law that (1) allows a person's criminal history to be considered at sentencing or (2) allows a person convicted of a given offense, and previously convicted of another specified offense, to receive a more severe penalty than that for the current offense alone. (2)

**Hands-off doctrine** ■ An historical policy of American courts not to intervene in prison management. Courts tended to follow the doctrine until the late 1960s. (10)

**Hedonistic calculus** ■ The idea that people are motivated by pleasure and pain and that the proper amount of punishment can deter crime. (3)

**Hospice** ■ An interdisciplinary, comfort-oriented care unit that allows seriously ill and dying prisoners to die with dignity and humanity in an environment that provides mental and spiritual preparation for the natural process of dying. (11)

**House arrest** ■ A sanction that requires an offender to remain in his or her home except for approved absences, such as work, school, or treatment programs. (6)

## I

**Importation theory** ■ The belief that inmate subcultures are brought into prisons from the outside world. (9)

**Incapacitation** ■ The use of imprisonment or other means to reduce an offender's capability to commit future offenses; a goal of criminal sentencing. (2)

**Indeterminate sentence** ■ A sentence in which a judge specifies a maximum length and a minimum length, and an administrative agency, generally a parole board, determines the actual time of release. (2)

**Industrial shop and school officers** ■ Those that ensure efficient use of training and educational resources within the prison. (8)

**Informational interviewing** ■ A process for obtaining firsthand information about a particular job or career. (16)

**Infraction** ■ A minor violation of state statute or local ordinance punishable by a fine or other penalty, but not by incarceration, or by a specified, usually very short term of incarceration. (1)

**Injunction** ■ A judicial order to do or refrain from doing a particular act. (10)

**Inmate roles** ■ Prison lifestyles; also, forms of ongoing social accommodation to prison life. (9)

**Inmate subculture** ■ (also prisoner subculture) The habits, customs, mores, values, beliefs, or superstitions of the body of inmates incarcerated in correctional institutions; also, the inmate social world. (9)

**Institutional corrections** ■ That aspect of the correctional enterprise that "involves the incarceration and rehabilitation of adults and juveniles convicted of offenses against the law, and the confinement of persons suspected of a crime awaiting trial and adjudication." (1)

**Institutional needs** ■ Prison administration interests recognized by the courts as justifying some restrictions on the constitutional rights of prisoners. Those interests are maintenance of institutional order, maintenance of institutional security, safety of prison inmates and staff, and rehabilitation of inmates. (10)

**Intake** ■ The first stage of the juvenile justice process. A court-appointed officer reviews the case and recommends a course of action—dismissal, informal disposition, formal disposition, or transfer to adult criminal court. (14)

**Intangible losses** ■ Costs such as fear, pain, suffering, and reduced quality of life that accrue to crime victims as a result of their victimization. (15)

**Integration model** ■ A combination of importation theory and deprivation theory. The belief that in childhood, some inmates acquired, usually from peers, values that support law-violating behavior, but that the norms and standards in a prison also affect an inmate. (9)

**Intensive-supervision probation (ISP)** ■ Control of offenders in the community, under strict conditions, by means of frequent reporting to a probation officer, whose caseload is generally limited to 30 offenders. (6)

**Intermediate sanctions** ■ New punishment options developed to fill the gap between traditional probation and traditional jail or prison sentences and to better match the severity of punishment to the seriousness of the crime. (6)

## J

**Jail accreditation** ■ The formal approval of a jail by a national accrediting body such as the American Correctional Association and the Commission on Accreditation. (4)

**Jails** ■ Locally operated correctional facilities that confine persons before or after conviction. Persons sentenced to jail usually receive a sentence of a year or less. (4)

**Job interview** ■ A meeting between two or more people for a mutual exchange of information regarding employment. (16)

**Judicial reprieve** ■ A nineteenth-century English forerunner of probation; a temporary suspension, or delay, of sentence. The suspended sentence was adopted in the United States and was used frequently until the Supreme Court found it unconstitutional in 1916. (5)

**Jurisdiction** ■ The power, right, or authority to interpret and apply the law. (10)

**Just deserts** ■ The punishment deserved. A just-deserts perspective on criminal sentencing holds that criminal acts are deserving of punishment and that justice is best served by the imposition of appropriate punishments on criminal-law violators. (2)

**Juvenile court** ■ Any court that has jurisdiction over matters involving juveniles. (14)

**Juvenile detention facility** ■ A facility for keeping juvenile offenders in secure custody, as necessary, through various stages of the juvenile justice process. (14)

## L

**Legitimate penological objectives** ■ The realistic concerns that correctional officers and administrators have for the integrity and security of the correctional institution and the safety of staff and inmates. (10)

## M

**Mandatory death penalty** ■ A death sentence that the legislature has required to be imposed upon persons convicted of certain offenses. (13)

**Mandatory minimum sentencing** ■ The imposition of sentences required by statute on those convicted of a particular crime or a particular crime with special circumstances, such as robbery with a firearm or selling drugs to a minor within 1000 feet of a school, or on those with a particular type of criminal history. (2)

**Mandatory release** ■ Early release after a time period specified by law. (12)

**Mandatory sentences** ■ Those that are required by law under certain circumstances—such as conviction of a specified crime or of a series of offenses of a specified type. (2)

**Manpower model** ■ An approach to private business partnerships with prisons in which the prison's role is similar to that of a temporary personnel service. (7)

**Maximum-security prison** ■ A prison designed, organized, and staffed to confine the most dangerous offenders for long periods. It has a highly secure perimeter, barred cells, and a

high staff-to-inmate ratio. It imposes strict controls on the movement of inmates and visitors, and it offers few programs, amenities, or privileges. (7)

**Medical model** ■ A philosophy of prisoner reform in which criminal behavior is regarded as a disease to be treated with appropriate therapy. (7)

**Medium-security prison** ■ A prison that confines offenders considered less dangerous than those in maximum security, for both short and long periods. It is also designed, organized, and staffed to prevent violence, escape, and disturbance but places fewer controls on inmates' and visitors' freedom of movement than a maximum-security facility. It, too, has barred cells and a fortified perimeter. The staff-to-inmate ratio is generally lower than in a maximum-security facility, and the level of amenities and privileges is slightly higher. (7)

**Minimization of penetration** ■ A form of diversion that keeps an offender from going further into the system. (5)

**Minimum-security prison** ■ A prison that confines the least dangerous offenders for both short and long periods. It allows as much freedom of movement and as many privileges and amenities as are consistent with the goals of the facility, while still following procedures to avoid escape, violence, and disturbance. It may have dormitory housing, and the staff-to-inmate ratio is relatively low. (7)

**Misdemeanor** ■ A relatively minor violation of the criminal law, such as petty theft or simple assault, punishable by confinement for one year or less. (1)

**Mitigating circumstances** ■ Factors that, although not justifying or excusing an action, may be considered as reducing the culpability of the offender. (13)

**Model of criminal sentencing** ■ A strategy or system for imposing criminal sanctions. (2)

**Mores** ■ Cultural restrictions on behavior that forbid serious violations of a group's values—such as murder, rape, and robbery. (1)

## N

**Net-widening** ■ Increasing the number of offenders sentenced to a greater level of restriction. It results in the sentencing of offenders to more restrictive sanctions than their offenses and characteristics warrant. (6)

**Networking** ■ An ongoing process of building professional contacts. (16)

**New offense violation** ■ Arrest and prosecution for the commission of a new crime by a parolee. (12)

**"No-frills" prisons and jails** ■ Correctional institutions that take away prisoner amenities and privileges. (11)

*Nolo contendere* ■ A plea of "no contest." A no-contest plea may be used where a defendant does not wish to contest conviction. Because the plea does not admit guilt, however, it cannot provide the basis for later civil suits. (1)

**Nominal damages** ■ Small amounts of money a court may award when inmates have sustained no actual damages, but there is clear evidence that their rights have been violated. (10)

**Noninstitutional corrections** (also community corrections) ■ That aspect of the correctional enterprise that includes pardon, probation, and parole activities, correctional administration not directly connectable to institutions, and miscellaneous activities not directly related to institutional care. (1)

## O

**Older inmates** ■ Inmates age 50 and older, as defined by the National Institute of Corrections. (11)

**Open institution** ■ A minimum-security facility that has no fences or walls surrounding it. (7)

**Operational capacity** ■ A measure of prison capacity. It is the number of inmates that a facility's staff, existing programs, and services can accommodate. (7) (11)

## P

**Pains of imprisonment** ■ Major problems new inmates face, such as loss of liberty and personal autonomy, lack of material possessions, loss of heterosexual relationships, and reduced personal security. (9)

**Pardon** ■ An executive act that legally excuses a convicted offender from a criminal penalty. (12)

*Parens patriae* ■ A Latin term that refers to the state as guardian of minors and incompetent people. (14)

**Parole eligibility date** ■ The earliest date on which an inmate might be paroled. (12)

**Parole** ■ The conditional release of a prisoner, prior to completion of the imposed sentence, under the supervision of a parole officer. (12)

**Parolee** ■ A person who is conditionally released from prison to community supervision. (12)

**Paroling authority** ■ A person or correctional agency (often called a parole board or parole commission) that has the authority to grant parole, to revoke parole, and to discharge from parole. (12)

**Penitentiary** ■ A place for reform of offenders through repentance and rehabilitation. The earliest form of large-scale incarceration, it punished criminals by isolating them so that they could reflect on their misdeeds, repent, and reform. (7)

**Pennsylvania system** ■ The first style of prison discipline, begun at the Walnut Street Jail to punish offenders with confinement instead of corporal punishment. Conceived by the American Quakers in 1790, it emphasized solitary confinement in silence. (7)

**Perimeter security officers** ■ Those assigned to security (or gun) towers, wall posts, and perimeter patrols. These officers are charged with preventing escapes and detecting and preventing intrusions. (8)

**Pleasure-pain principle** ■ The idea that actions are motivated primarily by a person's desire to seek pleasure and avoid pain. (2)

**Policy-centered approach** ■ A method of thinking about and planning for intermediate sanctions that draws together key stakeholders from inside and outside the corrections agency that will implement the sanction. (6)

**Precedent** ■ A previous judicial decision that judges should consider in deciding future cases. (10)

**Predisposition report** ■ A report that documents: (1) the juvenile's background; (2) educational history; (3) information gathered from interviews with the juvenile, family members, and others; (4) available placement options; and (5) recommended dispositions. (14)

**Presentence investigation report (PSI)** ■ A report, prepared by the probation department of a court, that provides a social and personal history as well as an evaluation of an offender as an aid to the court in determining a sentence and/or outlining a treatment plan. (2) (5)

**Principle of least eligibility** ■ The requirement that prison conditions—including the delivery of health care—must be a step below those of the working class and people on welfare. (7)

**Prison argot** ■ The special language of the inmate subculture. (9)

**Prison code** ■ A set of norms and values among prison inmates. It is generally antagonistic to the official administration and rehabilitation programs of the prison. (9)

**Prisoners' rights** ■ Constitutional guarantees of free speech, religious practice, due process, and other private and personal rights, as well as constitutional protections against cruel and unusual punishments, made applicable to prison inmates by the federal courts. (10)

**Prisonization** ■ The process by which inmates adapt to prison society; the taking on of the ways, mores, customs, and general culture of the penitentiary. (9)

**Probation** ■ The conditional release of a convicted offender into the community, under the supervision of a probation officer. It is conditional because it can be revoked if certain conditions are not met. The judge or the probation department usually imposes a set of restrictions on the offender's freedom. (5) (12)

**Profession** ■ An occupational group granted high social status by virtue of the personal integrity of its members. (1)

**Professional associations** ■ Organized groups of like-minded individuals who work to enhance the professional status of members of their occupational group. (1)

**Program staff** ■ Those staff members concerned with encouraging prisoners to participate in educational, vocational, and treatment programs. (8)

**Program-centered approach** ■ A method of planning intermediate sanctions in which planning for a program is usually undertaken by a single agency, which develops and funds the program. (6)

**Property crime** ■ Burglary, larceny, automobile theft, and arson as reported in the FBI's Uniform Crime Reports. (1)

**Proportionality** ■ The sentencing principle that the severity of punishment should match the seriousness of the crime for which the sentence is imposed. (2)

**Pseudofamilies** ■ Familylike structures, common in women's prisons, in which inmates assume roles similar to those in families in free society. (9)

**Public-accounts system** ■ The earliest form of prison industry, in which the warden was responsible for purchasing materials and equipment and for the manufacture, marketing, and sale of prison-made items. (7)

**Public-works system** ■ A system of prison industry in which prisoners were employed in the construction of public buildings, roads, and parks. (7)

**Punitive damages** ■ Money a court may award to punish the wrongdoer when a wrongful act was intentional and malicious or was done with reckless disregard for the rights of the inmate. (10)

## R

**Rabble management** ■ The control of persons whose noncriminal behavior is offensive to the community (for example, public nuisances, derelicts, junkies, drunks, vagrants, the mentally ill, and street people). According to John Irwin, rabble management is the purpose of jails. (4)

**Rated capacity** ■ A measure of prison capacity. It is the number of beds or inmates a rating official has assigned to a prison. (7) (11)

**Recidivism** ■ The repetition of criminal behavior; generally defined as re-arrest. The primary outcome measure for probation, as it is for all corrections programs. (5)

**Reentry court** ■ A court that manages the return to the community of individuals released from prison. (12)

**Reform school** ■ A penal institution to which especially young or first-time offenders are committed for training and reformation. (14)

**Rehabilitation** ■ The changing of criminal lifestyles into law-abiding ones by "correcting" the behavior of offenders through treatment, education, and training; a sentencing goal. (2)

**Reintegration** ■ The process of making the offender a productive member of the community. (2)

**Release on bail** ■ The release of a person upon that person's financial guarantee to appear in court. (4)

**Release on own recognizance (ROR)** ■ Pretrial release on the defendant's promise to appear for trial. It requires no cash guarantee. (4)

**Relief officers** ■ Experienced correctional officers who know and can perform almost any custody role within the institution, used to temporarily replace officers who are sick or on vacation or to meet staffing shortages. (8)

**Residential community center (RCC)** ■ A medium-security correctional setting that resident offenders are permitted to leave regularly—unaccompanied by staff—for work, for educational or vocational programs, or for treatment in the community. (6)

**Residential treatment center** ■ A residential facility that provides intensive treatment services to juveniles. (14)

**Restitution** ■ The practice of requiring an individual who has harmed another to repay the victim for the harm caused. Also, a court requirement that an alleged or convicted offender pay money or provide services to the victim of the crime or provide services to the community. (2) (15)

**Restoration** ■ The process of returning to their previous condition all those involved in or affected by crime—including victims, offenders, and society; a recent goal of criminal sentencing. (2)

**Resume** ■ A written summary of your education, interests, skills, achievements, and goals. (16)

**Retribution** ■ A sentencing goal that involves revenge against a criminal perpetrator. (2)

**Revocation hearing** ■ Administrative review to determine whether a violation of the conditions of parole warrants return to prison. (12)

**Right of allocution** ■ A statutory provision permitting crime victims to speak at the sentencing of convicted offenders. A federal right of allocution was established for victims of federal violent and sex crimes under the Violent

Crime Control and Law Enforcement Act of 1994. (15)

**Riot** ■ Seizure of control by inmates over all or part of a correctional facility with violence against staff and/or other prisoners. (11)

**Roles** ■ The normal patterns of behavior expected of those holding particular social positions. (8)

## S

**Salient factor score (SFS)** ■ Scale, developed from a risk-screening instrument, used to predict parole outcome. (12)

**Second-generation jail** ■ A jail where staff remain in a secure control booth surrounded by inmate housing areas called pods. Bars are replaced with reinforced glass. Although visual surveillance increases, verbal interaction with inmates is reduced. This design emerged in the 1960s. (4)

**Security threat groups (STGs)** ■ The current term for prison gangs. (11)

**Self-assessment** ■ A method of enhancing self-understanding—identifying your unique characteristics: what you do well (skills), what is important to you (values), and what you like to do (interests)—clearly and accurately. (16)

**Sentence** ■ The penalty a court imposes on a person convicted of a crime. (2)

**Sentencing commission** ■ A group assigned to create a schedule of sentences that reflect the gravity of the offenses committed and the prior record of the criminal offender. The commission often includes private citizens as well as representatives of the criminal justice system, including law enforcement, courts, and corrections. (2)

**Sentencing** ■ The imposition of a criminal sanction by a sentencing authority, such as a judge. (2)

**Social debt** ■ The sentencing principle that the severity of punishment should take into account the offender's prior criminal behavior. (2)

**Social order** ■ The smooth functioning of social institutions, the existence of positive and productive relations between individual members of society, and the orderly functioning of society as a whole. (2)

**Special master** ■ A person appointed by the court to act as its representative to oversee remedy of a violation and provide regular progress reports. (11)

**Special-needs inmates** ■ Prisoners who require special treatment or care because they suffer from mental illness, chemical dependency (drug or alcohol abuse), or communicable disease (especially HIV/AIDS and TB). (4)

**Specific deterrence** ■ The deterrence of the individual being punished from committing additional crimes. (2)

**Staff roles** ■ The patterns of behavior expected of correctional staff members in particular jobs. (8)

**Staff subculture** ■ The beliefs, values, and behavior of staff. They differ greatly from those of the inmate subculture. (8)

**State-use system** ■ A system of prison industry that employs prisoners to manufacture products consumed by state governments and their agencies, departments, and institutions. (7)

**Status offenses** ■ Acts that are law violations only for juveniles: e.g., running away, truancy, or ungovernability (sometimes referred to as incorrigibility or beyond parental control). (14)

**Statutory exclusion provisions** ■ Provisions under which adult criminal court jurisdiction for certain juvenile cases is established by state law. (14)

**Stress** ■ Tension in a person's body or mind, resulting from physical, chemical, or emotional factors. (8)

**Structured conflict** ■ The tensions between prison staff members and inmates that arise out of the correctional setting. (8)

**Structured sentencing** ■ A set of guidelines for determining an offender's sentence. (11)

**Subculture** ■ The beliefs, values, behavior, and material objects shared by a particular group of people within a larger society. (8)

**Supermax housing** ■ A free-standing facility, or a distinct unit within a facility, that provides for management and secure control of inmates who have been officially designated as exhibiting violent or serious and disruptive behavior while incarcerated. (11)

**Supervised pretrial release** ■ Nonfinancial pretrial release with more restrictive conditions (for example, participating in therapeutic or rehabilitative programs, reporting to a pretrial officer, and checking in regularly). (4)

**Supervision** ■ The second major role of probation officers, consisting of intervention, surveillance, and enforcement. (5)

## T

**Tangible losses** ■ Costs such as medical expenses, lost wages, and property losses that accrue to crime victims as a result of their victimization. (15)

**Technical violation** ■ A failure to fulfill the conditions of probation—attending counseling, paying restitution, contacting the probation officer—rather than the commission of a new offense. (5) (12)

**Teen courts** ■ Courts in which youths adjudicate and impose disposition for a juvenile offense. (14)

**Therapeutic community (TC)** ■ A highly structured residential treatment program within a prison or jail involving resocialization, intensive counseling, and an increasing level of inmate responsibility. (11)

**Third-generation jail,** sometimes called direct-supervision jail ■ A jail where inmates are housed in small groups in pods staffed 24 hours a day by specially trained officers. Officers interact with inmates to help change behavior. Bars and metal doors are absent, reducing noise and dehumanization. This approach to jail construction and inmate management emerged in the 1970s. (4)

**Tort** ■ A civil wrong, a wrongful act, or a wrongful breach of duty, other than a breach of contract, whether intentional or accidental, from which injury to another occurs. (10)

**Total institution** ■ A place where the same people work, play, eat, sleep, and recreate together on a continuous basis. The term was developed by the sociologist Erving Goffman to describe prisons and other facilities. (9)

**Totality of conditions** ■ A standard to be used in evaluating whether prison conditions are cruel and unusual. (10)

**True diversion** ■ A form of diversion that keeps an offender out of the system and avoids formal prosecution and labeling. (5)

**Truth in sentencing** ■ The sentencing principle that requires an offender to serve a substantial portion of the sentence and reduces the discrepancy between the sentence imposed and actual time spent in prison. (2)

## U

**Unconditional diversion** ■ The termination of criminal processing at any point before adjudication with no threat of later prosecution. It generally means that treatment, counseling, and other services are offered voluntarily. (5)

**Unit management system** ■ A method of controlling prisoners in self-contained living areas that include office space for unit staff, making staff and inmates accessible to each other. A unit team—typically composed of the unit manager, one or more case managers, two or more correctional counselors, and a unit secretary—is responsible for the inmates living in that unit. (7)

**Utilitarianism** ■ The principle that the highest objective of public policy is the greatest happiness for the largest number of people. (3)

## V

**Victim assistance program** ■ An organized program which offers services to victims of crime in the areas of crisis intervention and follow-up counseling, and which helps victims secure their rights under the law. (15)

**Victim compensation** ■ A form of victim assistance in which state-funded payments are made to victims to help them recover financial losses due to crime. (15)

**Victim-impact statement** ■ An assertion made by victims (and sometimes by friends or relatives of the victim) about the impact of the crime in question upon the victim and the victim's family. Also, a written document which describes the losses, suffering, and trauma experienced by a crime victim or by the victim's survivors. The judge considers it when sentencing the offender. (2) (5) (15)

**Victim notification** ■ Notification to victims of the release or pending release of convicted offenders who have harmed them. (15)

**Victim** ■ Someone who suffers direct or threatened physical, emotional, or financial harm as the result of the commission of a crime. The term victim also includes the immediate family of a minor or homicide victim. (15)

**Victims' rights** ■ The fundamental rights of victims to be equitably represented throughout the criminal justice process. (15)

**Violent crime** ■ Interpersonal crime that involves the use of force by offenders or results in injury or death to victims. In the FBI's Uniform Crime Reports, violent crimes are murder, forcible rape, robbery, and aggravated assault. (1)

## W

**Waiver provisions** ■ Provisions under which the juvenile court orders transfer of the case to adult criminal court. (14)

**Work detail supervisors** ■ Those that oversee the work of individual inmates and inmate work crews. (8)

**Writ of *certiorari*** ■ A writ issued by an appellate court to obtain from a lower court the record of its proceedings in a particular case. (1) (13)

**Writ of *habeus corpus*** ■ An order that directs the person detaining a prisoner to bring him or her before a judge, who will determine the lawfulness of the imprisonment. (10)

## Y

**Yard officers** ■ Those that supervise inmates in the prison yard. (8)

# Case Index

# Subject Index

# Photo Credits

# Text Credits

**2** P.H. Hahn, "Standardized Curriculum for Correctional Officers: History and Rationale," *The Keepers Voice*, Vol., 15, no. 4 (Fall 1994), pp. 8–10; **15** Reprinted with permission; **21** Reprinted with permission of the American Correctional Association; **24** Reprinted with permission; **26** Reprinted with permission; **27** Reprinted with permission of the Federal Bureau of Prisons; **38–39** Reprinted with permission; **54** Reprinted with permission; **55** Reprinted with permission; **66** Reprinted with permission; **67** Reprinted with permission. **77** Reprinted with permission; **87** Reprinted with permission; **92** Reprinted with permission of the American Jail Association; **95–97** W. Raymond Nelson, Cost Savings in New Generation Jails: The Direct Supervision Approach (Washington, DC: National Institute of Justice, June 1988), pp. 2–3; **98** Rocky Finocchio, "Oxbow Jail Division: Accepting the Challenge," *American Jails*, Vol. 10, No. 6, January-February 1997, p. 69, reprinted with permission; **105** Peter Finn, *The Orange County, Florida, Jail Educational and Vocational Programs* (Washington, DC: National Institute of Justice), p. 2; **109** Reprinted with permission; **117** Reprinted with permission of the American Jail Association; **132** Reprinted with permission of the American Correctional Association; **134** Reprinted with permission. **136** Reprinted with permission; **141-45** Reprinted with permission; **149** Reprinted with permission;

**156** H.G. Wells (1866–1946), *A Modern Utopia*, chapter 5, section 2 (1905), reprinted in *The Works of H.G. Wells*, Vol. 9 (1925); **158** Reprinted with permission of the American Jail Association; **161** Reprinted with permission; **169** Reprinted with permission; **171** Reprinted with permission; **173** Reprinted with permission; **197** Reprinted with permission of the American Correctional Association; **201** Reprinted with permission; **205** Peter Finn, *The Delaware Department of Correction Life Skills Program*, National Institute of Justice, Washington, DC, August 1998, p. 13; **214** Reprinted with permission; **222** Dora B. Schriro, "Women in Prison Keeping the Peace," *The Keeper's Voice*, Vol. 16, No. 2 (Spring 1995); **231** Reprinted with permission; **232** Peter Finn, *The Delaware Department of Correction Life Skills Program, National Institute of Justice*, Washington, DC, August 1998, p.9; **237** Reprinted with permission; **241** Reprinted with permission of the International Association of Correctional Officers; **248** Eldridge Cleaver, *Soul on Ice*, "On Becoming" (1968), written from Folsom Prison, June 25, 1965; **250** Reprinted with permission; **256** Reprinted with permission; **263** Reprinted with permission; **274** *Procunier* v. *Martinez*, 416 U.S. 396 (1974); **281** Reprinted with permission; **296–97** Reprinted with permission; **299** Reprinted with permission; **310** Jessica Mitford, *Kind and Usual Punishment: The Prison Business*, 1971; **312** Reprinted with permission; **319** Reprinted with permission of the American Correctional Association;

**331** Reprinted with permission; **332–34** Excerpted from an interview with Ann Seidlitz in "Fixin' to Die: Hospice Program Operates at LSP," National Prison Hospice Association, reprinted with permission; **346** Peter Finn, *Texas' Project RIO (Re-Integration of Offenders)* (Washington, DC: 1998), p. 3; **350** Reprinted with permission of the American Probation and Parole Association; **353** Reprinted with permission; **354** Reprinted with permission; **362** Reprinted with permission; **363** Peter Finn, *Texas' Project RIO (Re-Integration of Offenders)* (Washington, DC: 1998), p. 9; **378** Albert Camus (1913–1960), *Resistance, Rebellion and Death*, "Reflections on the Guillotine" (1961); **384** Mark Allen Jenkins, "Stop All the Violence," *On Wings of Hope*, Vol. 2, No. 1, Winter 1997, p. 3, reprinted with permission; **385** Reprinted with permission; **386** Reprinted with permission of the American Correctional Association; **390** Reprinted with permission; **402** Shay Bilchik, Administrator, Office of Juvenile Justice and Delinquency Prevention, U.S. Department of Justice; **410** Reprinted with permission; **412** Reprinted with permission; **415–16** Reprinted with permission; **418** Reprinted with permission; **428** President's Task Force on Victims of Crime, Final Report (Washington, D.C., U.S. Government Printing Office, December 1982). **436** Reprinted with permission; **439** Reprinted with permission; **473–75** "Getting Hired in Corrections," *Corrections Connection*, reprinted with permission.